Introduction to Artificial Intelligence and Expert Systems

Dan W. Patterson
University of Texas, El Paso

Prentice-Hall International, Inc.

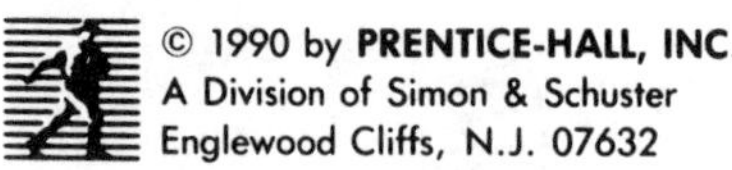

A Division of Simon & Schuster
Englewood Cliffs, N.J. 07632

Printed in the United States of America

10 9 8 7 6 5 4 3 2 1

ISBN 0-13-482928-X

Prentice-Hall International (UK) Limited, *London*
Prentice-Hall of Australia Pty. Limited, *Sydney*
Prentice-Hall Canada Inc., *Toronto*
Prentice-Hall Hispanoamericana, S.A., *Mexico*
Prentice-Hall of India Private Limited, *New Delhi*
Prentice-Hall of Japan, Inc., *Tokyo*
Simon & Schuster Asia Pte. Ltd., *Singapore*
Editora Prentice-Hall do Brasil, Ltda., *Rio de Janeiro*
Prentice-Hall, Inc., *Englewood Cliffs, New Jersey*

To Neslie

for her generous love and encouragement

Contents

Preface

A major turning point occurred in the field of artificial intelligence with the realization that "in knowledge lies the power." This realization led to the development of a new class of systems: knowledge-based systems. Knowledge-based systems use specialized sets of coded knowledge to "reason" and perform limited intelligent tasks. This is in constrast with more conventional type programs which rely on data and general algorithms (weak methods) to solve less intelligent tasks. Knowledge-based systems proved to be much more successful than the earlier, more general problem solving systems. They proved to be more effective in most areas of AI including computer vision, natural language understanding, planning, and problem solving using the newly developed rule-based expert systems.

In concert with the knowledge-base theme, this book is mainly about knowledge and the role it plays in creating effective AI programs. It focuses on all aspects of knowledge: knowledge representation methods, knowledge acquisition techniques, knowledge organization, and knowledge manipulation. It illustrates the basic knowledge-system approach and emphasizes the important use of knowledge in such systems.

This book was written as a text for my classes in artificial intelligence at the University of Texas at El Paso. These classes are for upper division undergraduate and first year graduate students. The courses assume prerequisites of basic computer science courses (like programming languages) and a general maturity in mathematics.

The material may be used as a one semester survey course in AI or as a two semester sequel with basic AI principles and tools being taught the first semester and special topics such as vision, natural language understanding, machine learning, and expert systems architectures taught the second semester.

The book is comprehensive in its coverage of all the important topic areas of AI, and no particular bias is given to any special area or approach. The treatment of knowledge acquisition and machine learning is much more comprehensive than that found in other introductory texts on AI. And computer vision, natural language processing, and pattern recognition are also covered in some depth. A significant part of the text is devoted to the important topics of knowledge representation, including methods of dealing with uncertain, incomplete, and vague knowledge (such as methods related to nonmonotonic logics and commonsense reasoning).

Currently, there is a debate being waged among artificial intelligence practitioners over the best approach to AI computations: the neural network approach vs. the symbolic computation approach. We recognize the importance of this debate because the future direction of AI will be determined by its outcome. But whatever the outcome, the successes of symbolic computation on knowledge structures suggest that this approach will last for some time to come. Because of that, most of the text has been devoted to this approach. Even so, the recent successes of the biologically inspired neural network approach suggests that there is an important place in AI for systems based on these paradigms. Consequently, we have included introductory material on this important subject as well.

This book is about the different areas of study which make up the field of AI, about the techniques and tools of AI, and about the products AI has produced. The book is also about knowledge, an essential component of AI. For this reason, the material has been organized around knowledge and the roles it plays in each of the component areas of study.

The book has been divided into five parts or general topic areas related to knowledge: Introduction to Artificial Intelligence, Knowledge Representation, Knowledge Organization and Manipulation, Perception and Communication, and Knowledge Acquisition.

Part I is a general introductory section composed of three chapters. Chapter 1 presents a general overview of AI in which the importance of the field is discussed, some important terms are introduced, and a brief summary of early work is presented. This is followed with a chapter which defines knowledge, what it is, and the important roles it plays in AI and in the development of knowledge-based systems. Chapter 3 offers a concise summary of the most important programming languages used by AI practitioners, with particular emphasis on LISP.

Part II covers the important areas of knowledge representation. It consists of five chapters. Chapter 4 presents the important topics of propositional and first order predicate logics. An area that has come to play a preeminent role in AI. Chapter 5 discusses problems and solutions for the representation of inconsistent and uncertain knowledge. Chapter 6 continues this theme with a treatment of fuzzy and modal logic. In Chapter 7, structured representation schemes are introduced with the notion of associative networks, conceptual graphs, and frames. Chapter 8 completes Part II with an introduction to systems which are based on object oriented representation structures.

Part III covers topics related to the organization and manipulation of knowledge. This part contains three chapters. Chapter 9 discusses the important problems associated with search and control. Chapter 10 presents a comprehensive treatment of matching techniques, an essential function of most AI programs. This part concludes with Chapter 11 which covers memory organization and management techniques.

Part IV contains three chapters related to perception and communication. The first chapter, Chapter 12 covers the subfield of natural language processing. Although only a single chapter has been devoted to this subject, the treatment is thorough. Chapter 13 presents a condensation of important topics from pattern recognition. Chapter 14 presents a comprehensive treatment of the important topic of computer vision. And, Chapter 15 has an introduction to Expert System architectures and related topics.

Part V, the final section, presents an up-to-date, comprehensive view of knowledge acquisition/machine learning. All of the important learning paradigms are covered in this part. Chapter 16 begins with general concepts related to knowledge acquisition. This is followed in Chapter 17 with a summary of early work in machine learning. Chapter 18 introduces inductive learning concepts and presents a detailed example of an inductive learning system. Chapter 19 continues inductive learning with examples of recent systems. Chapter 20, the final chapter, covers analogical and explanation-based learning paradigms.

We hope the reader will experience many enjoyable and rewarding sessions reading from the exciting material to be found in the text.

ACKNOWLEDGMENTS

In writing this text, a number of individuals have been helpful with their suggestions and comments. They include the following students: Teow Kiang Chew, Teck Huat Goh, Julie Lemen, Sergio Felix, Ricardo Martinez, Vincente Fresquez, Hun-Ming Hsu, Rudy Velasquez, and Jose Najera-Mora. Special thanks are given to E. Louise (Neslie) Patterson for proofreading most of the manuscript and offering many useful suggestions. Thanks are also given to the following reviewers for their valuable suggestions: Christopher K. Carlson, George Mason University; Daniel Chester, University of Delaware; Karen L. McGraw, Cognitive Technologies; and Gordon Novak, University of Texas, Austin. Finally, I wish to thank the Electrical Engineering and Computer Science Department of the University of Texas at El Paso for the generous use of their facilities.

PART 1
Introduction to Artificial Intelligence

1
Overview of Artificial Intelligence

Artificial Intelligence (AI), as we know it today, is a relatively new field. Even though some groundwork had been laid earlier, AI began in earnest with the emergence of the modern computer during the 1940s and 1950s. It was the ability of these new electronic machines to store large amounts of information and process it at very high speeds that gave researchers the vision of building systems which could emulate some human abilities.

During the past forty years, we have witnessed the realization of many of these early researchers' visions. We have seen computer systems shrink in size and cost by several orders of magnitude. We have seen memories increase in storage capacity to the point where they equal a significant fraction of the human brain's storage capacity. We have seen the speed and reliability of systems improve dramatically. And, we have seen the introduction of many impressive software tools.

Given these new hardware and software systems and our improved understanding of Homo sapiens, we are on the threshold of witnessing a whole new horizon of exciting innovations. During the next few decades, we will witness the introduction of many intelligent computer systems never dreamed of by the early visionaries. We will see the introduction of systems which equal or exceed human abilities, and see them become an important part of most business and government operations as well as our own daily activities.

1.1 WHAT IS AI?

What is AI exactly? As a beginning we offer the following definition:

> AI is a branch of computer science concerned with the study and creation of computer systems that exhibit some form of intelligence: systems that learn new concepts and tasks, systems that can reason and draw useful conclusions about the world around us, systems that can understand a natural language or perceive and comprehend a visual scene, and systems that perform other types of feats that require human types of intelligence.

Like other definitions of complex topics, an understanding of AI requires an understanding of related terms such as intelligence, knowledge, reasoning, thought, cognition, learning, and a number of computer-related terms. While we lack precise scientific definitions for many of these terms, we can give general definitions of them. And, of course, one of the objectives of this text is to impart special meaning to all of the terms related to AI, including their operational meanings.

Dictionaries define intelligence as the ability to acquire, understand and apply knowledge, or the ability to exercise thought and reason. Of course, intelligence is more than this. It embodies all of the knowledge and feats, both conscious and unconscious, which we have acquired through study and experience: highly refined sight and sound perception; thought; imagination; the ability to converse, read, write, drive a car, memorize and recall facts, express and feel emotions; and much more.

Intelligence is the integrated sum of those feats which gives us the ability to remember a face not seen for thirty or more years, or to build and send rockets to the moon. It is those capabilities which set Homo sapiens apart from other forms of living things. And, as we shall see, the food for this intelligence is knowledge.

Can we ever expect to build systems which exhibit these characteristics? The answer to this question is yes! Systems have already been developed to perform many types of intelligent tasks, and expectations are high for near term development of even more impressive systems. We now have systems which can learn from examples, from being told, from past related experiences, and through reasoning. We have systems which can solve complex problems in mathematics, in scheduling many diverse tasks, in finding optimal system configurations, in planning complex strategies for the military and for business, in diagnosing medical diseases and other complex systems, to name a few. We have systems which can "understand" large parts of natural languages. We have systems which can see well enough to "recognize" objects from photographs, video cameras and other sensors. We have systems which can reason with incomplete and uncertain facts. Clearly, with these developments, much has been accomplished since the advent of the digital computer.

In spite of these impressive achievements, we still have not been able to produce coordinated, autonomous systems which possess some of the basic abilities of a three-year-old child. These include the ability to recognize and remember numerous diverse objects in a scene, to learn new sounds and associate them with objects and concepts, and to adapt readily to many diverse new situations. These are the challenges now facing researchers in AI. And they are not easy ones. They will require important breakthroughs before we can expect to equal the performance of our three-year old.

To gain a better understanding of AI, it is also useful to know what AI is not. AI is not the study and creation of conventional computer systems. Even though one can argue that all programs exhibit some degree of intelligence, an AI program will go beyond this in demonstrating a high level of intelligence to a degree that equals or exceeds the intelligence required of a human in performing some task. AI is not the study of the mind, nor of the body, nor of languages, as customarily found in the fields of psychology, physiology, cognitive science, or linguistics. To be sure, there is some overlap between these fields and AI. All seek a better understanding of the human's intelligence and sensing processes. But in AI the goal is to develop working computer systems that are truly capable of performing tasks that require high levels of intelligence. The programs are not necessarily meant to imitate human senses and thought processes. Indeed, in performing some tasks differently, they may actually exceed human abilities. The important point is that the systems all be capable of performing intelligent tasks effectively and efficiently.

Finally, a better understanding of AI is gained by looking at the component areas of study that make up the whole. These include such topics as robotics, memory organization, knowledge representation, storage and recall, learning models, inference techniques, commonsense reasoning, dealing with uncertainty in reasoning and decision making, understanding natural language, pattern recognition and machine vision methods, search and matching, speech recognition and synthesis, and a variety of AI tools.

How much success have we realized in AI to date? What are the next big challenges? The answers to these questions form a large part of the material covered in this text. We shall be studying many topics which bear directly or indirectly on these questions in the following chapters. We only mention here that AI is coming of an age where practical commercial products are now available including a variety of robotic devices, vision systems that recognize shapes and objects, expert systems that perform many difficult tasks as well as or better than their human expert counterparts, intelligent instruction systems that help pace a student's learning and monitor the student's progress, ''intelligent'' editors that assist users in building special knowledge bases, and systems which can learn to improve their performance.

1.2 THE IMPORTANCE OF AI

Is AI important? Definitely! AI may be one of the most important developments of this century. It will affect the lives of most individuals in civilized countries by the end of the century. And countries leading in the development of AI by then will emerge as the dominant economic powers of the world.

The importance of AI became apparent to many of the world's leading countries during the late 1970s. Leaders in those countries who recognized the potential for AI were willing to seek approval for long-term commitments for the resources needed to fund intensive research programs in AI. The Japanese were the first to demonstrate their commitment. They launched a very ambitious program in AI research and development. Known as the Fifth Generation, this plan was officially announced in October 1981. It calls for the implementation of a ten-year plan to develop intelligent supercomputers. It is a cooperative effort between government and private companies having an interest in the manufacture of computer products, robotics, and related fields. With a combined budget of about one billion dollars, the Japanese are determined they will realize many of their goals, namely, to produce systems that can converse in a natural language, understand speech and visual scenes, learn and refine their knowledge, make decisions, and exhibit other human traits. If they succeed, and many experts feel they will, their success as a leading economic power is assured.

Following the Japanese, other leading countries of the world have announced plans for some form of AI program. The British initiated a plan called the Alvey Project with a respectable budget. Their goals are not as ambitious as the Japanese but are set to help the British keep abreast and remain in the race. The European Common Market countries have jointly initiated a separate cooperative plan named the ESPRIT program. The French too have their own plan. Other countries including Canada, the Soviet Union, Italy, Austria, and even the Irish Republic and Singapore have made some commitments in funded research and development.

The United States, although well aware of the possible consequences, has made no formal plan. However, steps have been taken by some organizations to push forward in AI research. First, there was the formation of a consortium of private companies in 1983 to develop advanced technologies that apply AI techniques (like VLSI). The consortium is known as the Microelectronics and Computer Technology Corporation (MCC) and is headquartered in Austin, Texas. Second, the Department of Defense Advanced Research Projects Agency (DARPA) has increased its funding for research in AI, including development support in three significant programs: (1) development of an autonomous land vehicle (ALV) (a driverless military vehicle); (2) the development of a pilot's associate (an expert system which provides assistance to fighter pilots), and (3) the Strategic Computing Program (an AI based military supercomputer project). In addition, most of the larger high-tech companies such as IBM, DEC, AT&T, Hewlett Packard, Texas Instruments, and Xerox have their own research programs. A number of smaller companies also have reputable research programs.

Who will emerge as the principal leaders in this race for superiority in the production and sale of that commodity known as knowledge? If forward vision and commitment to purpose are to be the determining factors, then surely the Japanese will be among the leaders if not the leader.

Just how the United States and other leading countries of the world will fare remains to be seen. One thing is clear. The future of a country is closely tied to the commitment it is willing to make in funding research programs in AI.

1.3 EARLY WORK IN AI

As noted above, AI began to emerge as a separate field of study during the 1940s and 1950s when the computer became a commercial reality. Prior to this time, a number of important areas of research that would later help to shape early AI work were beginning to mature. These developments all began to converge during this period. First, there was the work of logicians such as Alonzo Church, Kurt Godel, Emil Post, and Alan Turing. They were carrying on earlier work in logic initiated by Whitehead and Russell, Tarski, and Kleene. This work began in earnest during the 1920s and 1930s. It helped to produce formalized methods for reasoning, the form of logic known as propositional and predicate calculus. It demonstrated that facts and ideas from a language such as English could be formally described and manipulated mechanically in meaningful ways. Turing, sometimes regarded as the father of AI, also demonstrated, as early as 1936, that a simple computer processor (later named the Turing machine) could manipulate symbols as well as numbers.

Second, the new field of cybernetics, a name coined by Norbert Wiener, brought together many parallels between human and machine. Cybernetics, the study of communication in human and machine, became an active area of research during the 1940s and 1950s. It combined concepts from information theory, feedback control systems (both biological and machine), and electronic computers.

Third came the new developments being made in formal grammars. This work was an outgrowth of logic during the early 1900s. It helped to provide new approaches to language theories in the general field of linguistics.

Finally, during the 1950s, the electronic stored program digital computer became a commercial reality. This followed several years of prototype systems including the Mark I Harvard relay computer (1944), the University of Pennsylvania Moore School of Electrical Engineering's ENIAC electronic computer (1947), and subsequent development of the Aberdeen Proving Ground's EDVAC and Sperry-Rand's UNIVAC.

Other important developments during this early period which helped to launch AI include the introduction of information theory due largely to the work of Claude Shannon, neurological theories and models of the brain which were originated by psychologists, as well as the introduction of Boolean algebra, switching theory, and even statistical decision theory.

Of course AI is not just the product of this century. Much groundwork had been laid by earlier researchers dating back several hundred years. Names like Aristotle, Leibnitz, Babbage, Hollerith, and many others also played important roles in building a foundation that eventually led to what we now know as AI.

Work after 1950

During the 1950s several events occurred which marked the real beginning of AI. This was a period noted for the chess playing programs which were developed by researchers like Claude Shannon at MIT (Shannon, 1952, 1955) and Allen Newell at the RAND Corporation (Newell and Simon, 1972). Other types of game playing and simulation programs were also being developed during this time. Much effort was being expended on machine translation programs, and there was much optimism for successful language translation using computers (Weaver, 1955). It was felt that the storage of large dictionaries in a computer was basically all that was needed to produce accurate translations from one language to another. Although this approach proved to be too simplistic, it took several years before such efforts were aborted.

The mid-1950s are generally recognized as the official birth date of AI when a summer workshop sponsored by IBM was held at Dartmouth College. Attendees at this June 1956 seminar included several of the early pioneers in AI including Herbert Gelernter, Trenchard More, John McCarthy, Marvin Minsky, Allen Newell, Nat Rochester, Oliver Selfridge, Claude Shannon, Herbert Simon, and Ray Solomonoff (Newell and Simon, 1972). Much of their discussion focused on the work they were involved in during this period, namely automatic theorem proving and new programming languages.

Between 1956 and 1957 the Logic Theorist, one of the first programs for automatic theorem proving, was completed by Newell, Shaw, and Simon (Newell and Simon, 1972). As part of this development, the first list-processing language called IPL (Information Processing Language) was also completed. Other important events of this period include the development of FORTRAN (begun in 1954) and Noam Chomsky's work between 1955 and 1957 on the theory of generative grammars. Chomsky's work had a strong influence on AI in the area of computational linguistics or natural language processing.

Important events of the late 1950s were centered around pattern recognition and self-adapting systems. During this period Rosenblatt's perceptrons (Rosenblatt, 1958) were receiving much attention. Perceptrons are types of pattern recognition devices that have a simple learning ability based on linear threshold logic (described in detail in Chapter 17). This same period (1958) marked the beginning of the development of LISP by John McCarthy, one of the recognized programming languages of AI. It also marked the formation of the Massachusetts Institute of Technology's AI laboratory. Several important programming projects were also begun during the late 1950s, including the General Problem Solver (GPS) developed by Newell, Shaw, and Simon (Ernst and Newell, 1969) written in IPL, Gelernter's geometry theorem-proving machine written in FORTRAN at the IBM Research Center, and the Elementary Perceiver and Memorizer (EPAM) developed by Edward Feigenbaum and Herbert Simon and written in IPL.

GPS was developed to solve a variety of problems ranging from symbolic integration to word puzzles (such as the missionary-cannibal problem). GPS used a problem-solving technique known as means-end analysis discussed later in Chapter 9. The geometry theorem-proving machine of Gelernter was developed to solve high-school level plane geometry problems. From basic axioms in geometry, the system developed a proof as a sequence of simple subgoals. EPAM was written to study rote learning by machine. The system had a learning and performance component where pairs of nonsense words, a stimulus-response pair, were first learned through repetitive presentations (in different orders). The performance component was then used to demonstrate how well responses to the stimuli were learned.

Some significant AI events of the 1960s include the following.

1961–65 A. L. Samuel developed a program which learned to play checkers at a master's level.

1965 J. A. Robinson introduced resolution as an inference method in logic.

1965 Work on DENDRAL was begun at Stanford University by J. Lederberg, Edward Feigenbaum, and Carl Djerassi. DENDRAL is an expert system which discovers molecular structures given only information of the constituents of the compound and mass spectra data. DENDRAL was the first knowledge-based expert system to be developed.

1968 Work on MACSYMA was initiated at MIT by Carl Engleman, William Martin, and Joel Moses. MACSYMA is a large interactive program which solves numerous types of mathematical problems. Written in LISP, MACSYMA was a continuation of earlier work on SIN, an indefinite integration solving program.

References on early work in AI include McCorduck's *Machines Who Think* (1979), and Newell and Simon's *Human Problem Solving* (1972).

1.4 AI AND RELATED FIELDS

Fields which are closely related to AI and overlap somewhat include engineering, particularly electrical and mechanical engineering, linguistics, psychology, cognitive science, and philosophy. Robotics is also regarded by some researchers as a branch of AI, but this view is not common. Many researchers consider robotics as a separate interdisciplinary field which combines concepts and techniques from AI, electrical, mechanical, and optical engineering.

Psychologists are concerned with the workings of the mind, the mental and emotional processes that drive human behavior. As such, we should not be suprised to learn that researchers in AI have much in common with psychologists. During the past 20 years AI has adopted models of thinking and learning from psychology, while psychologists in turn have patterned many of their experiments on questions first raised by AI researchers. AI has given psychologists fresh ideas and enhanced their ability to model human cognitive functions on the computer. In their book *The Cognitive Computer*, Schank and Childers (1984) estimate that ". . . AI has contributed more to psychology than any other discipline for some time."

Because they share so many common interests, it has been claimed that AI researchers think less like computer scientists than they do psychologists and philosophers. As a consequence, researchers from AI and psychology have joined together at some universities to form a separate discipline known as *cognitive science*. This name has also been adopted by a few new companies offering AI services and products. Like AI researchers, cognitive scientists are interested in the computation processes required to perform certain human functions, and in the mental and computational states related to such processes. Like computer science, cognitive science is still searching for a theory and foundation that will qualify it as a science.

AI also has much in common with engineering, particularly electrical (EE) and mechanical engineering (ME). AI and EE are both interested in computational processes and systems, and how they relate to senses of perception such as vision and speech. ME and AI share common interests in their desire to build intelligent robots. Their goals are to build robots that can see and move around, perform mechanical tasks, and understand human speech.

The field of linguistics shares an interest in the theory of grammars and languages with AI. Both fields have a desire to build a well-founded theory, and to see the development of systems that understand natural languages, that can synthesize speech, and that are capable of language translations.

Finally, AI has some overlap with almost all fields in that it offers the potential for broad applications. Applications have already been proven in such areas as medicine, law, manufacturing, economics, banking, biology, chemistry, defense, civil engineering, and aerospace to name a few. And, it is only a matter of time before applications will permeate the home.

1.5 SUMMARY

In this introductory chapter, we have defined AI and terms closely related to the field. We have shown how important AI will become in the future as it will form the foundation for a number of new consumer commodities, all based on knowledge. It was noted that countries willing to commit appropriate resources to research in this field will emerge as the world's economic leaders in the not too distant future.

We briefly reviewed early work in AI, considering first developments prior to 1950, the period during which the first commercial computers were introduced. We then looked at post-1950 developments during which AI was officially launched as a separate field of computer science. Fields which overlap with and are closely related to AI were also considered, and the areas of commonality between the two presented.

2

Knowledge: General Concepts

The important role that knowledge plays in building intelligent systems is now widely accepted by practictioners in AI. Recognition of this important fact was necessary before successful, real-world systems could be built. Because of this importance, a significant amount of coverage is devoted to knowledge in this text. We will be looking at the important roles it plays in all of the subfields of AI. In this chapter, we attempt to set the stage for what follows by gaining some familiarity with knowledge, and a better appreciation of its power. As noted in Chapter 1, the whole text is in a sense all about knowledge, and is organized to reflect the way it dominates thinking and the direction of research in the field of AI.

2.1 INTRODUCTION

Early researchers in AI believed that the best approach to solutions was through the development of general purpose problem solvers, that is, systems powerful enough to prove a theorem in geometry, to perform a complex robotics task, or to develop a plan to complete a sequence of intricate operations. To demonstrate their theories, several systems were developed including several logic theorem provers and a general problem solver system (described in Chapter 9).

All of the systems developed during this period proved to be impotent as general problem solvers. They required much hand tailoring of problem descriptions and ad hoc guidance in their solution steps. The approaches they used proved to be too general to be effective. The systems became effective only when the solution methods incorporated domain specific rules and facts. In other words, they became effective as problem solvers only when specific knowledge was brought to bear on the problems. The realization that specific knowledge was needed to solve difficult problems gradually brought about the use of domain specific knowledge as an integral part of a system. It eventually led to what we now know as knowledge-based systems. Since the acceptance of this important fact, successful problem solvers in many domains have been developed.

2.2 DEFINITION AND IMPORTANCE OF KNOWLEDGE

Knowledge can be defined as the body of facts and principles accumulated by humankind or the act, fact, or state of knowing. While this definition may be true, it is far from complete. We know that knowledge is much more than this. It is having a familiarity with language, concepts, procedures, rules, ideas, abstractions, places, customs, facts, and associations, coupled with an ability to use these notions effectively in modeling different aspects of the world. Without this ability, the facts and concepts are meaningless and, therefore, worthless. The meaning of knowledge is closely related to the meaning of intelligence. Intelligence requires the possession of and access to knowledge. And a characteristic of intelligent people is that they possess much knowledge.

In biological organisms, knowledge is likely stored as complex structures of interconnected neurons. The structures correspond to symbolic representations of the knowledge possessed by the organism, the facts, rules, and so on. The average human brain weighs about 3.3 pounds and contains an estimated number of 10^{12} neurons. The neurons and their interconnection capabilities provide about 10^{14} bits of potential storage capacity (Sagan, 1977).

In computers, knowledge is also stored as symbolic structures, but in the form of collections of magnetic spots and voltage states. State-of-the-art storage in computers is in the range of 10^{12} bits with capacities doubling about every three to four years. The gap between human and computer storage capacities is narrowing rapidly. Unfortunately, there is still a wide gap between representation schemes and efficiencies.

A common way to represent knowledge external to a computer or a human is in the form of written language. For example, some facts and relations represented in printed English are

Joe is tall.
Bill loves Sue.
Sam has learned to use recursion to manipulate linked lists in several programming languages.

The first item of knowledge above expresses a simple fact, an attribute possessed by a person. The second item expresses a complex binary relation between two persons. The third item is the most complex, expressing relations between a person and more abstract programming concepts. To truly understand and make use of this knowledge, a person needs other world knowledge and the ability to reason with it.

Knowledge may be declarative or procedural. Procedural knowledge is compiled knowledge related to the performance of some task. For example, the steps used to solve an algebraic equation are expressed as procedural knowledge. Declarative knowledge, on the other hand, is passive knowledge expressed as statements of facts about the world. Personnel data in a database is typical of declarative knowledge. Such data are explicit pieces of independent knowledge.

Frequently, we will be interested in the use of heuristic knowledge, a special type of knowledge used by humans to solve complex problems. Heuristics are the knowledge used to make good judgments, or the strategies, tricks, or "rules of thumb" used to simplify the solution of problems. Heuristics are usually acquired with much experience. For example, in locating a fault in a TV set, an experienced technician will not start by making numerous voltage checks when it is clear that the sound is present but the picture is not, but instead will immediately reason that the high voltage flyback transformer or related component is the culprit. This type of reasoning may not always be correct, but it frequently is, and then it leads to a quick solution.

Knowledge should not be confused with data. Feigenbaum and McCorduck (1983) emphasize this difference with the following example. A physican treating a patient uses both knowledge and data. The data is the patient's record, including patient history, measurements of vital signs, drugs given, response to drugs, and so on, whereas the knowledge is what the physician has learned in medical school and in the years of internship, residency, specialization, and practice. Knowledge is what the physician now learns in journals. It consists of facts, prejudices, beliefs, and most importantly, heuristic knowledge.

Thus, we can say that knowledge includes and requires the use of data and information. But it is more. It combines relationships, correlations, dependencies, and the notion of gestalt with data and information.

Even with the above distinction, we have been using knowledge in its broader sense up to this point. At times, however, it will be useful or even necessary to distinguish between knowledge and other concepts such as belief and hypotheses. For such cases we make the following distinctions. We define *belief* as essentially any meaningful and coherent expression that can be represented. Thus, a belief may be true or false. We define a *hypothesis* as a justified belief that is not known to be true. Thus, a hypothesis is a belief which is backed up with some supporting evidence, but it may still be false. Finally, we define *knowledge* as true justified belief. Since these distinctions will be made more formal in later chapters, we need not attempt to give any further definitions of truth or justification at this time.

Two other knowledge terms which we shall occasionally use are epistemology and metaknowledge. *Epistemology* is the study of the nature of knowledge, whereas *metaknowldge* is knowledge about knowledge, that is, knowledge about what we know.

In this section we have tried to give a broader definition of knowledge than that commonly found in dictionaries. Clearly, we have not offered a scientific definition, nor will we in this text. That will have to wait. But, without a scientific definition, we are not able to measure knowledge. How then will we know when a system has enough knowledge to perform a specified task? Can we expect to build intelligent systems without having a more precise definition of either knowledge or intelligence? In spite of our ignorance about knowledge, the answer is definitely yes. We can and have built intelligent systems as we shall see in the following chapters.

As it happened, in 1950 Turing proposed a way to demonstrate if a machine can think and, therefore, exhibit intelligence. Known as the Turing test, it involves isolating a person in a room with only a computer teletype. If the person cannot distinguish between a man imitating a woman and a computer imitating a man imitating a woman on the teletype, the computer succeeded in passing the test. (Turing's test is often mistakenly understood to be simply a test of whether or not a person can distinguish between some other hidden person and a computer impersonating a person.) To date no one has developed a system able to pass the Turing test. Of course, it may be that no one has tried. Even so, systems need not pass such a test to be useful, and many systems have already been built that exhibit a high level of intelligence.

Finally, our overall picture of knowledge cannot be complete without also knowing the meaning of closely related concepts such as understanding, learning, thinking, remembering, and reasoning. These concepts all depend on the use of knowledge. But then just what is learning, or reasoning, or understanding? Here too we will find dictionary definitions lacking. And, as in the case of knowledge and intelligence, we cannot give scientific definitions for any of these terms either. But, we will gain a deeper understanding and appreciation for the concepts through our study of AI. In particular, we will see the difficulties encountered in attempting to implement such concepts in computer programs. For in programs, one must be precise.

The Importance of Knowledge

AI has given new meaning and importance to knowledge. Now, for the first time, it is possible to "package" specialized knowledge and sell it with a system that can use it to reason and draw conclusions. The potential of this important development is only now beginning to be realized. Imagine being able to purchase an untiring, reliable advisor that gives high level professional advice in specialized areas, such as manufacturing techniques, sound financial strategies, ways to improve one's health, top marketing sectors and strategies, optimal farming plans, and many other important matters. We are not far from the practical realization of this, and those who create and market such systems will have more than just an economic advantage over the rest of the world.

As noted in Chapter 1, the Japanese recognized the potential offered with these knowledge systems. They were the first to formally proceed with a plan to commit substantial resources toward an accelerated program of development for super-computers and knowledge-based systems. In their excellent book on the Fifth Generation, Feigenbaum and McCorduck (1983) present convincing arguments for the importance that should be ascribed to such programs. They argue that the time is right for the exploitation of AI and that the leaders in this field will become the leaders in world trade. By forging ahead in research and the development of powerful knowledge-based systems, the Japanese are assuring themselves of a leading role in the control and dissemination of packaged knowledge. Feigenbaum and McCorduck laud the Japanese for their boldness and farsightedness in moving ahead with this ambitious program.

2.3 KNOWLEDGE-BASED SYSTEMS

One of the important lessons learned in AI during the 1960s was that general purpose problem solvers which used a limited number of laws or axioms were too weak to be effective in solving problems of any complexity. This realization eventually led to the design of what is now known as knowledge-based systems, systems that depend on a rich base of knowledge to perform difficult tasks.

Edward Feigenbaum summarized this new thinking in a paper at the International Joint Conference on Artificial Intelligence (IJCAI) in 1977. He emphasized the fact that the real power of an expert system comes from the knowledge it possesses rather than the particular inference schemes and other formalisms it employs. This new view of AI systems marked the turning point in the development of more powerful problem solvers. It formed the basis for some of the new emerging expert systems being developed during the 1970s including MYCIN, an expert system developed to diagnose infectious blood diseases.

Since this realization, much of the work done in AI has been related to so-called knowledge-based systems, including work in vision, learning, general problem solving, and natural language understanding. This in turn has led to more emphasis being placed on research related to knowledge representation, memory organization, and the use and manipulation of knowledge.

Knowledge-based systems get their power from the expert knowledge that has been coded into facts, rules, heuristics, and procedures. The knowledge is stored in a knowledge base separate from the control and inferencing components (Figure 2.1). This makes it possible to add new knowledge or refine existing knowledge without recompiling the control and inferencing programs. This greatly simplifies the construction and maintenance of knowledge-based systems.

In the knowledge lies the power! This was the message learned by a few farsighted researchers at Stanford University during the late 1960s and early 1970s.

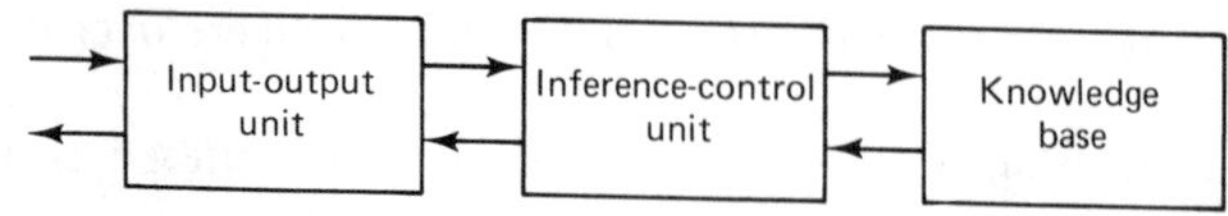

Figure 2.1 Components of a knowledge-based system.

The proof of their message was provided in the first knowledge-based expert systems which were shown to be more than toy problem solvers. These first systems were real world problem solvers, tackling such tasks as determining complex chemical structures given only the atomic constituents and mass spectra data from samples of the compounds, and later performing medical diagnoses of infectious blood diseases.

2.4 REPRESENTATION OF KNOWLEDGE

Given the fact that knowledge is important and in fact essential for intelligent behavior, the representation of knowledge has become one of AI's top research priorities. What exactly is meant by knowledge representation? As defined above, knowledge consists of facts, concepts, rules, and so forth. It can be represented in different forms, as mental images in one's thoughts, as spoken or written words in some language, as graphical or other pictures, and as character strings or collections of magnetic spots stored in a computer (Figure 2.2). The representations we shall be concerned with in our study of AI are the written ones (character strings, graphs, pictures) and the corresponding data structures used for their internal storage.

Any choice of representation will depend on the type of problem to be solved and the inference methods available. For example, suppose we wish to write a program to play a simple card game using the standard deck of 52 playing cards. We will need some way to represent the cards dealt to each player and a way to express the rules. We can represent cards in different ways. The most straightforward way is to record the suit (clubs, diamonds, hearts, spades) and face values (ace, 2, 3, . . . , 10, jack, queen, king) as a symbolic pair. So the queen of hearts might

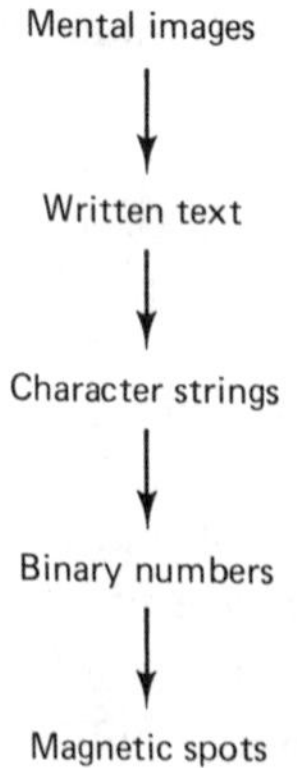

Figure 2.2 Different levels of knowledge representation.

be represented as <queen, hearts>. Alternatively, we could assign abbreviated codes (c6 for the 6 of clubs), numeric values which ignore suit (1, 2, . . . ,13), or some other scheme. If the game we wish to play is bridge, suit as well as value will be important. On the other hand, if the game is black jack, only face values are important and a simpler program will result if only numeric values are used.

To see how important a good representation is, one only needs to try solving a few simple problems using different representations. Consider the problem of discovering a pattern in the sequence of numbers 1 1 2 3 4 7. A change of base in the number from 10 to 2 transforms the number to

0 1 1 0 1 1 0 1 1 0 1 1 0 1 1 0 1 1.

Clearly a representation in the proper base greatly simplifies finding the pattern solution.

Sometimes, a state diagram representation will simplify solutions. For example, the Towers of Hanoi problem requires that n discs (say $n = 3$), each a different size, be moved from one of three pegs to a third peg without violating the rule a disc may only be stacked on top of a larger disc. Here, the states are all the possible disc-peg configurations, and a valid solution path can easily be traced from the initial state through other connected states to the goal state.

Later we will study several representation schemes that have become popular among AI practitioners. Perhaps the most important of these is first order predicate logic. It has become important because it is one of the few methods that has a well-developed theory, has reasonable expressive power, and uses valid forms of inferring. Its greatest weakness is its limitation as a model for commonsense reasoning. A typical statement in this logic might express the family relationship of fatherhood as FATHER(john, jim) where the predicate father is used to express the fact that John is the father of Jim.

Other representation schemes include frames and associative networks (also called semantic and conceptual networks), fuzzy logic, modal logics, and object-oriented methods. Frames are flexible structures that permit the grouping of closely related knowledge. For example, an object such as a ball and its properties (size, color, function) and its relationship to other objects (to the left of, on top of, and so on) are grouped together into a single structure for easy access. Networks also permit easy access to groups of related items. They associate objects with their attributes, and linkages show their relationship to other objects.

Fuzzy logic is a generalization of predicate logic, developed to permit varying degrees of some property such as tall. In classical two-valued logic, TALL(john) is either true or false, but in fuzzy logic this statement may be partially true. Modal logic is an extension of classical logic. It was also developed to better represent commonsense reasoning by permitting conditions such as likely or possible. Object oriented representations package an object together with its attributes and functions, therefore, hiding these facts. Operations are performed by sending messages between the objects.

Another representation topic covered more fully later is uncertainty. Not all knowledge is known with certainty. Knowledge may be vague, contradictory, or incomplete. Yet we would still like to be able to reason and make decisions. Humans do remarkably well with fuzzy, incomplete knowledge. We would also like our AI programs to demonstrate this versatility.

2.5 KNOWLEDGE ORGANIZATION

The organization of knowledge in memory is key to efficient processing. Knowledge-based systems may require tens of thousands of facts and rules to perform their intended tasks. It is essential then that the appropiate facts and rules be easy to locate and retrieve. Otherwise, much time will be wasted in searching and testing large numbers of items in memory.

Knowledge can be organized in memory for easy access by a method known as indexing. It amounts to grouping the knowledge in a way that key words can be used to access the group. The key words "point" to the knowledge groups. As a result, the search for some specific chunk of knowledge is limited to the group only, a fraction of the knowledge base rather than the whole memory.

The choice of representation can simplify the organization and access operations. For example, frames linked together in a network represent a versatile organization structure. Each frame will contain all closely associated information about an object and pointers to related object frames making it possible to quickly gain access to this information. Subsequent processing then typically involves only a few related frames.

2.6 KNOWLEDGE MANIPULATION

Decisions and actions in knowledge-based systems come from manipulation of the knowledge in specified ways. Typically, some form of input (from a user keyboard or sensors) will initiate a search for a goal or decision. This requires that known facts in the knowledge-base be located, compared (matched), and possibly altered in some way. This process may set up other subgoals and require further inputs, and so on until a final solution is found. The manipulations are the computational equivalent of reasoning. This requires a form of inference or deduction, using the knowledge and inferring rules.

All forms of reasoning require a certain amount of searching and matching. In fact, these two operations by far consume the greatest amount of computation time in AI systems. For this reason it is important to have techniques available that limit the amount of search and matching required to complete any given task. Much research has been done in these areas to find better methods. The research has paid off with methods which help to make many otherwise intractable problems solvable. They help to limit or avoid the so-called combinatorial explosion in problems which are so common in search.

2.7 ACQUISITON OF KNOWLEDGE

One of the greatest bottlenecks in building knowledge-rich systems is the acquisition and validation of the knowledge. Knowledge can come from various sources, such as experts, textbooks, reports, technical articles, and the like. To be useful, the knowledge must be accurate, presented at the right level for encoding, complete in the sense that all essential facts and rules are included, free of inconsistencies, and so on. Eliciting facts, heuristics, procedures, and rules from an expert is a slow, tedious process. Experience in building dozens of expert systems and other knowledge-based systems over the past fifteen years has shown this to be the single most time-consuming and costly part of the building process. This has led to the development of some sophisticated acquisition tools, including a variety of intelligent editors, editors which provide much assistance to the knowledge engineers and system users.

The acquisition problem has also stimulated much research in machine learning systems, that is, systems which can learn new knowledge autonomously without the aid of humans. Since knowledge-based systems depend on large quantities of high quality knowledge for their success, it is essential that better methods of acquisition, refinement, and validation be developed. The ultimate goal is to develop techniques that permit systems to learn new knowledge autonomously and continually improve the quality of the knowledge they possess.

2.8 SUMMARY

In this chapter we have defined and described the importance of knowledge in building intelligent AI computer systems. A definition of knowledge was given, and the differences between knowledge, belief, and hypotheses were described. The difference between knowledge and data was also clarified.

The recognition of the important role that knowledge plays in AI systems has led several countries to commit substantial resources to long-range research programs in AI. In particular, the Japanese government has undertaken a cooperative program with several industrial companies to develop intelligent supercomputers within a ten-year period.

Also in this chapter, we considered some of the basic research priorities related to knowledge-based systems: knowledge representation, knowledge organization, knowledge manipulation, and knowledge acquisition. These topics form the main theme of the remaining chapters.

EXERCISES

2.1 Define and describe the difference between knowledge, belief, hypotheses, and data.

2.2 What is the difference between declarative and procedural knowledge?

2.3 Look up the meaning of epistemology in a good encyclopedia and prepare a definition.

2.4 The Turing test has often been incorrectly interpreted as being a test of whether or not a person could distinguish between responses from a computer and responses from a person. How does this differ from the real Turing test? Are the two tests equivalent? If not, explain why they are not?

2.5 What important knowledge products are currently being marketed like other commodities? What are some new knowledge products likely to be sold within the next ten years?

2.6 Briefly describe the meaning of knowledge representation and knowledge acquisition.

2.7 Give four different ways to represent the fact that John is Bill's father.

3

LISP and Other AI Programming Languages

LISP is one of the oldest computer programming languages. It was invented by John McCarthy during the late 1950s, shortly after the development of FORTRAN. LISP (for *LIS*t *P*rocessing) is particularly suited for AI programs because of its ability to process symbolic information effectively. It is a language with a simple syntax, with little or no data typing and dynamic memory management. There are several dialects of LISP including FRANZLISP, INTERLISP, MACLISP, QLISP, SCHEME, and COMMON LISP. The COMMON LISP version is a recent attempt to standardize the language to make it more portable and easier to maintain.

LISP has become the language of choice for most AI practitioners. It was practically unheard of outside the research community until AI began to gain some popularity ten to fifteen years ago. Since then, special LISP processing machines have been built and its popularity has spread to many new sectors of business and government. In this chapter we give a summary of the important features of LISP and briefly introduce PROLOG and other AI languages.

3.1 INTRODUCTION TO LISP: SYNTAX AND NUMERIC FUNCTIONS

The basic building blocks of LISP are the atom, list, and the string. An atom is a number or string of contiguous characters, including numbers and special characters. A list is a sequence of atoms and/or other lists enclosed within parentheses. A string is a group of characters enclosed in double quotation marks. Examples of atoms, lists and strings are

VALID ATOMS	INVALID ATOMS[1]
this-is-a-symbolic-atom	(abc
bill	123abc
100004352	abcd'ef
mountain_top	(a b)
var	ab cde
block#6	
a12345	

VALID LISTS	INVALID LISTS
(this is a list)	this is not a list
(a (a b) c def)	(abcdef ghij
(father sam (joe bill sue))	)abck efg(
(mon tue wed thur fri sat sun)	(a b c (d e)
()	((a b) (

VALID STRINGS	INVALID STRINGS
"this is a string"	this is not a string
"a b c d e fgh #$%@!"	"neither is this
"please enter your name"	nor" this"

Since a list may contain atoms as well as other lists, we will call the basic unit members top elements. Thus, the top elements of the list (a b (c d) e (f)) are a, b, (c d), e, and (f). The elements c and d are top elements of the sublist (c d).

Atoms, lists, and strings are the only valid objects in LISP. They are called symbolic-expressions or s-expressions. Any s-expression is potentially a valid program. And those, believe it or not, are essentially the basic syntax rules for LISP. Of course, to be meaningful, a program must obey certain rules of semantics, that is, a program must have meaning.

LISP programs run either on an interpreter or as compiled code. The interpreter examines source programs in a repeated loop, called the read-evaluate-print loop. This loop reads the program code, evaluates it, and prints the values returned by the program. The interpreter signals its readiness to accept code for execution by printing a prompt such as the -> symbol. For example, to find the sum of the three numbers 5, 6, and 9 we type after the prompt the following function call:

```
-> (+ 5 6 9)
20
->
```

[1] Some dialects require that symbolic atoms begin with a letter and do not include parens or single quotes.

Note that LISP uses *prefix* notation, and the + symbol is the function name for the sum of the arguments that follow. The function name and its arguments are enclosed in parentheses to signify that it is to be evaluated as a function. The read-evaluate-print loop reads this expression, evaluates it, and prints the value returned (20). The interpreter then prints the prompt to signal its readiness to accept the next input. More complicated computations can be written as a single embedded expression. For example, to compute the centigrade equivalent of the Fahrenheit temperature 50, for the mathematical expression (50 * 9 / 5) + 32 we would write the corresponding LISP function

```
-> (+ (* (/ 9 5) 50) 32)
122
->
```

Each function call is performed in the order in which it occurs within the parentheses. But, in order to compute the sum, the argument (* (/ 9 5) 50) must first be evaluated. This requires that the product of 50 and 9/5 be computed, which in turn requires that the quotient 9/5 be evaluated. The embedded function (/ 9 5) returns the quotient 1.8 to the multiply function to give (* 1.8 50). This is then evaluated and the value 90 is returned to the top (sum) function to give (+ 90 32). The final result is the sum 122 returned to the read-evaluate-print loop for printing.

The basic numeric operations are +, -, *, and /. Arguments may be integers or real values (floating point), and the number of arguments a function takes will, of course, differ. For example, + and * normally take zero or more arguments, while - and / take two. These and a number of other basic functions are predefined in LISP. Examples of function calls and the results returned are given in Table 3.1. In addition to these basic calls, some LISP implementations include mnemonic names for arithmetic operations such as plus and times.

LISP tries to evaluate everything, including the arguments of a function. But, three types of elements are special in that they are constant and always evaluate to themselves, returning their own value: numbers, the letter *t* (for logical true), and

TABLE 3.1 PREDEFINED NUMERIC FUNCTIONS

Function call	Value returned	Remarks
(+ 3 5 8 4)	20	+ takes zero or more arguments. The sum of zero arguments is 0.
(− 10 12)	− 2	− takes two arguments.
(* 2 3 4)	24	* takes zero or more arguments. The product of no arguments is 1, and the product of 1 argument is the value of the argument.
(/ 25 2)	12.5	/ takes two arguments.

nil (for logical false). Nil is also the same as the empty list (). It is the only object in LISP that is both an atom and a list. Since these elements return their own value, the following are valid expressions.

```
->6
6
->t
T
->NIL
NIL
```

3.2 BASIC LIST MANIPULATION FUNCTIONS IN LISP

Sometimes we wish to take atoms or lists literally and not have them evaluated or treated as function calls as, for example, when the list represents data. To accomplish this, we precede the atom or the list with a single quotation mark, as in 'man or as in '(a b c d). The quotation mark informs the interpreter that the atom or list should not be evaluated, but should be taken literally as an atom or list.

Variables in LISP are symbolic (nonnumeric) atoms. They may be assigned values, that is, bound to values with the function setq. Setq takes two arguments, the first of which must be a variable. It is never evaluated and should not be in quotation marks. The second argument is evaluated (unless in quotation marks) and the result is bound to the first argument. The variable retains this value until a new assignment is made. When variables are evaluated, they return the last value bound to them. Trying to evaluate an undefined variable (one not previously bound to a value) results in an error. Some examples of the use of setq are as follows (note that comments in LISP code may be placed anywhere after a semicolon).

```
->(setq x 10)          ;the number 10 evaluates to itself
10                     ;is bound to x and 10 is returned
->x                    ;the variable x is evaluated to
10                     ;return the value it is bound to
->(setq x (+ 3 5))     ;x is reset to the value (+ 3 5)
8                      ;and that value returned
->(setq x '(+ 3 5))    ;x is reset to the literal value
(+ 3 5)                ;(+ 3 5), quote inhibits evaluation
->y                    ;the variable y was not previously
Unbound variable:Y     ;bound to a value, causing an error
```

Some basic symbol processing functions are car, cdr, cons, and list. Examples of these functions are given in Table 3.2. Car takes one argument, which must be a list. It returns the first top element of the list. Cdr also takes a list as its argument, and it returns a list consisting of all elements except the first. Cons takes two

TABLE 3.2 BASIC LIST MANIPULATION FUNCTIONS

Function call	Value returned	Remarks
(car '(a b c))	a	Car takes one argument, a list, and returns the first element.
(cdr '(a b c))	(b c)	Cdr takes one argument, a list, and returns a list with the first element removed.
(cons 'a '(b c))	(a b c)	Cons takes two arguments, an element, and a list and returns a list with the element inserted at the beginning.
(list 'a '(b c))	(a (b c))	List take any number of arguments and returns a list with the arguments as elements.

arguments, an element and a list. It constructs a new list by making the element the first member of the list. List takes any number of arguments, and makes them into a list, with each argument a top member.

Note the quotation marks preceding the arguments in the function calls of Table 3.2. As pointed out above, an error will result if they are not there because the interpreter will try to evaluate each argument before evaluating the function. Notice the difference in results with and without the quotation marks.

```
->(cons '(* 2 3) '(1))      ;the literal list (* 2 3) is
((* 2 3 ) 1)                ;"consed" to the list (1)
->(cons (* 2 3) '(1))       ;the evaluated list (* 2 3) is
(6 1)                       ;consed to the list (1)
->(setq x '(a b c))         ;x is bound to the literal list
(A B C)                     ;(a b c)
->'x                        ;the quote ' inhibits evaluation
X                           ;of x
->x                         ;but unquoted x evaluates to its
(A B C)                     ;previously bound value
```

The syntax for a function call is

```
(function-name arg1 arg2 ...)
```

where any number of arguments may be used. When a function is called, the arguments are first evaluated from left to right (unless within quotation marks) and then the function is executed using the evaluated argument values. Complete the list manipulation examples below.

```
->(car (cdr '(a b c d)))          ;extracts the second element
B
->(cdr car '((a b) c d))          ;extracts the list (b)
(B)
->(cons 'one '(two three))        ;inserts the element one in
(ONE TWO THREE)                   ;the list (two three)
->(cons (car '(a b c)             ;lists may continue on
   (cdr '(a b c)))                ;several lines, but parens
(A B C)                           ;must always balance!
->(list '(a b) 'c 'd))            ;makes a list of the top
((A B) C D)                       ;elements
->
```

Sequences of car and cdr functions may be abbreviated by concatenating the letter *a* for car and *d* for cdr within the letters *c*, and *r*. For example, to extract c from the list

$$(a\ (b\ c)\ d)$$

we write cadadr to abbreviate the sequence car cdr car cdr. Thus

```
->(cadadr '(a (b c) d))
C
->
```

Other useful list manipulation functions are append, last, member, and reverse. Append merges arguments of one or more lists into a single list. Last takes one argument, a list, and returns a list containing the last element. Member takes two arguments, the second of which must be a list. If the first argument is a member of the second one, the remainder of the second list is returned beginning with the member element. Reverse takes a list as its argument and returns a list with the top elements in reverse order from the input list. Table 3.3 summarizes these operations.

TABLE 3.3 ADDITIONAL LIST MANIPULATION FUNCTIONS

Function call	Value returned	Remarks
(append '(a) '(b c))	(a b c)	merges two or more lists into a single list.
(last '(a b c d))	(d)	returns a list containing the last element.
(member 'b '(a b d))	(b d)	returns remainder of second argument list starting with element matching first argument.
(reverse '(a (b c) d))	(d (b c) a)	returns list with top elements in reverse order.

Complete the practice examples below.

```
->(append '(a (b c)) '(d e))         ;returns a single list of
(A (B C) D E)                        ;top element input lists
->(append '(a) '(b c) '(d))
(A B C D)
->(last '(a b (c d) (e)))            ;returns the last top
((E))                                ;element as a list
->(member '(d) '(a (d) e f))         ;returns the tail of
((D) E F)                            ;list from member element
->(reverse '(a b (c d) e))           ;returns the list with top
(E (C D) B A)                        ;elements in reverse order
```

3.3 DEFINING FUNCTIONS, PREDICATES, AND CONDITIONALS

Defining Functions

Now that we know how to call functions, we should learn how to define our own. The function named defun is used to define functions. It requires three arguments: (1) the new function name, (2) the parameters for the function, and (3) the function body or LISP code which performs the desired function operations. The format is

```
(defun name (parm1 parm2 ...) body).
```

Defun does not evaluate its arguments. It simply builds a function which may be called like any other function we have seen. As an example, we define a function named averagethree to compute the average of three numbers.

```
->(defun averagethree (n1 n2 n3)
        (/ (+ n1 n2 n3) 3))
AVERAGETHREE
->
```

Note that defun returned the name of the function. To call averagethree, we give the function name followed by the actual arguments

```
->(averagethree 10 20 30)
20
->
```

When a function is called, the arguments supplied in the call are evaluated unless they are in quotation marks and bound to (assigned to) the function parameters. The argument values are bound to the parameters in the same order they were given in the definition. The parameters are actually dummy variables (n_1, n_2, n_3 in averagethree) used to make it possible to give a function a general definition.

Predicate Functions

Predicates are functions that test their arguments for some specific condition. Except for the predicate "member" (defined above), predicates return true (t) or false (nil), depending on the arguments. The most common predicates are

atom
equal
evenp
greaterp (or >)
<=
lessp (or <)
>=
listp
null
numberp
oddp
zerop

The predicate "atom" takes one argument. It returns t if the argument is an atom and nil otherwise. Equal takes two arguments and returns t if they evaluate to the same value, and nil otherwise. Evenp, numberp, oddp, and zerop are tests on a single numeric argument. They return t if their argument evaluates to an even number, a number, an odd number, or zero respectively. Otherwise they each return nil.

Greaterp and lessp each take one or more arguments. If there is only one argument, each returns t. If more than one argument is used, greaterp returns t if the arguments, from left to right, are successively larger; otherwise nil is returned. Lessp requires that the arguments be successively smaller from left to right to return t. Otherwise it returns nil. The predicates >= and <= have the same meaning as greaterp and lessp respectively, except they return t if successive elements are also equal. Finally listp and null both take a single argument. Listp returns t if its argument evaluates to a list, and nil otherwise. Null returns t if its argument evaluates to nil; otherwise it returns nil. Examples for calls using each of these predicates are given in Table 3.4.

TABLE 3.4 THE MOST COMMON PREDICATE CALLS

Function call	Value returned	Remarks
(atom 'aabb)	t	aabb is a valid atom
(equal 'a (car '(a b))	t	a equals a, but note that (equal 1 1.0) returns nil
(evenp 3)	nil	3 is not an even number
(numberp 10ab)	nil	10ab is not a number
(oddp 3)	t	3 is an odd number
(zerop .000001)	nil	argument is not zero
(greaterp 2 4 27)	t	arguments are succeedingly larger, from left to right
(lessp 5 3 1 2)	nil	arguments are not successively smaller, left to right
(listp '(a))	t	(a) is a valid list
(null nil)	t	nil is an empty list

The Conditional Cond

Predicates are one way to make tests in programs and take different actions based on the outcome of the test. However, to make use of the predicates, we need some construct to permit branching. Cond (for conditonal) is like the if..then..else construct.

The syntax for cond is

```
(cond   (<test_1>  <action_1>)
        (<test_2>  <action_2>)
           .           .
           .           .
           .           .
        (<test_k>  <action_k>))
```

Each (<test$_i$> <action$_i$>), i=1, . . ., k, is called a clause. Each clause consists of a test portion and an action or result portion. The first clause following the cond is executed by evaluating <test$_1$>. If this evaluates to non nil, the <action$_1$> portion is evaluated, its value is returned, and the remaining clauses are skipped over. If <test$_1$> evaluates to nil, control passes to the second clause without evaluating <action$_1$> and the procedure is repeated. If all tests evaluate to nil, cond returns nil.

We illustrate the use of cond in the following function maximum2 which returns the maximum of two numbers.

```
->(defun maximum2 (a b)
       (cond ((> a b) a)
             (t b)))
MAXIMUM2
->
```

When maximum2 is executed, it starts with the first clause following the cond. The test sequence is as follows: if (the argument bound to) a is greater than (that bound to) b, return a, else return b. Note the t in the second clause preceding b. This forces the last clause to be evaluated when the first clause is not.

```
->(maximum2 234 320)
320
->
```

A slightly more challenging use of cond finds the maximum of three numbers in the function maximum3.

```
->(defun maximum3 (a b c)
       (cond ((> a b) (cond ((> a c) a)
                            (t c)))
             ((> b c) b)
             (t c)))
->MAXIMUM3
```

Trying maximum3 we have

```
->(maximum3 20 30 25)
30
->
```

Common LISP also provides a form of the more conventional if..then..else conditional. It has the form

```
(if test <then-action> <else-action>)
```

For this form, test is first evaluated. If it evaluates to non nil, the <then-action> is evaluated and the result returned; otherwise the <else-action> is evaluated and its value returned. The <else-action> is optional. If omitted, then when test evaluates to nil, the if function returns nil.

Logical Functions

Like predicates, logical functions may also be used for flow of control. The basic logical operations are and, or, and not. Not is the simplest. It takes one argument and returns t if the argument evaluates to nil; it returns nil if its argument evaluates to non-nil. The functions and and or both take any number of arguments. For both, the arguments are evaluated from left to right. In the case of and, if all arguments evaluate to non-nil, the value of the last argument is returned; otherwise nil is returned. The arguments of or are evaluated until one evaluates to non-nil, in which case it returns the argument value; otherwise it returns nil.

Some examples of the operators and, or and not in expressions are

```
->(setq x '(a b c))
(A B C)
->(not (atom x))
T
->(not (listp x))
NIL
->(or (member 'e x) (member 'b x))
(B C)
->(or (equal 'c (car x)) (equal 'b (car x)))
NIL
->(and (listp x) (equal 'c (caddr x)))
C
->(or (and (atom x) (equal 'a x))
      (and (not (atom x)) (atom (car x))))
T
->
```

3.4 INPUT, OUTPUT, AND LOCAL VARIABLES

Without knowing how to instruct our programs to call for inputs and print messages or text on the monitor or a printer, our programs will be severely limited. The operations we need for this are performed with the input-output (I/O) functions. The most commonly used I/O functions are read, print, prinl, princ, terpri, and format.

Read takes no arguments. When read appears in a procedure, processing halts until a single s-expression is entered from the keyboard. The s-expression is then returned as the value of read and processing continues. For example, if we include a read in an arithmetic expression, an appropriate value should be entered when the interpreter halts.

```
->(+ 5 (read))
6
11
->
```

When the interpreter looked for the second argument for +, it found the read statement which caused it to halt and wait for an input from the keyboard. If we enter 6 as indicated, read returns this value, processing continues, and the sum 11 is then returned.

Print takes one argument. It prints the argument as it is received, and then returns the argument. This makes it possible to print something and also pass the same thing on to another function as an argument. When print is used to print an expression, its argument is preceded by the carriage-return and line-feed characters (to start a new line) and is followed by a space. In the following example, note the double printing. This occurs because print first prints its argument and then returns it, causing it to be printed by the read-evaluate-print loop.

```
->(print '(a b c))
(A B C)
(A B C)
->(print "hello there")
"hello there"
"hello there"
```

Notice that print even prints the double quotation marks defining the string.

Prinl is the same as print except that the new-line characters and space are not provided (this is not true for all implementations of Common LISP).

```
->((prin1 '(hello)) (prin1 '(hello)))
(HELLO)(HELLO)
->
```

We can avoid the double quotation marks in the output by using the printing function princ. It is the same as prinl except it does not print the unwanted quotation marks. For example, we use princ to print the following without the marks.

```
->(princ "hello there")
hello there "hello there"
->
```

Princ eliminated the quotes, but the echo still remains. Again, that is because princ returned its argument (in a form that LISP could read), and, since that was the last thing returned, it was printed by the read-evaluate-print loop. In a typical program, the returned value would not be printed on the screen as it would be absorbed (used) by another function.

The primitive function terpri takes no arguments. It introduces a new-line (carriage return and line feed) wherever it appears and then returns nil. Below is a program to compute the area of a circle which uses several I/O functions, including user prompts.

```
->(defun circle-area ()
     (terpri)
     (princ "Please enter the radius: ")
     (setq radius (read))
     (princ "The area of the circle is: ")
     (princ (* 3.1416 radius radius))
     (terpri))
CIRCLE-AREA
->(circle-area)
Please enter the radius: 4
The area of the circle is: 50.2656
->
```

Notice that princ permits us to print multiple items on the same line and to introduce a new-line sequence we use terpri.

The format function permits us to create cleaner output than is possible with just the basic printing functions. It has the form (format <destination> <string> arg1 arg2 . . .). Destination specifies where the output is to be directed, like to the monitor or some other external file. For our purposes, destination will always be *t* to signify the default output, the monitor. String is the desired output string, but intermixed with format directives which specify how each argument is to be represented. Directives appear in the string in the same order the arguments are to be printed. Each directive is preceded with a tilde character (~) to identify it as a directive. We list only the most common directives below.

~A The argument is printed as though princ were used.
~S The argument is printed as though prinl were used.

˜D The argument which must be an integer is printed as a decimal number.

˜F The argument which must be a floating-point number is printed as a decimal floating-point number.

˜C The argument is printed as character output.

˜% A new-line is printed.

The field widths for appropriate argument values are specified with an integer immediatly following the tilde symbol; for example, ˜5D specifies an integer field of width 5. As an example of format, suppose *x* and *y* have been bound to floating-point numbers 3.0 and 9.42 respectively. Using format, these numbers can be embedded within a string of text.

```
->(format t "Circle radius = ˜2F˜%Circle area = ˜3F" x y)
"Circle radius = 3.0
Circle area = 9.42"
->
```

Constructs for Local Variables

Frequently, it is desirable to designate local variables (variables which are defined only within a given procedure) rather than the global assignments which result from setq. Of course parameters named as arguments in a function definition are local. The values they are assigned within the function are accessible only within that function. For example, consider the variables *x* and *y* in the following:

```
->(setq y '(a b c))
(A B C)
->(setq x '(d e f))
(D E F)
->(defun local-var (x)
     (setq y (cons x y)))
LOCAL-VAR
->(local-var 6)
(6 A B C)
->x
(D E F)
->y
(A B C)
->
```

The variable *x* in the defun is local in scope. It reverts back to its previous value after the function local-var is exited. The variable *y*, on the other hand, is global. It is accessible from any procedure and retains its value unless reset with setq.

The let and prog constructs also permit the creation of local variables. The syntax for the let function is

(let ((var$_1$ val$_1$) (var$_2$ val$_2$)...) <s-expressions>)

where each var$_i$ is a different variable name and val$_i$ is an initial value assigned to each var$_i$, respectively. When let is executed, each val$_i$ is evaluated and assigned to the corresponding var$_i$, and the s-expressions which follow are then evaluated in order. The value of the last expression evaluated is then returned. If an initial value is not included with a var$_i$, it is assigned nil, and the parentheses enclosing it may be omitted.

```
->(let ((x 'a)
        (y 'b)
        (z 'c))
    (cons x (cons y (list z))))
(A B C)
->
```

The prog function is similar to let in that the first arguments following it are a list of local variables where each element is either a variable name or a list containing a variable name and its initial value. This is followed by the body of the prog, and any number of s-expressions.

Prog executes list s-expressions in sequence and returns nil unless it encounters a function call named return. In this case the single argument of return is evaluated and returned. Prog also permits the use of unconditional go statements and labels (atom labels) to identify the go-to transfer locations. With the go and label statements, prog permits the writing of unstructured programs and, therefore, is not recommended for general use. An example of a function like memb (member) which uses iteration, will illustrate this use. The main function memb requires two arguments, an element and a list.

```
->(defun memb (el 1st)
    (prog ()
      start
      (cond ((equal el (car 1st)) (return 1st)))
      (setq 1st (cdr 1st))
      (go start)))
MEMB
->
```

Note that prog used here requires no local variables. Also note the label start, the transfer (loop back) point for the go statement. The second clause of the cond executes when the first clause is skipped because setq is non-nil!

3.5 ITERATION AND RECURSION

Iteration Constructs

We saw one way to perform iteration using the prog construct in the previous section. In this section, we introduce a structured form of iteration with the do construct, which is somewhat like the while loop in Pascal.

The do statement has the form

```
(do(<var1 val1> <var-update1>)
   (<var2 val2> <var-update2>)
      .
      .
      .
   (<test> <return-value>)
   (<s-expressions>))
```

The val_i are initial values which are all evaluated and then bound to the corresponding variables var_i in parallel. Following each such statement are optional update statements which define how the var_i are to be updated with each iteration. After the variables are updated during an iteration, the test is evaluated, and if it returns non-nil (true), the return-value is evaluated and returned. The s-expressions forming the body of the construct are optional. If present, they are executed each iteration until an exit test condition is encountered. An example of the factorial function will illustrate the do construct.

```
>(defun factorial (n)
    (do ((count n (- count 1))
         (product n (* product (- count 1))
         ((equal 0 count) product)))
FACTORIAL
->
```

In this definition there is no need to include a body. All operations required to compute the factorial of *n* are contained in the initial values and the update procedures.

There is also a do* construct which is the same as do, except the assignment of initial values is made to each var_i sequentially before the next form is evaluated.

In addition to the do and prog constructs for iteration, one may use a loop function. Loop has the simple form

```
(loop <s-expressions>)
```

where the s-expressions are evaluated repeatedly until a call to a return is encountered.

Of course, let and other functions can be embedded within the loop construct if local variables are needed.

Recursion

For many problems, recursion is the natural method of solution. Such problems occur frequently in mathematical logic, and the use of recursion will often result in programs which are both elegant and simple. A recursive function is one which calls itself successively to reduce a problem to a sequence of simpler steps. Recursion requires a stopping condition and a recursive step.

We illustrate with a recursive version of factorial. The recursive step in factorial is the product of *n* and factorial(*n*-1). The stopping condition is reached when *n* = 0.

```
->(defun factorial (n)
     (cond ((zerop n) 1)
           (t (* n (factorial (- n 1))))))
FACTORIAL
->(factorial 6)
720
->
```

Note the stopping condition on the second line of the function definition, and the recursive step on the last line.

We present another example of recursion which defines the member function called newmember.

```
->(defun newmember (el 1st)
     (cond ((null 1st) nil)
           ((equal el (car 1st)) 1st)
           ((t (newmember el (cdr 1st)))))
NEWMEMBER
->
```

If the atom *c* and list (*a b c d*) are given as the arguments in the call to newmember, *c* gets bound to el and (*a b c d*) is bound to *lst*. With these bindings, the first cond test fails, since *lst* is not null. Consequently, the second test is executed. This also fails since *el*, bound to *c*, does not equal the car of *1st* which is *a*. The last test of the cond construct is forced to succeed because of the t test. This initiates a recursive call to newmember with the new arguments *el* (still bound to *c*) and the cdr of *lst* which is (*b c d*). Again, a match fails during the cond tests; so another recursive call is made, this time with arguments *el* (still bound to *c*) and *lst* now bound to (*c d*). When this call is executed, a match is found in the second cond test so the value of *lst* (*c d*) is returned.

3.6 PROPERTY LISTS AND ARRAYS

Property Lists

One of the unique and most useful features of LISP as an AI language is the ability to assign properties to atoms. For example, any object, say an atom which represents a person, can be given a number of properties which in some way characterize the person, such as height, weight, sex, color of eyes and hair, address, profession, family members, and so on. Property list functions permit one to assign such properties to an atom, and to retrieve, replace, or remove them as required.

The function putprop assigns properties to an atom. It takes three arguments: an object name (an atom), a property or attribute name, and property or attribute value. For example, to assign properties to a car, we can assign properties such as make, year, color, and style with the following statements:

```
->(putprop 'car 'ford 'make)
FORD
->(putprop 'car 1988 'year)
1988
->(putprop 'car 'red 'color)
RED
->(putprop 'car 'four-door 'style)
FOUR-DOOR
->
```

As you can see, the form of putprop is

```
(putprop object value attribute)
```

where value is returned. The object, car, will retain these properties until they are replaced with new ones or until removed with the remprop function which takes two arguments, the object and its attribute. In other words, properties are global assignments. To retrieve a property value, such as the color of car, we use the function get, which also takes the two arguments object and attribute.

```
->(get 'car 'color)
RED
->(get 'car 'make)
FORD
->(putprop 'car 'blue 'color)
BLUE
->(get 'car 'color)
BLUE
->(remprop 'car 'color)
BLUE
->(get 'car 'color)
NIL
->
```

The property value may be an atom or a list. For example, if Danny has pets named Schultz, Penny, and Etoile, they can be assigned as

```
->(putprop 'danny '(schultz penny etoile) 'pets)
(SCHULTZ PENNY ETOILE)
->(get 'danny 'pets)
(SCHULTZ PENNY ETOILE)
->
```

To add a new pet named Heidi without knowing the existing pets one can do the following:

```
->(putprop 'danny (cons 'heidi (get 'danny 'pets)) 'pets)
(HEIDI SCHULTZ PENNY ETOILE)
->
```

Items can be removed from a list of values in a similar manner.

Since some versions of Common LISP do not provide the putprop function, it may be necessary to define your own. This can be done with the following code.

```
->(defun putprop (object value property)
     (setf (get object property) value))
PUTPROP
->
```

The new function setf used in the above definition is like setq except it is more general. It is an assignment function which also takes two arguments, the first of which may be either an atom or an access function (like car, cdr, and get) and the second, the value to be assigned. When the first argument is an atom, setf behaves the same as setq. It simply binds the evaluated second argument to the first. When the first argument is an access function, setf places the second argument, the value, at the location accessed by the access function. For example, if (*a b c*) has been bound to *x*, the expression (setf (car x) 'd) will replace the *a* in (*a b c*) with *d*. Likewise, setf can be used directly to assign or replace a property value.

```
->(setf (get 'car 'color) 'pink)
PINK
->(get 'car 'color)
PINK
->
```

As we shall see in later chapters, property lists provide us with a convenient mechanism with which to represent knowledge. One such representation is the conceptual network where objects, their attributes, and relations to other objects are easily

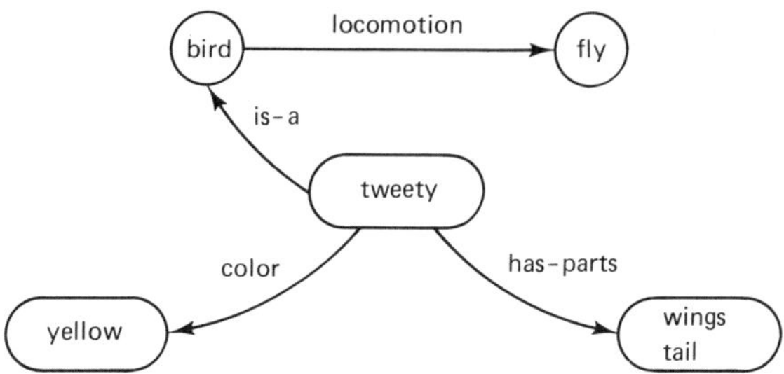


```
(putprop 'bird 'fly 'locomotion)
(putprop 'tweety 'bird 'is-a)
(putprop 'tweety '(wings tail) 'has-parts)
(putprop 'tweety 'yellow 'color)
```

Figure 3.1 Representation of facts and relations as a network.

expressed. In Figure 3.1 some facts about Tweety, the famous AI bird, have been represented as a network using property lists.

Arrays

Single- or multiple-dimension arrays may be defined in LISP using the make-array function. The items stored in the array may be any LISP object. For example, to create an array with ten cells named myarray, we bind the unquoted name to an array using setf (or setq) with the make-array function and a specification of the number of cells.

```
->(setf myarray (make-array '(10)))
#A(NIL NIL NIL NIL NIL NIL NIL NIL NIL NIL)
->
```

Note that the function returns the pound sign (#) followed by an A and the array representation with its cells initially set to nil.

To access the contents of cells, we use the function aref which takes two arguments, the name of the array and the index value. Since the cells are indexed starting at zero, an index value of 9 must be used to retrieve the contents of the tenth cell.

```
->(aref myarray 9)
NIL
->
```

To store items in the array, we use the function setf as we did above to store properties on a property list. So, to store the items 25, red, and (sam sue linda) in the first, second, and third cells of myarray, we write

```
->(setf (aref myarray 0) 25)
25
->(setf (aref myarray 1) 'red)
RED
->(setf (aref myarray 2) '(sam sue linda))
(SAM SUE LINDA)
->
```

3.7 MISCELLANEOUS TOPICS

We complete our presentation of LISP in this section with a few additional topics, including the functions mapcar, eval, lambda, trace and untrace, and a brief description of the internal representation of atoms and lists.

Mapping Functions

Mapcar is one of several mapping functions provided in LISP to apply some function successively to one or more lists of elements. The first argument of mapcar is a function, and the remaining argument(s) are lists of elements to which the named function is applied. The results of applying the function to successive members of the lists are placed in a new list which is returned. For example, suppose we wish to add 1 to each element of the list (5 10 15 20 25). We can do this quite simply with mapcar and the function 1+.

```
->(mapcar '1+ '(5 10 15 20 25))
(6 11 16 21 26)
->
```

If we wish to add the corresponding elements of two lists (even of unequal length), say (1 2 3 4 5 6) and (1 2 3 4), we use the + function with the lists to obtain the sum of the first four elements.

```
->(mapcar '+ '(1 2 3 4 5 6) '(1 2 3 4))
(2 4 6 8)
->
```

It should be clear that mapcar can be used in a variety of ways in lieu of iterative functions. And, the function being applied to the lists may be either user defined or built-in.

Lambda Functions

When a function is defined with defun, its name and address must be stored in a symbol table for retrieval whenever it is called in a program. Sometimes, however, it is desirable to use a function only once in a program. This will be the case when it is used in a mapping operation such as with mapcar, which must take a procedure as its first argument. LISP provides a method of writing unnamed or anonymous functions that are evaluated only when they are encountered in a program. Such functions are called lambda functions. They have the following form

```
(lambda (arguments) <function-body>)
```

We illustrate the use of a lambda function to compute the cubed value of a list of numbers. This will be accomplished by using mapcar to apply a lambda cube function to a list of numbers. When a function is called by another function, it should be preceded by the characters #' to indicate that the following item is a function. This is equivalent to preceding the function with a single quotation mark (') or the function named function in some LISP dialects. The lambda function we need to find the cube of a single number is just (lambda (x) (* x x x)). We use this with mapcar now to find the cubes of the numbers (1 2 3 4)

```
->(defun cube-list (lst)
     (mapcar #'(lambda (x) (* x x x)) lst))
CUBE-LIST
->(cubelist (1 2 3 4))
(1 8 27 64)
->
```

Internal Storage

As we have seen, lists are flexible data structures that can shrink or grow almost without limit. This is made possible through the use of linked cell structures in memory to represent lists. These can be visualized as storage boxes having two components which correspond to the car and cdr of a list. The cells are called cons-cells, because they are constructed with the cons function, where the left component points to the first element of a list (the car of the list) and the right component points to the remainder of the list (the cdr of the list). An example of the representation for the list (a (b c (d)) e f) is given in Figure 3.2.

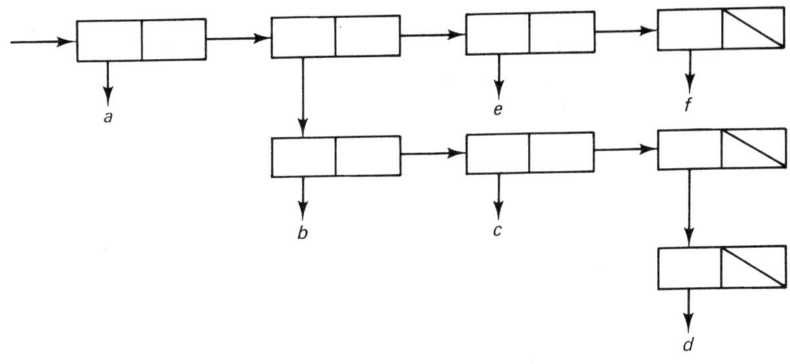

Figure 3.2 Representation for the list *(a (b c (d)) e f)*.

The boxes with the slash in the figure represent nil. When cons is used to construct a list, the cons-cells are created with pointers to the appropriate elements as depicted in Figure 3.2. The use of such structures permits lists to be easily extended or modified.

3.8 PROLOG AND OTHER AI PROGRAMMING LANGUAGES

PROLOG (for *PRO*gramming in *LOG*ic) was invented by Alain Colmerauer and his associates at the University of Marseilles during the early 1970s. PROLOG uses the syntax of predicate logic to perform symbolic, logical computations. It has a number of built-in features (particularly control features) that limit its flexibility but simplify many aspects of programming.

Programming in PROLOG is accomplished by creating a data base of facts and rules about objects, their properties, and their relationships to other objects. Queries can then be posed about the objects and valid conclusions will be determined and returned by the program. Responses to user queries are determined through a form of inferencing control known as resolution. This process is described in the next chapter.

Facts in PROLOG are declared with predicates and constants written in lowercase letters. The arguments of predicates are enclosed in parentheses and separated with commas. For example, some facts about family relationships could be written as

```
sister(sue,bill)
parent(ann,sam)
parent(joe,ann)
male(joe)
female(ann)
```

The first fact is the predicate sister with arguments sue and bill. This predicate has the intended meaning that Sue is the sister of Bill. Likewise, the next predicate has the meaning that Ann is the parent of Sam, and so on.

Rules in PROLOG are composed of a condition or ''if'' part, and a conclusion or ''then'' part separated by the symbol :- which is read as ''if'' (conclusion if conditions). Rules are used to represent general relations which hold when all of the conditions in the if part are satisfied. Rules may contain variables, which must begin with uppercase letters. For example to represent the general rule for grandfather, we write

```
grandfather(X,Z) :- parent(X,Y), parent(Y,Z), male(X)
```

This rule has the following meaning:

For all X, Y, and Z,
X is the grandfather of Z

IF X is the parent of Y, and
Y is the parent of Z, and
X is a male

Note that separate conditions in the rule are separated by commas. The commas act as conjunctions, that is, like and statements where all conditions in the right-hand side must be satisfied for the rule to be true.

Given a data base of facts and rules such as that above, we may make queries by typing after the query symbol -? statements such as

```
?- parent(X,sam)
X=ann
?- male(joe)
yes
?-grandfather(X,Y)
X=joe, Y=sam
?-female(joe)
no
```

Note that responses to the queries are given by returning the value a variable can take to satisfy the query or simply with yes (true) or no (false).

Queries such as these set up a sequence of one or more goals that are to be satisfied. A goal is satisfied if it can be shown to logically follow from the facts and rules in the data base. This means that a proper match must be found between predicates in the query and the database and that all subgoals must be satisfied through consistent substitutions of constants and variables for variable arguments. To determine if a consistent match is possible, PROLOG searches the data base and tries to make substitutions until a permissible match is found or failure occurs. For example, when the query

```
?-grandfather(X,sam)
```

is given, a search is made until the grandfather predicate is found in the data base. In this case, it is the head of the above grandfather rule. The constant Sam is substituted for Z, and an attempt is then made to satisfy the body of the rule. This requires that the three conditions (subgoals) in the body are satisfied. Attempts to satisfy these conditions are made from left to right in the body by searching and finding matching predicates and making consistent variable substitutions by (1) substituting Joe for X in the first subgoal parent(X,Y) and later in the third subgoal male(X), (2) substituting Sam for Z in the second subgoal parent(Y,Z), and (3) substituting Ann for Y in the first two subgoals parent(X,Y) and parent(Y,Z). Since consistent variable substitutions can be made in this case, PROLOG returns X = Joe, in response to the unknown X in the query. PROLOG will continue searching through the database until a consistent set of substitutions is found. If all substitutions cannot be found, failure is reported with the printout no.

Lists in PROLOG are similar to list data structures in LISP. A PROLOG list is written as a sequence of items separated by commas, and enclosed in square brackets. For example, a list of the students Tom, Sue, Joe, Mary, and Bill is written as

```
[tom,sue,joe,mary,bill]
```

A list is either empty [] or nonempty. If nonempty, a list is considered as an object with a head and a tail, corresponding to the car and cdr of a list in LISP. Thus, the head of the above list is Tom, and the tail is the remaining sublist [sue,joe,mary,bill]. Since the tail is a list, it too is either empty or it has a head and tail. This suggests a binary tree representation similar to linked LISP cons cells.

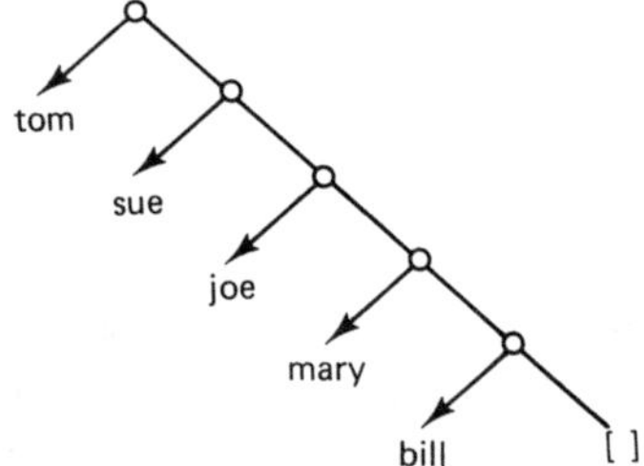

PROLOG provides a notation to separate the head and tail, the vertical bar |, as in [Head|Tail]. This permits one to define the Head of a list as any number of items followed by a | and the list of remaining items. Thus, the list [a,b,c,d] may be written as $[a,b,c,d]=[a|[b,c,d]]=[a,b|[c,d]]=[a,b,c,d|[]]$.

Matching with lists is accomplished as follows:

```
?-[Head|Tail] = [tom,sue,joe,mary].
Head = tom
Tail = [sue,joe,mary]
```

A number of list manipulation predicates are available in most PROLOG implementations, including append, member, conc (concatenate), add, delete, and so on. One can also define special predicates as needed from the basic definitions included. For example, a definition of the member function member(*X*,*L*), where *X* is an item and *L* is a list, can be written as a fact and a rule.

```
member(X,[X|Tail]).

member(X,[Head|Tail]) :-
    member(X,Tail).
```

The first condition states that X is a member of the list L if X is the head of L. Otherwise, the rule states that X is a member of L if X is a member of the tail of L. Thus,

```
?- member(c,[a,b,c,d])
yes
?- member(b,[a,[b,c],d])
no
```

PROLOG has numeric functions and relations, as well as list handling capabilities, which give it some similarity to LISP. In subsequent chapters, we will see examples of some PROLOG programs. For more details on the syntax, predicates, and other features of PROLOG the reader is referred to the two texts, Bratko (1986), and Clocksin and Mellish (1981).

Other programming languages used in AI include C, object oriented extensions to LISP such as Flavors, and languages like Smalltalk. The language C has been used by some practictioners in AI because of its popularity and its portability. Object oriented languages, although they have been introduced only recently, have been gaining much popularity. We discuss these languages in Chapter 8.

3.9 SUMMARY

In this chapter we introduced LISP, the programming language of AI. We defined LISP syntax and examined a number of built-in functions, including the numeric functions (+, -, *, /), and the list manipulation functions (car, cdr, cons, list, append, last, member, and reverse). We also defined a number of predicate functions such as equal, null, numberp, atom, listp, and so on. We then described how to define our own functions using defun. We saw how to use the conditional cond and the logical functions and, or, and not.

The input-output functions print, prinl, princ, read, terpri, and format were defined and example programs presented. We saw how to write iterative programs with the do, loop, and prog constructs. We saw how to define and use local variables with the let and prog functions. We discussed recursion, and saw examples of its use. We then looked at property lists, a valuable method with which to assign multiple values or properties to variable atoms. Array definitions and examples were briefly introduced, and a few miscellaneous topics such as mapping functions (mapcar), the lambda form, and internal list representations concluded our treatment of LISP.

Finally, we introduced the logic programming language PROLOG, and gave some simple examples of its use. We concluded the chapter with a few comments regarding other AI languages and noted that object oriented languages are described in detail in Chapter 8.

EXERCISES

3.1 Write a LISP program to convert centigrade temperatures to Fahrenheit.

3.2 Define a function called first-element that takes a list as its argument and returns the first top element of the list.

3.3 Define a function called number-of-elements that takes a list as its only argument and returns the number of top elements in the list.

3.4 Define a function called rotate that takes a list and rotates the elements by one position as in

```
(rotate '(a b c d)) returns (D A B C).
```

3.5 Define a function newlist that takes one argument and returns it as a list. If the argument is already a list, including the empty list, newlist returns it without change. If the argument is an atom, it returns it as a list.

3.6 Define a function named addlist that takes two arguments, an item and a list. If the item is in the list, the function returns the list unaltered. If the item is not in the list, the function returns the list with the item entered as the first element. For example,

```
(addlist 'c '(a b c d)) returns (a b c d) but
(addlist 'e '(a b c)) returns (e a b c).
```

3.7 Define a function construct-sentence which takes two lists as arguments. The lists are simple sentences such as

```
(the dog barked) or
(the dog chased the car).
```

The function should check to see if the subject of the sentence is the same in both sentences. If so, the function should return the compound sentence

```
(the dog barked and chased the car).
```

If the two sentences do not have the same subject, the function should return nil.

3.8 Write a function called word-member which takes one list as argument. The function should print a prompt to the user

```
(please type any word)
```

If the word typed is a member of the list the function should return *t*, otherwise nil. For example,

```
> (word-member '(the brown fox ran))
(please type any word) fox
T
```

3.9 Write a function talk that takes no arguments. It prints the prompt (without quotation marks or parentheses)

What is your name?

The function should then read an input from the same line two spaces following the question mark (e.g., Susan), issue a line feed and carriage return, and then print

Hello, Susan. What is your best friend's name?

As before, the user should type a name (e.g., Joe). The program should then respond with

Very interesting; Joe is my best friend too!

3.10 Write an iterative function named nth-item that takes two arguments, a positive integer and a list. The function returns the item in the nth position in the list. If the integer exceeds the number of elements in the list, it returns nil. For example,

(nth-item 3 '(a b c d e f)) returns c.

3.11 Write a recursive function named power that takes two numeric arguments, n and m. The function computes the nth power of m (m^n). Be sure to account for the the case where $n = 0$, that is $m^0 = 1$. For example,

(power 4 3) returns $4^3 = 64$.

3.12 Define a function called intersection which takes two lists as arguments. The function should return a list containing single occurrences of all elements which appear in both input lists. For example,

(intersection '(a b e g k l) '(a c e g x y))

should return (a e g).

3.13 Write a new function called new-reverse that takes a list as argument. The function should return the list in reversed order. Do not use the LISP function reverse to define new-reverse. For example,

(new-reverse '(a b (f e) l)) should return
(l (f e) b a).

3.14 Write an iterative function named sum-all using do that takes an integer n as argument and returns the sum of the integers from 1 to n. For example,

(sum-all 5) should return 15.

3.15 Write a function called sum-squares which uses mapcar to find the sum of the squares of a list of integers. The function takes a single list as its argument. Write a lambda function which mapcar uses to find the square of the integers in the list. For example,

```
(sum-squares (2 3 1 4)) should return 30.
```

3.16 Write a PROLOG program that answers questions about family members and relationships. Include predicates and rules which define sister, brother, father, mother, grandchild, grandfather, and uncle. The program should be able to answer queries such as the following:

```
?- father(X, bob).
?- grandson(X, Y).
?- uncle(bill, sue).
?- mother(mary, X).
```

3.17 Trace the search sequence PROLOG follows in satisfying the following goal:

```
?- member(c,[a,b,c,d]).
```

3.18 Write a function called match that takes two arguments, a pattern and a clause. If the first argument, the pattern, is a variable identified by a question mark followed by a lowercase letter (like ?x or ?y), the function should return a list giving the variable and the corresponding clause, since a variable matches anything. If the pattern is not a variable, it should return *t* only if the pattern and the clause are identical. Otherwise, the function should return nil.

PART 2
Knowledge Representation

4
Formalized Symbolic Logics

Starting with this chapter, we begin a study of some basic tools and methodologies used in AI and the design of knowledge-based systems. The first representation scheme we examine is one of the oldest and most important, First Order Predicate Logic (FOPL). It was developed by logicians as a means for formal reasoning, primarily in the areas of mathematics. Following our study of FOPL, we then investigate five additional representation methods which have become popular over the past twenty years. Such methods were developed by researchers in AI or related fields for use in representing different kinds of knowledge.

After completing these chapters, we should be in a position to best choose which representation methods to use for a given application, to see how automated reasoning can be programmed, and to appreciate how the essential parts of a system fit together.

4.1 INTRODUCTION

The use of symbolic logic to represent knowledge is not new in that it predates the modern computer by a number of decades. Even so, the application of logic as a practical means of representing and manipulating knowledge in a computer was not demonstrated until the early 1960s (Gilmore, 1960). Since that time, numerous systems have been implemented with varying degrees of success. Today, First Order Predicate Logic (FOPL) or Predicate Calculus as it is sometimes called, has assumed one of the most important roles in AI for the representation of knowledge.

A familiarity with FOPL is important to the student of AI for several reasons. First, logic offers the only formal approach to reasoning that has a sound theoretical foundation. This is especially important in our attempts to mechanize or automate the reasoning process in that inferences should be correct and logically sound. Second, the structure of FOPL is flexible enough to permit the accurate representation of natural language reasonably well. This too is important in AI systems since most knowledge must originate with and be consumed by humans. To be effective, transformations between natural language and any representation scheme must be natural and easy. Finally, FOPL is widely accepted by workers in the AI field as one of the most useful representation methods. It is commonly used in program designs and widely discussed in the literature. To understand many of the AI articles and research papers requires a comprehensive knowledge of FOPL as well as some related logics.

Logic is a formal method for reasoning. Many concepts which can be verbalized can be translated into symbolic representations which closely approximate the meaning of these concepts. These symbolic structures can then be manipulated in programs to deduce various facts, to carry out a form of automated reasoning.

In FOPL, statements from a natural language like English are translated into symbolic structures comprised of predicates, functions, variables, constants, quantifiers, and logical connectives. The symbols form the basic building blocks for the knowledge, and their combination into valid structures is accomplished using the syntax (rules of combination) for FOPL. Once structures have been created to represent basic facts or procedures or other types of knowledge, inference rules may then be applied to compare, combine and transform these "assumed" structures into new "deduced" structures. This is how automated reasoning or inferencing is performed.

As a simple example of the use of logic, the statement "All employees of the AI-Software Company are programmers" might be written in FOPL as

$$(\forall x)\ (\text{AI-SOFTWARE-CO-EMPLOYEE}(x) \rightarrow \text{PROGRAMMER}(x))$$

Here, $\forall x$ is read as "for all x" and $\rightarrow$ is read as "implies" or "then." The predicates AI-SOFTWARE-CO-EMPLOYEE(x), and PROGRAMMER(x) are read as "if *x* is an AI Software Company employee," and "*x* is a programmer" respectively. The symbol *x* is a variable which can assume a person's name.

If it is also known that Jim is an employee of AI Software Company,

$$\text{AI-SOFTWARE-CO-EMPLOYEE}(\text{jim})$$

one can draw the conclusion that Jim is a programmer.

$$\text{PROGRAMMER}(\text{jim})$$

The above suggests how knowledge in the form of English sentences can be translated into FOPL statements. Once translated, such statements can be typed into a knowledge base and subsequently used in a program to perform inferencing.

We begin the chapter with an introduction to Propositional Logic, a special case of FOPL. This will be constructive since many of the concepts which apply to this case apply equally well to FOPL. We then proceed in Section 4.3 with a more detailed study of the use of FOPL as a representation scheme. In Section 4.4 we define the syntax and semantics of FOPL and examine equivalent expressions, inference rules, and different methods for mechanized reasoning. The chapter concludes with an example of automated reasoning using a small knowledge base.

4.2 SYNTAX AND SEMANTICS FOR PROPOSITIONAL LOGIC

Valid statements or sentences in PL are determined according to the rules of propositional syntax. This syntax governs the combination of basic building blocks such as propositions and logical connectives. Propositions are elementary atomic sentences. (We shall also use the term *formulas* or *well-formed formulas* in place of sentences.) Propositions may be either true or false but may take on no other value. Some examples of simple propositions are

It is raining.
My car is painted silver.
John and Sue have five children.
Snow is white.
People live on the moon.

Compound propositions are formed from atomic formulas using the logical connectives not and or if . . . then, and if and only if. For example, the following are compound formulas.

It is raining and the wind is blowing.
The moon is made of green cheese or it is not.
If you study hard you will be rewarded.
The sum of 10 and 20 is not 50.

We will use capital letters, sometimes followed by digits, to stand for propositions; T and F are special symbols having the values true and false, respectively. The following symbols will also be used for logical connectives

~ for not or negation
& for and or conjunction

V for or or disjunction

→ for if . . . then or implication

↔ for if and only if or double implication

In addition, left and right parentheses, left and right braces, and the period will be used as delimiters for punctuation. So, for example, to represent the compound sentence "It is raining and the wind is blowing" we could write (*R* & *B*) where *R* and *B* stand for the propositions "It is raining" and "the wind is blowing," respectively. If we write (*R* V *B*) we mean "it is raining or the wind is blowing or both" that is, V indicates inclusive disjunction.

Syntax

The syntax of PL is defined recursively as follows.

T and F are formulas.

If *P* and *Q* are formulas, the following are formulas:

$$(\tilde{}P)$$

$$(P \;\&\; Q)$$

$$(P \vee Q)$$

$$(P \rightarrow Q)$$

$$(P \leftrightarrow Q)$$

All formulas are generated from a finite number of the above operations.

An example of a compound formula is

$$((P \;\&\; (\tilde{}Q \vee R) \rightarrow (Q \rightarrow S))$$

When there is no chance for ambiguity, we will omit parentheses for brevity: (˜(*P* & (˜*Q*))) can be written as ˜(*P* & ˜*Q*). When omitting parentheses, the precedence given to the connectives from highest to lowest is ˜, &, V, →, and ↔. So, for example, to add parentheses correctly to the sentence

$$P \;\&\; \tilde{}Q \vee R \rightarrow S \leftrightarrow U \vee W$$

we write

$$((((P \;\&\; \tilde{}(Q)) \vee R) \rightarrow S) \leftrightarrow (U \vee W))$$

Semantics

The semantics or meaning of a sentence is just the value true or false; that is, it is an assignment of a truth value to the sentence. The values true and false should not be confused with the symbols T and F which can appear within a sentence. Note however, that we are not concerned here with philosophical issues related to meaning but only in determining the truthfulness or falsehood of formulas when a particular interpretation is given to its propositions. An *interpretation* for a sentence or group of sentences is an assignment of a truth value to each propositional symbol. As an example, consider the statement (P & ~Q). One interpretation (I_1) assigns true to P and false to Q. A different interpretation (I_2) assigns true to P and true to Q. Clearly, there are four distinct interpretations for this sentence.

Once an interpretation has been given to a statement, its truth value can be determined. This is done by repeated application of semantic rules to larger and larger parts of the statement until a single truth value is determined. The semantic rules are summarized in Table 4.1 where t, and t' denote any true statements, f, and f' denote any false statements, and a is any statement.

TABLE 4.1 SEMANTIC RULES FOR STATEMENTS

Rule number	True statements	False statements
1.	T	F
2.	~f	~t
3.	t & t'	f & a
4.	$t \vee a$	a & f
5.	$a \vee t$	$f \vee f'$
6.	$a \rightarrow t$	$t \rightarrow f$
7.	$f \rightarrow a$	$t \leftrightarrow f$
8.	$t \leftrightarrow t'$	$f \leftrightarrow t$
9.	$f \leftrightarrow f'$	

We can now find the meaning of any statement given an interpretation I for the statement. For example, let I assign true to P, false to Q and false to R in the statement

((P & ~Q) → R) V Q

Application of rule 2 then gives ~Q as true, rule 3 gives (P & ~Q) as true, rule 6 gives (P & ~Q) → R as false, and rule 5 gives the statement value as false.

Properties of Statements

Satisfiable. A statement is satisfiable if there is some interpretation for which it is true.

Contradiction. A sentence is contradictory (unsatisfiable) if there is no interpretation for which it is true.

Valid. A sentence is valid if it is true for every interpretation. Valid sentences are also called tautologies.

Equivalence. Two sentences are equivalent if they have the same truth value under every interpretation

Logical consequences. A sentence is a logical consequence of another if it is satisfied by all interpretations which satisfy the first. More generally, it is a logical consequence of other statements if and only if for any interpretation in which the statements are true, the resulting statement is also true.

A valid statement is satisfiable, and a contradictory statement is invalid, but the converse is not necessarily true. As examples of the above definitions consider the following statements.

P is satisfiable but not valid since an interpretation that assigns false to P assigns false to the sentence P.

$P \vee \neg P$ is valid since every interpretation results in a value of true for $(P \vee \neg P)$.

$P \,\&\, \neg P$ is a contradiction since every interpretation results in a value of false for $(P \,\&\, \neg P)$.

P and $\neg(\neg P)$ are equivalent since each has the same truth values under every interpretation.

P is a logical consequence of $(P \,\&\, Q)$ since any interpretation for which $(P \,\&\, Q)$ is true, P is also true.

The notion of logical consequence provides us with a means to perform valid inferencing in PL. The following are two important theorems which give criteria for a statement to be a logical consequence of a set of statements.

Theorem 4.1. The sentence s is a logical consequence of $s_1, \ldots, s_n$ if and only if $s_1 \,\&\, s_2 \,\&\, \ldots \,\&\, s_n \rightarrow s$ is valid.

Theorem 4.2. The sentence s is a logical consequence of $s_1, \ldots, s_n$ if and only if $s_1 \,\&\, s_2 \,\&\, \ldots \,\&\, s_n \,\&\, \neg s$ is inconsistent.

The proof of theorem 4.1 can be seen by first noting that if s is a logical consequence of $s_1, \ldots, s_n$, then for any interpretation I in which $s_1 \,\&\, s_2 \,\&, \ldots, \&\, s_n$ is true, s is also true by definition. Hence $s_1 \,\&\, s_2 \,\&\, \ldots \,\&\, s_n \rightarrow s$ is true. On the other hand, if $s_1 \,\&\, s_2 \,\&\, \ldots \,\&\, s_n \rightarrow s$ is valid, then for any interpretation I if $s_1 \,\&\, s_2 \,\&\, \ldots \,\&\, s_n$ is true, s is true also.

The proof of theorem 4.2 follows directly from theorem 4.1 since s is a

TABLE 4.2 SOME EQUIVALENCE LAWS

Idempotency	P V P = P P & P = P
Associativity	(P V Q) V R = P V (Q V R) (P & Q) & R = P & (Q & R)
Commutativity	P V Q = Q V P P & Q = Q & P P ↔ Q = Q ↔ P
Distributivity	P & (Q V R) = (P & Q) V (P & R) P V (Q & R) = (P V Q) & (P V R)
De Morgan's laws	˜(P V Q) = ˜P & ˜Q ˜(P & Q) = ˜P V ˜Q
Conditional elimination	P → Q = ˜P V Q
Bi-conditional elimination	P ↔ Q = (P → Q) & (Q → P)

logical consequence of $s_1, \ldots, s_n$ if and only if $s_1 \,\&\, s_2 \,\&\, \ldots \,\&\, s_n \rightarrow s$ is valid, that is, if and only if $\tilde{}(s_1 \,\&\, s_2 \,\&\, \ldots \,\&\, s_n \rightarrow s)$ is inconsistent. But

$$\begin{aligned} \tilde{}(s_1 \,\&\, s_2 \,\&\, \ldots \,\&\, s_n \rightarrow s) &= \tilde{}(\tilde{}(s_1 \,\&\, s_2 \,\&\, \ldots \,\&\, s_n) \vee s) \\ &= \tilde{}\tilde{}\,(s_1 \,\&\, s_2 \,\&\, \ldots \,\&\, s_n) \,\&\, \tilde{}s) \\ &= s_1 \,\&\, s_2 \,\&\, \ldots \,\&\, s_n \,\&\, \tilde{}s \end{aligned}$$

When s is a logical consequence of $s_1, \ldots, s_n$, the formula $s_1 \,\&\, s_2 \,\&\, \ldots \,\&\, s_n \rightarrow s$ is called a theorem, with s the conclusion. When s is a logical consequence of the set $\mathbf{S} = \{s_1, \ldots, s_n\}$ we will also say **S** logically implies or logically entails s, written $\mathbf{S} \vdash s$.

It is often convenient to make substitutions when considering compound statements. If s_1 is equivalent to s_2, s_1 may be substituted for s_2 without changing the truth value of a statement or set of sentences containing s_2. Table 4.2 lists some of the important laws of PL. Note that the equal sign as used in the table has the same meaning as ↔; it also denotes equivalence.

One way to determine the equivalence of two sentences is by using truth tables. For example, to show that $P \rightarrow Q$ is equivalent to $\tilde{}P \vee Q$ and that $P \leftrightarrow Q$ is equivalent to the expression $(P \rightarrow Q) \,\&\, (Q \rightarrow P)$, a truth table such as Table 4.3, can be constructed to verify or disprove the equivalences.

TABLE 4.3 TRUTH TABLE FOR EQUIVALENT SENTENCES

P	Q	˜P	(˜P V Q)	(P → Q)	(Q → P)	(P → Q) & (Q → P)
true	true	false	true	true	true	true
true	false	false	false	false	true	false
false	true	true	true	true	false	false
false	false	true	true	true	true	true

Inference Rules

The inference rules of PL provide the means to perform logical proofs or deductions. The problem is, given a set of sentences $S = \{s_1, \ldots, s_n\}$ (the premises), prove the truth of s (the conclusion); that is, show that $S \vdash s$. The use of truth tables to do this is a form of semantic proof. Other syntactic methods of inference or deduction are also possible. Such methods do not depend on truth assignments but on syntactic relationships only; that is, it is possible to derive new sentences which are logical consequences of $s_1, \ldots, s_n$ using only syntactic operations. We present a few such rules now which will be referred to often throughout the text.

Modus ponens. From P and $P \rightarrow Q$ infer Q. This is sometimes written as

$$\frac{\begin{array}{c} P \\ P \rightarrow Q \end{array}}{Q}$$

For example

given: (joe is a father)
and: (joe is a father) → (joe has a child)
conclude: (joe has a child)

Chain rule. From $P \rightarrow Q$, and $Q \rightarrow R$, infer $P \rightarrow R$. Or

$$\frac{\begin{array}{c} P \rightarrow Q \\ Q \rightarrow R \end{array}}{P \rightarrow R}$$

For example,

given: (programmer likes LISP) → (programmer hates COBOL)
and: (programmer hates COBOL) → Programmer likes recursion)
conclude: (programmer likes LISP) → (programmer likes recursion)

Substitution. If s is a valid sentence, s' derived from s by consistent substitution of propositions in s, is also valid. For example, the sentence $P \vee \tilde{}P$ is valid; therefore $Q \vee \tilde{}Q$ is also valid by the substitution rule.

Simplification. From P & Q infer P.

Conjunction. From P and from Q, infer P & Q.

Transposition. From $P \rightarrow Q$, infer $\tilde{}Q \rightarrow \tilde{}P$.

We leave it to the reader to justify the last three rules given above.

We conclude this section with the following definitions.

Formal system. A formal system is a set of axioms S and a set of inference rules L from which new statements can be logically derived. We will sometimes denote a formal system as $<S, L>$ or simply a KB (for knowledge base).

Soundness. Let $<S, L>$ be a formal system. We say the inference procedures L are sound if and only if any statements s that can be derived from $<S, L>$ is a logical consequence of $<S, L>$.

Completeness. Let $<S, L>$ be a formal system. Then the inference procedure L is complete if and only if any sentence s logically implied by $<S, L>$ can be derived using that procedure.

As an example of the above definitions, suppose $S = \{P, P \rightarrow Q\}$ and L is the modus ponens rule. Then $<S, L>$ is a formal system, since Q can be derived from the system. Furthermore, this system is both sound and complete for the reasons given above.

We will see later that a formal system like *resolution* permits us to perform computational reasoning. Clearly, soundness and completeness are desirable properties of such systems. Soundness is important to insure that all derived sentences are true when the assumed set of sentences are true. Completeness is important to guarantee that inconsistencies can be found whenever they exist in a set of sentences.

4.3 SYNTAX AND SEMANTICS FOR FOPL

As was noted in the previous chapter, expressiveness is one of the requirements for any serious representation scheme. It should be possible to accurately represent most, if not all concepts which can be verbalized. PL falls short of this requirement in some important respects. It is too ''coarse'' to easily describe properties of objects, and it lacks the structure to express relations that exist among two or more entities. Furthermore, PL does not permit us to make generalized statements about classes of similar objects. These are serious limitations when reasoning about real world entities. For example, given the following statements, it should be possible to conclude that John must take the Pascal course.

All students in Computer Science must take Pascal.

John is a Computer Science major.

As stated, it is not possible to conclude in PL that John must take Pascal since the second statement does not occur as part of the first one. To draw the desired conclusion with a valid inference rule, it would be necessary to rewrite the sentences.

FOPL was developed by logicians to extend the expressiveness of PL. It is a generalization of PL that permits reasoning about world objects as relational entities as well as classes or subclasses of objects. This generalization comes from the introduction of predicates in place of propositions, the use of functions and the use of variables together with variable quantifiers. These concepts are formalized below.

The syntax for FOPL, like PL, is determined by the allowable symbols and rules of combination. The semantics of FOPL are determined by interpretations assigned to predicates, rather than propositions. This means that an interpretation must also assign values to other terms including constants, variables and functions, since predicates may have arguments consisting of any of these terms. Therefore, the arguments of a predicate must be assigned before an interpretation can be made.

Syntax of FOPL

The symbols and rules of combination permitted in FOPL are defined as follows.

Connectives. There are five connective symbols: ~(not or negation), & (and or conjunction), V (or or inclusive disjunction, that is, A or B or both A and B), → (implication), ↔ (equivalence or if and only if).

Quantifiers. The two quantifier symbols are ∃ (existential quantification) and ∀ (universal quantification), where (∃x) means for some x or there is an x and (∀x) means for all x. When there is no possibility of confusion, we will omit the parentheses for brevity. Furthermore, when more than one variable is being quantified by the same quantifier such as (∀x) (∀y) (∀z) we abbreviate with a single quantifier and drop the parentheses to get ∀xyz.

Constants. Constants are fixed-value terms that belong to a given domain of discourse. They are denoted by numbers, words, and small letters near the beginning of the alphabet such as a, b, c, 5.3, −21, flight-102, and john.

Variables. Variables are terms that can assume different values over a given domain. They are denoted by words and small letters near the end of the alphabet, such as aircraft-type, individuals, x, y, and z.

Functions. Function symbols denote relations defined on a domain D. They map n elements ($n \geq 0$) to a single element of the domain. Symbols f, g, h, and words such as father-of, or age-of, represent functions. An n place (n-ary) function is written as $f(t_1, t_2, \ldots, t_n)$ where the t_i are terms (constants, variables, or functions) defined over some domain. A 0-ary function is a constant.

Predicates. Predicate symbols denote relations or functional mappings from the elements of a domain D to the values true or false. Capital letters and capitalized words such as P, Q, R, EQUAL, and MARRIED are used to represent predicates. Like functions, predicates may have n ($n \geq 0$) terms for arguments written as $P(t_1, t_2, \ldots, t_n)$, where the terms t_i, $i = 1, 2, \ldots, n$ are defined over some domain. A 0-ary predicate is a proposition, that is, a constant predicate.

Constants, variables, and functions are referred to as *terms*, and predicates are referred to as atomic formulas or *atoms* for short. Furthermore, when we want to refer to an atom or its negation, we often use the word *literal*.

In addition to the above symbols, left and right parentheses, square brackets, braces, and the period are used for punctuation in symbolic expressions.

As an example of the above concepts, suppose we wish to represent the following statements in symbolic form.

E1: All employees earning $1400 or more per year pay taxes.
E2: Some employees are sick today.
E3: No employee earns more than the president.

To represent such expressions in FOPL, we must define abbreviations for the predicates and functions. We might, for example, define the following.

E(x) for x is an employee.
P(x) for x is president.
i(x) for the income of x (lower case denotes a function).
GE(u,v) for u is greater than or equal to v.
S(x) for x is sick today.
T(x) for x pays taxes.

Using the above abbreviations, we can represent E1, E2, and E3 as

E1′: ∀x ((E(x) & GE(i(x),1400)) → T(x))
E2′: ∃y (E(y) → S(y))
E3′: ∀xy ((E(x) & P(y)) → ˜GE(i(x),i(y)))

In the above, we read E1′ as "for all x if x is an employee and the income of x is greater than or equal to $1400 then x pays taxes." More naturally, we read E1′ as E1, that is as "all employees earning $1400 or more per year pay taxes."

E2′ is read as "there is an employee and the employee is sick today" or "some employee is sick today." E3′ reads "for all x and for all y if x is an employee and y is president, the income of x is *not* greater than or equal to the income of y." Again, more naturally, we read E3′ as, "no employee earns more than the president."

The expressions E1′, E2′, and E3′ are known as well-formed formulas or *wffs* (pronounced woofs) for short. Clearly, all of the wffs used above would be more meaningful if full names were used rather than abbreviations.

Wffs are defined recursively as follows:

An atomic formula is a wff.
If P and Q are wffs, then ˜P, P & Q, $P \vee Q$, $P \rightarrow Q$,

$P \leftrightarrow Q$, $\forall x\ P(x)$, and $\exists x\ P(x)$ are wffs.

Wffs are formed only by applying the above rules a finite number of times.

The above rules state that all wffs are formed from atomic formulas and the proper application of quantifiers and logical connectives.

Some examples of valid wffs are

```
MAN(john)
PILOT(father-of(bill))
∃xyz ((FATHER(x,y) & FATHER(y,z)) → GRANDFATHER(x,z))
∀x NUMBER(x) → (∃y GREATER-THAN(y,x))
∀x ∃y (P(x) & Q(y)) → (R(a) V Q(b))
```

Some examples of statements that are *not* wffs are:

```
∀P P(x) → Q(x)
MAN(~john)
father-of(Q(x))
MARRIED(MAN,WOMAN)
```

The first group of examples above are all wffs since they are properly formed expressions composed of atoms, logical connectives, and valid quantifications. Examples in the second group fail for different reasons. In the first expression, universal quantification is applied to the predicate $P(x)$. This is invalid in FOPL.[1] The second expression is invalid since the term John, a constant, is negated. Recall that predicates, and not terms are negated. The third expression is invalid since it is a function with a predicate argument. The last expression fails since it is a predicate with two predicate arguments.

Semantics for FOPL

When considering specific wffs, we always have in mind some domain D. If not stated explicitly, D will be understood from the context. D is the set of all elements or objects from which fixed assignments are made to constants and from which the domain and range of functions are defined. The arguments of predicates must be terms (constants, variables, or functions). Therefore, the domain of each n-place predicate is also defined over D.

For example, our domain might be all entities that make up the Computer Science Department at the University of Texas. In this case, constants would be professors (Bell, Cooke, Gelfond, and so on), staff (Martha, Pat, Linda, and so on), books, labs, offices, and so forth. The functions we may choose might be

[1] Predicates may be quantified in *second* order predicate logic as indicated in the example, but never in first order logic.

advisor-of(x), lab-capacity(y), dept-grade-average(z), and the predicates MARRIED(x), TENURED(y), COLLABORATE(x,y), to name a few.

When an assignment of values is given to each term and to each predicate symbol in a wff, we say an *interpretation* is given to the wff. Since literals always evaluate to either true or false under an interpretation, the value of any given wff can be determined by referring to a truth table such as Table 4.2 which gives truth values for the subexpressions of the wff.

If the truth values for two different wffs are the same under every interpretation, they are said to be *equivalent*. A predicate (or wff) that has no variables is called a *ground atom*.

When determining the truth value of a compound expression, we must be careful in evaluating predicates that have variable arguments, since they evaluate to true only if they are true for the appropriate value(s) of the variables. For example, the predicate $P(x)$ in $\forall x\ P(x)$, is true only if it is true for every value of x in the domain D. Likewise, the $P(x)$ in $\exists x\ P(x)$ is true only if it is true for at least one value of x in the domain. If the above conditions are not satisfied, the predicate evaluates to false.

Suppose, for example, we want to evaluate the truth value of the expression E, where

$$E:\ \forall x\ ((A(a,x) \lor B(f(x)))\ \&\ C(x)) \rightarrow D(x)$$

In this expression, there are four predicates: A, B, C, and D. The predicate A is a two-place predicate, the first argument being the constant a, and the second argument, a variable x. The predicates B, C, and D are all unary predicates where the argument of B is a function $f(x)$, and the argument of C and D is the variable x.

Since the whole expression E is quantified with the universal quantifier $\forall x$, it will evaluate to true only if it evaluates to true for all x in the domain D. Thus, to complete our example, suppose E is interpreted as follows: Define the domain $D = \{1,2\}$ and from D let the interpretation I assign the following values:

a = 2
f(1) = 2, f(2) = 1
A(2,1) = true, A(2,2) = false
B(1) = true, B(2) = false
C(1) = true, C(2) = false
D(1) = false, D(2) = true

Using a table such as Table 4.3 we can evaluate E as follows:

a. If $x = 1$, $A(2,1)$ evaluates to true, $B(2)$ evaluates to false, and $(A(2,1) \lor B(2))$ evaluates to true. $C(1)$ evaluates to true. Therefore, the expression in the outer parentheses (the antecedent of E) evaluates to true. Hence, since $D(1)$ evaluates to false, the expression E evaluates to false.

b. In a similar way, if $x = 2$, the expression can be shown to evaluate to true. Consequently, since E is not true for all x, the expression E evaluates to false.

4.4 PROPERTIES OF WFFS

As in the case of PL, the evaluation of complex formulas in FOPL can often be facilitated through the substitution of equivalent formulas. Table 4.3 lists a number of equivalent expressions. In the table F, G and H denote wffs not containing variables and $F\,[x]$ denotes the wff F which contains the variable x. The equivalences can easily be verified with truth tables such as Table 4.3 and simple arguments for the expressions containing quantifiers. Although Tables 4.4 and 4.3 are similar, there are some notable differences, particularly in the wffs containing quantifiers. For example, attention is called to the last four expressions which govern substitutions involving negated quantifiers and the movement of quantifiers across conjunctive and disjunctive connectives.

We summarize here some definitions which are similar to those of the previous section. A wff is said to be *valid* if it is true under every interpretation. A wff that is false under every interpretation is said to be *inconsistent* (or unsatisfiable). A wff that is not valid (one that is false for some interpretation) is *invalid*. Likewise, a wff that is not inconsistent (one that is true for some interpretation) is *satisfiable*. Again, this means that a valid wff is satisfiable and an inconsistent wff is invalid,

TABLE 4.4. EQUIVALENT LOGICAL EXPRESSIONS

˜(˜F) = F	(double negation)
F & G = G & F, F V G = G V F	(commutativity)
(F & G) & H = F & (G & H),	
(F V G) V H = F V (G V H)	(associativity)
F V (G & H) = (F V G) & (F V H),	
F & (G V H) = (F & G) V (F & H)	(distributivity)
˜(F & G) = ˜F V ˜G,	
˜(F V G) = ˜F & ˜G	(De Morgan's Laws)
F → G = ˜F V G	
F ↔ G = (˜F V G) & (˜G V F)	
∀x F[x] V G = ∀x (F[x] V G),	
∃x F[x] V G = ∃x (F[x] V G)	
∀x F[x] & G = ∀x (F[x] & G),	
∃x F[x] & G = ∃x (F[x] & G)	
˜(∀x) F[x] = ∃x (˜F[x]),	
˜(∃x) F[x] = ∀x (˜F[x])	
∀x F[x] & ∀x G[x] = ∀x (F[x] & G[x])	
∃x F[x] V ∃x G[x] = ∃x (F[x] V G[x])	

but the respective converse statements do not hold. Finally, we say that a wff Q is a *logical consequence* of the wffs $P_1, P_2, \ldots, P_n$ if and only if whenever P_1 & P_2 & . . . & P_n is true under an interpretation, Q is also true.

To illustrate some of these concepts, consider the following examples:

a. P & ˜P is inconsistent and $P \vee$ ˜P is valid since the first is false under every interpretation and the second is true under every interpretation.

b. From the two wffs

CLEVER(bill) and
∀x CLEVER(x) → SUCCEED(x)

we can show that SUCCEED(bill) is a logical consequence. Thus, assume that both

CLEVER(bill) and
∀x CLEVER(x) → SUCCEED(x)

are true under an interpretation. Then

CLEVER(bill) → SUCCEED(bill)

is certainly true since the wff was assumed to be true for all x, including x = bill. But,

CLEVER(bill) → SUCCEED(bill)
=˜CLEVER(bill) V SUCCEED(bill)

are equivalent and, since CLEVER(bill) is true, ˜CLEVER(bill) is false and, therefore, SUCCEED(bill) must be true. Thus, we conclude SUCCEED-(bill) is a logical consequence of

CLEVER(bill) and ∀x CLEVER(x) → SUCCEED(x).

Suppose the wff $F[x]$ contains the variable x. We say x is *bound* if it follows or is within the scope of a quantifier naming the variable. If a variable is not bound, it is said to be free. For example, in the expression $\forall x\ (P(x) \rightarrow Q(x,y))$, x is bound, but y is free since every occurrence of x follows the quantifier and y is not within the scope of any quantifier. Clearly, an expression can be evaluated only when all the variables in that expression are bound. Therefore, we shall require that all wffs contain only bound variables. We will also call such expressions a sentence.

We conclude this section with a few more definitions. Given wffs F_1, F_2,

. . . , F_n each possibly consisting of the disjunction of literals only, we say F_1 & F_2 & . . . & F_n is in *conjunctive normal form* (CNF). On the other hand if each F_i, $i = 1, \ldots, n$ consists only of the conjunction of literals, we say $F_1 \lor F_2 \lor \ldots \lor F_n$ is in *disjunctive normal form* (DNF). For example, the wffs (~$P \lor Q \lor R$) & (~$P \lor$ ~Q) & ~R and (P & Q & R) $\lor$ (Q & R) $\lor$ P are in conjunctive and disjunctive normal forms respectively. It can be shown that *any* wff can be transformed into either normal form.

4.5 CONVERSION TO CLAUSAL FORM

As noted earlier, we are interested in mechanical inference by programs using symbolic FOPL expressions. One method we shall examine is called *resolution*. It requires that all statements be converted into a normalized clausal form. We define a *clause* as the disjunction of a number of literals. A *ground clause* is one in which no variables occur in the expression. A *Horn clause* is a clause with at most one positive literal.

To transform a sentence into clausal form requires the following steps:

eliminate all implication and equivalence symbols,

move negation symbols into individual atoms,

rename variables if necessary so that all remaining quantifiers have different variable assignments,

replace existentially quantified variables with special functions and eliminate the corresponding quantifiers,

drop all universal quantifiers and put the remaining expression into CNF (disjunctions are moved down to literals), and

drop all conjunction symbols writing each clause previously connected by the conjunctions on a separate line.

These steps are described in more detail below. But first, we describe the process of eliminating the existential quantifiers through a substitution process. This process requires that all such variables be replaced by something called Skolem functions, arbitrary functions which can always assume a correct value required of an existentially quantified variable.

For simplicity in what follows, assume that all quantifiers have been properly moved to the left side of the expression, and each quantifies a different variable. Skolemization, the replacement of existentially quantified variables with Skolem functions and deletion of the respective quantifiers, is then accomplished as follows:

1. If the first (leftmost) quantifier in an expression is an existential quantifier, replace all occurrences of the variable it quantifies with an arbitrary constant not appearing elsewhere in the expression and delete the quantifier. This same procedure should be followed for all other existential quantifiers not preceded by a universal quantifier, in each case, using different constant symbols in the substitution.

2. For each existential quantifier that is preceded by one or more universal quantifiers (is within the scope of one or more universal quantifiers), replace all occurrences of the existentially quantified variable by a function symbol not appearing elsewhere in the expression. The arguments assigned to the function should match all the variables appearing in each universal quantifier which precedes the existential quantifier. This existential quantifier should then be deleted. The same process should be repeated for each remaining existential quantifier using a different function symbol and choosing function arguments that correspond to all universally quantified variables that precede the existentially quantified variable being replaced.

An example will help to clarify this process. Given the expression

$$\exists u\ \forall v\ \forall x\ \exists y\ P(f(u), v, x, y) \rightarrow Q(u,v,y)$$

the Skolem form is determined as

$$\forall v\ \forall x\ P(f(a),v,x,g(v,x)) \rightarrow Q(a,v,g(v,x)).$$

In making the substitutions, it should be noted that the variable u appearing after the first existêntial quantifier has been replaced in the second expression by the arbitrary constant a. This constant did not appear elsewhere in the first expression. The variable y has been replaced by the function symbol g having the variables v and x as arguments, since both of these variables are universally quantified to the left of the existential quantifier for y. Replacement of y by an arbitrary function with arguments v and x is justified on the basis that y, following v and x, may be functionally dependent on them and, if so, the arbitrary function g can account for this dependency. The complete procedure can now be given to convert any FOPL sentence into clausal form.

Clausal Conversion Procedure

Step 1. Eliminate all implication and equivalency connectives (use $\tilde{}P \vee Q$ in place of $P \rightarrow Q$ and $(\tilde{}P \vee Q)$ & $(\tilde{}Q \vee P)$ in place of $P \leftrightarrow Q$.

Step 2. Move all negations in to immediately precede an atom (use P in place of $\tilde{}(\tilde{}P)$, and DeMorgan's laws, $\exists x\ \tilde{}F[x]$ in place of $\tilde{}(\forall x)\ F[x]$ and $\forall x\ \tilde{}F[x]$ in place of $\tilde{}(\exists x)\ F[x]$).

Step 3. Rename variables, if necessary, so that all quantifiers have different variable assignments; that is, rename variables so that variables bound by one quantifier are not the same as variables bound by a different quantifier. For example, in the expression $\forall x\ (P(x) \rightarrow (\exists x\ (Q(x)))$ rename the second "dummy" variable x which is bound by the existential quantifier to be a different variable, say y, to give $\forall x\ (P(x) \rightarrow (\exists y\ Q(y)))$.

Step 4. Skolemize by replacing all existentially quantified variables with Skolem functions as described above, and deleting the corresponding existential quantifiers.

Step 5. Move all universal quantifiers to the left of the expression and put the expression on the right into CNF.

Step 6. Eliminate all universal quantifiers and conjunctions since they are retained implicitly. The resulting expressions (the expressions previously connected by the conjunctions) are clauses and the set of such expressions is said to be in clausal form.

As an example of this process, let us convert the expression

$$\exists x\ \forall y\ (\forall z\ P(f(x),y,z) \rightarrow (\exists u\ Q(x,u)\ \&\ \exists v\ R(y,v)))$$

into clausal form. We have after application of step 1

$$\exists x\ \forall y\ (\sim(\forall z)\ P(f(x),y,z)\ V\ (\exists u\ Q(x,u)\ \&\ (\exists v)\ R(y,v)))).$$

After application of step 2 we obtain

$$\exists x\ \forall y\ (\exists z\ \sim P(f(x),y,z)\ V\ (\exists u\ Q(x,u)\ \&\ (\exists v)\ R(y,v))).$$

After application of step 4 (step 3 is not required)

$$\forall y\ (\sim P(f(a),y,g(y))\ V\ (Q(a,h(y))\ \&\ R(y,l(y))).$$

After application of step 5 the result is

$$\forall y\ ((\sim P(f(a),y,g(y))\ V\ Q(a,h(y))\ \&\ (\sim P(f(a),y,g(y))\ V\ R(y,l(y))).$$

Finally, after application of step 6 we obtain the clausal form

$$\sim P(f(a),y,g(y))\ V\ Q(a,h(y))$$
$$\sim P(f(a),y,g(y)\ V\ R(y,l(y))$$

The last two clauses of our final form are understood to be universally quantified in the variable y and to have the conjunction symbol connecting them.

It should be noted that the set of clauses produced by the above process are not *equivalent* to the original expression, but *satisfiability* is retained. That is, the set of clauses are satisfiable if and only if the original sentence is satisfiable.

Having now labored through the tedious steps above, we point out that it is often possible to write down statements directly in clausal form without working through the above process step-by-step. We illustrate how this may be done in Section 4.7 when we create a sample knowledge base.

4.6 INFERENCE RULES

Like PL, a key inference rule in FOPL is modus ponens. From the assertion "Leo is a lion" and the implication "all lions are ferocious" we can conclude that Leo is ferocious. Written in symbolic form we have

assertion: LION(leo)
implication: $\forall$x LION(x) $\rightarrow$ FEROCIOUS(x)
conclusion: FEROCIOUS(leo)

In general, if a has property P and all objects that have property P also have property Q, we conclude that a has property Q.

$$\frac{\begin{array}{c}P(a)\\ \forall x\, P(x) \rightarrow Q(x)\end{array}}{Q(a)}$$

Note that in concluding $Q(a)$, a substitution of a for x was necessary. This was possible, of course, since the implication $P(x) \rightarrow Q(x)$ is assumed true for all x, and in particular for $x = a$. Substitutions are an essential part of the inference process. When properly applied, they permit simplifications or the reduction of expressions through the cancellation of complementary literals. We say that two literals are *complementary* if they are identical but of opposite sign; that is, P and $\tilde{}P$ are complementary.

A *substitution* is defined as a set of pairs t_i and v_i where v_i are distinct variables and t_i are terms not containing the v_i. The t_i replace or are substituted for the corresponding v_i in any expression for which the substitution is applied. A set of substitutions $\{t_1/v_1, t_2/v_2, \ldots, t_n/v_n\}$ where $n \geq 1$ applied to an expression will be denoted by Greek letters α, β, and δ. For example, if $\beta = \{a/x, g(b)/y\}$, then applying β to the clause $C = P(x,y) \vee Q(x,f(y))$ we obtain $C' = C\beta = P(a,g(b)) \vee Q(a,f(g(b)))$.

Unification

Any substitution that makes two or more expressions equal is called a *unifier* for the expressions. Applying a substitution to an expression E produces an *instance* E' of E where $E' = E\beta$. Given two expressions that are unifiable, such as expressions C_1 and C_2 with a unifer β with $C_1\beta = C_2$, we say that β is a *most general unifer* (mgu) if any other unifer α is an instance of β. For example two unifiers for the literals $P(u,b,v)$ and $P(a,x,y)$ are $\alpha = \{a/u,b/x,v/y\}$ and $\beta = \{a/u,b/x,c/v,c/y\}$. The former is an mgu whereas the latter is not since it is an *instance* of the former.

Unification can sometimes be applied to literals within the same single clause. When an mgu exists such that two or more literals within a clause are unified, the clause remaining after deletion of all but one of the unified literals is called a *factor* of the original clause. Thus, given the clause $C = P(x) \vee Q(x,y) \vee P(f(z))$ the factor $C' = C\beta = P(f(z)) \vee Q(f(z),y)$ is obtained where $\beta = \{f(z)/x\}$.

Let **S** be a set of expressions. We define the *disagreement set* of **S** as the set obtained by comparing each symbol of all expressions in **S** from left to right and extracting from **S** the subexpressions whose first symbols do not agree. For example, let $\mathbf{S} = \{P(f(x),g(y),a), P(f(x),z,a), P(f(x),b,h(u))$. For the set **S**, the disagreement set is $\{g(y),a,b,z,h(u)\}$. We can now state a unification algorithm which returns the mgu for a given set of expressions **S**.

Unification algorithm:

1. Set $k = 0$ and $\sigma_k = e$ (the empty set).
2. If the set $\mathbf{S}\sigma_k$ is a singleton, then stop; σ_k is an mgu of **S**. Otherwise, find the disagreement set D_k of $\mathbf{S}\sigma_k$.
3. If there is a variable v and term t in D_k such that v does not occur in t, put $\sigma_{k+1} = \sigma_k\{t/v\}$, set $k = k + 1$, and return to step 2. Otherwise, stop. **S** is not unifiable.

4.7 THE RESOLUTION PRINCIPLE

We are now ready to consider the resolution principle, a syntactic inference procedure which, when applied to a set of clauses, determines if the set is unsatisfiable. This procedure is similar to the process of obtaining a proof by contradiction. For example, suppose we have the set of clauses (axioms) $C_1, C_2, \ldots, C_n$ and we wish to deduce or prove the clause D, that is, to show that D is a logical consequence of $C_1 \& C_2 \& \ldots \& C_n$. First, we negate D and add $\sim D$ to the set of clauses C_1, $C_2, \ldots, C_n$. Then, using resolution together with factoring, we can show that the set is unsatisfiable by deducing a contradiction. Such a proof is called a proof by refutation which, if successful, yields the empty clause denoted by [ ].[2] Resolution with factoring is *complete* in the sense that it will always generate the empty clause from a set of unsatisfiable clauses.

Resolution is very simple. Given two clauses C_1 and C_2 with no variables in common, if there is a literal 1_1 in C_1 which is a complement of a literal 1_2 in C_2, both 1_1 and 1_2 are deleted and a disjuncted C is formed from the remaining reduced clauses. The new clause C is called the *resolvent* of C_1 and C_2. Resolution is the process of generating these resolvents from a set of clauses. For example, to resolve the two clauses

$$(\sim P \vee Q) \text{ and } (\sim Q \vee R)$$

[2] The empty clause [ ] is always false since no interpretation can satisfy it. It is derived from combining contradictory clauses such as P and $\sim P$.

we write

$$\frac{\tilde{}P \vee Q,\ \tilde{}Q \vee R}{\tilde{}P \vee R}$$

Several types of resolution are possible depending on the number and types of parents. We define a few of these types below.

Binary resolution. Two clauses having complementary literals are combined as disjuncts to produce a single clause after deleting the complementary literals. For example, the binary resolvent of

$$\tilde{}P(x,a) \vee Q(x) \quad \text{and} \quad \tilde{}Q(b) \vee R(x)$$

is just

$$\tilde{}P(b,a) \vee R(b).$$

The substitution $\{b/x\}$ was made in the two parent clauses to produce the complementary literals $Q(b)$ and $\tilde{}Q(b)$ which were then deleted from the disjunction of the two parent clauses.

Unit resulting (UR) resolution. A number of clauses are resolved simultaneously to produce a unit clause. All except one of the clauses are unit clauses, and that one clause has exactly one more literal than the total number of unit clauses. For example, resolving the set

{~MARRIED(x,y) V ~MOTHER(x,z) V FATHER(y,z),
MARRIED(sue,joe), ~FATHER(joe,bill)}

where the substitution $\beta = \{\text{sue}/x,\ \text{joe}/y,\ \text{bill}/z\}$ is used, results in the unit clause ~MOTHER(sue,bill).

Linear resolution. When each resolved clause C_i is a parent to the clause C_{i+1} $(i = 1, 2, \ldots, n - 1)$ the process is called linear resolution. For example, given a set **S** of clauses with $C_0 \subseteq S$, C_n is derived by a sequence of resolutions, C_0 with some clause B_0 to get C_1, then C_1 with some clause B_1 to get C_2, and so on until C_n has been derived.

Linear input resolution. If one of the parents in linear resolution is always from the original set of clauses (the B_i), we have linear input resolution. For example, given the set of clauses $S = \{P \vee Q,\ \tilde{}P \vee Q,\ P \vee \tilde{}Q,\ \tilde{}P \vee \tilde{}Q\}$ let $C_0 = (P \vee Q)$. Choosing $B_0 = \tilde{}P \vee Q$ from the set S and resolving this with C_0 we obtain the resolvent $Q = C_1$. B_1 must now be chosen from S and the resolvent of C_1 and B_1 becomes C_2 and so on.

Unification and resolution give us one approach to the problem of mechanical inference or automated reasoning, but without some further refinements, resolution can be intolerably inefficient. Randomly resolving clauses in a large set can result in inefficient or even impossible proofs. Typically, the curse of combinatorial explosion occurs. So methods which constrain the search in some way must be used.

When attempting a proof by resolution, one ideally would like a minimally unsatisfiable set of clauses which includes the conjectured clause. A *minimally unsatisfiable set* is one which is satisfiable when any member of the set is omitted. The reason for this choice is that irrelevant clauses which are not needed in the proof but which participate are unnecessary resolutions. They contribute nothing toward the proof. Indeed, they can sidetrack the search direction resulting in a dead end and loss of resources. Of course, the set must be unsatisfiable otherwise a proof is impossible.

A minimally unsatisfiable set is ideal in the sense that all clauses are essential and no others are needed. Thus, if we wish to prove B, we would like to do so with a set of clauses $S = \{A_1, A_2, \ldots, A_k\}$ which become minimally unsatisfiable with the addition of $\tilde{}B$.

Choosing the order in which clauses are resolved is known as a search strategy. While there are many such strategies now available, we define only one of the more important ones, the set-of-support strategy. This strategy separates a set which is unsatisfiable into subsets, one of which is satisfiable.

Set-of-support strategy. Let S be an unsatisfiable set of clauses and T be a subset of S. Then T is a set-of-support for S if $S - T$ is satisfiable. A set-of-support resolution is a resolution of two clauses not both from $S - T$. This essentially means that given an unsatisfiable set $\{A_1, \ldots, A_k\}$, resolution should not be performed directly among the A_i as noted above.

Example of Resolution

The example we present here is one to which all AI students should be exposed at some point in their studies. It is the famous "monkey and bananas problem," another one of those complex real life problems solvable with AI techniques. We envision a room containing a monkey, a chair, and some bananas that have been hung from the center of the ceiling, out of reach from the monkey. If the monkey is clever enough, he can reach the bananas by placing the chair directly below them and climbing on top of the chair. The problem is to use FOPL to represent this monkey-banana world and, using resolution, prove the monkey can reach the bananas.

In creating a knowledge base, it is essential first to identify all relevant objects which will play some role in the anticipated inferences. Where possible, irrelevant objects should be omitted, but never at the risk of incompleteness. For example, in the current problem, the monkey, bananas, and chair are essential. Also needed is some reference object such as the floor or ceiling to establish the height relationship between monkey and bananas. Other objects such as windows, walls or doors are not relevant.

The next step is to establish important properties of objects, relations between them, and any assertions likely to be needed. These include such facts as the chair is tall enough to raise the monkey within reach of the bananas, the monkey is dexterous, the chair can be moved under the bananas, and so on. Again, all important properties, relations, and assertions should be included and irrelevant ones omitted. Otherwise, unnecessary inference steps may be taken.

The important factors for our problem are described below, and all items needed for the actual knowledge base are listed as axioms. These are the essential facts and rules. Although not explicitly indicated, all variables are universally quantified.

Relevant factors for the problem

CONSTANTS

{floor, chair, bananas, monkey}

VARIABLES

{x, y, z}

PREDICATES

```
{can_reach(x,y)       ; x can reach y
dexterous (x)         ; x is a dexterous animal
close(x,y)            ; x is close to y
get_on(x,y)           ; x can get on y
under(x,y)            ; x is under y
tall(x)               ; x is tall
in_room(x)            ; x is in the room
can_move(x,y,z)       ; x can move y near z
can_climb(x,y)}       ; x can climb onto y
```

AXIOMS

```
{in_room(bananas)
in_room(chair)
in_room(monkey)
dexterous(monkey)
tall(chair)
~close(bananas,floor)
can_move(monkey,chair,bananas)
can_climb(monkey,chair)
(dexterous(x) & close(x,y) → can-reach(x,y)
((get_on(x,y) & under(y,bananas) & tall(y) →
   close(x,bananas))
((in_room(x) & in_room(y) & in_room(z) & can_move(x,y,z))
     → close(z,floor) V under(y,z))
(can_climb(x,y) → get_on(x,y))}
```

Using the above axioms, a knowledge base can be written down directly in the required clausal form. All that is needed to make the necessary substitutions are the equivalences

$$P \rightarrow Q = \tilde{}P \vee Q$$

and De Morgan's laws. To relate the clauses to a LISP program, one may prefer to think of each clause as being a list of items. For example, number 9, below, would be written as

```
(or (~can_climb(?x ?y) get_on(?x ?y))
```

where ?*x* and ?*y* denote variables.

Note that clause 13 is not one of the original axioms. It has been added for the proof as required in refutation resolution proofs.

Clausal form of knowledge base

1. in_room(monkey)
2. in_room(bananas)
3. in_room(chair)
4. tall(chair)
5. dexterous(monkey)
6. can_move(monkey, chair, bananas)
7. can_climb(monkey,chair)
8. ~close(bananas,floor)
9. ~can_climb(x,y) V get_on(x,y)
10. ~dexterous(x) V ~close(x,y) V can_reach(x,y)
11. ~get_on(x,y) V ~under(y,bananas) V ~tall(y) V close(x,bananas)
12. ~in_room(x) V ~in_room(y) V ~in_room(z) V ~can_move(x,y,z) V close(y,floor) V under(y,z)
13. ~can_reach(monkey,bananas)

Resolution proof. A proof that the monkey can reach the bananas is summarized below. As can be seen, this is a refutation proof where the statement to be proved (can_reach(monkey,bananas)) has been negated and added to the knowledge base (number 13). The proof then follows when a contradiction is found (see number 23, below).

14. ~can_move(monkey,chair,bananas) V close(bananas,floor) V under (chair,bananas) ; 14 is a resolvent of 1,2,3 and 12 with substitution {monkey/*x*, chair/*y*, bananas/*z*}

15. close(bananas,floor) V under (chair,bananas) ; this is a resolvent of 6 and 14

16. under(chair,bananas) ; this is a resolvent of 8 and 15

17. ~get_on(x,chair) V ~tall(chair) V close(x,bananas) ; this is a resolvent of 11 and 16 with substitution {chair/y}

18. ~get_on(x,chair) V close(x,bananas) ; a resolvent of 4 and 17

19. get_on(monkey,chair) ; a resolvent of 7 and 9

20. close(monkey,bananas) ; a resolvent of 18 and 19 with substitution {monkey/x}

21. ~close(monkey,y) V can_reach (monkey,y) ; a resolvent of 10 and 5 with substitution {monkey/x}

22. reach(monkey,bananas) ; a resolvent of 20 and 21 with substitution {bananas/y}

23. [ ] ; a resolvent of 13 and 22

In performing the above proof, no particular strategy was followed. Clearly, however, good choices were made in selecting parent clauses for resolution. Otherwise, many unnecessary steps may have been taken before completing the proof. Different forms of resolution were completed in steps 14 through 23. One of the exercises requires that the types of resolutions used be identified.

The Monkey-Banana Problem in PROLOG

Prolog was introduced in the previous chapter. It is a logic programming language that is based on the resolution principle. The refutation proof strategy used in PROLOG is resolution by selective linear with definite clauses or SLD resolution. This is just a form of linear input resolution using definite Horn clauses (clauses with exactly one positive literal). In finding a resolution proof, PROLOG searches a data base of clauses in an exhaustive manner (guided by the SLD strategy) until a chain of unifications have been found to produce a proof.

Next, we present a PROLOG program for the monkey-banana problem to illustrate the ease with which many logic programs may be formulated.

```
% Constants:
% {floor, chair, bananas, monkey}

% Variables:
% {X, Y, Z}

% Predicates:
% {can-reach(X,Y)          ; X can reach Y
%  dexterous(X)            ; X is a dexterous animal
%  close(X,Y)              ; X is close to Y
```

```
% get-on(X,Y)             ; X can get on Y
% under(X,Y)              ; X is under Y
% tall(X)                 ; X is tall
% in-room(X)              ; X is in the room
% can-move(X,Y,Z)         ; X can move Y near Z
% can-climb(X,Y)}         ; X can climb onto Y

% Axioms :

in-room(bananas).

in-room(chair).

in-room(monkey).

dexterous(monkey).

tall(chair).

can-move(monkey, chair, bananas).

can-climb(monkey, chair).

can-reach(X,Y) :–

        dexterous(X), close(X,Y).

close(X,Z) :–

        get-on(X,Y),

        under(Y,Z),

        tall(Y).

get-on(X,Y) :–

        can-climb(X,Y).

Under(Y,Z) :–

        in-room(X),

        in-room(Y),

        in-room(Z),

        can-move(X,Y,Z).
```

This completes the data base of facts and rules required. Now we can pose various queries to our theorem proving system.

```
| ?- can-reach(X,Y).

X = monkey,

Y = bananas

| ?- can-reach(X,bananas).

X = monkey

| ?- can-reach(monkey,Y).

Y = bananas

| ?- can-reach(monkey,bananas).

yes

| ?- can-reach(lion,bananas).

no

| ?- can-reach(monkey,apple).

no
```

4.8 NONDEDUCTIVE INFERENCE METHODS

In this section we consider three nondeductive forms of inferencing. These are not valid forms of inferencing, but they are nevertheless very important. We use all three methods often in every day activities where we draw conclusions and make decisions. The three methods we consider here are abduction, induction, and analogical inference.

Abductive Inference

Abductive inference is based on the use of known causal knowledge to explain or justify a (possibly invalid) conclusion. Given the truth of proposition Q and the implication $P \rightarrow Q$, conclude P. For example, people who have had too much to drink tend to stagger when they walk. Therefore, it is not unreasonable to conclude that a person who is staggering is drunk even though this may be an incorrect conclusion. People may stagger when they walk for other reasons, including dizziness from twirling in circles or from some physical problem.

We may represent abductive inference with the following, where the c over the implication arrow is meant to imply a possible causal relationship.

$$\begin{array}{ll} \text{assertion} & Q \\ \text{implication} & P^c \rightarrow Q \\ \hline \text{conclusion} & P \end{array}$$

Abductive inference is useful when known causal relations are likely and deductive inferencing is not possible for lack of facts.

Inductive Inference

Inductive inferencing is based on the assumption that a recurring pattern, observed for some event or entity, implies that the pattern is true for all entities in the class. Given instances $P(a_1), P(a_2), \ldots, P(a_k)$, conclude that $\forall x\, P(x)$. More generally, given $P(a_1) \rightarrow Q(b_1), P(a_2) \rightarrow Q(b_2), \ldots, P(a_k) \rightarrow Q(b_k)$, conclude $\forall x,y\, P(x) \rightarrow Q(y)$.

We often make this form of generalization after observing only a few instances of a situation. It is known as the *inductive leap*. For example, after seeing a few white swans, we incorrectly infer that all swans are white (a type of Australian swan is black), or we conclude that all Irishmen are stubborn after discussions with only a few.

We can represent inductive inference using the following description:

$$\frac{P(a_1), \ldots, P(a_k)}{\forall x\, P(x)}$$

Inductive inference, of course, is not a valid form of inference, since it is not usually the case that all objects of a class can be verified as having a particular property. Even so, this is an important and commonly used form of inference.

Analogical Inference

Analogical inference is a form of experiential inference. Situations or entities which are alike in some respects tend to be similar in other respects. Thus, when we find that situation (object) A is related in certain ways to B, and A' is similar in some context to A, we conclude that B' has a similar relation to A' in this context. For example, to solve a problem with three equations in three unknowns, we try to extend the methods we know in solving two equations in two unknowns.

Analogical inference appears to be based on the use of a combination of three other methods of inference, abductive, deductive and inductive. We depict this form of inference with the following description, where the r above the implication symbol means is related to.

$$\frac{p^r \rightarrow Q}{p'^r \rightarrow Q'}$$

Analogical inference, like abductive and inductive is a useful but invalid form of commonsense inference.

4.9 REPRESENTATIONS USING RULES

Rules can be considered a subset of predicate logic. They have become a popular representation scheme for expert systems (also called rule-based systems). They were first used in the General Problem Solver system in the early 1970s (Newell and Simon, 1972).

Rules have two component parts: a left-hand side (LHS) referred to as the antecedent, premise, condition, or situation, and a right-hand side (RHS) known as the consequent, conclusion, action, or response. The LHS is also known as the if part and the RHS as the then part of the rule. Some rules also include an else part. Examples of rules which might be used in expert systems are given below.

IF: The temperature is greater than 95 degrees C,
THEN: Open the relief valve.

IF: The patient has a high temperature,
and the stain is gram-positive,
and the patient has a sore throat,
THEN: The organism is streptococcus.

IF: The lights do not come on,
and the engine does not turn over,
THEN: The battery is dead or the cable is loose.

IF: $A \& B \& C$
THEN: D
$A \& B \& (C \lor D) \rightarrow D$

The simplest form of a rule-based production system consists of three parts, a knowledge base (KB) consisting of a set of rules (as few as 50 or as many as several thousand rules may be required in an expert system), a working memory, and a rule interpreter or inference engine. The interpreter inspects the LHS of each rule in the KB until one is found which matches the contents of working memory. This causes the rule to be activated or to "fire" in which case the contents of working memory are replaced by the RHS of the rule. The process continues by scanning the next rules in sequence or restarting at the beginning of the knowledge base.

INTERNAL FORM

```
RULE047
     Premise: (($and (same cntxt site blood)
                     (notdefinite contxt ident)
                     (same cntxt morph rod)
                     (same cntxt burn t))
      Action: (conclude cntxt ident pseudonomas 0.4))
```

ENGLISH TRANSLATION

IF: 1) The site of the culture is blood, and
2) The identity of the organism is not known with certainty, and
3) The stain of the organism is gramneg, and
4) The morphology of the organism is rod, and
5) The patient has been seriously burned

THEN: There is weakly suggestive evidence (0.4) that the identity of the organism is pseudonomas.

Figure 4.1 A rule from the MYCIN system.

Each rule represents a chunk of knowledge as a conditional statement, and each invocation of the rules as a sequence of actions. This is essentially an inference process using the chain rule as described in Section 4.2. Although there is no established syntax for rule-based systems, the most commonly used form permits a LHS consisting of a conjunction of several conditions and a single RHS action term.

An example of a rule used in the MYCIN[3] expert system (Shortliffe, 1976) is illustrated in Figure 4.1.

In RULE047, the quantity 0.4 is known as a confidence factor (CF). Confidence factors range from −1.0 (complete disbelief) to 1.0 (certain belief). They provide a measure of the experts' confidence that a rule is applicable or holds when the conditions in the LHS have all been satisfied.

We will see further examples of rules and confidence factors in later chapters.

4.10 SUMMARY

We have considered propositional and first order predicate logics in this chapter as knowledge representation schemes. We learned that while PL has a sound theoretical foundation, it is not expressive enough for many practical problems. FOPL, on the

[3] MYCIN was one of the earliest expert systems. It was developed at Stanford University in the mid-1970s to demonstrate that a system could successfully perform diagnoses of patients having infectious blood diseases.

other hand, provides a theoretically sound basis and permits a great latitude of expressiveness. In FOPL one can easily code object descriptions and relations among objects as well as general assertions about classes of similar objects. The increased generality comes from the joining of predicates, functions, variables, and quantifiers. Perhaps the most difficult aspect in using FOPL is choosing appropriate functions and predicates for a given class of problems.

Both the syntax and semantics of PL and FOPL were defined and examples given. Equivalent expressions were presented and the use of truth tables was illustrated to determine the meaning of complex formulas. Rules of inference were also presented, providing the means to derive conclusions from a basic set of facts or axioms. Three important syntactic inference methods were defined: modus ponens, chain rule and resolution. These rules may be summarized as follows.

MODUS PONENS	CHAIN RULE	RESOLUTION
$\dfrac{P \quad P \rightarrow Q}{Q}$	$\dfrac{P \rightarrow Q \quad Q \rightarrow R}{P \rightarrow R}$	$\dfrac{P \lor \sim Q,\ Q \lor R}{P \lor R}$

A detailed procedure was given to convert any complex set of formulas to clausal normal forms. To perform automated inference or theorem proving, the resolution method requires that the set of axioms and the conjecture to be proved be in clausal form. Resolution is important because it provides the means to mechanically derive conclusions that are valid. Programs using resolution methods have been developed for numerous systems with varying degrees of success, and the language PROLOG is based on the use of such resolution proofs. FOPL has without question become one of the leading methods for knowledge representation.

In addition to valid forms of inference based on deductive methods, three invalid, but useful types of inferencing were also presented, abductive, inductive, and analogical.

Finally, rules, a subset of FOPL, were described as a popular representation scheme. As will be seen in Chapter 15, many expert systems use rules for their knowledge bases. Rules provide a convenient means of incrementally building a knowledge base in an easily understood language.

EXERCISES

4.1 Construct a truth table for the expression (A & ($A \lor B$)). What single term is this expression equivalent to?

4.2 Prove the following rules from Section 4.2.
  (a) Simplification: From P & Q, infer P
  (b) Conjunction: From P and Q, infer P & Q
  (c) Transposition: From $P \rightarrow Q$, infer $\sim Q \rightarrow \sim P$

4.3 Given the following PL expressions, place parentheses in the appropriate places to form fully abbreviated wffs.

(a) $\sim P \vee Q \,\&\, R \rightarrow S \rightarrow U \,\&\, Q$

(b) $\sim P \,\&\, Q \vee P \leftrightarrow U \rightarrow \sim R$

(c) $Q \vee P \vee \sim R \,\&\, S \rightarrow \sim U \,\&\, P \leftrightarrow R$

4.4 Translate the following axioms into predicate calculus wffs. For example, A_1 below could be given as

∀x,y,z CONNECTED(x,y,z) & Bikesok(z) → GETTO(x,y)

A1. If town x is connected to town y by highway z, and bicycles are allowed on z, you can get to y from x by bike.
A2. If town x is connected to y by z, y is connected to x by z.
A3. If you can get to y from x, and you can get to z from y, you can get to z from x.
A4. Town-A is connected to Town-B by Road-1.
A5. Town-B is connected to Town-C by Road-2.

4.5 Convert axioms A1-A5 from Problem 4.4 to clausal form and write axioms A6-A13, below, directly into clausal form.
A6. Town-A is connected to Town-C by Road-3.
A7. Town-D is connected to Town-E by Road-4.
A8. Town-D is connected to Town-B by Road-5.
A9-A11. Bikes are allowed on Road-3, Road-4, and Road-5.
A12. Bikes are always allowed on either Road-2 or Road-1 (each day it may be different but one road is always possible).
A13. Town-A and Town-E are not connected by Road-3.

4.6 Use the clauses from Problem 4.5 to answer the following questions:

(a) What can be deduced from clauses 2 and 13?

(b) Can GETTO(Town-D, Town-B) be deduced from the above clauses?

4.7 Find the meaning of the statement

$$(\sim P \vee Q) \,\&\, R \rightarrow S \vee (\sim R \,\&\, Q)$$

for each of the interpretations given below.

(a) I_1: P is true, Q is true, R is false, S is true.

(b) I_2: P is true, Q is false, R is true, S is true.

4.8 Transform each of the following sentences into disjunctive normal form.

(a) $\sim(P \,\&\, Q) \,\&\, (P \vee Q)$

(b) $\sim(P \vee \sim Q) \,\&\, (R \rightarrow S)$

(c) $P \rightarrow ((Q \,\&\, R) \leftrightarrow S)$

4.9 Transform each of the following sentences into conjunctive normal form.

(a) $(P \rightarrow Q) \rightarrow R$

(b) $P \vee (\sim P \,\&\, Q \,\&\, R)$

(c) $(\sim P \,\&\, Q) \vee (P \,\&\, \sim Q) \,\&\, S$

4.10 Determine whether each of the following sentences is

(a) satisfiable

(b) contradictory

(c) valid

S_1: $(P \ \& \ Q) \lor \,\tilde{}(P \ \& \ Q)$ S_2: $(P \lor Q) \rightarrow (P \ \& \ Q)$
S_3: $(P \ \& \ Q) \rightarrow R \lor \,\tilde{}Q$ S_4: $(P \lor Q) \ \& \ (P \lor \,\tilde{}Q) \lor P$
S_5: $P \rightarrow Q \rightarrow \,\tilde{}P$ S_6: $P \lor Q \ \& \ \tilde{}P \lor \,\tilde{}Q \ \& \ P$

4.11 Given the following wffs $P \rightarrow Q$, $\tilde{}Q$, and $\tilde{}P$, show that $\tilde{}P$ is a logical consequene of the two preceding wffs:
(a) Using a truth table
(b) Using Theorem 4.1.

4.12 Given formulas S_1 and S_2 below, show that $Q(a)$ is a logical consequence of the two.

$$S_1: (\forall x)(P(x) \rightarrow Q(x)) \qquad S_2: P(a)$$

4.13 Transform the following formula to prenex normal form

$$\forall xy \ (\exists z \ P(x,z) \ \& \ P(y,z)) \rightarrow \exists u \ Q(x,y,u)$$

4.14 Prove that the formula $\exists x \ P(x) \rightarrow \forall x \ P(x)$ is always true if the domain D contains only one element.

4.15 Find the standard normal form for the following statement.

$$\forall x \ (\tilde{}P(x,0) \rightarrow (\exists y \ (P(y,g(x)) \ \& \ \forall z \ (P(z,g(x)) \rightarrow P(y,z))$$

4.16 Referring to Problems 4.4 and 4.5, use resolution to show (by refutation) that you can get from Town-E to Town-C.

4.17 Write a LISP resolution program to answer different queries about a knowledge base where the knowledge base and queries are given in clausal form. For example,

```
(setq KB (A1 to A13))
(query (GETTO Town-E Town-C))
```

4.18 Given the following information for a database:
A1. If x is on top of y, y supports x.
A2. If x is above y and they are touching each other, x is on top of y.
A3. A cup is above a book.
A4. A cup is touching a book.
(a) Translate statements A1 through A4 into clausal form.
(b) Show that the predicate supports (book, cup) is true using resolution.

4.19 Write a PROLOG program using A1 to A4 of Problem 4.18, and show that SUPPORTS (book cup) is true.

5

Dealing with Inconsistencies and Uncertainties

The previous chapter considered methods of reasoning under conditions of certain, complete, unchanging, and consistent facts. It was implicitly assumed that a sufficient amount of reliable knowledge (facts, rules, and the like) was available with which to deduce confident conclusions. While this form of reasoning is important, it suffers from several limitations.

1. It is not possible to describe many envisioned or real-world concepts; that is, it is limited in expressive power.
2. There is no way to express uncertain, imprecise, hypothetical or vague knowledge, only the truth or falsity of such statements.
3. Available inference methods are known to be inefficient.
4. There is no way to produce new knowledge about the world. It is only possible to add what is derivable from the axioms and theorems in the knowledge base.

In other words, strict classical logic formalisms do not provide realistic representations of the world in which we live. On the contrary, intelligent beings are continuously required to make decisions under a veil of uncertainty.

Uncertainty can arise from a variety of sources. For one thing, the information we have available may be incomplete or highly volatile. Important facts and details which have a bearing on the problems at hand may be missing or may change rapidly. In addition, many of the "facts" available may be imprecise, vague, or fuzzy. Indeed, some of the available information may be contradictory or even unbelievable. However, despite these shortcomings, we humans miraculously deal with uncertainties on a daily basis and usually arrive at reasonable solutions. If it were otherwise, we would not be able to cope with the continually changing situations of our world.

In this and the following chapter, we shall discuss methods with which to accurately represent and deal with different forms of inconsistency, uncertainty, possibility, and beliefs. In other words, we shall be interested in representations and inference methods related to what is known as commonsense reasoning.

5.1 INTRODUCTION

Consider the following real-life situation. Timothy enjoys shopping in the mall only when the stores are not crowded. He has agreed to accompany Sue there on the following Friday evening since this is normally a time when few people shop. Before the given date, several of the larger stores announce a one-time, special sale starting on that Friday evening. Timothy, fearing large crowds, now retracts the offer to accompany Sue, promising to go on some future date. On the Thursday before the sale was to commence, weather forecasts predicted heavy snow. Now, believing the weather would discourage most shoppers, Timothy once again agreed to join Sue. But, unexpectedly, on the given Friday, the forecasts proved to be false; so Timothy once again declined to go.

This anecdote illustrates how one's beliefs can change in a dynamic environment. And, while one's beliefs may not fluctuate as much as Timothy's, in most situations, this form of belief revision is not uncommon. Indeed, it is common enough that we label it as a form of commonsense reasoning, that is, reasoning with uncertain knowledge.

Nonmonotonic Reasoning

The logics we studied in the previous chapter are known as monotonic logics. The conclusions derived using such logics are valid deductions, and they remain so. Adding new axioms increases the amount of knowledge contained in the knowledge base. Therefore, the set of facts and inferences in such systems can only grow larger; they can not be reduced; that is, they increase monotonically. The form of reasoning performed above by Timothy, on the other hand, is nonmonotonic. New facts became known which contradicted and invalidated old knowledge. The old knowledge was retracted causing other dependent knowledge to become invalid, thereby requiring further retractions. The retractions led to a shrinkage or nonmonotonic growth in the knowledge at times.

More formally, let KBL be a formal first order system consisting of a knowledge base and some logic L. Then, if KB1 and KB2 are knowledge bases where

$$\begin{aligned}&\text{KB1} = \text{KBL}\\&\text{KB2} = \text{KBL} \cup \text{F, for some wff F, then}\\&\text{KB1} \subseteq \text{KB2}\end{aligned}$$

In other words, a first order KB system can only grow monotonically with added knowledge.

When building knowledge-based systems, it is not reasonable to expect that all the knowledge needed for a set of tasks could be acquired, validated, and loaded into the system at the outset. More typically, the initial knowledge will be incomplete, contain redundancies, inconsistencies, and other sources of uncertainty. Even if it were possible to assemble complete, valid knowledge initially, it probably would not remain valid forever, not in a continually changing environment.

In an attempt to model real-world, commonsense reasoning, researchers have proposed extensions and alternatives to traditional logics such as PL and FOPL. The extensions accommodate different forms of uncertainty and nonmonotony. In some cases, the proposed methods have been implemented. In other cases they are still topics of research. In this and the following chapter, we will examine some of the more important of these methods.

We begin in the next section with a description of truth maintenance systems (TMS), systems which have been implemented to permit a form of nonmonotonic reasoning by permitting the addition of changing (even contradictory) statements to a knowledge base. This is followed in Section 5.3 by a description of other methods which accommodate nonmonotonic reasoning through default assumptions for incomplete knowledge bases. The assumptions are plausible most of the time, but may have to be retracted if other conflicting facts are learned. Methods to constrain the knowledge that must be considered for a given problem are considered next. These methods also relate to nonmonotonic reasoning. Section 5.4 gives a brief treatment of modal and temporal logics which extend the expressive power of classical logics to permit representations and reasoning about necessary and possible situations, temporal, and other related situations. Section 5.5 concludes the chapter with a brief presentation of a relatively new method for dealing with vague and imprecise information, namely fuzzy logic and language computation.

5.2 TRUTH MAINTENANCE SYSTEMS

Truth maintenance systems (also known as belief revision and revision maintenance systems) are companion components to inference systems. The main job of the TMS is to maintain consistency of the knowledge being used by the problem solver and not to perform any inference functions. As such, it frees the problem solver from any concerns of consistency and allows it to concentrate on the problem solution aspects. The TMS also gives the inference component the latitude to perform nonmonotonic inferences. When new discoveries are made, this more recent information can displace previous conclusions that are no longer valid. In this way, the set of beliefs available to the problem solver will continue to be current and consistent.

Figure 5.1 illustrates the role played by the TMS as part of the problem solver. The inference engine (IE) solves domain problems based on its current belief set, while the TMS maintains the currently active belief set. The updating process is incremental. After each inference, information is exchanged between the two components. The IE tells the TMS what deductions it has made. The TMS, in turn, asks questions about current beliefs and reasons for failures. It maintains a consistent set of beliefs for the IE to work with even if new knowledge is added and removed.

For example, suppose the knowledge base (KB) contained only the propositions P, $P \rightarrow Q$, and modus ponens. From this, the IE would rightfully conclude Q and add this conclusion to the KB. Later, if it was learned that $\tilde{}P$ was appropriate, it would be added to the KB resulting in a contradiction. Consequently, it would be necessary to remove P to eliminate the inconsistency. But, with P now removed, Q is no longer a justified belief. It too should be removed. This type of belief revision is the job of the TMS.

Actually, the TMS does not discard conclusions like Q as suggested. That could be wasteful, since P may again become valid, which would require that Q and facts justified by Q be rederived. Instead, the TMS maintains dependency records for all such conclusions. These records determine which set of beliefs are current (which are to be used by the IE). Thus, Q would be removed from the current belief set by making appropriate updates to the records and not by erasing Q. Since Q would not be lost, its rederivation would not be necessary if P became valid once again.

The TMS maintains complete records of reasons or justifications for beliefs. Each proposition or statement having at least one valid justification is made a part of the current belief set. Statements lacking acceptable justifications are excluded from this set. When a contradiction is discovered, the statements responsible for the contradiction are identified and an appropriate one is retracted. This in turn may result in other retractions and additions. The procedure used to perform this process is called dependency-directed backtracking. This process is described later.

The TMS maintains records to reflect retractions and additions so that the IE

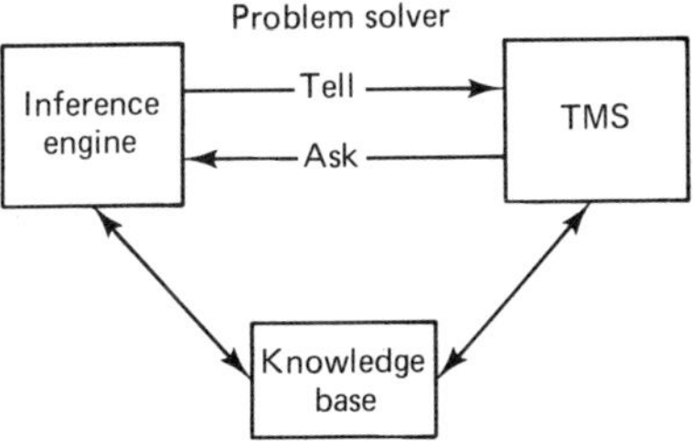

Figure 5.1 Architecture of the problem solver with a TMS.

will always know its current belief set. The records are maintained in the form of a dependency network. The nodes in the network represent KB entries such as premises, conclusions, inference rules, and the like. Attached to the nodes are justifications which represent the inference steps from which the node was derived. Nodes in the belief set must have valid justifications. A premise is a fundamental belief which is assumed to be always true. Premises need no justifications. They form a base from which all other currently active nodes can be explained in terms of valid justifications.

There are two types of justification records maintained for nodes: support lists (SL) and conceptual dependencies (CP). SLs are the most common type. They provide the supporting justifications for nodes. The data structure used for the SL contains two lists of other dependent node names, an in-list and an out-list. It has the form

(SL <in-list> <out-list>)

In order for a node to be active and, hence, labeled as IN the belief set, its SL must have at least one valid node in its in-list, and all nodes named in its out-list, if any, must be marked OUT of the belief set. For example, a current belief set that represents Cybil as a nonflying bird (an ostrich) might have the nodes and justifications listed in Table 5.1.

Each IN-node given in Table 5.1 is part of the current belief set. Nodes n1 and n5 are premises. They have empty support lists since they do not require justifications. Node n2, the belief that Cybil *can* fly is out because n3, a valid node, is in the out-list of n2.

Suppose it is discovered that Cybil is not an ostrich, thereby causing n5 to be retracted (marking its status as OUT). Then n3, which depends on n5, must also be retracted. This, in turn, changes the status of n2 to be a justified node. The resultant belief set is now that the bird Cybil can fly.

To represent a belief network, the symbol conventions shown in Figure 5.2 are sometimes used. The meanings of the nodes shown in the figure are (1) a premise is a true propositon requiring no justification, (2) an assumption is a current belief that could change, (3) a datum is either a currently assumed or IE derived belief, and (4) justifications are the belief (node) supports, consisting of supporting antecedent node links and a consequent node link.

TABLE 5.1 EXAMPLE NODES IN A DEPENDENCY NETWORK

Node	Status	Meaning	Support list	Comments
n1	IN	Cybil is a bird	(SL ( ) ( ))	a premise
n2	OUT	Cybil can fly	(SL (n1) (n3))	unjustified belief
n3	IN	Cybil cannot fly	(SL (n5) (n4))	justified belief
n4	OUT	Cybil has wings	(SL ( ) ( ))	retracted premise
n5	IN	Cybil is an Ostrich	(SL ( ) ( ))	a premise

Figure 5.2 Belief network node meanings.

An example of a typical network representation is given in Figure 5.3. Note that nodes T, U, and W are OUT since they lack needed support from P. If the node labeled P is made IN for some reason, the TMS would update the network by propagating the "inness" support provided by node P to make T, U, and W IN.

As noted earlier, when a contradiction is discovered, the TMS locates the source of the contradiction and corrects it by retracting one of the contributing sources. It does this by checking the support lists of the contradictory node and going directly to the source of the contradiction. It goes directly to the source by examining the dependency structure supporting the justification and determining the offending nodes. This is in contrast to the naive backtracking approach which would search a deduction tree sequentially, node-by-node until the contradictory node is reached. Backtracking directly to the node causing the contradiction is known as dependency-directed backtracking (DDB). This is clearly a more efficient search strategy than chronological backtracking. This process is illustrated in Figure 5.4 where it is assumed that A and D are contradictory. By backtracking directly to

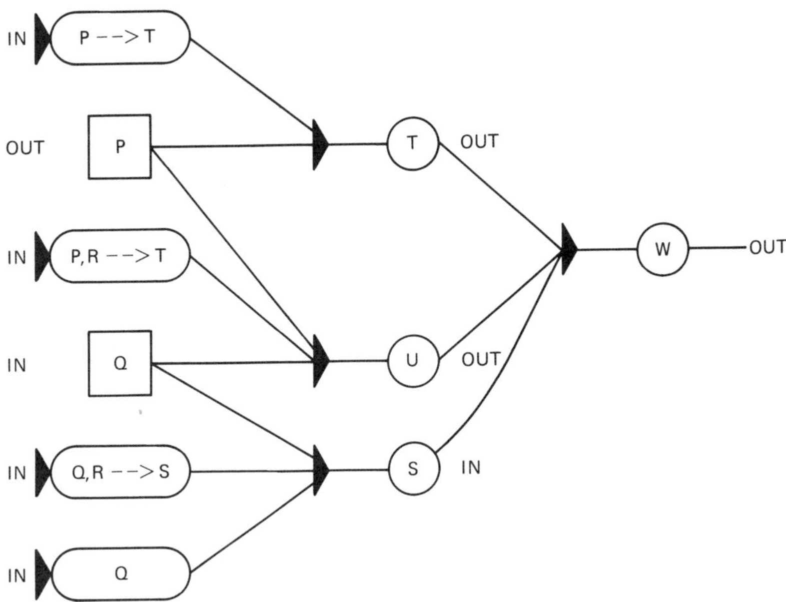

Figure 5.3 Typical fragment of a belief network.

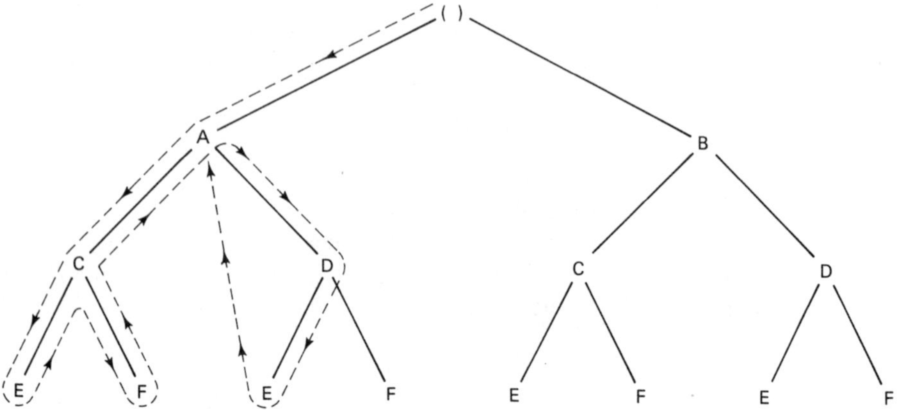

Figure 5.4 Dependency-directed backtracking in a TMS.

the source of a contradiction (the dashed line from E to A), extra search time is avoided.

CP justifications are used less frequently than the SLs. They justify a node as a type of valid hypothetical argument. The internal form of a CP justification is as follows:

(CP <consequent><inhypotheses><outhypotheses>)

A CP is valid if the consequent node is IN whenever each node among the in-hypotheses is IN and each node among the out-hypotheses is OUT. Two separate lists of hypotheses are used, since nodes may be derived from both nodes that are IN and other nodes that are OUT.

CPs correspond to conditional proofs typically found in deduction systems. The hypotheses used in such a conditional proof correspond to the in-hypotheses in the CP. Since the functions of the CP are somewhat complex, we clarify their main functions with an example.

Suppose a system is being used to schedule aircraft and crews for commercial airline flights. The type of aircraft normally scheduled for a given flight is a 737, and the crew required is class A. The nodes and justifications for these facts might be

n1	IN	type(aircraft) = 737	(SL ( ) (n2))
n2	OUT	type(aircraft) = L400	
n3	IN	class(crew) = A	(SL (n8, . . . , n22) ( ))

where the justifications for n1 is n2 (with OUT status) and for n3 is nodes n8, . . . , n22 which relate to the availability of a captain, copilot, and other crew members qualified as class A. Now suppose it is learned that a full class A crew is not available. To complete a schedule for the flight, the system must choose an alternative aircraft, say an L400. To do this the IE changes the status of n2 to IN. But this results in a contradiction and, hence, creation of the node

n4	IN	contradiction	(SL (n1,n3) ( ))

The contradiction now initiates the DDB procedure in the TMS to locate the offending assumptions. Since there is only one such node, n1, its retraction is straightforward. For this, the TMS creates a "nogood" node with a CP justification as

n5	IN	nogood n1	(CP n4 (n1,n3) ( ))

To correct the inconsistency, the TMS next makes n2 an IN node by justifying it with n5 as follows

n2	IN	type(aircraft) = L400	(SL (n5) ( ))

This in turn causes n1 to become OUT (as an assumption n1 has a nonempty out-list). Also, since n4 was justified by n1, it too must become OUT. This gives the following set of nodes

n1	OUT	type(aircraft) = 737	(SL ( ) (n2))
n2	IN	type(aircraft) = L400	(SL (n5) ( ))
n3	IN	class(crew) = A	(SL (n8, . . . , n22) ( ))
n4	OUT	contradiction	(SL (n1,n3) ( ))
n5	IN	nogood n1	(CP n4 (n1,n3) ( ))

Note that a CP justification was needed for the "nogood" node to prevent a circular retraction of n2 from occurring. Had an SL been used for n5 with an n4 node in-list justification, n5 would have become OUT after n4, again causing n2 to become OUT.

The procedures for manipulating CPs are quite complicated, and, since they are usually converted into SLs anyway, we only mention their main functions here. For a more detailed account see Doyle (1979).

We have briefly described the JTMS here since it is the simplest and most widely used truth maintenance system. This type of TMS is also known as a nonmonotonic TMS (NMTMS). Several other types have been developed to correct some of the deficiencies of the JTMS and to meet other requirements. They include the logic-based TMS (the LTMS), and the assumption-based TMS (the ATMS), as well as others (de Kleer, 1986a and 1986b).

5.3 DEFAULT REASONING AND THE CLOSED WORLD ASSUMPTION

Another form of uncertainty occurs as a result of incomplete knowledge. One way humans deal with this problem is by making plausible default assumptions; that is, we make assumptions which typically hold but may have to be retracted if new information is obtained to the contrary. For example, if you have an acquaintance named Pat who is over 20 years old, you would normally assume that this person would drive a car. Later, if you learned Pat had suffered from blackouts until just recently, you would be forced to revise your beliefs.

Default Reasoning

Default reasoning is another form of nonmonotonic reasoning; it eliminates the need to explicitly store all facts regarding a situation. Reiter (1980) develops a theory of default reasoning within the context of traditional logics. A default is expressed as

$$\frac{a(x):\mathrm{M}b_1(x), \ldots, \mathrm{M}b_k(x)}{c(x)} \tag{5.1}$$

where $a(x)$ is a precondition wff for the conclusion wff $c(x)$, M is a consistency operator and the $b_i(x)$ are conditions, each of which must be separately consistent with the KB for the conclusion $c(x)$ to hold. As an example, suppose we wish to make the statement, "If x is an adult and it is consistent to assume that x can drive, then infer that x can drive." Using the above formula this would be represented as

$$\frac{\mathrm{ADULT}(x):\mathrm{MDRIVE}(x)}{\mathrm{DRIVE}(x)}$$

Default theories consist of a set of axioms and set of default inference rules with schemata like formula 5.1. The theorems derivable from a default system are those that follow from first-order logic and the assumptions assumed from the default rules.

Suppose a KB contains only the statements

$$\frac{\mathrm{BIRD}(x):\mathrm{MFLY}(x)}{\mathrm{FLY}(x)}$$

$$\mathrm{BIRD}(\mathrm{tweety})$$

A default proof of FLY(tweety) is possible. But if KB also contains the clauses

$$\mathrm{OSTRICH}(\mathrm{tweety})$$

$$\mathrm{OSTRICH}(x) \rightarrow {}^{\sim}\mathrm{FLY}(x)$$

FLY(tweety) would be blocked since the default is now inconsistent.

Default rules are especially useful in hierarchial KBs. Because the default rules are transitive, property inheritance becomes possible. For example, in a heirarchy of living things, any animal could inherit the property has-heart from the rule

$$\forall x\ \mathrm{ANIMAL}(x) \rightarrow \mathrm{HAS\text{-}HEART}(x)$$

Transitivity can also be a problem in KBs with many default rules. Rule interactions can make representations very complex. Therefore caution is needed in implementing such systems.

Closed World Assumption

Another form of assumption, made with regard to incomplete knowledge, is more global in nature than single defaults. This type of assumption is useful in applications where most of the facts are known, and it is, therefore, reasonable to assume that if a proposition cannot be proven, it is false. This is known as the closed world assumption (CWA) with failure as negation (failure to prove a statement F results in assuming its negation, $\tilde{}F$). This means that in a KB if the ground literal $P(a)$ is not provable, then $\tilde{}P(a)$ is assumed to hold.

A classic example where this type of assumption is reasonable is in an airline KB application where city-to-city flights, not explicitly entered or provable, are assumed not to exist. Thus, ˜CONNECT(boston,van-horn) would be inferred whenever CONNECT(boston,van-horn) could not be derived from the KB. This seems reasonable since we would not want to enter all pairs of cities which do not have intercity flights.

By augmenting a KB with an assumption (a metarule) which states that if the ground atom $P(a)$ cannot be proved, assume its negation $\tilde{}P(a)$, the CWA completes the theory with respect to KB. (Recall that a formal KB system is complete if and only if every ground atom or its negation is in the system.) Augmenting a KB with the negation of all ground atoms of the language which are not derivable, gives us a complete theory. For example, a KB containing only the clauses

$$P(a)$$

$$P(b)$$

$$P(a) \rightarrow Q(a)$$

and modus ponens is not complete, since neither $Q(b)$ nor $\tilde{}Q(b)$ is inferrable from the KB. This KB can be completed, however, by adding either $Q(b)$ or $\tilde{}Q(b)$.

In general, a KB augmented with CWA is not consistent. This is easily seen by considering the KB consisting of the clause

$$P(a) \vee Q(b)$$

Now, since none of the ground literals in this clause are derivable, the augmented KB becomes

$$P(a) \vee Q(b)$$

$$\tilde{}P(a),\ \tilde{}Q(b)$$

which is inconsistent.

It can be shown that consistency can be maintained for a special type of

CWA. This is a KB consisting of Horn clauses. If a KB is consistent and Horn, then its CWA augmentation is consistent. (Recall that Horn clauses are clauses with at most one positive literal.)

It may appear that the global nature of the negation as failure assumption is a serious drawback of CWA. And indeed there are many applications where it is not appropriate. There is a way around this using completion formulas which we discuss in the next section. Even so, CWA is essentially the formalism under which Prolog operates and Prolog has been shown to be effective in numerous applications.

5.4 PREDICATE COMPLETION AND CIRCUMSCRIPTION

Limiting default assumptions to only portions of a KB can be achieved through the use of completion or circumscription formulas. Unlike CWA, these formulas apply only to specified predicates, and not globally to the whole KB.

Completion Formulas

Completion formulas are axioms which are added to a KB to restrict the applicability of specific predicates. If it is known that only certain objects should satisfy given predicates, formulas which make this knowledge explicit (complete) are added to the KB. This technique also requires the addition of the unique-names assumption (UNA); that is, formulas which state that distinguished named entities in the KB are unique (different).

As an example of predicate completion, suppose we have the following KB:

OWNS(joe,ford)
STUDENT(joe)
OWNS(jill,chevy)
STUDENT(jill)
OWNS(sam,bike)
PROGRAMMER(sam)
STUDENT(mary)

If it is known that Joe is the only person who owns a Ford, this fact can be made explicit with the following completion formula:

$$\forall x \; OWNS(x,ford) \rightarrow EQUAL(x,joe) \tag{5.2}$$

In addition, we add the inequality formula

$$\neg EQUAL(a,joe) \tag{5.3}$$

which has the meaning that this is true for all constants a which are different from Joe.

Likewise, if it is known that Mary also has a Ford, and only Mary and Joe have Fords, the completion and corresponding inequality formulas in this case would be

$$\forall x \text{ OWNS(ford,x)} \rightarrow \text{EQUAL(x,joe)} \vee \text{EQUAL(x,mary)}$$
$$\sim\text{EQUAL(a,joe)}$$
$$\sim\text{EQUAL(a,mary)}$$

Once completion formulas have been added to a KB, ordinary first order proof methods can be used to prove statements such as ~OWNS(jill,ford). For example, to obtain a refutation proof using resolution, we put the completion and inequality formulas 5.2 and 5.3 in clausal form respectively, negate the query ~OWNS(jill,ford) and add it to the KB. Thus, resolving with the following clauses

1. ~OWNS(x,ford) V EQUAL(x,joe)
2. ~EQUAL(a,joe)
3. OWNS(jill,ford)

from 1 and 3 we obtain

4. EQUAL(jill,joe)

and from 2 and 4 (recall that *a* is any constant not = Joe) we obtain the empty clause [ ], proving the query.

The need for the inequality formulas should be clearer now. They are needed to complete the proof by restricting the objects which satisfy the completed predicates.

Predicate completion performs the same function as CWA but with respect to the completed predicates only. However with predicate completion, it is possible to default both negative as well as positive statements.

Circumscription

Circumscription is another form of default reasoning introduced by John McCarthy (1980). It is similar to predicate completion in that all objects that can be shown to have some property *P* are in fact the only objects that satisfy *P*. We can use circumscription, like predicate completion, to constrain the objects which must be considered in any given situation. Suppose we have a university world situation in which there are two known CS students. We wish to state that the known students are the only students, to "circumscribe" the students

CSSTUDENT(a)
CSSTUDENT(b)

Let x be a tuple, that is $x = (x_1, \ldots, x_n)$, and let ϕ denote a relation of the same arity as P. Also let KB($\phi(x)$) denote a KB with every occurrence of P in KB replaced by ϕ. The usual form of circumscribing P in KB, denoted as CIR(KB:P), is given by

$$\text{CIR(KB:P)} = \text{KB} \ \& \ [\forall\phi(\text{KB}(\phi) \ \& \ (\forall x\phi(x) \rightarrow \text{P}(x))] \rightarrow \forall x[\text{P}(x) \rightarrow \phi(x)]$$

This amounts to replacing KB with a different KB in which some expression ϕ (in this example $\phi = (x = a \lor x = b))$ replaces each occurrence of P (here CSSTUDENT). The first conjunct inside the bracket identifies the required substitution. The second conjunct, $\forall x\phi(x) \rightarrow \text{P}(x)$, states that objects which satisfy ϕ also satisy P, while the conclusion states that ϕ and P are then equivalent.

Making the designated substitution in our example we obtain the circumscriptive inference

From CSSTUDENT(a) & CSSTUDENT(b), infer

$$\forall x(\text{CSSTUDENT}(x) \rightarrow (x = a \lor x = b)$$

Note that ϕ has been quantified in the circumscription schema above, making it a second order formula. This need not be of too much concern since in many cases the formula can be rewritten in equivalent first order form.

An interesting example used by McCarthy in motivating circumscription, related to the task of getting across a river when only a row boat was available. For problems such as this, it should only be necessary to consider those objects named as being important to the task completion and not innumerable other contingencies, like a hole in the boat, lost oars, breaking up on a rock, or building a bridge.

5.5 MODAL AND TEMPORAL LOGICS

Modal logics were invented to extend the expressive power of traditional logics. The original intent was to add the ability to express the necessity and possibility of propositions P in PL and FOPL. Later, other modal logics were introduced to help capture and represent additional subjective mood concepts (supposition, desire) in addition to the standard indicative mood (factual) concept representations given by PL and FOPL.

With modal logics we can also represent possible worlds in addition to the actual world in which we live. Thus, unlike traditional logics, where an interpretation of a wff results in an assignment of true or false (in one world only), an interpretation in modal logics would be given for each possible world. Consequently, the wff may be true in some worlds and false in others.

Modal logics are derived as extensions of PL and FOPL by adding modal operators and axioms to express the meanings and relations for concepts such as consistency, possibility, necessity, obligation, belief, known truths, and temporal situations, like past, present, and future. The operators take predicates as arguments and are denoted by symbols or letters such as L (it is necessary that), M (it is possible that), and so on. For example, MCOLDER-THAN(denver,portland) would be used to represent the statement ''it is possible that Denver is colder than Portland.''

Modal logics are classified by the type of modality they express. For example, alethic logics are concerned with necessity and possibility, deontic logics with what is obligatory or permissible, epistemic logics with belief and (known) knowledge, and temporal logics with tense modifiers like sometimes, always, what has been, what will be, or what is. In what follows, we shall be primarily concerned with alethic and temporal logics.

It is convenient to refer to an *agent* as the conceptualization of our knowledge-based system (a robot or some other KB system). We may adopt different views regarding the world or environment in which the agent functions. For example, one view may regard an agent as having a set of basic beliefs which consists of all statements that are derivable from the knowlege base. This was essentially the view taken in PL and FOPL. Note, however, that the statements we now call beliefs are not the same as known factual knowledge of the previous chapter. They may, in fact be erroneous.

In another view, we may treat the agent as having a belief set that is determined by possible worlds which are accessible to the agent. In what follows, we will adopt this latter view. But before describing the modal language of our agent, we should explain further the notion of possible worlds.

Possible Worlds

In different knowledge domains it is often productive to consider possible situations or events as alternatives to actual ones. This type of reasoning is especially useful in fields where an alternative course of action can lead to a significant improvement or to a catastrophic outcome. It is a common form of reasoning in areas like law, economics, politics, and military planning to name a few. Indeed, we frequently engage our imaginations to simulate possible situations which predict outcomes based on different scenarios. Our language has even grown to accommodate hypothetical concepts with statements like "if this were possible," or "suppose we have the following situation." On occasion, we may also wish to think of possible worlds as corresponding to different distributed knowledge bases.

Next, we wish to establish a relationship between an agent A and A's possible worlds. For this, we make use of a binary *accessibility* relation R. R is used to define relative possibilities between worlds for agent A. Let $W = \{w_0, w_1, \ldots\}$ denote a set of possible worlds where w_0 refers to the actual world. Let the relation $R(A: w_i, w_j)$ be defined on W such that for any $w_i, w_j \in W$, w_j is accessible from w_i for agent A whenever R is satisfied. This means that a proposition P is true in w_i if and only if P is true in all worlds accessible from w_i.

Since R is a relation, it can be characterized with relational properties such as reflexivity, transitivity, symmetry, and equivalence. Thus for any $w_i, w_j, w_k \in W$, the following properties are defined.

Reflexive. R is reflexive if $(w_i, w_i) \in R$ for each $w_i \in W$. In other words, all worlds are possible with respect to themselves.

Transitive. R is transitive if when $(w_i,w_j) \in R$, and $(w_j,w_k) \in R$ then $(w_i,w_k) \in R$. If w_j is accessible from w_i and w_k is accessible from w_j, then w_k is accessible from w_i.

Symmetric. R is symmetric if when $(w_i,w_j) \in R$ then $(w_j,w_i) \in R$. If w_j is accessible from w_i, then w_i is accessible from w_j.

Equivalence. R is an equivalence relation if R is reflexive, transitive, and symmetric.

These properties can also be described pictorially as illustrated in Figure 5.5.

Modal Operators and Logics

As suggested above, different operators are used to obtain different modalities. We begin with the standard definitions of a traditional logic, say PL, and introduce appropriate operators and, as appropriate, introduce certain axioms. For example, to define one first order modal logic we designate as L_{LM}, the operators L and M noted above would be included. We also add a necessity axiom which states that if the proposition P is a logical axiom then infer LP (that is, if P is universally valid, it is necessary that P is true). We also define LP = ˜M˜P or it is necessary that P is true as equivalent to it is not possible that P is not true.

Different modal logics can be obtained from L_{LM} by adding different axioms. Some axioms can also be related to the accessibility relations. Thus, for example, we can say that

> If R is reflexive, add LP → P. In other words, if it is necessary that P is true in w_i, then P is true in w_i.
>
> If R is transitive, add LP → LLP. This states that if P is true in all w_j accessible from some w_i, then P is true in all w_k accessible from w_j.

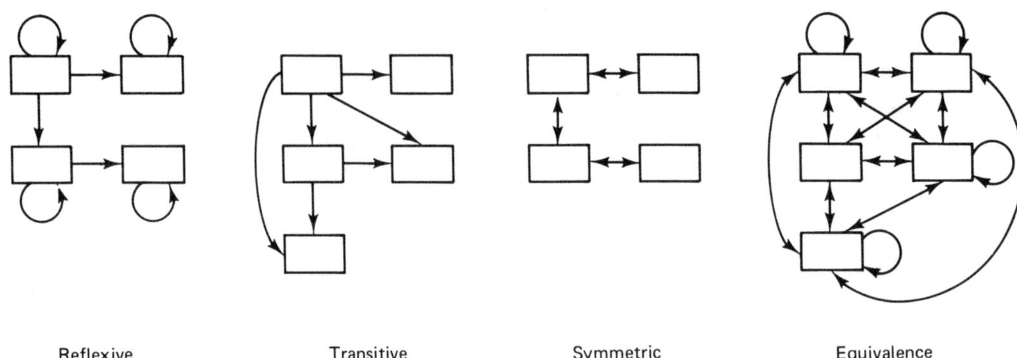

Figure 5.5 Accessibility relation properties.

If R is symmetric, then add P → LMP. This states that if P is true in w_i, then MP is true in all w_j accessible from w_i.
If R is an equivalence relation, add LP → P and MP → LMP.

To obtain a formal system from any of the above, it is necessary to add appropriate inference rules. Many of the inference rules defined in Chapter 4 would apply here as well, (modus ponens, universal substitution, and others). Thus, for a typical modal system based on propositional logic, the following axioms could apply:

A. The basic propositional logic assumptions (Chapter 4) including modus ponens,
B. Addition of the operators L (necessity) and M (possibility), and
C. Some typical modal axioms such as
   1. MP = ~L~P (possible P is equivalent to the statement it is not necessary that not P),
   2. L(P → Q) → (LP → LQ) (if it is necessary that P implies Q, then if P is necessary, Q is necessary),
   3. LP → P (if P is necessary then P), and
   4. LP → LLP (if P is necessary, then it is necessary that P is necessary).

Axioms C3 and C4 provide the reflexivity and transitivity access relations, respectively. If other relations are desired, appropriate axioms would be added to those given above; for example, for the symmetric access relation P → LMP would be added.

As an example of a proof in modal logic, suppose some assertions are added to a knowledge base for which the above assumptions and axioms apply:

D. Assertions:
   1. (sam is a man)
   2. M(sam is a child)
   3. L[(sam is a child) → L(sam is a child)]
   4. L[(sam is a man) → ~(sam is a child)]

A simple proof that ~(sam is a child) would proceed as follows. From C3 and D4 infer that

(sam is a man) → ~(sam is a child)

From D1 and E1 using modus ponens conclude

~(sam is a child)

Temporal Logics

Temporal logics use modal operators in relation to concepts of time, such as past, present, future, sometimes, always, preceeds, succeeds, and so on. An example of two operators which correspond to necessity and possibility are always (A) and sometimes (S). A propositional temporal logic system using these operators would include the propositional logic assumptions of Chapter 4, the operators A and S, and appropriate axioms. Typical formulas using the A and S operators with the predicate Q would be written as

$AQ \rightarrow SQ$	(if always Q then sometimes Q)
$AQ \rightarrow Q$	(if always Q then Q)
$Q \rightarrow SQ$	(if Q then sometimes Q)
$SQ \rightarrow \tilde{}A\tilde{}Q$	(if sometimes Q then not always not Q)

A combination of propositional and temporal logic inference rules would then be added to obtain a formal system.

In addition to the above operators, the tense operators past (P) and future (F) have also been used. For example, tense formulas for the predicate (tweety files) would be written as

(tweety flies)	present tense.
P(tweety flies)	past tense: Tweety flew.
F(tweety flies)	future tense: Tweety will fly.
FP(tweety flies)	future perfect tense: Tweety will have flown.

It is also possible to define other modalities from the ones given above. For example, to express the concepts it has always been and it will always be the operators H and G may be defined respectively as

$HQ = \tilde{}P\tilde{}Q$	(it has always been the case that Q)
$GQ = \tilde{}F\tilde{}Q$	(it will always be the case that Q)

The four operators P, F, H, and G were used by the logician Lemmon (1965) to define a propositional tense logic he called KT. The language used consisted of propositional logic assumptions, the four tense operators P, F, H, and G, and the following axioms:

$$G(Q \rightarrow R) \rightarrow (GQ \rightarrow GR)$$
$$H(Q \rightarrow R) \rightarrow (HQ \rightarrow HR)$$
$$\tilde{}G\tilde{}HQ \rightarrow Q$$
$$\tilde{}H\tilde{}GQ \rightarrow Q$$

To complete the formal system, inference rules of propositional logic such as modus ponens and the two rules

$$\frac{Q}{HQ} \qquad \frac{Q}{GQ}$$

were added. These rules state that if Q is true, infer that Q has always been the case and Q will always be the case, respectively.

The semantics of a temporal logic is closely related to the frame problem. The frame problem is the problem of managing changes which occur from one situation to another or from frame to frame as in a moving picture sequence.

For example, a KB which describes a robot's world must know which facts change as a result of some action taken by the robot. If the robot throws out the cat, turns off the light, leaves the room, and locks the door, some, but not all facts which describe the room in the new situation must be changed.

Various schemes have been proposed for the management of temporally changing worlds including other modal operators and time and date tokens. This problem has taken on increased importance and a number of solutions have been offered. Still much work remains to find a comprehensive solution.

5.6 FUZZY LOGIC AND NATURAL LANGUAGE COMPUTATIONS

We have already noted several limitations of traditional logics in dealing with uncertain and incomplete knowledge. We have now considered methods which extend the expressive power of the traditional logics and permit different forms of nonmonotonic reasoning. All of the extensions considered thus far have been based on the truth functional features of traditional logics. They admit interpretations which are either true or false only. The use of two valued logics is considered by some practitioners as too limiting. They fail to effectively represent vague or fuzzy concepts.

For example, you no doubt would be willing to agree that the predicate "TALL" is true for Pole, the seven foot basketball player, and false for Smidge the midget. But, what value would you assign for Tom, who is 5 foot 10 inches? What about Bill who is 6 foot 2, or Joe who is 5 foot 5? If you agree 7 foot is tall, then is 6 foot 11 inches also tall? What about 6 foot 10 inches? If we continued this process of incrementally decreasing the height through a sequence of applications of modus ponens, we would eventually conclude that a three foot person is tall. Intuitively, we expect the inferences should have failed at some point, but at what point? In FOPL there is no direct way to represent this type of concept. Furthermore, it is not easy to represent vague statements such as "slightly more beautiful," "not quite as young as . . . ," "not very expensive, but of questionable reliability," "a little bit to the left," and so forth.

Theory of Fuzzy Sets

In standard set theory, an object is either a member of a set or it is not. There is no in between. The natural numbers 3, 11, 19, and 23 are members of the set of prime numbers, but 10, blue, cow, and house are not members. Traditional logics are based on the notions that P(a) is true as long as a is a member of the set belonging to class P and false otherwise. There is no partial containment. This amounts to the use of a characteristic function f for a set A, where $f_A(x) = 1$ if x is in A; otherwise it is 0. Thus, f is defined on the universe U and for all $x \in U$, $f: U \rightarrow \{0,1\}$.

We may generalize the notion of a set by allowing characteristic functions to assume values other than 0 and 1. For example, we define the notion of a fuzzy set with the characteristic function u which maps from U to a number in the real interval [0,1]; that is $u: U \rightarrow [0,1]$. Thus, we define the fuzzy set $\tilde{A}$ as follows (the ˜ symbol is omitted but assumed when a fuzzy set appears in a subscript):

Definition. Let U be a set, denumerable or not, and let x be an element of U. A fuzzy subset $\tilde{A}$ of U is a set of ordered pairs $\{(x, u_A(x))\}$, for all x in U, where $u_A(x)$ is a membership characteristic function with values in [0,1], and which indicates the degree or level of membership of x in $\tilde{A}$.

A value of $u_A(x) = 0$ has the same meaning as $f_A(x) = 0$, that x is not a member of $\tilde{A}$, whereas a value of $u_A(x) = 1$ signifies that x is completely contained in $\tilde{A}$. Values of $0 < u_A(x) < 1$ signify that x is a partial member of $\tilde{A}$.

Characteristic functions for fuzzy sets should not be confused with probabilities. A probability is a measure of the degree of uncertainty, likelihood, or belief based on the frequency or proportion of occurrence of an event. Whereas a fuzzy characteristic function relates to vagueness and is a measure of the feasibility or ease of attainment of an event. Fuzzy sets have been related to possibility distributions which have some similarities to probability distributions, but their meanings are entirely different.

Given a definition of a fuzzy set, we now have a means of expressing the notion TALL(x) for an individual x. We might for example, define the fuzzy set $\tilde{A}$ = {tall} and assign values of $u_A(0) = u_A(10) = \ldots = u_A(40) = 0$, $u_A(50) = 0.2$, $u_A(60) = 0.4$, $u_A(70) = 0.6$, $u_A(80) = 0.9$, $u_A(90) = u_A(100) = 1.0$. Now we can assign values for individuals noted above as TALL(Pole) = 1.0, and TALL (Joe) = 0.5. Of course, our assignment of values for $u_A(x)$ was purely subjective. And to be complete, we should also assign values to other fuzzy sets associated with linguistic variables such as very short, short, medium, etc. We will discuss the notions of linguistic variables and related topics later.

Operations on fuzzy sets are somewhat similar to the operations of standard set theory. They are also intuitively acceptable.

$\tilde{A} = \tilde{B}$ if and only if $u_A(x) = u_B(x)$ for all $x \in U$	equality
$\tilde{A} \subseteq \tilde{B}$ if and only if $u_A(x) \leq u_B(x)$ for all $x \in U$	containment
$u_{A \cap B}(x) = \min_x\{u_A(x), u_B(x)\}$	intersection
$u_{A \cup B}(x) = \max_x\{u_A(x), u_B(x)\}$	union
$u_{A'}(x) = 1 - u_A(x)$	complement set

The single quotation mark denotes the complement fuzzy set, A'. Note that the intersection of two fuzzy sets $\tilde{A}$ and $\tilde{B}$ is the largest fuzzy subset that is a subset of both. Likewise, the union of two fuzzy sets $\tilde{A}$ and $\tilde{B}$ is the smallest fuzzy subset having both $\tilde{A}$ and $\tilde{B}$ as subsets.

With the above definitions, it is possible to derive a number of properties which hold for fuzzy sets much the same as they do for standard sets. For example, we have

$$\tilde{A} \cup (\tilde{B} \cap \tilde{C}) = (\tilde{A} \cup \tilde{B}) \cap (\tilde{A} \cup \tilde{C}) \qquad \text{distributivity}$$

$$\tilde{A} \cap (\tilde{B} \cup \tilde{C}) = (\tilde{A} \cap \tilde{B}) \cup (\tilde{A} \cap \tilde{C})$$

$$(\tilde{A} \cup \tilde{B}) \cup \tilde{C} = \tilde{A} \cup (\tilde{B} \cup \tilde{C}) \qquad \text{associativity}$$

$$(\tilde{A} \cap \tilde{B}) \cap \tilde{C} = \tilde{A} \cap (\tilde{B} \cap \tilde{C})$$

$$\tilde{A} \cap \tilde{B} = \tilde{B} \cap \tilde{A}, \quad \tilde{A} \cup \tilde{B} = \tilde{B} \cup \tilde{A} \qquad \text{commutativity}$$

$$\tilde{A} \cap \tilde{A} = \tilde{A}, \quad \tilde{A} \cup \tilde{A} = \tilde{A} \qquad \text{idempotency}$$

There is also a form of DeMorgan's laws:

$$u_{(A \cap B)'}(x) = u_{A' \cup B'}(x)$$

$$u_{(A \cup B)'}(x) = u_{A' \cap B'}(x)$$

Note however, that

$$\tilde{A} \cap \tilde{A}' \neq \emptyset, \tilde{A} \cup \tilde{A}' \neq U$$

since in general for $u_A(x) = a$, with $0 < a < 1$, we have

$$u_{A \cup A'}(x) = \max[a, 1 - a] \neq 1$$

$$u_{A \cap A'}(x) = \min[a, 1 - a] \neq 0$$

On the other hand the following relations do hold:

$$\tilde{A} \cap \emptyset = \emptyset \qquad \tilde{A} \cup \emptyset = \tilde{A}$$

$$\tilde{A} \cap U = \tilde{A} \qquad \tilde{A} \cup U = U$$

The universe from which a fuzzy set is constructed may also be uncountable. For example, we can define values of u for the fuzzy set $\tilde{A} = \{\text{young}\}$ as

$$u_A(x) = \begin{cases} 1.0 & \text{for } 0 \leq x \leq 20 \\ \left[1 + \left(\dfrac{x - 20}{10}\right)^2\right]^{-1} & \text{for } x > 20 \end{cases}$$

The values of $u_A(x)$ are depicted graphically, in Figure 5.6.

A number of operations that are unique to fuzzy sets have been defined. A few of the more common operations include

Dilation. The dilation of $\tilde{A}$ is defined as

$$\text{DIL}(\tilde{A}) = [u_A(x)]^{1/2} \qquad \text{for all } x \text{ in } U$$

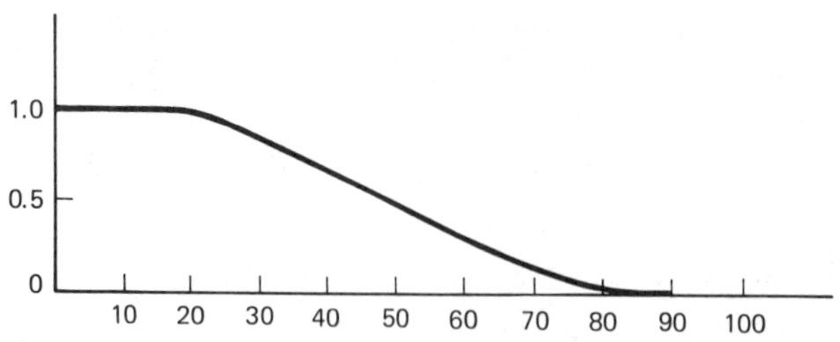

Figure 5.6 Degrees of membership for young age.

Concentration. The concentration of $\tilde{A}$ is defined as

$$\text{CON}(\tilde{A}) = [u_A(x)]^2 \qquad \text{for all } x \text{ in } U$$

Normalization. The normalization of $\tilde{A}$ is defined as

$$\text{NORM}(\tilde{A}) = u_A(x) \; / \; \max_x\{u_A(x)\} \qquad \text{for all } x \text{ in } U$$

These three operations are depicted graphically in Figure 5.7. Note that dilation tends to increase the degree of membership of all partial members x by spreading out the characteristic function curve. The concentration is the opposite of dilation. It tends to decrease the degree of membership of all partial members, and concentrates the characteristic function curve. Normalization provides a means of normalizing all characteristic functions to the same base much the same as vectors can be normalized to unit vectors.

In addition to the above, a number of other operations have been defined including fuzzification. Fuzzification permits one to fuzzify any normal set. These operations will not be required here. Consequently we omit their definitions.

Lotfi a. Zadeh of the University of California, Berkeley, first introduced fuzzy sets in 1965. His objectives were to generalize the notions of a set and propositions to accommodate the type of fuzziness or vagueness we have discussed above. Since its introduction in 1965, much research has been conducted in fuzzy set theory and logic. As a result, extensions now include such concepts as fuzzy arithmetic, possibility distributions, fuzzy statistics, fuzzy random variables, and fuzzy set functions.

Many researchers in AI have been reluctant to accept fuzzy logic as a viable alternative to FOPL. Still, successful systems which employ fuzzy logic have been

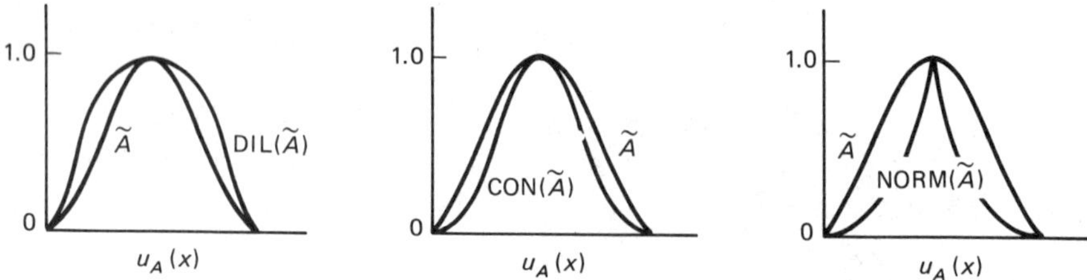

Figure 5.7 Dilation, concentration, and normalization of u.

developed, and a fuzzy VLSI chip has been produced by Bell Telephone Laboratories, Inc., of New Jersey (Togai and Watanabe, 1986).

Reasoning with Fuzzy Logic

The characteristic function for fuzzy sets provides a direct linkage to fuzzy logic. The degree of membership of x in $\tilde{A}$ corresponds to the truth value of the statement x is a member of $\tilde{A}$ where $\tilde{A}$ defines some propositional or predicate class. When $u_A(x) = 1$, the proposition A is completely true, and when $u_A(x) = 0$ it is completely false. Values between 0 and 1 assume corresponding values of truth or falsehood.

In Chapter 4 we found that truth tables were useful in determining the truth value of a statement or wff. In general this is not possible for fuzzy logic since there may be an infinite number of truth values. One could tabulate a limited number of truth values, say those corresponding to the terms false, not very false, not true, true, very true, and so on. More importantly, it would be useful to have an inference rule equivalent to a fuzzy modus ponens.

Generalized modus ponens for fuzzy sets have been proposed by a number of researchers. They differ from the standard modus ponens in that statements which are characterized by fuzzy sets are permitted and the conclusion need not be identical to the implicand in the implication. For example, let $\tilde{A}$, $\tilde{A}1$, $\tilde{B}$, and $\tilde{B}1$ be statements characterized by fuzzy sets. Then one form of the generalized modus ponens reads

Premise: x is $\tilde{A}1$

Implication: If x is $\tilde{A}$ then y is $\tilde{B}$

Conclusion: y is $\tilde{B}1$

An example of this form of modus ponens is given as

Premise: This banana is very yellow

Implication: If a banana is yellow then the banana is ripe

Conclusion: This banana is very ripe

Although different forms of fuzzy inference have been proposed, we present only Zadeh's original compositional rule of inference.

First, recall the definition of a relation. For two sets A and B, the Cartesian product $A \times B$ is the set of all ordered pairs (a,b), for $a \subseteq A$ and $b \subseteq B$. A binary relation on two sets A and B is a subset of $A \times B$. Likewise, we define a binary fuzzy relation $\tilde{R}$ as a subset of the fuzzy Cartesian product $\tilde{A} \times \tilde{B}$, a mapping of $\tilde{A} \rightarrow \tilde{B}$ characterized by the two parameter membership function $u_R(a,b)$. For example, let $\tilde{A} = \tilde{B} = \mathbb{R}$ the set of real numbers, and let $\tilde{R}:=$ much larger than. A membership function for this relation might then be defined as

$$u_R(a,b) = \begin{cases} 0 & \text{for } a \leq \text{b} \\ (1 + (a - b)^{-2})^{-1} & \text{for } a > \text{b} \end{cases}$$

Now let X and Y be two universes and let $\tilde{A}$ and $\tilde{B}$ be fuzzy sets in X and $X \times Y$ respectively. Define fuzzy relations $\tilde{R}_A(x)$, $\tilde{R}_B(x,y)$, and $\tilde{R}_C(y)$ in X, $X \times Y$ and Y, respectively. Then the compositional rule of inference is the solution of the relational equation

$$\tilde{R}_C(y) = \tilde{R}_A(x) \text{ o } \tilde{R}_B(x,y) = \max_x \min\{u_A(x), u_B(x,y)\}$$

where the symbol o signifies the composition of $\tilde{A}$ and $\tilde{B}$. As an example, let

$$X = Y = \{1,2,3,4\}$$

$$\tilde{A} = \{\text{little}\} = \{(1 / 1),(2 / .6),(3 / .2),(4 / 0)$$

$\tilde{R}$ = approximately equal, a fuzzy relation defined by

$\tilde{R}$: x \ y	1	2	3	4
1	1	.5	0	0
2	.5	1	.5	0
3	0	.5	1	.5
4	0	0	.5	1

Then applying the max-min composition rule

$$\begin{aligned}\tilde{R}_C(y) &= \max_x \min\{u_A(x), u_R(x,y)\}\\ &= \max_x \{\min[(1,1),(.6,.5),(.2,0),(0,0)],\\ &\qquad \min[(1,.5),(.6,1),(.2,.5),(0,0)],\\ &\qquad \min[(1,0),(.6,.5),(.2,1),(0,.5)],\\ &\qquad \min[(1,0),(.6,0),(.2,.5),(0,1)]\}\\ &= \max_x\{[1,.5,0,0],[.5,.6,.2,0],[0,.5,.2,0],[0,0,.2,0]\}\\ &= \{[1],[.6],[.5],[.2]\}\end{aligned}$$

Therefore the solution is

$$\tilde{R}_C(y) = \{(1 / 1),(2 / .6),(3 / .5),(4 / .2)\}.$$

Stated in terms of a fuzzy modus ponens, we might interpret this as the inference

Premise: x is little

Implication: x and y are approximately equal

Conclusion: y is more or less little

The above notions can be generalized to any number of universes by taking the Cartesian product and defining relations on various subsets.

Natural Language Computations

Earlier, we mentioned linguistic variables without really defining them. Linguistic variables provide a link between a natural or artifical language and representations which accommodate quantification such as fuzzy propositions. In this section, we formally define a linguistic variable and show how they are related to fuzzy logic.

Informally, a linguistic variable is a variable that assumes a value consisting of words or sentences rather than numbers. For example, the variable AGE might assume values of very young, young, not young, or not old. These values, which are themselves linguistic variables, may in turn, each be given meaning through a base universe of elapsed time (years). This is accomplished through appropriately defined characteristic functions.

As an example, let the linguistic variable AGE have possible values {very young, young, not young, middle-aged, not old, old, very old}. To each of these variables, we associate a fuzzy set consisting of ordered tuples $\{(x/u_A(x))\}$ where $x \in U = [0,110]$ the universe (years). The variable AGE, its values, and their corresponding fuzzy sets are illustrated in Figure 5.8.

A formal, more elegant definition of a linguistic variable is one which is based on language theory concepts. For this, we define a linguistic variable as the quintuple

$$(x,T(x),U,G,M)$$

where

x is the name of the variable (AGE in the above example),

$T(x)$ is the terminal set of x (very-young, young, etc.),

U is the universe of discourse (years of life),

G is a set of syntactic rules, the grammer which generates the values of x, and

M is the semantic rule which associates each value of x with its meaning $M(x)$, a fuzzy subset of U.

The grammar G is further defined as the tuple (V_N,V_T,P,S) where V_N is the set of nonterminal symbols, V_T the set of terminal symbols from the alphabet of G, P is

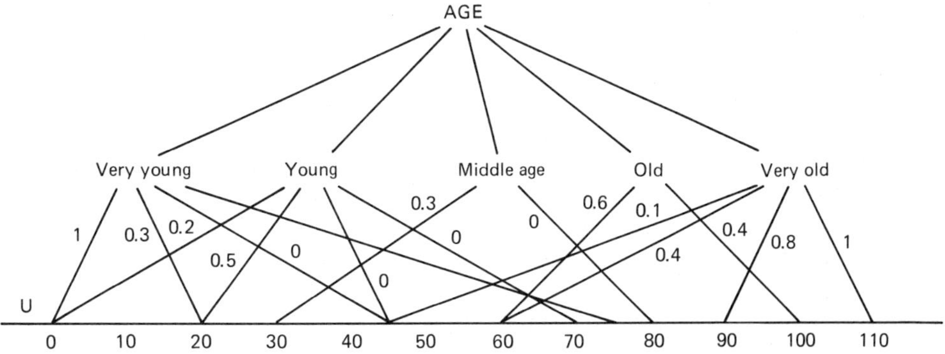

Figure 5.8 The linguistic variable *age*.

a set of rewrite (production) rules, and S is the start symbol. The language $L(G)$ generated by the grammar G is the set of all strings w derived from S consisting of symbols in V_T. Thus, for example, using $V_N = \{A,B,C,D,E,S\}$ and the following rules in P, we generate the terminal string "not young and not very old."

P:	$S \rightarrow A$	$A \rightarrow A$ and B	$C \rightarrow D$	$D \rightarrow$ young
	$S \rightarrow$ S or A	$B \rightarrow C$	$C \rightarrow$ very C	$E \rightarrow$ old
	$A \rightarrow B$	$B \rightarrow$ not C	$C \rightarrow E$	

This string is generated through application of the following rules:

$S \rightarrow A \rightarrow A$ and $B \rightarrow A$ and not $C \rightarrow A$ and not very $C \rightarrow A$ and not very $E \rightarrow A$ and not very old $\rightarrow B$ and not very old $\rightarrow$ not C and not very old $\rightarrow$ not D and not very old $\rightarrow$ not young and not very old

The semantic rule M gives meaning to the values of AGE. For example, we might have $M(\text{old}) = \{(x \,/\, u_{\text{old}}(x)) \mid x \in [0,110]\}$ where $u_{\text{old}}(x)$ is defined as

$$u_{\text{old}}(x) = \begin{cases} 0 & \text{for } 0 \leq x \leq 50 \\ \left(1 + \left(\dfrac{x - 50}{5}\right)^{-2}\right)^{-1} & \text{for } x > 50 \end{cases}$$

In this section we have been able to give only a brief overview of some of the concepts and issues related to the expanding fields based on fuzzy set theory. The interested reader will find numerous papers and texts available in the literature. We offer a few representative references here which are recent and have extensive bibliographies: (Zadeh, 1977, 1981, 1983), (Kandel, 1982), (Gupta et al., (1985), and (Zimmerman, 1985).

5.7 SUMMARY

Commonsense reasoning is nonmonotonic in nature. It requires the ability to reason with incomplete and uncertain knowledge, replacing outmoded or erroneous beliefs with new ones to better model current situations.

In this chapter, we have considered various methods of representing and dealing with uncertainty and inconsistencies. We first described truth maintenance systems which permit nonmonotonic forms of reasoning by maintaining a consistent, but changing, belief set. The type of TMS we considered in detail, was the justification based TMS or JTMS. It maintained a belief network consisting of nodes representing facts and rules. Attached to each node was a justification, a data structure which characterized the In or Out status of the node and its support. The JTMS maintains the current belief set for the problem solver, but does not perform inferencing functions. That is the job of the IE.

Other methods of dealing with nonmonotonic reasoning include default reasoning and CWA. In both cases, assumptions are made regarding knowledge or beliefs which are not directly provable. In CWA, if P can not be proved, then assume ~P is true. Default reasoning is based on the use of typical assumptions about an object or class of objects which are plausible. The assumptions are regarded as valid unless new contrary information is learned.

Predicate completion and circumscription are methods which restrict the values a predicate or group of predicates may assume. They allow the predicates to take on only those values the KB says they must assume. Both methods are based on the use of completion formulas. Like CWA, they are also a form of nonmonotonic reasoning.

Modal logics extend the expressiveness of classical logics by permitting the notions of possibility, necessity, obligation, belief, and the like. A number of different modal logics have been formalized, and inference rules comparable to propositional and predicate logic are available to permit different forms of nonmonotonic reasoning.

Like modal logics, fuzzy logic was introduced to generalize and extend the expressiveness of traditional logics. Fuzzy logic is based on fuzzy set theory which permits partial set membership. This, together with the ability to use linguistic variables, makes it possible to represent such notions as Sue is not very tall, but she is quite pretty.

EXERCISES

5.1 Give an example of nonmonotonic reasoning you have experienced at some time.

5.2 Draw the TMS belief network for the following knowledge base of facts. The question marks under output status means that the status must be determined for these datum nodes.

INPUTS

Premises	Status	Assumptions	Status
$Q \rightarrow S$	IN	Q	OUT
$Q, R \rightarrow U$	IN	R	IN
$P, R \rightarrow T$	IN		. . .
P	IN		
	. . .		

OUTPUTS

Datum	Status	Conditions
S	?	If Q, $Q \rightarrow S$ then S
U	?	If Q; $Q, R \rightarrow U, R$ then U
T	?	If R; $P, R \rightarrow T$; P then T

5.3 Draw a TMS belief network for the aircraft example described in Section 5.2 and show how the network changes with the selection of an alternate choice of aircraft.

5.4 Write schemata for default reasoning using the following statements:

(a) If someone is an adult and it is consistent to assume that adults can vote, infer that that person can vote.

(b) If one is at least 18 years old and it is consistent to assume that one who is physically fit and who passes a test may obtain a pilots license, infer that such a person can obtain a pilots license.

5.5 Show that a Horn clause data base that is consistent is consistent under the CWA assumption. Give an example of a simple Horn clause CWA data base to illustrate consistency.

5.6 For the following database facts, write a completion formula that states that Bill is the only person that lives in Dallas.

LIVESIN(bill,dallas)

LIVESIN(joe,denver)

LIVESIN(sue,phoenix)

OWNS(bill,computer)

STUDENT(sue)

5.7 Determine whether the following modal statements have accessibility relations that are reflexive, transitive, or symmetric:

(a) Bill Brown is alive in the current world.

(b) In the current world and in all worlds in the future of the current world, if Jim Jones is dead in that world, then he will be dead in all worlds in the future of that world.

(c) In the current world or in some world in the future of the current world, John Jones is dead.

5.8 Write modal propositional statements for the following using the operators L and M as described in Section 5.4.

(a) It is necessarily true that the moon is made of green cheese or it is not made of green cheese.

(b) It is possible that if Kennedy were born in Spain Kennedy would speak Spanish.

(c) It is necessarily true that if n is divisible by 4 then n is divisible by 2.

5.9 Show that the dilation of the fuzzy set $\tilde{A} = \text{CON}(\tilde{B})$ is the fuzzy set $\tilde{B}$.

5.10 Give three examples of inferencing with English statements using fuzzy modus ponens (see the example in Section 5.6 under Reasoning with Fuzzy Logic).

5.11 Draw a pictorial definition for the linguistic variable TALL (similar to the variable AGE of Figure 5.8) giving your own subjective values for TALL variables and their values.

5.12 Define a reasonable, real valued fuzzy function for the linguistic variable SHORT (see the function for $u_{\text{old}}(x)$).

6

Probabilistic Reasoning

The previous chapter considered methods of representation which extend the expressiveness of classical logic and permit certain types of nonmonotonic reasoning. Representations for vague and imprecise concepts were also introduced with fuzzy set theory and logic. There are other types of uncertainty induced by random phenomena which we have not yet considered. To round out the approaches which are available for commonsense reasoning in AI, we continue in this chapter with theory and methods used to represent probabilistic uncertainties.

6.1 INTRODUCTION

We saw in the previous chapter that a TMS deals with uncertainty by permitting new knowledge to replace old knowledge which is believed to be outdated or erroneous. This is not the same as inferring directly with knowledge that can be given a probability rating based on the amount of uncertainty present. In this chapter, we want to examine methods which use probabilistic representations for all knowledge and which reason by propagating the uncertainties from evidence and assertions to conclusions. As before, the uncertainties can arise from an inability to predict outcomes due to unreliable, vague, incomplete, or inconsistent knowledge.

The probability of an uncertain event A is a measure of the degree of likelihood of occurrence of that event. The set of all possible events is called the sample space, S. A probability measure is a function $P(\cdot)$ which maps event outcomes E_1, E_2, . . . , from S into real numbers and which satisfies the following axioms of probability:

1. $0 \leq P(A) \leq 1$ for any event $A \subseteq S$.
2. $P(S) = 1$, a certain outcome.
3. For $E_i \cap E_j = \varnothing$, for all $i \neq j$ (the E_i are mutually exclusive), $P(E_1 \cup E_2 \cup E_3 \cup \ldots) = P(E_1) + P(E_2) + P(E_3) + \ldots$

From these three axioms and the rules of set theory, the basic laws of probability can be derived. Of course, the axioms are not sufficient to compute the probability of an outcome. That requires an understanding of the underlying distributions which must be established through one of the following approaches:

1. use of a theoretical argument which accurately characterizes the processes,
2. using one's familiarity and understanding of the basic processes to assign subjective probabilities, or
3. collecting experimental data from which statistical estimates of the underlying distributions can be made.

Since much of the knowledge we deal with is uncertain in nature, a number of our beliefs must be tenuous. Our conclusions are often based on available evidence and past experience, which is often far from complete. The conclusions are, therefore, no more than educated guesses. In a great many situations it is possible to obtain only partial knowledge concerning the possible outcome of some event. But, given that knowledge, one's ability to predict the outcome is certainly better than with no knowledge at all. We manage quite well in drawing plausible conclusions from incomplete knowledge and past experiences.

Probabilistic reasoning is sometimes used when outcomes are unpredictable. For example, when a physician examines a patient, the patient's history, symptoms, and test results provide some, but not conclusive, evidence of possible ailments. This knowledge, together with the physician's experience with previous patients, improves the likelihood of predicting the unknown (disease) event, but there is still much uncertainty in most diagnoses. Likewise, weather forecasters "guess" at tomorrow's weather based on available evidence such as temperature, humidity, barometric pressure, and cloud coverage observations. The physical relationships which govern these phenomena are not fully understood; so predictability is far from certain. Even a business manager must make decisions based on uncertain predictions when the market for a new product is considered. Many interacting factors influence the market, including the target consumer's lifestyle, population growth, potential consumer income, the general economic climate, and many other dependent factors.

In all of the above cases, the level of confidence placed in the hypothesized conclusions is dependent on the availability of reliable knowledge and the experience of the human prognosticator. Our objective in this chapter is to describe some approaches taken in AI systems to deal with reasoning under similar types of uncertain conditions.

6.2 BAYESIAN PROBABILISTIC INFERENCE

The form of probabilistic reasoning described in this section is based on the Bayesian method introduced by the clergyman Thomas Bayes in the eighteenth century. This form of reasoning depends on the use of conditional probabilities of specified events when it is known that other events have occurred. For two events H and E with the probability $P(E) > 0$, the conditional probability of event H, given that event E has occurred, is defined as

$$P(H|E) = P(H \,\&\, E) \,/\, P(E) \tag{6.1}$$

This expression can be given a frequency interpretation by considering a random experiment which is repeated a large number of times, n. The number of occurrences of the event E, say No. (E), and of the joint event H and E, No. (H & E), are recorded and their relative frequencies rf computed as

$$rf(H \,\&\, E) = \frac{\text{No. } (A \,\&\, E)}{n} \qquad rf(E) = \frac{\text{No. } (E)}{n} \tag{6.2}$$

When n is large, the two expressions (6.2) approach the corresponding probabilities respectively, and the ratio

$$rf(H \,\&\, E) \,/\, rf(E) \simeq P(H \,\&\, E) \,/\, P(E)$$

then represents the proportion of times event H occurs relative to the occurrence of E, that is, the approximate conditional occurrence of H with E.

The conditional probability of event E given that event H occurred can likewise be written as

$$P(E|H) = P(H \,\&\, E) \,/\, P(H) \tag{6.3}$$

Solving 6.3 for $P(H \,\&\, E)$ and substituting this in equation 6.1 we obtain one form of Bayes' Rule

$$P(H|E) = P(E|H)P(H) \,/\, P(E) \tag{6.4}$$

This equation expresses the notion that the probability of event H occurring when it is known that event E occurred is the same as the probability that E occurs when it is known that H occurred, multiplied by the ratio of the probabilities of the two events H and E occurring. As an example of the use of equation 6.4, consider the problem of determining the probability that a patient has a certain disease $D1$, given that a symptom E was observed. We wish to find $P(D1|E)$.

Suppose now it is known from previous experience that the prior (unconditional) probabilities $P(D1)$ and $P(E)$ for randomly chosen patients are $P(D1) = 0.05$, and $P(E) = 0.15$, respectively. Also, we assume that the conditional probability of the observed symptom given that a patient has disease $D1$ is known from experience to be $P(E|D1) = 0.95$. Then, we easily determine the value of $P(D1|E)$ as

$$P(D1|E) = P(E|D1)P(D1)/P(E) = (0.95 \times 0.05)/0.15$$
$$= 0.32$$

It may be the case that the probability $P(E)$ is difficult to obtain. If that is the case, a different form of Bayes' Rule may be used. To see this, we write equation 6.4 with $\tilde{}H$ substituted in place of H to obtain

$$P(\tilde{}H|E) = \frac{P(E|\tilde{}H)P(\tilde{}H)}{P(E)}$$

Next, we divide equation 6.4 by this result to eliminate $P(E)$ and get

$$\frac{P(H|E)}{P(\tilde{}H|E)} = \frac{P(E|H)P(H)}{P(E|\tilde{}H)P(\tilde{}H)} \tag{6.5}$$

Note that equation 6.5 has two terms that are ratios of a probability of an event to the probability of its negation, $P(H|E) / P(\tilde{}H|E)$ and $P(H) / P(\tilde{}H)$. The ratio of the probability of an event E divided by the probability of its negation is called the *odds* of the event and are denoted as $O(E)$. The remaining ratio $P(E|H) / P(E|\tilde{}H)$ in equation 6.5 is known as the likelihood ratio of E with respect to H. We denote this quantity by $L(E|H)$. Using these two new terms, the odds-likelihood form of Bayes' Rule for equation 6.5 may be written as

$$O(H|E) = L(E|H)\cdot O(H)$$

This form of Bayes' Rule suggests how to compute the posterior odds $O(H|E)$ from the prior odds on H, $O(H)$. That value is proportional to the likelihood $L(E|H)$. When $L(E|H)$ is equal to one, the knowledge that E is true has no effect on the odds of H. Values of $L(E|H)$ less than or greater than one decrease or increase the odds correspondingly. When $L(E|H)$ cannot be computed, estimates may still be made by an expert having some knowledge of H and E. Estimating the ratio rather than the individual probabilities appears to be easier for individuals in such cases. This is sometimes done when developing expert systems where more reliable probabilities are not available.

In the example cited above, $D1$ is either true or false, and $P(D1|E)$ is the interpretation which assigns a measure of confidence that $D1$ is true when it is known that E is true. There is a similarity between E, $P(D1|E)$ and modus ponens discussed in Chapter 4. For example, when E is known to be true and $D1$ and E are known to be related, one concludes the truth of $D1$ with a confidence level $P(D1|E)$.

One might wonder if it would not be simpler to assign probabilities to as many ground atoms $E_1, E_2, \ldots, E_k$ as possible, and compute inferred probabilities (probabilities of $E_j \rightarrow H$ and H) directly from these. The answer is that in general this is not possible. To compute an inferred probability requires a knowledge of the joint distributions of the ground predicates participating in the inference. From the joint distributions, the required marginal distributions may then be computed. The distributions and computations required for that approach are, in general, much more complex than the computations involving the use of Bayes' Rule.

Consider now two events A and $\tilde{}A$ which are mutually exclusive ($A \cap \tilde{}A = \emptyset$) and exhaustive ($A U \tilde{}A$) = S. The probability of an arbitrary event B can always be expressed as

$$P(B) = P(B \ \& \ A) + P(B \ \& \ \tilde{}A) = P(B|A)P(A) + P(B|\tilde{}A)P(\tilde{}A)$$

Using this result, equation 6.4 can be written as

$$P(H|E) = P(E|H)P(H) \ / \ [P(E|H)P(H) + P(E|\tilde{}H)P(\tilde{}H)] \tag{6.6}$$

Equation 6.6 can be generalized for an arbitrary number of hypotheses H_i, $i = 1, \ldots, k$. Thus, suppose the H_i partition the universe; that is, the H_i are mutually exclusive and exhaustive. Then for any evidence E, we have

$$P(E) = \sum_{i=1}^{k} P(E \ \& \ H_i) = \sum_{i=1}^{k} P(E|H_i)P(H_i)$$

and hence,

$$P(H_i|E) = \frac{P(E|H_i)P(H_i)}{\sum_{j=1}^{k} P(E|H_j)\, P(H_j)} \tag{6.7}$$

Finally, to be more realistic and to accommodate multiple sources of evidence $E_1, E_2, \ldots, E_m$, we generalize equation 6.7 further to obtain

$$P(H_i|E_1, E_2, \ldots, E_m) = \frac{P(E_1, E_2, \ldots, E_m|H_i)P(H_i)}{\sum_{j=1}^{k} P(E_1, E_2, \ldots, E_m|H_j)\, P(H_j)} \tag{6.8}$$

If there are several plausible hypotheses and a number of evidence sources, equation 6.8 can be fairly complex to compute. This is one of the serious drawbacks of the Bayesian approach. A large number of probabilities must be known in advance in order to apply an equation such as 6.8. If there were k hypotheses, H_i, and m sources of evidence, E_j, then $k + m$ prior probabilities must be known in addition to the k likelihood probabilities. The real question then is where does one obtain such a large number of reliable probabilities?

To simplify equation 6.8, it is sometimes assumed that the E_j are statistically independent. In that case, the numerator and denominator probability terms $P(E_1, E_2, \ldots, E_m|H_j)$ factor into

$$P(E_1|H_j)P(E_2|H_j) \ . \ . \ . \ P(E_m|H_j)$$

resulting in a somewhat simpler form. But, even though the computations are straightforward, the number of probabilities required in a moderately large system can still be prohibitive, and one may be forced to simply use subjective probabilities when more reliable values are not available. Furthermore, the E_j are almost never completely independent. Consequently, this assumption may introduce intolerable errors.

The formulas presented above suggest how probabilistic evidence would be combined to produce a likelihood estimate for any given hypothesis. When a number of individual hypotheses are possible and several sources of evidence are available, it may be necessary to compute two or more alternative probabilities and select among them. This may mean that none, one, or possibly more than one of the hypotheses could be chosen. Normally, the one having the largest probability of occurrence would be selected, provided no other values were close. Before accepting such a choice, however, it may be desirable to require that the value exceed some threshold to avoid selecting weakly supported hypotheses. In Section 6.5 we describe a typical system which combines similar values and chooses only those conclusions that exceed a threshold of 0.2.

Bayesian Networks

Network representations of knowledge have been used to graphically exhibit the interdependencies which exist between related pieces of knowledge. Much work has been done in this area to develop a formal syntax and semantics for such representations. We discuss related topics in some detail in Chapter 7 when we consider associative networks and conceptual graphs. Here, however, we are more interested in network representations which depict the degrees of belief of propositions and the causal dependencies that exist between them. Inferencing in a network amounts to propogating the probabilities of given and related information through the network to one or more conclusion nodes.

Network representations for uncertain dependencies are further motivated by observations made earlier. If we wish to represent uncertain knowledge related to a set of propositional variables $x_1, \ldots, x_n$ by their joint distribution $P(x_1, \ldots, x_n)$, it will require some 2^n entries to store the distribution explicitly. Furthermore, a determination of any of the marginal probabilities x_i requires summing $P(x_1, \ldots, x_n)$ over the remaining $n - 1$ variables. Clearly, the time and storage requirements for such computations quickly become impractical. Inferring with such large numbers of probabilities does not appear to model the human process either. On the contrary, humans tend to single out only a few propositions which are known to be causally linked when reasoning with uncertain beliefs. This metaphor leads quite naturally to a form of network representation.

One useful way to portray the problem domain is with a network of nodes which represent propositional variables x_i, connected by arcs which represent causal

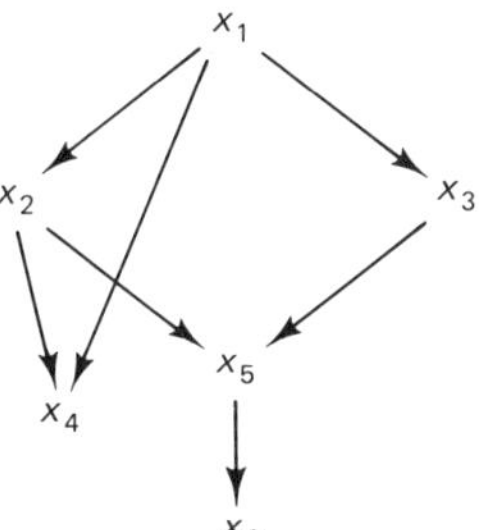

Figure 6.1 Example of Bayesian belief network.

influences or dependencies among the nodes. The strengths of the influences are quantified by conditional probabilities of each variable. For example, to represent causal relationships between the propositional variables $x_1, \ldots, x_6$ as illustrated in Figure 6.1, one can write the joint probability $P(x_1, \ldots, x_6)$ by inspection as a product of (chain) conditional probabilities

$$P(x_1, \ldots, x_6) = P(x_6|x_5)P(x_5|x_2,x_3)P(x_4|x_1,x_2)\,P(x_3\,|x_1)P(x_2|x_1\,)P(x_1)$$

Once such a network is constructed, an inference engine can use it to maintain and propagate beliefs. When new information is received, the effects can be propagated throughout the network until equilibrium probabilities are reached. Pearl (1986, 1987) has proposed simplified methods for updating networks (trees and, more generally, graphs) of this type by fusing and propagating the effects of new evidence and beliefs such that equilibrium is reached in time proportional to the longest path through the network. At equilibrium, all propositions will have consistent probability assignments. Methods for graphs are more difficult. They require the use of dummy variables to transform them to equivalent tree structures which are then easier to work with.

To use the type of probabilistic inference we have been considering, it is first necessary to assign probabilities to all basic facts in the knowledge base. This requires the definition of an appropriate sample space and the assignment of a priori and conditional probabilities. In addition, some method must be chosen to compute the combined probabilities when pooling evidence in a sequence of inference steps (such as Pearl's method). Finally, when the outcome of an inference chain results in one or more proposed conclusions, the alternatives must be compared, and one or more selected on the basis of its likelihood.

6.3 POSSIBLE WORLD REPRESENTATIONS

In Section 5.4 the notion of possible worlds was introduced as a formalism through which an agent could view a set of propositions as being true in some worlds and false in others. We use the possible world concepts in this section to describe a method proposed by Nilsson (1986) which generalizes first order logic in the modelling of uncertain beliefs. The method assigns truth values ranging from 0 to 1 to possible

TABLE 6.1 TRUTH VALUE ASSIGNMENTS FOR THE SET $\{P, P \rightarrow Q, Q\}$

Consistent			Inconsistent		
P	Q	$P \rightarrow Q$	P	Q	$P \rightarrow Q$
true	true	true	true	true	false
true	false	false	true	false	true
false	true	true	false	true	false
false	false	true	false	false	false

worlds. Each set of possible worlds corresponds to a different interpretation of sentences contained in a knowledge base denoted as KB.

Consider first the simple case where a KB contains only the single sentence S. S may be either true or false. We envision S as being true in one set of possible worlds W_1, and false in another set W_2. The actual world, the one we are in, must be in one of the two sets, but we are uncertain which one. Our uncertainty is expressed by assigning a probability P to W_1 and $1 - P$ to W_2. We can say then that the probability of S being true is P.

When our KB contains L sentences, $S_1, \ldots, S_L$, more sets of possible worlds are required to represent all consistent truth value assignments. There are 2^L possible truth assignments for L sentences. Some of the assignments may be inconsistent (impossible), however. For example, the set of sentences $\{P, P \rightarrow Q, Q)$ has 2^3 possible truth assignments, only four of which are consistent as depicted in Table 6.1.

If K of the truth assignments are consistent, K sets of possible worlds $W_1, W_2, \ldots, W_K$ are used to model the corresponding interpretations. A probability distribution is then defined over the possible worlds, where P_i is the probability that W_i is the actual world, and $\Sigma_i P_i = 1$. The probability or belief in any sentence S_j can then be determined by summing the P_i over all W_i in which S_j is true.

These notions can be represented using vector notation. We use the matrix $\mathbf{V}$ with L columns and K rows to represent the truth values of the L sentences in each of the K sets W_i. The ith column of $\mathbf{V}$ contains a one in row j if sentence S_j is true in W_i and a zero if it is false. Also let the K-dimensional column vector $\mathbf{p}$ with components p_i, $i = 1, \ldots, K$, represent the possible world probabilities. With this notation, the product of $\mathbf{V}$ and $\mathbf{p}$ is a vector $\mathbf{q}$ which contains the probabilities q_j of sentence S_j, for $j = 1, \ldots, L$, that is

$$\mathbf{q} = \mathbf{V}p \tag{6.9}$$

The jth component q_j of $\mathbf{q}$ is the sum of probabilities of the sets of possible worlds in which S_j is true, or the probabilistic truth value of S_j. As an example of this notation, the matrix equation for the consistent truth value assignments given in Table 6.1 is

$$\mathbf{q} = \begin{bmatrix} 1 & 1 & 0 & 0 \\ 1 & 0 & 1 & 1 \\ 1 & 0 & 1 & 0 \end{bmatrix} \begin{bmatrix} p_1 \\ p_2 \\ p_3 \\ p_4 \end{bmatrix}$$

where p_1, p_2, p_3, and p_4 are the probabilities for the corresponding W_i. Thus, the sentence probabilities are computed as

$$\begin{aligned} q_1 &= \boldsymbol{p}(S_1) = p_1 + p_2 \\ q_2 &= \boldsymbol{p}(S_2) = p_1 + p_3 + p_4 \\ q_3 &= \boldsymbol{p}(S_3) = p_1 + p_3 \end{aligned}$$

Given a KB of sentences with known probabilities (obtained from an expert or other source), we wish to determine the probability of any new sentence S deduced from KB. Alternatively, we may wish to recompute some sentence probabilities in KB if new information has been gained which changes one or more of the original sentences in KB. To compute the probability of S requires that consistent truth values first be determined for S for all sets of possible worlds. A new augmented matrix **V** can then be formed by adding a bottom row of ones and zeros to the original **V** where the ones and zeros correspond to the truth assignments.

No methods have been developed for the computation of exact solutions for the KB sentence probabilities, although methods for determining approximations were presented for both small and large matrices **V**. We do not consider those methods here. They may be found in Nilsson (1986). They are based on the use of the probability constraints

$$0 \leq p_i \leq 1, \text{ and } \Sigma_i \, p_i = 1,$$

and the fact that consistent probability assignments are bounded by the hyperplanes of a certain convex hull. Suggestions have also been made for the partitioning of larger matrices into smaller ones to simplify the computations.

6.4 DEMPSTER-SHAFER THEORY

As noted in the previous section, the assumption of conditional independence is probably not warranted in many problems. There are other serious drawbacks in using Bayesian theory as a model of uncertain reasoning as well. To begin with, the probabilities are described as a single numeric point value. This can be a distortion of the precision that is actually available for supporting evidence. It amounts to an overstatement of the evidence giving support to many of our beliefs. When we assert with probability 0.7 that the dollar will fall against the Japanese Yen over the next six months, what we really mean is we have a fairly strong conviction there is a chance of about 0.6 to 0.8 say, that it will fall.

Another problem with traditional theory is that there is no way to differentiate between ignorance and uncertainty. These are distinctly different concepts and should be treated as such. For example, suppose we are informed that one of three terrorist groups, A, B, or C has planted a bomb in a certain government building. We may have some evidence to believe that group C is the guilty one and be willing to assign a measure of this belief equal to $P(C) = 0.8$. On the other hand, without more knowledge of the other two groups, we would not want to say that the probability is 0.1 that each one of them is guilty. Yet, traditional theory would have us distribute an equal amount of the remaining probability to each of the other groups. In fact, we may have no knowledge to justify either the amount of uncertainty nor the equal division of it.

Finally, with classical probability theory, we are forced to regard belief and disbelief as functional opposites. That is, if some proposition A is assigned the probability $P(A) = 0.3$, then we must assign $\tilde{}A$ the probability $P(\tilde{}A) = 0.7$ since we must have $P(A) + P(\tilde{}A) = 1$. This forces us to make an assignment that may be conflicting since it is possible to both believe and disbelieve some propositions by the same amount, making this requirement awkward.

In an attempt to remedy the above problems, a generalized theory has been proposed by Arthur Dempster (1968) and extended by his student Glenn Shafer (1976). It has come to be known as the Dempster-Shafer theory of evidence. The theory is based on the notion that separate probability masses may be assigned to all subsets of a universe of discourse rather than just to indivisible single members as required in traditional probability theory. As such, it permits the inequality $P(A) + P(\tilde{}A) \leq 1$.

In the Dempster-Shafer theory, we assume a universe of discourse U and a set corresponding to n propositions, exactly one of which is true. The propositions are assumed to be exhaustive and mutually exclusive. Let 2^U denote all subsets of U including the empty set and U itself (there are 2^n such subsets). Let the set function m (sometimes called a basic probability assignment) defined on 2^U, be a mapping to [0,1],

$$m{:}2^U \rightarrow [0,1], \text{ be such that for all subsets } A \subseteq U$$
$$m(\emptyset) = 0$$
$$\sum_{A \subseteq U} m(A) = 1$$

The function m defines a probability distribution on 2^U (not just on the singletons of U as in classical theory). It represents the measure of belief committed exactly to A. In other words, it is possible to assign belief to each subset A of U without assigning any to anything smaller.

A belief function, Bel, corresponding to a specific m for the set A, is defined as the sum of beliefs committed to every subset of A by m. That is, Bel(A) is a measure of the total support or belief committed to the set A and sets a minimum value for its likelihood. It is defined in terms of all belief assigned to A as well as to all proper subsets of A. Thus,

$$\text{Bel}(A) = \sum_{B \subseteq A} m(B)$$

For example, if U contains the mutually exclusive subsets A, B, C, and D then

$$\text{Bel}(\{A,C,D\}) = m(\{A,C,D\}) + m(\{A,C\}) + m(\{A,D\}) + m(\{C,D\}) + m(\{A\}) + m(\{C\}) + m(\{D\})$$

In Dempster-Shafer theory, a belief interval can also be defined for a subset A. It is represented as the subinterval [Bel(A), Pl(A)] of [0,1]. Bel(A) is also called the *support* of A, and $P\text{l}(A) = 1 - \text{Bel}(\tilde{\ }A)$, the *plausibility* of A.

We define Bel $(\varnothing) = 0$ to signify that no belief should be assigned to the empty set and Bel(U) = 1 to show that the truth is contained within U. The subsets A of U are called the *focal elements* of the support function Bel when $m(A) > 0$.

Since Bel(A) only partially describes the beliefs about proposition A, it is useful to also have a measure of the extent one believes in ˜A, that is, the *doubts* regarding A. For this, we define the doubt of A as $D(A) = \text{Bel}(\tilde{\ }A)$. From this definition it will be seen that the upper bound of the belief interval noted above, Pl(A), can be expressed as $P\text{l}(A) = 1 - D(A) = 1 - \text{Bel}(\tilde{\ }A)$. Pl(A) represents an upper belief limit on the proposition A. The belief interval, [Bel(A),Pl(A)], is also sometimes referred to as the *confidence* in A, while the quantity $P\text{l}(A) - \text{Bel}(A)$ is referred to as the *uncertainty* in A. It can be shown that (Prade 1983)

$$P\text{l}(\varnothing) = 0,\ P\text{l}(U) = 1$$

For all A,

$$P\text{l}(A) \geq \text{Bel}(A),$$
$$\text{Bel}(A) + \text{Bel}(\tilde{\ }A) \leq 1,$$
$$P\text{l}(A) + P\text{l}(\tilde{\ }A) \geq 1, \text{ and}$$

For $A \subseteq B$,

$$\text{Bel}(A) \leq \text{Bel}(B),\ P\text{l}(A) \leq P\text{l}(B)$$

In interpreting the above definitions, it should be noted that a portion of belief may be committed to a set of propositions, but need not be, and if committed, it is not necessary to commit any belief to its negation. However, a belief committed to a proposition is committed to any other proposition it implies.

A few specific interval belief values will help to clarify the intended semantics. For example,

[0,1]	represents no belief in support of the proposition
[0,0]	represents the belief the proposition is false
[1,1]	represents the belief the proposition is true
[.3,1]	represents partial belief in the proposition
[0,.8]	represents partial disbelief in the proposition
[.2,.7]	represents belief from evidence both for and against the proposition

When evidence is available from two or more independent knowledge sources Bel_1 and Bel_2, one would like to pool the evidence to reduce the uncertainty. For this, Dempster has provided such a combining function denoted as $\text{Bel}_1 \circ \text{Bel}_2$.

Given two basic probability assignment functions, m_1 and m_2 corresponding to the belief functions Bel_1 and Bel_2, let $A_1, \ldots, A_k$ be the focal elements for Bel_1 and $B_1, \ldots, B_p$ be the focal elements for Bel_2. Then $m_1(A_i)$ and $m_2(B_j)$ each assign probability masses on the unit interval. They can be orthogonally combined as depicted with the square illustrated in Figure 6.2 (Garvey et al., 1981).

The unit square in Figure 6.2 represents the total probability mass assigned by both m_1 and m_2 for all of their common subsets. A particular subrectangle within the square, shown as the intersection of the sets A_i and B_j, has committed to it the measure $m_1(A_i)m_2(B_j)$. Likewise, any subset C of U may have one, or more than one, of these rectangles committed to it. Therefore, the total probability mass committed to C will be

$$\sum_{A_i \cap B_j = C} m_1(A_i)m_2(B_j) \tag{6.9}$$

where the summation is over all i and j.

The sum in equation 6.9 must be normalized to account for the fact that some intersections $A_i \cap B_j = \varnothing$ will have positive probability which must be discarded. The final form of Dempster's rule of combination is then given by

$$m_1 \circ m_2 = \frac{\sum_{A_i \cap B_j} m_1(A_i)m_2(B_j)}{\sum_{A_i \cap B_j \neq 0} m_1(A_i)m_2(B_j)} \tag{6.10}$$

where the summations are taken over all i and j.

As an example of the above concepts, recall once again the problem of identifying the terrorist group or groups responsible for a certain attack in some country. Suppose any of four known terrorist organizations A, B, C, and D could have been responsible for the attack. The possible subsets of U in this case form a lattice of sixteen subsets (Figure 6.3).

Assume one piece of evidence supports the belief that groups A and C were

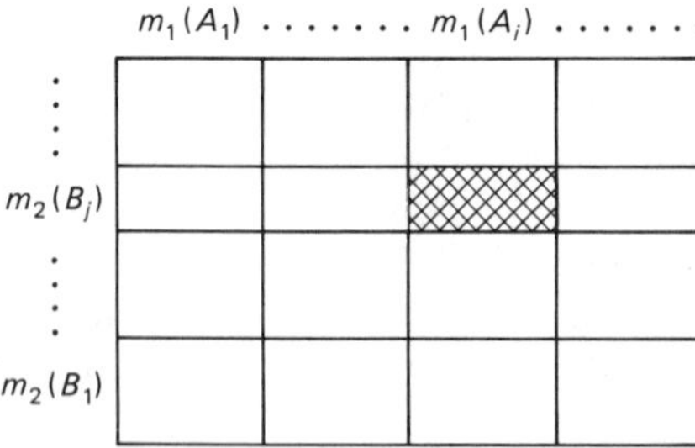

Figure 6.2 Composition of probability mass from sources Bel_1 and Bel_2.

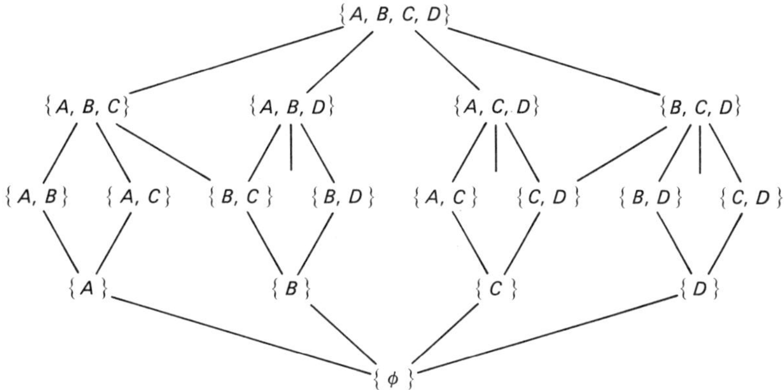

Figure 6.3 Lattice of subsets of the universe U.

responsible to a degree of $m_1(\{A,C\}) = 0.6$, and another source of evidence disproves the belief that C was involved (and therefore supports the belief that the three organizations, A, B, and D were responsible; that is $m_2(\{A,B,D\}) = 0.7$. To obtain the pooled evidence, we compute the following quantities (summarized in Table 6.2).

$$m_1 o m_2(\{A\}) = (0.6)*(0.7) = 0.42$$
$$m_1 o m_2(\{A,C\}) = (0.6)*(0.3) = 0.18$$
$$m_1 o m_2(\{A,B,D\}) = (0.4)*(0.7) = 0.28$$
$$m_1 o m_2(\{U\}) = (0.4)*(0.3) = 0.12$$
$$m_1 o m_2 = 0 \text{ for all other subsets of U}$$
$$\text{Bel}_1(\{A,C\}) = m(\{A,C\}) + m(\{A\}) + m(\{C\})$$

TABLE 6.2 TABLEAU OF COMBINED VALUES OF BELIEF FOR m_1 AND m_2

		m_2: $\{A,B,D\}$ (0.7)	m_2: U (0.3)
m_1	$\{A,C\}$ (0.6)	$\{A\}$ (0.42)	$\{A,C\}$ (0.18)
	U (0.4)	$\{A,B,D\}$ (0.28)	U (0.12)

6.5 AD HOC METHODS

The so-called ad hoc methods of dealing with uncertainty are methods which have no formal theoretical basis (although they are usually patterned after probabilistic concepts). These methods typically have an intuitive, if not a theoretical, appeal.

They are chosen over formal methods as a pragmatic solution to a particular problem, when the formal methods impose difficult or impossible conditions.

Different ad hoc procedures have been employed successfully in a number of AI systems, particularly in expert systems. We illustrate the basic ideas with the belief measures used in the MYCIN system, one of the earliest expert systems developed to diagnose meningitis and infectious blood diseases (Buchanan and Shortliffe, 1984).

MYCIN's knowledge base is composed of if . . . then rules which are used to assess various forms of patient evidence with the ultimate goal being the formulation of a correct diagnosis and recommendation for a suitable therapy. A typical rule has the form

> IF: The stain of the organism is gram positive, and
> The morphology of the organism is coccus, and
> The growth conformation of the organism is chains
>
> THEN: There is suggestive evidence (0.7) that the identity of the organism is streptococcus

This is a rule that would be used by the inference mechanism to help identify the offending organism. The three conditions given in the IF part of the rule refer to attributes that help to characterize and identify organisms (the stain, morphology, and growth conformation). When such an identification is relatively certain, an appropriate therapy may then be recommended.

The numeric value (0.7) given in the THEN part of the above rule corresponds to an expert's estimate of degree of belief one can place in the rule conclusion when the three conditions in the IF part have been satisfied. Thus, the belief associated with the rule may be thought of as a (subjective) conditional probability $P(H|E_1,E_2,E_3) = 0.7$, where H is the hypothesis that the organism is streptococcus, and E_1, E_2, and E_3 correspond to the three pieces of joint evidence given in the IF part, respectively.

MYCIN uses measures of both belief and disbelief to represent degrees of confirmation and disconfirmation respectively in a given hypothesis. The basic measure of belief, denoted by $MB(H,E)$, is actually a measure of the *increased* belief in hypothesis H due to the evidence E. This is roughly equivalent to the estimated increase in probability of $P(H|E)$ over $P(H)$ given by an expert as a result of the knowledge gained by E. A value of 0 corresponds to no increase in belief and 1 corresponds to maximum increase or absolute belief. Likewise, $MD(H,E)$ is a measure of the increased disbelief in hypothesis H due to evidence E. MD ranges from 0 to +1 also, with +1 representing maximum increase in disbelief, (total disbelief) and 0 representing no increase. In both measures, the evidence E may be absent or may be replaced with another hypothesis, $MB(H_1,H_2)$. This represents the increased belief in H_1 given H_2 is true.

In an attempt to formalize the uncertainty measure in MYCIN, definitions of MB and MD have been given in terms of prior and conditional probabilities. It should be remembered, however, the actual values are often subjective probability estimates provided by a physician. We have for the definitions

$$MB(H,E) = \begin{cases} 1 & \text{if } P(H) = 1 \\ \dfrac{max[P(H|E),P(H)] - P(H)}{max[1,0] - P(H)} & \text{otherwise} \end{cases} \quad (6.11)$$

$$MD(H,E) = \begin{cases} 1 & \text{if } P(H) = 0 \\ \dfrac{min[P(H|E),P(H)] - P(H)}{min[1,0] - P(H)} & \text{otherwise} \end{cases} \quad (6.12)$$

Note that when $0 < P(H) < 1$, and E and H are independent (so $P(H|E) = P(H)$), then $MB = MD = 0$. This would be the case if E provided no useful information.

The two measures MB and MD are combined into a single measure called the certainty factor (CF), defined by

$$CF(H,E) = MB(H,E) - MD(H,E) \quad (6.13)$$

Note that the value of CF ranges from -1 (certain disbelief) to $+1$ (certain belief). Furthermore, a value of $CF = 0$ will result if E neither confirms nor unconfirms H (E and H are independent).

In MYCIN, each rule hypothesis H_i has an associated MB and MD initially set to zero. As evidence is accumulated, they are updated using intermediate combining functions, and, when all applicable rules have been executed, a final CF is calculated for each H_i. These are then compared and the largest cumulative confirmations or disconfirmations are used to determine the appropriate therapy. A threshold value of $|CF| > 0.2$ is used to prevent the acceptance of a weakly supported hypothesis.

In the initial assignment of belief values an expert will consider all available confirming and disconfirming evidence, $E_1, \ldots, E_k$, and assign appropriate, consistent values to both. For example, in the assignment process, a value of 1 should be made if and only if a piece of evidence logically implies H ($\tilde{}H$) with certainty. Additional rules related to the assignment process must also be carefully followed when using such methods.

Ad hoc methods have been used in a large number of knowledge-based systems, more so than have the more formal methods. This is largely because of the difficulties encountered in acquiring large numbers of reliable probabilities related to the given domain and to the complexities of the ensuing calculations. But, in bypassing the formal approaches one should question what end results can be expected. Are they poorer than would be obtained using formal methods? The answer to this question seems to be not likely. Sensitivity analyses (Buchanan et al., 1984) seem to indicate that the outcomes are not too sensitive to either the method nor the actual values used for many systems. However, much work remains to be done in this area before a useful theory can be formulated.

6.6 HEURISTIC REASONING METHODS

The approaches to uncertainty described so far seem to lack an AI flavor. The uncertainty in a given hypothesis is represented as a number which is combined with and compared to other numbers until a final number is translated into a weighted conclusion. Once the uncertainties have been translated into numbers, the cause of the uncertainty, its relative importance, necessity, and other factors are lost. Furthermore, this does not appear to be the process with which humans reason about uncertainty. Although we do weigh evidence both pro and con, we usually do not arrive at a net numeric estimate of a conclusion, only whether or not the conclusion is justified. In place of numbers, our reasoning appears to depend more on heuristics when reasoning with uncertain, incomplete knowledge. In this section we briefly consider this type of approach.

Heuristic methods are based on the use of procedures, rules, and other forms of encoded knowledge to achieve specified goals under uncertainty. Using both domain specific and general heuristics, one of several alternative conclusions may be chosen through the strength of positive versus negative evidence presented in the form of justifications or endorsements. The endorsement weights employed in such systems need not be numeric. Some form of ordering or preference selection scheme must be used, however.

For example, in a prototype system (named SOLOMON) developed by Paul Cohen (1985), endorsements in the form of domain and general heuristics are used to reason about uncertainties associated with a client's investment portfolio. In selecting investments for clients, there are many sources of uncertainty to contend with. First, there is uncertainty related to the client's lifestyle and financial status as well as his or her objectives. Secondly, there are varying degrees of uncertainty related to all types of investments. Some important factors which influence an investor's status include age, preretirement income expected, net worth, income needs, retirement programs, and tax bracket. Factors related to investments include corporate earnings, dividends, bond and money market yields, the direction of the market, and the rate of inflation, to name a few.

Endorsements in the SOLOMON system are justifications or reasons for believing or disbelieving a proposition or an inference. They are provided by experts as heuristics in place of numeric probability estimates. They are expressed as rules about the properties and relationships of domain objects. For example, heuristics used to reason about the uncertainties related to a client's status might take the form of rules such as

IF: Client income need is high and net worth is medium to high,
THEN: Risk-tolerance level is medium.

IF: Client tax bracket is high and risk-tolerance level is low,
THEN: Tax-exempt mutual-funds are indicated.

IF: Client age is high and income needs are high and retirement income is medium,

THEN: Risk-tolerance is low.
IF: Two positive endorsements are medium or high and one negative endorsement is high,
THEN: Then favor the positive choice.

Endorsements are used to control the reasoning process in at least two different ways. First, preference is given to rules which are strongly supported. Second, endorsements permit the condition or left-hand side of a rule to be satisfied (or rejected) without finding an exact match in the KB. The SOLOMON system is goal driven and uses a form of backward rule chaining. A goal is achieved when all of the inference conditions in the left-hand side of the goal rule have been proved. This requires proving subgoals and sub-subgoals until the chain of inferences is completed.

The control structure in SOLOMON is based on the use of an agenda where tasks derived from rules are ordered for completion on the strength of their endorsements. Strongly endorsed tasks are scheduled ahead of weakly endorsed ones. And when a task is removed for execution, endorsements are checked to see if they are still worth completing.

Endorsements are propagated over inferences $P \rightarrow Q$ by combining, replacing, or dropping endorsements E_P associated with antecedents P, endorsements of the implication itself, and other evidential relationships between Q and conclusions in the KB.

The SOLOMON system borrowed several design features from another heuristic reasoning system developed by Douglas Lenat called AM (Davis and Lenat, 1982). AM discovers basic concepts in mathematics by investigating examples of a newly generated conjecture and looking for regularities and extreme or boundary values in the examples. With an exponential number of available tasks, the system is always uncertain about what to work on next. For this, AM also uses an agenda to schedule its tasks for further investigation. Here again, heuristics are used to control the reasoning process. The system does this by developing a numerical "interest" factor rating for tasks which is used to determine the task's position on the agenda. Like the SOLOMON system, AM gives more strength to rules which have supportive evidence.

Although both AM and SOLOMON take into account the importance of the evidence, SOLOMON differs in one respect. SOLOMON also accounts for the accuracy of the evidence just as the testimony of an eyewitness is more convincing than circumstantial evidence. AM is unable to assess accuracy as such.

6.7 SUMMARY

Commonsense reasoning is nonmonotonic in nature. It requires the ability to reason with incomplete, and uncertain knowledge. Many AI systems model uncertainty with probabilities or levels of confidence and probability inference computations.

Each belief is assigned a degree of truthfulness or plausibility. Evidence is pooled through combining functions which compute a combined belief probability. Two popular approaches were considered in this chapter: the Bayesian probability method and the Dempster-Shafer approach.

The Bayesian approach depends on the use of known-prior and likely probabilities to compute conditional probabilities. The Dempster-Shafer approach on the other hand is a generalization of classical probability theory which permits the assignment of probability masses (beliefs) to all subsets of the universe and not just to the basic elements. A measure of belief for an assertion is then computed as a subinterval of [0,1], where the length of the interval measures the uncertainty.

In addition to methods based on formal theories the more pragmatic ad hoc approaches to uncertain reasoning were examined. In particular, the procedures used in MYCIN which combine measures of belief and disbelief into certainty factors were described. Because of its success, a number of expert systems designs have been patterned after this method.

Finally, heuristic, nonnumeric approaches to the uncertainty problem were considered. Here, endorsements for a given alternative would outweigh negative factors if general rules, data, and other domain knowledge provided stronger support. The SOLOMON and AM systems use a form of heuristic control to reason with uncertain knowledge.

EXERCISES

6.1 Find the probability of the event A when it is known that some event B occurred. From experiments it has been determined that $P(B|A) = 0.84$, $P(A) = 0.2$, and $P(B) = 0.34$.

6.2 Prove that if A and B are independent, $P(A|B) = P(A)$. (Note that A and B are independent if and only if $P(A \& B) = P(A)P(B)$).

6.3 From basic set theory prove that $P(\tilde{}A) = 1 - P(A)$, and that $P(\tilde{}B|A) = 1 - P(B|A)$.

6.4 Is it possible to compute $P(A|\tilde{}B)$ when you are only given $P(A)$, $P(B|A)$, and $P(B)$? Explain your answer.

6.5 Write the joint distribution of x_1, x_2, x_3, x_4, x_5, and x_6 as a product of the chain conditional probabilities for the following causal network:

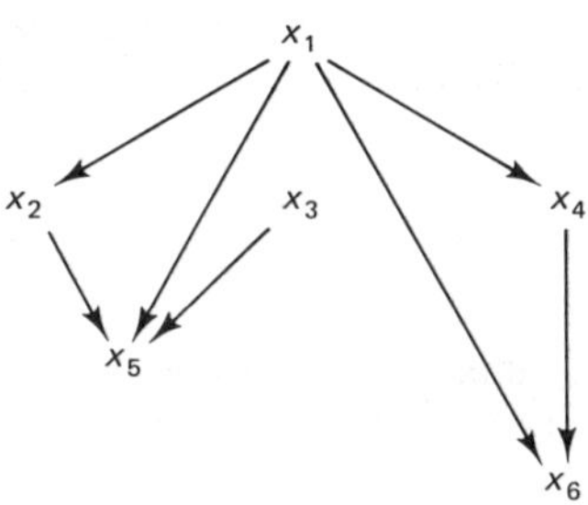

6.6 Define the sentences S_1, S_2, and S_3 as $S_1 = P$, $S_2 = Q$, and $S_3 = P \rightarrow Q$. Determine the probabilistic truth values of S_1, S_2, and S_3 when it is known that the probabilities of the possible worlds are given by $P(W_1) = 1/4$, $P(W_2) = 1/8$, $P(W_3) = 1/8$, and $P(W_4) = 1/2$.

6.7 Write a LISP program that computes certainty factors for rules based on the ad hoc MYCIN model.

6.8 Dempster-Shafer computations were given for four terrorist organizations A, B, C, and D in Section 6.4. Suppose now that new evidence (m_3) indicates that organization C was indeed responsible to a degree of 0.8. This requires that values for $m_3 \circ m_4$ be computed, where $m_4 = m_1 + m_2$. Compute a new intersection tableau for the new evidence, that is compute $m_3(C)$ and $m_3(U)$ versus $m_4(A)$, $m_4(C,A)$, $m_4(A,B,D)$, and $m_4(U)$.

6.9 In what ways do endorsement justifications differ from probabilistic justifications?

6.10 In what ways do endorsement justifications differ from fuzzy logic justifications?

7

Structured Knowledge: Graphs, Frames, and Related Structures

The representations considered up to this point focused primarily on expressiveness, validity, consistency, inference methods, and related topics. Little consideration was given to the way in which the knowledge was structured and how it might be viewed by designers, or to the type of data structures that should be used internally. Neither was much consideration given to effective methods of organizing the knowledge structures in memory. In this, and the following two chapters, we address such problems.

In this chapter, we first look at associative networks as a form of representation and see examples of their use and flexibility. Next, we look at frames, a generalized structure recently introduced as a method of grouping and linking related chunks of knowledge. Finally, we consider structures closely related to frames known as scripts and memory organization packets. We compare them with the frame structures and see how they are used in reasoning systems.

7.1 INTRODUCTION

The representations studied in Chapter 4 are suitable for the expression of fairly simple facts. They can be written in clausal form as independent units and placed in a KB in any order. Inference is straightforward with a procedure such as chaining

```
PROFESSION(bob,professor)
FACULTY(bob,engineering)
      .
      .
      .
MARRIED(bob,sandy)
FATHER-OF(bob,sue,joe)
DRIVES(bob,buick)
OWNS(bob,house)
~MARRIED(x,y) V MARRIED(y,x)
      .
      .
      .
```

Figure 7.1 Facts in a KB given in clausal form.

or resolution. For example, facts about Bob, a university professor, might be entered as clauses in a KB as depicted in Figure 7.1.

The entries in the KB of Figure 7.1 have no particular order or grouping associated with them. Furthermore, in representing various facts about Bob, it was necessary to repeat Bob's name for each association given. All facts appear independently, without any linkage to other facts, even though they may be closely related conceptually (Bob is married, owns a house, has children, drives a Buick, and so forth).

For small KBs, the representation used in Figure 7.1 presents no problem. Adding, or otherwise changing facts in the KB is easy enough, and a search of all clauses in the KB can be made if necessary when performing inferences. When the quantity of information becomes large and more complex, however, the acquisition, comprehension, use, and maintenance of the knowledge can become difficult or even intractible. In such cases, some form of knowledge structuring and organization becomes a necessity.

Real-world problem domains typically involve a number and variety of different objects interacting with each other in different ways. The objects themselves may require extensive characterizations, and their interaction relationships with other objects may be very complex.

7.2 ASSOCIATIVE NETWORKS

Network representations provide a means of structuring and exhibiting the structure in knowledge. In a network, pieces of knowledge are clustered together into coherent semantic groups. Networks also provide a more natural way to map to and from natural language than do other representation schemes. Network representations give a pictorial presentation of objects, their attributes and the relationships that exist between them and other entities. In this section, we describe general associative

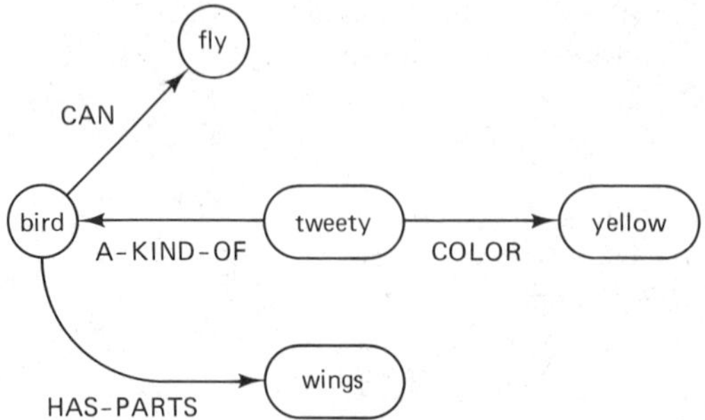

Figure 7.2 Fragment of an associative network.

networks (also known as semantic networks) and conceptual graphs and give some of their properties.

Associative networks are directed graphs with labeled nodes and arcs or arrows. The language used in constructing a network is based on selected domain primitives for objects and relations as well as some general primitives. A fragment of a simple network is illustrated in Figure 7.2. In the figure, a class of objects known as Bird is depicted. The class has some properties and a specific member of the class named Tweety is shown. The color of Tweety is seen to be yellow.

Associative networks were introduced by Quillian (1968) to model the semantics of English sentences and words. He called his structures semantic networks to signify their intended use. He developed a system which ''found'' the meanings between words by the paths connecting them. The connections were determined through a kind of ''spreading activation'' between the two words.

Quillian's model of semantic networks has a certain intuitive appeal in that related information is clustered and bound together through relational links. The knowledge required for the performance of some task is typically contained within a narrow domain or ''semantic vicinity'' of the task. This type of organization in some way, resembles the way knowledge is stored and retrieved in humans.

The graphical portrayal of knowledge can also be somewhat more expressive than other representation schemes. This probably accounts for the popularity and the diversity of representation models for which they have been employed. They have, for example, been used in a variety of systems such as natural language understanding, information retrieval, deductive data bases, learning systems, computer vision, and in speech generation systems.

Syntax and Semantics of Associative Networks

Unlike FOPL, there is no generally accepted syntax nor semantics for associative networks. Such rules tend to be designer dependent and vary greatly from one implementation to another. Most network systems are based on PL or FOPL with extensions, however. The syntax for any given system is determined by the object and relation primitives chosen and by any special rules used to connect nodes. Some efforts have been made toward the establishment of acceptable standards by

Schubert, Goebel, and Cercone (1979), Shapiro (1979), Hendrix (1979), and Brachman (1979). Later in this section we will review one formal approach to graphical representations which was recently proposed by John Sowa (1984).

Basically, the language of associative networks is formed from letters of the alphabet, both upper- and lowercase, relational symbols, set membership and subset symbols, decimal digits, square and oval nodes, and directed arcs of arbitrary length. The word symbols used are those which represent object constants and *n*-ary relation constants. Nodes are commonly used for objects or nouns, and arcs (or arc nodes) for relations. The direction of an arc is usually taken from the first to subsequent arguments as they appear in a relational statement. Thus, OWNS(bobs,house) would be written as

Figure 7.3 depicts graphically some additional concepts not expressed in Figure 7.1.

A number of arc relations have become common among users. They include such predicates as ISA, MEMBER-OF, SUBSET-OF, AKO (a-kind-of), HAS-

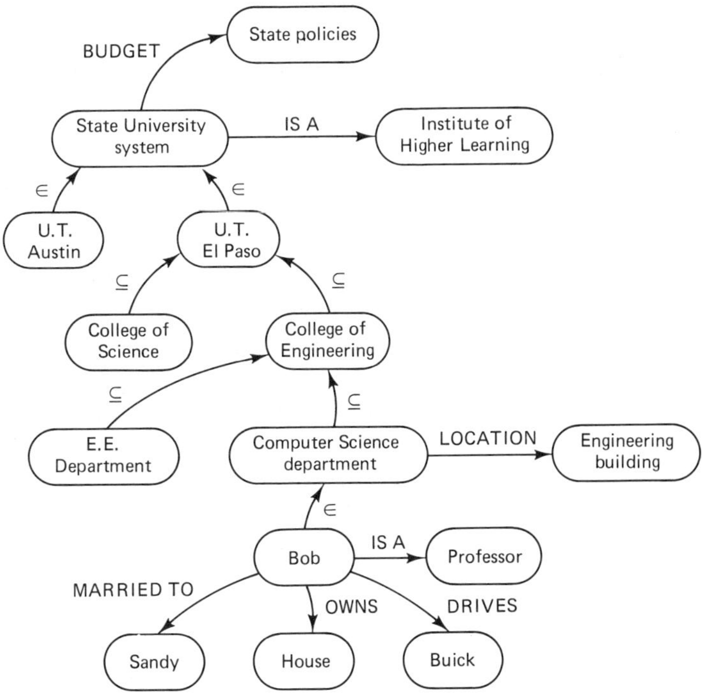

Figure 7.3 Associative network node and arc types.

PARTS, INSTANCE-OF, AGENT, ATTRIBUTES, SHAPED-LIKE, and so forth. Less common arcs have also been used to express modality relations (time, manner, mood), linguistics case relations (theme, source, goal), logical connectives (or, not, and, implies), quantifiers (all, some), set relations (superset, subset, member), attributes, and quantification (ordinal, count).

One particular arc or link, the ISA (is a) link, has taken on a special meaning. It signifies that Bob is a professor and that the state university system is an institute of higher learning. ISA relationships occur in many representations of worlds: Bill is a student, a cat is a furry animal, a tree is a plant, and so on. The ISA link is most often used to represent the fact that an object is of a certain type (predication) or to express the fact that one type is a subtype of another (for example, conditional quantification).

Brachman (1979, 1983) has given an interesting description of the background and uses of this now famous link. For example, the ISA predicate has been used to exhibit the following types of structures:

GENERIC-GENERIC RELATIONSHIPS

Subset-Superset (fighting ships-battleships)
Generalization-Specialization (restaurant-fast-foods)
AKO (an elephant is a kind of mammal)
Conceptual containment (a triangle is a polygon)
Sets and their type (an elephant and a set of elephants)
Role value restrictions (an elephant trunk is a cylinder 1.3 meters in length)

GENERIC-INDIVIDUAL RELATIONSHIPS

Set membership (Clyde is a camel)
Predication (predicate application to individual as in BROWN(camel))
Conceptual containment (king and the King of England)
Abstraction (the ''eagle'' in ''the eagle is an endangered species'')

Figure 7.3 illustrates some important features associative networks are good at representing. First, it should be apparent that networks clearly show an entity's attributes and its relationships to other entities. This makes it easy to retrieve the properties an entity shares with other entities. For this, it is only necessary to check direct links tied to that entity. Second, networks can be constructed to exhibit any hierarchical or taxonomic structure inherent in a group of entities or concepts. For example, at the top of the structure in Figure 7.3 is the Texas State University System. One level down from this node are specific state universities within the system. One of these universities, the University of Texas at El Paso, is shown with some of its subparts, colleges, which in turn have subparts, the different departments. One member of the Computer Science Department is Bob, a professor who owns a house and is married to Sandy. Finally, we see that networks depict the way in which knowledge is distributed or clustered about entities in a KB.

Associative network structures permit the implementation of property inheritance, a form of inference. Nodes which are members or subsets of other nodes may inherit properties from their higher level ancester nodes. For example, from the network of Figure 7.4, it is possible to infer that a mouse has hair and drinks milk.

Property inheritance of this type is recognized as a form of default reasoning. The assumption is made that unless there is information to the contrary, it is reasonable for an entity to inherit characteristics from its ancestor nodes. As the name suggests, this type of inheritance is called default inheritance. When an object does not or cannot inherit certain properties, it would be assigned values of its own which override any inherited ones.

Data structures patterned after associative networks also permit the efficient storage of information since it is only necessary to explicitly store objects and shared properties once. Shared properties are attached only to the highest node in a structure to which they apply. For example, in LISP, Bob's associations (Figure 7.3) can be implemented with property lists where all of Bob's properties are linked to one atom.

```
(putprop 'bob 'cs-dept 'member-of)
(putprop 'bob 'professor 'isa)
(putprop 'bob 'sandy 'married-to)
(putprop 'bob 'house 'owns)
(putprop 'bob 'buick 'drives)
```

The semantics of associative networks are sometimes defined along the same lines as that of traditional logics. In fact, some network system definitions provide a means of mapping to and from PL or FOPL expressions. For these systems, the semantics are based on interpretations. Thus, an interpretation satisfies a portion of a network if and only if all arc relations hold in the given portion.

Inference procedures for networks can also parallel those of PL and FOPL. If a class A of objects has some property P, and a is a member of A, we infer that a has property P. Syntactic inference in networks can also be defined using parallels to traditional logics such as unification, chaining, modus ponens, and even resolution.

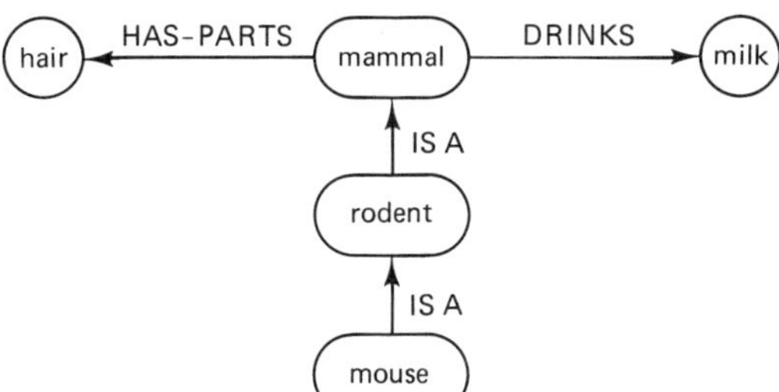

Figure 7.4 Property inheritance in a heirarchical network.

These procedures are implemented through node and arc matching processes and operators which insert, erase, copy, simplify, and join networks. We examine some typical inferencing procedures in more detail below.

Conceptual Graphs

Although there are no commonly accepted standards for a syntax and semantics for associative networks, we present an approach in this section which we feel may at least become a de facto standard in the future. It is based on the use of the conceptual graph as a primitive building block for associative networks. The formalism of these graphs has been adopted as a basic representation by a number of AI researchers and a variety of implementations using conceptual graphs are currently under development. Much of the popularity of these graphs has been due to recent work by John Sowa (1984) and his colleagues.

A conceptual graph is a graphical portrayal of a mental perception which consists of basic or primitive concepts and the relationships that exist between the concepts. A single conceptual graph is roughly equivalent to a graphical diagram of a natural language sentence where the words are depicted as concepts and relationships. Conceptual graphs may be regarded as formal building blocks for associative networks which, when linked together in a coherent way, form a more complex knowledge structure. An example of such a graph which represents the sentence "Joe is eating soup with a spoon" is depicted in Figure 7.5.

In Figure 7.5, concepts are enclosed in boxes and relations between the concepts are enclosed in ovals. The direction of the arrow corresponds to the order of the arguments in the relation they connect. The last or *n*th arc (argument) points away from the circle relation and all other arcs point toward the relation.

Concept symbols refer to entities, actions, properties, or events in the world. A concept may be individual or generic. Individual concepts have a type field followed by a referrent field. The concept [PERSON:joe] has type PERSON and referrent Joe. Referrents like joe and food in Figure 7.5 are called individual concepts since they refer to specific entities. EAT and SPOON have no referrent fields since they are generic concepts which refer to unspecified entities. Concepts like AGENT, OBJECT, INSTRUMENT, and PART are obtained from a collection of standard concepts. New concepts and relations can also be defined from these basic ones.

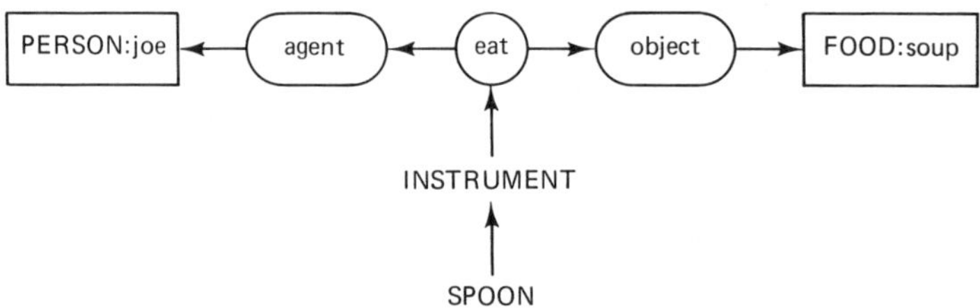

Figure 7.5 A conceptual graph.

A linear conceptual graph form which is easier to present as text can also be given. The linear form equivalent to the above sentence is

```
[PERSON:joe] ←(AGENT) ←[EAT]–
                              (OBJECT) →[FOOD:soup]
                              (INSTRUMENT) →[SPOON]
```

where square brackets have replaced concept boxes and parentheses have replaced relation circles.

The language of conceptual graphs is formed from upper- and lowercase letters of the alphabet, boxes and circles, directed arcs, and a number of special characters including -, ?, !, *, #, @, ∀, ˜, ", :, [,], (,), →, ←, {, and }. Some symbols are used to exhibit the structure of the graph, while others are used to determine the referrents.

The dash signifies continuation of the linear graph on the next line. The question mark is used to signify a query about a concept when placed in the referrent field: [HOUSE:?] means which house? The exclamation mark is used for emphasis to draw attention to a concept. The asterisk signifies a variable or unspecified object: [HOUSE:*x] means a house or some house. The pound sign signifies a definite article known to the speaker. For example, [House:#432] refers to a specific house, house number 432. The @ symbol relates to quantification: [HOUSE:@n] means n houses. ∀ signifies every or all, the same as in FOPL. The tilde is negation. Double quotation marks delimit literal strings. And the colon, brackets, parentheses, and directed arcs are used to construct graph structures as illustrated above.

Since conceptual graphs and FOPL are both a form of logical system, one might expect that it is possible to map from one representation to the other. Indeed this is the case, although some mappings will, in general, result in second order FOPL statements.

To transform a conceptual graph to a predicate logic statement requires that unique variable names be assigned to every generic concept of the graph. Thus, the concepts EAT and FOOD of Figure 7.5 would be assigned the variable names x and y, respectively. Next, all type labels such as PERSON and FOOD are converted to unary predicates with the same name. Conceptual relations such as AGENT, OBJECT, and INSTRUMENT are converted to predicates with as many arguments as there are arcs connected to the relation. Concept referrents such as Joe and soup become FOPL constants. Concepts with extended referrents such as ∀ map to the universal quantifier ∀. Generic concepts with no quantifier in the referrent field have an existential quantifier, ∃, placed before the formula for each variable, and conjunction symbols, &, are placed between the predicates.

As an example, one could convert the sentence "Every car has an engine" from its conceptual graph representation given by

[CAR:∀] →(PART) →(ENGINE]

to its equivalent FOPL representation. Using the rules outlined above, the equivalent FOPL representation derived is just

$$\forall x \exists y \text{ (CAR(x)} \rightarrow \text{(ENGINE(y) \& PART(x,y)))}$$

Mapping the other way, that is from FOPL statements to conceptual graphs, begins by putting the FOPL formula into prenex normal form, and converting all logical connectives to negation and conjunction. Next, every occurrence of universal quantification $\forall x$ is replaced with the equivalent form $\tilde{}\exists\tilde{}x$ (in graph notation this is ˜[ ]x˜[with the subsequent addition of balancing brackets]] to close off the expression). Every variable x and every occurrence of $\exists x$ is then replaced with the most general type concept denoted as [T:*x]. And finally, every n-ary predicate symbol is replaced with an n-ary concept relation whose ith arc is attached to the concept in the ith argument place in the predicate.

Implication in a conceptual graph can be represented with negation and conjunction. For example, the FOPL equivalent of $P \rightarrow Q$ can be written as ˜[P ˜[Q]] (recall that $P \rightarrow Q$ = (˜P V Q) = ˜(P & ˜Q)). In this expression, ˜[is read *as if* and the nested ˜[is read *as then*. More generally, we write the implication as ˜[*p˜[*q]] where *p and *q are themselves any conceptual graph.

Inference can be accomplished by modifying and combining graphs through the use of operators and basic graph inference rules. Four useful graph formation operators are copy, restrict, join, and simplify. These operators are defined as follows.

Copy. Produces a duplicate copy of a CG.

Restrict. Modifies a graph by replacing a type label of a concept with a subtype or a specialization from generic to individual by inserting a referrent of the same concept type.

Join. Combines two identical graphs C_1 and C_2 by attaching all relation arcs from C_2 to C_1 and then erasing C_2.

Simplify. Eliminates one of two identical relations in a conceptual graph when all connecting arcs are also the same.

As an example of the use of the formation rules, consider the sentence "Tweety ate a fat worm." This sentence can be broken down into five basic or cannonical conceptual graphs corresponding to the five words in the sentence.

Tweety:	[BIRD:tweety]
ate:	[Animal] ← (AGENT) ← [ATE] → (Patient) → [ENTITY]
a:	[T: *]
fat:	[FAT] ← (ATTRIBUTE) ← [PHYSICAL-OBJECT]
worm:	[WORM]

The [T:*] signifies that something of an unspecified type exists (T is the most general type of all concepts).

From these basic graphs a single conceptual graph can be constructed using the formation operators. First, the subgraph from "a fat worm" is constructed by *restricting* PHYSICAL-OBJECT in the fat graph to WORM and then *joining* it to the graph for worm to get [FAT] ← [ATTRIBUTE] ← [WORM]. Next, ENTITY in the graph for ate is *restricted* to WORM and *joined* to the graph just completed. This gives

[ANIMAL] ← (AGENT) ← [ATE] → (PATIENT) → [WORM] ← (ATTRIBUTE) → [FAT].

The final conceptual graph is obtained by *restricting* ANIMAL to BIRD with referrent Tweety, *joining* the graphs and labeling the whole graph with PAST (for past tense).

(PAST) → [[BIRD: tweety] ← (AGENT) ← [EAT] → (PATIENT) – [WORM] → (ATTRIBUTE) → [FAT]]

In forming the above graph, concept specialization occurred (e.g., when restriction took place as in PHYSICAL-OBJECT to WORM). Thus, the formation rules and their inverses provide one method of inference. When rules for handling negation and other basic inference rules are combined with the formation rules, a complete inference system is obtained. This system is truth preserving. The inference rules needed which are the equivalent of those in a PL system are defined as follows.

Erasure. Any conceptual graph enclosed by an even number of negations may be erased.

Insertion. Any conceptual graph may be inserted into another graph context which is enclosed by an odd number of negations.

Iteration. A copy of any conceptual graph C may be inserted into a graph context in which C occurs or in which C is dominated by another concept.

Deiteration. Any conceptual graph which could be the result of iteration may be erased from a conceptual graph context.

Double Negation. A double negation may be erased or drawn before any conceptual graph or set of graphs.

As an example of some of the above rules, any graph w may be inserted in the implication $\sim[u \sim[v]]$ to derive $\sim[u\ w \sim[v]]$. Any graph w may be erased from the consequent of an implication $\sim[u \sim[v\ w]]$ to derive $\sim[u \sim[v]]$. Any graph w may be erased from the antecedent of an implication only if it has been independently asserted. Thus if u and $\sim[u\ v \sim[w]]$ then derive $\sim[v \sim w]]$.

Note that deiteration and double negation are equivalent to modus ponens, that is, given p and $\sim[p \sim[q]]$, deiteration permits erasure of p inside the first bracket to get $\sim[\sim[q]]$. Double negation then permits erasure of $\sim[\sim$ to obtain the final result q.

Other inference methods including inheritance (if all *A* have property *P* and all *B* are *A*, all *B* have property *P*) and default reasoning are also possible with conceptual graphs. The implementation of modal logic formalisms with these graphs is possible by using concepts such as possible and necessary. Heuristic reasoning can be accomplished within the theory of conceptual graphs.

In summary, conceptual graphs offer the means to represent natural language statements accurately and to perform many forms of inference found in common sense reasoning.

7.3 FRAME STRUCTURES

Frames were first introduced by Marvin Minsky (1975) as a data structure to represent a mental model of a stereotypical situation such as driving a car, attending a meeting, or eating in a restaurant. Knowledge about an object or event is stored together in memory as a unit. Then, when a new situation is encountered, an appropriate frame is selected from memory for use in reasoning about the situation.

Frames are general record-like structures which consist of a collection of slots and slot values. The slots may be of any size and type. Slots typically have names and values or subfields called facets. Facets may also have names and any number of values. An example of a simple frame for Bob is depicted in Figure 7.6 and a general frame template structure is illustrated in Figure 7.7.

From Figure 7.7 it will be seen that a frame may have any number of slots, and a slot may have any number of facets, each with any number of values. This gives a very general framework from which to build a variety of knowledge structures.

The slots in a frame specify general or specific characteristics of the entity for which the frame represents, and sometimes they include instructions on how to apply or use the slot values. Typically, a slot contains information such as attribute value pairs, default values, conditions for filling a slot, pointers to other related frames, and procedures that are activated when needed for different purposes. For example, the Ford frame illustrated in Figure 7.8 has attribute-value slots (COLOR: silver, MODEL: 4-door, and the like), a slot which takes default values for GAS-MILEAGE, and a slot with an attached *if-needed* procedure.

```
(bob
      (PROFESSION (VALUE professor))
      (AGE (VALUE 42))
      (WIFE (VALUE sandy))
      (CHILDREN (VALUE sue joe))
      (ADDRESS (STREET (VALUE 100 elm))
               (CITY (VALUE dallas))
               (STATE (VALUE tx))
               (ZIP (VALUE 75000))))
```

Figure 7.6 A simple instantiated person frame.

```
(<frame name>
    (<slot1> (<facet1><value1>....<valuek1>)
             (<facet2><value1>....<valuek2>)
                  .
                  .
                  .
    (< slot2> (<facet1><value1>....<valuekm>)
          .
          .
          . )
```

Figure 7.7 A general frame structure.

The value fget in the GAS-MILEAGE slot is a function call to fetch a default value from another frame such as the general car frame for which Ford is a-kind-of (AKO). When the value of this slot is evaluated, the fget function is activated. When fget finds no value for gas mileage it recursively looks for a value from ancestor frames until a value is found.

The if-needed value in the Range slot is a procedure name that, when called, computes the driving range of the Ford as a function of gas mileage and fuel capacity. Slots with attached procedures such as fget and if-needed are called procedural attachments or demons. They are done automatically when a value is needed but not provided for in a slot. Other types of demons include *if-added* and *if-removed* procedures. They would be triggered, for example, when a value is added or removed from a slot and other actions are needed such as updating slots in other dependent frames.

Like associative networks, frames are usually linked together in a network through the use of special pointers such as the AKO pointer in Figure 7.8. Hierarchies of frames are typical for many systems where entities have supertype-subtype or generic-instance relationships. Such networks make it possible to easily implement property inheritance and default reasoning as depicted in Figure 7.8. This is illustrated

```
(ford (AKO (VALUE car))
      (COLOR (VALUE silver))
      (MODEL (VALUE 4-door))
      (GAS-MILEAGE (DEFAULT fget))
      (RANGE (VALUE if-needed))
      (WEIGHT (VALUE 2600))
      (FUEL-CAPACITY (VALUE 18))
         .
         .
         .
```

Figure 7.8 A Ford frame with various slot types.

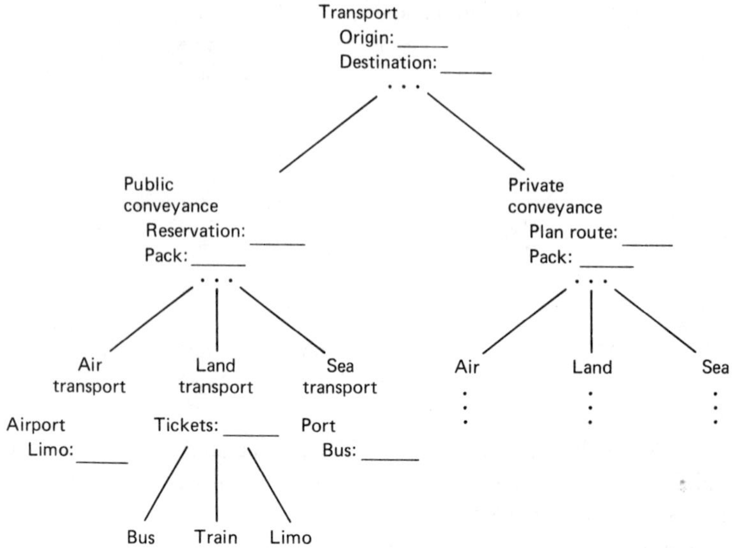

Figure 7.9 Network of frames for transportation methods.

in the network of frames which represents various forms of transportation for people (Figure 7.9).

Frame-Based Representation Languages

Frame representations have become popular enough that special high level frame-based representation languages have been developed. Most of these languages use LISP as the host language. They typically have functions to create, access, modify, update, and display frames. For example, a function which defines a frame might be called with

```
(fdefine f-name <parents><slots>)
```

where fdefine is a frame definition function, f-name is the name assigned to the new frame, <parents> is a list of all parent frames to which the new frame is linked, and <slots> is a list of slot names and initial values. Using the function fdefine to create a train frame we might provide the following details.

```
(fdefine general-train land-transport
   (type (VALUE passenger))
   (class  (VALUE first-class second-class sleeper))
   (food (restaurant (VALUE hot-meals))
         (fast-food (VALUE cold-snacks))
              . . .
              . . .
```

A few other functions typically provided in a frame language include

```
(fget f-name slot-name facet-name)        ;returns data from
                                          ;specified location
(fslots f-name)                           ;returns names of
                                          ;slots
(ffacets f-name slot-name)                ;returns names of
                                          ;facets
(fput f-name slot-name facet-name)        ;adds data to a
                                          ;specified location
(fremove f-name slot-name facet-name)     ;removes data from
                                          ;specified location
```

Several frame languages have now been developed to aid in building frame-based systems. They include the Frame Representation Language (FRL) (Bobrow et al., 1977), Knowledge Representation Language (KRL), which served as a base language for a scheduling system called NUDGE (Goldstein et al., 1977) and KLONE (Brachman, 1978).

Implementation of Frame Structures

One way to implement frames is with property lists. An atom is used as the frame name and slots are given as properties. Facets and values within slots become lists of lists for the slot property. For example, to represent a train frame we define the following putprop.

```
(putprop 'train ((type (VALUE passenger))
                 (class(VALUE first second sleeper))
                 (food (restaurant (VALUE hot-meals))
                       (fast-food (VALUE cold snacks)))
                          'land-transport)
```

Another way to implement frames is with an association list (an a-list), that is, a list of sublists where each sublist contains a key and one or more corresponding values. The same train frame would be represented using an a-list as

```
(setq train '((AKO land-transport)
              (type (VALUE passenger))
              (class(VALUE first second sleeper))
              (food (restaurant (VALUE hot-meals))
                    (fast-food (VALUE cold snacks))))
```

It is also possible to represent frame-like structures using object-oriented programming extensions to LISP languages such as FLAVORS (described in Chapter 8).

7.4 CONCEPTUAL DEPENDENCIES AND SCRIPTS

Scripts are another structured representation scheme introduced by Roger Schank (1977). They are used to represent sequences of commonly occurring events. They were originally developed to capture the meanings of stories or to "understand" natural language text. In that respect they are like a script for a play.

A script is a predefined frame-like structure which contains expectations, inferences, and other knowledge that is relevant to a stereotypical situation. Scripts are constructed using basic primitive concepts and rules of formation somewhat like the conceptual graphs described in Section 7.2. Before proceeding with a description of the script, we describe the primitives and related rules used in building them. They are known as conceptual dependencies (not to be confused with conceptual graphs).

Conceptual Dependencies

Conceptual dependency (CD) theory is based on the use of a limited number of primitive concepts and rules of formation to represent any natural language statement. The theory states that different sentences which have the same meaning should have the same unique CD representation. Furthermore, representations for any sentence should be unambiguous as the speaker intends, even though it may have syntactic ambiguity, as in "I saw the Golden Gate Bridge flying into San Francisco this afternoon." It is the contention that any concept, like dreaming, thinking, bellowing, or scheming can be described in terms of these primitives.

In CD theory five different types of ontological (state of being) building blocks are distinguished. Each of these types, in turn, has several subtypes. The types are made up of entities, actions, conceptual cases, conceptual dependencies, and conceptual tenses.

ENTITIES

Picture producers (PP) are actors or physical objects (including human memory) that perform different acts.

Picture aiders (PA) are supporting properties or attributes of producers.

ACTIONS

Primitive actions (ACTs) as listed in Figure 7.10.

Action aiders (AA) are properties or attributes of primitive actions.

Primitive actions	Intended meaning
ATRANS	Transfer of an abstract entity
ATTEND	Focusing attention on an object
CONC	To think about something
EXPEL	Expulsion of anything from the body
GRASP	Grasping or holding an object tightly
INGEST	Ingesting something
MBUILD	Building on information
MOVE	Moving a part of the body
MTRANS	Transfer of mental information
PROPEL	Application of force
PTRANS	Physical transfer from one location to another
SPEAK	Emitting a sound

Figure 7.10 Conceptual dependency primitive actions.

CONCEPTUAL CASES (ALL ACTIONS INVOLVE ONE OR MORE OF THESE)

Objective Case
Directive Case
Instrumental Case
Recipient Case

CONCEPTUAL DEPENDENCIES

Semantic rules for the formation of dependency structures such as the relationship between an actor and an event or between a primitive action and an instrument, (see Figure 7.11).

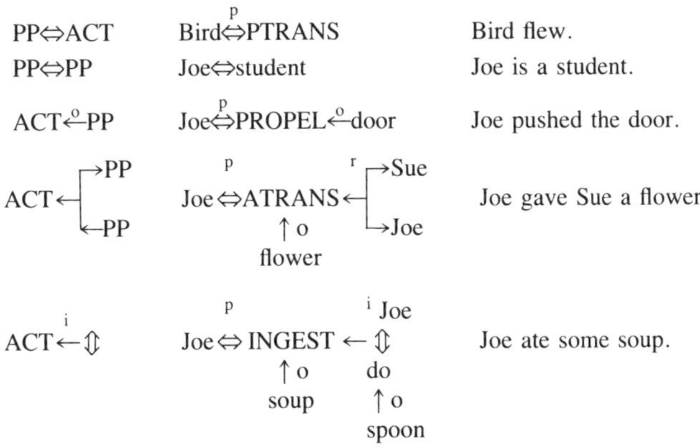

Figure 7.11 Some typical conceptual dependency structures.

CONCEPTUAL TENSES (TIME OF ACTION OR STATE OF BEING)

Conditional (c)
Continuing (k)
Finished Transition (tf)
Future (f)
Interrogative (?)
Negative (/)
Past (p)
Present (nil)
Start Transition (ts)
Timeless (delta)
Transition (t)

Conceptual structures in the form of a graph are used to represent the meanings of different English (or other language) sentences. The graphs are constructed from elementary structures in accordance with basic syntax rules. Some of the basic concept rules are as follows.

PP ACT	Some picture producers perform primitive actions.
PP PA	Picture producers have attributes.
ACT ← O—PP	Primitive actions have objects.
→ PP ACT ← R— ← pp	Primitive actions have recipients.
→ LOC ACT ← D— ← LOC	Primitive actions have directions.
T	Conceptualizations have times.
LOC	Conceptualizations have locations.
ACT ← I —⇕	Primitive actions have instruments.

Using these syntactic elements, structures which represent any sentence can be constructed. Some examples of simple graphs and their corresponding sentences are illustrated in Figure 7.11.

More complex sentence representations are constructed from the basic building blocks given above. Note the similarities between CD theory and the conceptual graphs of the previous section. Both have primitive concepts and relations defined, and both have a syntax for graphical representation. Conceptual graphs differ from CDs mainly in that the conceptual graph is logic based, whereas CD theory is mainly concerned with the semantics of events. We now turn to the event representation structure which uses CDs, the script.

Scripts

Scripts are frame-like structures used to represent commonly occurring experiences such as going to the movies, shopping in a supermarket, eating in a restaurant, or visiting a dentist. Like a script for a play, the script structure is described in terms

SCRIPT-NAME:	food market
TRACK :	supermarket
ROLES :	shopper deli attendant seafood attendant checkout clerk sacking clerk other shoppers
ENTRY CONDITIONS :	shopper needs groceries food market open
PROPS :	shopping cart display aisles market items checkout stands cashier money
SCENE1 :	Enter Market shopper PTRANS shopper into market shopper PTRANS shopping-cart to shopper
SCENE2 :	Shop For Items shopper MOVE shopper through aisles shopper ATTEND eyes to display items shopper PTRANS items to shopping cart
SCENE3 :	Check Out shopper MOVE shopper to checkout stand shopper WAIT shopper turn shopper ATTEND eyes to charges shopper ATRANS money to cashier sacker ATRANS bags to shopper
SCENE4 :	Exit Market shopper PTRANS shopper to exit market
RESULTS :	shopper has less money shopper has grocery items market has less grocery items market has more money

Figure 7.12 A supermarket script structure.

of actors, roles, props, and scenes. Slots in a script which correspond to parts of the event are filled with CD primitives as defined above. An example of a supermarket script is illustrated in Figure 7.12. This script has four scenes which correspond to the main events which commonly occur in a supermarket shopping experience.

Reasoning with Scripts

Since scripts contain knowledge that people use for common every day activities, they can be used to provide an expected scenario for a given situation.

Reasoning in a script begins with the creation of a partially filled script named to meet the current situation. Next, a known script which matches the current situation is recalled from memory. The script name, preconditions, or other key words provide index values with which to search for the appropriate script. Inference is accomplished by filling in slots with inherited and default values that satisfy certain conditions. For example, if it is known that Joe-PTRANS-Joe into a supermarket and Joe-ATRANS-cashier money, it can be inferred that Joe needed groceries, shopped for items, paid the cashier, checked out, and left the market with groceries but with less money than when he entered.

Scripts have now been used in a number of language understanding systems (English as well as other languages) at Yale University by Schank and his colleagues. One such system is SAM (Script Applier Mechanism) which reads and reasons with text to demonstrate an ''understanding'' of stories (such as car accident stories from newspapers) that were script based. Other programs developed at Yale include PAM, POLITICS, FRUMP, IPP, BORIS, BABEL, and CYRUS. All of these programs deal with reading, planning, explaining, or in some way understanding stories. They all used some form of script representation scheme.

7.5 SUMMARY

In this chapter we have investigated different types of structured knowledge representation methods. We first considered associative networks, a representation based on a structure of linked nodes (concepts) and arcs (relations) connecting the nodes. With these networks we saw how related concepts could be structured into cohesive units and exhibited as a graphical representation.

Next, we looked at conceptual graphs, a structured formalism based on traditional logics and which uses primitive building blocks for concepts and relationships between the concepts. How conceptual graphs and formulas in FOPL could be mapped from one to the other and how inferring with conceptual graphs compared to logical inference were demonstrated.

We then considered frame structures as general methods of representing units of knowledge. Frames are composed of any number of slots, each with any number of facets, and they in turn, contain any number of values. The contents of a slot may be attributes which characterize the frame entity, pointers to related frames, procedures, or even other subframes. Inference with frames is accomplished through property inheritance, default values, embedded procedures, and the use of heuristics.

Finally, we described a special frame-like structure called a script. Scripts are used to represent stereotypical patterns for commonly occurring events. Conceptual dependency theory provides primitive building blocks for actions and states that occur within a script. Like a play, a script contains actors, roles, props, and scenes which combine to represent a familiar situation. Scripts have been used in a number of programs which read and "understand" language in the form of stories.

EXERCISES

7.1 Express the following concepts as an associative network structure with interconnected nodes and labeled arcs.

Company ABC is a software development company. Three departments within the company are Sales, Administration, and Programming. Joe is the manager of Programming. Bill and Sue are programmers. Sue is married to Sam. Sam is an editor for Prentice Hall. They have three children, and they live on Elm street. Sue wears glasses and is five feet four inches tall.

7.2 Write LISP expressions which represent the associative network of Problem 7.1.
   a. using property lists, and
   b. using a-lists.

7.3 Write PROLOG expressions which represent the associative network of Problem 7.1.

7.4 Transform the FOPL statements given below into equivalent conceptual graphs.
   a. $\forall x$ NORMAL(x) & GROWN(x)→WALK(x).
   b. ∀x,y MARRIED(x,y) → MARRIED(y,x).
   c. ∀x HASWINGS(x) & LAYSEGGS(x) → ISBIRD(x).

7.5 Transform the following conceptual graphs into equivalent FOPL statements.
   a. [PERSON:sue] ←(AGENT) ←[DRINK]-
      (OBJECT)→ [FOOD:milk]
      (INSTRUMENT)→ [GLASS]
   b. (PAST)→ [[CAMEL:clyde] ←(AGENT) ←[DRINK]→ (OBJECT)-
      [WATER]→ (ATTRIBUTE)→ [50-GALLONS]]

7.6 The original primitives of conceptual dependency theory developed by Schank fail to represent some important concepts directly. What additional primitives can you discover that would be useful?

7.7 Create a movie script similar to the supermarket script of Figure 7.11.

7.8 What are the main differences between scripts and frame structures?

7.9 Express the following sentences as conceptual dependency structures.
   a. Bill is a programmer.
   b. Sam gave Mary a box of candy.
   c. Charlie drove the pickup fast.

7.10 Create a frame network for terrestrial motor vehicles (cars, trucks, motorcycles) and give one complete frame in detail for cars which includes the slots for the main component parts, their attributes, and relations between parts. Include an as-needed slot for the gas of each type mileage.

7.11 Write a LISP program to create a frame data structure which represents the car frame of Problem 7.10.

7.12 Compare the inference process using frames to that of inference in FOPL. Give examples of both.

8

Object-Oriented Representations

The previous chapter marked a departure from the approaches to knowledge representation of earlier chapters in that the methods there focused on adding structure to the knowledge. Structure was added by linking concepts through relations and clustering together all related knowledge about an object. In some cases, as with frames, procedures related to the knowledge were also attached to the knowledge cluster. The approach in grouping knowledge and related procedures together into a cohesive unit is carried even further with object-oriented systems which we examine in some detail in this chapter.

8.1 INTRODUCTION

Grouping related knowledge together in AI systems gains some of the same cognitive advantages realized in the human brain. The knowledge required for a given cognitive task is usually quite limited in domain and scope. Therefore, access and processing can be made more efficient by grouping or partitioning related knowledge together as an unit. We saw how this notion was implemented with linked frames in the previous chapter. We shall see in this chapter, that object-oriented systems share a number of similarities with the frame implementations.

In procedural programming languages such as Pascal or FORTRAN, a program consists of a procedural part and a data part. The procedural part consists of the set of program instructions, and the data part, the numbers and character strings that are manipulated by the instructions. Programs typically contain several modules of instructions that perform computations on the same data set. When some change is made to the format of the data, every module that uses it must then be modified to accommodate the newly revised format. This places a heavy burden on the software maintenance process and makes these types of programs more prone to errors.

In an object-oriented system (OOS) the emphasis between data and procedures is reversed. Data becomes the primary object and procedures are secondary. For example, everything in the universe of an OOS is an object, and objects are inaccessible to outside procedures. This form of structuring is sometimes called encapsulation or data hiding. It is a well known system design principle used to make systems more modular and robust. With encapsulation, objects are associated with their own procedures and, as such, are responsible for their own actions. Thus, when some change is required in the data or procedure, only the changed object need be modified. Other objects are not affected and therefore require no modifications.

In object-oriented systems there is a simplicity in structure because almost everything is an object. For example, a car can be regarded as an object consisting of many interacting components or subobjects: an engine, electrical system, fuel system, drive train, controls, and so on. To model such a system using an object-oriented approach requires that all parts be declared as objects, each one characterized by its own attributes and its own operational behavior. Even a simple windshield wiper would be described as an object with given attributes and operations. As such, it might be described as the structure presented in Figure 8.1.

This object has a name, a class characterization, several distinguishing attributes, and a set of operations. Since all characteristics of the wiper object, including its operations, are contained within a single entity, only this entity needs changing when some design change is made to this part of the car. Other objects that interact with it are not affected, provided the communication procedures between the objects were not changed. To initiate the task of cleaning moisture from the windshield requires only that a message be sent to the object. This message can remain the

OBJECT NAME	left wiper
AKO	wiper
ATTRIBUTES	made of rubber and metal length: 14 inches color: black and silver location: lower left windshield function: rub moisture from windshield
OPERATIONS	turn-on switch: move in arc on windshield repeating clockwise then counter-clockwise turn-off switch: move to home position

Figure 8.1 Object description for a windshield wiper.

same even though the structure of the wiper or its mode of operation may have changed.

Because there is more than one wiper, each with similar attributes and operations, some savings in memory and procedures can be realized by creating a generic class which has all the characteristics which are common to the left, right, and rear wipers. The three instances retain some characteristics unique to themselves, but they inherit common attributes and operations from the more general wiper class.

The object paradigm described above seems to model real-world systems more closely than the procedural programming models where objects (data) and procedures are separated. In object-oriented systems, objects become individual, self-contained units that exhibit a certain behavior of their own and interact with other objects only through the passing of messages. Tasks get performed when a message is sent to an object that can perform the task. All the details of the task are rightfully hidden from other objects. For example, when your car needs repairing, you send a message to the repair shop. The repair shop, in turn, may need parts from one or more manufacturers for which they must send messages. When the car has been repaired, the repair shop sends you a message informing you of that fact.

In having the shop repair your car, you probably are not interested in all the details related to the repair, the fact that messages were sent to other organizations for parts, that they were obtained by Federal Express, and that certain detailed procedures were taken to complete the repair process. Your primary concern is that the repair operation was properly completed and your car returned in working order. The need to model operational behavior such as this has prompted the development of object-oriented systems.

8.2 OVERVIEW OF OBJECT-ORIENTED SYSTEMS

The basic idea behind an OOS is the notion of classes of objects interacting with each other to accomplish some set of tasks. The objects have well-defined behaviors. They interact with each other through the use of messages. When a task needs to be performed, an object is passed a message which specifies the task requirements. The receiving object then takes appropriate action in response to the message and responds by returning a message to the sender. In performing the required task, the receiver may need assistance from other objects, thereby prompting further messages to be sent.

These ideas are illustrated in Figure 8.2 which depicts the simulation of a seaport facility. Ocean ships arrive for docking, unloading, loading, and departing. When the facilities (tugboats, berths, and loading and unloading equipment and crews) are busy, arriving ships must queue and wait at sea until space and other facilities are available. The harbor master coordinates the arrivals and departures by assigning tugs and other resources to the arriving ships. The objects in this example are, of course, the individual ships, the tugs, the docks, the harbor master,

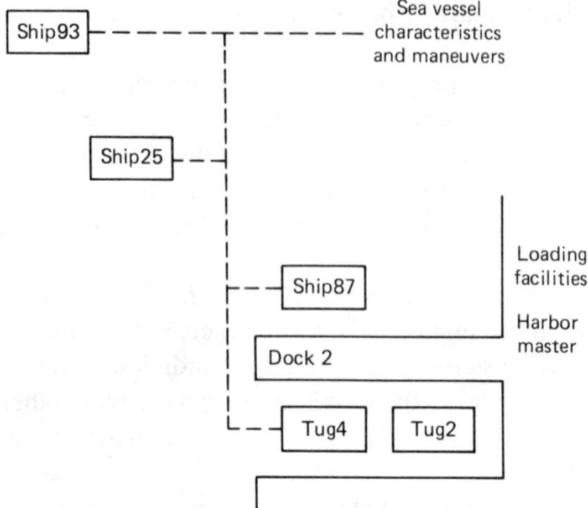

Figure 8.2 Objects communicating to complete a task.

and the cargo handling facilities. Actions are initiated by message passing between these objects. The dashed lines connecting members of the class of sea vessels depict the way common characteristics and operational behaviors are shared by members of the same class (they all have a coordinate position, a maximum cruising speed, cargo capacity, and so on).

Tasks are performed when a message is sent from one object to another. For exmaple, the harbor master may send a message to a tug to provide assistance to ship 87 in deberthing from dock 2. This would then result in a sequence of actions from the tug having received the message.

In general, a task may consist of any definable operation, such as changing an object's position, loading cargo, manipulating a character string, or popping up a prompt window. A complete program would then be a sequence of the basic tasks such as the simulated movement of ships into and out of the seaport after discharging and taking on cargo.

8.3 OBJECTS, CLASSES, MESSAGES, AND METHODS

In this section we present definitions for the basic concepts that make up an OOS: the object, message, class, methods, and class hierarchies. There are probably as many as fifty different OOS languages, and the examples presented in this section may not comply exactly with any one in particular. The examples are representative of all OOS however, and are based mainly on material from the Smalltalk family, including Smalltalk 80 (Goldberg and Robson, 1983, and Kaehler and Patterson, 1986), Smalltalk/V (Digitalk, Inc., 1986), and Little Smalltalk (Budd, 1987). Specialized OOS languages are considered in Section 8.5.

Objects

Objects are the basic building blocks in object-oriented systems. All entities except parts of a message, comments, and certain punctuation symbols are objects. An object consists of a limited amount of memory which contains other objects (data and procedures). They are encapsulated together as a unit and are accessible to that object only. Examples of objects are numbers such as 5, 31, 6.213, strings like 'this is a string,' arrays such as #(23 'a string' 311 (3 4 5)), the Turtle (a global graphics object originally used in LOGO), a windshield wiper as described above, a ship, and so on. Objects are characterized by attributes and by the way they behave when messages are sent to them. All objects belong to some class. They are created by declaring them as instances of an existing class and instantiating instance variables. The class to which an object belongs can be determined by sending it the message "class."

Messages

Actions are performed in an OOS by sending messages to an object. This corresponds to a function or procedure call in other languages. The messages are formatted strings composed of three parts: a receiver object, a message selector, and a sequence of zero or more arguments. The format of a message is given as

<object><selector><arg_1 arg_2. . .>

The object identifies the receiver of the message. This field may contain an object item or another message which evaluates to an object. The selector is a procedure name. It specifies what action is required from the object. The arguments are objects used by the receiver object to complete some desired task. Messages may also be given in place of an argument since a message always elicits an object as a response.

When an object receives a valid message, it responds by taking appropriate actions (such as executing a procedure or sending messages to other objects) and then returning a result. For example, the message 9 − 5 causes the receiver object 9 to respond to the selector − by subtracting 5 from 9 and returning the object 4.

There are three types of messages: unary, binary, and keyword (*n*-ary). All three types parse from left to right, but parentheses may be used to determine the order of interpretation. A unary message requires no arguments. For example, each of the following are unary messages:

```
5 sign
10 factorial
'once upon a time' size
#(a b c d) reversed
68 asCharacter
```

In each of these examples, the first item in the message is the receiver object, and the second item the selector. The first example returns the integer +1 to signify a positive algebraic sign for the number 5. The second example returns 3628800 the factorial value of the integer 10. The third example returns 16, the length of the string. The fourth returns the array #(*d c b a*), and the fifth returns *D*, the ASCII character equivalent of 68.

Binary messages take one argument. Arithmetic operations are typical of binary messages, where the first operand is the receiver, the selector is the arithmetic operation to be performed, and the second operand is the argument. Examples of binary messages are

```
10 + 32                "an addition message"
13 - 9                 "a subtraction message"
22 * 7                 "multiplication message"
54 / 2                 "rational division message"
#(a b c), #(d e f)     "the comma concatenates two arrays"
7 < 9                  "relational test message"
7 @ 12                 "an x-y coordinate point reference"
```

Comments may be placed anywhere within an OOS program using the double quotation marks as seen in the above examples. Note that the last three examples are nonarithmetic binary messages. They result in the combining of two arrays into one, a boolean relational test, and the creation of a graphics coordinate point at column 7, row 12, respectively.

The third and most general type of message is the keyword message. These messages have selectors which consist of one or more keyword identifiers, where each is followed by a colon and an argument. The argument can be an object or any message, but if it is another keyword message, it must be enclosed in parentheses to avoid ambiguity. Examples of keyword messages are

```
5 between: 4 and: 10              "a Boolean test"

'aecdb' copyFrom: 2 to: 5         "copies position 2 of the
                                  string to position 5"

#(a b c x) at: 4 put: #(d e)      "the elements of #(d e)
                                  replace x in the array"

'texas' size between: 2 + 2 and: 4 factorial

set1 add: (i + 1)                 "add new element to set 1"
```

The last two examples above contain messages within messages, while the last example has a message delimited with parentheses. In executing a message without parentheses, the execution proceeds left to right with unary messages taking precedence followed by binary, and then keyword. Therefore, the messages 'texas' size and 4 factorial are completed before the keyword part between:and: in the last example above.

Methods

Procedures are called methods. They determine the behavior of an object when a message is sent to the object. Methods are the algorithms or sequence of instructions executed by an object. For example, in order to respond to the message 5 + 7, the object 5 must initiate a method to find the sum of the integer numbers 5 and 7. On completion of the operation, the method returns the object 12 to the sending object.

Methods are defined much like procedures in other programming languages using the constructs and syntax of the given OOS. The constructs used to build higher level methods are defined in terms of a number of primitive operations and basic methods provided as part of the OOS. The primitives of an OOS are coded in some host language such as an assembler language or C. For example, the operation for integer addition used in some versions of Smalltalk would be written as

```
+ aNumber
   ^  <SameTypeOfObject self aNumber>
      ifTrue: [<IntegerAddition self aNumber>]
      ifFalse: [super + aNumber]
```

The name of this method is + and the argument is an object of type aNumber. The primitive operation SameTypeOfObject tests whether the two object arguments are of the same type (instances of the same class). The variable self is a temporary variable of an instance of the class it belongs to, Integer. If the two objects are of the same type, the primitive IntegerAddition in the ifTrue block of code is executed and the sum returned. Otherwise, a search for an appropriate method is made by checking the superclass of this class (the class Number) . The up-arrow ^ signifies the quantity to be returned by the method.

A typical OOS may have as many as a few hundred predefined primitives and basic methods combined. We will see examples of some typical methods in the next section.

Classes and Hierarchies

A class is a general object that defines a set of individual (instance) objects which share common characteristics. For example, the class of rabbits contains many individual rabbit objects, each with four legs, long ears, whiskers, and short bushy tails. The class of natural numbers contains many instance objects such as 43,91,2, ... All objects are instances of some class and classes are subclasses of some higher class, except for a most general root class. The root class for an OOS is the class named Object.

Classes can often be divided into subclasses or merged into superclasses. The class of fruit can be divided into citrus and noncitrus, both of which can be further divided. Fruit is part of the superclass of plant-grown foods which in turn is part of the class of all foods. Classes permit the formation of hierarchies of objects which can be depicted as a tree or taxonomic structure as illustrated in Figure 8.3.

Objects belonging to the same class have the same variables and the same methods. They also respond to the same set of messages called the *protocol* of the class. Each class in a hierarchy inherits the variables and methods of all of its parents or superclasses of the class.

When a message is sent to an object, a check is first made to see if the methods for the object itself or its immediate class can perform the required task. If not, the methods of the nearest superclass are checked. If they are not adequate, the search process continues up the hierarchy recursively until methods have been found or the end of a chain has been reached. If the required methods are not found, an error message is printed.

Some OOSs permit classes to have two or more direct superclasses (Stefik and Bobrow, 1986). For example, StereoSystem may have superclasses of Appliances, LuxuryGoods, and FragileCommodity. As such, a stereo object may inherit characteristics and methods from all three superclasses. When this is the case, an inheritance precedence must be defined among the superclasses. One approach would be to try the leftmost superclass path in the hierarchy first. If applicable methods are not found up this path, the next leftmost path is taken. This process continues progressively shifting to the right until a method is found or failure occurs.

An OOS will have many predefined classes. For example, a few of the classes for the Smalltalk family and their hierarchical structure are depicted in Figure 8.4.

Each of the classes depicted in Figure 8.4 has a number of methods that respond to the protocol for the class. A class may also inherit methods from a superclass. For example, all classes inherit the method "== anObject" which answers true if the receiver and anObject are the same, and answers false otherwise.

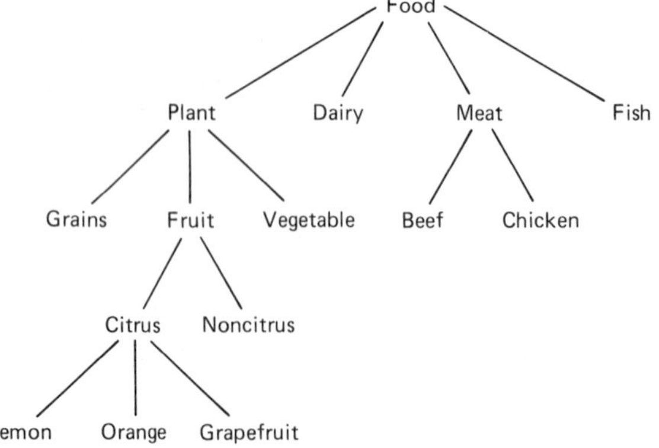

Figure 8.3 A class hierarchy of foods.

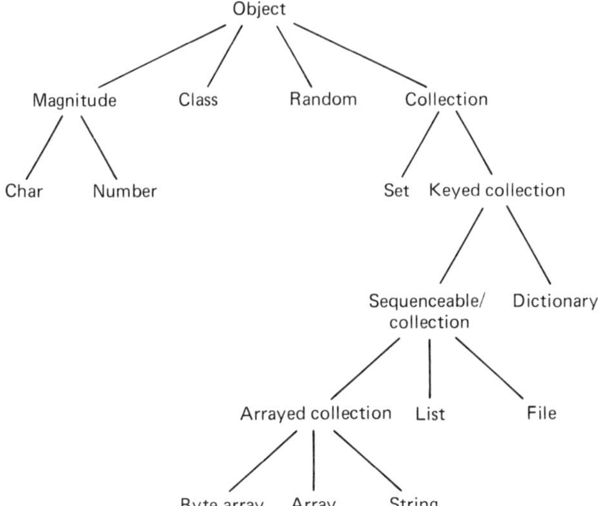

Figure 8.4 Partial hierarchy of predefined OOS classes.

Polymorphism is the capability for different objects to respond to the same message protocols but exhibit their own unique behaviors in response. For example, a message containing the selector moveForward could invoke the forward movement of a ship as well as advancing a piece in a game such as checkers. Both classes use the same message template but respond differently. The only requirement is that the message protocol for the two classes be implemented as required for the given class.

8.4 SIMULATION EXAMPLE USING AN OOS PROGRAM

In this section, we present a simple example of an OOS program to demonstrate some of the features defined above. The example is a program to simulate the seaport operations described in Section 8.2. Before we begin however, we define some additional syntax and operations used in an OOS.

An OOS will have most of the basic programming constructs of a procedural language such as Pascal, including arithmetic and string manipulation operations, assignment and conditional statements, logical expressions, iteration, and so on. A few examples will help to illustrate some of the basic constructs and syntactical conventions.

1. A period is used as a statement separator, not as a terminator.

2. A block object is a sequence of OOS statements (messages) enclosed within square brackets. A block is like an in-line procedure that, when evaluated, returns the last value executed within the block. Blocks are instances of the Block class that execute when sent the message value, value: or value:value:, depending on whether the block has zero, one, or two arguments.

3. Variable assignment is made with := as in Pascal. Some OOS implementations use the back arrow ← like Algol for assignment

```
index := 1     (or index ← 1).
```

4. The vertical bar is used as a delimiter to identify a set of temporary variables used in methods as well as a separator of method definitions within a class.

5. An up arrow which immediately precedes an item signifies that the item is to be returned in response to a message.

6. Boolean relational tests use the relational symbols and syntax of the OOS such as

```
5 < 'string' size
('camel' at: 3) isVowel.
```

7. Conditional statements follow the test condition as in

```
a < b   ifTrue: [a print]
        ifFalse: [b print].
```

8. Typical logical expressions are given by

```
a >= b and: [c <= d]
x isDigit or: [$F <= y and: [y <= $L]]
```

The dollar sign preceding a character identifies character objects.

9. Typical iteration constructs are whileTrue, whileFalse, timesRepeat, and do.

```
i := 1.
[i print. i := i + 2. i <= 10] whileTrue.

1 to: 10 do [[:j| array at: j] print].

paths := 6.
paths timesRepeat [ship move: 100; turn: 360//paths].
```

10. The variable self in a method refers to the receiver object of the message that invokes the method. The variable super is used in a method to invoke a search for a method in an object's superclass.

In addition to the above examples, an OOS will have many special methods for the definition of classes and objects and for the definition of class behaviors and class related tasks.

Simulation of Seaport Operations

An event driven simulation of the seaport operation described in Section 8.2 is a computed sequence of the events of interest which occur at discrete time points.

This system would have as a minimum the three events: (1) cargo ship arrivals, (2) ship berthing operations, and (3) cargo transfer and ship departures. These events are symbolized by the following expressions which will be used in our program.

```
shipArrival
shipDocking
shipDeparture
```

In the interest of clarity, several simplifying assumptions are made for the simulation problem. First, we limit our objects of interest to three classes, namely the class of ships (three types of cargo ships), the group of entities which make up the harbor operations (tugs, docks, cranes, crews, and the like) treated collectively as one object class called HarborOperations, and the class called Simulator. The Simulator class is defined to permit separate simulation runs, that is, separate instances of Simulator.

Second, we assume that ships arriving to find all berths full depart immediately from the system. Ships arriving when at least one of the eight berths is available are scheduled for docking and cargo transfer. Once a ship has been docked, its departure is then scheduled.

To add some realistic randomness to the operation, the time between ship arrivals is assumed to be exponentially distributed with a mean value of 3 time units. The time to dock is assumed to be uniformly distributed with a range of 0.5 to 2.0 time units, and the time to transfer cargo is assumed to be exponentially distributed with a mean of 14 time units. Finally, to simulate three different types of ships, a newly arriving ship is randomly assigned a cargo weight of 10, 20, or 30 thousand tons from an empirical distribution with probabilities 0.2, 0.5, and 0.3, respectively.

The three types of simulated events may occur at any discrete time point, and they may even occur concurrently. To manage these events, we require a system clock to assign scheduled event times and a data structure in which to record all pending events. At any time during the run, the pending event list could include a scheduled ship arrival at current time t_{now} plus some time increment t_1, the berthing of a ship at time $t_{\text{now}} + t_2$, and the departures of one or more ships at $t_{\text{now}} + t_3$, $t_{\text{now}} + t_4$, and so on. Scheduled events are removed from the list of pending events in the order of smallest time value first.

Pending events are held in a dictionary data structure which contains index-value pairs of objects. And, since multiple events may occur at the same time points, we use a set to hold all events indexed by the same time value. Thus, pending events will be stored in a dictionary of indexed sets with each set containing one or more of the basic events.

Messages required to access sets and dictionary objects (collectively referred to as collections) are needed in the program. The messages and the corresponding actions they elicit are as follows.

MESSAGE	RESULTING ACTION
add:	adds an element to the receiver collection, like a list
at:	returns the item in the dictionary whose key matches the argument
at: ifAbsent:	returns the element given by the key in the first argument and evaluates the second argument if no argument exists
at:put:	places the second argument into the receiver collection under the key given by the first argument
first	returns the first element from a Set
includesKey:	returns true if the key is valid for the receiver
isEmpty	returns true if the receiver collection contains no elements
keysDo:	evaluates each key element of the one argument block which follows according to the procedure given in the block
remove:	removes the argument object from the receiver collection
removeKey:	removes the object with the given key from the receiver collection

For output from the simulation, we print the arrival time of each ship, indicating whether it docks or not, each ship departure, and the total cargo transferred at the end of the run.

With the above preliminaries, we now define the three classes and their corresponding methods. We begin with the class Simulator which is the most complicated. To define a class, the word Class is given followed by the class name and (optionally) by the class's immediate superclass; if no superclass is given, the default class Object is assumed. This is followed by a list of local variables within vertical bar delimiters. The method protocol for the class is defined next, with the methods separated by vertical bars. The message template for each method is given as the first item following the vertical bar. When local variables for a method are needed, they follow the message template, also given within vertical bars.

```
Class Simulator
|currentTime eventsPending|
[
  new
    eventsPending := Dictionary new.
    currentTime := 0
|
  time
    ^currentTime
|
  addEvent: event at: eventTime
    (eventsPending includesKey: eventTime)
      ifTrue: [(eventsPending at: eventTime) add: event]
```

```
            ifFalse: [eventsPending at: eventTime
                    put: (Set new ; add: event)]
    |
      addEvent: event next: delayTime
        self addEvent: event at: currentTime + delayTime
    |
      proceed   |minTime eventSet event|
        mintime := 99999.
        eventsPending keysDo:
          [:x| (x < minTime) ifTrue: [minTime := x ]].
        currentTime := minTime.
        eventSet:= eventsPending at:
                        minTime ifAbsent: [^ nil].
        event := eventSet first.
        eventSet remove: event.
        (eventSet isEmpty)
             ifTrue: [eventsPending removeKey: minTime].
        self processEvent: event
    ]
```

The method responding to the message addEvent checks to see if a time value (key) exists in the dictionary. If so, it adds the new event to the set under the key. If the time does not already exist, a new set is created, and the event is added to the set and the set put in eventsPending. The proceed method finds the smallest event time (key) and retrieves and removes the first element of the set located there. If the resultant set is empty, the key for the empty set is removed. A message is then sent to the processEvent object in the class HarborOperations which is defined next.

```
    Class HarborOperation :Simulator
    |totalCargo arrivalDistribution dockingDistribution
      serviceDistribution remainingBerths|
    [
      new
        totalCargo := 0.
        remainingBerths := 8.
        arrivalDistribution := Exponential new: 3.
        shipDistribution := DiscreteProb new: #(0.2 0.5 0.3)
        dockingDistribution := Uniform new: #(0.5 2.0).
        serviceDistribution := Exponential new: 14.
        self scheduleArrival
    |
      scheduleArrival  |newShip time|
        newShip := Ship new.
        self addEvent: [self shipArrival: newShip]
              at: (self time + (arrivalDistribution next))
    |
```

```
    processEvent: event
      event value.
      ('ship arrived at', self time) print.
      totalCargo := totalCargo + (shipSize * 10).
      self scheduleArrival
  |
    reportCargo
      ('total cargo transferred', totalCargo) print
  ]
```

The method new initializes some variables, including the arrival, docking, and service distributions. A sample from a distribution is obtained by sending the distribution the message next. (The programming details for the generation of random samples from all distributions have been omitted in the interest of presenting a more readable example.) The scheduleArrival method sends a message to the Ship class to create a new ship and then adds the event block

```
[self shipArrival: newShip]
```

to the pending event list at the arrival time value. The processEvent method is activated from the proceed method in the Simulator class. It initiates evaluation of the event block stored in the pending list, prints a ship arrival message, and computes the new total for the cargo discharged.

Next, we define the class Ship.

```
Class ship
|shipSize|
[
  new
    shipSize := shipDistribution next
|
  shipSize
    ^ shipSize
]
```

With the object classes defined, we can now write the statements for the three object events. The arrival event is initiated from the HarborOperation class. This event then schedules the next operation (docking), which in turn schedules the ship departure event.

```
shipArrival: ship
  (remainingBerths > 0)
    ifTrue: [remainingBerths := remainingBerths - 1.
            self addEvent: [self shipDocking: ship]
              at: (self time + dockingDistribution next)].
    ifFalse: ['all berths occupied, ship departs' print]
```

```
shipDocking: ship
  totalCargo := totalCargo + shipSize.
  self addEvent: [self shipDepart: ship]
          next: (serviceDistribution next)

shipDepart: ship
  'ship departs after cargo transfer' print.
  remainingBerths := remainingBerths + 1
```

To run the simulation program we simply execute the following statements.

```
Simulator new.
port := HarborOperation new
[port time < 720] whileTrue: [port proceed]
```

Note that the message ''port proceed'' in the whileTrue block is sent to Harbor-Operation. Since there is no method proceed in this class, it must be inherited from the Simulator class.

An environment for an OOS will usually include all of the basic primitives, class and method definitions, an editor, a browser, window and mouse facilities, and a graphics output.

8.5 OBJECT-ORIENTED LANGUAGES AND SYSTEMS

In addition to the Smalltalk family of OOS languages, a number of other languages have been developed, including object-oriented extensions to LISP dialects and special purpose languages. Typical of the LISP extensions is the FLAVORS add-ons.

OOS with Lisp Extensions

In FLAVORS, classes are created with the defflavor form, and methods of the flavor are created with defmethod. An instance of a flavor is created with a make-instance type of function. For example, to create a new flavor (class) of ships with instance variables x-position, y-position, x-velocity, y-velocity, and cargo-capacity, the following expression is evaluated:

```
(defflavor ship (x-position y-position x-velocity
                 y-velocity cargo-capacity))
```

Methods for the ship flavor are written in a similar manner with a defmethod, say for the ship's speed, as

```
(defmethod (ship :speed) ()
(sqrt (+ (* x-velocity x-velocity)
         (* y-velocity y-velocity))))
```

To create an instance of ship one then uses the form

```
(setf ship42 (make-instance 'ship))
```

In addition to user defined methods, three additional predefined methods are available for a flavor. They are used to assign values to instance variables, to initialize variable values, and to get values of the variables. These options are specified in the defflavor statement when the flavor is created. For example, to include these optional methods, the following form is used:

```
(defflavor ship (x-position y-position x-velocity
                 y-velocity cargo-capacity)
  ( )
 :gettable-instance-variables
 :settable-instance-variables
 :inittable-instance-variables)
```

Values for the ship instance variables can now be assigned either with a message or when an instance of the ship is created.

```
(send ship42 :set-cargo-capacity 22.5) or

(setf ship42 (make-instance 'ship :x-position 5.0
                                  :y-position 8.0))
```

Variable assignments can be examined with the describe method, one of the base methods provided with the system.

```
(describe ship42)
#<SHIP 1234567>, an object of flavor SHIP,
has instance variable values:
     X-POSITION          5.0
     Y-POSITION          8.0
     X-VELOCITY          unbound
     Y-VELOCITY          unbound
     CARGO-CAPACITY      22.5
```

Default values can also be assigned to instance variables with the defvar statement.

```
(defvar *default-x-velocity* 12.0)
```

Thus, unless *x*-velocity is explicitly assigned a value in a make-instance or defflavor statement, it will be given the default value 12.0.

Flavors are defined hierarchically by including one or more superclasses in the second subform of the defflavor statement, thereby permitting flavors to be ''mixed.'' Inheritance of methods is then achieved much the same as in the Smalltalk case. For example, to create a ship flavor which has two superclass flavors named moving-object and pleasure-craft, the following form would be used:

```
(defflavor ship (x-position y-position passenger-capacity)
                (moving-object pleasure-craft)
   :gettable-instance-variables)
```

If the flavor moving-object has a method for speed, it will be inherited unless a method for speed has been defined explicitly for the ship flavor.

The base flavor for FLAVOR extensions is the vanilla-flavor. This flavor will typically have a number of base methods including a :print-self and describe method as used above. Generic instance variables are also defined for the vanilla-flavor. Through method inheritance and other forms, methods may be combined to give a variety of capabilities for flavors including the execution of some methods just prior to or just after a main method.

Special Purpose OOS Languages

A typical special purpose OOS language is ROSS (for Rand OOS) developed by the Rand Corporation for military battle simulations (Klahr et al, 1980, 1982). This system has been implemented in several dialects of LISP as an interactive simulation system which includes a movie generator and graphics facility. Visual representations can be generated as the simulation is running, and on-the-fly changes can easily be made to a program. It has been used to simulate both air and ground battles.

Messages are sent to objects in ROSS with an ''ask'' form having the following structure.

```
(ask <object><message>)
```

For example, to send a message to a fighter-base requesting that a fighter be sent to intercept a penetrator, the following message might be sent:

```
(ask fighter-basel send fighter2 guided by radar3
          to penetrator2)
```

In response to this message, a method associated with the fighter-base class would be evaluated and appropriate actions would then be initiated through direct computations and embedded message transmissions to other objects.

Object hierarchies which provide variable and method inheritance in much the same way as FLAVORS or Smalltalk can also be created. A simulation program in ROSS would be created in a similar manner to that of the example presented in the previous section, but with a number of basic methods for simulation behaviors

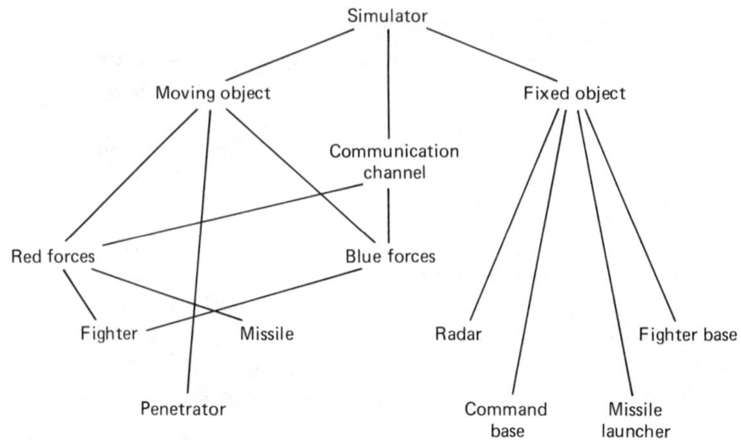

Figure 8.5 An example of a battle class hierarchy.

already predefined. A typical class hierarchy for a battle simulation might be defined as the structure illustrated in Figure 8.5.

8.6 SUMMARY

Object-oriented systems are useful in modeling many real-world situations in which real objects can be put in a one-to-one correspondence with program classes and objects. In an OOS all entities are objects, and objects are protected from other entities. They interact with other objects through an interface which recognizes a set of messages called the protocol for the class. Each class within an OOS will have its own unique behavior which is governed by a set of class methods. Methods and instance variables may be inherited by a class of objects from its parents or superclasses. Multiple inheritance is also supported by many systems.

OOS languages are well suited for certain types of system simulation problems because of the natural way in which OOS programs model real systems. To build a simulation program in an OOS such as Smalltalk, one first defines the object classes required, their hierarchical relationship with each other, and the behaviors of the objects within each class. The events of importance are also defined and the sequence in which they may occur. Message formats for class protocols are then defined, and the specific methods are then coded.

OOS capabilities have been developed for several LISP sytems as add-ons such as found in FLAVORS. Special purpose OOS languages have also been developed such as the ROSS system which was developed to provide capabilities not available in other simulation languages.

EXERCISES

8.1. Show the order of evaluation for the subexpressions given in the following expression: 9/2 between: 8 + 19 sqrt and: 4 * 5

8.2. What values will be printed after the following sequences?

a. *i* := 17
j := [*i* := *i* + 1]
i print

b. *j* value print (after the sequence in a above)

c. *i* value print (after the sequence in b above)

8.3. What is the class of Class? What is the superclass of Class?

8.4. What is the result from typing the following expression?

```
3 + (4 print) ; + 6
```

8.5. A bag is like a set except the same item may occur more than once. One way to implement the class Bag is with a dictionary, where the value contained in the dictionary is the number of times the item occurs in the bag. A partial implementation for a bag is given below. Complete the implementation, keeping in mind that instances of dictionary respond to first and next with values and not keys. The current key is accessible, however, if currentKey is used.

```
Class Bag :Collection
| dict count|
[
      new
         dict:=Dictionary new
|. . . some methods go here. . . .
|     first
         (count:=dict first) isNil ifTrue:[ ^ nil].
          count:=count - 1.
          ^ dict currentKey
|     next
         [count notNil] whileTrue:
            [(count>0)
              ifTrue:[count:=count - 1. ^ dict currentKey]
              ifFalse:[count:=dict next]].
         nil
]
```

8.6. One method of defining a discrete probability distribution is to provide the actual sample space elements in a collection. A random sample can then be obtained from the collection entries. Produce a class description for a class called SampleSpace which will be used to randomly select points using the following:

```
    sample := SampleSpace new ; define: #(12 9 14 19 11 21)
    sample first
12
```

8.7. Modify the simulation program given in Section 8.4 to collect use statistics on the tugs; at the end of the run a printout of average tug usage should be made.

PART 3
Knowledge Organization and Manipulation

9
Search and Control Strategies

In the next three chapters we examine the organization and manipulation of knowledge. This chapter is concerned with search, an operation required in almost all AI programs. Chapter 10 covers the comparison or matching of data structures and in particular pattern matching, while Chapter 11 is concerned with the organization of knowledge in memory.

Search is one of the operational tasks that characterize AI programs best. Almost every AI program depends on a search procedure to perform its prescribed functions. Problems are typically defined in terms of states, and solutions correspond to goal states. Solving a problem then amounts to searching through the different states until one or more of the goal states are found. In this chapter we investigate search techniques that will be referred to often in subsequent chapters.

9.1 INTRODUCTION

Consider the process of playing a game such as chess. Each board configuration can be thought of as representing a different state of the game. A change of state occurs when one of the players moves a piece. A goal state is any of the possible board configurations corresponding to a checkmate.

It has been estimated that the game of chess has more than 10^{120} possible states. (To see this, just note that there are about 20 alternative moves for each board configuration and more than 100 different configurations. Thus, there are more than $20^{100} = 10^{100} * 2^{100} > 10^{120}$). This is another example of the combinatorial explosion problem. The number of states grows exponentially with the number of basic elements. Winning a game amounts to finding a sequence of states through this maze of possible states that leads to one of the goal states.

An "intelligent" chess playing program certainly would not play the game by exploring all possible moves (it would never finish in our lifetime nor in your distant descendent's lifetimes). Like a human, the program must eliminate many questionable states when playing. But, even with the elimination of numerous states, there is still much searching to be done since finding good moves at each state of the game often requires looking ahead a few moves and evaluating the consequences.

This type of problem is not limited to games. Search is ubiquitous in AI. For every interesting problem there are numerous alternatives to consider. When attempting to understand a natural language, a program must search to find matching words that are known (a dictionary), sentence constructions, and matching contexts. In vision perception, program searches must be performed to find model patterns that match input scenes. In theorem proving, clauses must be found by searching axioms and assertions which resolve together to give the empty clause. This requires a search of literals which unify and then a search to find resolvable clauses. In planning problems, a number of potential alternatives must be examined before a good workable plan can be formulated. As in learning, many potential hypotheses must be considered before a good one is chosen.

9.2 PRELIMINARY CONCEPTS

Problems can be characterized as a space consisting of a set of states (not necessarily finite) and a set of operators that map from one state to other states. Three types of states may be distinguished: one or more initial states, a number of intermediate states, and one or more goal states. A solution to a problem is a sequence of operators that map an initial state to a goal state. A "best" or good solution is one that requires the fewest operations or the least cost to map from an initial state to a goal state. The performance of a particular solution method is judged by the amount of time and memory space required to complete the mapping. Thus, a solution based on some algorithm A_1 is considered better than one using algorithm A_2 if the time and space complexity of A_1 is less than that of A_2.

Time and Space Complexity

Time and space complexities of algorithms may be defined in terms of their best, their average, or their worst-case performance in completing some task. In evaluating different search strategies, we follow the usual convention of considering worst-case performances and look for ways to improve on them. For this, we need the O (for order) notation.

Let f and g be functions of n, where algorithm A has size n. The size can be the number of problem states, the number of input characters which specify the problem or some similar number. Let $f(n)$ denote the time (or space) required to solve a given problem using algorithm A. We say "f is big O of g" written $f = O(g)$, if and only if there exists a constant $c > 0$ and an integer n_0, such that $f(n) \leq cg(n)$ for all $n \geq n_0$. Stated more simply, algorithm A solves a problem in at most $cg(n)$ units or steps for all but a finite number of steps. Based on this definition, we say an algorithm is of linear time if it is $O(n)$. It is of quadratic time if it is $O(n^2)$, and of exponential time if it is $O(2^{kn})$ for some constant k (or if it is $O(b^{kn})$ for any real number $b > 1$).

For example, if a knowledge base has ten assertions (clauses), with an average of five literals per clause, and a resolution proof is being performed with no particular strategy, a worst-case proof may require as many as 1125 comparisons ($5^2 \times 10(9)/2$) for a single resolution and several times this number for a complete proof.

Graph and Tree Representations

It is customary to represent a search space as a diagram of a directed graph or a tree. Each node or vertex in the graph corresponds to a problem state, and arcs between nodes correspond to transformations or mappings between the states. The immediate successors of a node are referred to as children, siblings, or offspring, and predecessor nodes are ancestors. An immediate ancestor to a node is a parent.

A tree is a graph in which each node has at most one parent. One node, the root or starting node, has no parent. Leaf or terminal nodes are nodes without children. The number of successors emanating from a node is called the branching degree of that node (denoted as b). A path is a sequence of nodes $n_1, \ldots, n_k$, where each n_i is a successor of n_{i-1} for $i = 1, \ldots, k$.

It is always possible to convert a directed graph into a tree with multiple labeled nodes. This can be done by opening up all but one of the several alternate paths connecting two nodes and creating duplicate copies of the end node, one for each different path from the parent. We will find it more convenient, however, to use both types of representations in the following discussion.

An And-Or graph or tree is a special type of representation for problems which can be reduced to a set of subproblems, all of which must be solved. The requirement for the solution of all subproblems is depicted as an And node, a node with all arcs emanating from it connected by a curved line. Or nodes have no line connecting its arcs to signify that any emanating path may be taken for a solution. For example, if a robot is given the task of painting a table, it may complete the task by scraping, sanding, and painting the table, or it may choose the simpler solution and send it to a paintshop (Figure 9.1).

In what follows, we assume simple Or graphs or trees as the problem space

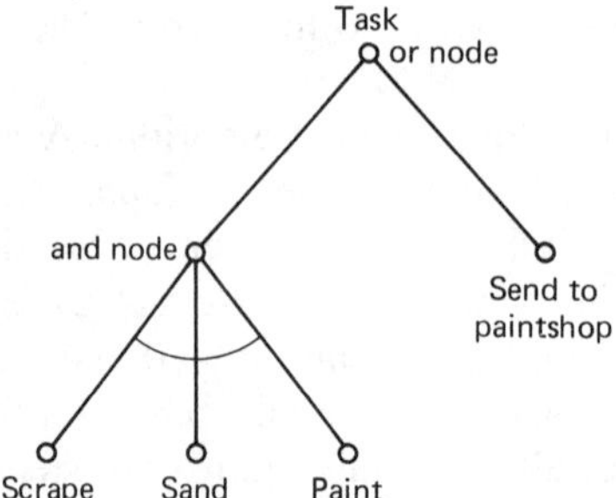

Figure 9.1 Example of an and-or graph.

representation unless noted otherwise. And-Or graph searches are covered in Section 9.6.

Graph and Search Trees

Search can be characterized as finding a path through a graph or tree structure. This requires moving from node to node after successively expanding and generating connected nodes. Node generation is accomplished by computing the identification or representation code of children nodes from a parent node. Once this is done, a child is said to be *generated* and the parent is said to be *explored*. The process of generating all of the children of a parent is also known as *expanding* the node. A search procedure is a strategy for selecting the order in which nodes are generated and a given path selected.

Search problems may be classified by the information used to carry out a given strategy. In *blind or uninformed search*, no preference is given to the order of successor node generation and selection. The path selected is blindly or mechanically followed. No information is used to determine the preference of one child over another.

In *informed or directed search*, some information about the problem space is used to compute a preference among the children for exploration and expansion. Before proceeding with a comparison of strategies, we consider next some typical search problems.

9.3 EXAMPLES OF SEARCH PROBLEMS

In this section we describe three typical problems which illustate the concepts defined above and which are used in subsequent sections to portray different search techniques. The problems considered are the often-used examples, the eight puzzle and the traveling salesman problem.

The Eight Puzzle

The eight puzzle consists of a 3-by-3 square frame which holds eight movable square tiles which are numbered from 1 to 8. One square is empty, permitting tiles

3	8	1
6	2	5
	4	7

A start configuration

1	2	3
8		4
7	6	5

A goal configuration

Figure 9.2 The eight puzzle game.

to be shifted (Figure 9.2). The objective of the puzzle is to find a sequence of tile movements that leads from a starting configuration to a goal configuration such as that shown in Figure 9.2.

The states of the eight puzzle are the different permutations of the tiles within the frame. The operations are the permissible moves (one may consider the empty space as being moveable rather than the tiles): up, down, left, and right. An optimal or good solution is one that maps an initial arrangement of tiles to the goal configuration with the smallest number of moves.

The search space for the eight puzzle problem may be depicted as the tree shown in Figure 9.3.

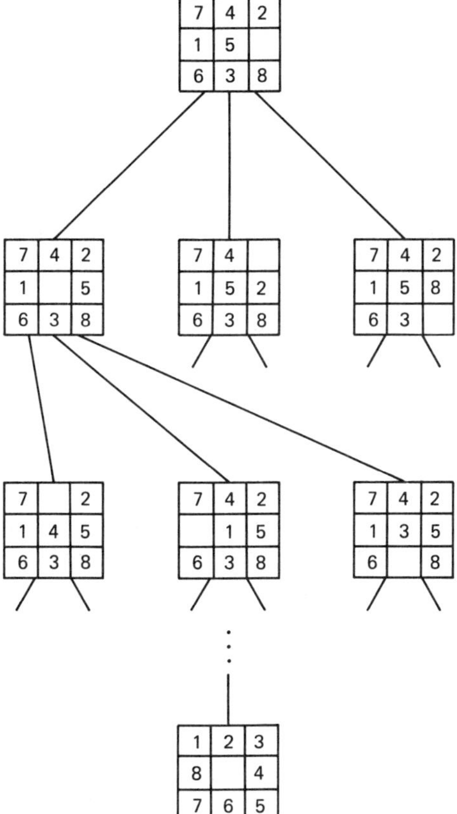

Figure 9.3 A tree diagram for the eight puzzle.

In the figure, the nodes are depicted as puzzle configurations. The root node represents a randomly chosen starting configuration, and its successor nodes correspond to the three single tile movements that are possible from the root. A path is a sequence of nodes starting from the root and progressing downward to the goal node.

Traveling Salesman Problem

The traveling salesman problem involves *n* cities with paths connecting the cities. A tour is any path which begins with some starting city, visits each of the other cities exactly once, and returns to the starting city. A typical tour is depicted in Figure 9.4.

The objective of a traveling salesman problem is to find a minimal distance tour. To explore all such tours requires an exponential amount of time. For example, a minimal solution with only 10 cities is tractable (3,628,000 tours). One with 20 or more cities is not, since a worst-case search requires on the order of 20! (about 23×10^{17}) tours. The state space for the problem can also be represented as a graph as depicted in Figure 9.5.

Without knowing in advance the length of a minimum tour, it would be necessary to traverse each of the distinct paths shown in Figure 9.5 and compare their lengths. This requires some $O(n!)$ traverses through the graph, an exponential number.

General Problem Solver

The General Problem Solver was developed by Newell, Simon, and Shaw (Ernst and Newell, 1969) in the late 1950s. It was important as a research tool for several reasons and notable as the first AI system which cleanly separated the task knowledge from the problem solving part.

General Problem Solver was designed to solve a variety of problems that could be formulated as a set of objects and operators, where the operators were applied to the objects to transform them into a goal object through a sequence of applications.

Given an initial object (state) and a goal object (state), the system attempted to transform the initial object to the goal object through a series of operator application transformations. It used a set of methods similar to those discussed in Chapter 8 for each goal type, to achieve that goal by recursively creating and solving subgoals. The basic method is known as means-end analysis, which we now describe.

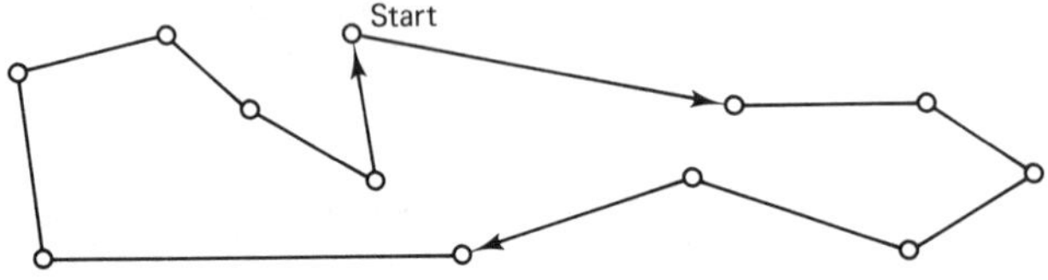

Figure 9.4 A typical tour for the traveling salesman problem.

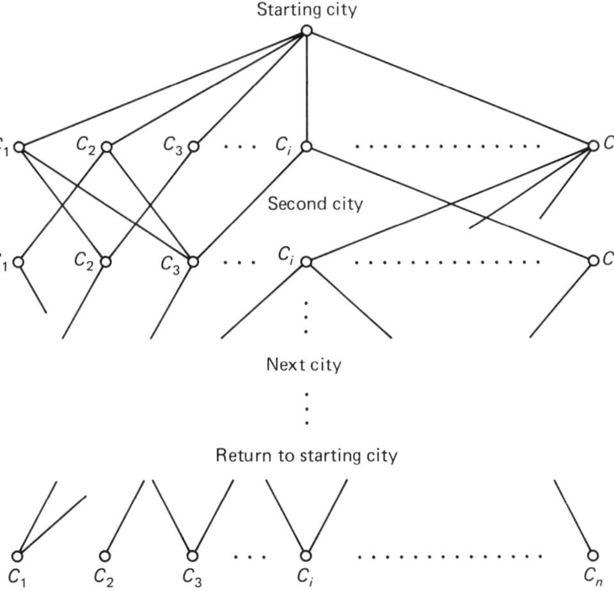

Figure 9.5 State space representation for the TSP.

Means-end analysis. The problem space of means-end analysis has an initial state (object) and one or more goal states (objects), a set of operators O_k with given preconditions for their application, and a difference function that computes the difference between two states S_i and S_j. A problem is solved using means-end analysis by:

1. Comparing the current state S_i to a goal state S_g and computing the difference D_{ig}.
2. An operator O_k is then selected to reduce the difference D_{ig}.
3. The operator O_k is applied if possible. If not, the current state is saved, a subgoal is created and means-end analysis is applied recursively to reduce the subgoal.
4. If the subgoal is solved, the saved state is restored and work is resumed on the original problem.

In carrying out these methods, the General Problem Solver may transform some S_i into an intermediate state S_k, to reduce the difference D_{ij} between states S_i and S_j, then apply another operator O_k to the S_k, and so on until the state S_j is obtained. Differences that may occur between objects will, of course, depend on the task domain.

As an example, in proving theorems in propositional logic, some common differences that occur are a variable may appear in one object and not in the other,

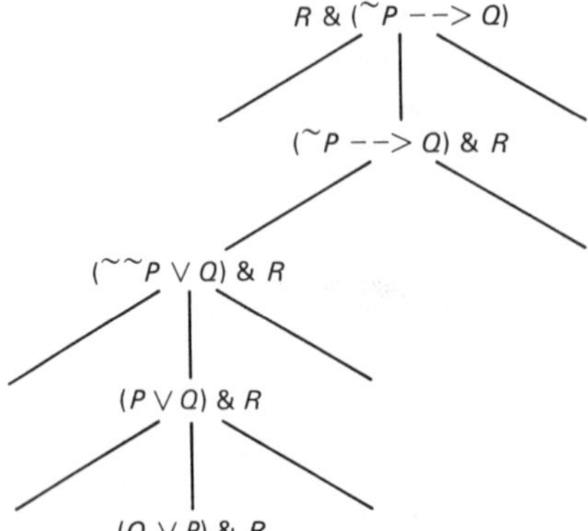

Figure 9.6 A typical solution tree for GPS.

a variable may occur a different number of times between two objects, objects will have different signs or different connectives, associative groupings will differ, and so on.

To illustrate the search process, we assume the General Problem Solver operators are rewrite rules of the following form:

R1: (A V B) → (B V A)
R2: (A & B) → (B & A)
R3: (A → B) → (˜B → ˜A)
R4: (A → B) → (˜A V B)
.
.
.

As a simple example, we suppose General Problem Solver is given the initial propositional logic object L_i = $(R \ \& \ (\tilde{}P \rightarrow Q))$ and goal object L_g = $((Q \vee P) \ \& \ R)$. To determine L_g from L_i requires a few simple transformations. The system first determines the difference between the two expressions and then systematically reduces these differences until L_g is obtained from L_i or failure occurs. For example, a comparison of L_i and L_g reveals the difference that R is on the left in L_i but on the right in L_g. This causes a subgoal to be set up to reduce this difference. The subgoal, in turn, calls for an application of the reduction method, namely to rewrite L_i in the equivalent form L'_i = $((\tilde{}P \rightarrow Q) \ \& \ R)$. The rest of the solution process follows the path indicated in the tree of Figure 9.6.

9.4 UNINFORMED OR BLIND SEARCH

As noted earlier, search problems can be classified by the amount of information that is available to the search process. Such information might relate to the problem space as a whole or to only some states. It may be available a priori or only after a node has been expanded.

In a worst case situation the only information available will be the ability to distinguish goal from nongoal nodes. When no further information is known a priori, a search program must perform a blind or uninformed search. A blind or uninformed search algorithm is one that uses no information other than the initial state, the search operators, and a test for a solution. A blind search should proceed in a systematic way by exploring nodes in some predetermined order or simply by selecting nodes at random. We consider only systematic search procedures in this section.

Search programs may be required to return only a solution value when a goal is found or to record and return the solution path as well. To simplify the descriptions that follow, we assume that only the goal value is returned. To also return the path requires making a list of nodes on the path or setting back-pointers to ancestor nodes along the path.

Breadth-First Search

Breadth-first searches are performed by exploring all nodes at a given depth before proceeding to the next level. This means that all immediate children of nodes are explored before any of the children's children are considered. Breadth first tree search is illustrated in Figure 9.7. It has the obvious advantage of always finding a minimal path length solution when one exists. However, a great many nodes may need to be explored before a solution is found, especially if the tree is very full.

An algorithm for the breadth-first search is quite simple. It uses a queue structure to hold all generated but still unexplored nodes. The order in which nodes are placed on the queue for removal and exploration determines the type of search. The breadth-first algorithm proceeds as follows.

BREADTH-FIRST SEARCH

1. Place the starting node s on the queue.
2. If the queue is empty, return failure and stop.
3. If the first element on the queue is a goal node g, return success and stop. Otherwise,

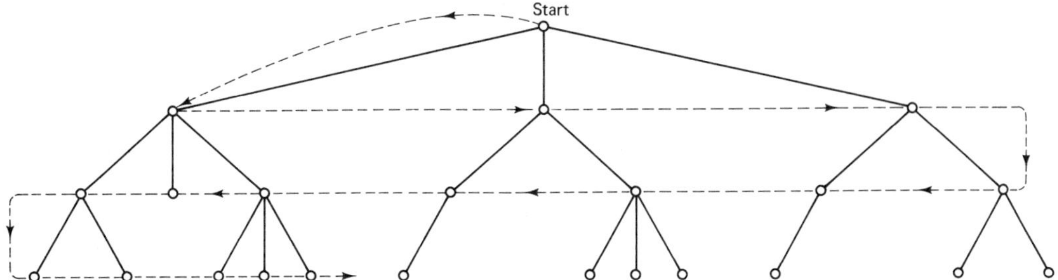

Figure 9.7 Breadth-first search of a tree.

4. Remove and expand the first element from the queue and place all the children at the end of the queue in any order.
5. Return to step 2.

The time complexity of the breadth-first search is $O(b^d)$. This can be seen by noting that all nodes up to the goal depth d are generated. Therefore, the number generated is $b + b^2 + \ldots + b^d$ which is $O(b^d)$. The space complexity is also $O(b^d)$ since all nodes at a given depth must be stored in order to generate the nodes at the next depth, that is, b^{d-1} nodes must be stored at depth $d - 1$ to generate nodes at depth d, which gives space complexity of $O(b^d)$. The use of both exponential time and space is one of the main drawbacks of the breadth-first search.

Depth-First Search

Depth-first searches are performed by diving downward into a tree as quickly as possible. It does this by always generating a child node from the most recently expanded node, then generating that child's children, and so on until a goal is found or some cutoff depth point d is reached. If a goal is not found when a leaf node is reached or at the cutoff point, the program backtracks to the most recently expanded node and generates another of its children. This process continues until a goal is found or failure occurs.

An example of a depth-first search is illustrated in Figure 9.8.

An algorithm for the depth-first search is the same as that for breadth-first except in the ordering of the nodes placed on the queue. Depth-first places the newly generated children at the head of the queue so that they will be chosen first. The search proceeds as follows.

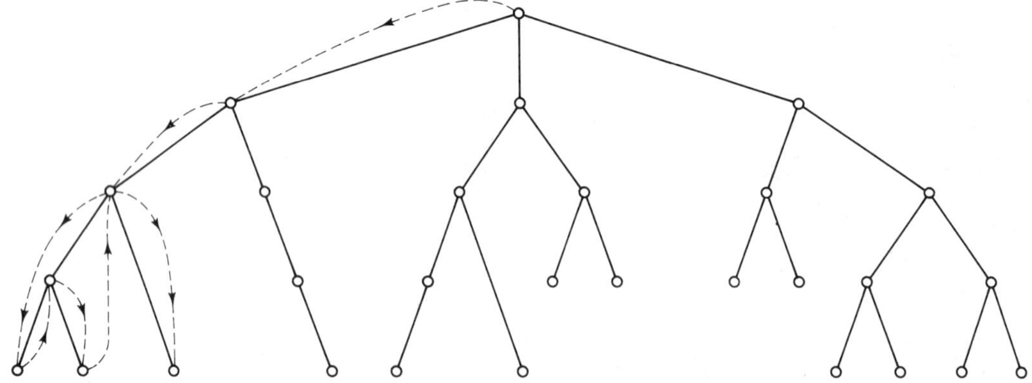

Figure 9.8 Depth-first search of a tree.

DEPTH-FIRST SEARCH

1. Place the starting node *s* on the queue.
2. If the queue is empty, return failure and stop.
3. If the first element on the queue is a goal node *g*, return success and stop. Otherwise,
4. Remove and expand the first element, and place the children at the front of the queue (in any order).
5. Return to step 2.

The depth-first search is preferred over the breadth-first when the search tree is known to have a plentiful number of goals. Otherwise, depth-first may never find a solution. The depth cutoff also introduces some problems. If it is set too shallow, goals may be missed; if set too deep, extra computation may be performed.

The time complexity of the depth-first tree search is the same as that for breadth-first, $O(b^d)$. It is less demanding in space requirements, however, since only the path from the starting node to the current node needs to be stored. Therefore, if the depth cutoff is d, the space complexity is just $O(d)$.

Depth-First Iterative Deepening Search

Depth-first iterative deepening searches are performed as a form of repetitive depth first search moving to a successively deeper depth with each iteration. It begins by performing a depth-first search to a depth of one. It then discards all nodes generated and starts over doing a search to a depth of two. If no goal has been found, it discards all nodes generated and does a depth-first search to a depth of three. This process continues until a goal node is found or some maximum depth is reached.

Since the depth-first iterative deepening search expands all nodes at a given depth before expanding nodes at a greater depth, it is guaranteed to find a shortest-path solution. The main disadvantage of this method is that it performs wasted computations before reaching a goal depth. Even so, it has been shown to be asymptotically optimal over depth and breadth first search in terms of time and space complexity (Korf, 1985). That is, depth- and breadth-first searches take at least as much time and memory as depth-first iterative deepening searches for increasingly large searches. The time and space complexities of this search are $O(b^d)$ and $O(d)$ respectively.

This search algorithm works basically the same as the depth first search algorithm given above for a single iteration. However, it terminates the search at depth d on each iteration if no goal has been found, removes all nodes from the queue, increments d by one, and initiates the search again.

Bidirectional Search

When a problem has a single goal state that is given explicitly, and all node generation operators have inverses, bidirectional search can be used. (This is the case with the eight puzzle described above, for example). Bidirectional search is performed by searching forward from the initial node and backward from the goal node simultaneously. To do so, the program must store the nodes generated on both search frontiers until a common node is found. With some modifications, all three of the blind search methods described above may be used to perform bidirectional search.

For example, to perform bidirectional depth-first iterative deepening search to a depth of k, the search is made from one direction and the nodes at depth k are stored. At the same time, a search to a depth of k and $k + 1$ is made from the other direction and all nodes generated are matched against the nodes stored from the other side. These nodes need not be stored, but a search of the two depths is needed to account for odd-length paths. This process is repeated for lengths $k = 0$ to $d/2$ from both directions.

The time and space complexities for bidirectional depth-first iterative deepening search are both $O(b^{d/2})$ when the node matching is done in constant time per node.

Since the number of nodes to be searched using the blind search methods described above increase as b^d with depth d, such problems become intractable for large depths. It, therefore, behooves us to consider alternative methods. Such methods depend on some knowledge to limit the number of problem states visited. We turn to these methods now in the next section.

9.5 INFORMED SEARCH

When more information than the initial state, the operators, and the goal test is available, the size of the search space can usually be constrained. When this is the case, the better the information available, the more efficient the search process will be. Such methods are known as informed search methods. They often depend on the use of heuristic information. In this section, we examine search strategies based on the use of some problem domain information, and in particular, on the use of heuristic search functions.

Heuristic Information

Information about the problem (the nature of the states, the cost of transforming from one state to another, the promise of taking a certain path, and the characteristics of the goals) can sometimes be used to help guide the search more efficiently. This information can often be expressed in the form of a heuristic evaluation function $f(n,g)$, a function of the nodes n and/or the goals g.

Recall that a heuristic is a rule of thumb or judgmental technique that leads to a solution some of the time but provides no guarantee of success. It may in fact end in failure. Heuristics play an important role in search strategies because of the exponential nature of most problems. They help to reduce the number of alternatives from an exponential number to a polynomial number and, thereby, obtain a solution in a tolerable amount of time. When exhaustive search is impractical, it is necessary to compromise for a constrained search which eliminates many paths but offers the promise of success some of the time. Here, success may be considered to be finding an optimal solution a fair proportion of the time or just finding good solutions much of the time. In this regard, any policy which uses as little search effort as possible to find any qualified goal has been called a *satisficing policy*.

Consider for example, the traveling salesman problem described above. A simple heuristic for choosing the next city at any point in a tour is one which picks the nearest unvisited neighbor. This policy gives no guarantee of an optimal solution, but its solutions are often good, and the time required is only $O(n^2)$. Likewise, for the eight puzzle, using a heuristic function, which selects moves that produce the smallest number of tiles out of place from the goal configuration, can result in a worthwhile time saving. In solving a problem in propositional logic, such as proving a theorem in the General Problem Solver, the time complexity can often be reduced from exponential to polynomial time through the application of a simple heuristic strategy. In General Problem Solver this is accomplished by first planning a solution by breaking the main problem down into several subproblems of lesser complexity. This often has the effect of reducing the overall complexity by several orders of magnitude.

Hill Climbing Methods

Search methods based on hill climbing get their names from the way the nodes are selected for expansion. At each point in the search path, a successor node that appears to lead most quickly to the top of the hill (the goal) is selected for exploration. This method requires that some information be available with which to evaluate and order the most promising choices.

Hill climbing is like depth-first searching where the most promising child is selected for expansion. When the children have been generated, alternative choices are evaluated using some type of heuristic function. The path that appears most promising is then chosen and no further reference to the parent or other children is retained. This process continues from node-to-node with previously expanded nodes being discarded. A typical path is illustrated in Figure 9.9 where the numbers by a node correspond to the computed estimates of the goal distance for alternative paths.

Hill climbing can produce substantial savings over blind searches when an informative, reliable function is available to guide the search to a global goal. It suffers from some serious drawbacks when this is not the case. Potential problem types named after certain terrestrial anomalies are the foothill, ridge, and plateau traps.

The foothill trap results when local maxima or peaks are found. In this case the children all have less promising goal distances than the parent node. The search is essentially trapped at the local node with no indication of goal direction. The only way to remedy this problem is to try moving in some arbitrary direction a few generations in the hope that the real goal direction will become evident, backtrack-

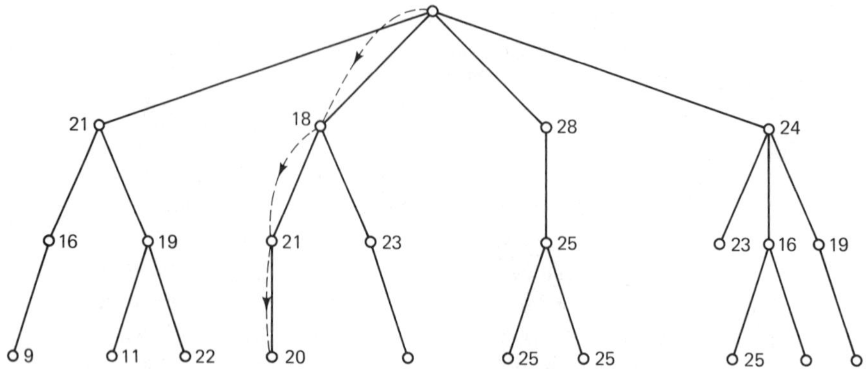

Figure 9.9 Search with hill climbing.

ing to an ancestor node and trying a secondary path choice, or altering the computation procedure to expand ahead a few generations each time before choosing a path.

A second potential problem occurs when several adjoining nodes have higher values than surrounding nodes. This is the equivalent of a ridge. It too is a form of local trap and the only remedy is to try to escape as in the foothill case above.

Finally, the search may encounter a plateau type of structure, that is, an area in which all neighboring nodes have the same values. Once again, one of the methods noted above must be tried to escape the trap.

The problems encountered with hill climbing can be avoided using a best-first search approach.

Best-First Search

Best-first search also depends on the use of a heuristic to select most promising paths to the goal node. Unlike hill climbing, however, this algorithm retains all estimates computed for previously generated nodes and makes its selection based on the best among them all. Thus, at any point in the search process, best-first moves forward from the most promising of all the nodes generated so far. In so doing, it avoids the potential traps encountered in hill climbing. The best-first process is illustrated in Figure 9.10 where numbers by the nodes may be regarded as estimates of the distance or cost to reach the goal node.

The algorithm we give for best first search differs from the previous blind search algorithms only in the way the nodes are saved and ordered on the queue. The algorithm reads as follows.

BEST-FIRST SEARCH

1. Place the starting node s on the queue.
2. If the queue is empty, return failure and stop.

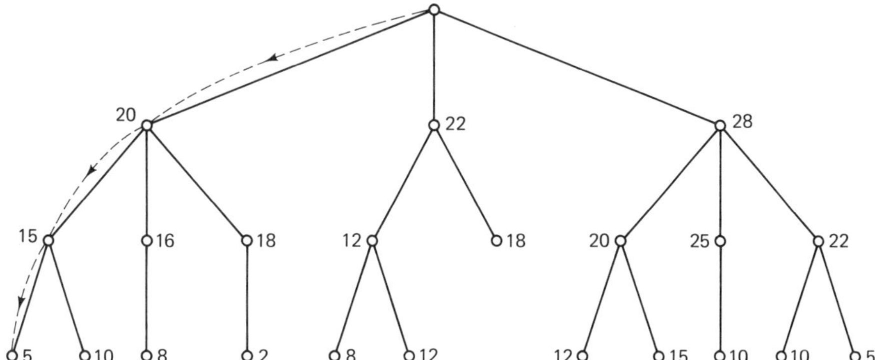

Figure 9.10 Best-first search of a tree.

3. If the first element on the queue is a goal node g, return success and stop. Otherwise,
4. Remove the first element from the queue, expand it and compute the estimated goal distances for each child. Place the children on the queue (at either end) and arrange all queue elements in ascending order corresponding to goal distance from the front of the queue.
5. Return to step 2.

Best-first searches will always find good paths to a goal, even when local anomalies are encountered. All that is required is that a good measure of goal distance be used.

Branch-and-Bound Search

The branch-and-bound search strategy applies to problems having a graph search space where more than one alternative path may exist between two nodes. This strategy saves all path lengths (or costs) from a node to all generated nodes and chooses the shortest path for further expansion. It then compares the new path lengths with all old ones and again chooses the shortest path for expansion. In this way, any path to a goal node is certain to be a minimal length path. This process is illustrated in Figure 9.11.

An algorithm for the branch-and-bound strategy which uses a queue data structure to hold partial paths developed during the search is as follows.

BRANCH-AND-BOUND SEARCH

1. Place the start node of zero path length on the queue.
2. Until the queue is empty or a goal node has been found: (a) determine if the first path in the queue contains a goal node, (b) if the first path contains a goal node exit with success, (c) if the first path does not contain a goal node,

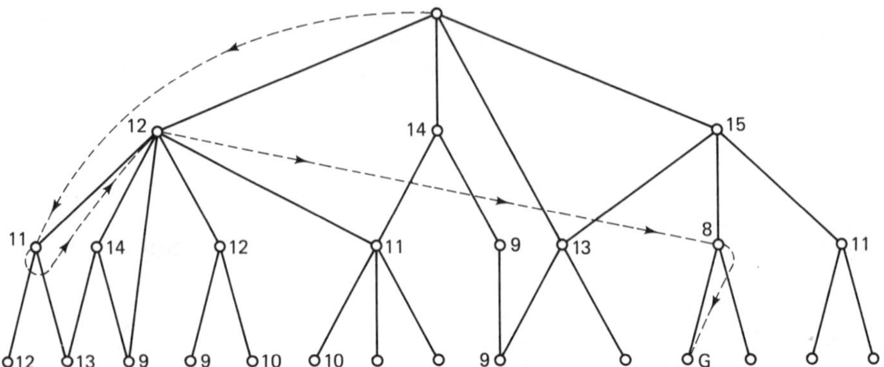

Figure 9.11 Branch-and-bound search of a tree.

remove the path from the queue and form new paths by extending the removed path by one step, (d) compute the cost of the new paths and add them to the queue, (e) sort the paths on the queue with lowest-cost paths in front.

3. Otherwise, exit with failure.

Always extending the lowest-cost path in branch-and-bound search insures that a lowest-cost path will be found if one exists. Of course, this is at the expense of computing and remembering all competing paths. We next look at a special case of branch-and-bound search which estimates the total cost to a goal node, and selects the least cost path at each stage in the search.

Optimal Search and A*

The previous heuristic methods offer good strategies but fail to describe how the shortest distance to a goal should be estimated. The A* algorithm is a specialization of best-first search. It provides general guidelines with which to estimate goal distances for general search graphs.

At each node along a path to the goal, the A* algorithm generates all successor nodes and computes an estimate of the distance (cost) from the start node to a goal node through each of the successors. It then chooses the successor with the shortest estimated distance for expansion. The successors for this node are then generated, their distances estimated, and the process continues until a goal is found or the search ends in failure.

The form of the heuristic estimation function for A* is

$$f^*(n) = g^*(n) + h^*(n)$$

where the two components $g^*(n)$ and $h^*(n)$ are estimates of the cost (or distance) from the start node to node n and the cost from node n to a goal node, respectively. The asterisks are used to designate estimates of the corresponding true values $f(n)$

$= g(n) + h(n)$. For state space tree problems $g^*(n) = g(n)$ since there is only one path and the distance $g^*(n)$ will be known to be the true minimum from the start to the current node n. This is not true in general for graphs, since alternate paths from the start node to n may exist.

For this type of problem, it is convenient to maintain two lists of node types designated as open and closed. Nodes on the open list are nodes that have been generated but not yet expanded while nodes on the closed list are nodes that have been expanded and whose children are, therefore, available to the search program. The A* algorithm proceeds as follows.

A* SEARCH

1. Place the starting node s on open.
2. If open is empty, stop and return failure.
3. Remove from open the node n that has the smallest value of $f^*(n)$. If the node is a goal node, return success and stop. Otherwise,
4. Expand n, generating all of its successors n' and place n on closed. For every successor n', if n' is not already on open or closed attach a back-pointer to n, compute $f^*(n')$ and place it on open.
5. Each n' that is already on open or closed should be attached to back-pointers which reflect the lowest $g^*(n')$ path. If n' was on closed and its pointer was changed, remove it and place it on open.
6. Return to step 2.

Next, we consider some desirable properties of heuristic search algorithms. They are summarized in the following definitions.

Admissibility condition. Algorithm A is *admissible* if it is guaranteed to return an optimal solution when one exists.

Completeness condition. Algorithm A is *complete* if it always terminates with a solution when one exists.

Dominance property. Let A_1 and A_2 be admissible algorithms with heuristic estimation functions h^*_1 and h^*_2, respectively. A_1 is said to be more *informed* than A_2 whenever $h^*_1(n) > h^*_2(n)$ for all n. A_1 is also said to dominate A_2.

Optimality Property. Algorithm A is *optimal* over a class of algorithms if A dominates all members of the class.

The admissibility condition for an algorithm has led to a corresponding definition for a heuristic function h^*; h^* is said to be admissible if $h^* \leq h$ for all n. It can be shown that if A_1 and A_2 are admissible, and A_1 is more informed than A_2, then A_1 never expands a node not expanded by A_2. In general then, it is desirable to find admissible heuristic functions that approximate h as closely as possible. This will insure that few if any nodes off the optimal path are expanded. Of course, if $h^* = h$ only nodes on the optimal path will be expanded. The cost of computing such a function should also be taken into account, however. It may not be cost effective if the computation cost is too high.

It has been shown that the A* algorithm is both complete and admissible. Thus, A* will always find an optimal path if one exists. The efficiency of an A* algorithm depends on how closely h^* approximates h and the cost of the computing f^*.

Iterative Deepening A*

By combining a heuristic evaluation function with a modified version of the iterative deepening search method presented earlier, we obtain iterative deepening A* or IDA*.

IDA* performs a depth search at each iteration and eliminates or trims all branches whose estimated cost $(g^* + h^*)$ exceeds a given threshold $T(i)$ where $i = 0,1,2 \ldots$ is the iteration number. The initial threshold $T(0)$ is the estimated cost of the initial state. After that, the threshold increases with each iteration. The value of T on iteration $i + 1$ is taken as the minimum of the costs which exceed T on iteration i.

Like A*, it can be shown that IDA* always finds a cheapest path if h^* is admissible. Furthermore, IDA* expands the same number of nodes as A* (asymptotically).

9.6 SEARCHING AND-OR GRAPHS

The depth-first and breadth-first strategies given earlier for Or trees and graphs can easily be adapted for And-Or trees. The main difference lies in the way termination conditions are determined, since all goals following an And node must be realized, whereas a single goal node following an Or node will do. Consequently, we describe a more general optimal strategy that subsumes these types, the AO* (O for ordered) algorithm.

As in the case of the A* algorithm, we use the open list to hold nodes that have been generated but not expanded and the closed list to hold nodes that have been expanded (successor nodes that are available). The algorithm is a variation of the original given by Nilsson (1971). It requires that nodes traversed in the tree be labeled as solved or unsolved in the solution process to account for And node solutions which require solutions to all successor nodes. A solution is found when the start node is labeled as solved.

THE AO* ALGORITHM

1. Place the start node s on open.
2. Using the search tree constructed thus far, compute the most promising solution tree T_0.

3. Select a node n that is both on open and a part of T_0. Remove n from open and place it on closed.
4. If n is a terminal goal node, label n as solved. If the solution of n results in any of n's ancestors being solved, label all the ancestors as solved. If the start node s is solved, exit with success where T_0 is the solution tree. Remove from open all nodes with a solved ancestor.
5. If n is not a solvable node (operators cannot be applied), label n as unsolvable. If the start node is labeled as unsolvable, exit with failure. If any of n's ancestors become unsolvable because n is, label them unsolvable as well. Remove from open all nodes with unsolvable ancestors.
6. Otherwise, expand node n generating all of its successors. For each such successor node that contains more than one subproblem, generate their successors to give individual subproblems. Attach to each newly generated node a back pointer to its predecessor. Compute the cost estimate h^* for each newly generated node and place all such nodes that do not yet have descendents on open. Next, recompute the values of h^* at n and each ancestor of n.
7. Return to step 2.

It can be shown that AO* will always find a minimum-cost solution tree if one exists, provided only that $h^*(n) \leq h(n)$, and all arc costs are positive. Like A*, the efficiency depends on how closely h^* approximates h.

9.7 SUMMARY

Search is characteristic of almost all AI problems. We find search in natural language understanding and generation, in machine vision, in planning and problem solvers, in expert systems, in game playing programs, and in machine learning. It should not be too surprising then that much effort has been devoted to finding efficient search strategies.

Search strategies can be compared by their time and space complexities using big O notation. It is important to determine the complexity of a given strategy before investing too much programming effort, since many search problems are intractable. Search spaces are usually represented as a graph or tree structure, and a search is finding a path from some start node to a goal node.

In a blind search, nodes in the space are explored mechanically until a goal is found, a time limit has been reached, or failure occurs. In a worst case, it may be necessary to explore the whole space before finding a solution. Examples of blind searches are depth-first, breadth-first, and depth-first iterative deepening searches.

When some information is available about the goals, the problem states, or the problem in general, it may be possible to guide the search process and eliminate a number of implausible paths. This is the case in informed searches where cost or another function is used to select the most promising path at each point in the search. Heuristic evaluation functions are used in best-first search strategies to find good solution paths. A solution is not always guaranteed with this type of search, but in most practical cases, good or acceptable solutions are often found.

We saw several examples of informed searches, including general best-first, hill climbing, branch-and-bound, A*, and finally, the optimal And-Or heuristic search known as the OA* algorithm. Desirable properties of heuristic search methods were also defined.

EXERCISES

9.1. Games and puzzles are often used to describe search problems because they are easy to describe. One such puzzle is the farmer-fox-goose-grain puzzle. In this puzzle, a farmer wishes to cross a river taking his fox, goose, and grain with him. He can use a boat which will accommodate only the farmer and one possession. If the fox is left alone with the goose, the goose will be eaten. If the goose is left alone with the grain it will be eaten. Draw a state space search tree for this puzzle using leftbank and rightbank to denote left and right river banks respectively.

9.2. For the search tree given below, use breadth-first searching and list the elements of the queue just before selecting and expanding each next state until a goal node is reached. (Goal states designated with *.)

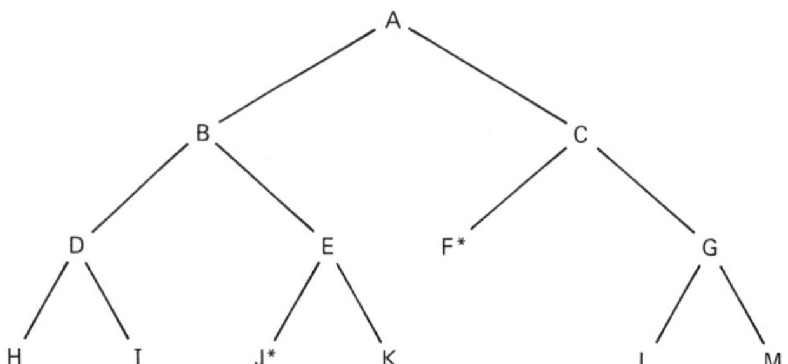

9.3. Repeat Problem 9.2 using a depth-first search.

9.4. Repeat Problem 9.2 using a depth-first iterative deepening search.

9.5. Describe and compare three primary uninformed search methods described in this chapter.

9.6. Show that a worst-case algorithm to solve the traveling salesman problem is of exponential complexity, but an algorithm that chooses a tour through the nearest neighbor of each city is of lower order. Give an example to show the nearest neighbor algorithm is not, in general, optimal, but still often good.

9.7. Fifteen puzzle is like eight puzzle except there are fifteen tiles instead of eight. What is the branching factor of the search tree for fifteen puzzle?

9.8. Describe a problem for which means-end analysis could be successfully applied. Give an example of a few solution steps.

9.9. Give three different heuristics for an $h^*(n)$ to be used in solving the eight puzzle.

9.10. Using the search tree given below, list the elements of the queue just before the next node is expanded. Use best-first search where the numbers correspond to estimated cost-to-goal for each corresponding node.

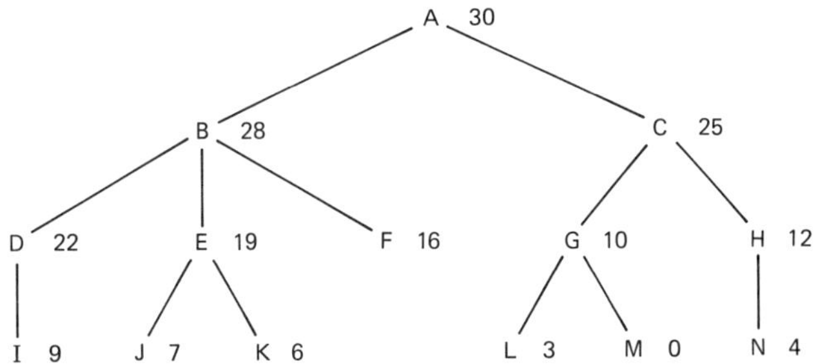

9.11. Repeat Problem 9.10 when the cost of node B is changed to 18.

9.12. Give the time and space complexities for the search methods of Problems 9.2 and 9.3.

9.13. Discuss some of the potential problems when using hill climbing search. Give examples of the problems cited.

9.14. Discuss and compare hill climbing and best-first search techniques.

9.15. Give an example of an admissible heuristic for the eight puzzle.

9.16. Give two examples of problems in which solutions requiring the minimum search are more appropriate than optimal solutions. Give reasons for your choices.

9.17. Write a LISP program to perform a breadth-first search on a solution space tree constructed using property lists. For example, children nodes e, f, and g of node D of the tree would be constructed with the LISP function

```
(putprop 'D '(E F G) 'children)
```

9.18. Write a LISP program to perform a depth-first search on the tree constructed in Problem 9.17.

10

Matching Techniques

Matching is a basic function that is required in almost all AI programs. It is an essential part of more complex operations such as search and control. In many programs it is known that matching consumes a large fraction of the processing time. For example, it has been estimated that matching operations in many production systems account for as much as 90% of the total computation time. Consequently, the AI practitioner will find it is essential to learn efficient matching techniques. In this chapter we examine such techniques and their application to different AI programs.

10.1 INTRODUCTION

Matching is the process of comparing two or more structures to discover their likenesses or differences. The structures may represent a wide range of objects including physical entities, words or phrases in some language, complete classes of things, general concepts, relations between complex entities, and the like. The representations will be given in one or more of the formalisms like FOPL, networks, or some other scheme, and matching will involve comparing the component parts of such structures.

Matching is used in a variety of programs for different reasons. It may serve to control the sequence of operations, to identify or classify objects, to determine the best of a number of different alternatives, or to retrieve items from a data base. It is an essential operation in such diverse programs as speech recognition, natural language understanding, vision, learning, automated reasoning, planning, automatic programming, and expert systems, as well as many others.

In its simplest form, matching is just the process of comparing two structures or patterns for equality. The match fails if the patterns differ in any aspect. For example, a match between the two character strings acdebfba and acdebeba fails on an exact match since the strings differ in the sixth character positions.

In more complex cases the matching process may permit transformations in the patterns in order to achieve an equality match. The transformation may be a simple change of some variables to constants, or it may amount to ignoring some components during the match operation. For example, a pattern matching variable such as ?x may be used to permit successful matching between the two patterns (a b (c d) e) and (a b ?x e) by binding ?x to (c d). Such matchings are usually restricted in some way, however, as is the case with the unification of two clauses where only consistent bindings are permitted. Thus, two patterns such as

(a b (c d) e f) and (a b ?x e ?x)

would not match since ?x could not be bound to two different constants.

In some extreme cases, a complete change of representational form may be required in either one or both structures before a match can be attempted. This will be the case, for example, when one visual object is represented as a vector of pixel gray levels and objects to be matched are represented as descriptions in predicate logic or some other high level statements. A direct comparison is impossible unless one form has been transformed into the other.

In subsequent chapters we will see examples of many problems where exact matches are inappropriate, and some form of partial matching is more meaningful. Typically in such cases, one is interested in finding a best match between pairs of structures. This will be the case in object classification problems, for example, when object descriptions are subject to corruption by noise or distortion. In such cases, a measure of the degree of match may also be required.

Other types of partial matching may require finding a match between certain key elements while ignoring all other elements in the pattern. For example, a human language input unit should be flexible enough to recognize any of the following three statements as expressing a choice of preference for the low-calorie food item.

I prefer the low-calorie choice.

I want the low-calorie item.

The low-calorie one please.

Recognition of the intended request can be achieved by matching against key words in a template containing ''low-calorie'' and ignoring other words except, perhaps, negative modifiers.

Finally, some problems may obviate the need for a form of fuzzy matching where an entity's degree of membership in one or more classes is appropriate. Some classification problems will apply here if the boundaries between the classes are not distinct, and an object may belong to more than one class.

Figure 10.1 illustrates the general match process where an input description is being compared with other descriptions. As stressed earlier, the term *object* is used here in a general sense. It does not necessarily imply physical objects. All objects will be represented in some formalism such as a vector of attribute values, propositional logic or FOPL statements, rules, frame-like structures, or other scheme. Transformations, if required, may involve simple instantiations or unifications among clauses or more complex operations such as transforming a two-dimensional scene to a description in some formal language. Once the descriptions have been transformed into the same schema, the matching process is performed element-by-element using a relational or other test (like equality or ranking). The test results may then be combined in some way to provide an overall measure of similarity. The choice of measure will depend on the match criteria and representation scheme employed.

The output of the matcher is a description of the match. It may be a simple yes or no response or a list of variable bindings, or as complicated as a detailed annotation of the similarities and differences between the matched objects.

To summarize then, matching may be exact, used with or without pattern variables, partial, or fuzzy, and any matching algorithm will be based on such factors as

Choice of representation scheme for the objects being matched,

Criteria for matching (exact, partial, fuzzy, and so on),

Choice of measure required to perform the match in accordance with the chosen criteria, and

Type of match description required for output.

In the remainder of this chapter we examine various types of matching problems and their related algorithms. We begin with a description of representation structures

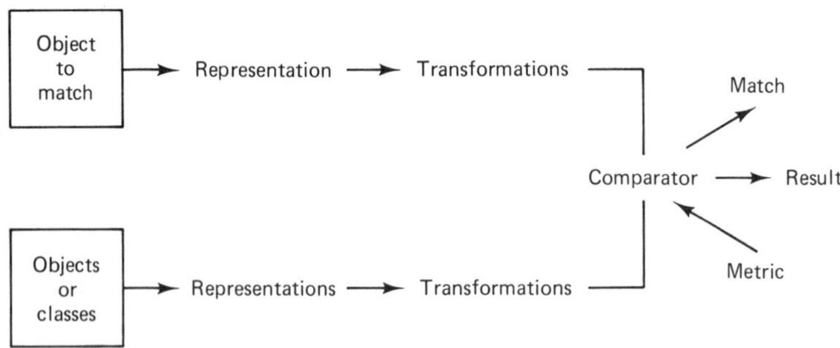

Figure 10.1 Typical matching process.

and measures commonly found in matching problems. We next look at various matching techniques based on exact, partial, and fuzzy approaches. We conclude the chapter with an example of an efficient match algorithm used in some rule-based expert systems.

10.2 STRUCTURES USED IN MATCHING

We are already familiar with many of the representation structures used in matching programs. Typically, they will be some type of list structures that represent clauses in propositional or predicate logic such as

```
(or ~(MARRIED ?x ?y) ~(DAUGHTER ?z ?y) (MOTHER ?y ?z)),
```

or rules, such as

```
(and ((cloudy-sky) (low-bar-pressure) (high-humidity))
                   (conclude (rain-likely)),
```

or fragments of associative networks (Figure 10.2) and frames or frame-like structures (Figure 10.3).

In addition to these, other common structures include strings of characters $a_1a_2 \ldots a_k$, where the a_i belong to a given alphabet A, vectors $\mathbf{X} = (x_1,x_2, \ldots, x_n)$, where the x_i represents attribute values, matrices **M** (rows of vectors), general graphs, trees, and sets.

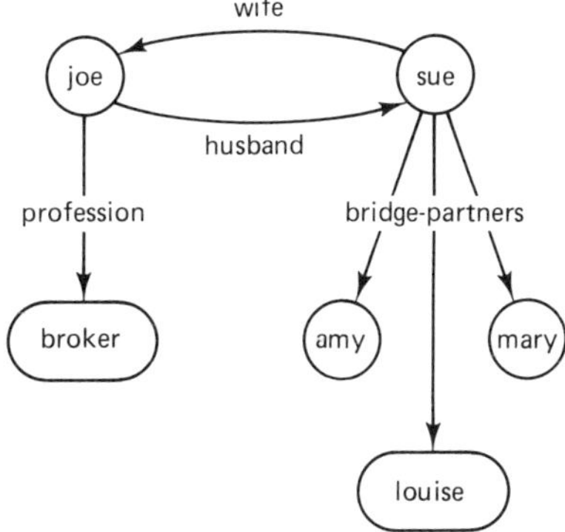


```
(putprop 'joe '(sue) 'wife)
(putprop 'sue '(joe) 'husband)
(putprop 'joe '(broker) 'profession)
(putprop 'sue '(amy louise mary) 'bridge-partners)
```

Figure 10.2 Fragment of associative network and corresponding LISP code.

```
          name: data-structures
           ako: university-course
    department: computer-science
       credits: 3-hours
 prerequisites:(if-needed check catalog)
```

(a)

```
(data-structures (ako (value university-course))
                 (department (value computer-science))
                 (credits (value 3-hours))
                 (prerequisites (:if-needed check-catalog))))
```

(b)

Figure 10.3 (a) Frame structure and (b) corresponding A-list code.

Variables

All of the structures we shall consider here are constructed from basic atomic elements, numbers, and characters. Character string elements may represent either constants or variables. If variables, they may be classified by either the type of match permitted or by their value domains.

We can classify match variables by the number of items that can replace them (one or more than one). An *open variable* can be replaced by a single item, while a *segment variable* can be replaced by zero or more items. Open variables are labeled with a preceding question mark (?*x*, ?*y*, ?class). They may match or assume the value of any single string element or word, but they are sometimes subject to consistency constraints. For example, to be consistent, the variable ?x can be bound only to the same top level element in any single structure. Thus (*a* ?*x d* ?*x e*) may match (*a b d b e*), but not (*a b d a e*). Segment variable types will be preceded with an asterisk (*x, *z, *words). This type of variable can match an arbitrary number or segment of contiguous atomic elements (any sublist including the empty list). For example, (**x d* (*e f*) **y*) will match the patterns

(*a* (*b c*) *d* (*e f*) *g* h), (*d* (*e f*) (*g*))

or other similar patterns. Segment variables may also be subject to consistency constraints similar to open variables.

Variables may also be classified by their value domains. This distinction will be useful when we consider similarity measures below. The variables may be either quantitative, having a meaningful origin or zero point and a meaningful interval difference between two values, or they may be qualitative in which there is no origin nor meaningful interval value difference. These two types may be further subdivided as follows.

Nominal variables. Qualitative variables whose values or states have no order nor rank. It is only possible to distinguish equality or inequality between two such objects. Of course each state can be given a numerical code. For example, "marital status" has states of married, single, divorced, or widowed. These states have no numerical significance, and no particular order nor rank. The states could be assigned numerical codes however, such as married = 1, single = 2, divorced = 3, and widowed = 4.

Ordinal variables. Qualitative variables whose states can be arranged in a rank order, but the difference between two distinct values has no significance. Ordinal variables may also be assigned numerical values. For example, the states very tall, tall, medium, short, and very short can be arranged in order from tallest to shortest and be assigned an arbitrary scale of 5 to 1. However, the difference between successive values does not necessarily have any quantitative meaning.

Binary variable. Qualitative discrete variables which may assume only one of two values, such as 0 or 1, good or bad, yes or no, high or low.

Interval (metric) variables. Quantitative variables which take on numeric values and for which equal differences between values have the same significance. For example, real numbers corresponding to temperature or integers corresponding to an amount of money are considered as interval variables.

Graphs and Trees

Two other structures we shall consider in this section are graphs and trees. One type of graph we are already familiar with is the associative network (Chapter 6). Such structures provide a rich variety of representation schemes. More generally, a graph $G = (V, E)$ is an ordered pair of sets V and E. The elements of V are nodes or vertices and the elements of E are a subset of $V \times V$ called edges (or arcs or links). An edge joints two distinct vertices in V.

Directed graphs, or digraphs, have directed edges or arcs with arrows. If an arc is directed from node n_i to n_j, node n_i is said to be a parent or successor of n_j, and n_j is the child or successor of n_i. Undirected graphs have simple edges without arrows connecting the nodes. A path is a sequence of edges connecting two nodes where the endpoint of one edge is the start of its successor. A cycle is a path in which the two end points coincide. A connected graph is a graph for which every pair of vertices is joined by a path. A graph is complete if every element of $V \times V$ is an edge.

A tree is a connected graph in which there are no cycles, and each node has, at most, one parent. A node with no parent is called the root node, and nodes with no children are called leaf nodes. The *depth* of the root node is defined as zero. The depth of any other node is defined to be the depth of its parent plus 1. Pictorial representations of some graphs and a tree are given in Figure 10.4.

Recall that graph representations typically use labeled nodes and arcs where

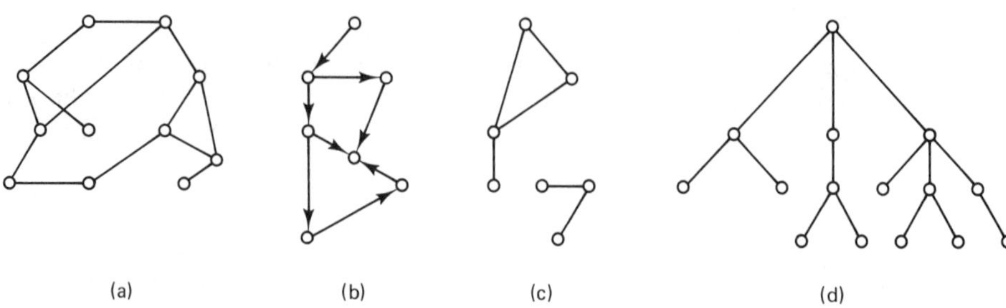

Figure 10.4 Examples of (a) general connected graph, (b) digraph, (c) disconnected graph and (d) tree of depth 3.

the nodes correspond to entities and the arcs to relations. Labels for the nodes and arcs are attribute values.

Sets and Bags

A set is represented as an unordered list of unique elements such as the set (*a d f c*) or (black red blue green). A bag is a set which may contain more than one copy of the same member; for example, the list *a d e a b d* represents a bag with members *a*, *b*, *d*, and *e*. Sets and bags are structures frequently used in matching operations.

10.3 MEASURES FOR MATCHING

Next, we turn to the problem of comparing structures without the use of pattern matching variables. This requires consideration of measures used to determine the likeness or similarity between two or more structures. The similarity between two structures is a measure of the degree of associaton or likeness between the object's attributes and other characteristic parts. If the describing variables are quantitative, a distance metric is often used to measure the proximity.

Distance Metrics

For all elements x, y, z, of the set E, the function d is a metric if and only if

$$\begin{aligned} &\text{a. } d(x,x) = 0 \\ &\text{b. } d(x,y) \geq 0 \\ &\text{c. } d(x,y) = d(y,x) \\ &\text{d. } d(x,y) \leq d(x,z) + d(z,y) \end{aligned} \tag{10.1}$$

The Minkowski metric is a general distance measure satisfying the above assumptions. It is given by

$$d_p = \left[\sum_{i=1}^{n} |x_i - y_i|^p \right]^{1/p}$$

For the case $p = 2$, this metric is the familiar Euclidean distance. When $p = 1$, d_p is the so-called absolute or city block distance.

Probabilistic Measures

In some cases, the representation variables should be treated as random variables. Then one requires a measure of the distance between the variates, their distributions, or possibly between a variable and distribution. One such measure is the Mahalanobis distance which gives a measure of the separation between two distributions. Given the random vectors **X** and **Y** let C be their covariance matrix. Then the Mahalanobis distance is given by

$$D = \mathbf{X}'C^{-1}\mathbf{Y}$$

where the prime (′) denotes transpose (row vector) and C^{-1} is the inverse of C. The **X** and **Y** vectors may be adjusted for zero means by first subtracting the vector means u_x and u_y.

Another popular probability measure is the product moment correlation r, given by

$$r = \frac{\mathrm{Cov}(\mathbf{X},\mathbf{Y})}{[\mathrm{Var}(\mathbf{X}) * \mathrm{Var}(\mathbf{Y})]^{1/2}}$$

where Cov and Var denote covariance and variance respectively. The correlation r, which ranges between -1 and $+1$, is a measure of similarity frequently used in vision applications.

Other probabilistic measures often used in AI applications are based on the scatter of attribute values. These measures are related to the degree of clustering among the objects. In addition, conditional probabilities are sometimes used. For example, they may be used to measure the liklihood that a given **X** is a member of class C_i, $P(C_i|\mathbf{X})$, the conditional probability of C_i given an observed **X**. These measures can establish the proximity of two or more objects. These and related measures are discussed further in Chapter 12.

Qualitative Measures

A number of distance measures based on qualitative variables (nominal, ordinal, and binary) have also been defined as well as methods which deal with mixtures of variables (Anderberg, 1973). We describe only a few such measures here to illustrate the basic forms they take.

Measures between binary variables are best described using contingency tables like Table 10.1. The table entries there give the number of objects having attribute X or Y with corresponding value of 1 or 0. For example, if the objects are animals,

TABLE 10.1 CONTINGENCY TABLE FOR BINARY VARIABLES

	Variable X	1	0	Totals
Variable Y	1	a	b	a + b
	0	c	d	c + d
	Totals	a + c	b + d	n

X might be horned and Y might be long tailed. In this case, the entry a is the number of animals having both horns and long tails. Note that $n = a + b + c + d$, the total number of objects.

Various measures of association for such binary variables have been defined. For example

$$\frac{a}{a+b+c+d} = \frac{a}{n}, \qquad \frac{a+d}{n}$$

$$\frac{a}{a+b+c}, \qquad \frac{a}{b+c}$$

Contingency tables are also useful for describing other qualitative variables, both ordinal and nominal. Since the methods are similar to those for binary variables, we omit the details here.

Whatever the variable types used in a measure, they should all be properly scaled or normalized to prevent variables having large values from negating the effects of smaller valued variables. This could happen when one variable is scaled in millimeters and another variable in meters.

Similarity Measures

For many problems, distance metrics are not appropriate. Instead, a measure of similarity satisfying conditions different from those of Table 10.1 may be more appropriate. Of course, measures of dissimilarity (or similarity), like distance, should decrease (or increase) as objects become more alike. There is strong evidence, however, to suggest that similarities are not in general symmetric (Tversky, 1977) and hence, any similarity measure between a subject description A and its referrent B, denoted by $s(A,B)$, is not necessarily equal; that is, in general, $s(A,B) \neq s(B,A)$ or "A is like B" may not be the same as "B is like A."

Tests on subjects have shown that in similarity comparisons, the focus of attention is on the subject and, therefore, subject features are given higher weights than the referrent. For example, in tests comparing countries, statements like "North Korea is similar to Red China" and "Red China is similar to North Korea" or "the

USA is like Mexico'' and ''Mexico is like the USA'' were not rated as symmetrical or equal. The likenesses and differences in these cases are directional. Moreover, like many interpretations in AI, similarities may depend strongly on the context in which the comparisons are made. They may also depend on the purpose of the comparison.

An interesting family of similarity measures which takes into account such factors as asymmetry and has some intuitive appeal has recently been proposed (Tversky, 1977). Such measures may be adapted to give more realistic results for similarity measures in AI applications where context and purpose should influence the similarity comparisons.

Let $O = \{o_1, o_2, \ldots\}$ be the universe of objects of interest and let A_i be the set of attributes or features used to represent o_i. A similarity measure s which is a function of three disjoint sets of attributes common to any two objects A_i and A_j is given as

$$s(A_i,A_j) = F(A_i \,\&\, A_j, A_i - A_j, A_j - A_i) \tag{10.2}$$

where $A_i \,\&\, A_j$ is the set of features common to both o_i and o_j, $A_i - A_j$ is the set of features belonging to o_i and not o_j, and $A_j - A_i$ is the set of features belonging to o_j and not o_i. The function F is a real valued nonnegative function. Under fairly general assumptions equation 10.2 can be written as

$$s(A_i,A_j) = af(A_i \,\&\, A_j) - bf(A_i - A_j) - cf(A_j - A_i) \tag{10.3}$$

for some $a,b,c \geq 0$ and where f is an additive interval metric function. The function $f(A)$ may be chosen as any nonnegative function of the set A, like the number of attributes in A or the average distance between points in A. Equation 10.3 may be normalized to give values of similarity ranging between 0 and 1 by writing

$$S(A_i,A2_j) = \frac{f(A_i \,\&\, A_j)}{f(A_i \,\&\, A_j) + af(A_i - A_j) + bf(A_j - A_i)} \tag{10.4}$$

for some $a,b \geq 0$.

When the representations are graph structures, a similarity measure based on the cost of transforming one graph into the other may be used. For example, a procedure to find a measure of similarity between two labled graphs (described in Section 10.5) decomposes the graphs into basic subgraphs and computes the minimum cost to transform either graph into the other one, subpart-by-subpart.

Fuzzy Measures

Finally, we can define a distance between the two fuzzy sets $\tilde{A}$ and $\tilde{B}$ as

$$d(\tilde{A},\tilde{B}) = \frac{1}{n}\left[\sum_{i=1}^{n} (u_A(x_i) - u_B(x_i))^2\right]^{1/2} \tag{10.5}$$

where the total number of objects x_i in the universe is n.

Equation 10.5 measures the mean square difference in universe membership scores between $\tilde{A}$ and $\tilde{B}$. A score of 1 implies that the distance is maximal, whereas a score near zero can signify that either $\tilde{A}$ and $\tilde{B}$ are very similar or that most objects have low membership scores in both fuzzy sets. Therefore, care must be exercised when interpreting such measures.

Fuzzy similarity measures can be defined with inverse functions of fuzzy distances such as the measure defined in equation 10.5 above. An even simpler measure is, of course, the characteristic function u itself, which may be regarded as a measure of the distance of an object x_i with respect to some reference fuzzy set. In that case, distance is interpreted as a function of the inverse of degree of membership.

Rather than the distance or similarity between two sets or a set and an object, we may be interested in the distance or similarity between objects (x_i) themselves where the fuzzy sets represent traits or characteristics of the objects. One such similarity measure for this is

$$s(x_i,x_j) = \frac{1}{K}\sum_{k=1}^{K} (1 - |u_A(x_i) - u_A(x_j)|) \tag{10.6}$$

which gives the mean trait membership difference between two objects x_i and x_j. Of course $s(x_i,x_i) = 0$ corresponds to equal likeness or maximal similarity, and $s(x_i,x_j) = 1$ for $i \neq j$ corresponds to maximum dissimilarity.

10.4 MATCHING LIKE PATTERNS

In this section we consider procedures which amount to performing a complete match between two structures. The match will be accomplished by comparing the two structures and testing for equality among the corresponding parts. Pattern variables will be used for instantiations of some parts subject to restrictions as noted below.

Matching Substrings

Since many of the representation structures are just character strings, a basic function required in many match algorithms is to determine if a substring S_2 consisting of m characters occurs somewhere in a string S_1 of n characters, $m \leq n$. A direct approach to this problem is to compare the two strings character-by-character, starting with the first characters of both S_1 and S_2. If any two characters disagree, the process is repeated, starting with the second character of S_1 and matching again against S_2 character-by-character until a match is found or disagreement occurs again. This process continues until a match occurs or S_1 has no more characters.

Let i and j be position indices for string S_1 and k a position index for S_2. We can perform the substring match with the following algorithm.

```
i:=0
while i≤(n−m+1) do
begin
  i:=i+1; j:=i; k:=1;
  while S1(j)=S2(k) do
  begin
    if k=m writeln('success')
    else do
     begin
      j:=j+1; k:=k+1
    end
   end
  end
 writeln('fail')
end.
```

This algorithm requires $m(n - m)$ comparisons in the worst case. A more efficient algorithm will not repeat the same comparisons over and over again. One such algorithm uses two indices, i and j, where i indexes (counts) the character positions in S_1 and j is set to a "match state" value ranging from 0 to m (like the states in a finite automaton). The state 0 corresponds to no matched characters between the strings, while the state 1 corresponds to the first letter in S_2 matching character i in S_2. State 2 corresponds to the first two consecutive letters in S_2 matching letters i and $i + 1$ in S_1 respectively, and so on, with state m corresponding to a successful match. Whenever consecutive letters fail to match, the state index is reduced accordingly. We leave the actual details as an exercise.

Matching Graphs

Two graphs G_1 and G_2 match if they have the same labeled nodes and same labeled arcs and all node-to-node arcs are the same. More generally, we wish to determine if G_2 with m nodes is a subgraph of G_1 with n nodes, where $n \geq m$. In a worst-case match, this will require $n!/(n - m)!$ node comparisons and $O(m^2)$ arc comparisons. Consequently, we will see that most graph matching applications deal with small manageable graphs only or use some form of heuristics to limit the number of comparisons.

Finding subgraph isomorphisms is also an important matching problem. An isomorphism between the graphs G_1 and G_2 with vertices (nodes) $V1$, $V2$ and edges $E1$, $E2$, that is, $(V1,E1)$ and $(V2,E2)$, respectively, is a one-to-one mapping to f between $V1$ and $V2$, such that for all $v1 \in V1$, $f(v1) = v2$, and for each arc $e1 \in E1$ connecting $v1$ and $v1'$, there is a corresponding arc $e2 \in E2$ connecting $f(v1)$ and $f(v1')$. An example of an application in which graph isomorphisms are used to determine the similarity between two graphs is given in the next section.

Matching Sets and Bags

An exact match of two sets having the same number of elements requires that their intersection also have that number of elements. Partial matches of two sets can also be determined by taking their intersection. If the two sets have the same number of elements and all elements are of equal importance, the degree of match can be the proportion of the total members which match. If the number of elements differ between the sets, the proportion of matched elements to the minimum of the total number of members can be used as a measure of likeness. When the elements are not of equal importance, weighting factors can be used to score the matched elements. For example, a measure such as

$$s(S1,S2) = \left(\sum_{i=1}^{m} w_i N(a_i)\right)/m \tag{10.7}$$

could be used, where $w_i = 1$ and $N(a_i) = 1$ if a_i is in the intersection; otherwise it is 0.

An efficient way to find the intersection of two sets of symbolic elements (nonnumeric atoms) in LISP is to work through one set marking each element on the elements property list and then saving all elements from the other list that have been marked. The resultant list of saved elements is the required intersection.

Matching two bags is similar to matching two sets except that counts of the number of occurrences of each element must also be made. For this, a count of the number of occurrences can be used as the property mark for elements found in one set. This count can then be used to compare against a count of elements found in the second set.

Matching to Unify Literals

One of the best examples of nontrivial pattern matching is in the unification of two FOPL literals. Recall the procedure for unifying two literals, both of which may contain variables (see Chapter 4). For example, to unify $P(f(a,x),y,y)$ and $P(x,b,z)$ we first rename variables so that the two predicates have no variables in common. This can be done by replacing the x in the second predicate with u to give $P(u,b,z)$. Next, we compare the two symbol-by-symbol from left to right until a disagreement is found. Disagreements can be between two different variables, a nonvariable term and a variable, or two nonvariable terms. If no disagreement is found, the two are identical and we have succeeded.

If a disagreement is found and both are nonvariable terms, unification is impossible; so we have failed. If both are variables, one is replaced throughout by the other. (After any substitution is made, it should be recorded in a substitution worklist for later use.) Finally, if the disagreement is a variable and a nonvariable term, the variable is replaced by the entire term. Of course, in this last step, replacement is possible only if the term does not contain the variable that is being replaced. This matching process is repeated until the two are unified or until a failure occurs.

For the two predicates P, above, a disagreement is first found between the term $f(a,x)$ and variable u. Since $f(a,x)$ does not contain the variable u, we replace u with $f(a,x)$ everywhere it occurs in the literal. This gives a substitution set of $\{f(a,x)/u\}$ and the partially matched predicates $P(f(a,x),y,y)$ and $P(f(a,x),b,z)$.

Proceeding with the match, we find the next disagreement pair, y and b, a variable and term, respectively. Again, we replace the variable y with the term b and update the substitution list to get $\{f(a,x)/u,\ b/y\}$. The final disagreement pair is two variables. Replacing the variable in the second literal with the first we get the substitution set $\{f(a,x)/u,b/y,y/z\}$ or, equivalently, $\{f(a,x)/u,b/y,b/z\}$. Note that this procedure can always give the most general unifier.

We conclude this section with an example of a LISP program which uses both the open and the segment pattern matching variables to find a match between a pattern and a clause.

```
(defun match (pattern clause)
  (cond   ((equal pattern clause) t)            ;return t if
          ((or (null pattern) (null clause)) nil) ;equal, nil
                                                 ;if not.
          ((or (equal (car pattern) (car clause)) ;not. ?x
                                                 ;binds
               (equal (car pattern) '?x))        ;to single
           (match (cdr pattern) (cdr clause)))   ;term,*y
                                                 ;binds
          ((equal (car pattern) '*y)             ;to several
           (or (match (cdr pattern) (cdr clause)) ;contiguous
               (match pattern (cdr clause))))))  ;terms.
```

Notice that when a segment variable is encountered (the $*y$), match is recursively executed on the cdrs of both pattern and clause or on the cdr of clause and pattern as $*y$ matches one or more than one item respectively.

10.5 PARTIAL MATCHING

For many AI applications complete matching between two or more structures is inappropriate. For example, input representations of speech waveforms or visual scenes may have been corrupted by noise or other unwanted distortions. In such cases, we do not want to reject the input out of hand. Our systems should be more tolerant of such commonly occurring problems. Instead, we want our systems to be able to find an acceptable or best match between the input and some reference description.

Compensating for Distortions

Finding an object in a photograph given only a general description of the object is a common problem in vision applications. For example, the task may be to locate a human face or human body in photographs without the necessity of storing hundreds of specific face templates. A better approach in this case would be to store a single reference description of the object. Matching between photograph regions and corresponding descriptions then could be approached using either a measure of correlation or, alternatively, by altering the image to obtain a closer fit. If nothing is known about the noise and distortion characteristics, correlation methods can be ineffective or even misleading. In such cases, methods based on mechanical distortion may be more appropriate.

Imagine that our reference image is on a transparent rubber sheet. This sheet is moved over the input image and at each location is stretched to get the best match alignment between the two images. The match between the two can then be evaluated by how well they correspond and how much push-and-pull distortion is needed to obtain the best correspondence.

In practice, a discrete version of the stretchable model is needed for computer implementation. One way this can be accomplished is to use a number of rigid pieces (like templates) connected with springs. The pieces can correspond to low level areas such as pixels or even larger area segments (Figure 10.5).

To model any restrictions such as the relative positions of body parts (eyes must be above nose, legs below torso, and so on), nonlinear cost functions of piece displacements can be used. The costs can correspond to different spring tensions which reflect the constraints. For example, the cost of displacing some pieces might be zero for no displacement, one unit for single increment displacements in any one of the permissible directions (left, right, up, down), two units for two position

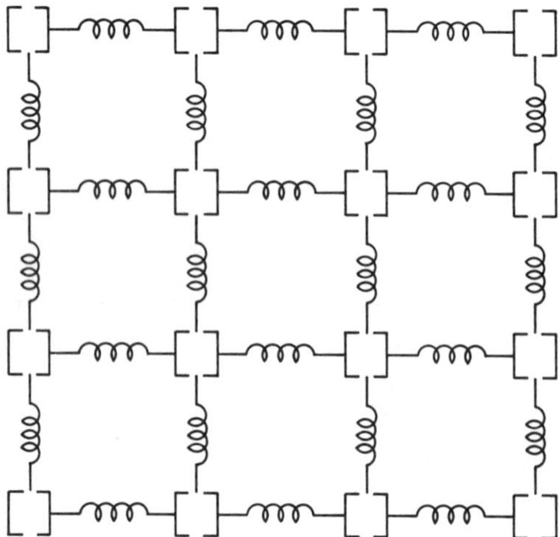

Figure 10.5 Discrete version of stretchable overlay image.

displacements and infinite cost for displacements of more than two increments. Other pieces would be assigned higher costs for unit and larger position displacements when stronger constraints were applicable.

The matching problem here is to find a least cost location and distortion pattern for the reference sheet with regard to the sensed picture. Attempting to compare each component of some reference to each primitive part of a sensed picture is a combinatorially explosive problem. However, in using the template-spring reference image and heuristic methods (based on dynamic programming techniques) to compare against different segments of the sensed picture, the search and match process can be made tractible.

Any matching metric used in the least cost comparison would need to take into account the sum of the distortion costs C_d, the sum of the costs for reference and sensed component dissimilarities C_c, and the sum of penalty costs for missing components C_m. Thus, the total cost is given by

$$C_t = C_d + C_c + C_m \tag{10.8}$$

Finding Match Differences

Distortions occurring in representations are not the only reasons for partial matches. For example, in problem solving or analogical inference, differences are expected. In such cases the two structures are matched to isolate the differences in order that they may be reduced or transformed. Once again, partial matching techniques are appropriate. The problem is best illustrated with another example.

In a vision application (Eshera and Fu, 1984), an industrial part may be described using a graph structure where the set of nodes correspond to rectangular or cylindrical block subparts. The arcs in the graph correspond to positional relations between the subparts. Labels for rectangular block nodes contain length, width, and height, while labels for cylindrical block nodes give radius and height. The arc labels give location and distances between block nodes, where location can be above, to the right of, behind, inside, and so on.

Figure 10.6 illustrates a segment of such a graph. In the figure the following abbreviations are used:

R = rectangular block $\quad l_i$ = length of subpart
C = cylindrical block $\quad w_i$ = width of subpart
J = joint $\quad h_i$ = height of subpart
T = to-the-right-of $\quad r_i$ = radius of subpart
V = above $\quad d_i$ = distance between subparts

Interpreting the graph, we see it is a unit consisting of subparts, made up of rectangular and cylindrical blocks with dimensions specified by attribute values. The cylindrical block n_1 is to the right of n_2 by d_1 units and the two are connected by a joint. The blocks n_1 and n_2 are above the rectangular block n_3 by d_2 and d_3 units respectively, and so on.

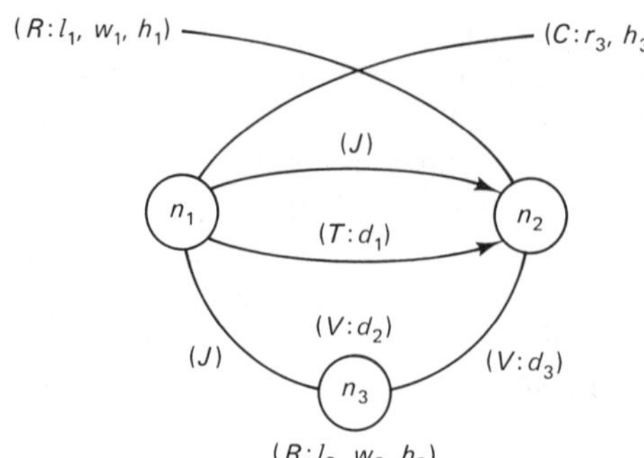

Figure 10.6 Segment of an attributed relational graph.

Graphs such as this are called attributed relational graphs (ATRs). Such a graph G is defined formally as a sextuple

$$G = (N,B,A,G_n,G_b)$$

where $N = \{n_1, n_2, \ldots, n_k\}$ is a set of nodes, $A = \{an_1, an_2, \ldots, an_k\}$ is an alphabet of node attributes, $B = \{b_1, b_2, \ldots, b_m\}$ is a set of directed branches ($b = (n_i,n_j)$), and G_n and G_b are functions for generating node and branch attributes respectively.

When the representations are graph structures like ARGs, a similarity measure may be computed as the total cost of transforming one graph into the other. For example, the similarity of two ARGs may be determined with the following steps: (1) Decompose the ARGs into basic subgraphs, each having a depth of one, (2) compute the minimum cost to transform either basic ARG into the other one subgraph-by-subgraph, and (3) compute the total transformation cost from the sum of the subgraph costs.

An ARG may be transformed by the three basic operations of node or branch deletions, insertions, or substitutions, where each operation is given a cost based on computation time or other factors.

Finding the minimal cost to transform one ARG into another is known to be an NP complete problem. However, heuristic solutions using dynamic programming methods have been developed which have time complexity of $O(m^2n^2(m + n))$ where m and n are the number of nodes in the two ARGs. For details regarding such computation procedures the reader is referred to Eshera and Fu (1984).

10.6 FUZZY MATCHING ALGORITHMS

Fuzzy matching is accomplished by computing a fuzzy distance or similarity measure between two objects such as those given in Section 10.3. A similarity score of 1 corresponds to an identical match while a score near 0 corresponds to maximal dissimilarity. For example, suppose two objects say o_1 and o_2, are each described by the same set of k attributes A_i, $i = 1, \ldots, k$. Each attribute may be regarded as a fuzzy set, and a metric similar to equation 10.6 may then be used to match compare the two objects based on their attribute memberships.

If the attributes represent linguistic variables such as height, weight, facial-appearance, color-of-eyes, and type-of-hair, each variable may be assigned a limited number of values. For example, a reasonable assignment for height would be the integers 10 to 96 corresponding to height in inches. Eye colors could be assigned brown, black, blue, hazel, and so on. An object description of tall, slim, pretty, blue-eyed, blonde will have characteristic function values for the five attributes of $u_{Aj}(o_1)$ and $u_{Aj}(o_2)$ for objects o_1 and o_2 respectively. A measure of fuzzy similarity between the two objects can then be defined as

$$s(o_1,o_2) = 1 \,/\, (1 - d),$$

where

$$d = \frac{1}{k}\left[\sum_{i=1}^{k}(u_{Ai}(o_1) - u_{Ai}(o_2))^2\right]^{1/2} \qquad (10.9)$$

For an accurate match, the quantity d in equation 10.9 should be computed for several different values of each linguistic variable (very short, short, medium, tall, and very tall) and the average taken. This will be done at the expense of much computation, however.

Note that it is always possible to define the attribute domains as discrete finite approximations to any domain as we have done for height, and the characteristic values for tall might be $u_{tall}(10) = \ldots u_{tall}(50) = 0, \ldots, u_{tall}(66) = 0.5. \ldots$

The number (k) of attributes and domain values chosen for each attribute will depend on the specific application. Furthermore, it should be noted that the characteristic values will be subjective ones. Even so, selecting only a few relevant attributes and assigning a modest number of values for each domain can give a good approximation to fuzzy likenesses.

10.7 THE RETE MATCHING ALGORITHM

Production (or rule-based) systems are described in Chapter 15. They are popular architectures for expert systems. A typical system will contain a Knowledge Base which contains structures representing the domain expert's knowledge in the form of rules or productions, a working memory which holds parameters for the current problem, and an inference engine with rule interpreter which determines which rules are applicable for the current problem (Figure 10.7).

The basic inference cycle of a production system is match, select, and execute as indicated in Figure 10.7. These operations are performed as follows:

Match. During the match portion of the cycle, the conditions in the left hand side (LHS) of the rules in the knowledge base are matched against the contents

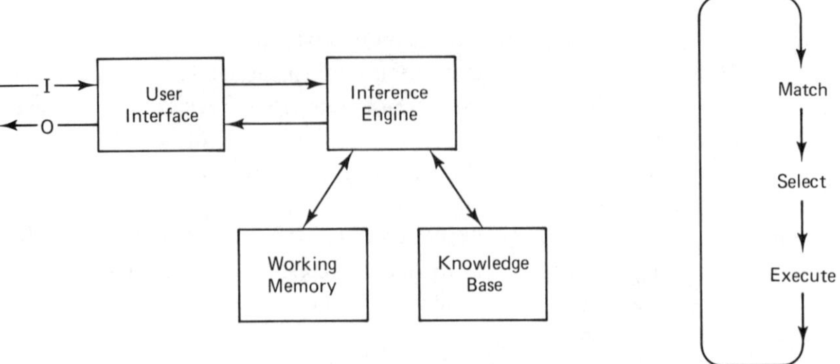

Figure 10.7 Production system components and basic cycle.

of working memory to determine which rules have their LHS conditions satisfied with consistent bindings to working memory terms. Rules which are found to be applicable (that match) are put in a conflict set.

Select. From the conflict set, one of the rules is selected to execute. The selection strategy may depend on recency of useage, specificity of the rule, or other criteria.

Execute. The rule selected from the conflict set is executed by carrying out the action or conclusion part of the rule, the right hand side (RHS) of the rule. This may involve an I/O operation, adding, removing or changing clauses in Working Memory or simply causing a halt.

The above cycle is repeated until no rules are put in the conflict set or until a stopping condition is reached.

A typical knowledge base will contain hundreds or even thousands of rules and each rule will contain several (perhaps as many as ten or more) conditions. Working memories typically contain hundreds of clauses as well. Consequently, exhaustive matching of all rules and their LHS conditions against working-memory clauses may require tens of thousands of comparisons. This accounts for the claim made in the introductory paragraph that as much as 90% of the computing time for such systems can be related to matching operations.

To eliminate the need to perform thousands of matches per cycle, an efficient match algorithm called RETE has been developed (Forgy, 1982). It was initially developed as part of the OPS family of programming languages (Brownston, et al., 1985). This algorithm uses several novel features, including methods to avoid repetitive matching on successive cycles. The main time-saving features of RETE are as follows.

1. In most expert systems, the contents of working memory change very little from cycle to cycle. There is a persistence in the data known as temporal redundancy.

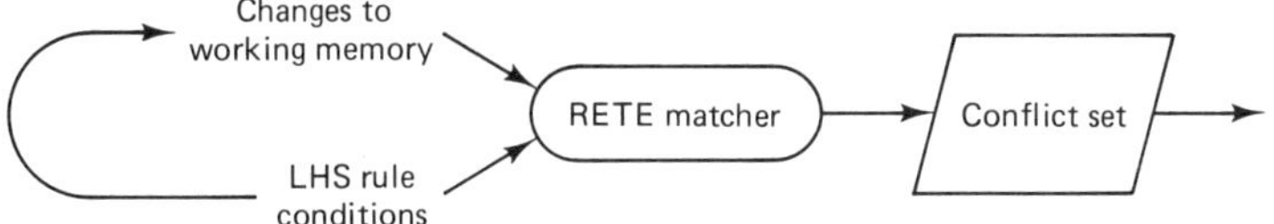

Figure 10.8 Changes to working memory are mapped to the conflict set.

This makes exhaustive matching on every cycle unnecessary. Instead, by saving match information, it is only necessary to compare working memory changes on each cycle. In RETE, additions to, removals from, and changes to working memory are translated directly into changes to the conflict set (Figure 10.8). Then, when a rule from the conflict set has been selected to fire, it is removed from the set and the remaining entries are saved for the next cycle. Consequently, repetitive matching of all rules against Working Memory is avoided. Furthermore, by indexing rules with the condition terms appearing in their LHS (described below), only those rules which could match Working Memory changes need to be examined. This greatly reduces the number of comparisons required on each cycle.

2. Many rules in a knowledge base will have the same conditions occurring in their LHS. This is just another way in which unnecessary matching can arise. Repeated testing of the same conditions in those rules could be avoided by grouping rules which share the same conditions and linking them to their common terms. It would then be possible to perform a single set of tests for all the applicable rules. A description of this linking process is given below.

When the rules are first loaded into the knowledge base, they are examined and processed by a rule compiler. The compiler checks the LHS conditions and forms an association between rule names and their LHS condition terms. In addition, the compiler builds a network structure which connects all rules having common conditions in their LHS. The network is then used during run time to locate and test rule conditions which might be satisfied with consistent bindings to new working-memory clauses. Figure 10.9 illustrates how rules sharing common LHS terms are grouped together and indexed with these common condition terms.

One way to form the associations and indices using LISP is with property lists. For example,

```
(putprop 'R6 'father 'cond-1)
(putprop 'R6 'father 'cond-2)
(putprop 'R12 'father 'cond-1)
```

sets up a link between rules and their LHS conditions, whereas statements like

```
(putprop 'father (cons R6 (get 'father 'cond-1) 'cond-1))
```

link specific LHS terms to all rules which contain the term in the same LHS positions. When a change is made to working memory, such as the addition of the clause

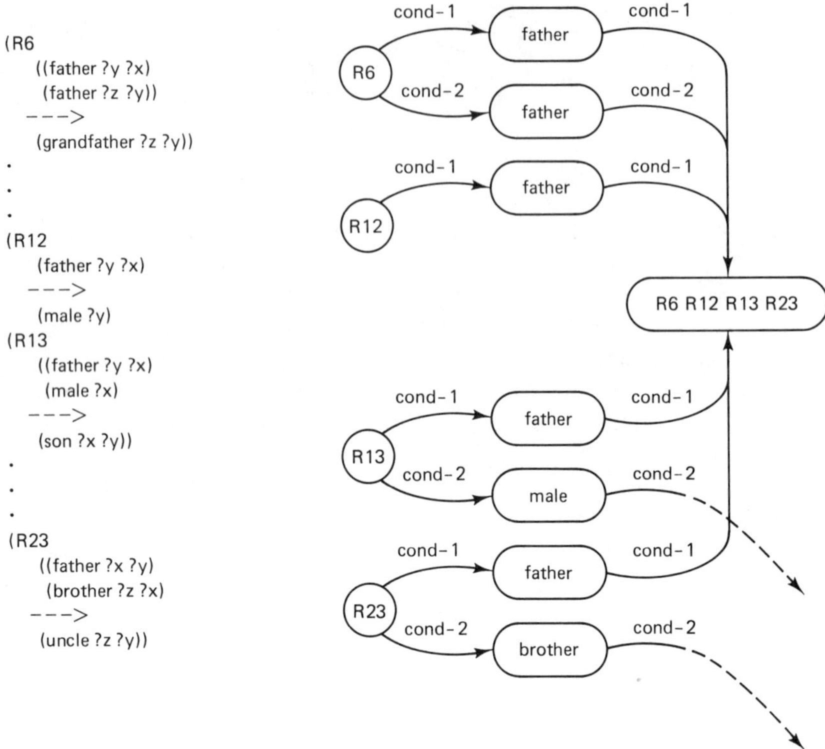
(R6
((father ?y ?x)
(father ?z ?y))
--->
(grandfather ?z ?y))
(R12
(father ?y ?x)
--->
(male ?y)
(R13
((father ?y ?x)
(male ?x)
--->
(son ?x ?y))
(R23
((father ?x ?y)
(brother ?z ?x)
--->
(uncle ?z ?y))
R6
R12
R13
R23
cond-1
cond-2
father
male
brother
R6 R12 R13 R23

Figure 10.9 Typical rules and a portion of a compiled network.

(father bill joe), all rules which contain father as an LHS condition are easily identified and retrieved.

In RETE, the retrieval and subsequent testing of rule conditions is initiated with the creation of a token which is passed to the network constructed by the rule compiler. The network provides paths for all applicable tests which can lead to consistent bindings and hence to complete LHS satisfaction of rules. The matcher traverses the network finding all rules which newly match or no longer match Working Memory elements. The output from the matcher are data structures which consist of pairs of elements: a rule name and list of working-memory elements that match its LHS, like (R6 ((father bob sam) (father mike bob)).

The reader will notice that the indexing methods described above are similar to those presented in the following chapter. Other time-saving tricks are also employed in RETE; however, the ones noted above are the most important. They provide a substantial saving over exhaustive matching of hundreds or even tens of thousands of conditions.

10.8 SUMMARY

In this chapter we have examined representation structures used in match comparison operations, and considered various measures of similarity and distance between two or more such structures.

We began by reviewing some representation structures such as FOPL expressions, rules, frames, fuzzy sets, and networks. We added to this group general graphs, trees, sets, and bags. We defined pattern variables as open or segment based on the number of constant terms they could bind with. We also defined variables as a function of their domains, nominal, ordinal, binary, and interval.

Next, we considered various measures that could be used in assessing the likeness or proximity of two or more objects. These included Euclidean distance, probabilistic measures, qualitative measures, various similarity measures, and fuzzy measures.

We then examined matching algorithms for exact matches where the structures were required to be identical, be transformable, or be capable of binding to pattern variables with certain constraints.

We also considered partial matching problems and saw two examples in which partial matches were more realistic than exact matches. Fuzzy matching procedures for objects were also described and appropriate measures presented.

Finally, we concluded the chapter with a description of an important matching algorithm used in the OPS programming languages. This is the RETE algorithm which takes advantage of the fact that the contents of working memory change little from cycle to cycle, and many rules share the same conditions in their LHS. By properly indexing predicates and rules and saving match information, RETE is able to eliminate exhaustive matching on every cycle and update the conflict set only as needed.

EXERCISES

10.1. Indicate whether or not consistent substitutions can be made which result in matches for the following pairs of clauses. If substitutions can be made, given examples of valid ones.

a. P(a,f(x,b),g(f(a,y)),z), P(a,f(a,y),g(f(x,y)),c)
b. P(a,x) V Q(b,y,f(y)) V R(x,y),
   P(x,a) V Q(f(y),y,b) V R(y,x)
c. R(a,b,c) V Q(x,y,z) V P(f(a,x,b),
   P(z) V Q(x,y,b) V R(x,y,z)

10.2. State what variable bindings, if any, will make the following lists match.

a. (a b c (d a) f), (?x b c (d ?y) ?z)
b. (*x a b (c d) *x), ((e f) a b *y e f)
c. (?x *y a b c (d e)), (a (j k (f)) a b c *z)

10.3. Write a LISP function called "match" that takes two arguments and returns T if the two are identical, returns the two arguments if one is a variable and the other a term and returns nil, otherwise.

10.4. Identify the following variables as nominal, ordinal, binary or interval:

temperature	sex
wavelength	university class
population	intelligence
quality of restaurant	

10.5. What is the difference between a bag and a set? Give examples of both. How could a program determine whether a data structure was either a bag or a set?

10.6. Compute the Mahalanobis distance between two normal distributions having zero means, variances of 4 and 9, and a covariance of 5.

10.7. Give three different examples of functions f that can be used in the similarity equations 10.3 and 10.4.

10.8. Choose two simple objects $O1$ and $O2$ that are somewhat similar in their features $A1$ and $A2$, respectively, and compute the similarity of the two using a form of equation 10.4.

10.9. Define two fuzzy sets "tall" and "short" and compute the distance between them using equation 10.5.

10.10. For the two sets defined in Problem 10.9, compute the similarity of the two using equation 10.6.

10.11. Write a LISP function to find the intersection of two sets using the marking method described in the subsection entitled Matching Sets and Bags.

10.12. Write a LISP function that determines if two sets match exactly.

10.13. Write pseudocode to unify two FOPL literals.

10.14. Write a LISP program based on the pseudocode developed in Problem 10.13.

10.15. Write pseudocode to find the similarity between two attributed relational graphs (AGRs).

10.16. Suppose an expert system working memory has m clauses each with an average of four if . . . then conditions per clause and a knowledge base with 200 rules. Each rule has an avereage of five conditions. What is the time complexity of a matching algorithm which performs exhaustive matching?

10.17. Estimate the average time savings if the RETE algorithm was used in the previous problem.

10.18. Write a PROLOG program that determines if two sets match exactly.

10.19. Write a PROLOG program that determines if two sets match except possibly for the first elements of each set.

11

Knowledge Organization and Management

We have seen how important the choice of a suitable representation can be in the solution of knowledge-based problems. When a good representation is chosen for a class of problems, the solution process can be greatly simplified. A poor representation can lead to excessive effort or even failure. Another factor which can have a significant impact on the ease with which problems are solved is the accessibility of the knowledge. By accessibility, we mean the ease and the reliability with which a specific set of knowledge can be selectively found and retrieved for use over extended periods of time.

The problem of access is closely related to and dependent on the way in which the knowledge is organized and maintained in memory. Through appropriate structuring of the knowledge, the retrieval process can be greatly expedited. But a memory organization for an intelligent system must not be a static one. In order to be effective, it must be dynamic, since knowledge will continually change with modifications to the environment. New knowledge must be integrated with the old, and outmoded knowledge must be modified or forgotten. This requires continual reorganization of the knowledge.

Knowledge-based systems tend to require large amounts of knowledge. And, as knowledge bases increase in size and complexity, the access problem becomes more difficult. The time to search, test, select, and retrieve a minimal amount of requisite knowledge from a large body of knowledge can be very time consuming if the knowledge is poorly organized. Such problems can easily become intractible or at best intolerable.

In this chapter, we investigate various approaches to the effective organization of knowledge within memory. We recognize that while the representation of knowledge is still an important factor, we are more concerned here with the broader problem, that of organization and maintenance for efficient storage and recall as well as for its manipulation.

11.1 INTRODUCTION

The advantages of using structured knowledge representation schemes (frames, associative networks, or object-oriented structures) over unstructured ones (rules or FOPL clauses) should be understood and appreciated at this point. Structured schemes group or link small related chunks of knowledge together as a unit. This simplifies the processing operations, since knowledge required for a given task is usually contained within a limited semantic region which can be accessed as a unit or traced through a few linkages.

But, as suggested earlier, representation is not the only factor which affects efficient manipulation. A program must first locate and retrieve the appropriate knowledge in an efficient manner whenever it is needed. One of the most direct methods for finding the appropriate knowledge is exhaustive search or the enumeration of all items in memory. This is also one of the least efficient access methods. More efficient retrieval is accomplished through some form of indexing or grouping. We consider some of these processes in the next section where we review traditional access and retrieval methods used in memory organizations. This is followed by a description of less commonly used forms of indexing.

A "smart" expert system can be expected to have thousands or even tens of thousands of rules (or their equivalent) in its KB. A good example is XCON (or R1), an expert system which was developed for the Digital Equipment Corporation to configure their customers' computer systems. XCON has a rapidly growing KB which, at the present time, consists of more than 12,000 production rules. Large numbers of rules are needed in systems like this which deal with complex reasoning tasks. System configuration becomes very complex when the number of components and corresponding parameters is large (several hundred). If each rule contained about four or five conditions in its antecedent or If part and an exhaustive search was used, as many as 40,000–50,000 tests could be required on each recognition cycle. Clearly, the time required to perform this number of tests is intolerable. Instead, some form of memory management is needed. We saw one way this problem was solved using a form of indexing with the RETE algorithm described in the preceding chapter. More direct memory organization approaches to this problem are considered in this chapter.

We humans live in a dynamic, continually changing environment. To cope with this change, our memories exhibit some rather remarkable properties. We are able to adapt to varied changes in the environment and still improve our performance. This is because our memory system is continuously adapting through a reorganization process. New knowledge is continually being added to our memories, existing knowledge is continually being revised, and less important knowledge is gradually being forgotten. Our memories are continually being reorganized to expand our recall and reasoning abilities. This process leads to improved memory performance throughout most of our lives.

When developing computer memories for intelligent systems, we may gain some useful insight by learning what we can from human memory systems. We would expect computer memory systems to possess some of the same features. For example, human memories tend to be limitless in capacity, and they provide a uniform grade of recall service, independent of the amount of information stored. For later use, we have summarized these and other desirable characteristics that we feel an effective computer memory organization system should possess.

1. It should be possible to add and integrate new knowledge in memory as needed without concern for limitations in size.
2. Any organizational scheme chosen should facilitate the remembering process. Thus, it should be possible to locate any stored item of knowledge efficiently from its content alone.
3. The addition of more knowledge to memory should have no adverse effects on the accessibility of items already stored there. Thus, the search time should not increase appreciably with the amount of information stored.
4. The organization scheme should facilitate the recognition of similar items of knowledge. This is essential for reasoning and learning functions. It suggests that existing knowledge be used to determine the location and manner in which new knowledge is integrated into memory.
5. The organization should facilitate the process of consolidating recurrent incidents or episodes and "forgetting" knowledge when it is no longer valid or no longer needed.

These characteristics suggest that memory be organized around *conceptual clusters* of knowledge. Related clusters should be grouped and stored in close proximity to each other and be linked to similar concepts through associative relations. Access to any given cluster should be possible through either direct or indirect links such as concept pointers indexed by meaning. Index keys with synonomous meanings should provide links to the same knowledge clusters. These notions are illustrated graphically in Figure 11.1 where the clusters represent arbitrary groups of closely related knowledge such as objects and their properties or basic conceptual categories. The links connecting the clusters are two-way pointers which provide relational associations between the clusters they connect.

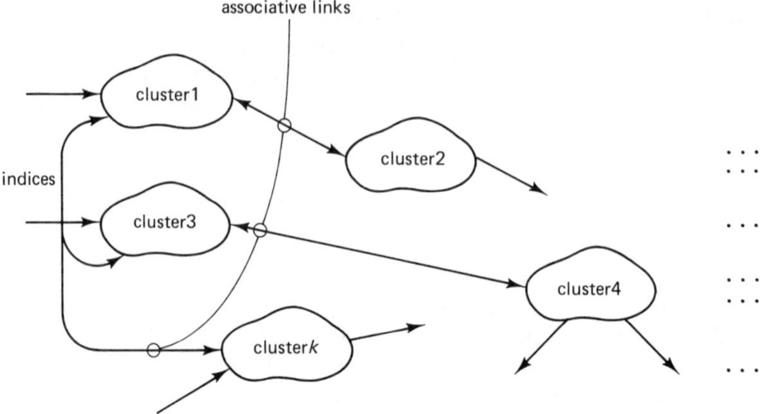

Figure 11.1 Indexed clusters of linked knowledge.

The Frame Problem

One tricky aspect of systems that must function in dynamic environments is due to the so-called frame problem. This is the problem of knowing what changes have and have not taken place following some action. Some changes will be the direct result of the action. Other changes will be the result of secondary or side effects rather than the result of the action. For example, if a robot is cleaning the floors in a house, the location of the floor sweeper changes with the robot even though this

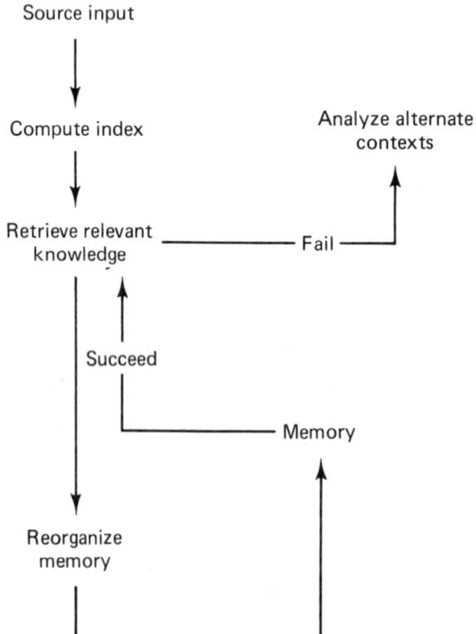

Figure 11.2 Memory organization functions.

is not explicitly stated. Other objects not attached to the robot remain in their original places. The actual changes must somehow be reflected in memory, a feat that requires some ability to infer. Effective memory organization and management methods must take into account effects caused by the frame problem.

In the remainder of this chapter we consider three basic problems related to knowledge organization: (1) classifying and computing indices for input information presented to a system, (2) access and retrieval of knowledge from memory through the use of the computed indices, and (3) the reorganization of memory structures when necessary to accommodate additions, revisions, and forgetting. These functions are depicted in Figure 11.2.

11.2 INDEXING AND RETRIEVAL TECHNIQUES

When a knowledge base is too large to be held in main memory, it must be stored as a file in secondary storage (disk, drum or tape). Storage and retrieval of information in secondary memory is then performed through the transfer of equal-size physical blocks consisting of between 2^8 (256) and 2^{12} (4096) bytes. When an item of information is retrieved or stored, at least one complete block must be transferred between main and secondary memory. The time required to transfer a block typically ranges between 10 ms. and 100 ms., about the same amount of time required to sequentially search the whole block for an item. Clearly, then, grouping related knowledge together as a unit can help to reduce the number of block transfers, and hence the total access time.

An example of effective grouping alluded to above, can be found in some expert system KB organizations. Grouping together rules which share some of the same conditions (propositions) and conclusions can reduce block transfer times since such rules are likely to be needed during the same problem-solving session. Consequently, collecting rules together by similar conditions or content can help to reduce the number of block transfers required. As noted before, the RETE algorithm, described in the previous chapter, is an example of this type of organization.

Indexed Organization

While organization by content can help to reduce block transfers, an indexed organization scheme can greatly reduce the time to determine the storage location of an item. Indexing is accomplished by organizing the information in some way for easy access. One way to index is by segregating knowledge into two or more groups and storing the locations of the knowledge for each group in a smaller index file. To build an indexed file, knowledge stored as units (such as records) is first arranged sequentially (sorted) by some key value. The key can be any chosen field or fields that uniquely identify the record. A second file containing indices for the record locations is created while the sequential knowledge file is being loaded. Each physical block in this main file results in one entry in the index file. The index file entries are pairs of record key values and block addresses. The key value is the key of the first record stored in the corresponding block. To retrieve an item of knowledge from the main file, the index file is searched to find the desired record key and obtain the corresponding block address. The block is then accessed using this address. Items within the block are then searched sequentially for the desired record.

An indexed file contains a list of the entry pairs (k,b) where the values k are the keys of the first record in each block whose starting address is b. Figure 11.3 illustrates the process used to locate a record using the key value of 378. The largest key value less than 378 (375) gives the block address (800) where the item will be found. Once the 800 block has been retrieved, it can be searched linearly to locate the record with key value 378. This key could be any alphanumeric string that uniquely identifies a block, since such strings usually have a collation order defined by their code set.

If the index file is large, a binary search can be used to speed up the index file search. A binary search will significantly reduce the search time over linear search when the number of items is not too small. When a file contains n records, the average time for a linear search is proportional to $n/2$ compared to a binary search time on the order of $\ln_2(n)$.

Further reductions in search time can be realized using secondary or higher order (hierarchically) arranged index files. In this case the secondary index file would contain key and block-address pairs for the primary index file. Similar indexing would apply for higher order hierarchies where a separate file is used for each level. Both binary search and hierarchical index file organization may be needed when the KB is a very large file.

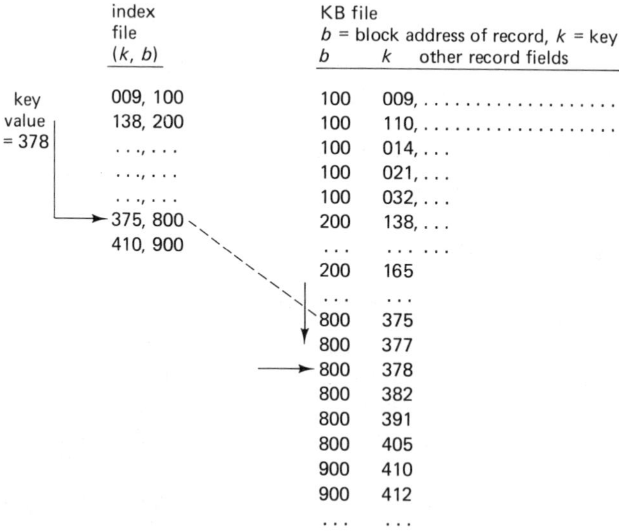

Figure 11.3 Indexed file organization.

When the total number of records in a KB file is n with r records stored per block giving a total of b blocks ($n = r * b$), the average search time for a nonindexed, sequential search is $b / 2$ block access times plus $n / 2$ record tests. This compares with an index search time of $b / 2$ index tests, one block access, and $r / 2$ record tests. A binary index search on the other hand would require only $\ln_2(b)$ index tests, one block access, and $r / 2$ record tests. Therefore, we see that for large n, and moderately large r (30 to 80), the time savings possible using binary indexed access can be substantial.

Indexing in LISP can be implemented with property lists, A-lists, and/or hash-tables. For example, a KB can be partitioned into segments by storing each segment as a list under the property value for that segment. Each list indexed in this way can be found with the get property function and then searched sequentially or sorted and searched with binary search methods. A hash-table is a special data structure in LISP which provides a means of rapid access through key hashing. We review the hashing process next.

Hashed Files

Indexed organizations that permit efficient access are based on the use of a hash function. A hash function, h, transforms key values k into integer storage location indices through a simple computation. When a maximum number of items or categories C are to be stored, the hashed values $h(k)$ will range from 0 to $C - 1$. Therefore, given any key value k, $h(k)$ should map into one of $0 \ldots C - 1$.

An effective, but simple hash function can be computed by choosing the largest prime number p less than or equal to C, converting the key value k into an integer k' if necessary, and then using the value $k' \bmod p$ as the index value h. For example, if C is 1000, the largest prime less than C is $p = 997$. Thus, if the record key value is 123456789 (a social security number), the hashed value is $h = (k \bmod 997) = 273$.

When using hashed access, the value of C should be chosen large enough to accommodate the maximum number of categories needed. The use of the prime number p in the algorithm helps to insure that the resultant indices are somewhat uniformly distributed or hashed throughout the range $0 \ldots C - 1$.

This type of organization is well suited for groups of items corresponding to C different categories. When two or more items belong to the same category, they will have the same hashed values. These values are called *synonyms*. One way to accommodate collisions (simultaneous attempts to access synonyms) is with data structures known as buckets. A bucket is a linked list of one or more items, where each item is a record, block, list or other data structure. The first item in each bucket has an address corresponding to the hashed address. Figure 11.4 illustrates a form of hashed memory organization which uses buckets to hold all items with the same hashed key value. The address of each bucket in this case is the indexed location in an array.

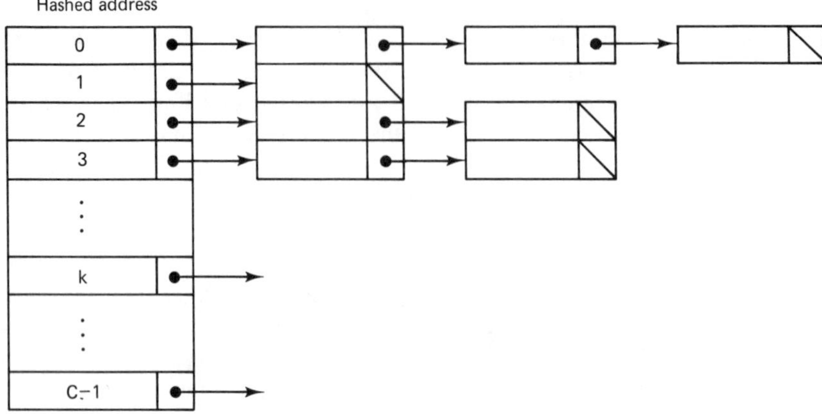

Figure 11.4 Hashed memory file organization.

Conceptual Indexing

The indexing schemes described above are based on lexical ordering, where the collation order of a key value determines the relative location of the record. Keys for these items are typically chosen as a coded field (employee number, name, part number, and so on) which uniquely identifies the item. A better approach to indexed retrieval is one which makes use of the content or meaning associated with the stored entities rather than some nonmeaningful key value. This suggests the use of indices which name and define or otherwise describe the entity being retrieved. Thus, if the entity is an object, its name and characteristic attributes would make meaningful indices. If the entity is an abstract object such as a concept, the name and other defining traits would be meaningful as indices.

How are structures indexed by meaning, and how are they organized in memory for retrieval? One straightforward and popular approach uses associative networks (see Chapter 7) similar to the structures illustrated in Figure 11.1. Nodes within the network correspond to different knowledge entities, whereas the links are indices or pointers to the entities. Links connecting two entities name the association or relationship between them. The relationship between entities may be defined as a hierarchical one or just through associative links.

As an example of an indexed network, the concept of computer science (CS) should be accessible directly through the CS name or indirectly through associative links like a university major, a career field, or a type of classroom course. These notions are illustrated in Figure 11.5.

Object attributes can also serve as indices to locate items or categories based on the attribute values. In this case, the best attribute keys are those which provide the greatest discrimination among objects within the same category. For example, suppose we wish to organize knowledge by object types. In this case, the choice of attributes should depend on the use intended for the knowledge. Since objects

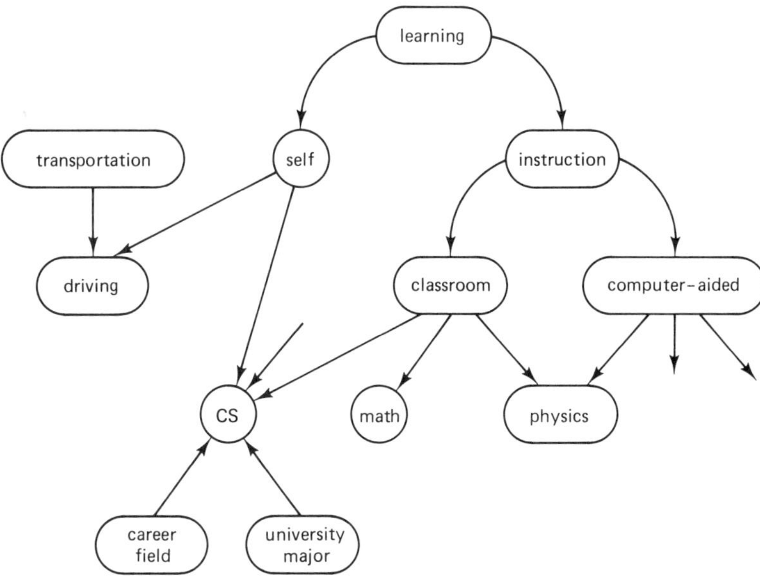

Figure 11.5 Associative network indexing and organization.

may be classified with an unlimited number of attributes (color, size, shape, markings, and so on), those attributes which are most discriminable with respect to the concept meaning should be chosen. Alternatively, object features with the most predictive power make the best indices. A good index for bird types is one based on individual differences like feet, size, beak shape, sounds emitted, special markings, and so forth. Attribute values possessed by all objects are useful for forming categories but poor for identifying an object within the category.

Truly intelligent methods of indexing will be content associative and usually require some inferring. Like humans, a system may fail to locate an item when it has been modified in memory. In such cases, cues related to the item may be needed. For example, you may fail to remember whether or not you have ever discussed American politics with a foreigner until you have considered under what circumstances you may have talked with foreigners (at a university, while traveling or living abroad, or just a chance meeting). An example of this type of indexing strategy is discussed in Section 11.4.

11.3 INTEGRATING KNOWLEDGE IN MEMORY

Integrating new knowledge in traditional data bases is accomplished by simply adding an item to its key location, deleting an item from a key directed location, or modifying fields of an existing item with specific input information. When an item in inventory is replaced with a new one, its description is changed accordingly. When an item is added to memory, its index is computed and it is stored at the corresponding address.

More sophisticated memory systems will continuously monitor a knowledge base and make inferred changes as appropriate. We have seen one example of memory reorganization in the truth maintenance systems (TMS) described in Chapter 5. The primary purpose of those systems, however, is maintaining consistency among the knowledge units, not reorganization and recall. A more comprehensive management system will perform other functions as well, including (1) the formation of new conceptual structures, (2) the computation and association of causal linkages between related concepts, (3) generalization of items having common features and the formation of specialized conceptual categories, and (4) specialization of concepts that have been over-generalized. Examples of these notions are given in the following section under memory organization with E-MOPs.

Hypertext

Hypertext systems are interesting examples of information organized through associative links, somewhat like semantic or associative networks. These systems are interactive window systems connected to a data base through associative links. Unlike normal text which is read in a linear fashion, hypertext can be browsed in a nonlinear way by moving through a network of information nodes which are linked bidirectionally through associative relationships. Users of hypertext systems can wander through the data base scanning text and graphics, creating new information nodes and linkages or modify existing ones. This approach to documentation use is said to more closely match the cognitive process. It provides a new approach to information access and organization for authors, researchers, and other users of large bodies of information.

11.4 MEMORY ORGANIZATION SYSTEMS

HAM, a Model of Memory

One of the earliest computer models of memory was the Human Associative Memory (HAM) system developed by John Anderson and Gordon Bower (1973). This memory is organized as a network of propositional binary trees. An example of a simple tree which represents the statement ''In a park a hippie touched a debutante'' is illustrated in Figure 11.6. When an *informant* asserts this statement to HAM, the system parses the sentence and builds a binary tree representation. Nodes in the tree are assigned unique numbers, while links are labeled with the following functions:

C: context for tree fact	P: predicate
e: set membership	R: relation
F: a fact	S: subject
L: a location	T: time
O: object	

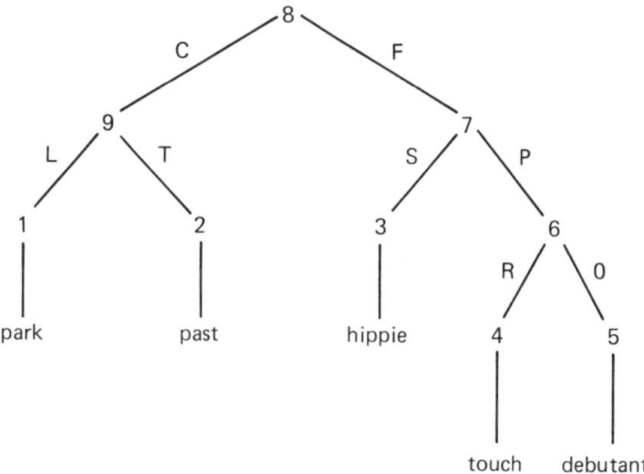

Figure 11.6 Organization of knowledge in HAM.

As HAM is informed of new sentences, they are parsed and formed into new tree-like memory structures or integrated with existing ones. For example, to add the fact that the hippie was tall, the following subtree is attached to the tree structure of Figure 11.6 by merging the common node hippie (node 3) into a single node.

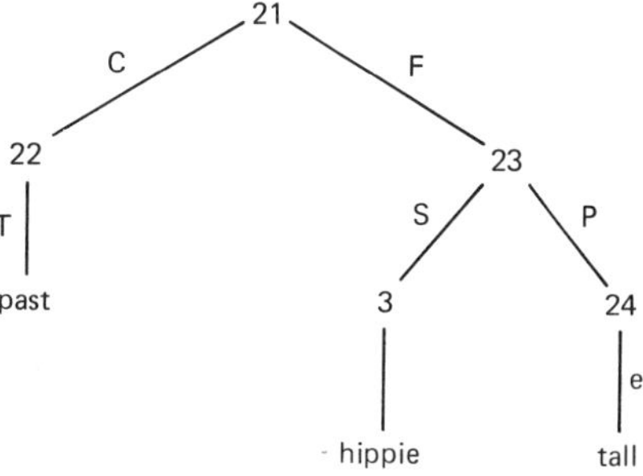

When HAM is posed with a query, it is formed into a tree structure called a probe. This structure is then matched against existing memory structures for the best match. The structure with the closest match is used to formulate an answer to the query.

Matching is accomplished by first locating the leaf nodes in memory that match leaf nodes in the probe. The corresponding links are then checked to see if they have the same labels and in the same order. The search process is constrained by searching only node groups that have the same relation links, based on recency of usage. The search is not exhaustive and nodes accessed infrequently may be forgotten. Access to nodes in HAM is accomplished through word indexing in LISP (node words in tree structures are accessed directly through property lists or A-lists).

Memory Organization with E-MOPs

Roger Schank and his students at Yale University have developed several computer systems which perform different functions related to the use of natural language text, knowledge representation, and memory organization. One system of particular interest was developed by Janet Kolodner (1983a, 1983b, 1984) to study problems associated with the retrieval and organization of reconstructive memory. Her system, called CYRUS (Computerized Yale Retrieval and Updating System) stores episodes from the lives of former secretaries of state Cyrus Vance and Edmund Muskie. The episodes are indexed and stored in long-term memory for subsequent use in answering queries posed in English. The system has many of the features we have described above under conceptual indexing.

The basic memory model in CYRUS is a network consisting of Episodic Memory Organization Packets (E-MOPs). Each such E-MOP is a frame-like node structure which contains conceptual information related to different categories of episodic events. E-MOPs are indexed in memory by one or more distinguishing features. For example, there are basic E-MOPs for diplomatic meetings with foreign dignitaries, specialized political conferences, traveling, sightseeing, negotiations, state dinners, as well as other basic events related to diplomatic state functions. The diplomatic-meeting E-MOP, called $MEET, contains information which is common to all diplomatic meeting events. The common information which characterizes such an E-MOP is called its content. For example, $MEET might contain the following information:

actor	:	Cyrus Vance
participants	:	foreign diplomats
topics	:	international contracts
actions	:	participants talk to each other
goals	:	to resolve disputed contract

A second type of information contained in E-MOPs are the indices which index either individual episodes or other E-MOPs which have become specializations of their parent E-MOPs. For instance, specific diplomatic meetings are indexed by features unique to the individual meetings such as location, actual topic discussed, or the actual meeting participants. A typical $MEET E-MOP which has indices to two particular event meetings EV1 and EV2, is illustrated in Figure 11.7.

One of the meetings indexed was between Vance and Gromyko of the USSR in which they discussed SALT (arms limit talks). This is labeled as event EV1 in the figure. The second meeting was between Vance and Begin of Israel in which they discussed Arab-Israeli peace. This is labeled as event EV2. Note that each of these events can be accessed through more than one feature (index). For example, EV1 can be located from the $MEET event through a topic value of "Arab-Israel peace," through a participants' nationality value of "Israel," through a participants' occupation value of "head of state," and so on.

As new diplomatic meetings are entered into the system, they are either integrated with the $MEET E-MOP as a separately indexed event or merged with another event to form a new specialized meeting E-MOP. When several events belonging

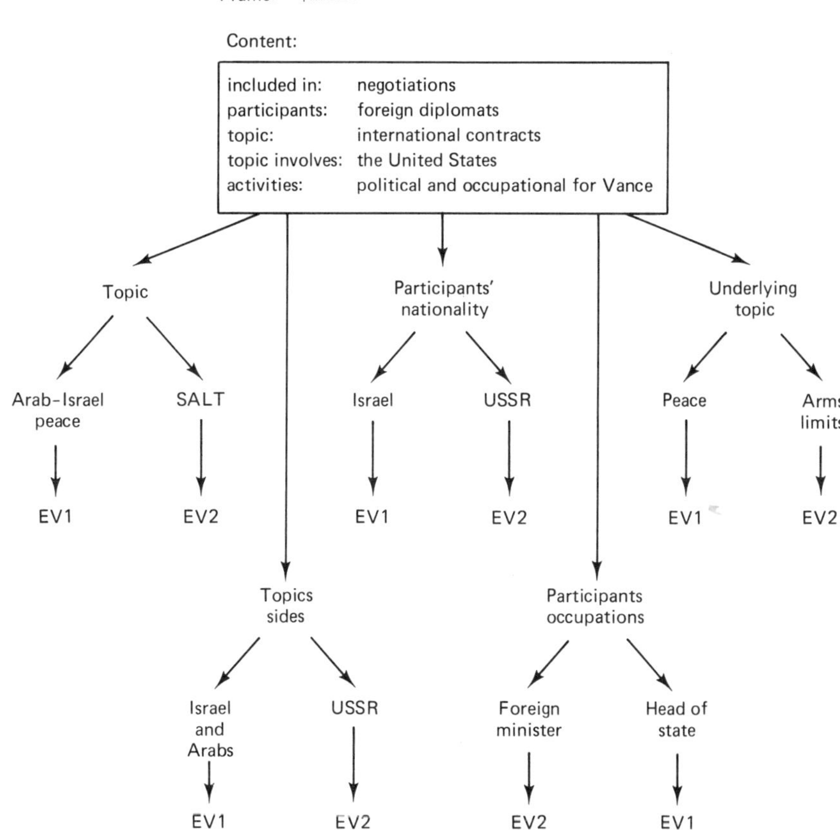

Figure 11.7 An example of an EMOP with two indexed events EV1 and EV2.

to the same MOP category are entered, common event features are used to generalize the E-MOP. This information is collected in the frame contents. Specialization may also be required when over-generalization has occurred. Thus, memory is continually being reorganized as new facts are entered. This process prevents the addition of excessive memory entries and much redundancy which would result if every event entered resulted in the addition of a separate event. Reorganization can also cause forgetting, since originally assigned indices may be changed when new structures are formed. When this occurs, an item cannot be located; so the system attempts to derive new indices from the context and through other indices by reconstructing related events.

To see how CYRUS builds and maintains a memory organization, we briefly examine how a basic E-MOP grows and undergoes revision with time. Initially, the $MEET E-MOP of Figure 11.7 would consist of the content part of the frame only. Then, after a first meeting occurred, indices relevant and unique to that meeting are established and recorded, and pointers are set to the corresponding event. Subsequent meeings also result in the determination of new event indices, or, if two or more of the new meetings have some features in common, a new sub-E-MOP would be formed with indices established and pointers set to the new E-MOP. This process continues with new indices to events added or new E-MOPs formed and indexed as new meetings occur. Furthermore, the content portion of all E-MOPs is continually monitored and modified to better describe the common events it indexes. Thus, when a number of meeting events exhibit some new property, the frame content is generalized to include this property and new indices are determined. When overgeneralization occurs, subsequent events will result in a correction through some specialization and recomputation of indices.

After the two diplomatic meetings described above had been entered, indices are developed by the system to index the events (EV1 and EV2) using features which discriminate between the two meetings (Figure 11.7). If a third meeting is now entered, say one between Vance and Sadat of Egypt, which is also about Arab-Israeli peace, new E-MOPs will be formed since this meeting has some features in common with the Begin (V1) meeting. One of the new E-MOPs that is formed is indexed under the previous topic index. It has the following structure:

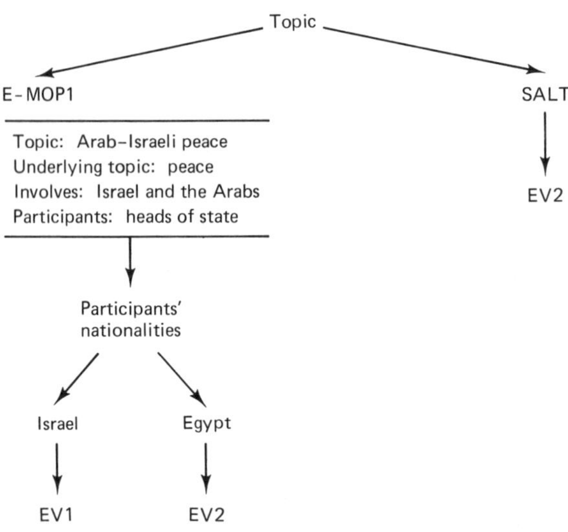

The key issues in this type of organization are the same as those noted earlier. They are (1) the selection and computation of good indices for new events so that similar events can be located in memory for new event integration, (2) monitoring and reorganization of memory to accommodate new events as they occur, and (3) access of the correct event information when provided clues for retrieval.

11.5 SUMMARY

Effective memory organization can facilitate remembering (knowledge retrieval and access), memory management (knowledge reorganization), and forgetting. These are important components of the overall knowledge manipulation process. They are essential adjuncts to the reasoning and learning functions.

Popular forms of intelligent knowledge organization schemes are associative networks, networks of frames, or other structured representation schemes. These schemes will permit the effective organization and revision of knowledge into meaningful categories. Items within each category should share common features and individual items are best indexed by their differences. Access to categories and items can then be made through indices determined by content rather than meaningless keys. The best type of indices are those with good predictive power. Thus, relevant features determined by content and uniqueness to an item are good sources for index determination.

The CYRUS system is a good example of "intelligent" memory organization. It exhibits many of the desirable features possessed by human memories as described in this chapter. They include integrating and indexing events by context, memory reorganization by generalization or specialization, and the formation of new memory structures. Reorganization is performed to reflect commonalities and unique differences among events.

E-MOPs are the basic organization unit within CYRUS. They organize events by indexing them according to their differences. Similarities between events make up the generalized episode descriptions, and separate E-MOPs are associated by causal links.

EXERCISES

11.1. What important characteristics should a computer memory organization system possess?

11.2. Explain why each of the characteristics named in Problem 11.1 are important.

11.3. What basic operations must a program perform in order to access specific chunks of knowledge?

11.4. Suppose 64-byte records are stored in blocks of size 2^8 bytes. Describe a suitable index file to access the records using the following keys (start with block address 1000).

rabbit	dog	cat	duck
chicken	pig	cow	rat
horse	ox	mule	parrot
gopher	mouse	deer	elk

11.5. If ten chunks of knowledge were each stored in records of 64 bytes and the records randomly stored in eight blocks of secondary memory, what would be the access time when a block can be located and read on the average within 60 ms. and the time to search each record is one ms. per block? Compare this time to the time required to search a single block for the same information.

11.6. Referring to Problem 11.4, describe how a hashing method could be applied to search for the indicated records.

11.7. Draw a conceptual indexing tree structure using the same keys as those given in Problem 11.4, but with the addition of a generalized node named farm-animals.

11.8. Using the same label links as those used in HAM, develop propositional trees for the following sentences.
The birds were singing in the park.
John and Mary went dancing at the prom.
Do not drink the water.

11.9. For the previous problem, add the sentence "There are lots of birds and they are small and yellow."

11.10. Develop an E-MOP for a general episode to fill up a car with gasoline using the elements Actor, Participant, Objects, Actions, and Goals.

11.11. Show how the E-MOP of Problem 11.10 would be indexed and accessed for the two events of filling the car at a self-service and at a full-service location.

11.12. Are the events of Problem 11.11 good candidates for specialized E-MOPs? Explain your answer.

11.13. Give an example of a hashing function that does not distribute key values uniformly over the key space.

11.14. Draw a small hypertext network that you might want to browse where the general network subject of artificial intelligence is used. Make up your own subtopics and show all linkages which you feel are useful, including link directions between subtopics.

11.15. Show how the E-MOP of Figure 11.7 would be generalized when peace was one of the topics discussed at every meeting.

11.16. Modify the E-MOP of Figure 11.7 to accommodate a new meeting between Vance and King Hussain of Jordan. The topic of their meeting is Palestinian refugees.

PART 4
Perception, Communication, and Expert Systems

12

Natural Language Processing

Perception and communication are essential components of intelligent behavior. They provide the ability to effectively interact with our environment. Humans perceive and communicate through their five basic senses of sight, hearing, touch, smell, and taste, and their ability to generate meaningful utterances. Two of the senses, sight and hearing are especially complex and require concious inferencing. Developing programs that understand natural language and that comprehend visual scenes are two of the most difficult tasks facing AI researchers.

Developing programs that understand a natural language is a difficult problem. Natural languages are large. They contain an infinity of different sentences. No matter how many sentences a person has heard or seen, new ones can always be produced. Also, there is much ambiguity in a natural language. Many words have several meanings such as can, bear, fly, and orange, and sentences can have different meanings in different contexts. This makes the creation of programs that ''understand'' a natural language, one of the most challenging tasks in AI. It requires that a program transform sentences occurring as part of a dialog into data structures which convey the intended meaning of the sentences to a reasoning program. In general, this means that the reasoning program must know a lot about the structure of the language, the possible semantics, the beliefs and goals of the user, and a great deal of general world knowledge.

12.1 INTRODUCTION

Developing programs to understand natural language is important in AI because a natural form of communication with systems is essential for user acceptance. Furthermore, one of the most critical tests for intelligent behavior is the ability to communicate effectively. Indeed, this was the purpose of the test proposed by Alan Turing (see Chapter 2). AI programs must be able to communicate with their human counterparts in a natural way, and natural language is one of the most important mediums for that purpose.

Before proceeding further, a definition of understanding as used here should be given. We say a program *understands* a natural language if it behaves by taking a (predictably) correct or acceptable action in response to the input. For example, we say a child demonstrates understanding if it responds with the correct answer to a question. The action taken need not be an external response. It may simply be the creation of some internal data structures as would occur in learning some new facts. But in any case, the structures created should be meaningful and correctly interact with the world model representation held by the program. In this chapter we explore many of the important issues related to natural language understanding and language generation.

12.2 OVERVIEW OF LINGUISTICS

An understanding of linguistics is not a prerequisite to the study of natural language understanding, but a familiarity with the basics of grammar is certainly important. We must understand how words and sentences are combined to produce meaningful word strings before we can expect to design successful language understanding systems. In a natural language, the sentence is the basic language element. A sentence is made up of words which express a complete thought. To express a complete thought, a sentence must have a subject and a predicate. The subject is what the sentence is about, and the predicate says something about the subject.

Sentences are classified by structure and usage. A simple sentence has one independent clause comprised of a subject and predicate. A compound sentence consists of two or more independent clauses connected by a conjunction or a semicolon. A complex sentence consists of an independent clause and one or more dependent clauses. Sentences are used to assert, query, and describe. The way a sentence is used determines its mood, declarative, imperative, interrogative, or exclamatory.

A word functions in a sentence as a part of speech. Parts of speech for the English language are nouns, pronouns, verbs, adjectives, adverbs, prepositions, conjunctions, and interjections.

A noun is a name for something (person, place, or thing). Pronouns replace nouns when the noun is already known. Verbs express action, being, or state of being. Adjectives are used to modify nouns and pronouns, and adverbs modify verbs, adjectives, or other adverbs. Prepositions establish the relationship between a noun and some other part of the sentence. Conjunctions join words or groups of words together, and interjections are used to express strong feelings apart from the rest of the sentence.

Phrases are made up of words but act as a single unit within a sentence. These form the building blocks for the syntactic structures we consider later.

Levels of Knowledge Used in Language Understanding

A language understanding program must have considerable knowledge about the structure of the language including what the words are and how they combine into phrases and sentences. It must also know the meanings of the words and how they contribute to the meanings of a sentence and to the context within which they are being used. Finally, a program must have some general world knowledge as well as knowledge of what humans know and how they reason. To carry on a conversation with someone requires that a person (or program) know about the world in general, know what other people know, and know the facts pertaining to a particular conversational setting. This all presumes a familiarity with the language structure and a minimal vocabulary.

The component forms of knowledge needed for an understanding of natural language are sometimes classified according to the following levels.

Phonological. This is knowledge which relates sounds to the words we recognize. A phoneme is the smallest unit of sound. Phones are aggregated into word sounds.

Morphological. This is lexical knowledge which relates to word constructions from basic units called morphemes. A morpheme is the smallest unit of meaning; for example, the construction of friendly from the root *friend* and the suffix *ly*.

Syntactic. This knowledge relates to how words are put together or structured to form grammatically correct sentences in the language.

Semantic. This knowledge is concerned with the meanings of words and phrases and how they combine to form sentence meanings.

Pragmatic. This is high-level knowledge which relates to the use of sentences in different contexts and how the context affects the meaning of the sentences.

World. World knowledge relates to the language a user must have in order to understand and carry on a conversation. It must include an understanding of the other person's beliefs and goals.

The approaches taken in developing language understanding programs generally follow the above levels or stages. When a string of words has been detected, the sentences are parsed or analyzed to determine their structure (syntax) and grammatical correctness. The meanings (semantics) of the sentences are then determined and appropriate representation structures created for the inferencing programs. The whole process is a series of transformations from the basic speech sounds to a complete set of internal representation structures.

Understanding written language or text is easier than understanding speech. To understand speech, a program must have all the capabilities of a text understanding program plus the facilities needed to map spoken sounds (often corrupted by noise) into textual form. In this chapter, we focus on the easier problem, that of natural language understanding from textual input and information processing. The process of translating speech into written text is considered in Chapter 13 under Pattern Recognition and the process of generating text is considered later in this chapter.

General Approaches to Natural Language Understanding

Essentially, there have been three different approaches taken in the development of natural language understanding programs, (1) the use of keyword and pattern matching, (2) combined syntactic (structural) and semantic directed analysis, and (3) comparing and matching the input to real world situations (scenario representations).

The keyword and pattern matching approach is the simplest. This approach was first used in programs such as ELIZA described in Chapter 10. It is based on the use of sentence templates which contain key words or phrases such as "_______ my mother _______," "I am ___________," and, "I don't like _______," that are matched against input sentences. Each input template has associated with it one or more output templates, one of which is used to produce a response to the given input. Appropriate word substitutions are also made from the input to the output to produce the correct person and tense in the response (I and me into you to give replies like "Why are you _______"). The advantage of this approach is that ungrammatical, but meaningful sentences are still accepted. The disadvantage is that no actual knowledge structures are created; so the program does not really understand.

The third approach is based on the use of structures such as the frames or scripts described in Chapter 7. This approach relies more on a mapping of the input to prescribed primitives which are used to build larger knowledge structures. It depends on the use of constraints imposed by context and world knowledge to develop an understanding of the language inputs. Prestored descriptions and details for commonly occurring situations or events are recalled for use in understanding a new situation. The stored events are then used to fill in missing details about the current scenario. We will be returning to this approach later in this chapter. Its advantage is that much of the computation required for syntactical analysis is bypassed. The disadvantage is that a substantial amount of specific, as well as general world knowledge must be prestored.

The second approach is one of the most popular approaches currently being used and is the main topic of the first part of this chapter. With this approach, knowledge structures are constructed during a syntactical and semantical analysis of the input sentences. Parsers are used to analyze individual sentences and to build structures that can be used directly or transformed into the required knowledge formats. The advantage of this approach is in the power and versatility it provides. The disadvantage is the large amount of computation required and the need for still further processing to understand the contextual meanings of more than one sentence.

12.3 GRAMMARS AND LANGUAGES

A language L can be considered as a set of strings of finite or infinite length, where a string is constructed by concatenating basic atomic elements called symbols. The finite set v of symbols of the language is called the alphabet or vocabulary. Among all possible strings that can be generated from v are those that are well-formed, the sentences (such as the sentences found in a language like English). Well-formed sentences are constructed using a set of rules called a grammar. A grammar G is a formal specification of the sentence structures that are allowable in the language, and the language generated by the grammar G is denoted by L(G).

More formally, we define a grammar G as

$$G = (v_n, v_t, s, p)$$

where v_n is a set of nonterminal symbols, v_t a set of terminal symbols, s is a starting symbol, and p is a finite set of productions or rewrite rules. The alphabet v is the union of the disjoint sets v_n and v_t which includes the empty string e. The terminals v_t, are symbols which cannot be decomposed further (such as adjectives, nouns or verbs in English), whereas the nonterminals can be decomposed (such as a noun or verb phrase).

A general production rule from P has the form

$$xyz \longrightarrow xwz$$

where x, y, z, and w are strings from v. This rule states that y should be rewritten as w in the context of x to z where x and z can be any string including the empty string e.

As an example of a simple grammar G, we choose one which has component parts or constituents from English with vocabulary Q given by

$$Q_N = \{S, NP, N, VP, V, ART\}$$
$$Q_T = \{boy, popsicle, frog, ate, kissed, flew, the, a\}$$

and rewrite rules given by

$$
\begin{aligned}
P: \quad \mathrm{S} &\rightarrow \mathrm{NP\ VP} \\
\mathrm{NP} &\rightarrow \mathrm{ART\ N} \\
\mathrm{VP} &\rightarrow \mathrm{V\ NP} \\
\mathrm{N} &\rightarrow \mathrm{boy} \mid \mathrm{popsicle} \mid \mathrm{frog} \\
\mathrm{V} &\rightarrow \mathrm{ate} \mid \mathrm{kissed} \mid \mathrm{flew} \\
\mathrm{ART} &\rightarrow \mathrm{the} \mid \mathrm{a}
\end{aligned}
$$

where the vertical bar indicates alternative choices.

S is the initial symbol (for sentence here), NP stands for noun phrase, VP stands for verb phrase, N stands for noun, V is an abbreviation for verb, and ART stands for article.

The grammar G defined above generates only a small fraction of English, but it illustrates the general concepts of generative grammars. With this G, sentences such as the following can be generated.

The boy ate a popsicle.
The frog kissed a boy.
A boy ate the frog.

To generate a sentence, the rules from P are applied sequentially starting with S and proceeding until all nonterminal symbols are eliminated. As an example, the first sentence given above can be generated using the following sequence of rewrite rules:

$$
\begin{aligned}
\mathrm{S} &\rightarrow \mathrm{NP\ VP} \\
&\rightarrow \mathrm{ART\ N\ VP} \\
&\rightarrow \mathrm{the\ N\ VP} \\
&\rightarrow \mathrm{the\ boy\ VP} \\
&\rightarrow \mathrm{the\ boy\ V\ NP} \\
&\rightarrow \mathrm{the\ boy\ ate\ NP} \\
&\rightarrow \mathrm{the\ boy\ ate\ ART\ N} \\
&\rightarrow \mathrm{the\ boy\ ate\ a\ N} \\
&\rightarrow \mathrm{the\ boy\ ate\ a\ popsicle}
\end{aligned}
$$

It should be clear that a grammar does not guarantee the generation of meaningful sentences, only that they are structurally correct. For example, a gramatically correct, but meaningless sentence like "The popsicle flew a frog" can be generated with this grammar.

We learn a language by learning its structure and not by memorizing all of the sentences we have ever heard, and we are able to use the language in a variety of ways because of this familiarity. Therefore, a useful model of language is one which characterizes the permissible structures through the generating grammars. Unfortunately, it has not been possible to formally characterize natural languages with a simple grammar. In other words, it has not been possible to classify natural languages in a mathematical sense as we did in the example above. More constrained languages (formal programming languages) have been classified and studied through the use of similar grammars, including the Chomsky classes of languages (1965).

The Chomsky Hierarchy of Generative Grammars

Noam Chomsky defined a hierarchy of grammars he called types 0, 1, 2, and 3. Type 0 grammar is the most general. It is obtained by making the simple restriction that y cannot be the empty string in the rewrite form $xyz \rightarrow xwz$. This broad generality requires that a computer having the power of a Turing machine be used to recognize sentences of type 0.

The next level down in generality is obtained with type 1 grammars which are called context-sensitive grammars. They have the added restriction that the length of the string on the right-hand side of the rewrite rule must be at least as long as the string on the left-hand side. Furthermore, in productions of the form $xyz \rightarrow xwz$, y must be a single nonterminal symbol and w, a nonempty string. Typical rewrite rules for type 1 grammars take the forms

$$\begin{aligned} S &\rightarrow aS \\ S &\rightarrow aAB \\ AB &\rightarrow BA \\ aA &\rightarrow ab \\ aA &\rightarrow aa \end{aligned}$$

where the capitalized letters are nonterminals and the lower case letters terminals.

The third type, the type 2 grammar, is known as a context-free grammar. It is characterized by rules with the general form <symbol> → <symbol1> . . . <symbolk> where $k \geq 1$ and where the left-hand side is a single nonterminal symbol, A → xyz where A is a single nonterminal. Productions for this type take forms such as

$$\begin{aligned} S &\rightarrow aS \\ S &\rightarrow aSb \\ S &\rightarrow aB \\ S &\rightarrow aAB \\ A &\rightarrow a \\ B &\rightarrow b \end{aligned}$$

The final and most restrictive type is type 3. It is also called a finite state or regular grammar, whose rules are characterized by the forms

$$\begin{aligned} A &\rightarrow aB \\ A &\rightarrow a \end{aligned}$$

The languages generated by these grammars are also termed types 0, 1 (context-sensitive), 2 (context-free), and 4 (regular) corresponding to the grammars which generate them.

The regular and context-free languages have been the most widely studied and best understood. For example, formal programming languages are typically based on context-free languages. Consequently, much of the work in human language understanding has been related to these two types. This is understandable since type 0 grammars are too general to be of much practical use, and type 1 grammars are not that well understood yet.

Structural Representations

It is convenient to represent sentences as a tree or graph to help expose the structure of the constituent parts. For example, the sentence "The boy ate a popsicle" can be represented as the tree structure depicted in Figure 12.1. Such structures are also called phrase markers because they help to mark or identify the phrase structures in a sentence.

The root node of the tree in Figure 12.1 corresponds to the whole sentence S, and the constituent parts of S are subtrees. For this example, the left subtree is a noun phrase, and the right subtree a verb phrase. The leaf or terminal nodes contain the terminal symbols from v_t.

A tree structure such as the above represents a large number of English sentences. It also represents a large class of ill-formed strings that are nonsentences like "The popsicle flew a tree." This satisfies the above structure, but has no meaning.

For purposes of computation, a tree must be represented as a record, a list or similar data structure. We saw in earlier chapters that a list can always be used to represent a tree structure. For example, the tree in Figure 12.1 could be represented as the list

```
(S  (NP  ((ART the)
          (N boy))
    (VP  (V ate)
         (NP  (ART a)
              (N popsicle)))))
```

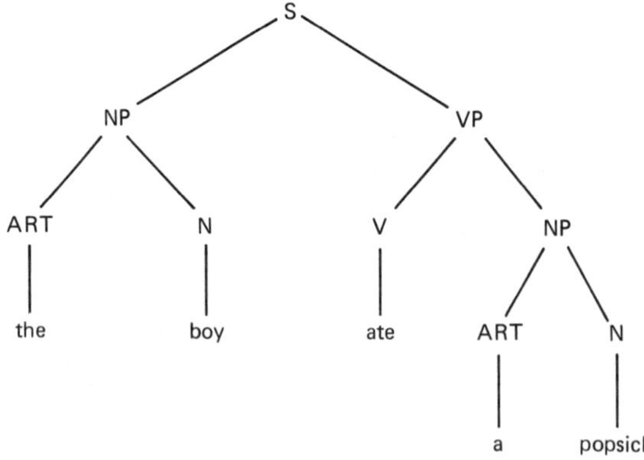

Figure 12.1 A phrase marker or syntactic tree.

A more extensive English grammar than the one given above can be obtained with the addition of other constituents such as prepositional phrases PP, adjectives ADJ, determiners DET, adverbs ADV, auxiliary verbs AUX, and so on. Additional rewrite rules permitting the use of these constituents could include some of the following:

$$
\begin{aligned}
\text{PP} &\rightarrow \text{PREP NP} \\
\text{VP} &\rightarrow \text{V ADV} \\
\text{VP} &\rightarrow \text{V PP} \\
\text{VP} &\rightarrow \text{V NP PP} \\
\text{VP} &\rightarrow \text{AUX V NP} \\
\text{DET} &\rightarrow \text{ART ADJ} \\
\text{DET} &\rightarrow \text{ART}
\end{aligned}
$$

These extensions broaden the types of sentences that can be generated by permitting the added constituents in sentence forms such as

The mean boy locked the dog in the house.

The cute girl worked to make some extra money.

These sentences have the form S → NP VP PP.

Transformational Grammars

The generative grammars described above generally produce different structures for sentences having different syntactical forms even though they may have the same semantic content. For example, the active and passive forms of a sentence will result in two different phrase marker structures. The sentences ''Joe kissed Sue'' (active voice) and ''Sue was kissed by Joe'' (passive voice) result in the structures depicted in Figure 12.2 where the subject and object roles for Joe and Sue are switched.

Obtaining different structures from sentences having the same meaning is undesirable in language understanding systems. Sentences with the same meaning should always map to the same internal knowledge structures. In an attempt to repair these shortcomings in generative grammars, Chomsky (1965) extended them by incorporating two additional components to the basic syntactic component. The added components provide a mechanism to produce single representations for sentences having the same meanings through a series of transformations. This extended grammar is called a transformational generative grammar. Its additions include a semantic component and a phonological component. They are used to interpret the output of the syntactic component by producing meanings and sound sequences. The transformations are essentially tree manipulation rules which depend on the use of an extended lexicon (dictionary) containing a number of semantic features for each word.

Using a transformational generative grammar, a sentence is analyzed in two stages. In one stage the basic structure of the sentence is analyzed to determine the

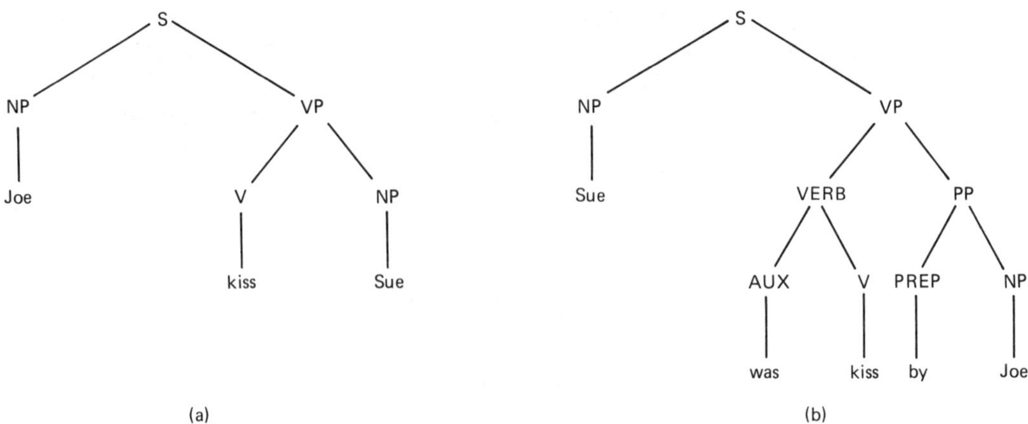

Figure 12.2 Structures for (a) active and (b) passive voice.

grammatical constituent parts. This reveals the surface structure of the sentence, the way the sentence is used in speech or in writing. This structure can be transformed into another one where the deeper semantic structure of the sentence is determined.

Application of the transformation rules can produce a change from passive voice to active voice, change a question to declarative form, and handle negations, subject-verb agreement, and so on. For example, the structure in 12.2(b) could be transformed to give the same basic structure as that of 12.2(a) as is illustrated in Figure 12.3.

Transformational grammars were never widely adopted as computational models of natural language. Instead, other grammars, including case grammars, have had more influence on such models.

Case Grammars

A case relates to the semantic role that a noun phrase plays with respect to verbs and adjectives. Case grammars use the functional relationships between noun phrases and verbs to reveal the deeper case of a sentence. These grammars use the fact

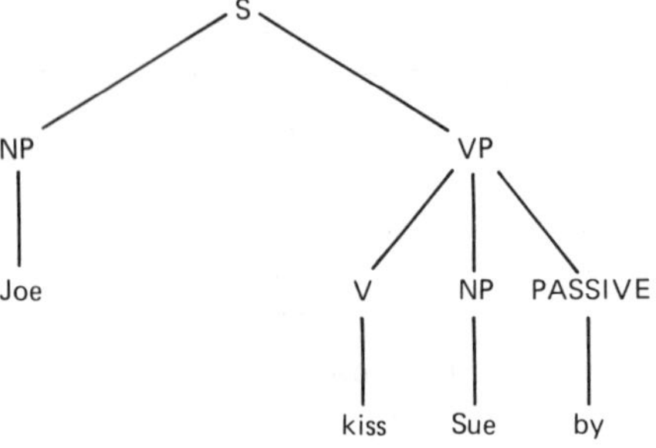

Figure 12.3 Passive voice transformed to active voice.

that verbal elements provide the main source of structure in a sentence since they describe the subject and objects.

In inflected languages like Latin, nouns generally have different ending forms for different cases. In English these distinctions are less pronounced and the forms remain more constant for different cases. Even so, they provide some constraints. English cases are the nominative (subject of the verb), possessive (showing possession or ownership), and objective (direct and indirect objects). Fillmore (1968, 1977) revived the notion of using case to extract the meanings of sentences. He extended the transformational grammars of Chomsky by focusing more on the semantic aspects of a sentence.

In case grammars, a sentence is defined as being composed of a proposition P, a tenseless set of relationships among verbs and noun phrases and a modality constituent M, composed of mood, tense, aspect, negation, and so on. Thus, a sentence can be represented as

$$S \rightarrow M + P$$

where P in turn consists of one or more distinct cases C1, C2, . . . , Ck,

$$P \rightarrow C1 + C2 + . . . + Ck.$$

The number of cases suggested by Fillmore were relatively few. For example, the original list contained only some six cases. They relate to the actions performed by agents, the location and direction of actions, and so on. For example, the case of an instigator of an action is the agentive (or agent), the case of an instrument or object used in an action is the instrumental, and the case of the object receiving the action or change is the objective. Thus, in sentences like "The soldier struck the suspect with the rifle butt" the soldier is the agentive case, the suspect the objective case, and the rifle butt the instrumental case. Other basic cases include dative (an animate entity affected by an action), factitive (the case of the object or of being that which results from an event), and locative (the case of location of the event). Additional cases or substitutes for those given above have since been introduced, including beneficiary, source, destination, to or from, goal, and time.

Case frames are provided for verbs to identify allowable cases. They give the relationships which are required and those which are optional. For the above sentence, a case frame for the verb struck might be

STRUCK[OBJECTIVE (AGENTIVE) (INSTRUMENTAL)]

This may be interpreted as stating that the verb struck must occur in sentences with a noun phrase in the objective case and optionally (parentheses indicate optional use) with noun phrases in the agentive and instrumental cases.

A tree representation for a case grammar will identify the words by their modality and case. For example, a case grammar tree for the sentence "Sue did not take the car" is illustrated in Figure 12.4.

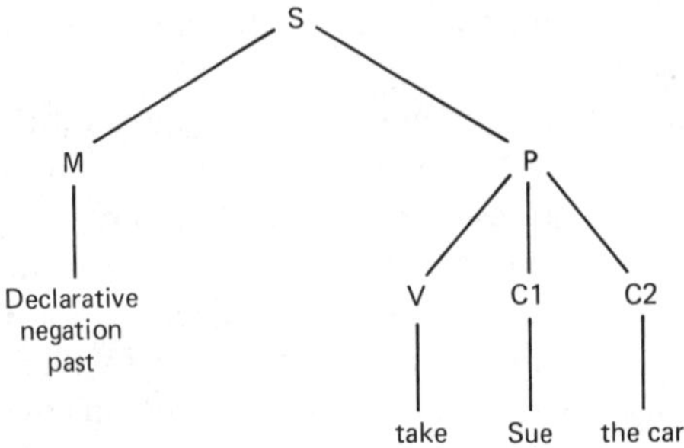

Figure 12.4 Case grammar tree representation.

To build a tree structure like this requires that a word lexicon with sufficient information be available in which to determine the case of sentence elements.

Systemic Grammars

Systemic grammars emphasize function and purpose in the analysis of language. They attempt to account for the personal and social aspects which influence communication through language. As such, context and pragmatics play a more important role in systemic grammars.

Systemic grammars were introduced by Michael Halliday (1961) and Winograd (1972) in an attempt to account for the principles that underlie the organization of different structures. He classifies language by three functions which relate to content, purpose, and coherence.

1. The *ideational function* relates to the content intended by the speaker. This function provides information about the kinds of activities being described, who the actors are, whether there are other participants, and the circumstances related to time and place. These concepts bear some similarity to the case grammars described above.

2. The *interpersonal function* is concerned with the purpose and mood of the statements, whether a question is being asked, an answer being given, a request being made, an opinion being offered, or information given.

3. The *textual function* dictates the necessity for continuity and coherence between the current and previously stated expressions. This function is concerned with the theme of the conversation, what is known, and what is newly expressed.

Halliday proposed a model of language which consisted of four basic categories.

Language units. A hierarchy for sentences based on the sentence, clause, phrase group, word, and morpheme.

Role structure of units. A unit consists of one or more units of lower rank based on its role, such as subject, predicate, complement, or adjunct.

Classification of units. Units are classified by the role they play at the next higher level. For example, the verbal serves as the predicate, the nominal serves as the subject or complement, and so on.

System constraints. These are constraints in combining component features. For example, the network structure given below depicts the constraints in an interpretation.

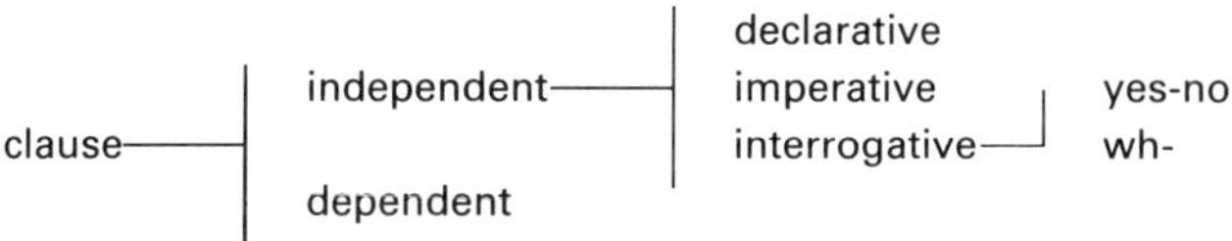

Given these few principles, it is possible to build a grammar which combines much semantic information with the syntactic. Many of the ideas from systemic grammars were used in the successful system SHRDLU developed by Terry Winograd (1972). This system is described later in the chapter.

Semantic Grammars

Semantic grammars encode semantic information into a syntactic grammar. They use context-free rewrite rules with nonterminal semantic constituents. The constituents are categories or metasymbols such as attribute, object, present (as in display), and ship, rather than NP, VP, N, V, and so on. This approach greatly restricts the range of sentences which can be generated and requires a large number of rewrite rules.

Semantic grammars have proven to be successful in limited applications including LIFER, a data base query system distributed by the Navy which is accessible through ARPANET (Hendrix et al., 1978), and a tutorial system named SOPHIE which is used to teach the debugging of circuit faults. Rewrite rules in these systems essentially take the forms

S → What is <OUTPUT-PROPERTY> of <CIRCUIT-PART>?
OUTPUT-PROPERTY → the <OUTPUT-PROP>
OUTPUT-PROPERTY → < OUTPUT-PROP>
CIRCUIT-PART → C23
CIRCUIT-PART → D12
OUTPUT-PROP → voltage
OUTPUT-PROP → current

In the LIFER system, there are rules to handle numerous forms of wh-queries such as

What is the name and location of the carrier nearest to New York
Who commands the Kennedy

Which convoy escorts have inoperative radar units

When will they be repaired

What Soviet ship has hull number 820

These sentences are analyzed and words matched to metasymbols contained in lexicon entries. For example, the input statement "Print the length of the Enterprise" would fit with the LIFER top grammar rule (L.T.G.) of the form

<L.T.G.> → <PRESENT> the <ATTRIBUTE> of <SHIP>

where print matches <PRESENT>, length matches <ATTRIBUTE>, and the Enterprise matches <SHIP>. Other typical lexicon entries that can match <ATTRIBUTE> include CLASS, COMMANDER, FUEL, TYPE, BEAM, LENGTH, and so on.

LIFER can also accommodate elliptical (incomplete) inputs. Given the query "What is the length of the Kennedy?" a subsequent query consisting of the abbreviated form "of the Enterprise?" will elicit a proper response (see also the third and fourth example queries above).

Semantic grammars are suitable for use in systems with restricted grammars since computation is limited. They become unwieldy when used with general purpose language understanding systems, however.

12.4 BASIC PARSING TECHNIQUES

Before the meaning of a sentence can be determined, the meanings of its constituent parts must be established. This requires a knowledge of the structure of the sentence, the meanings of individual words and how the words modify each other. The process of determining the syntactical structure of a sentence is known as parsing.

Parsing is the process of analyzing a sentence by taking it apart word-by-word and determining its structure from its constituent parts and subparts. The structure of a sentence can be represented with a syntactic tree or a list as described in the previous section. The parsing process is basically the inverse of the sentence generation process since it involves finding a grammatical sentence structure from an input string. When given an input string, the lexical parts or terms (root words) must first be identified by type, and then the role they play in a sentence must be determined. These parts can then be combined successively into larger units until a complete tree structure has been completed.

To determine the meaning of a word, a parser must have access to a lexicon. When the parser selects a word from the input stream it locates the word in the lexicon and obtains the word's possible function and other features, including semantic information. This information is then used in building a tree or other representation structure. The general parsing process is illustrated in Figure 12.5.

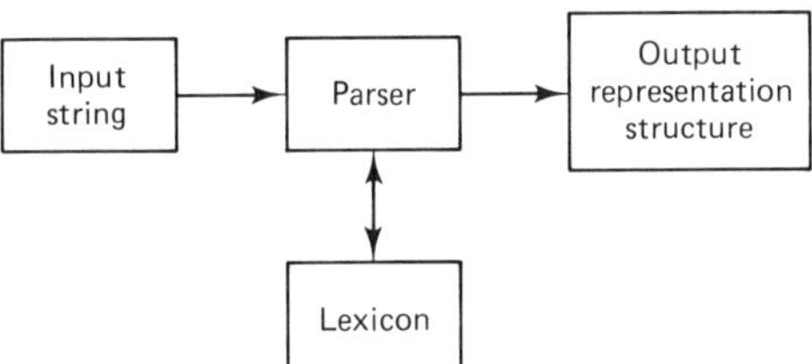

Figure 12.5 Parsing an input to create an output structure.

The Lexicon

A lexicon is a dictionary of words (usually morphemes or root words together with their derivatives), where each word contains some syntactic, semantic, and possibly some pragmatic information. The information in the lexicon is needed to help determine the function and meanings of the words in a sentence. Each entry in a lexicon will contain a root word called the head. Different derivatives of the word, if any, will also be given, and the roles it can play in a sentence (e.g. its part of speech and sense). A fragment of a simplified lexicon is illustrated in Figure 12.6.

The abbreviations 1s, 2s, . . . , 3p in Figure 12.6 stand for first person singular, second person singular, . . . , third person plural, respectively. Note that some words have more than one type such as can which is both a noun and a verb, and orange which is both an adjective and a noun. A lexicon may also be organized to contain separate entries for words with more than one function by giving them separate identities, can1 and can2. Alternatively, the entries in a lexicon could be grouped and given by word category (by articles, nouns, pronouns, verbs,

Word	Type	Features
a	Determiner	{3s}
be	Verb	Trans: intransitive
boy	Noun	{3s}
can	Noun	{1s, 2s, 3s, 1p, 2p, 3p}
	Verb	Trans: intransitive
carried	Verb	Form: past, past participle
.	.	.
.	.	.
.	.	.
orange	Adjective	
	Noun	{3s}
the	Determiner	{3s, 3p}
to	Preposition	
we	Pronoun	{ 1p}
		Case: subjective
yellow	Adjective	
.	.	.
.	.	.
.	.	.

Figure 12.6 Typical entries in a lexicon.

and so on), and all words contained within the lexicon listed within the categories to which they belong.

The organization and entries of a lexicon will vary from one implementation to another, but they are usually made up of variable length data structures such as lists or records arranged in alphabetical order. The word order may also be given in terms of usage frequency so that frequently used words like a, the, and an will appear at the beginning of the list facilitating the search.

Access to the words may be facilitated by indexing, with binary searches, hashing, or combinations of these methods. A lexicon may also be partitioned to contain a base lexicon set of general, frequently used words and domain specific components of words.

Transition Networks

Transition networks are another popular method used to represent formal and natural language structures. They are based on the application of directed graphs (digraphs) and finite state automata. A transition network consists of a number of nodes and labeled arcs. The nodes represent different states in traversing a sentence, and the arcs represent rules or test conditions required to make the transition from one state to the next. A path through a transition network corresponds to a permissible sequence of word types for a given grammar. Thus, if a transition network can be successfully traversed, it will have recognized a permissible sentence structure. For example, a network used to recognize a sentence consisting of a determiner, a noun and a verb (''The child runs'') would be represented by the three-node graph as follows.

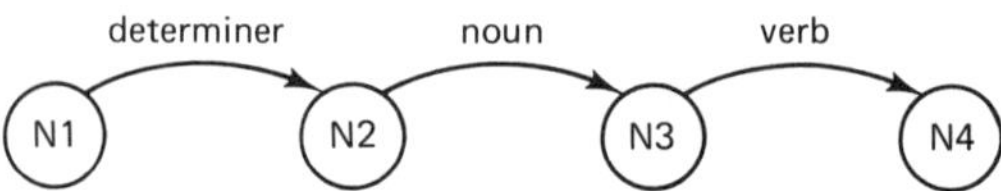

Starting at node N1, the transition from node N1 to N2 will be made if a determiner is the first input word found. If successful, state N2 is entered. The transition from N2 to N3 can then be made if a noun is found next. The final transition (from N3 to N4) will be made if the last word is a verb. If the three-word category sequence is not found, the parse fails. Clearly, this type of network is very limited since it will only recognize simple sentences of the form DET N V.

The utility of a network such as this could be increased if more than a single choice were permitted at some of the nodes. For example, if several arcs were constructed between nodes N1 and N2 where each arc represented a different noun phrase, the number of permissible sentence types would be increased substantially. Individual arcs could be a noun, a pronoun, a determiner followed by a noun, a determiner followed by an adjective followed by a noun, or some other type of noun phrase which we wish the parser to be capable of recognizing. These alternatives are depicted in Figure 12.7.

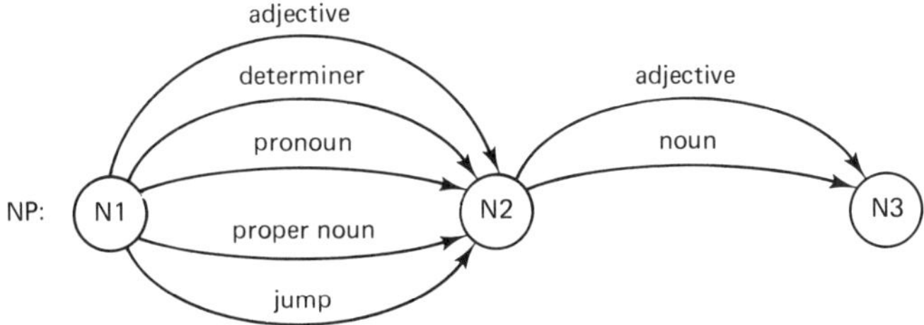

Figure 12.7 A noun phrase segment of a transition network.

To move from state N1 to N2 in this transition network, it is necessray to first find an adjective, a determiner, a pronoun, a proper noun, or none of these by "jumping" directly to N2. This network extends the possible types of sentences that can be recognized substantially over the simple network given above. For example, it will recognize noun phrases having forms such as

Big white fluffy clouds
Our bright children
A large beautiful white flower
Large green leaves
Buildings
Boston's best seafood restaurants

Top-Down versus Botton-up Parsing

Parsers may be designed to process a sentence using either a top-down or a bottom-up approach. A top-down parser begins by hypothesizing a sentence (the symbol S) and successively predicting lower level constituents until individual preterminal symbols are written. These are then replaced by the input sentence words which match the terminal categories. For example, a possible top-down parse of the sentence "Kathy jumped the horse" would be given by

S → NP VP
→ NAME VP
→ Kathy VP
→ Kathy V NP
→ Kathy jumped NP
→ Kathy jumped ART N
→ Kathy jumped the N
→ Kathy jumped the horse

A bottom-up parse, on the other hand, begins with the actual words appearing in the sentence and is, therefore, data driven. A possible bottom-up parse of the same sentence might proceed as follows.

→ Kathy jumped the horse
→ NAME jumped the horse
→ NAME V the horse
→ NAME V ART horse
→ NAME V ART N
→ NP V ART N
→ NP V NP
→ NP VP
→ S

Words in the input sentence are replaced with their syntactic categories and those in turn are replaced by constitutents of the same or smaller size until S has been rewritten or until failure occurs.

Deterministic versus Nondeterministic Parsers

Parsers may also be classified as deterministic or nondeterministic depending on the parsing strategy employed. A deterministic parser permits only one choice (arc) for each word category. Thus, each arc will have a different test condition. Consequently, if an incorrect test choice is accepted from some state, the parse will fail since the parser cannot backtrack to an alternative choice. This may occur, for example, when a word satisfies more than one category such as a noun and a verb or an adjective, noun, and verb. Clearly, in deterministic parsers, care must be taken to make correct test choices at each stage of the parsing. This can be facilitated with a look-ahead feature which checks the categories of one or more subsequent words in the input sentence before deciding in which category to place the current word. Some researchers prefer to use deterministic parsing since they feel it more closely models the way humans parse input sentences.

Nondeterministic parsers permit different arcs to be labeled with the same test. Consequently, the next test from any given state may not be uniquely determined by the state and the current input word. The parser must guess at the proper constituent and then backtrack if the guess is later proven to be wrong. This will require saving more than one potential structure during parts of the network traversal. Examples of both deterministic and nondeterministic parsers are presented in Figure 12.8.

Suppose the following sentence is given to a deterministic parser with the grammar given by the network of Figure 12.8(a): ''The strong bear the loads.'' If the parser chose to recognize strong as an adjective and bear as a noun, the parse would fail, since there is no verb following bear. A nondeterministic parser, on the other hand, would simply recover by backtracking when failure was detected and then taking another arc which accepted strong as a noun.

Example of a Simple Parser in Prolog

The reader may have noticed the close similarity between rewrite rules and Horn clauses, especially when the Horn clauses are written in the form of PROLOG

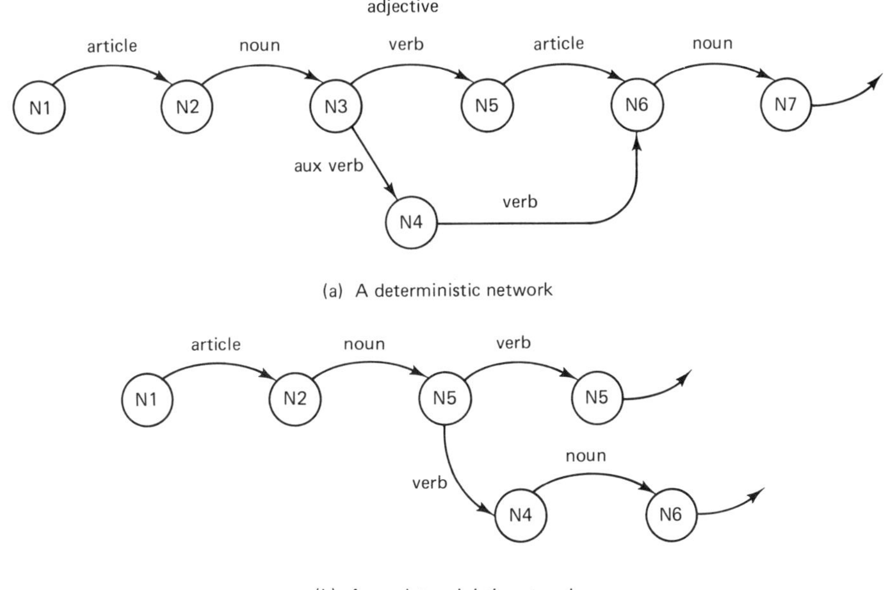

Figure 12.8 Deterministic and nondeterministic networks.

rules. This similarity makes it a straightforward task to write parsers in a language like PROLOG. For example, the grammar rule that states that S is a sentence if it is a noun phrase followed by a verb phrase (S → NP VP) may be written in PROLOG as

```
sentence(A,C) :-nounPhrase(A,B), verbPhrase(B,C)
```

The variables A, B, and C in this statement represent lists of words. The argument A is the whole list of words to be tested as a sentence, and C is the list of remaining words, if any. Similar assumptions hold for A, B, and C in the noun and verb phrase conditions respectively.

Rule definitions which rewrite the noun phrases and verb phrases must also be defined. Thus, an NP may be defined with statements such as the following:

```
nounPhrase(A,C) :=article(A,B), noun(B,C).
nounPhrase(A,B) :=noun(A,B).
```

Like the above rule, these rules state that (1) a noun phrase can be either an article which consists of a list A and remaining list B (if any) and a noun which is a list B and remaining list C or (2) a noun consisting of the list A with remaining list B (if any). Similarly, a verb phrase may be defined with rules like the following:

```
verbPhrase(A,B) := verb(A,B).
verbPhrase(A,C) := verb(A,B), nounPhrase(B,C).
verbPhrase(A,C) := verb(A,B), prepositionPhrase(B,C).
```

Definitions for the prepositional phrase as well as lexical terminals must also be given. These can include the following:

```
prepositionPhrase(A,C) := preposition(A,B), nounPhrase(B,C).

preposition([at|X],X).
article([a|X],X).
article([the|X],X).
noun([dog| X],X).
noun([cow|X],X).
noun([moon| X],X).
verb([barked|X],X).
verb([winked|X],X).
```

With this simple parser we can determine if strings of the following type are grammatically correct.

The dog barked at the cow.
The moon winked at the dog.
A cow barked at a moon.

To do so, we must enter sentence queries as lists such as the following for the PROLOG interpreter:

```
?- sentence([the,dog,barked,at,the,moon],X]).
X = [ ]
?- sentence([barked,a,moon,dog,the],X].
no
```

Since the remainder of the sentence bound to X is the empty set, it is recognized as correct. The second sentence failed since it could not instantiate with the correct constituent parts.

Of course, for a parser to be of much practical use, other constituents and a great many more words should be defined. The example illustrates the utility of using PROLOG as a basic parser.

Recursive Transition Networks

The simple networks described above are not powerful enough to recognize the variety of sentences a human language system could be expected to cope with. In fact, they fail to recognize all languages that can be generated by a context-free grammar. Other extensions are needed to accept a wider range of sentences but still avoid the necessity for large complex networks. We can achieve such extensions by labeling some arcs as a separate network state (such as an NP) and then constructing a subnetwork which recognizes the different noun phrases required. In this way, a single subnetwork for an NP can be called from several places in a sentence. Similar arcs can be labeled for other sentence constituents including VP, PP (prepositional phrases) and others. With these additions, complex sentences having embedded phrases can be parsed with relatively simple networks. This leads directly to the notion of using recursion in a network.

A recursive transition network (RTN) is a transition network which permits arc labels to refer to other networks (including the network's own name), and they in turn may refer back to the referring network rather than just permitting word categories used previously. For example, an RTN described by William Woods (1970) is illustrated in Figure 12.9 where the main network calls two subnetworks and an NP and PP network as illustrated in 12.9(b) and (c).

The top network in the figure is the top level (sentence) network, and the lower level networks are for NP and PP arc states. The arcs corresponding to these states will be traversed only if the corresponding subnetworks (b) or (c) are successfully traversed.

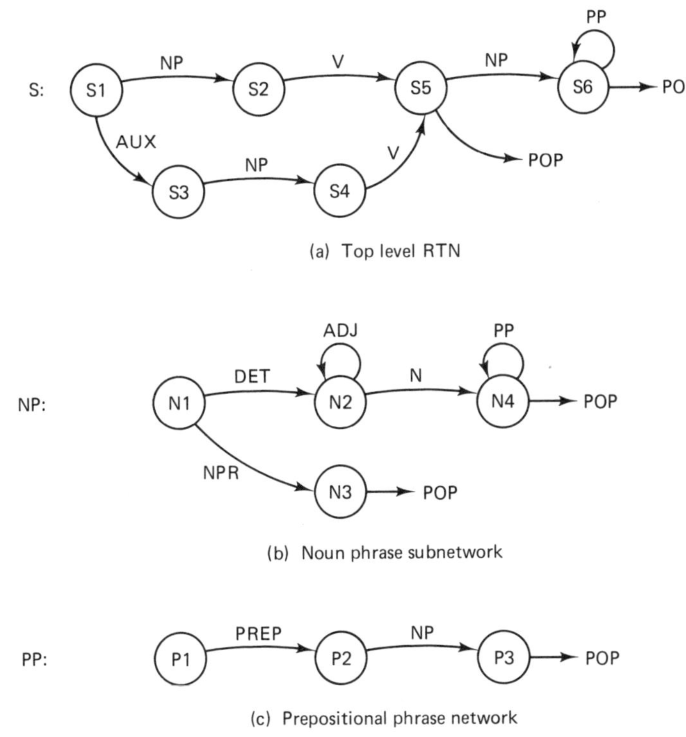

Figure 12.9 Recursive transition network.

In traversing a network, it is customary to test the arcs in a clockwise order. Thus, in the top level RTN, the NP arc will be called first. If this arc fails, the arc labeled AUX will be tested next.

During the traversal of an RTN, a record must be maintained of the word position in the input sentence and the current state or node position and return nodes to be used as return points when control has been transferred to a lower level network. This information can be maintained as a triple like POS CND RLIST where POS is the current input word position, CND is the current node, and RLIST is the list of return points. The RLIST can be maintained as a stack data structure.

In Figure 12.9, the arc named POP is used as a dummy arc to signal the successful completion of the subnetwork and a return to the node following the arc from which it was called. Some other arc types that will be useful in what follows are summarized in Table 12.1.

The CAT arc represents a test for a specific word category such as a noun or a verb. When the input word is of the specified category, the CAT test succeeds and the input pointer is advanced to the next word. The JUMP arc may be traversed without satisfying any test condition in which case the word pointer is not advanced when a JUMP arc is traversed. An arc labeled with a state, such as NP or PP, is defined as a PUSH arc. This arc initiates a call to another network with the indicated state (such as an NP or PP). When a PUSH arc is taken, a return state must be saved. This is accomplished by pushing the return pointer onto a stack. The POP arc, as noted above, is a dummy test which pops the top return node pointer that was previously pushed onto the stack. A TEST arc allows the use of an arbitrary test to determine if the arc is to be taken. For example, TEST can be used to determine if a sentence is declarative or interrogative, if one or more negatives occur, and so on. A WORD arc corresponds to a specific word test such as to, from, and at. (In some systems a list of words may apply rather than a single word.)

To see how an interpreter operates with the grammar given for the RTN of Figure 12.6, we apply it to the following sentence (the subscripted numbers give the word positions):

$$_1\text{The}_2\text{big}_3\text{tree}_4\text{shades}_5\text{the}_6\ \text{old}_7\text{house}_8\text{by}_9\text{the}_{10}\text{stream}_{11}.$$

TABLE 12.1 ARC LABELS FOR TRANSITION NETWORKS

Type of arc	Purpose of arc	Example
CAT	a test label for the current word category	V
JUMP	requires no test to succeed	jump
POP	a label for the end of a network	pop
PUSH	a label for a call to a network	NP
TEST	a label for an arbitrary test	negatives
WORD	a label for a specific word type	from

Starting with CND set to S1, POS set to 1, and RLIST set to nil, the first arc test (NP) would be completed. Since this test is for a state, the parser would PUSH the return node S2 onto RLIST, set CND to N1, and call the NP network. Trying the first test DET (a CAT test) in the NP network, a match would be found with word position 1. This would result in CND being updated to N2 and POS to position 2. The next word (big) satisfies the ADJ test causing CND to be updated to N2 again, and POS to be updated to position 3. The ADJ test is then repeated for the word tree, but it fails. Hence, the arc test for N is made next with no change made to POS and CND. This time the test succeeds resulting in updates of N4 to CND and position 4 to POS. The next test is the POP which signals a successful completion of the NP network and causes the return node (S1) to be retrieved from the RLIST stack and CND to be updated with S2. POP does not cause an advance in the word position POS.

The only possible test from S2 is for category V which succeeds on the word "shades" with resultant updates of S5 to CND and 5 to POS. At S5, the only possible test is the NP. This again invokes a call to the lower level NP network which is traversed successfully with the noun phrase "the old house." After a return to the main network, CND is set to S6 and POS is set to position 8. At this point, the lower PP network is called with CND being set to P1 and S6 pushed onto RLIST. From P1, the CAT test for PREP passes with CND being set to P2 and POS being set to 9. NP is then called with CND being set to N1 and P2 being pushed onto RLIST. As before, the NP network is traversed with the noun phrase "the stream" resulting in a POS value of 11, P3 being popped from RLIST and a return to that node. The test at P3 (POP) results in S6 being popped from RLIST and a return to the S6 node. Finally, the POP test at N6, together with the period at position 11 results in a successful traversal and acceptance of the sentence.

During a network traversal, a parse can fail if (1) the end of the input sentence (a period) has been reached when the test from the CND node value is not a terminal (POP) value or (2) if a word in the input sentence fails to satisfy any of the available arc tests from some node in the network.

The number of sentences accepted by an RTN can be extended if backtracking is permitted when a failure occurs. This requires that states having alternative transitions be remembered until the parse progresses past possible failure points. In this way, if a failure occurs at some point, the interpreter can backtrack and try alternative paths. The disadvantage with this approach is that parts of a sentence may be parsed more than one time resulting in excessive computations.

Augmented Transition Networks

The networks considered so far are not very useful for language understanding. They have only been capable of accepting or rejecting a sentence based on the grammar and syntax of the sentence. To be more useful, an interpreter must be able to build structures which will ultimately be used to create the required knowledge entities for an AI system. Furthermore, the resulting data structures should contain more information than just the syntactic information dictated by the grammar alone. Semantic information should also be included. For example, a number of sentence features can also be established and recorded, such as the subject NP, the object NP, the subject-verb number agreement, the mood (declarative or interrogative), tense, and so on. This means that additional tests must be performed to determine the possible semantics a sentence may have. Without these additional tests, much ambiguity will still be present and incorrect or meaningless sentences accepted.

We can achieve the additional capabilities required by augmenting an RTN with the ability to perform additional tests and store immediate results as a sentence is being parsed. When an RTN is given these additional features, it is called an augmented transition network or ATN.

When building a representation structure, an ATN uses a number of different registers as temporary storage to hold the different sentence constituents. Thus, one set of registers would be used for an NP network, one for a PP network, one for a V, and so on. Using the register contents, an ATN builds a partial structural description of the sentence as it moves from state to state in the network. These registers provide temporary storage which is easily modified, switched, or discarded until the final sentence structure is constructed. The registers also hold flags and other indicators used in conjunction with some arcs. When a partial structure has been stored in registers and a failure occurs, the interpreter can clear the registers, backtrack, and start a new set of tests. At the end of a successful parse, the contents of the registers are combined to form the final sentence data structure required for output.

An ATN Specification Language

A specification language developed by Woods (1970, 1986) for ATNs takes the form of an extended context-free grammar. This language is given in Figure 12.10 where the vertical bar indicates alternative choices for a construction and the * (Kleene star) signifies repeatable (zero or more) elements. All nonterminals are enclosed in angle brackets. Some of the capitalized words appearing in the language were defined earlier as arc tests and actions. The other words in uppercase correspond to functions which perform many of the tasks related to the construction of the structure using the registers.

The specification language is read the same as rewrite rules. Thus, it specifies that a transition network is composed of a list of arc sets, where each arc set is in turn a list with first element being a state name and the remaining elements being arcs which emanate from that state. An arc can be any of the forms CAT, JUMP, PUSH, TEST, WORD or POP. For example, as noted earlier, the TEST arc corresponds to an arbitrary test which determines whether the arc is to be traversed or not. Note that a sequence of actions is associated with the arc tests. These actions are executed during the arc traversals. They are used to build pieces of structures such as a tree or a list. The terminal action of any arc specifies the state to which control is passed to complete the transition.

```
<transition net> → (<arc set><arc set>*)
<arc set> → (<state><arc>*)
<arc> → (CAT <category name><test><action>*<term act>)|
        (PUSH <state><test><action>*<term act>)|
        (TST (arbitrary label><test><action>*<term act>)|
        (POP <form><test>)
<action> → (SETR <register><form>)|
           (SENDR <register><form>)|
           (LIFTR <register><form>)
<term act> → (TO <state>)|
             (JUMP <state>)
<form> → (GETR <register>)|
         @|
         (GETF <feature>)|
         (BUILDQ <fragment><register>*)|
         (LIST <form>*)|
         (APPEND <form><form>)|
         (QUOTE <arbitrary structure>)
```

Figure 12.10 A specification language for ATNs.

Among other things, an action can be any of the three function forms SETR, SENDR, and LIFTR which cause the indicated register values to be set to the value of form. Terminal actions can be either TO or JUMP where TO requires that the input sentence pointer should be advanced, and JUMP requires that the pointer remain fixed and the input word continue to be scanned. Finally, a construction form can be any of the seven alternatives in the bottom group of Figure 12.10, including the symbol @ which is a terminal symbol placeholder for form.

The function SETR causes the contents of the indicated registers to be set equal to the value of the corresponding form. This is done at the current level in the network, while SENDR causes it to be done by sending it to the next lower level of computation. LIFTR returns information to the next higher level of computation. The function GETR returns the value of the indicated register, and GETF returns the value of a specified feature for the current input word. As noted before, the value of @ is usually an input word. The function BUILDQ takes lists from the indicated registers (which represent fragments of a parse tree with marked nodes) and builds the sentence structures.

An ATN network similar to the RTN illustrated in Figure 12.9 is presented in Figure 12.11. Note that the arcs in this network have some of the tests described above. These tests will have the basic forms given in Figure 12.10, together with the indicated actions. The actions include building the final sentence structure which may contain more features than those considered thus far, as well as certain semantic features.

Using the specification language, we can represent this particular network with the constituent abbreviations and functions described above in the form of a LISP program. For example, a partial description of the network is depicted in

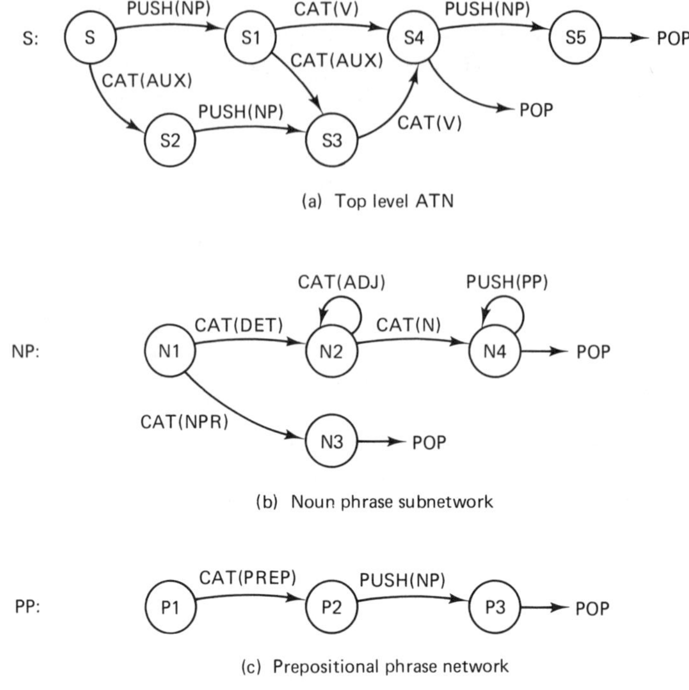

(a) Top level ATN

(b) Noun phrase subnetwork

(c) Prepositional phrase network

Figure 12.11 Augmented transition network.

Figure 12.12 (where T in the expressions is the equivalent of non-nil or true in LISP).

From the language of Figure 12.12, it can be seen that the ATN begins building a sentence representation in which the first constituent is either type declarative (DCL) or type interrogative (Q for question), depending on whether the first successful test is an NP or AUX, respectively. The next constituent is the subject (SUBJ) NP, and the third is either an auxiliary verb (AUX) or nil. The fourth constituent is a VP. An ATN is traversed much the same as the RTN described above.

An example of its operation will help to demonstrate how the structure is built during a parse of the sentence

"The big dog likes the small boy."

1. Starting with state S, PUSH down a level to the NP network. If an NP is found (T for true), execute lines 2, 3, and 4.

2. In the lower level NP network, the noun phrase "the big dog" is found with successive CAT tests for determiner, adjective, and noun. During these tests, NP registers are set to indicate the word constituents. When the terminal node

```
 1. (S/ (PUSH NP/ T
 2.        (SETR SUBJ @)
 3.        (SETR TYPE (QUOTE DCL))
 4.        (TO S1)
 5.     (CAT AUX T
 6.        (SETR AUX @)
 7.        (SETR TYPE (QUOTE Q))
 8.        (TO S2)))
 9. (S1 (CAT V T
10.        (SETR AUX NIL)
11.        (SETR V @)
12.        (TO S4)))
13.     (CAT AUX T
14.        (SETR AUX @)
15.        (TO S3)))
16. (S2 (PUSH NP/ T
17.        (SETR SUBJ @)
18.        (TO S3)))
19. (S3 (CAT V T
20.        (SETR V @)
21.        (TO S4)))
22. (S4 (POP BUILDQ (S+++(VP+)) TYPE SUBJ AUX V) T)
23.     (PUSH NP/ T
24.        (SETR VP BUILDQ (VP (V+) @) V))
25.        (TO S5)))
26. (S5 (POP (BUILDQ (S++++) TYPE SUBJ AUX VP) T)
27.     (PUSH PP/ T
28.        (SETR VP (APPEND (GETR VP) (LIST @)))
29.        (TO S5)))
    . . .
    . . .
```

Figure 12.12 An ATN specification language.

(N4) is tested and the PP test subsequently fails, POP is executed and a return of control is made to statement 2.

3. The register SUBJ is set to the value of @ which is the list structure (NP (dog (big) DEF)) returned from the NP registers. DEF signifies that the determiner is definite.

4. In line 3, register TYPE is set to DCL (for declarative).

5. Control is transferred to S1 with the statement TO in line 4 and the input pointer is moved past the noun phrase to the verb "likes."

6. If an auxiliary verb had been found at the beginning of the sentence instead of an NP, control would have been passed to line 5 where statements 5, 7, and 8 would have been executed. This would have resulted in registers AUX and TYPE being set to the values @ and Q respectively.

7. At S1, a category test is made for a V. Since this succeeds (is T), statements 11, 12, and 13 are executed. This results in register AUX being set to nil, and register V being set to the contents of @, to give (V likes). Control is then passed to S4 and the input pointer is moved to the word "the."

8. If the test for V had failed, and an auxiliary verb had been found, statements 14 and 15 would have been executed.

9. Since S4 is a terminal node, a sentence structure can be built there. This will be the case if the end of the sentence has been reached. If so, the BUILDQ function creates a list structure with first element S, followed by the values of the three registers TYPE, SUBJ, AUX, corresponding to the three plus (+) signs. These are then followed with VP and the contents of the V register. For example, with an input sentence of,

The boy can whistle.

the structure (S DCL (NP (boy) DEF) (AUX can) (VP whistle)) would be constructed from the four registers TYPE, SUBJ, AUX, and V.

10. Because more input words remain, the BUILDQ in line 22 is not executed, and control drops to the next line where a push is made to the lower NP network. As before, the NP succeeds with the structure (NP (boy (small) DEF)) being returned as the value of @. Register VP is then set to the list returned by BUILDQ (line 24) which consists of VP followed by the verb phrase and control is passed to S5.

11. Since S5 is a terminal node and the end of the input sentence has been reached, BUILDQ will build the final sentence structure from the TYPE, SUBJ, AUX, and VP register contents. The final structure constructed is

```
(S DCL (NP (dog (big) DEF))
       (VP (V likes)(NP (boy (small) DEF))))
```

The use of recursion, arc tests, and a variety of arc and node combinations give the ATNs the power of a Turing Machine. This means that an ATN can recognize any language that a general purpose computer can recognize. This versatility also makes it possible to build deep sentence structures rather than just structures with surface features only. (Recall that surface features relate to the form of words, phrases, and sentences, whereas deep features relate to the content or meaning of these elements). The ability to build deep structures requires that other appropriate tests be included to check pronoun references, tense, number agreement, and other features.

Because of their power and versatility, ATNs have become popular as a model for general purpose parsers. They have been used successfully in a number of natural language systems as well as front ends for databases and expert systems.

12.5 SEMANTIC ANALYSIS AND REPRESENTATION STRUCTURES

We have now seen how the structure of a complex sentence can be determined and how a representation of that structure can be constructed using different types of parsers. In particular, it should now be clear how an ATN can be used to build structures for different grammars, like those described in Section 12.3. But, we have not yet explained how the final semantic knowledge structures are created to satisfy the requirements of a knowledge base used to represent some particular world model. Experience has shown the semantic interpretation to be the most difficult stage in the transformation process.

As an example of some of the difficulties encountered in extracting the full intended meaning of some utterances, consider the following situation.

> It turned into a black day. In his haste to catch the flight, he backed over Tom's bicycle. He should never have left it there. It was damaged beyond repair. That caused the tailpipe to break. It would be impossible to make it now. . . . It was all because of that late movie. He would be heartbroken when he found out about it.

Although a car was never explicitly mentioned, it must be assumed that a car was the object which was backed over Tom's bicycle. A program must be able to infer this. The "black day" metaphor also requires some inference. Days are not usually referred to by color. And sorting out the pronoun references can also be an onerous task for a program. Of the seven uses of it, two refer to the bicycle, two to the flight, two refer to the situation in general, and one to the status of the day. There are also four uses of he referring to two different people and a that which refers to the accident in general. The placement of the pronouns is almost at random making it difficult to give any rule of association. Words that point back or refer to people, places, objects, events, times, and so on that occurred before, are called anaphors. Their interpretation may require the use of heuristics, syntactic and semantic constraints, inference, and other forms of object analysis within the discourse content.

This example should demonstrate again that language cannot be separated from intelligence and reasoning. To fully understand the above situation requires that a program be able to reason about people's goals, beliefs, motives, and facts about the world in general.

The semantic structures constructed from utterances such as the above, must account for all aspects of meaning in what is known as the domain, context, and the task. The *domain* refers to the knowledge that is part of the world model the system knows about. This includes object descriptions, relationships, and other relevant concepts. The *context* relates to previous expressions, the setting and time of the utterances, and the beliefs, desires, and intentions of the speakers. A *task* is part of the service the system offers, such as retrieving information from a data base, providing expert advice, or performing a language translation. The domain, context, and task are what we have loosely referred to before as semantics, pragmatics, and world knowledge.

Semantic interpretations require that utterances be transformed into coherent expressions in the form of FOPL clauses, associative networks, frames, or script-like structures that can be manipulated by the understanding program. There are a number of different approaches to the transformation problem. The approach we have been following up to this point is one in which the transformation is made in stages. In the first stage, a syntactic analysis is performed and a tree-like structure is produced using a parser. This stage is followed by use of a semantic analyzer to produce either an intermediate or final semantic structure.

Another approach is to transform the sentences directly into the target structures with little syntactical analysis. Such approaches typically depend on the use of constraints given by semantic grammars or place strong reliance on the use of key words to extract meaning.

Between these two extremes, are approaches which perform syntactic and semantic analyses concurrently, using semantic information to guide the parse, and the structure learned through the syntactical analysis is used to help determine meaning.

Another dimension related to semantic interpretation is the approach taken in extracting the meaning of an expression, (1) whether it can or should be derived by paraphrasing input utterances and transforming them into structures containing a few generic terms or (2) whether meanings are best derived by composing the meanings of clauses and larger units from the meanings of their constituent parts. These two methods of approach are closely tied to the form of the target semantic structures.

The first of these approaches we call unit or *lexical semantics* to emphasize the role played by the special primitive words used to represent the meanings of all expressions. In this approach the meaning is constructed through a restatement of the expression in terms of linked primitive generic words such as those used in Shank's conceptual dependency theory (Chapter 7).

The second approach is called *compositonal semantics* since the meaning of an expression is derived from the meanings ascribed to the constituent parts. The structures created through this approach are usually characterized as logical formulae in some calculus such as FOPL or an extended FOPL.

Lexical Semantics Approaches

The semantic grammars described in Section 12.2 are one form of approach based on the use of lexical semantics. With this approach, input sentences are transformed through the use of domain dependent semantic rewrite rules which create the target knowledge structures. A second example of an informal lexical-semantic approach is one which uses conceptual dependency theory. Conceptual dependency structures provide a form of linked knowledge that can be used in larger structures such as scenes and scripts.

The construction of conceptual dependency structures is accomplished without performing any direct syntactic analysis. Making the jump between utterances and

ACTOR: (a PP with animate attributes)
OBJECT: (a PP)
ACTION: (one of the primitive acts with tense)
DIRECTION: (from-to direction of the action)
INSTRUMENT: (object with which the act is performed)
LOCATION: (event location information)
TIME: (time of the event information)

Figure 12.13 Conceptual dependency structure.

these structures requires that more information be contained in the lexicon. The lexicon entries must include word sense and other information which relate the words to a number of primitive semantic categories as well as some syntactic information.

Recall from Chapter 7 that conceptualizations are either events or object states. Event structures include objects and their attributes, picture producers (PPs) or actors, actions, direction of action (to or from) and sometimes instruments that participate in the actions, and the location and time of the event. These items are collected together in a slot-filler structure as depicted in Figure 12.13.

Verbs in the input string are a dominant factor in building conceptual dependency structures because they denote the event action or state. Consequently, lexicon entries for verbs will be more extensive than other entry types. They will contain all possible senses, tense, and other information. Each verb maps to one of the primitive actions: ATRANS, ATTEND, CONC, EXPEL, GRASP, INGEST, MBUILD, MOVE, MTRANS, PROPEL, PTRANS, and SPEAK. Each primitive action will also have an associated tense: past, present, future, conditional, continuous, interrogative, end, negation, start, and timeless.

The basic process followed in building conceptual dependency structures is simply the three steps listed below.

1. Obtain the next lexical item (a word or phrase).
2. Access the lexical entry for the item and obtain the associated tests and actions.
3. Perform the specified actions given with the entry.

Three types of tests are performed in Step 2.

1. If a certain lexical entry is found, the indicated action is performed. This corresponds to true (non-nil in LISP).
2. Specific word orderings are checked as the structure is being built and actions initiated as a result of the orderings. For example, if a PP follows the last word parsed, action is initiated to fill the object slot.
3. Checks are made for specific words or phrases and, if found, specified actions taken. For example, if an intransitive verb such as listen is found, an action

would be initiated to look for associated words which complete the phrase beginning with to or for.

For the above tests, there are four types of actions taken.

1. Adding additional structure to a partially built conceptual dependency.
2. Filling a slot with a substructure.
3. Activating another action.
4. Deactivating an action.

These actions build up the conceptual dependency structure as the input string is parsed. For example, the action taken for a verb like drank would be to build a substructure for the primitive action INGEST with unfilled slots for ACTOR, OBJECT, and TENSE.

```
(INGEST (ACTOR nil)
        (OBJECT nil)
        (TENSE past))
```

Subsequent words in the input string would initiate actions to add to this structure and fill in the empty ACTOR and OBJECT slots. Thus, a simple sentence like

The boy drank a soda

would be transformed through a series of test and action steps to produce a structure such as the following.

```
(INGEST (ACTOR (PP (NAME boy) (CLASS PHYS-OBJ)
                   (TYPE ANIMATE) (REF DEF)))
        (OBJECT (PP (NAME soda) (CLASS PHYS-OBJ)
                    (TYPE INANIMATE) (REF INDEF)))
        (TENSE  PAST))
```

Compositional Semantics Approaches

In the compositional semantics approach, the meaning of an expression is derived from the meanings of the parts of the expression. The target knowledge structures constructed in this approach are typically logic expressions such as the formulas of FOPL. The LUNAR system developed by Woods (1978) uses this approach. The input strings are first parsed using an ATN from which a syntactic tree is output. This becomes the input to a semantic interpreter which interprets the meaning of the syntactic tree and creates the semantic representations.

As an example, suppose the following declaration is submitted to LUNAR.

Sample24 contains silicon

This would be parsed, and the following tree structure would be output from the ATN:

```
(S DCL
   (NP  (N (Sample24)))
   (AUX (TENSE (PRESENT)))
   (VP  (V (contain))
        (NP (N (silicon))))
```

Using this structure, the semantic interpreter would produce the predicate clause

```
(CONTAIN sample24 silicon)
```

which has the FOPL meaning you would expect.

The interpreter used in LUNAR is driven by semantic pattern → action interpretation rules. The rule that builds the CONTAIN predicate is selected whenever the input tree has a verb of the form have or contain and a sample as the subject and either chemical element, isotope, or oxide as an object. The action of the rule states that such a sentence is to be interpreted as an instance of the schema (CONTAIN *x y*) with *x* and *y* being replaced by the ATN's interpretation of subject noun phrase and object respectively.

LUNAR is also capable of performing quantification of variables in expressions. The quantifiers are an elaboration of those used in FOPL. They include the standard existential and universal quantifiers "for every" and "for some," as well as others such as "for the," "exactly," "the single," "more than," "at least," and so on. For example, an expression with universal quantification would appear as

```
(For Every X/(SEQ samples):CONTAIN X Overall silicon)
```

12.6 NATURAL LANGUAGE GENERATION

It is sometimes claimed that language generation is the exact inverse of language understanding. While it is true the two processes have many differences, it is an over simplification to claim that they are exact opposites.

The generation of natural language is more difficult than understanding it, since a system must not only decide what to say, but how the utterances should be stated. A generation system must decide which form is better (active or passive), which words and structures best express the intent, and when to say what. To produce expressions that are natural and close to humans requires more than rules of syntax, semantics, and discourse. In general, it requires that a coherent plan be developed to carry out multiple goals. A great deal of sophistication goes into the simplest types of utterances when they are intended to convey different shades of meanings and emotions. A participant in a dialog must reason about a hearer's understanding and his or her knowledge and goals. During the dialog, the system must maintain proper focus and formulate expressions that either query, explain, direct, lead or just follow the conversation as appropriate.

The study of language generation falls naturally into three areas: (1) the determination of content, (2) formulating and developing a text utterance plan, and (3) achieving a realization of the desired utterances.

Content determination is concerned with what details to include in an explanation, a request, a question or argument in order to convey the meanings set forth by the goals of the speaker. This means the speaker must know what the hearer already knows, what the hearer needs to know, and what the hearer wants to know. These topics are related to the domain, task, and discourse context described above. *Text planning* is the process of organizing the content to be communicated so as to best achieve the goals of the speaker. *Realization* is the process of mapping the organized content to actual text. This requires that specific words and phrases be chosen and formulated into a syntactic structure.

Until about 1980, not much work had been done beyond single sentence generation. Understanding and generation was performed with a single piece of isolated text without much regard given to context and consideration of the hearer. Following this early work, a few comprehensive systems were developed. To complete this section, we describe the basic ideas behind two of these systems. They take different approaches to those taken by the lexical and compositional semantics understanding described in the previous section.

Language Planning and Generation with KAMP

KAMP is a knowledge and modalities planner developed for the generation of natural language text. Developed by Douglas Appelt (1985), KAMP simulates the behavior of an expert robot named Rob (a terminal) assisting John (a person) in the disassembly and repair of air compressors.

KAMP uses a planner and a data base of knowledge in (modal) logical form. The knowledge includes domain knowledge, world knowledge, linguistic knowledge, and knowledge about the hearer. A description of actions and action summaries are available to the planner. Given a goal, the planner uses heuristics to build and refine a plan in the form of a procedural network. Other procedures act as critics of the plans and help to refine them. If a plan is completed, a deduction system is used to prove that the sequence of actions do, in fact, achieve the goal. If the plan fails, the planner must do further searching for a sequence of actions that will work. A completed plan states the knowledge and intentions of the agent, the robot

Rob. This is the first step in producing the output text. The process can be summarized as follows.

Suppose KAMP has determined the immediate goal to be the removal of the compressor pump from the platform.

True(˜Attached(pump platform))

KAMP first formulates and refines a plan that John adopt Rob's plan to remove the pump from the platform. The first part of Rob's plan suggests a request for John to remove the pump leading to the expression

INTENDS(john, REMOVE(pump platform))

After axioms are used to prove that actions in the initial summary plan are successful, the request is expanded to include details for the pump removal. Rob decides that John will know he is near the platform and that he knows where the toolbox is located, but that he does not know what tool to use. Rob, therefore, determines that John will not need to be told about the platform, but that he must be informed, with an imperative statement, to remove the pump with a wrench in the toolbox.

```
INTENDS(john, REMOVE(pump platform))
LOCATION(john) = LOCATION(platform)

DO(john, REMOVE(pump platform))

DO(rob, REQUEST(john, REMOVE(pump platform)))
DO(rob, COMMAND(john, REMOVE(pump platform)))

DO(rob, INFORM(john (TOOL(wrench))))
DO(rob, INFORM(john LOCATION (wrench) =
                              LOCATION(tool-box)))
```

The next step is for Rob to plan speech acts to realize the request. This requires linguistic knowledge of the structure to use for an imperative request, in this case, that the sentence should have the form V NP (PP)* (recall that * stands for optional repetition). Words to complete the output string are then selected and ordered accordingly.

```
DO(rob REQUEST(john, REMOVE(pump platform)))
DO(rob COMMAND(john, REMOVE(pump platform)))
DO(rob INFORM(john, TOOL(wrench)))
DO(rob INFORM(john, LOCATION(wrench) =
                              LOCATION(tool-box)))
```

This leads to the generation of a sentence with the following tree structure.

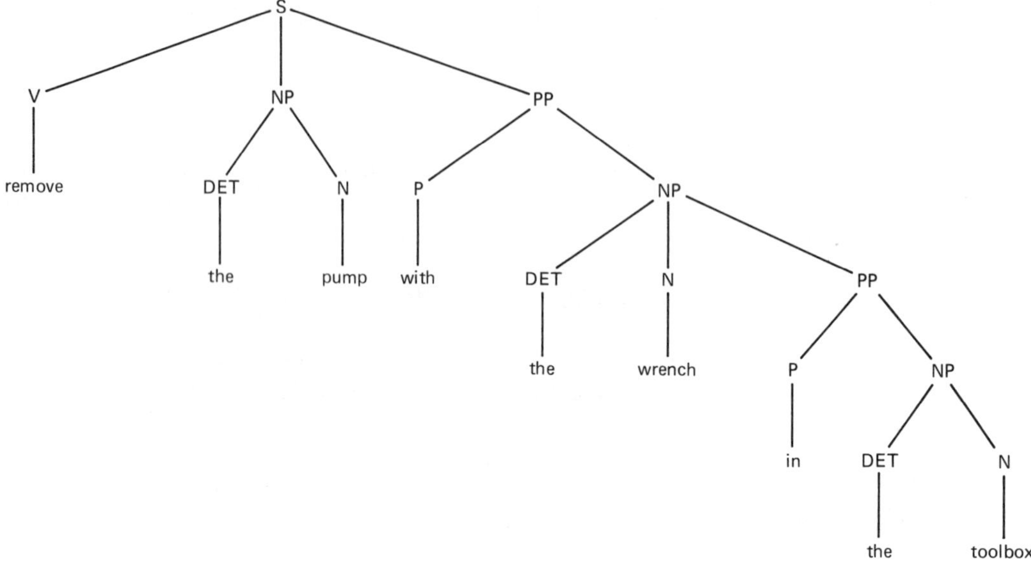

The overall process of planning and formulating the final sentence "Remove the pump with the wrench in the toolbox" is very involved and detailed. It requires planning and plan verification for content, selecting the proper structures, selecting senses, mood, tense, the actual words, and a final ordering. All of the steps must be constrained toward the realization of the (possibly multiple) goals set forth. It is truly amazing we accomplish such acts with so little effort.

Generation from Conceptual Dependency Structures

Niel Goldman (Schank et al., 1973) developed a generation component called BABEL which was used as part of several language understanding systems built by Schank and his students (SAM, MARGIE, QUALM, and so on). This component worked in conjunction with an inference component to determine responses to questions about short news and other stories.

Given the general content or primitive event for the response, BABEL selects and builds an appropriate conceptual dependency structure which includes the intended word senses. A modified ATN is then used to generate the actual word string for output.

To determine the proper word sense, BABEL uses a discrimination net. For example, suppose the system is told a story about Joe going into a fast-food restaurant, ordering a sandwich and a soft drink in a can, paying, eating, and then leaving. After the understanding part of the system builds the conceptual dependency and script structures for the story, questions about the events could be posed. If asked what Joe had in the restaurant, BABEL would first need to determine the conceptual

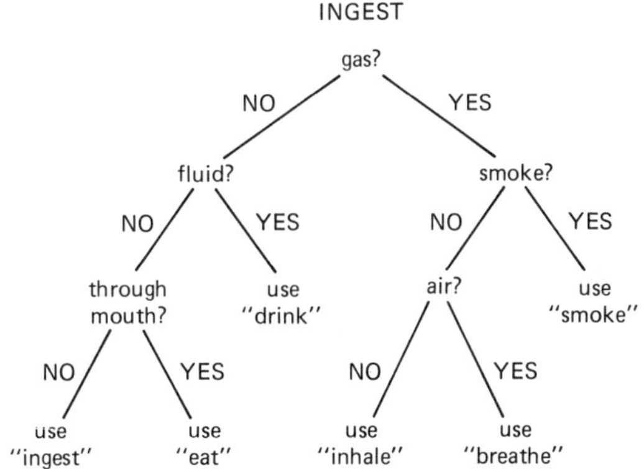

Figure 12.14 Discrimination net for INGEST.

category of the question in order to select the proper conceptual dependency pattern to build. The verb in the query determines the appropriate primitive categories of eat and drink as being INGEST. To determine the correct sense of INGEST as eat and drink a discrimination net like that depicted in Figure 12.14 would be used. A traversal of the discrimination net leads to eat and drink, using the relation from have and sandwich as being taken through the mouth and soft drink as fluid.

Once a conceptual dependency framework has been selected, the appropriate words must be chosen and the slots filled. Functions are used to operate on the net to complete it syntactically to obtain the correct tense, mood, form, and voice. When completed, a modified ATN is then used to transform the conceptual dependency structure into a surface sentence structure for output.

The final conceptual dependency structure passed to the ATN would appear as follows.

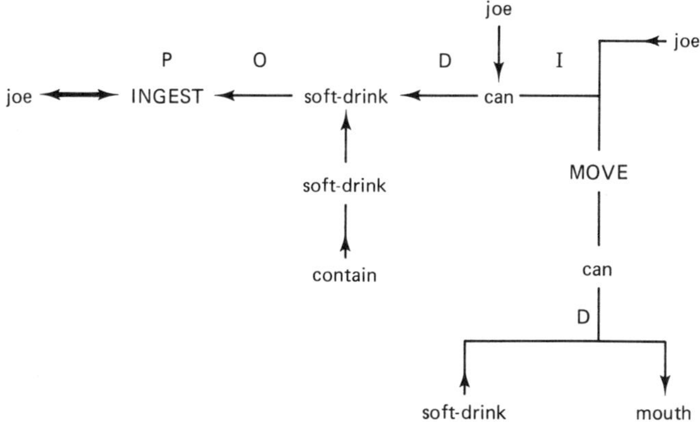

An ATN used for text generation differs from one used for analysis. In particular, the registers and arcs must be different. The value of the register contents (denoted as @ in the previous section) corresponds to a node or arc in the conceptual dependency (or other type) network rather than the next word in the input sentence. Registers will be present to hold tense, voice, and the like. For example, a register named FORM might be set to past and a register VOICE set to active when generating an active sentence like "Joe bought candy." Following an arc such as a CAT/V arc means there must be a word in the lexicon corresponding to the node in the conceptual dependency. The tense of the word then follows from the FORM register contents.

12.7 NATURAL LANGUAGE SYSTEMS

In this section, we briefly describe a few of the more successful natural language understanding systems. They include LUNAR, LIFER, and SHRDLU.

The LUNAR System

The LUNAR system was designed as a language interface to give geologists direct access to a data base containing information on lunar rock and soil compositions obtained during the NASA Apollo-11 moon landing mission. The design objective was to build a system that could respond to natural queries received from geologists such as

What is the average concentration of aluminum in high-alkali rocks?
What is the average of the basalt?
In which samples has apatite been identified?

LUNAR has three main components:

1. A general purpose grammar and an ATN parser capable of handling a large subset of English. This component produces a syntactic parse tree of the input sentence.
2. A rule-driven semantic interpreter which transforms the syntactic representation into a logical form suitable for querying the data base. The rules have the general form of pattern → action as described in Section 12.5. The rules produce disposable programs to carry out different tasks such as answering a query.
3. A data base retrieval and inference component which is used to determine answers to queries and to make changes to the data base.

The system has a dictionary of some 3500 words, an English grammar and two data bases. One data base contains a table of chemical analyses of about 13,000 entries, and the other contains 10,000 indexed document topics. LUNAR uses a meaning representation language which is an extended form of FOPL. The language uses (1) designators which name objects or classes of objects like nouns, variables, and classes with range quantifiers, (2) propositions that can be true or false, that are connected with logical operators and, or, not, and quantification identifiers, and (3) commands which carry out specific actions (like TEST which tests the truth value of propositions against given arguments (TEST (CONTAIN sample24 silicon))).

Although never fully implemented, the LUNAR project was considered an operational success since it related to a real world problem in need of a solution. It failed to parse or find the correct semantic interpretation on only about 10% of the questions presented to it.

The LIFER System

LIFER (Language Interface Facility with Ellipsis and Recursion) was described briefly in Section 12.2 under semantic grammars. It was developed by Gary Hendrix (1978) and his associates to be used as a development aid and run-time language interface to other systems such as a data base management system. Among its special features are spelling corrections, processing of elliptical inputs, and the ability of the run-time user to extend the language through the use of paraphrase.

LIFER consists of two major components, a set of interactive functions for language specifications and a parser. The specification functions are used to define an application language as a subset of English that is capable of interacting with existing software. Given the language specification, the parser interprets the language inputs and translates them into appropriate structures that interact with the application software.

In using a semantic grammar, LIFER systems incorporate much semantic information within the syntax. Rather than using categories like NP, VP, N, and V, LIFER uses semantic categories like <SHIP-NAME> and <ATTRIBUTE> which match ship names or attributes. In place of syntactic patterns like NP VP, semantic patterns like What is the <ATTRIBUTE> of <SHIP>? are used. For each such pattern, the language definer supplies an expression with which to compute the interpretations of instances of the pattern. For example, if LIFER were used as the front end for a database query system, the interpretation would be for a database retrieval command.

LIFER has proven to be effective as a front end for a number of systems. The main disadvantage, as noted earlier, is the potentially large number of patterns that may be required for a system which requires many, diverse patterns.

The SHRDLU System

SHRDLU was developed by Terry Winograd as part of his doctoral work at M.I.T. (1972, 1986). The system simulates a simple robot arm that manipulates blocks on a table. During a dialog which is interactive, the system can be asked to manipulate the block objects and build stacks or put things into a box. It can be questioned about the configuration of things on the table, about events that have transpired during the dialog, and even about its reasoning. It can also be told facts which are added to its knowledge base for later reasoning.

The unique aspect of the system is that the meanings of words and phrases are encoded into procedures that are activated by input sentences. Furthermore, the syntactic and semantic analysis, as well as the reasoning process are more closely integrated.

The system can be roughly divided into four component domains: (1) a syntactic parser which is governed by a large English (systemic type) grammar, (2) a semantic component of programs that interpret the meanings of words and structures, (3) a cognitive deduction component used to examine consequences of facts, carry out commands, and find answers, and (4) an English response generation component. In addition, there is a knowledge base containing blocks world knowledge, and a model of its own reasoning process, used to explain its actions.

Knowledge is represented with FOPL-like statements which give the state of the world at any particular time and procedures for changing and reasoning about the state. For example, the expressions

```
(IS b1 block)
(IS b2 pyramid)
(AT b1 (LOCATION 120 120 0))
(SUPPORT b1 b2)
(CLEARTOP b2)
(MANIPULATE b1)
(IS blue color)
```

contain facts describing that b1 is a block, b2 is a pyramid, and b1 supports b2. There are also procedural expressions to perform different tasks such as clear the top or manipulate an object. The CLEARTOP expression is essentially a procedure that first checks to see if the object X supports an object Y. If so, it goes to GET-RID-OF Y and checks again. Integrating the parts of the understanding process with procedural knowledge has resulted in an efficient and effective understanding system. Of course, the domain of SHRDLU is very limited and closed, greatly simplifying the problem.

12.8 SUMMARY

Understanding and generating human language is a difficult problem. It requires a knowledge of grammar and language, of syntax and semantics, of what people know and believe, their goals, the contextual setting, pragmatics, and world knowledge.

We began this chapter with an overview of topics in linguistics, including sentence types, word functions, and the parts of speech. The different forms of knowledge used in natural language understanding were then presented: phonological, morphological, syntactic, semantic, pragmatic, and world. Three general approaches have been followed in developing natural language systems: keyword and pattern matching, syntactic and semantic directed analysis, and matching real world scenarios. Most of the material in this chapter followed the syntactic and semantic directed approach.

Grammars were formally introduced, and the Chomsky hierarchy was presented. This was followed with a description of structural representations for sentences, the phrase marker. Four additional extended grammars were briefly described. One was the transformational grammars, an extension of generative grammars. Transformational grammars include tree manipulation rules that permit the construction of deeper semantic structures than the generative grammars. Case, semantic, and systemic grammars were given as examples of grammars that are also more semantic oriented than the generative grammars.

Lexicons were described, and the role they play in NL systems given. Basic parsing techniques were examined. We looked at simple transition networks, recursive transition networks, and the versatile ATN. The ATN includes tests and actions as part of the arc components and special registers to help in building syntactic structures. With an ATN, extensive semantic analysis is even possible. We defined top-down, bottom-up, deterministic, and nondeterministic parsing methods, and an example of a simple PROLOG parser was also discussed.

We next looked at the semantic interpretation process and discussed two broad approaches, namely the lexical and compositional semantic approaches. These approaches are also identified with the type of target knowledge structures generated. In the compositional semantics approach, logical forms were generated, whereas in the lexical semantics approach, conceptual dependency or similar network structures are created.

Language generation is approximately the opposite of the understanding analysis process, although more difficult. Not only must a system decide what to say but how to say it. Generation falls naturally into three areas, content determination, text planning, and text realization. Two general approaches were presented. They are like the inverses of the lexical and compositional semantic analysis processes. The KAMP system uses an elaborate planning process to determine what, when, and how to state some concepts. The system simulates a robot giving advice to a human helper in the repair of air compressors. At the other extreme, the BABEL system generates output text from conceptual dependency and script structures.

We concluded the chapter with a look at three systems of somewhat disparate architectures: the LUNAR, LIFER, and SHRDLU systems. These systems typify the state-of-the-art in natural language processing systems.

EXERCISES

12.1. Derive a parse tree for the sentence "Bill loves the frog," where the following rewrite rules are used.

S → NP VP
NP → N
NP → DET N
VP → V NP

DET → the
V → loves
N → bill | frog

12.2. Develop a parse tree for the sentence "Jack slept on the table" using the following rules.

S → NP VP
NP → N
NP → DET N
VP → V PP
PP → PREP NP
N → jack | table
V → slept
DET → the
PREP → on

12.3. Give an example of each of the four types 0, 1, 2, and 3 for Chomsky's hierarchy of grammers.

12.4. Modify the grammer of Problem 12.1 to allow the NP (noun phrase) to have zero to many adjectives.

12.5. Explain the main differences between the following three grammars and describe the principal features that could be used to develop specifications for a syntactical recognition program. Consult additional references for more details regarding each grammar.
Chomsky's Transformational Grammar
Fillmore's Case Grammar
Systemic Grammars

12.6. Draw an ATN to implement the grammer of Problem 12.1.

12.7. Given the following parse tree, write down the corresponding context free grammer.

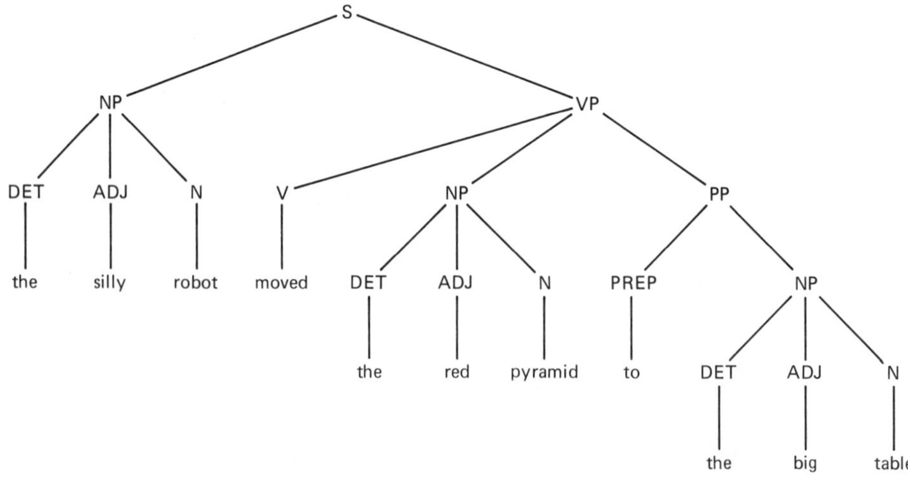

12.8. Create a LISP data structure to model a simple lexicon similar to the one depicted in Figure 12.6.

12.9. Write a LISP match program which checks an input sentence for matching words in the lexicon of the previous problem.

12.10. Derive an ATN for the parse tree of Problem 12.7.

12.11. Derive an ATN (graph) to implement the parse tree of Problem 12.1.

12.12. Determine if the following sentences will be accepted by the grammar of Problem 12.6.
(a) The green green grass of the home
(b) The red car drove in the fast lane.

12.13. Write PROLOG rules to implement the grammar used to derive the parse tree of Problem 12.7. Omit rules for the individual word categories (like noun ([ball | X],X)). Generate a syntax tree using one output parameter.

12.14. Write a PROLOG program that will take grammar rules in the following format:

$$NT \rightarrow (NT \mid T)^*$$

where NT is any nonterminal, T is any terminal, and Kleene star (*) signifies any number of repetitions, and generate the corresponding top-down parser; that is,

```
sentence → noun_phrase, verb_phrase
determiner → [the]
```

will generate the following:

```
sentence(I,O) :- noun_phrase(I,R), verb_phrase(R,O).
determiner([the|X],X) :-!.
```

12.15. Modify the program in Problem 12.12 to accept extra arguments used to return meaningful knowledge structures.

```
sentence(sentence(NP,VP)) → noun_phrase(NP), verb_phrase (VP).
```

12.16. Write a LISP program which uses property lists to create the recursive transition network depicted in Figure 12.9. Each node should be given a name such as S1, N1, and P1 and associated with a list of arc and node pairs emanating from the node.

12.17. Write a recursive program in LISP which tests input sentences for the RTN developed in the previous problem. The program should return *t* if the sentence is acceptable, and nil if not.

12.18. Modify the program of Problem 12.15 to accept sentences of the type depicted in Figure 12.12

12.19. Write an ATN type of program as depicted in Figure 12.12 which builds structures like those of Figure 12.13.

12.20. Describe in detail the differences between language understanding and language generation. Explain the problems in developing a program which is capable of carrying on a dialog with a group of people.

12.21. Give the processing steps required and corresponding data structures needed for a robot named Rob to formulate instructions for a helper named John to complete a university course add-drop request form.

12.22. Give the conceptual dependency graph for the sentence ''Mary drove her car to school'' and describe the steps required for a program to transform the sentence to an internal conceptual dependency structure.

13

Pattern Recognition

One of the most basic and essential characteristics of living things is the ability to recognize and identify objects. Certainly all higher animals depend on this ability for their very survival. Without it they would be unable to function even in a static, unchanging environment.

In this chapter we consider the process of computer pattern recognition, a process whereby computer programs are used to recognize various forms of input stimuli such as visual or acoustic (speech) patterns. This material will help to round out the topic of natural language understanding when speech, rather than text, is the language source. It will also serve as an introduction to the following chapter where we take up the general problem of computer vision.

Although some researchers feel that pattern recognition should no longer be considered a part of AI, we believe many topics from pattern recognition are essential to an understanding and appreciation of important concepts related to natural language understanding, computer vision, and machine learning. Consequently, we have included in this chapter a selected number of those topics believed to be important.

13.1 INTRODUCTION

Recognition is the process of establishing a close match between some new stimulus and previously stored stimulus patterns. This process is being performed continually throughout the lives of all living things. In higher animals this ability is manifested in many forms at both the conscious and unconscious levels, for both abstract as well as physical objects. Through visual sensing and recognition, we identify many special objects, such as home, office, school, restaurants, faces of people, handwriting, and printed words. Through aural sensing and recognition, we identify familiar voices, songs and pieces of music, and bird and other animal sounds. Through touch, we identify physical objects such as pens, cups, automobile controls, and food items. And through our other senses we identify foods, fresh air, toxic substances and much else.

At more abstract levels of cognition, we recognize or identify such things as ideas (electromagnetic radiation phenomena, model of the atom, world peace), concepts (beauty, generosity, complexity), procedures (game playing, making a bank deposit), plans, old arguments, metaphors, and so on.

Our pervasive use of and dependence on our ability to recognize patterns has motivated much research toward the discovery of mechanical or artificial methods comparable to those used by intelligent beings. The results of these efforts to date have been impressive, and numerous applications have resulted. Systems have now been developed to reliably perform character and speech recognition; fingerprint and photograph identifications; electroencephelogram (EEG), electrocardiogram (ECG), oil log-well, and other graphical pattern analyses; various types of medical and system diagnoses; resource identification and evaluation (geological, forestry, hydrological, crop disease); and detection of explosive and hostile threats (submarine, aircraft, missile) to name a few.

Object classification is closely related to recognition. The ability to classify or group objects according to some commonly shared features is a form of class recognition. Classification is essential for decision making, learning, and many other cognitive acts. Like recognition, classification depends on the ability to discover common patterns among objects. This ability, in turn, must be acquired through some learning process. Prominent feature patterns which characterize classes of objects must be discovered, generalized, and stored for subsequent recall and comparison.

We do not know exactly how humans learn to identify or classify objects, however, it appears the following processes take place:

> New objects are introduced to a human through activation of sensor stimuli. The sensors, depending on their physical properties, are sensitive in varying degrees to certain attributes which serve to characterize the objects, and the sensor output tends to be proportional to the more prominent attributes. Having perceived a new object, a cognitive model is formed from the stimuli patterns and stored in memory. Recurrent experiences in perceiving the same or similar objects strengthen and refine the similarity

patterns. Repeated perception results in the formation of generalized or archetype models of object classes which become useful in matching, and hence recognition, of similar objects.

13.2 THE RECOGNITION AND CLASSIFICATION PROCESS

In artificial or mechanical recognition, essentially the same steps as noted above must be performed. These steps are illustrated in Figure 13.1 and summarized below:

Step 1. Stimuli produced by objects are perceived by sensory devices. The more prominent attributes (such as size, shape, color, and texture) produce the strongest stimuli. The values of these attributes and their relations are used to characterize an object in the form of a pattern vector **X**, as a string generated by some grammar, as a classification tree, a description graph, or some other means of representation. The range of characteristic attribute values is known as the measurement space M.

Step 2. A subset of attributes whose values provide cohesive object grouping or clustering, consistent with some goals associated with the object classifications, are selected. Attributes selected are those which produce high intraclass and low interclass groupings. This subset represents a reduction in the attribute space dimensionality and hence simplifies the classification process. The range of the subset of attribute values is known as the feature space F.

Step 3. Using the selected attribute values, object or class characterization models are learned by forming generalized phototype descriptions, classification rules, or decision functions. These models are stored for subsequent recognition. The range of the decision function values or classification rules is known as the decision space D.

Step 4. Recognition of familiar objects is achieved through application of the rules learned in Step 3 by comparison and matching of object features with the stored models. Refinements and adjustments can be performed continually thereafter to improve the quality and speed of recognition.

There are two basic approaches to the recognition problem, (1) the decision-theoretic approach and (2) the syntactic approach.

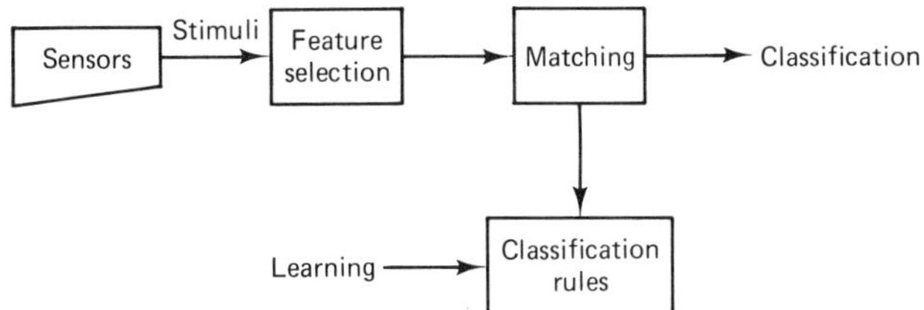

Figure 13.1 The pattern recognition process.

Decision Theoretic Classification

The decision theoretic approach is based on the use of decision functions to classify objects. A decision function maps pattern vectors **X** into decision regions of D. More formally, this problem can be stated as follows.

1. Given a universe of objects $0 = \{o_1, o_2, \ldots, o_n\}$, let each o_i have k observable attributes and relations expressable as a vector $\mathbf{V} = (v_1, v_2, \ldots, v_k)$.
2. Determine (a) a subset of $m \leq k$ of the v_i, say $\mathbf{X} = (x_1, x_2, \ldots, x_m)$ whose values uniquely characterize the o_i, and (b) $c \geq 2$ groupings or classifications of the o_i which exhibit high intraclass and low interclass similarities such that a decision function $d(\mathbf{X})$ can be found which partitions D into c disjoint regions. The regions are used to classify each o_i as belonging to at most one of the c classes.

Determining the feature attributes and decision regions requires stipulating or learning mappings from the measurement space M to the feature space F and then a mapping from F to the classification or decision space D,

$$\mathrm{M} \rightarrow \mathrm{F} \rightarrow \mathrm{D}$$

When there are only two classes, say C_1 and C_2, the values of the object's pattern vectors may tend to cluster into two disjoint groups. In this case, a linear decision function $d(\mathbf{X})$ can often be used to determine an object's class. For example, when the classes are clustered as depicted in Figure 13.2, a linear decision function d is adequate to classify unknown objects as belonging to either C_1 or C_2, where

$$d(\mathbf{X}) = w_1x_1 + w_2x_2 + w_3$$

The constants w_i in d are parameters or weights that are adjusted to find a separating line for the classes. When a function such as d is used, an object is classified as belonging to C_1 if its pattern vector is such that $d(\mathbf{X}) < 0$, and as

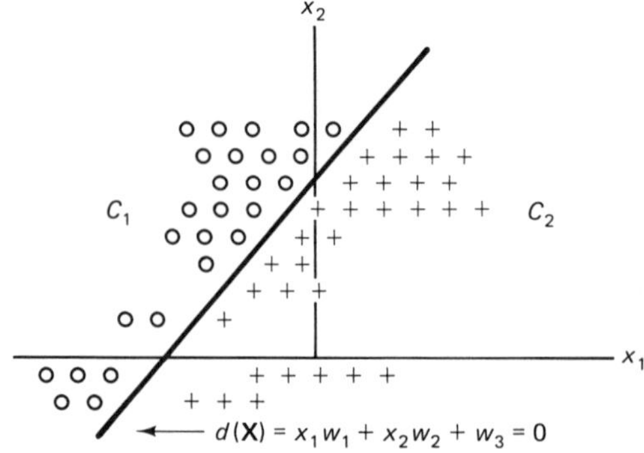

Figure 13.2 A linear decision function.

belonging to class C_2 when $d(\mathbf{X}) > 0$. When $d(\mathbf{X}) = 0$ the classification is indeterminate, so either (or neither) class may be selected.

When class reference vectors, prototypes $\mathbf{R}_j$, $j = 1, \ldots, c$ are available, decision functions can be defined in terms of the distance of the $\mathbf{X}$ from the reference vectors. For example, the distance

$$d_i(\mathbf{X}) = (\mathbf{X} - \mathbf{R}_i)'(\mathbf{X} - \mathbf{R}_i)$$

could be computed for each class C_i, and class C_k would then be chosen when $d_k = \min_i\{C_i\}$.

For the general case of $c \geq 2$ classes, $C_1, C_2, \ldots, C_c$, a decision function may be defined for each class $d_1, d_2, \ldots, d_c$. A class decision rule in this case would be defined to select class C_j when

$$d_j(\mathbf{X}) < d_i(\mathbf{X}) \text{ for } i,j = 1, 2, \ldots, c, \text{ and } i \neq j.$$

When a line d (or more generally a hyperplane in n-space) can be found that separates classes into two or more groups as in the case of Figure 13.2, we say the classes are linearly separable. Classes that overlap each other or surround one another, as in Figure 13.3, cannot generally be classified with the use of simple linear decison functions. For such cases, more general nonlinear (or piecewise-linear) functions may be required. Alternatively, some other selection technique (like heuristics) may be needed.

The decision function approach described above is an example of deterministic recognition since the x_i are deterministic variables. In cases where the attribute values are affected by noise or other random fluctuations, it may be more appropriate to define probabilistic decision functions. In such cases, the attribute vectors $\mathbf{X}$ are treated as random variables, and the decision functions are defined as measures of likelihood of class inclusion. For example, using Bayes' rule, one can compute the conditional probability $P(C_i|\mathbf{X})$ that the class of an object o_j is C_i given the observed value of $\mathbf{X}$ for o_j. This approach requires a knowledge of the prior probability $P(C_i)$, the probability of the occurrence of samples from C_i, as well as $P(\mathbf{X}|C_i)$.

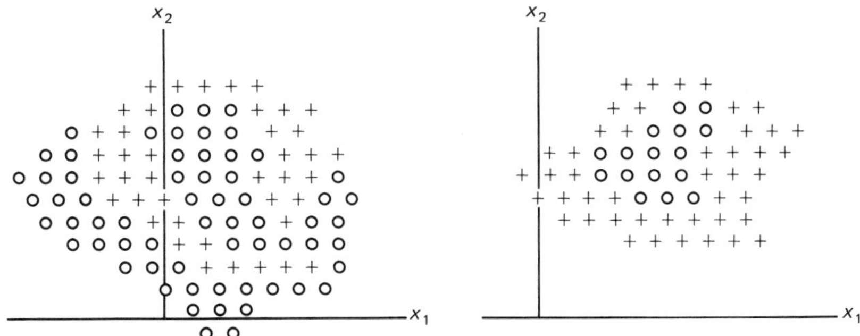

Figure 13.3 Examples of nonlinearly separable classes.

(Note that the C_i are treated like random variables here. This is equivalent to the assumption made in Bayesian classification where the distribution parameter Θ is assumed to be a random variable since C_i may be regarded as a function of Θ). A decision rule for this case is to choose class C_j if

$$P(C_j \mid \mathbf{X}) > P(C_i \mid \mathbf{X}) \text{ for all } i \neq j.$$

A more comprehensive probabilistic approach is one which is based on the use of a loss or risk Bayesian function where the class is chosen on the basis of minimum loss or risk. Let the loss function L_{ij} denote the loss incurred by incorrectly classifying an object actually belonging to class C_i as belonging to C_j. When L_{ij} is a constant for all $i, j, i \neq j$, a decision rule can be formulated using the likelihood ratio defined as (see Chapter 6)

$$\frac{P(\mathbf{X} \mid C_k)}{P(\mathbf{X} \mid C_j)}$$

The rule is to choose class C_k whenever the relation

$$\frac{P(\mathbf{X} \mid C_k)}{P(\mathbf{X} \mid C_j)} > \frac{P(C_j)}{P(C_k)} \quad \text{holds for all } j \neq k.$$

Probabilistic decision rules may be constructed as either parametric or nonparametric depending on knowledge of the distribution forms, respectively. For a comprehensive treatment of these methods see (Duda and Hart, 1973) or (Tou and Gonzales, 1974).

Syntactic Classification

The syntactic recognition approach is based on the uniqueness of syntactic "structure" among the object classes. With this approach, a grammar similar to the grammars defined in Chapter 10 or the generative grammars of Chapter 12 is defined for object descriptions. Instead of defining the grammar in terms of an alphabet of characters or terminal words, the vocabulary is based on shape primitives. For example, the objects depicted in Figure 13.4 could be defined using the grammar $G(v_n, v_t, p, s)$, where the terminals v_t consist of the following shape primitives.

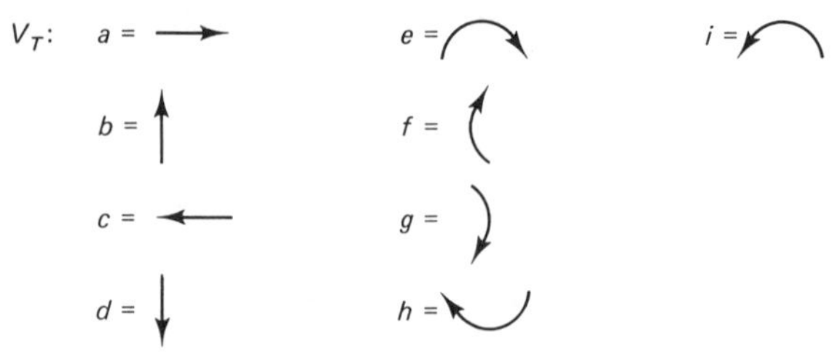

V_T: a = b = c = d = e = f = g = h = i =

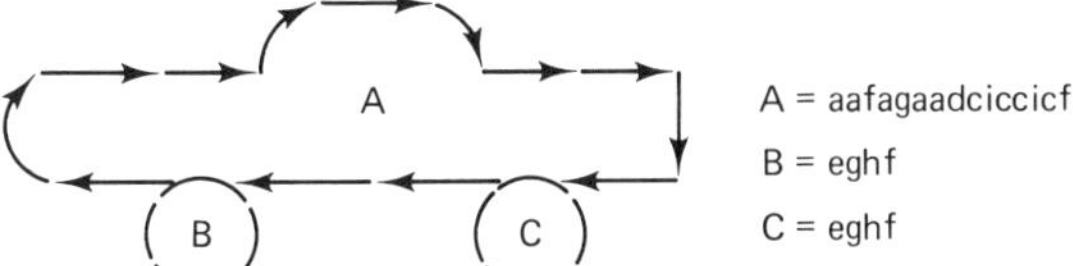

Figure 13.4 Syntactic characterization of objects.

Using syntactic analysis, that is parsing and analyzing the string structures, classification is accomplished by assigning an object to class C_i when the string describing it has been generated by the grammar G_i. This requires that the string be recognized as a member of the language $L(G_i)$. If there are only two classes, it is sufficient to have a single grammar G (two grammars are needed when strings of neither class can occur).

When classification for $c \geq 2$ classes is required, $c - 1$ (or c) different grammars are needed for class recognition. The decision functions in this case are based on grammar recognition functions which choose class C_j if the pattern string is found to be generated by grammar G_j, that is, if it is a member of $L(G_j)$. Patterns not recognized as a member of a defined language are indeterminate.

When patterns are noisy or subject to random fluctuations, ambiguities may occur since patterns belonging to different classes may appear to be the same. In such cases, stochastic or fuzzy grammars may be used. Classification for these cases may be made on the basis of least cost to transform an input string into a valid recognizable string, by the degree of class set inclusion or with a similarity measure using one of the methods described in Chapter 10.

13.3 LEARNING CLASSIFICATION PATTERNS

Before a system can recognize objects, it must possess knowledge of the characteristic features for those objects. This means that the system designer must either build the necessary discriminating rules into the system or the system must learn them. In the case of a linear decision function, the weights that define class boundaries must be predefined or learned. In the case of syntactic recognition, the class grammars must be predefined or learned.

Learning decision functions, grammars, or other rules can be performed in either of two ways, through supervised learning or unsupervised learning. Supervised learning is accomplished by presenting training examples to a learning unit. The examples are labeled beforehand with their correct identities or class. The attribute values and object labels are used by the learning component to inductively extract and determine pattern criteria for each class. This knowledge is used to adjust parameters in decision functions or grammar rewrite rules. Supervised learning concepts are discussed in some detail in Part V. Therefore, we concentrate here on some of the more important notions related to unsupervised learning.

In unsupervised learning, labeled training examples are not available and little is known beforehand regarding the object population. In such cases, the system must be able to perceive and extract relevant properties from the otherwise unknown objects, find common patterns among them, and formulate descriptions or descrimination criteria consistent with the goals of the recognition process.

This form of learning is known as *clustering*. It is the first step in any recognition process where discriminating features of objects are not known in advance.

Learning through Clustering

Clustering is the process of grouping or classifying objects on the basis of a close association or shared characteristics. The objects can be physical or abstract entities, and the characteristics can be attribute values, relations among the objects, and combinations of both. For example, the objects might be streets, freeways, and other pathways connecting two points in a city, and the classifications, the pathways which provide fast or slow traversal between the points. At a more abstract level, the objects might be some concept such as the quality of the items purchased. The classifications in this case might be made on the basis of some subjective criteria, such as poor, average, or good.

Clustering is essentially a discovery learning process in which similarity patterns are found among a group of objects. Discovery of the patterns is usually influenced by the environment or context and motivated by some goal or objective (even if only for economy in cognition). For example, finding short-cuts between two frequently visited points is motivated by a desire to reduce the planning effort and transit time between the points. Likewise, developing a notion of quality is motivated by a desire to save time and money or to improve one's appearance.

Given different objectives, the same set of objects would, in general, be clustered differently. If the objective given above for the streets, freeways, and the like were modified to include safe for bicycle riding, a different object classification would, in general, result.

Finding the most meaningful cluster groupings among a set of unknown objects o_i requires that similarity patterns be discovered in the feature space. Clustering is usually performed with the intent of capturing any gestalt properties of a group of objects and not just the commonality of certain attribute values. This is one of the basic requirements of *conceptual* clustering (Chapter 19) where the objects are grouped together as members of a concept class. Procedures for conceptual clustering are based on more than simple distance measures. They must also take into account the context (environment) of the objects as well as the goals or objectives of the clustering.

The clustering problem gives rise to several subproblems. In particular, before an implementation is possible, the following questions must be addressed.

1. What set of attributes and relations are most relevant, and what weights should be given to each? In what order should attributes be observed or measured? (If the observation process is sequential, ordering may influence the effectiveness of the attributes in discriminating among objects.)

2. What representation formalism should be used to characterize the objects?

3. What representation scheme should be used to describe the cluster groupings or classifications? Usually, some simplification results if the single representation trick can be used (the use of a single representation method for both object and cluster descriptions).

4. What clustering criteria is most consistent with and effective in achieving the objectives relative to the context or domain? This requires consideration of an appropriate distance or similarity measure compatible with the description domains noted in 2, above.

5. What clustering algorithms can best meet the criteria in 2 within acceptable time and space complexity bounds?

By now questions such as these should be familiar. They are by no means trivial, but they must be addressed when designing a system. They depend on many complex factors for which the tools of earlier chapters become essential. These problems have been addressed elsewhere; therefore, we focus our attention here on the clustering process.

The clustering process must be performed with a limited set of observations, and checking all possible object groupings for patterns is not feasible except with a small number of objects. This is due to the combinatorial explosion which results in arranging n objects into an unknown number m of clusters.[1] Consequently, methods which examine only the more promising groupings must be used. Establishing such groupings requires the use of some measure of similarity, association, or degree of fit among a set of objects.

When the attribute values are real valued, cluster groupings can sometimes be found with the use of point-to-point or point-to-set distances, probability measures (like using the covariance matrix between two populations), scatter matrices, the sum of squared error distance between objects, or other means (see Chapter 10). In these cases, an object is clustered in class C_i if its proximity to other members of C_i is within some threshold or limiting value.

Many clustering algorithms have been proposed for different tasks. One of the most popular algorithms developed at the Stanford Research Institute by G. H. Ball and D. J. Hall (Anderberg, 1973) is known as the ISODATA method. This method requires that the number of clusters m be specified, and threshold values t_1, t_2, and t_3 be given or determined for use in splitting, merging, or discarding

[1] The number of ways in which n objects can be arranged into m groups is an exponential quantity.

$$S_m = \left(\frac{1}{m!}\right) \sum_k (-1)^{m-k} \binom{m}{k} k^n.$$

When m is unknown, the number of arrangements increases as the sum of the S_m, that is, as S^m. For example when $n = 25$, the number of arrangements is more than $4*10^{18}$.

clusters respectively. During the clustering process, the thresholds are used to determine if a cluster should be split into two clusters, merged with other clusters or discarded (when too small). The algorithm is given with the following steps.

1. Select m samples as seed points for initial cluster centers. This can be done by taking the first m points, selecting random points or by taking the first m points which exceed some mutual minimum separation distance d.
2. Group each sample with its nearest cluster center.
3. After all samples have been grouped, compute new cluster centers for each group. The center can be defined as the centroid (mean value of the attribute vectors) or some similar central measure.
4. If the split threshold t_1 is exceeded for any cluster, split it into two parts and recompute new cluster centers.
5. If the distance between two cluster centers is less than t_2, combine the clusters and recompute new cluster centers.
6. If a cluster has fewer than t_3 members, discard the cluster. It is ignored for the remainder of the process.
7. Repeat steps 3 through 6 until no change occurs among cluster groupings or until some iteration limit has been exceeded.

Measures for determining distances and the center location need not be based on ordered variates. They may be one of the measures described in Chapter 10 (including probabilistic or fuzzy measures) or some measure of similarity between graphs, strings, and even FOPL descriptions. In any case, it is assumed each object o_i is described by a unique point or event in the feature space F.

Up to this point we have ignored the problem of attribute scaling. It is possible that a few large valued variables may completely dominate the other variables in a similarity measure. This could happen, for example, if one variable is measured in units of meters and another variable in millimeters or if the range and scale of variation for two variables are widely different. This problem is closely related to the feature selection problem, that is, in the assignment of weights to feature variables on the basis of their importance or relevance. One simple method for adjusting the scales of such variables is to use a diagonal weight matrix $\mathbf{W}$ to transform the representation vector $\mathbf{X}$ to $\mathbf{X}' = \mathbf{WX}$. Thus, for all of the measures described above, one should assume the representation vectors $\mathbf{X}$ have been appropriately normalized to account for scale variations.

To summarize the above process, a subset of characteristic features which represent the o_i are first selected. The features chosen should be good discriminators in separating objects from different classes, relevant, and measurable (observable) at reasonable cost. Feature variables should be scaled as noted above to prevent any swamping effect when combined due to large valued variables. Next, a suitable metric which measures the degree of association or similarity between objects should be chosen, and an appropriate clustering algorithm selected. Finally, during the clustering process, the feature variables may need to be weighted to reflect the relative importance of the feature in affecting the clustering.

13.4 RECOGNIZING AND UNDERSTANDING SPEECH

Developing systems that understand speech has been a continuing goal of AI researchers. Speech is one of our most expedient and natural forms of communication, and so understandably, it is a capability we would like AI systems to possess. The ability to communicate directly with programs offers several advantages. It eliminates the need for keyboard entries and speeds up the interchange of information between user and system. With speech as the communication medium, users are also free to perform other tasks concurrently with the computer interchange. And finally, more untrained personnel would be able to use computers in a variety of applications.

The recognition of continuous waveform patterns such as speech begins with sampling and digitizing the waveforms. In this case the feature values are the sampled points $x_i = f(t_i)$ as illustrated in Figure 13.5.

It is known from information theory that a sampling rate of twice the highest speech frequency is needed to capture the information content of the speech waveforms. Thus, sampling requirements will normally be equivalent to 20K to 30K bytes per second. While this rate of information in itself is not too difficult to handle, this, added to the subsequent processing, does place some heavy requirements on real time understanding of speech.

Following sample digitization, the signals are processed at different levels of abstraction. The lowest level deals with phones (the smallest unit of sound), allophones (variations of the phoneme as they actually occur in words), and syllables. Higher level processing deals with words, phrases, and sentences.

The processing approach may be from the bottom, top, or a combination of both. When bottom processing is used the input signal is segmented into basic speech units and a search is made to match prestored patterns against these units. Knowledge about the phonetic composition of words is stored in a lexicon for comparisons. For the top approach, syntax, semantics (the domain), and pragmatics (context) are used to anticipate which words the speaker is likely to have said and

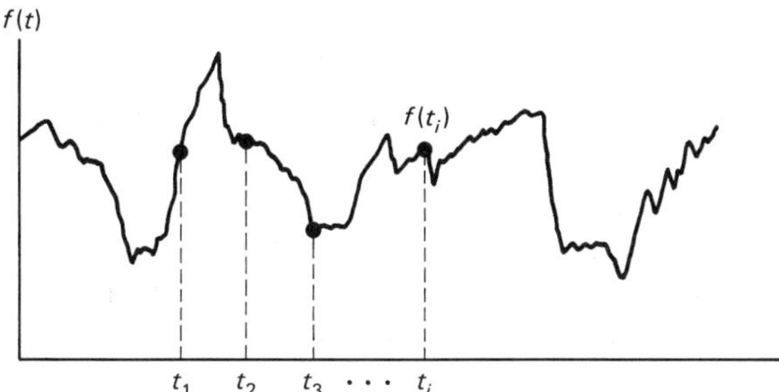

Figure 13.5 Sampling a continuous waveform.

direct the search for recognizable patterns. A combined approach which uses both methods has also been applied successfully.

Early research in speech recognition concentrated on the recognition of isolated words. Patterns of individual words were prestored and then compared to the digitized input patterns. These early systems met with limited success. They were unable to tolerate variations in speaker voices and were highly susceptible to noise. Although important, this early work helped little with the general problem of continuous speech understanding since words appearing as part of a continuous stream differ significantly from isolated words. In continuous speech, words are run together, modified, and truncated to produce a great variation of sounds. Thus, speech analysis must be able to detect different sounds as being part of the same word, but in different contexts. Because of the noise and variability, recognition is best accomplished with some type of fuzzy comparison.

In 1971 the Defense Advanced Research Projects Agency (DARPA) funded a five year program for continuous speech understanding research (SUR). The objective of this research was to design and implement systems that were capable of accepting continuous speech from several cooperative speakers using a limited vocabulary of some 1000 words. The systems were expected to run at slower than real time speeds. A product of this research were several systems including HEARSAY I and II, HARPY, and HWIM. While the systems were only moderately successful in achieving their goals, the research produced other important byproducts as well, particularly in systems architectures, and in the knowledge gained regarding control.

The HEARSAY system was important for its introduction of the blackboard architecture (Chapter 15). This architecture is based on the cooperative efforts of several specialist knowledge components communicating by way of a blackboard in the solution of a class of problems. The specialists are each expert in a different area. For example, speech analysis experts might each deal with a different level of the speech problem. The solution process is opportunistic, with each expert making a contribution when it can. The solution to a given problem is developed as a data structure on the blackboard. As the solution is developed, this data structure is modified by the contributing expert. A description of the systems developed under SUR is given in Barr and Feigenbaum (1981).

13.5 SUMMARY

Pattern recognition systems are used to identify or classify objects on the basis of their attribute and attribute-relation values. Recognition may be accomplished with decision functions or structural grammars. The decision functions as well as the grammars may be deterministic, probabilistic, or fuzzy.

Before recognition can be accomplished, a system must learn the criteria for object recognition. Learning may be accomplished by direct designer encoding, supervised learning, or unsupervised learning. When unsupervised learning is required, some form of clustering may be performed to learn the object class characteristics.

Speech understanding first requires recognition of basic speech patterns. These patterns are matched against lexicon patterns for recognition. Basic speech units such as phonemes are the building blocks for longer units such as syllables and words.

EXERCISES

13.1. Choose three common objects and determine five of their most discriminating visual attributes.

13.2. For the previous problem, determine three additional nonvisual attributes for the objects which are most discriminating.

13.3. Find a linear decision function which separates the following $x-y$ points into two distinct classes.

−1,8	−5,−1	−3,3	−3,0	1,3	−1,1
0,1	3,4	0,0	2,3	−4,−1	−2,3

13.4. Describe how you would design a pattern recognition program which must validate hand written signatures. Identify some potential problem areas.

13.5. Compare the deterministic decision function approach to the probabilistic decision function apporoach in pattern recognition applications. Give examples when each would be the appropriate function to use.

13.6. Define a set of rewrite rules for a grammar for syntactic generation (recognition) of objects such as the object of Figure 13.4.

13.7. Give two examples of unsupervised learning in humans in which they learn to recognize objects through clustering. Describe how different goals can influence the learning process.

13.8. Apply the ISODATA algorithm to find three different clusters among the following $x-y$ data points.

−2,1	−1,3	−1,2	−1,0	0,2	1,7	1,2	1,1
1,0	2,9	2,8	2,5	2,0	3,9	3,7	3,6
4,8	4,6	4,3	4,2	5,4	5,3	5,2	6,3
6,3	7,7	7,5	7,4	7,2	7,0	−1,6	−2,6

13.9. Consider a cluster algorithm which builds clusters of objects by forming small regions in normalized attribute space (spheres in n-dimensional space) about each object, and includes them in a cluster if and only if the sphere overlaps with at least one other neighboring object sphere. Show how such a scheme could be used to partition the attribute space into subspace with nonlinear boundaries.

13.10. Define an alphabet of shape primitives for a syntactic recognition grammar which can be used to recognize the integer characters 0, 1, 2, 3, 4, 5, 6, 7, 8, and 9. Check to see that the resultant character strings for each character are unique.

13.11. Give two examples where the single representation trick simplifies clustering among unknown objects.

13.12. Compute the number of ways five objects can be arranged into 1, 2, 3, and 4 groups. From this, try to develop an inductive proof of arranging n objects into m groups.

13.13. Read "High Level Knowledge Sources in Usable Speech Recognition Systems" by Sheryl Young, Alexander Hauptmann, Wayne Ward, Edward Smith, and Philip Werner, in *Communications of the ACM,* Vol. 32, Number 2, Feb., 1989. Summarize some of the more complicated problems associated with general speech recognition.

14

Visual Image Understanding

Vision is perhaps the most remarkable of all of our intelligent sensing capabilities. Through our visual system, we are able to acquire information about our environment without direct contact. Vision permits us to acquire information at a phenomenal rate and at resolutions that are most impressive. For example, one only needs to compare the resolution of a TV camera system to that of a human to see the difference. Roughly speaking, a TV camera has a resolution on the order of 500 parts per square cm, while the human eye has a limiting resolution on the order of some 25×10^6 parts per square cm. Thus, humans have a visual resolution several orders of magnitude better (more than 10,000 times finer) than that of a TV camera. What is even more remarkable is the ease with which we humans sense and perceive a variety of visual images. It is so effortless, we are seldom conscious of the act.

In this chapter, we examine the processes and the problems involved in building computer vision systems. We look at some of the approaches taken thus far and at some of the more successful vision systems constructed to date.

14.1 INTRODUCTION

Because of its wide ranging potential, computer vision has become one of the most intensely studied areas of AI and engineering during the past few decades. Some typical areas of application include the following.

MANUFACTURING

Parts inspection for quality control
Assembly, sorting, dispensing, locating, and packaging of parts

MEDICAL

Screening x-ray, tomographic, ultrasound, and other medical images

DEFENSE

Photo reconnaisance, analysis, and scene interpretation
Target detection, identification, and tracking
Microbe detection and identification
Weapons guidance
Remote and local site monitoring

BUSINESS

Visual document readers
Design tools for engineers and architects
Inspection of labels for identification
Inspection of products for contents and packaging

ROBOTICS

Guidance of welders and spray paint nozzles
Sorting, picking, and bin packing of items
Autonomous guidance of land, air and sea vehicles

SPACE EXPLORATION

Discovery and interpretation of astronomical images
Terrestial image mapping and interpretation for plant disease, mineral deposits, insect infestations, and soil erosion

Vision in an organic system is the process of sensing a pattern of light energy, and developing an interpretation of those patterns. The sensing part of the process consists of selectively gathering light from some area of the environment, focusing and projecting it onto a light sensitive surface, and converting the light into electrochemical patterns of impulses. The perception part of the process involves the transformation and comparison of the transmitted impulse patterns to other prestored patterns

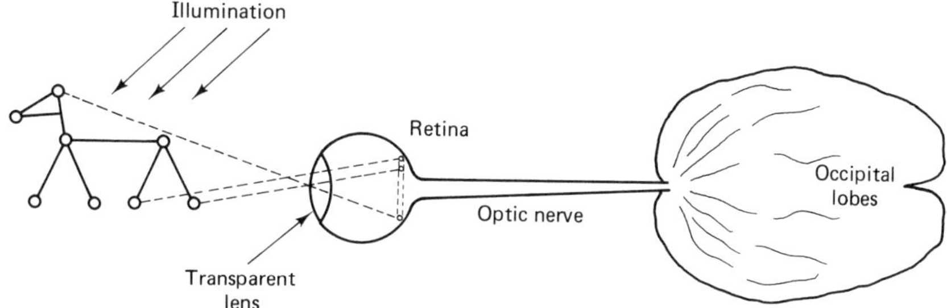

Figure 14.1 The human process of visual interpretation.

together with some form of inference. The basic vision process as it occurs in humans is depicted in Figure 14.1.

Light from illuminated objects is collected by the transparent lens of the eye, focused, and projected onto the retina where some 250 million light sensitive sensors (cones and rods) are excited. When excited, the sensors send impulses through the optic nerve to the visual cortex of the occipital lobes of the brain where the images are interpreted and recognized.

Computer vision systems share some similarities with human visual systems, at least as we now understand them. They also have a number of important differences. Although artificial vision systems vary widely with the specific application, we adopt a general approach here, one in which the ultimate objective is to determine a high-level description of a three-dimensional scene with a competency level comparable to that of human vision systems. Before proceeding farther we should distinguish between a scene and an image of a scene. A scene is the set of physical objects in a picture area, whereas an image is the projection of the scene onto a two-dimensional plane.

With the above objectives in mind, a typical computer vision system should be able to perform the following operations:

1. Image formation, sensing, and digitization
2. Local processing and image segmentation
3. Shape formation and interpretation
4. Semantic analysis and description.

The sequence of these operations is depicted in Figure 14.2.

As we proceed through the processing stages of computer vision, the reader will no doubt be impressed by the similarities and parallels one can draw between vision processing and natural language processing. The image-sensor stage in vision corresponds to speech recognition in language understanding, the low and intermediate processing levels of vision correspond to syntactic and semantic language processing respectively, and high level processing, in both cases, corresponds to the process of building and interpreting high level knowledge structures.

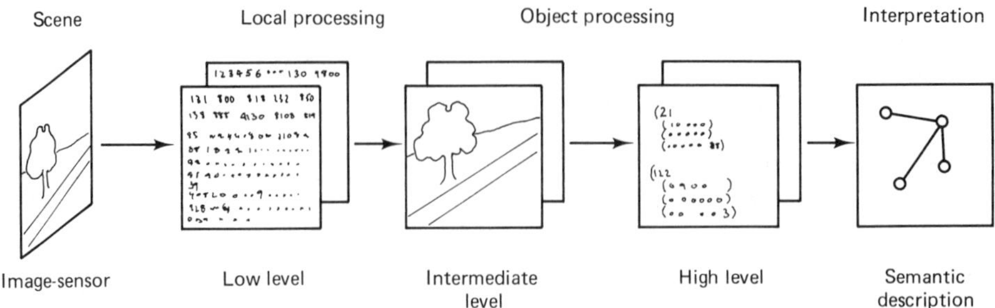

Figure 14.2 Processing stages in computer vision systems.

Vision Processing Overview

The input to a vision system is a two dimensional image collected on some form of light sensitive surface. This surface is scanned by some means to produce a continuous voltage output that is proportional to the light intensity of the image on the surface. The output voltage $f(x, y)$ is sampled at a discrete number of x and y points or pixel (picture element) positions and converted to numbers. The numbers correspond to the gray level intensity for black and white images. For color images, the intensity value is comprised of three separate arrays of numbers, one for the intensity value of each of the basic colors (red, green, and blue).

Thus, through the digitization process, the image is transformed from a continuous light source into an array of numbers which correspond to the local image intensities at the corresponding x-y pixel positions on the light sensitive surface.

Using the array of numbers, certain low level operations are performed, such as smoothing of neighboring points to reduce noise, finding outlines of objects or edge elements, thresholding (recording maximum and minimum values only, depending on some fixed intensity threshold level), and determining texture, color, and other object features. These initial processing steps are ones which are used to locate and accentuate object boundaries and other structure within the image.

The next stage of processing, the intermediate level, involves connecting, filling in, and combining boundaries, determining regions, and assigning descriptive labels to objects that have been accentuated in the first stage. This stage builds higher level structures from the lower level elements of the first stage. When complete, it passes on labeled surfaces such as geometrical objects that may be capable of identification.

High-level image processing consists of identifying the important objects in the image and their relationships for subsequent description as well-defined knowledge structures and hence, for use by a reasoning component.

Special types of vision systems may also require three dimensional processing and analysis as well as motion detection and analysis.

The Objectives of Computer Vision Systems

The ultimate goals of computer image understanding is to build systems that equal or exceed the capabilities of human vision systems. Ideally, a computer vision system would be capable of interpreting and describing any complex scene in complete detail. This means that the system must not only be able to identify a myriad of complex objects, but must also be able to reason about the objects, to describe their function and purpose, what has taken place in the scene, why any visible or implied events occurred, what is likely to happen, and what the objects in the scene are capable of doing.

Figure 14.3 presents an example of a complex scene that humans can interpret well with little effort. It is the objective of many researchers in computer vision to build systems capable of interpreting, describing, and reasoning about scenes of this type in real time. Unfortunately, we are far from achieving this level of competency. To be sure, some interesting vision systems have been developed, but they are quite crude compared to the elegant vision systems of humans.

Like natural language understanding, computer vision interpretation is a difficult problem. The amount of processing and storage required to interpret and describe a complex scene can be enormous. For example, a single image for a high resolution aerial photograph may result in some four to nine million pixels (bytes) of information and require on the average some 10 to 20 computations per pixel. Thus, when several frames must be stored during processing, as many as 100 megabytes of storage may be needed, and more than 100 million computations performed.

Figure 14.3 Example of a complex scene. (THE FAR SIDE COPYRIGHT 1984 UNIVERSAL PRESS SYNDICATE. Reprinted by permission. All rights reserved.)

14.2 IMAGE TRANSFORMATION AND LOW-LEVEL PROCESSING

In this section, we examine the first stages of processing. This includes the process of forming an image and transforming it to an array of numbers which can then be operated on by a computer. In this first stage, only local processing is performed on the numbers to reduce noise and other unwanted picture elements, and to accentuate object boundaries.

Transforming Light Energy to Numbers

The first step in image processing requires a transformation of light energy to numbers, the language of computers. To accomplish this, some form of light sensitive transducer is used such as a vidicon tube or charge-coupled device (CCD).

A vidicon tube is the type of sensor typically found in home or industrial video systems. A lens is used to project the image onto a flat surface of the vidicon. The tube surface is coated with a photoconductive material whose resistance is inversely proportional to the light intensity falling on it. An electron gun is used to produce a flying-spot scanner with which to rapidly scan the surface left to right and top to bottom. The scan results in a time varying voltage which is proportional to the scan spot image intensity. The continuously varying output voltage is then fed to an analog-to-digital converter (ADC) where the voltage amplitude is periodically sampled and converted to numbers. A typical ADC unit will produce 30 complete digitized frames consisting of 256×256, or 512×512 (or more) samples of an image per second. Each sample is a number (or triple of numbers in the case of color systems) ranging from 0 to 64 (six bits) or 0 to 255 (eight bits). The image conversion process is depicted in Figure 14.4.

A CCD is typical of the class of solid state sensor devices known as charge transfer devices that are now being used in many vision systems. A CCD is a rectangular chip consisting of an array of capacitive photodetectors, each capable of storing an electrostatic charge. The charges are scanned like a clock-driven shift register and converted into a time varying voltage which is proportional to the incident light intensity on the detectors. This voltage is sampled and converted to integers using an ADC unit as in the case of the vidicon tube. The density of the

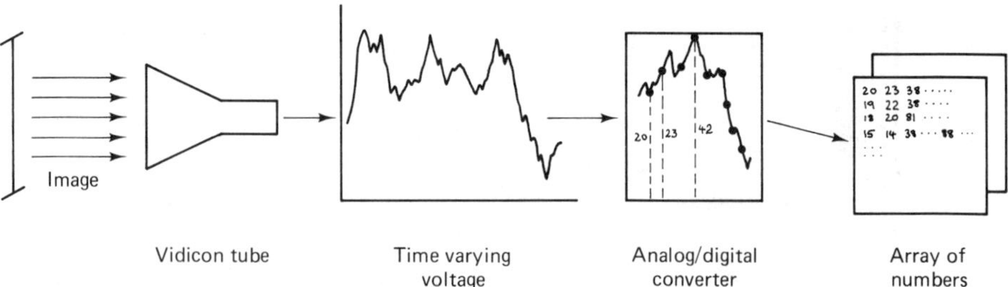

Figure 14.4 Transforming the image to numbers.

detectors on the chip is quite high. For example, a CCD chip of about five square centimeters in area may contain as many as 1000 by 1000 detectors.

The numeric outputs from the ADC units are collected as arrays of numbers which correspond to the light intensity of the image on the surface of the transducer. This is the input to the next stage of processing illustrated in Figure 14.4.

Processing the Quantized Arrays

The array of numbers produced from the image sensing device may be thought of as the lowest, most primitive level of abstraction in the vision understanding process. The next step in the processing hierarchy is to find some structure among the pixels such as pixel clusters which define object boundaries or regions within the image. Thus, it is necessary to transform the array of raw pixel data into regions of discontinuities and homogeneity, to find edges and other delimiters of these object regions.

A raw digitized image will contain some noise and distortion. Therefore, computations to reduce these effects may be necessary before locating edges and regions. Depending on the particular application, low level processing will often require local smoothing of the array to eliminate this noise. Other low level operations include threshold processing to help define homogeneous regions, and different forms of edge detection to define boundaries. We examine some of these low level methods next.

Thresholding is the process of transforming a gray level representation to a binary representation of the image. All digitized array values above some threshold level T are set equal to the maximum gray-level value (black), and values less than or equal to T are set equal to zero (white). For simplicity, assume gray-level values have been normalized to range between zero and one, and suppose a threshold level of $T = 0.7$ has been chosen. Then all array values $g(x,y) > 0.7$ are set equal to 1 and values $g(x,y) \leq 0.7$ are set equal to 0. The result is an array of binary 0 and 1 values. An example of an image that has been thresholded at 0.7 to produce a binary image is illustrated in Figure 14.5.

Thresholding is one way to segment the image into sharpen object regions by enhancing some portions and reducing others like noise and other unwanted features. Thresholding can also help to simplify subsequent processing steps. And in many cases, the use of several different threshold levels may be necessary since low intensity object surfaces will be lost to high threshold levels, and unwanted background will be picked up and enhanced by low threshold levels. Thresholding at several levels may be the best way to determine different regions in the image when it is necessary to compensate for variations in illumination or poor contrast.

Selecting one or more appropriate threshold level settings T_i will require additional computations, such as first producing a histogram of the image gray-level intensities. A histogram gives the frequencies of occurrence of different intensity (or some other feature) levels within the image. An analysis of a histogram can reveal where concentrations of different intensity levels occur, where peaks and broad flat levels occur and where abrupt differences in level occur. From this informa-

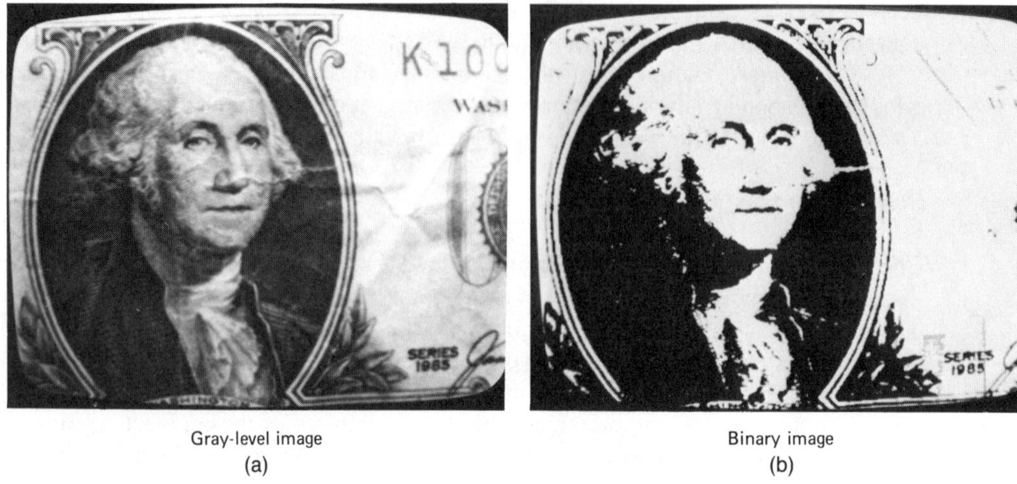

Gray-level image
(a)

Binary image
(b)

Figure 14.5 Threshold transformation of an image.[1]

tion the best choice of T_i values are often made apparent. For example, a histogram with two or more clear separations between intensity levels that have a relatively high frequency of occurrence will usually suggest the best threshold levels for object identification and separation. This is seen in Figure 14.6.

Next, we turn to the question of image smoothing. *Smoothing* is a form of digital filtering. It is used to reduce noise and other unwanted features and to enhance certain image features. Smoothing is a form of image transformation that tends to eliminate spikes and flaten widely fluctuating intensity values. Various forms of smoothing techniques have been employed, including local averaging, the use of models, and parametric form fitting.

One common method of smoothing is to replace each pixel in an array with a weighted average of the pixel and its neighboring values. This can be accomplished with the use of filter masks which use some configuration of neighboring pixel values to compute a smoothed replacement value. Two typical masks consist of either four or eight neighboring pixels whose intensity values are used in the weighting

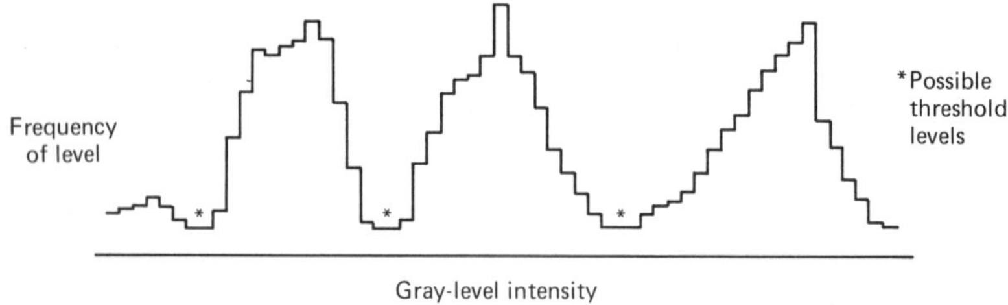

Figure 14.6 Histogram of light intensity levels.

[1] Courtesy of Kenneth Chapman and INTELLEDEX, INC.

computation. If smoothing is being performed at pixel location (x,y), the neighboring pixels are at the eight locations: $(x + 1,y - 1)$, $(x + 1,y)$, $(x + 1,y + 1)$, $(x,y + 1)$, $(x,y - 1)$, $(x - 1,y - 1)$, $(x - 1,y)$, and $(x - 1,y - 1)$. From these, either the four immediate neighbors (top, bottom, left, and right) or all eight neighbors are sometimes chosen.

Examples of smoothing masks for four and eight neighborhood pixels are as follows:

$$\begin{bmatrix} 1/32 & 3/32 & 1/32 \\ 3/32 & \underline{1/2} & 3/32 \\ 1/32 & 3/32 & 1/32 \end{bmatrix} \qquad \begin{bmatrix} & 1/8 & \\ 1/8 & \underline{1/2} & 1/8 \\ & 1/8 & \end{bmatrix}$$

The underlined number in each array identifies the pixel being smoothed. (Note that the filter weights in a mask should sum to one to avoid distortions.) Applying a mask to an image array has the effect of reducing spurious noise as well as sharp boundaries. It reduces sharp spikes but also tends to blur the image. For example, when the eight mask filter given above is applied to the array shown in Figure 14.7, the blurring effects are quite pronounced.

The degree of smoothing and hence blurring can, of course, be controlled with the use of appropriate weighting values in the mask. Weighted smoothing of this type over a region is known as convolution. Convolution is sometimes used to smooth an image prior to the application of differential operators which detect edges. We return to the subject of convolution smoothing after we look at the edge detection problem.

Local edge detection is the process of finding a boundary or delimiter between two regions. An edge will show up as a relatively thin line or arc which appears as a measurable difference in contrast between two otherwise homogeneous regions.

Original image array

(a)

Smoothed image array

(b)

Figure 14.7 Application of a smoothing mask.[2]

[2] Courtesy of Kenneth Chapman and INTELLEDEX, INC.

Regions belonging to the same object are usually distinguishable by one or more features which are relatively homogeneous throughout, such as color, texture, three-dimensional flow effects, or intensity.

Boundaries which separate adjoining regions represent a discontinuity in one or more of these features, a fact that can be exploited by measuring the rate of change of a feature value over the image surface. For example, the rate of change or gradient in intensity in the horizontal and vertical directions can be measured with difference functions D_x and D_y defined as

$$D_x = f(x,y) - f(x - n,y)$$

$$D_y = f(x,y) - f(x,y - n)$$

where n is a small integer greater than or equal to 1.

When an image is scanned horizontally or vertically, D_x and D_y will vary little over homogeneous regions, and show a sharp increase or decrease at locations where discontinuities occur. They are the discrete equivalents of the continuous differential operators used in the calculus. The rate of change of the gradient can also be useful in finding local edges as we will see below. For discrete functions, second order difference operators provide the rate of change of gradient, comparable to second order differential operators.

Since we are interested in locating edges with any given orientation, a better gradient measure is one which is sensitive to intensity changes in any direction. We can achieve this with a directional norm of D_x and D_y such as the vector gradient.

$$D_{xy} = (D_x^2 + D_y^2)^{1/2}$$

$$\theta_{xy} = \tan^{-1}(D_y/D_x)$$

For $n = 1$, D_x and D_y are most easily computed by application of the equivalent weighting masks; the two element masks are $(-1\ \underline{1})$ and $\begin{bmatrix} 1 \\ \hline -1 \end{bmatrix}$ respectively.

An example of the application of these two masks to an image array is illustrated in Figure 14.8 where a vertical edge is seen to be quite pronounced. Masks such as these have been generalized to measure gradients over wider regions covering several pixels. This has the effect of reducing spurious noise and other sharp spikes.

Two masks deserving particular attention are the Prewitt (1970) and Sobel (1970) masks as depicted in Figure 14.9. These masks are used to compute a broadened normalized gradient than the simple masks given above. We leave the details of the computations as one of the exercises at the end of this chapter.

We return now to the methods of edge detection which employ smoothing followed by an application of the gradient. For this, the continuous case is considered first.

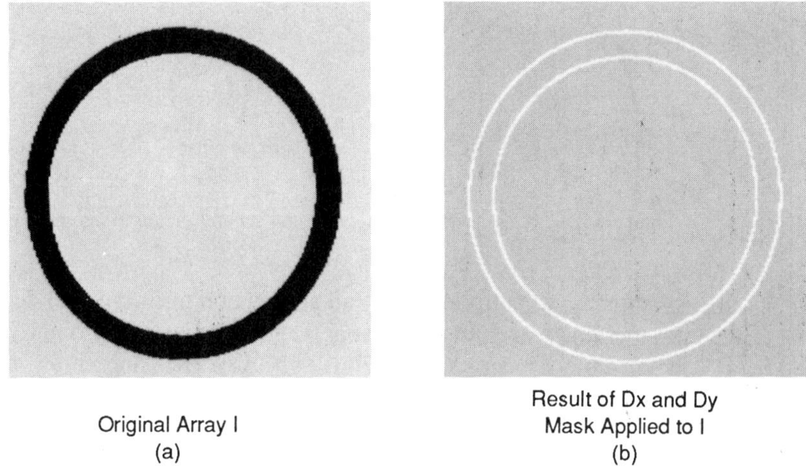

Figure 14.8 Application of difference functions to an image.

The continuous analog of discrete smoothing in one dimension is the convolution of two functions f and g (written $f * g$) where

$$h(y) = f * g = \int f(x)g(y - x)dx$$

Convolving the two functions f and g is similar to computing the cross correlation, a process that reduces random noise and enhances coherent or structural changes.

One particular form of weighting function g has a symmetric bell shape or normal form, that is the Gaussian distribution. The two dimensional form of this function is given by

$$g(u,v) = ce^{-(u^2+v^2)/2}$$

where c is a normalizing constant.

Because of their rotational symmetry, Gaussian filters produce desirable effects

$$P_x = \begin{bmatrix} -1 & 0 & 1 \\ -1 & \underline{0} & 1 \\ -1 & 0 & 1 \end{bmatrix} \qquad S_x = \begin{bmatrix} -1 & 0 & 1 \\ -2 & \underline{0} & 2 \\ -1 & 0 & 1 \end{bmatrix}$$

$$P_y = \begin{bmatrix} 1 & 1 & 1 \\ 0 & \underline{0} & 0 \\ -1 & -1 & -1 \end{bmatrix} \qquad S_y = \begin{bmatrix} 1 & 2 & 1 \\ 0 & \underline{0} & 0 \\ -1 & -2 & -1 \end{bmatrix}$$

Prewitt Masks Sobel Masks

Figure 14.9 Generalized edge detection masks.

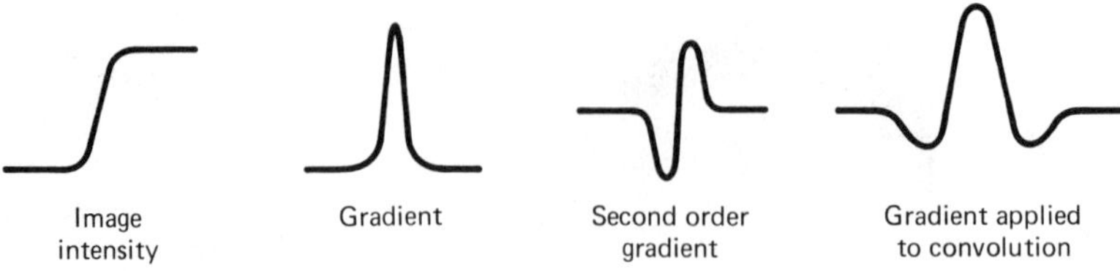

Figure 14.10 Application of Gaussian and second degree differential operators.

as an edge detector when followed by an application of the second degree differential (gradient) operator. Over discontinuous regions, the transformed intensity results in a zero crossing as depicted in Figure 14.10. The smoothing and differencing operations may be combined into a single operator and approximated with a digital mask of the types given above (Marr and Hildreth, 1980).

There is some psychological evidence to support the belief that the human eye uses a form of Gaussian transformation called lateral inhibition which has the effect of enhancing the contrast between gradually changing objects, such as an object and its background.

Another approach used to filter the digitized image applies frequency domain transforms such as the Fourier transform. Since edges represent higher frequency components, the transformed image can be analyzed on the basis of its frequency distribution. For this, the Fourier transform has become one of the most popular transform methods, since an efficient computation algorithm has been developed. It is known as the Fast Fourier transform. The discrete two-dimensional version of the Fourier transform is given by

$$F(u,v) = \frac{1}{n} \sum_{x=0}^{n-1} \sum_{y=0}^{n-1} f(x,y)\, e^{-2i(xu+yv)/n}$$

Applying this transform to an array of intensity values produces an array of complex numbers that correspond to the spatial frequency components of the image (sums of sine and cosine terms). The transformed array will contain all of the information in the original intensity image, but in a form that is more easily used to identify regions that contain different frequency components. Filtering with the Fourier transform is accomplished by setting the high (or low) values of u and v equal to zero. For example, the value $F(v,v) = F(0,0)$ corresponds to the zero frequency or the DC component, and higher values of u and v correspond to the high frequency components. As with intensity image arrays, thresholding of transformed arrays can be used to separate different frequency components.

The original intensity image with any modifications, is recovered with the inverse transform given by

$$f(x,y) = \frac{1}{n} \sum_{u=0}^{n-1} \sum_{v=0}^{n-1} F(u,v) \exp\left[\frac{2i}{n}(xu + yv)\right]$$

Another method of edge detection is model fitting. This is accomplished by locally fitting a parametric profile of edges to the image array. A model in the form of a mask is shifted over a region and compared to the corresponding gray levels. If the fit between the model and the gray-level pattern scores high enough, an edge with the given orientation is labeled appropriately. Model fitting methods usually require heavy computations. We omit the details here.

Texture and Color

As suggested earlier, texture and color are also used to identify regions and boundaries. Texture is a repeated pattern of elementary shapes occurring on an object's surface. Texture may appear to be regular and periodic, random, or partially periodic. Figure 14.11 illustrates some examples of textured surfaces.

The structure in texture is usually too fine to be resolved, yet still course enough to cause noticeable variation in the gray levels. Even so, methods of analysis for texture have been developed. They are commonly based on statistical analyses of small groups of pixels, the application of pattern matching, the use of Fourier transforms, or modeling with special functions known as fractals. These methods are beyond the scope of our goals in this chapter.

The use of color to identify and interpret regions requires more than three times as much processing as gray-level processing. First, the image must be separated into its three primary colors with red, green, and blue filters (Figure 14.12).

The separate color images must then be processed by sampling the intensities and producing three arrays or a single array of tristimulus values. The arrays are then processed separately (in some cases jointly) to determine common color regions and corresponding boundaries. The processes used to find boundaries and regions, and to interpret color images is similar to that of gray-level systems.

Although the additional computation required in color analysis can be significant, the added information gained from separate color intensity arrays may be warranted, depending on the application. In complex scene analysis, color may be the most effective method of segmentation and object identification. In Section 14.6 we describe

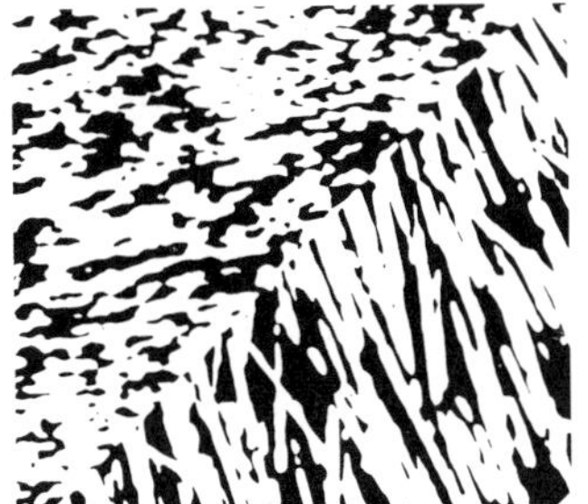
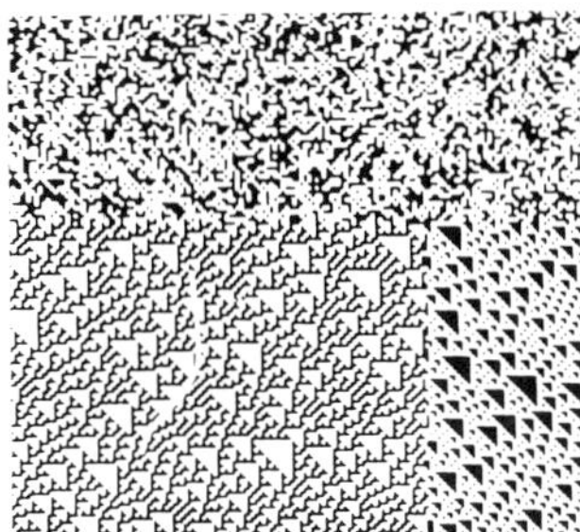

Figure 14.11 Examples of textured surfaces.

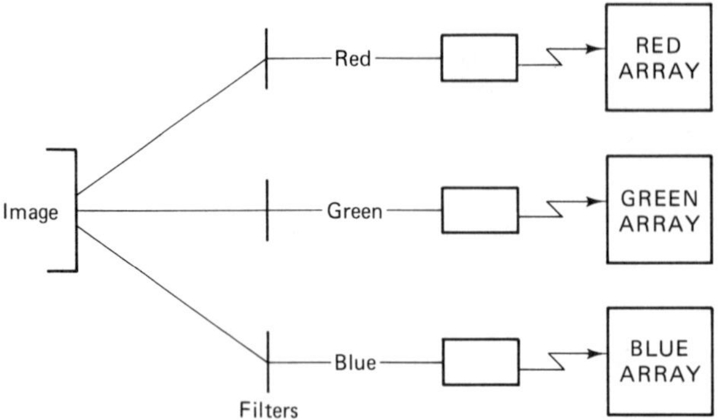

Figure 14.12 Color separation and processing.

an interesting color scene analyser which is based on a rule based inferencing system (Ohta, 1985).

Stereo and Optic Flow

A stereoscopic vision system requires two displaced sensors to obtain two views of objects from different perspectives. The differences between the views makes it possible to estimate distances and derive a three-dimensional model of a scene. The displacement of a pixel from one image to a different location in another image is known as the disparity. It is the dispatity between the two views that permit the estimation of the distance to objects in the scene. The human vision system is somehow able to relate the two different images and form a correspondence that translates to a three-dimensional interpretation. Figure 14.13 illustrates the geometric relationships used to estimate distances to objects in stereoscopic systems.

The distance k from the lens to the object can be estimated from the relationships that hold between the sides of the similar triangles. Using the relations $i_1 / e_1 = f / k$, $i_2 / e_2 = f / k$, and $d = e_1 + e_2$ we can write

$$k = fd / (i_1 + i_2)$$

Since f and d are relatively constant, the distance k is a function of the disparity, or sum of the distances i_1 and i_2.

In computer vision systems, determining the required correspondence between the two displaced images is perhaps the most difficult part in determining the disparity.

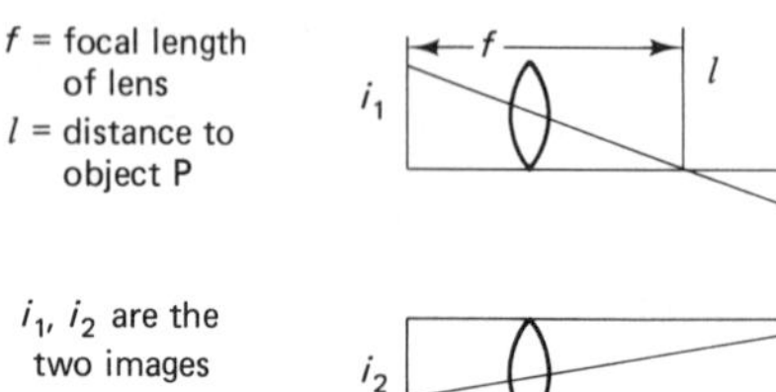

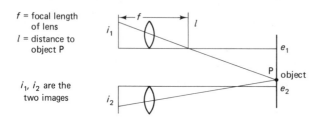

Figure 14.13 Disparity in stereoscopic systems.

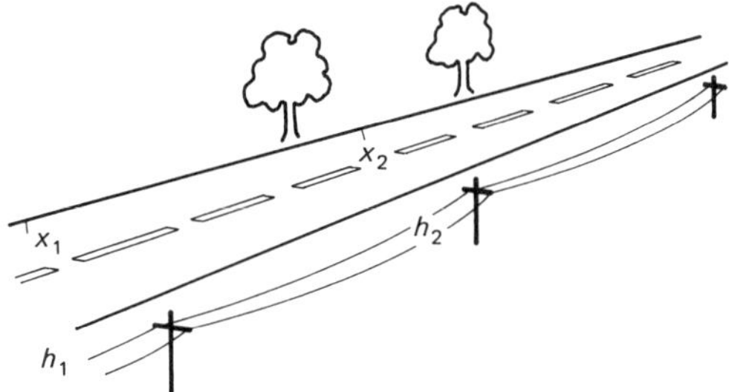

Figure 14.14 Example of optical flow in a scene.

Corresponding pixel groupings in the two images must be located to determine the disparity from which the distance can be estimated. In practice, methods based on correlation, gray-level matching, template matching, and edge contour comparisons have been used to estimate the disparity between stereo images.

Optic flow is an alternative approach to three-dimensional scene analysis which is based on the relative motion of a sensor and objects in the scene. If a sensor is moving (or objects are moving past a sensor), the apparent continuous flow of the objects relative to the sensor is known as optical flow. Distances can be estimated from the change in flow or relative velocity of the sensor and the objects. For example, in Figure 14.14 if the velocity of the sensor is constant, the change in distance dx between points x_1 and x_2 is proportional to the change in size of the power lines h, through the relation

$$dx / dt = k(dh / dt)$$

This relationship is equivalent to the change in size of regular flowing objects with distance from the observer such as highways, railroad tracks, or power lines, as depicted in Figure 14.14.

14.3 INTERMEDIATE-LEVEL IMAGE PROCESSING

The next major level of analysis builds on the low-level or early processing steps described above. It concentrates on segmenting the image space into larger global structures using homogeneous features in pixel regions and boundaries formed from pieces of edges discovered during the low-level processing. This level requires that pieces of edges be combined into contiguous contours which form the outline of objects, partitioning the image into coherent regions, developing models of the segmented objects, and then assigning labels which characterize the object regions.

One way to begin defining a set of objects is to draw a silhouette or sketch of their outlines. Such a sketch has been called the raw primal sketch by Marr (1982). It requires connecting up pieces of edges which have a high likelihood of forming a continuous boundary. For example, the problem is to decide whether two edge pieces such as

```
(edge (location 21 103)        (edge (location 18 98)
      (intensity 0.8)                (intensity 0.6)
      (direction 46))                (direction 41))
```

should be connected. This general process of forming contours from pieces of edges is called *segmentation*.

Graphical Edge Finding

Graphical methods can be used to link up pieces of edges. One approach is to use a minimum spanning tree (MST). Starting at any cluster of pixels known to be part of an edge, this method performs a search in the neighborhood of the cluster for groupings with similar feature values. Each such grouping corresponds to a node in an edge tree. When a number of such nodes have been found they are connected using the MST algorithm.

An MST is found by connecting an arc between the first node selected and its closest neighbor node and labeling the two nodes accordingly. Neighborhoods of both connected nodes are then searched. Any node found closest to either of the two connected nodes (below some threshold distance) is then used to form the next branch in the tree. A second arc is constructed between the newly found node and the closest connected node, again labeling the new node. This process is repeated until all nodes having arc distances less than some value (such as a function of the average arc distances) have been connected. An example of an MST is given in Figure 14.15.

Another graphical approach is based on the assignment of a cost or other measure of merit to pixel groupings. The cost assignment can be based on a simple function of features, such as intensity, orientation, or color. A best-first (branch-and-bound) or other form of graph search is then performed using some heuristic function to determine a least-cost path which represents the edge contour.

Other edge finding approaches are based on fitting a low degree polynomial to a number of edge pieces which have been found through local searches. The resultant polynomial curve segment is then taken as the edge boundary. This approach is similar to one which compares edge templates to short groupings of pieces. If a particular matching template scores above some threshold, the template pattern is then used to define the contour.

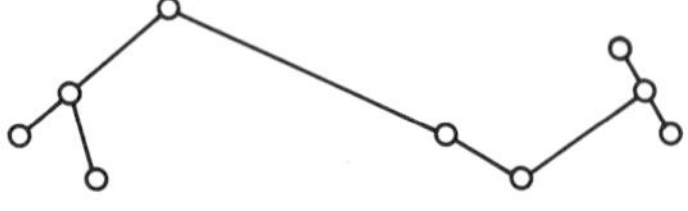

Figure 14.15 Edge finding using a minimum spanning tree.

Edge Finding with Dynamic Programming

Edge following can also be formulated as a dynamic programming problem since picking a best edge path is a type of sequential optimizion problem. Candidate edge pieces are assigned a local cost value based on some feature such as intensity, and the path having minimum cost is defined as the edge contour.

Assume that a starting point E_s has been selected. Dynamic programming begins with a portion of the problem and finds an optimal solution for this subproblem. The subproblem is then enlarged, and an optimal solution is found for the enlarged problem. This process continues step-by-step until a global optimum for the whole problem has been found (a path to the terminal edge point E_t).

The process can be described mathematically as a recursive process. Let $C_n(s,t_n)$ be the total cost of the best path for the remaining path increments, given the search is at position (state) s and ready to select t_n as the next move direction. Let $t_n{}^*$ be the value of t_n that minimizes C_n, and $C_n{}^*$ the corresponding minimum of C_n. Thus, at each stage, the following values are computed:

$$C_n{}^*(s) = \min_{t_n} C_n(s,t_n) = C_n(s,t_n{}^*)$$

where

$$\begin{aligned} C_n(s,t_n) &= \text{(cost at stage } n\text{)} \\ &\quad + \text{(minimum costs for stages } n + 1 \text{ onwards)} \\ &= K(s,t_n) + C_{n+1}{}^*(t_n) \end{aligned}$$

where $K(s,t_n)$ is the cost at stage n, and $C_{n+1}{}^*(t_n)$ is the minimum cost for stages $n + 1$ to the terminal stage.

The computation process is best understood through an example. Consider the following 5×5 array of pixel cost values.

$$\begin{bmatrix} 9 & 7 & 6 & 5 & 1 \\ 3 & 7 & 2 & 7 & 1 \\ 4 & 1 & 5 & 2 & 7 \\ 6 & 6 & 3 & 7 & 7 \\ 8 & 7 & 2 & 2 & 3 \end{bmatrix}$$

Suppose we wish to find the optimal cost path from the lower left to the upper right corner of the array. We could work from either direction, but we arbitrarily choose to work forward from the lower left pixel with cost value 8. We first set all values except 8 equal to some very large number, say M, and compute the minimum cost of moving from the position with the 8 to all other pixels in the bottom row by adding the cost of moving from pixel to neighboring pixel. This results in the following cost array.

$$\begin{bmatrix} M & M & M & M & M \\ M & M & M & M & M \\ M & M & M & M & M \\ M & M & M & M & M \\ 8 & 15 & 17 & 19 & 22 \end{bmatrix}$$

Next, we compute the minimum neighbor path cost for the next to the last row to obtain

$$\begin{bmatrix} M & M & M & M & M \\ M & M & M & M & M \\ M & M & M & M & M \\ 14 & 14 & 17 & 24 & 29 \\ 8 & 15 & 17 & 19 & 22 \end{bmatrix}$$

Note that the minimum cost path to the second, third and fourth positions in this row is the diagonal path (position 5,1 to 4,2) followed by a horizontal right traversal in the same row, whereas the minimum cost path for the last position in this row is the path passing through the rightmost position of the bottom row. The remaining minimum path costs are computed in a similar fashion, row by row, to obtain the final cost array.

$$\begin{bmatrix} 27 & 24 & 23 & 22 & 21 \\ 18 & 22 & 17 & 24 & 20 \\ 18 & 15 & 19 & 19 & 26 \\ 14 & 14 & 17 & 24 & 29 \\ 8 & 15 & 17 & 19 & 22 \end{bmatrix}$$

From this final minimum cost array, the least cost path is easily found to be

$$(5,1) \rightarrow (4,1) \text{ or } (4,2) \rightarrow (3,2) \rightarrow (2,3) \rightarrow (1,4) \rightarrow (1,5)$$

as depicted with the double line path.

$$\begin{bmatrix} 27 & 24 & 23 & 22 = & 21 \\ 18 & 22 & 17 & 24 & 20 \\ 18 & 15 & 19 & 19 & 26 \\ 14 & 14 & 17 & 24 & 29 \\ 8 & 15 & 17 & 19 & 22 \end{bmatrix}$$

Dynamic programming methods usually result in considerable savings over exhaustive search methods which require an exponential number of computations and comparisons (see Chapter 9), whereas the number of dynamic programming computations for the same size of problem is of linear order.

Region Segmentation through Splitting and Merging

Rather than defining regions with edges, it is possible to build them. For example, global structures can be constructed from groups of pixels by locating, connecting, and defining regions having homogeneous features such as color, texture, or intensity. The resulting segmented regions are expected to correspond to surfaces of objects in the real world. Such coherent regions do not always correspond to meaningful regions, but they do offer another viable approach to the segmentation of an image. When these methods are combined with other segmentation techniques, the confidence level that the regions represent meaningful objects will be high.

Once an image has been segmented into disjointed object areas, the areas can be labeled with their properties and their relationships to other objects, and then identified through model matching or description satisfaction.

Region segmentation may be accomplished by region splitting, by region growing (also called region merging), or by a combination of the two. When splitting is used, the process proceeds in a top-down manner. The image is split successively into smaller and smaller homogeneous pieces until some criteria are satisfied. When growing regions, the process proceeds in a bottom-up fashion. Individual pixels or small groups of pixels are successively merged into contiguous, homogeneous areas. A combined splitting-growing approach will use both bottom-up and top-down techniques.

Regions are usually assumed to be disjointed entities which partition the image such that (1) a given pixel can appear in a single region only, (2) subregions are composed of connected pixels, (3) different regions are disjoint areas, and (4) the complete image area is given by the union of all regions. Regions are usually defined by some homogeneous property such that all pixels belonging to the region satisfy the property, and pixels not satisfying the property lie in a different region. Note that a region need not consist of contiguous pixels only since some objects may be split or covered by occluding surfaces. Condition 2 is needed to insure that all regions are accounted for and that they fill up the complete image area.

In region splitting, the process begins with an entire image which is successively divided into smaller regions which exhibit some coherence in features. One effective method is to apply multiple thresholding levels which can isolate regions having homogeneous features. Histograms are first obtained to establish the threshold levels. This may require masking portions of the image to achieve effective separation of complex objects. Each threshold level can then produce a binary image consisting of all of the objects which exceed the thresholded level. Once the binary regions are formed, they are easily delineated, separated, and marked for subsequent processing. This whole process of masking, computing, and analyzing a histogram, thresholding, defining an area, masking, and so on can be performed in a recursive manner. The process terminates when the masks produce monomodal histograms with the image fully partitioned.

Segmentation techniques based on region growing start with small atomic regions (one or a few pixels) and build coherent pixel regions in a bottom-up fashion.

Local features such as the intensity of a group of pixels relative to the average intensity of neighboring pixels are used as criteria for the merging operation. A low level of contrast between contiguous groups gives rise to the merging of areas, while a higher level of contrast, such as found at boundaries, provides the criteria for region segregation.

Split-and-merge techniques attempt to gain the advantages of both methods. They combine top-down and bottom-up processing using both region splitting and merging until some split-merge criterion no longer exists. At each step in the process, split and merge threshold values can be compared and the appropriate operation performed. In this way, over-splitting and under-merging can be avoided.

14.4 DESCRIBING AND LABELING OBJECTS

We continue in this section with further intermediate-level processing steps all aimed at building higher levels of abstraction. The processing steps here are related to describing and labeling the regions.

Once the image has been segmented into disjointed regions, their shapes, spatial interrelationships, and other characteristics can be described and labeled for subsequent interpretation. This process requires that the outlines or boundaries, vertices, and surfaces of the objects be described in some way. It should be noted, however, that a description for a region can be based on a two- or three-dimensional image interpretation. Initially, we focus on the two-dimensional interpretation.

Typically, a region description will include attributes related to size, shape, and general appearance. For example, some or all of the following features might be included.

Region area
Contour length (perimeter) and orientation
Location of the center of mass
Minimum bounding rectangle
Compactness (area divided by perimeter squared)
Fitted scatter matrix of pixels
Number and characteristics of holes or internal occlusions
Minimum bounding rectangle
Degree and type of texture
Average intensity (or average intensities of base colors)
Type of boundary segments (sharp, fuzzy, and so on) and their locations
Boundary contrast
Chain code (described below)
Shape classification number (task specific)
Position and types of vertices (number of adjoining segments)

Some of the above features are illustrated in Figure 14.16.

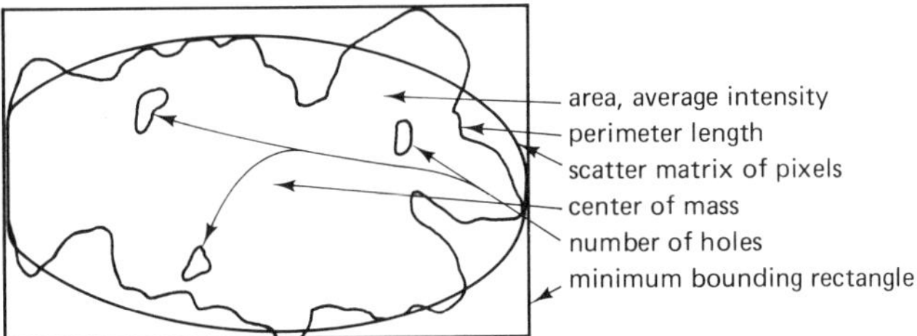

Figure 14.16 Descriptive features for a region.

In addition to these characteristics, the relationships between regions may also be important, particularly adjacent regions. Relations between regions can include their relative positions and orientations, distances between boundaries, intervening regions, relative intensities or contrasts in color, degree of abutment, and degree of connectivity or concentration. When the image domain is known, domain or task specific features may also be useful.

Next, we examine some of the definitions and methods used for region descriptions.

Describing Boundaries

Boundaries can be described as linked straight-line segments, fitted polynomial curves, or in a number of other ways. One simple method of fitting straight-line segments to an arbitrary boundary is by successive linear segmentation fitting. This method permits any degree of fit accuracy at the expense of computation time. The fitting procedure is illustrated in Figure 14.17.

The fitting begins by connecting a single straight line to the two end points and using this as an approximation to the curve (a). Additional lines are then constructed using the points on the curve at maximum perpendicular distances to the fitted lines (b, c,and d).

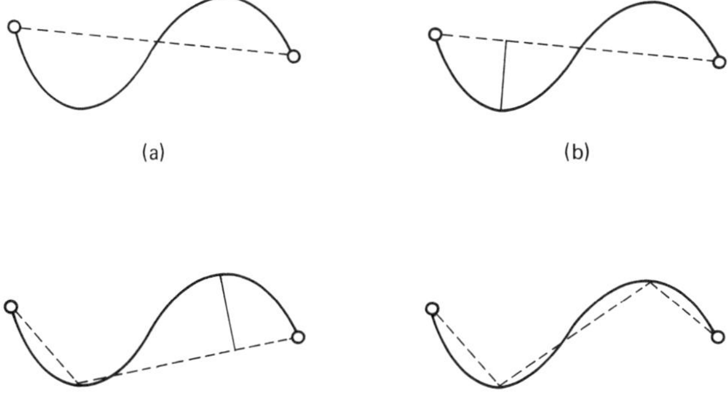

Figure 14.17 Curve fitting with linear segments.

An algorithm to perform the fitting would proceed as follows.

1. Starting with the two end points of the boundary curve, construct a straight line between the points.
2. At successive intervals along the curve, compute the perpendicular distance to the constructed line. If the maximum distance is within some specified limit, stop and use the segmented line as an approximation to the boundary.
3. Otherwise, choose the point on the curve at which the largest distance occurs and use this as a breakpoint with which to construct two new line segments which connect to the two endpoints. Continue the process recursively with each subcurve until the stopping condition of Step 2 is satisfied.

Chain Codes

Another method used for boundary descriptions is known as chain coding. A *chain code* is a sequence of integers which describe the boundary of a region in terms of displacements from some starting point. A chain code is specified by four or more direction numbers which give a trace of the directional displacements of successive unit line segments. An example of a four direction chain code is presented in Figure 14.18.

Chain code descriptions are useful for certain types of object matchings. If the starting position is ignored, the chain code is independent of object location. A derivative or difference (mod 4) for a chain code can also be useful since it is invariant under object rotation. The derivative is found by counting the number of 90 degree counterclockwise rotations made from segment to segment. Thus, the derivative for the chain code of Figure 14.18 is the code

10000303001000103000300003000000000.

Other Descriptive Features

Some other descriptive features include the area, intensity, orientation, center of mass, and bounding rectangle. These descriptions are determined in the following way.

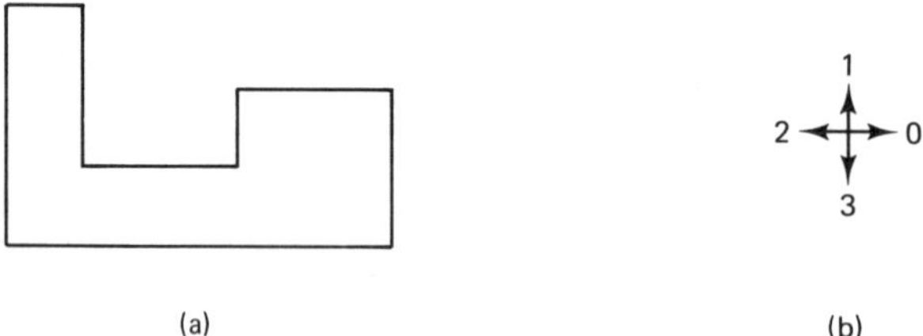

(c) Chain code: 111110033300001100003333322222222222

Figure 14.18 (a) Region boundary, (b) direction numbers, and (c) chain code for region boundary.

1. The area of a region can be given by a count of the number of pixels contained in the region.
2. The average region intensity is just the average gray-level intensity taken over all pixels in the region. If color is used in the image, the average is given as the three base color intensity averages.
3. The center of mass M_c for a region can be computed as the average x-y vector position (denoted as P_i), that is

$$M_c = (1/n) \sum_{i=1}^{n} P_i$$

4. The scatter matrix S_m is an elliptical area which approximates the shape of the region. It may be computed as the average distance from the center of the region mass as follows.

$$S_m = \sum_{i=1}^{n} (P_i - M_c)\,(P_i - M_c)^t$$

   where t denotes matrix transposition.
5. The minimum bounding rectangle is found as the rectangular area defined by the intersection of the horizontal and vertical lines which pass through the maximum and minimum pixel positions of the region.

Three-Dimensional Descriptions

Up to this point, we have been mainly concerned with developing two-dimensional descriptions for images. But for many applications, an analysis which produces a three-dimensional scene description will be required. When a stereo system is being used, the methods described in the previous section for stereo analysis can be applied to estimate such parameters as depths, volumes, and distances of objects. When a two-dimensional image is being used as the source, this information must be determined by other means.

Several programs capable of interpreting images consisting of three-dimensional polyhedral blocks world objects were written beginning in the early 1960s (Roberts, 1965, Guzman, 1969, Huffman, 1971, Clowes, 1971 and Waltz, 1975). The experience gained from this work has led to algorithms and techniques with which to classify and identify regular complex polyhedral types of objects from two-dimensional images.

Roberts wrote a program which began by finding lines in the image which corresponded to the edges of the polyhedral objects. It then used descriptions of the lines to match against stored models of primitive objects such as wedges, cubes, and prisms. To perform the match operation, it was necessary to transform the objects by scaling and performing rotations and translations until a best match was possible. Once a match was obtained and all objects identified, the program demonstrated its "understanding" of the scene by producing a graphic display of it on a monitor screen.

Guzman wrote a program called SEE which examined how surfaces from the same object were linked together. The geometric relationships between different types of line junctions (vertices) helped to determine the object types. Guzman identified eight commonly occurring edge junctions for his three-dimensional blocks world objects. The junctions were used by heuristic rules in his program to classify the different object by type (Figure 14.19).

Huffman and Clowes, working independently, extended this work by developing a line labeling scheme which systematized the classification of polyhedral objects. Their scheme was used to classify edges as either concave, convex, or occluding. Concave edges are produced by two adjacent touching surfaces which produce a concave (less than 180°) depth change. Conversely, convex edges produce a convexly viewed depth change (greater than 180°), and an occluding edge outlines a surface that obstructs other objects.

To label a concave edge, a minus sign is used. Convex edges are labeled with a plus sign, and a right or left arrow is used to label the occluding or boundary edges. By restricting vertices to be the intersection of three object faces (trihedral vertices), it is possible to reduce the number of basic vertex types to only four: the L, the T, the Fork, and the Arrow (Figure 14.20). Different label combinations assigned to these four types then assist in the classification and identification of objects.

When a three-dimensional object is viewed from all possible positions, the four junction types, together with the valid edge labels, give rise to eighteen different permissible junction configurations as depicted in Figure 14.20. From a dictionary of these valid junction types, a program can classify objects by the sequence of bounding vertices which describe it. Impossible object configurations such as the one illustrated in Figure 14.21 can also be detected.

Geometric constraints, together with a consistent labeling scheme, can greatly simplify the object identification process. A set of labeling rules which greatly facilitates this process can be developed for different classes of objects. For example, using the labels described above, the following rules will apply for many polyhedral

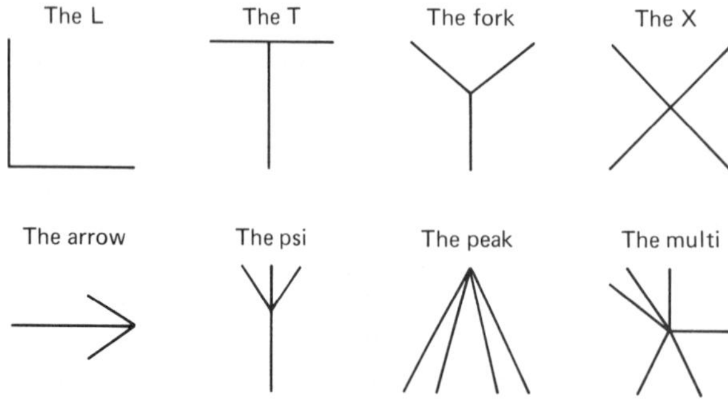

Figure 14.19 Three-dimensional polyhedral junction types.

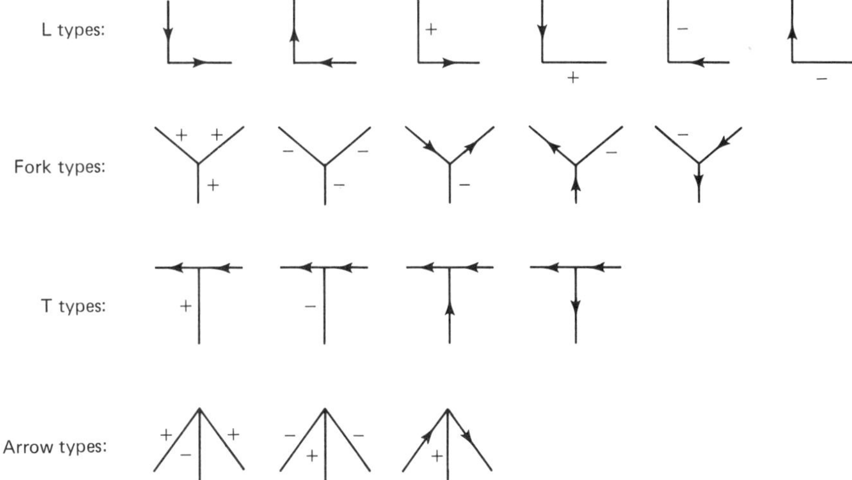

Figure 14.20 Valid junction labels for three-dimensional shapes.

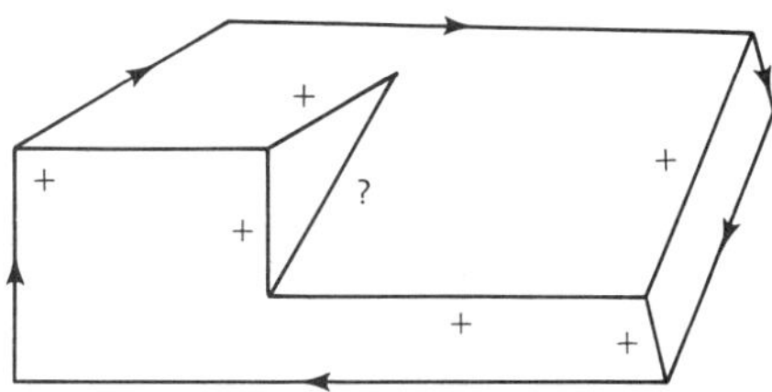

Figure 14.21 Example of an impossible object.

objects: (1) the arrow should be directed to mark boundaries by traversing the object in a clockwise direction (the object face appears on the right of the arrow), (2) unbroken lines should have the same label assigned at both ends, (3) when a fork is labeled with a + edge, it must have all three edges labeled as +, and (4) arrow junctions which have a $\rightarrow$ label on both barb edges must also have a + label on the shaft.

These rules can be applied to a polygonal object as illustrated in Figure 14.22.

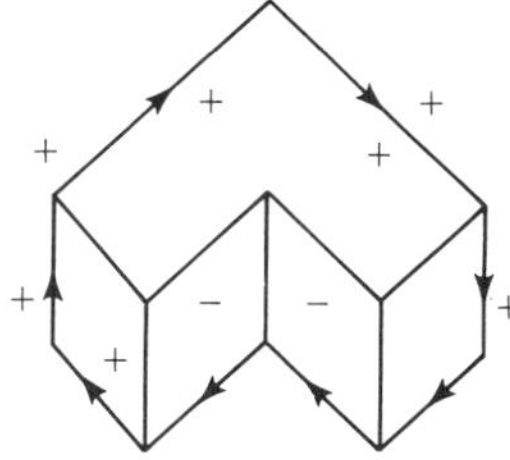

Figure 14.22 Example of object labeling.

Starting with any edge having an object face on its right, the external boundary is labeled with the → in a clockwise direction. Interior lines are then labeled with + or − consistent with the other labeling rules.

Filtering with Constraint Satisfaction

Continuing with this early work, David Waltz developed a method of vertex constraint propagation which establishes the permissible types of vertices that can be associated with a certain class of objects. He broadened the class of images that could be analyzed by relaxing lighting conditions and extending the labeling vocabulary to accommodate shadows, some multiline junctions and other types of interior lines. His constraint satisfaction algorithm was one of his most important contributions.

To see how this procedure works, consider the image drawing of a pyramid as illustrated in Figure 14.23. At the right side of the pyramid are all possible labelings for the four junctions A, B, C, and D.

Using these labels as mutual constraints on connected junctions, permissible labels for the whole pyrimid can be determined. The constraint satisfaction procedure works as follows.

1. Starting at an arbitrary junction, say A, a record of all permissible labels is made for that junction. An adjacent junction is then chosen, say B, and labels which are inconsistent with the line AB are then eliminated from the permissible A and B lists. In this case, the line joining B can only be a +, −, or an up-arrow

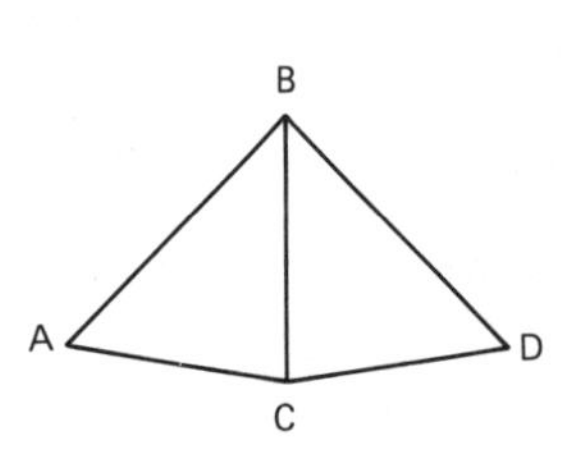

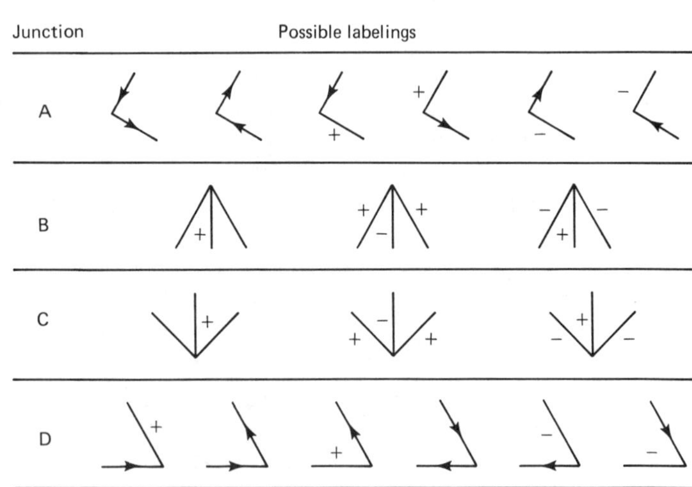

Figure 14.23 Possible labelings for an object.

→. Consequently, two of the possible A labelings can be eliminated with the remaining four being

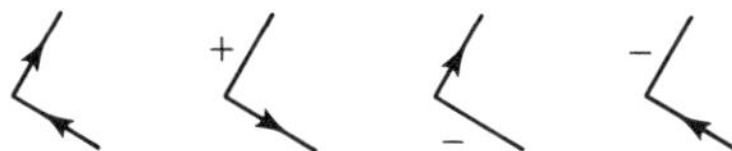

2. Choosing junction C next, we find that the BC constraints are satisfied by all of the B and C labelings; so no reduction is possible with this step. On the other hand, the line AC must be labeled as − or as an up-left-arrow ← to be consistent. Therefore, an additional label for A can be eliminated to reduce the remainder to the following.

3. This new restriction on A now permits the elimination of one B labeling to maintain consistency. Thus, the permissible B labelings remaining are now

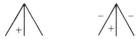

This reduction in turn, places a new restriction on BC, permitting the elimination of one C label, since BC must now be labeled as a + only. This leaves the remaining C labels as

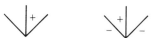

4. Moving now to junction D, we see that of the six possible D labelings, only three satisfy the BD constraint of a − or a down-arrow. Therefore, the remaining permissible labelings for D are now

Continuing with the above procedure, it will be found that further label eliminations are not possible since all constraints have been satisfied. The above process is completed by finding the different combinations of unique labelings that can be assigned to the figure. This can be accomplished through a tree search process. A simple enumeration of the remaining labels shows that it is possible to find only three different labelings. We leave the labeling as an exercise at the end of this chapter.

The process of constraint satisfaction described here has been called Waltz filtering. It is a special form of a more general solution process called relaxation in which constraints are iteratively reduced or eliminated until equilibrium is reached. Such processes can be very effective in reducing large search spaces to manageable ones.

Template Matching

Template matching is the process of comparing patterns found in an image with prestored templates that are already named. The matching process may occur at lower levels using individual or groups of pixels using correlation techniques or at higher image processing levels using labeled region structures. Comparisons between object and template may be based on an exact or on a partial match; and, the matching process may use whole or component pieces when comparing the two. Rigid or flexible templates may also be used. (An example of flexible template matching was described in Section 10.5, Partial Matching, where the idea of a rubber mask template was introduced.)

Template matching can be effective only when the search process is constrained in some way. For example, the types of scenes and permissible objects should be known in advance, thereby limiting the possible pattern-template pairs. The use of some form of informed search can help restrict the size of the search space.

14.5 HIGH-LEVEL PROCESSING

Before proceeding with a discussion of the final (high-level) steps in vision processing, we shall briefly review the processing stages up to this point. We began with an image of gray-level or tristimulus color intensity values and digitized this image to obtain an array of numerical pixel values. Next, we used masks or some other transform (such as Fourier) to perform smoothing and edge enhancement operations to reduce the effects of noise and other unwanted features. This was followed by edge detection to outline and segment the image into coherent regions. The product of this step is a primal sketch of the objects. Region splitting and/or merging, the dual of edge finding, can also be used separately or jointly with edge finding as part of the segmentation process.

Histogram computations of intensity values and subsequent analyses were an important part of the segmentation process. They help to establish threshold levels which serve as cues for object separation. Other techniques such as minimum spanning tree or dynamic programming are sometimes used in these early processing stages to aid in edge finding.

Following the segmentation process, regions are analyzed and labeled with their characteristic features. The results of these final steps in intermediate-level processing is a set of region descriptions (data structures). Such structures are used as the input to the final high-level image processing stage. A summary of the data structures produced from the lowest processing stage to the final interpretation stage then can be depicted as follows.

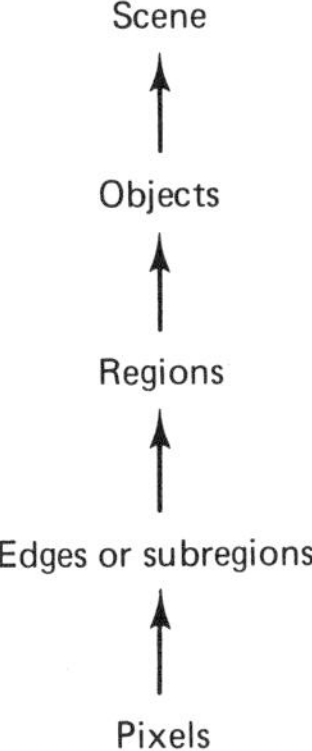

Marr's Theory of Vision

David Marr and his colleagues (1982, 1980, and 1978) proposed a theory of vision which emphasized the importance of the representational scheme used at each stage of the processing. His proposal was based on the assumption that processing would be carried out in several steps similar to the summary description given above. The steps, and the corresponding representations are summarized as follows.

1. Gray-level image. The lowest level in processing consists of the two-dimensional array of pixel intensity levels. These levels correspond to important physical properties of world objects, the illumination, orientation with respect to the observer, geometry, surface reflectances, and object discontinuities. Processing at this stage is local with structure being implicit only. The key aspect of representation at this level is that it facilitate local and first-order statistical transformations.

2. Raw primal sketch. The primal sketch is a two-dimensional representation which makes object features more iconic and explicit. It consists of patterns of edge segments, intensity changes, and local features such as texture. The representation at this stage should emphasize pictorial image descriptions and facilitate transformations to the next stage where surface features and volumes are described.

3. The $2\frac{1}{2}$-dimensional sketch. This sketch is an explicit representation of a three-dimensional scene in which objects are given a viewer-centered coordinate system. The models here provide distance, volume, and surface structure. Three-dimensional spatial reconstruction requires the use of various tools including stereopsis, shape contours, shape from shading and texture, and other tools described earlier.

4. The three-dimensional models. The representations at the three-dimensional model level are symbolic ones giving attribute, relational, and geometric descriptions of the scene. The use of generalized cones and cylinders help to represent many object types, and hierarchical descriptions facilitate processing.

High-Level Processing

High-level processing techniques are less mechanical than either of the preceeding image processing levels. They are more closely related to classical AI symbolic methods. In the high-level processing stage, the intermediate-level region descriptions are transformed into high-level scene descriptions in one of the knowledge representation formalisms described earlier in Part II (associative nets, frames, FOPL statements, and so on; see Figure 14.24).

The end objective of this stage is to create high-level knowledge structures which can be used by an inference program. Needless to say, the resulting structures should uniquely and accurately describe the important objects in an image including their interrelationships. In this regard, the particular vision application will dictate the appropriate level of detail, and what is considered to be important in a scene description.

There are various approaches to the scene description problem. At one extreme, it will be sufficient to simply apply pattern recognition methods to classify certain objects within a scene. This approach may require no more than application of the methods described in the preceding chapter. At the other extreme, it may be desirable to produce a detailed description of some general scene and provide an interpretation of the function, purpose, intent, and expectations of the objects in the scene. Although this requirement is beyond the current state-of-the-art, we can say that it will require a great many prestored pattern descriptions and much general world knowledge. It will also require improvements on many of the processing techniques described in this chapter.

```
(region6
   (mass-center 23 48)
   (shape-code 24)
   (area 245)
   (number-boundary-segments 6)
   (chain-code 1133300011. . .)
   (orientation 85)
   (borders (region4 (position left-of) (contrast 5))
            (region7 (position above) (contrast 2))
               . . .
   (mean-intensity 0.6)
   (texture light regular)
       .
       .
       .
```

Figure 14.24 Typical description of a segmented region.

Before a scene can be described in terms of high-level structures, prestored model descriptions of the objects must be available. These descriptions must be compared with the region descriptions created during the intermediate-level stage. The matching process can take the form of rule instantiations, segmented graph or network matchings, frame instantiations, traversal of a discrimination network (decision tree), or even response to message patterns in an object oriented system. The type of matching will naturally be influenced by the representation scheme chosen for the final structures.

To round out this section, we consider some of the approaches used in the high-level processing stage. In the following section, we consider some complete vision system architectures.

Associative networks have become a popular representation scheme for scene descriptions since they show the relationships among the objects as well as object characteristics. A simple example of an outdoor scene representation is illustrated in Figure 14.25.

Scene descriptions such as this can be formulated by interpreting region descriptions of the type shown in Figure 14.16. The interpretation knowledge will be encoded in production rules or other representation scheme. For example, a rule used to identify a sky region in an outdoor color scene would be instantiated with sky properties such as intensity, color, shape, and so forth. A rule to identify houses in an aerial photograph would be instantiated with conditions of area, compactness, texture, type of border, and so on, as illustrated in Figure 14.26. Rule conditions will sometimes have fuzzy or probability predicates to allow for similarity or partial

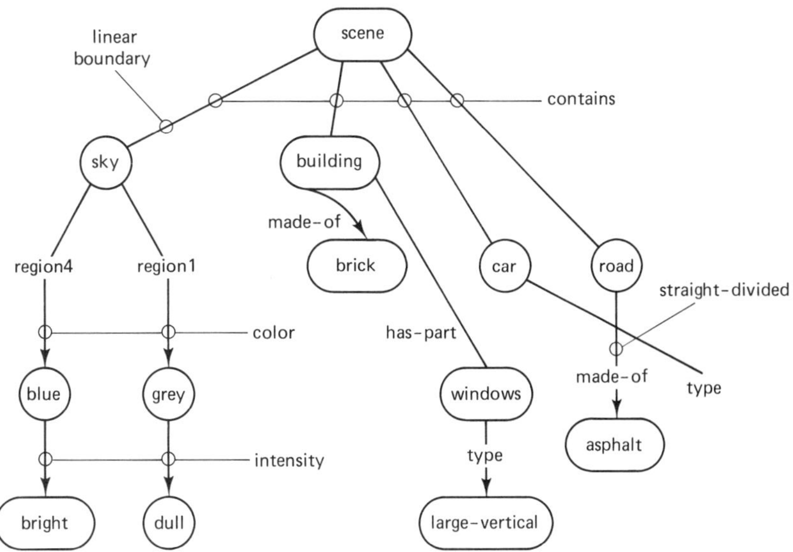

Figure 14.25 Associative network scene representation.

matches rather than absolute ones. Rule conclusions will be rated by likelihood or certainty factors instead of complete certainty. Identification of objects can then be made on the basis of a likelihood score. In Figure 14.26 (a) pairs of numbers are given in the antecedent to suggest acceptable condition levels comparable to Dempster-Shafer probabilities (the values in the figure are arbitrarily chosen with a scale of 0 to 1.0)

When rule-based identification is used, the vision system may be given an initial goal of identifying each region. This can be accomplished with a high-level goal statement of the following type.

```
(label region
   (or (*rgn = building)
       (*rgn = bushes)
       (*rgn = car)
       (*rgn = house)
       (*rgn = road)
       (*rgn = shadow)
       (*rgn = tree)))
```

Other forms of matching may also be used in the interpretation process. For example, a decision tree may be used in which region attributes and relation values determine the branch taken at each node when descending the tree. The leaves of the decision tree are labeled with the object identities as in Figure 14.27.

```
(R10-sky
    (and (location upper *rgn)
         (intensity *rgn bright (0.4 0.8))
         (color *rgn (or (blue grey)) (0.7 1.0))
         (textural *rgn low (0.8 1.0))
         (linear-boundary *rgn rgn2 (0.4 0.7)))
      →
         (label *rgn sky))
```

(a) Sky Identification Rule

```
(R32-building
    (and (intensity-avg *rgn > image)
         (area >= 60)
         (area <= 250)
         (compactness >= 0.6)
         (texture-variation <= 64.0)
         (percent border-planer >= 60)
      →
         (label region HOUSE (0.9))))
```

(b) Building Identification Rule

Figure 14.26 Interpretation rules for a sky and a building.

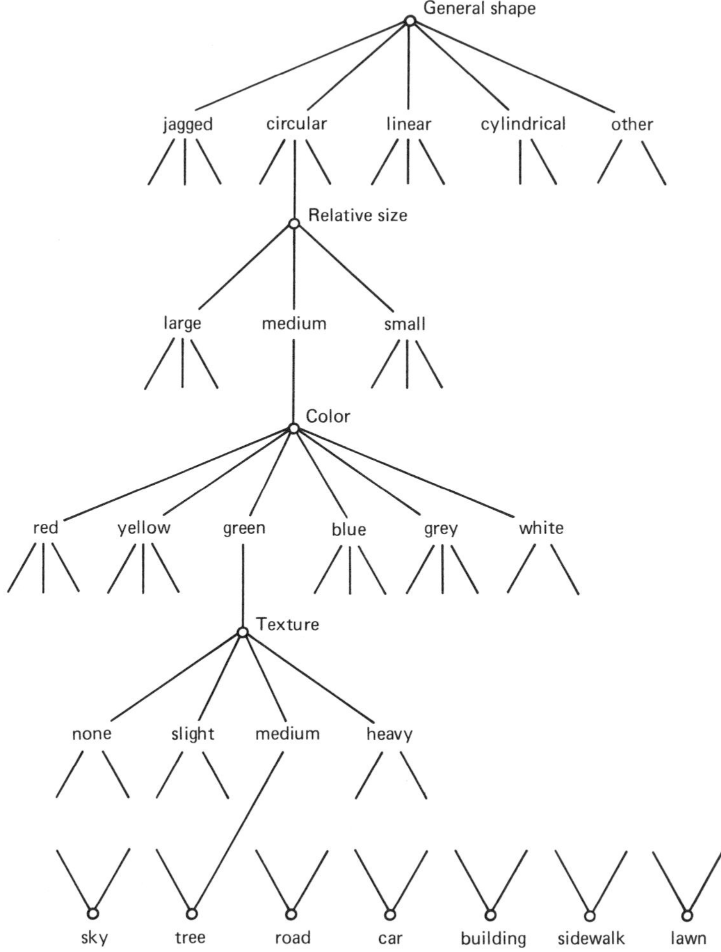

Figure 14.27 Object identification tree.

Objects, with their attributes and relations are then used to construct an associative net scene, a frame network, or other structure.

14.6 VISION SYSTEM ARCHITECTURES

In this section we present two vision systems which are somewhat representative of complete system architectures. The first system is a model-based system, one of the earliest successful vision systems. The second is a color region analyzer recently developed at the University of Kyoto, Japan.

The ACRONYM System

The ACRONYM system is a model-based, domain independent system developed by Rodney Brooks (1981) while at Stanford University during the late 1970s. The system takes user descriptions of sets of objects as models or patterns which are then used to assist in the identification of structures appearing in monocular images. Figure 14.28 illustrates the main components of the system.

The user prepares descriptions of objects or general classes of objects and their spatial relationships and subclass relationships in the form of LISP statements. For example, to model a class of screwdrivers with lengths between 1 and 10 inches, descriptions like the following are specified.

```
(user-variable DRIVER-LENGTH (* 10.0 INCHES))
(user-variable HANDLE-LENGTH (* 4.0 INCHES))
(user-constant HANDLE-RADIUS (* 0.5 INCHES))
(user-constant SHAFT-RADIUS (* 0.125 INCHES))
(define object SCREWDRIVER having
            subpart SHAFT
            subpart HANDLE)
(define object SHAFT having cone-descriptor
  (define cone having main-cone
    (define simple-cone having
       cross-section (define cross-section having
                         type CIRCLE
                         radius SHAFT-RADIUS)
      spine (define spine having
          type STRAIGHT
          length (- DRIVER-LENGTH HANDLE-LENGTH))
      sweeping-rule CSW)))
(affix HANDLE to SCREWDRIVER)
(affix SHAFT to HANDLE with pos HANDLE-LENGTH 0 0)
. . .
```

The user descriptions are parsed and transformed by the system into geometric and algebraic network representations. These representations provide volumetric descriptions in local coordinate systems. A graphic presentation, the system's interpretation of the input models created by the user, provides feedback to the user during the modeling process. The completed representations are used by the system to predict what features (e.g. shape, orientation, and position) of the modeled objects can be observed from the input image components. The predicted models are stored as prediction graphs.

The visual input consists of gray-level image processing arrays, a line finder, and an edge linker. This part of the system provides descriptions of objects as defined by segmented edge structures. The descriptions created from this unit are represented as observation graphs. One output from the predictor serves as an input

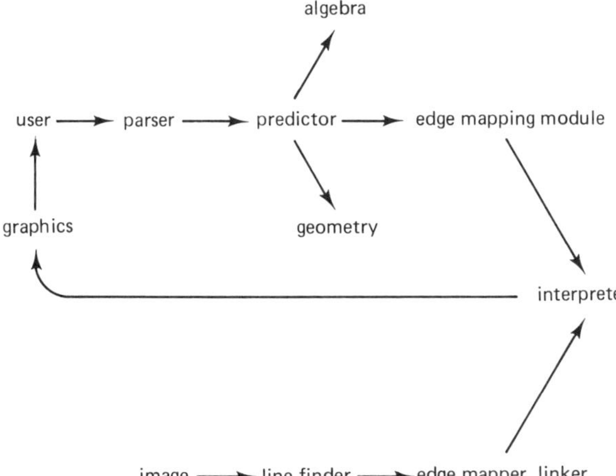

Figure 14.28 Main functional components of ACRONYM.

to the edge mapping and linking module. This unit uses the predicted information (predicted edges, ribbons, or ellipses in the modeled objects) to assist in finding and identifying image objects appearing in the input image. Outputs from both the predictor and the edge mapper and linker serve as inputs to the interpreter. The interpreter is essentially a graph matcher. It tries to find the most matches among subgraphs of the image observation graph and the prediction graph. Each match becomes an interpretation graph. Partial matching is accommodated in the interpretation process through consistency checks.

The basic interpretation process is summarized in Figure 14.29 where models are given for two wide bodied aircraft, (a Boeing 747 and a Lockheed L-1011), and the interpretation of an aircraft from gray-level image to ACRONYM's interpretation is shown.

Ohta's Color Scene Analyzer

Yuichi Ohta of Kyoto University recently developed a vision system which performs region analysis on outdoor color scenes (1986). Outdoor scenes typically include objects such as trees, bushes, sky, roads, buildings, and other objects which are more naturally defined as regions rather than edges. His system makes use of the role color can play in the segmentation process.

Starting with tricolor (red, green, and blue) intensity arrays, digitized images are produced from which regions are defined by a segmentation splitting process. The output of the segmentation process is a two-dimensional array which identifies regions as commonly numbered pixel areas. This array is then transformed into a structured data network which contains descriptive elements for regions such as boundary segments, vertices, and the like. With this network, the system constructs a semantic description of the scene using model knowledge in the form of production rules. Figure 14.30 illustrates the main processing steps carried out by the system.

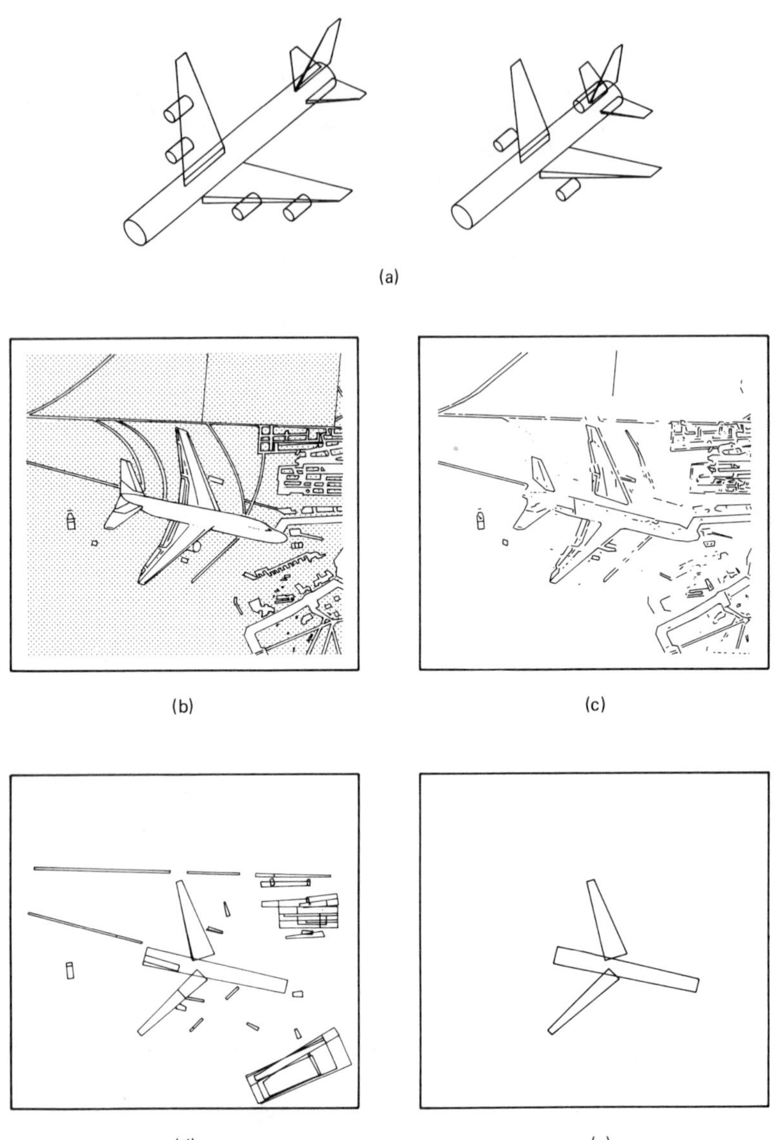

Figure 14.29 Models and stages of interpretation in ACRONYM. (Courtesy of Rodney A. Brooks.)

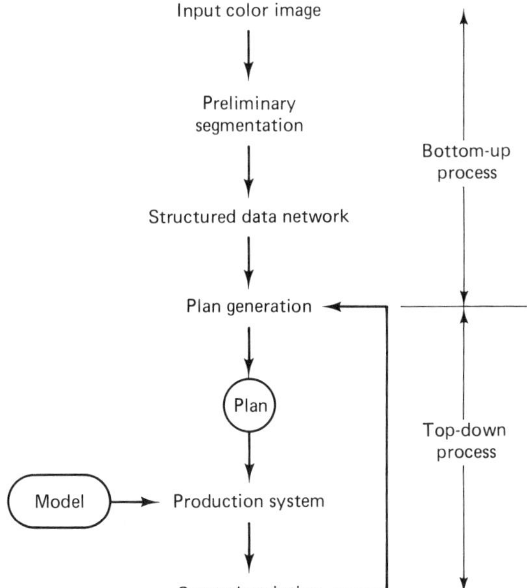

Figure 14.30 Color scene region analyzer.

In the preliminary segmentation stage, the image is segmented into coherent regions using region splitting methods based on color information. Multihistograms serve as cues for thresholding and region splitting. Color features are selected based on results from the Karhunen-Loeve transformation (Devijver and Kittler, 1982) which amounts to choosing those features having the greatest discriminating power (essentially the greatest variance). These segmented regions become the atomic elements from which the structured data network is built.

Regions are characterized by their boundary segments, vertices, line segments, and holes. These basic descriptions are formed during the preliminary segmentation phase. From these, other features are derived including the area, mean color intensities (red, green, blue), degree of texture, contour length, position of mass center, number of holes, minimum bounding rectangle, distance from origin, and orientation. These, and region relationships are described in a data structure known as a patchery data structure. Elements in the data network are essentially matched against model knowledge described in the form of production rules. The rule actions then effectively construct the scene description.

A *plan* is a representation of the crude structure of the input scene given as object labels and their degree of correctness. It is generated by the bottom-up process to provide clues concerning which knowledge can be applied to different parts of the scene.

Knowledge of the task world is represented by sets of production rules. One set is used in the bottom-up process and the other in the top-down process. Each rule in the bottom-up set has a fuzzy predicate which describes properties of relations between objects. The rules also have weights which indicate the level of uncertainty of the knowledge. Each rule in the top-down set is a condition-action pair, where the condition is a fuzzy predicate which examines the situation of the data base. The action part includes operations to construct the scene description. An agenda manages the activation of production rules and schedules the executable actions. Examples of a typical property rule and a relation rule are as follows:

```
[(GEN (or  (*blue *sk) (*gray *sk)) (1.0 . 0.2)) (*sk)]

[GEN (and (linear-boundary *bl *sk)
          (not (position up *bl *sk)))
            (1.0 . 0.5) for sky) (*bl *sk)]
```

The first rule is a property rule about the color of the sky (blue or gray). The second rule is a relation rule about the boundary between a building and the sky. The boundary between the two has a lot of linear parts, and the building is not on the upper side of that boundary.

The final product of the analyzer is, of course, a description of the scene. This is constructed as a hierarchical network as illustrated in Figure 14.31.

Ohta's system has demonstrated that it can deal with fairly complex scenes, including objects with substructures. To validate this claim, a number of outdoor scenes from the Kyoto University campus were analyzed correctly by the system.

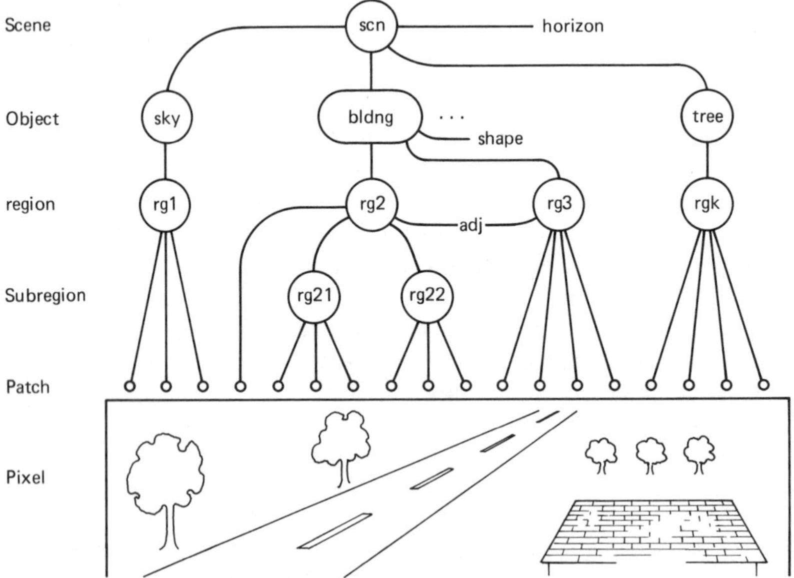

Figure 14.31 Basic structure of the scene description.

14.7 SUMMARY

Computer vision is a computation intensive process. It involves multiple transformations starting with arrays of low level pixels and progressing to high level scene descriptions. The transformation process can be viewed as three stages of processing: low- or early-level processing, intermediate-, and high- or late-level processing. Low-level processing is concerned with the task of finding structure among thousands of atomic gray-level (or tristimulus) pixel intensity values. The goal of this phase is to find and define enough structure in the raw image to permit its segmentation into coherent regions which correspond to definable objects from the source scene. Intermediate-level processing is concerned with the task of accurately forming and describing the segmented regions. The atomic units of this phase are regions and subregions. Finally, high-level processing requires that the segmented regions from the intermediate stage be transformed into scene descriptions. This stage of processing is less mechanical than the two previous stages and relies more on classical AI methods of symbolic processing.

Low-level processing usually involves some form of smoothing operation on the digitized arrays. Smoothing helps to reduce noise and other unwanted features. This is followed by some form of edge detection such as the application of difference operators to the arrays. Edge fragments must then be joined to form continuous contours which outline objects. Various techniques are available for these operations.

The dual-of-the-edge-finding approach is region segmentation, which may be accomplished by region splitting, region growing, or a combination of both. Multihistograms and thresholding are commonly used techniques in the segmentation process. They are applied to one or more image features such as intensity, color, texture, shading, or optical flow in the definition of coherent regions. The end product of the segmentation process will be homogeneous regions. The properties of these regions and their interrelationships must be described in order that they may be identified in the high level processing stage. Regions can be described by boundary segments, vertices, number of holes, compactness, location, orientation, and so on.

The final stage is the knowledge application stage, since the regions must be interpreted and explained. This requires task or domain specific knowledge as well as some general world knowledge. The current state-of-the-art in computer vision does not permit the interpretation of arbitrary complex scenes such as that depicted in Figure 14.1. Much work still remains before that degree of sophistication can be realized.

EXERCISES

14.1. Visual continuity in TV systems is maintained through the generation of 15 frames per second. What characteristics must an ADC unit have to match this same level of continuity for a vision system with a 1024×1024 pixel resolution?

14.2. Describe the types of world knowledge a vision system must have to "comprehend" the scene portrayed in Figure 14.3.

14.3. Suppose the CPU in a vision system takes 200 nanoseconds to perform memory/register transfers and 500 nanoseconds to perform basic arithmetic operations. Estimate the time required to produce a binary image for a system with a resolution of 256 × 256 pixels.

14.4. How much memory is required to produce and compare five different binary images, each with a different threshold level? Assume a system resolution of 512 × 512. Can the binary images be compressed in some way to reduce memory requirements?

14.5. Find the binary image for the array given below when the threshold is set at 35.

$$\begin{bmatrix} 23 & 1 & 32 & 35 \\ 36 & 30 & 42 & 38 \\ 2 & 9 & 34 & 36 \\ 37 & 36 & 35 & 33 \end{bmatrix}$$

14.6. Given the following histogram, what are the most likely threshold points? Explain why you chose the given points and rejected others.

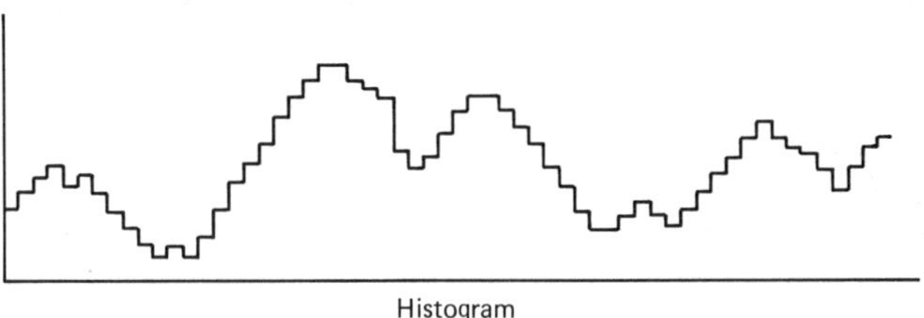

Histogram

14.7. What is the value of the smoothed pixel for the associated mask?

$$\text{MASK} \begin{bmatrix} & 3/16 & \\ 3/16 & 1/4 & 3/16 \\ & 3/16 & \end{bmatrix} \qquad \text{PIXELS} \begin{bmatrix} 7 & 8 & 9 \\ 5 & 4 & 6 \\ 4 & 6 & 2 \end{bmatrix}$$

14.8. Compare the effects of the eight- and four-neighbor filters described in Section 14.2 when applied to the following array of pixel gray-level values.

$$\begin{bmatrix} 5 & 8 & 8 & 10 & 12 & 29 & 32 & 30 \\ 4 & 7 & 8 & 9 & 10 & 9 & 30 & 29 \\ 5 & 8 & 7 & 8 & 11 & 33 & 31 & 34 \\ 6 & 9 & 8 & 10 & 34 & 31 & 29 & 33 \\ 6 & 8 & 9 & 32 & 30 & 29 & 5 & 6 \\ 8 & 7 & 31 & 32 & 32 & 28 & 6 & 7 \\ 7 & 8 & 33 & 33 & 29 & 7 & 8 & 7 \\ 9 & 30 & 32 & 31 & 28 & 8 & 8 & 9 \end{bmatrix}$$

14.9. Low noise systems should use little or no filtering to avoid unnecessary blurring. This means that more weight should be given to the pixel being smoothed. Define two low-noise filters, one a four-neighbor and one an eight-neighbor filter, and compare their effects on the array of Problem 14.5.

14.10. Using a value of $n = 1$, apply D_x and D_y (horizontally) to the array of Problem 14.5 and comment on the trace of any apparent edges.

14.11. Apply the vector gradient to the array of Problem 14.5 and compare the results to those of Problem 14.7.

14.12. This problem relates to the application of template matching using correlation techniques. The objective is to try to match an unknown two-dimensional curve or waveform with a known waveform. Assume that both waveforms are discrete and are represented as arrays of unsigned numbers. Write a program in any suitable language to match the unknown waveform to the known waveform using the correlation function given as

$$C_i = \frac{< \mathbf{X},\mathbf{Z}_i >}{\|\mathbf{X}\| \; \|\mathbf{Z}_i\|}$$

where $\mathbf{X}$ is the unknown pattern vector, $\mathbf{Z}_i$ is the known pattern vector at position i, $< \mathbf{X},\mathbf{Z}_i >$ denotes the inner product of $\mathbf{X}$ and $\mathbf{Z}_i$, and $\|\mathbf{X}\|$ is the norm of $\mathbf{X}$.

$$\|\mathbf{X}\| = [\Sigma_i x_i^2]^{1/2}$$

14.13 Write a program to apply the Sobel edge detection mask to an array consisting of 256×256 pixel gray level values.

14.14 Color and texture are both potentially useful in defining regions. Describe an algorithm that could be used to determine regions that are homogenious in color.

14.15 Referring to Problem 14.14, develop an algorithm that can be used to define regions that are homogeneous in texture.

14.16 Referring to the two previous problems, develop an algorithm that determines regions on the basis of homogeniety in both color and texture.

15

Expert Systems Architectures

This chapter describes the basic architectures of knowledge-based systems with emphasis placed on expert systems. Expert systems are a recent product of artificial intelligence. They began to emerge as university research systems during the early 1970s. They have now become one of the more important innovations of AI since they have been shown to be successful commercial products as well as interesting research tools.

Expert systems have proven to be effective in a number of problem domains which normally require the kind of intelligence possessed by a human expert. The areas of application are almost endless. Wherever human expertise is needed to solve problems, expert systems are likely candidates for application. Application domains include law, chemistry, biology, engineering, manufacturing, aerospace, military operations, finance, banking, meteorology, geology, geophysics, and more. The list goes on and on.

In this chapter we explore expert system architectures and related building tools. We also look at a few of the more important application areas as well. The material is intended to acquaint the reader with the basic concepts underlying expert systems and to provide enough of the fundamentals needed to build basic systems or pursue further studies and conduct research in the area.

15.1 INTRODUCTION

An expert system is a set of programs that manipulate encoded knowledge to solve problems in a specialized domain that normally requires human expertise. An expert system's knowledge is obtained from expert sources and coded in a form suitable for the system to use in its inference or reasoning processes. The expert knowledge must be obtained from specialists or other sources of expertise, such as texts, journal articles, and data bases. This type of knowledge usually requires much training and experience in some specialized field such as medicine, geology, system configuration, or engineering design. Once a sufficient body of expert knowledge has been acquired, it must be encoded in some form, loaded into a knowledge base, then tested, and refined continually throughout the life of the system.

Characteristic Features of Expert Systems

Expert systems differ from conventional computer systems in several important ways.

1. Expert systems use knowledge rather than data to control the solution process. ''In the knowledge lies the power'' is a theme repeatedly followed and supported throughout this book. Much of the knowledge used is heuristic in nature rather than algorithmic.

2. The knowledge is encoded and maintained as an entity separate from the control program. As such, it is not compiled together with the control program itself. This permits the incremental addition and modification (refinement) of the knowledge base without recompilation of the control programs. Furthermore, it is possible in some cases to use different knowledge bases with the same control programs to produce different types of expert systems. Such systems are known as expert system shells since they may be loaded with different knowledge bases.

3. Expert systems are capable of explaining how a particular conclusion was reached, and why requested information is needed during a consultation. This is important as it gives the user a chance to assess and understand the system's reasoning ability, thereby improving the user's confidence in the system.

4. Expert systems use symbolic representations for knowledge (rules, networks, or frames) and perform their inference through symbolic computations that closely resemble manipulations of natural language. (An exception to this is the expert system based on neural network architectures.)

5. Expert systems often reason with metaknowledge; that is, they reason with knowledge about themselves, and their own knowledge limits and capabilities.

Background History

Expert systems first emerged from the research laboratories of a few leading U.S. universities during the 1960s and 1970s. They were developed as specialized problem solvers which emphasized the use of knowledge rather than algorithms and general search methods. This approach marked a significant departure from conventional AI systems architectures at the time. The accepted direction of researchers then was to use AI systems that employed general problem solving techniques such as hill-climbing or means-end analysis (Chapter 9) rather than specialized domain knowledge and heuristics. This departure from the norm proved to be a wise choice. It led to the development of a new class of successful systems and special system designs.

The first expert system to be completed was DENDRAL, developed at Stanford University in the late 1960s. This system was capable of determining the structure of chemical compounds given a specification of the compound's constituent elements and mass spectrometry data obtained from samples of the compound. DENDRAL used heuristic knowledge obtained from experienced chemists to help constrain the problem and thereby reduce the search space. During tests, DENDRAL discovered a number of structures previously unknown to expert chemists.

As researchers gained more experience with DENDRAL, they found how difficult it was to elicit expert knowledge from experts. This led to the development of Meta-DENDRAL, a learning component for DENDRAL which was able to learn rules from positive examples, a form of inductive learning described later in detail (Chapters 18 and 19).

Shortly after DENDRAL was completed, the development of MYCIN began at Stanford University. MYCIN is an expert system which diagnoses infectious blood diseases and determines a recommended list of therapies for the patient. As part of the Heuristic Programming Project at Stanford, several projects directly related to MYCIN were also completed including a knowledge acquisition component called THEIRESIUS, a tutorial component called GUIDON, and a shell component called EMYCIN (for Essential MYCIN). EMYCIN was used to build other diagnostic systems including PUFF, a diagnostic expert for pulmonary diseases. EMYCIN also became the design model for several commercial expert system building tools.

MYCIN's performance improved significantly over a several year period as additional knowledge was added. Tests indicate that MYCIN's performance now equals or exceeds that of experienced physicians. The initial MYCIN knowledge base contained about only 200 rules. This number was gradually increased to more than 600 rules by the early 1980s. The added rules significantly improved MYCIN's performance leading to a 65% success record which compared favorably with experienced physicians who demonstrated only an average 60% success rate (Lenat, 1984). (An example of MYCIN's rules is given in Section 4.9, and the treatment of uncertain knowledge by MYCIN is described in Section 6.5.)

Other early expert system projects included PROSPECTOR, a system that assists geologists in the discovery of mineral deposits, and R1 (aka XCON), a system used by the Digital Equipment Corporation to select and configure components of complex computer systems. Since the introduction of these early expert systems, numerous commercial and military versions have been completed with a high degree of success. Some of these application areas are itemized below.

Applications

Since the introduction of these early expert systems, the range and depth of applications has broadened dramatically. Applications can now be found in almost all areas of business and government. They include such areas as

Different types of medical diagnoses (internal medicine, pulmonary diseases, infectious blood diseases, and so on)
Diagnosis of complex electronic and electromechanical systems
Diagnosis of diesel electric locomotion systems
Diagnosis of software development projects
Planning experiments in biology, chemistry, and molecular genetics
Forecasting crop damage
Identification of chemical compound structures and chemical compounds
Location of faults in computer and communications systems
Scheduling of customer orders, job shop production operations, computer resources for operating systems, and various manufacturing tasks
Evaluation of loan applicants for lending institutions
Assessment of geologic structures from dip meter logs
Analysis of structural systems for design or as a result of earthquake damage
The optimal configuration of components to meet given specifications for a complex system (like computers or manufacturing facilities)
Estate planning for minimal taxation and other specified goals
Stock and bond portfolio selection and management
The design of very large scale integration (VLSI) systems
Numerous military applications ranging from battlefield assessment to ocean surveillance
Numerous applications related to space planning and exploration
Numerous areas of law including civil case evaluation, product liability, assault and battery, and general assistance in locating different law precedents
Planning curricula for students
Teaching students specialized tasks (like trouble shooting equipment faults)

Importance of Expert Systems

The value of expert systems was well established by the early 1980s. A number of successful applications had been completed by then and they proved to be cost effective. An example which illustrates this point well is the diagnostic system developed by the Campbell Soup Company.

Campbell Soup uses large sterilizers or cookers to cook soups and other canned products at eight plants located throughout the country. Some of the larger cookers hold up to 68,000 cans of food for short periods of cooking time. When difficult maintenance problems occur with the cookers, the fault must be found and corrected quickly or the batch of foods being prepared will spoil. Until recently, the company had been depending on a single expert to diagnose and cure the more difficult problems, flying him to the site when necessary. Since this individual will retire in a few years taking his expertise with him, the company decided to develop an expert system to diagnose these difficult problems.

After some months of development with assistance from Texas Instruments, the company developed an expert system which ran on a PC. The system has about 150 rules in its knowledge base with which to diagnose the more complex cooker problems. The system has also been used to provide training to new maintenance personnel. Cloning multiple copies for each of the eight locations cost the company only a few pennies per copy. Furthermore, the system cannot retire, and its performance can continue to be improved with the addition of more rules. It has already proven to be a real asset to the company. Similar cases now abound in many diverse organizations.

15.2 RULE-BASED SYSTEM ARCHITECTURES

The most common form of architecture used in expert and other types of knowledge-based systems is the production system, also called the rule-based system. This type of system uses knowledge encoded in the form of production rules, that is, if . . . then rules. We may remember from Chapter 4 that rules have an antecedent or condition part, the left-hand side, and a conclusion or action part, the right-hand side.

```
  IF: Condition-1 and Condition-2 and Condition-3
THEN: Take Action-4

  IF: The temperature is greater than 200 degrees, and
      The water level is low
THEN: Open the safety valve.

A & B & C & D → E & F
```

Each rule represents a small chunk of knowledge relating to the given domain of expertise. A number of related rules collectively may correspond to a chain of inferences which lead from some initially known facts to some useful conclusions. When the known facts support the conditions in the rule's left side, the conclusion or action part of the rule is then accepted as known (or at least known with some degree of certainty). Examples of some typical expert system rules were described in earlier sections (for example see Sections 4.9, 6.5, and 10.6).

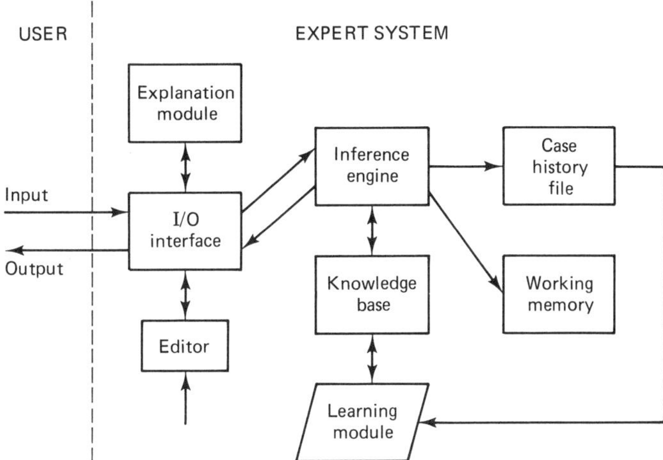

Figure 15.1 Components of a typical expert system.

Inference in production systems is accomplished by a process of chaining through the rules recursively, either in a forward or backward direction, until a conclusion is reached or until failure occurs. The selection of rules used in the chaining process is determined by matching current facts against the domain knowledge or variables in rules and choosing among a candidate set of rules the ones that meet some given criteria, such as specificity. The inference process is typically carried out in an interactive mode with the user providing input parameters needed to complete the rule chaining process.

The main components of a typical expert system are depicted in Figure 15.1. The solid lined boxes in the figure represent components found in most systems whereas the broken lined boxes are found in only a few such systems.

The Knowledge Base

The knowledge base contains facts and rules about some specialized knowledge domain. An example of a simple knowledge base giving family relationships is illustrated in Figure 15.2. The rules in this figure are given in the same LISP format as those of Section 10.6 which is similar to the format given in the OPS5 language as presented by Bronston, Farrell, Kant, and Martin (1985). Each fact and rule is identified with a name (*a*1, *a*2, . . . , *r*1, *r*2, . . .). For ease in reading, the left side is separated from the right by the implication symbol →. Conjuncts on the left are given within single parentheses (sublists), and one or more conclusions may follow the implication symbol. Variables are identified as a symbol preceded by a question mark. It should be noted that rules found in real working systems may have many conjuncts in the LHS. For example, as many as eight or more are not uncommon.

```
((a1 (male bob))
 (a2 (female sue))
 (a3 (male sam))
 (a4 (male bill))
 (a5 (female pam))
 (r1 ((husband ?x ?y))
     →
     (male ?x))
 (r2 ((wife ?x ?y))
     →
     (female ?x))
 (r3 ((wife ?x ?y))
     →
     (husband ?y ?x))
 (r4 ((mother ?x ?y)
      (husband ?z ?x))
     →
     (father ?z ?y))
 (r5 ((father ?x ?y))
      (wife ?z ?x))
     →
     (mother ?z ?y))
 (r6 ((husband ?x ?y))
     →
     (wife ?y ?x))
 (r7 ((father ?x ?z)
      (mother ?y ?z))
     →
     (husband ?x ?y))
 (r8 ((father ?x ?z)
      (mother ?y ?z))
     →
     (wife ?y ?z))
 (r9 ((father ?x ?y)
      (father ?y ?z))
     →
     (grandfather ?x ?z)))
```

Figure 15.2 Facts and rules in a simple knowledge base.

In PROLOG, rules are written naturally as clauses with both a head and body. For example, a rule about a patient's symptoms and the corresponding diagnosis of hepatitis might read in English as the rule

IF: The patient has a chronic disorder, and
the sex of the patient is female, and
the age of the patient is less than 30, and
the patient shows condition A, and
test B reveals biochemistry condition C

THEN: conclude the patient's diagnosis is autoimmune-chronic-hepatitis.

This rule could be written straightaway in PROLOG as

```
conclude(patient, diagnosis, autoimmune_chronic_hepatitis):-
        same(patient, disorder, chronic),
        same(patient, sex, female),
        lessthan(patient, age, 30),
        same(patient, symptom_a, value_a),
        same(patient, biochemistry, value_c).
```

Note that PROLOG rules have at most one conclusion clause.

The Inference Process

The inference engine accepts user input queries and responses to questions through the I/O interface and uses this dynamic information together with the static knowledge (the rules and facts) stored in the knowledge base. The knowledge in the knowledge base is used to derive conclusions about the current case or situation as presented by the user's input.

The inferring process is carried out recursively in three stages: (1) match, (2) select, and (3) execute. During the match stage, the contents of working memory are compared to facts and rules contained in the knowledge base. When consistent matches are found, the corresponding rules are placed in a conflict set. To find an appropriate and consistent match, substitutions (instantiations) may be required. Once all the matched rules have been added to the conflict set during a given cycle, one of the rules is selected for execution. The criteria for selection may be most recent use, rule condition specificity, (the number of conjuncts on the left), or simply the smallest rule number. The selected rule is then executed and the right-hand side or action part of the rule is then carried out. Figure 15.3 illustrates this match-select-execute cycle.

As an example, suppose the working memory contains the two clauses

```
(father bob sam)
(mother sue sam)
```

When the match part of the cycle is attempted, a consistent match will be made between these two clauses and rules r7 and r8 in the knowledge base. The match is made by substituting Bob for $?x$, Sam for $?z$, and Sue for $?y$. Consequently, since all the conditions on the left of both r7 and r8 are satisfied, these two rules will be placed in the conflict set. If there are no other working memory clauses to match, the selection step is executed next. Suppose, for one or more of the selection criteria stated above, r7 is the rule chosen to execute. The clause on the right side of r7 is instantiated and the execution step is initiated. The execution step may result in the right-hand clause (husband bob sue) being placed in working memory or it may be used to trigger a message to the user. Following the execution step, the match-select-execute cycle is repeated.

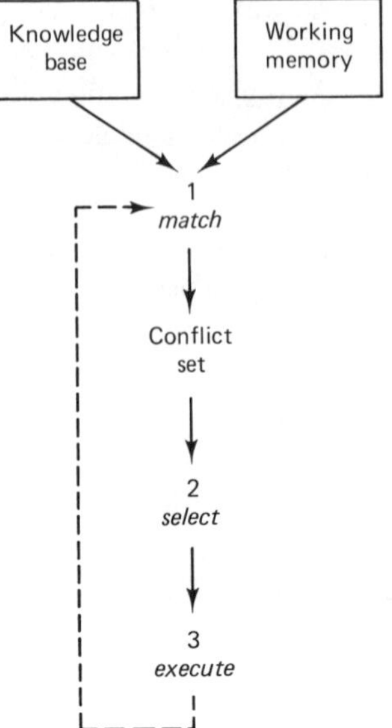

Figure 15.3 The production system inference cycle.

As another example of matching, suppose the two facts (a6 (father sam bill)) and (a7 (father bill pam)) have been added to the knowledge base and the immediate goal is a query about Pam's grandfather. When made, assume this query has resulted in placement of the clause (grandfather ?x pam) into working memory. For this goal to succeed, consistent substitutions must be made for the variables ?*x* and ?*y* in rule r9 with a6 and a7. This will be the case if Sam and Bill are substituted for ?*x* and ?*y* in the subgoal left-hand conditions of r9. The right hand side will then correctly state that Pam's grandfather is Sam.

When the left side of a sequence of rules is instantiated first and the rules are executed from left to right, the process is called forward chaining. This is also known as data-driven inference since input data are used to guide the direction of the inference process. For example, we can chain forward to show that when a student is encouraged, is healthy, and has goals, the student will succeed.

ENCOURAGED(student) → MOTIVATED(student)
MOTIVATED(student) & HEALTHY(student) → WORKHARD(student)
WORKHARD(student) & HASGOALS(student) → EXCELL(student)
EXCELL(student) → SUCCEED(student)

On the other hand, when the right side of the rules is instantiated first, the left-hand conditions become subgoals. These subgoals may in turn cause sub-subgoals to be established, and so on until facts are found to match the lowest subgoal conditions. When this form of inference takes place, we say that backward chaining is performed. This form of inference is also known as goal-driven inference since an initial goal establishes the backward direction of the inferring.

For example, in MYCIN the initial goal in a consultation is ''Does the patient have a certain disease?'' This causes subgoals to be established such as ''are certain bacteria present in the patient?'' Determining if certain bacteria are present may require such things as tests on cultures taken from the patient. This process of setting up subgoals to confirm a goal continues until all the subgoals are eventually satisfied or fail. If satisfied, the backward chain is established thereby confirming the main goal.

When rules are executed, the resulting action may be the placement of some new facts in working memory, a request for additional information from the user, or simply the stopping of the search process. If the appropriate knowledge has been stored in the knowledge base and all required parameter values have been provided by the user, conclusions will be found and will be reported to the user. The chaining continues as long as new matches can be found between clauses in the working memory and rules in the knowledge base. The process stops when no new rules can be placed in the conflict set.

Some systems use both forward and backward chaining, depending on the type of problem and the information available. Likewise, rules may be tested exhaustively or selectively, depending on the control structure. In MYCIN, rules in the KB are tested exhaustively. However, when the number of rules exceeds a few hundred, this can result in an intolerable amount of searching and matching. In such cases, techniques such as those found in the RETE algorithm (Chapter 10) may be used to limit the search.

Many expert systems must deal with uncertain information. This will be the case when the evidence supporting a conclusion is vague, incomplete, or otherwise uncertain. To accommodate uncertainties, some form of probabilities, certainty factors, fuzzy logic, heuristics, or other methods must be introduced into the inference process. These methods were introduced in Chapters 5 and 6. The reader is urged at this time to review those methods to see how they may be applied to expert systems.

Explaining How or Why

The explanation module provides the user with an explanation of the reasoning process when requested. This is done in response to a how query or a why query.

To respond to a how query, the explanation module traces the chain of rules fired during a consultation with the user. The sequence of rules that led to the conclusion is then printed for the user in an easy to understand human-language style. This permits the user to actually see the reasoning process followed by the system in arriving at the conclusion. If the user does not agree with the reasoning steps presented, they may be changed using the editor.

To respond to a why query, the explanation module must be able to explain why certain information is needed by the inference engine to complete a step in the reasoning process before it can proceed. For example, in diagnosing a car that will not start, a system might be asked why it needs to know the status of the distributor spark. In response, the system would reply that it needs this information to determine if the problem can be isolated to the ignition system. Again, this information allows the user to determine if the system's reasoning steps appear to be sound. The explanation module programs give the user the important ability to follow the inferencing steps at any time during the consultation.

Building a Knowledge Base

The editor is used by developers to create new rules for addition to the knowledge base, to delete outmoded rules, or to modify existing rules in some way. Some of the more sophisticated expert system editors provide the user with features not found in typical text editors, such as the ability to perform some types of consistency tests for newly created rules, to add missing conditions to a rule, or to reformat a newly created rule. Such systems also prompt the user for missing information, and provide other general guidance in the KB creation process.

One of the most difficult tasks in creating and maintaining production systems is the building and maintaining of a consistent but complete set of rules. This should be done without adding redundant or unnecessary rules. Building a knowledge base requires careful planning, accounting, and organization of the knowledge structures. It also requires thorough validation and verification of the completed knowledge base, operations which have yet to be perfected. An ''intelligent'' editor can greatly simplify the process of building a knowledge base.

TEIRESIAS (Davis, 1982) is an example of an intelligent editor developed to assist users in building a knowledge base directly without the need for an intermediary knowledge engineer. TEIRESIUS was developed to work with systems like MYCIN in providing a direct user-to-system dialog. TEIRESIUS assists the user in formulating, checking, and modifying rules for inclusion in the performance program's knowledge base. For this, TEIRESIUS uses some metaknowledge, that is, knowledge about MYCIN's knowledge. The dialog is carried out in a near English form so that the user needs to know little about the internal form of the rules.

The I/O Interface

The input-output interface permits the user to communicate with the system in a more natural way by permitting the use of simple selection menus or the use of a restricted language which is close to a natural language. This means that the system must have special prompts or a specialized vocabulary which encompasses the terminology of the given domain of expertise. For example, MYCIN can recognize many medical terms in addition to various common words needed to communicate. For this, MYCIN has a vocabulary of some 2000 words.

Personal Consultant Plus, a commercial PC version of the MYCIN architecture, uses menus and English prompts to communicate with the user. The prompts, written in standard English, are provided by the developer during the system building stage. How and why explanations are also given in natural language form.

The learning module and history file are not common components of expert systems. When they are provided, they are used to assist in building and refining the knowledge base. Since learning is treated in great detail in later chapters, no description is given here.

15.3 NONPRODUCTION SYSTEM ARCHITECTURES

Other, less common expert system architectures (although no less important) are those based on nonproduction rule-representation schemes. Instead of rules, these systems employ more structured representation schemes like associative or semantic networks, frame and rule structures, decision trees, or even specialized networks like neural networks. In this section we examine some typical system architectures based on these methods.

Associative or Semantic Network Architectures

Associative or semantic network representation schemes were discussed in Chapter 7. From the description there, we know that an associative network is a network made up of nodes connected by directed arcs. The nodes represent objects, attributes, concepts, or other basic entities, and the arcs, which are labeled, describe the relationship between the two nodes they connect. Special network links include the ISA and HASPART links which designate an object as being a certain type of object (belonging to a class of objects) and as being a subpart of another object, respectively.

Associative network representations are especially useful in depicting hierarchical knowledge structures, where property inheritance is common. Objects belonging to a class of other objects may inherit many of the characteristics of the class. Inheritance can also be treated as a form of default reasoning. This facilitates the storage of information when shared by many objects as well as the inferencing process.

Associative network representations are not a popular form of representation for standard expert systems. More often, these network representations are used in natural language or computer vision systems or in conjunction with some other form of representation.

One expert system based on the use of an associative network representation is CASNET (Causal Associational Network), which was developed at Rutgers University during the early 1970s (Weiss et al., 1978). CASNET is used to diagnose and recommend treatment for glaucoma, one of the leading causes of blindness.

The network in CASNET is divided into three planes or types of knowledge as depicted in Figure 15.4. The different knowledge types are

Patient observations (tests, symptoms, other signs)
Pathophysiological states
Disease categories

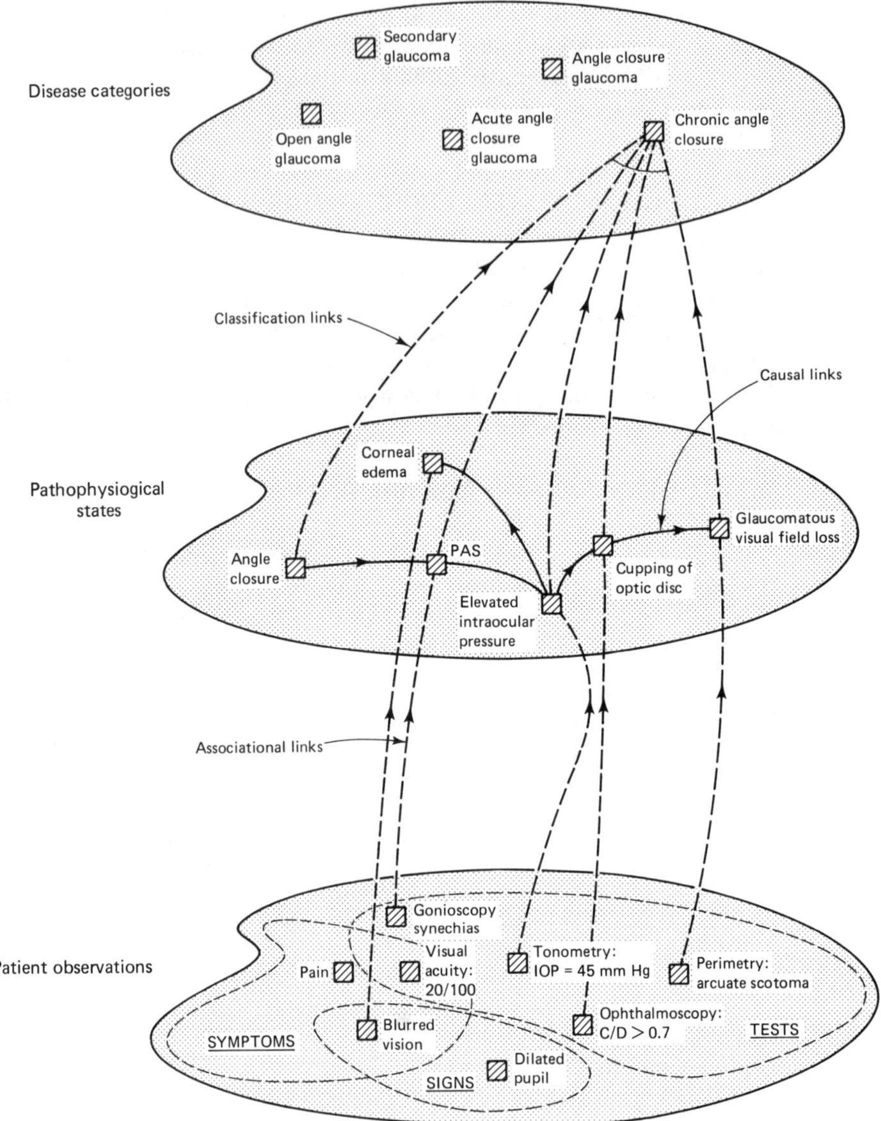

Figure 15.4 Levels of network description in CASNET. (From Artificial Intelligence Journal, Vol. II p. 148, 1978. By permission.)

Patient observations are provided by the user during an interactive session with the system. The system presents menu type queries, and the user selects one of several possible choices. These observations help to establish an abnormal condition caused by a disease process. The condition is established through the causal network model as part of the cause and effect relationship relating symptoms and other signs to diseases.

Inference is accomplished by traversing the network, following the most plausible paths of causes and effects. Once a sufficiently strong path has been determined through the network, diagnostic conclusions are inferred using classification tables that interpret patterns of the causal network. These tables are similar to rule interpretations.

The CASNET system was never used much beyond the initial research stage. At the time, physicians were reluctant to use computer systems in spite of performance tests in which CASNET scored well.

Frame Architectures

Frame representations were described in Chapter 7. Frames are structured sets of closely related knowledge, such as an object or concept name, the object's main attributes and their corresponding values, and possibly some attached procedures (if-needed, if-added, if-removed procedures). The attributes, values, and procedures are stored in specified slots and slot facets of the frame. Individual frames are usually linked together as a network much like the nodes in an associative network. Thus, frames may have many of the features of associative networks, namely, property inheritance and default reasoning. Several expert systems have been constructed with frame architectures, and a number of building tools which create and manipulate frame structured systems have been developed.

An example of a frame-based system is the PIP system (Present Illness Program) developed at M.I.T. during the late 1970s and 1980s (Szolovits and Pauker, 1978). This system was used to diagnose patients using low cost, easily obtained information, the type of information obtained by a general practitioner during an office examination.

The medical knowledge in PIP is organized in frame structures, where each frame is composed of categories of slots with names such as

Typical findings
Logical decision criteria
Complimentary relations to other frames
Differential diagnosis
Scoring

The patient findings are matched against frames, and when a close match is found, a trigger status occurs. A trigger is a finding that is so strongly related to a disorder that the system regards it as an active hypothesis, one to be pursued further. A special is-sufficient slot is used to confirm the presence of a disease when key findings correlate with the slot contents.

Decision Tree Architectures

Knowledge for expert systems may be stored in the form of a decision tree when the knowledge can be structured in a top-to-bottom manner. For example, the identification of objects (equipment faults, physical objects, diseases, and the like) can be made through a decision tree structure. Initial and intermediate nodes in the tree correspond to object attributes, and terminal nodes correspond to the identities of objects. Attribute values for an object determine a path to a leaf node in the tree which contains the object's identification. Each object attribute corresponds to a nonterminal node in the tree and each branch of the decision tree corresponds to an attribute value or set of values.

A segment of a decision tree knowledge structure taken from an expert system used to identify objects such as liquid chemical waste products is illustrated in Figure 15.5 (Patterson, 1987). Each node in the tree corresponds to an identifying attribute such as molecular weight, boiling point, burn test color, or solubility test results. Each branch emanating from a node corresponds to a value or range of values for the attribute such as 20–37 degrees C, yellow, or nonsoluble in sulphuric acid.

An identification is made by traversing a path through the tree (or network) until the path leads to a unique leaf node which corresponds to the unknown object's identity.

The knowledge base, which is the decision tree for an identification system, can be constructed with a special tree-building editor or with a learning module. In either case, a set of the most discriminating attributes for the class of objects being identified should be selected. Only those attributes that discriminate well among different objects need be used. Permissible values for each of the attributes are grouped into separable sets, and each such set determines a branch from the attribute node to the next node.

New nodes and branches can be added to the tree when additional attributes

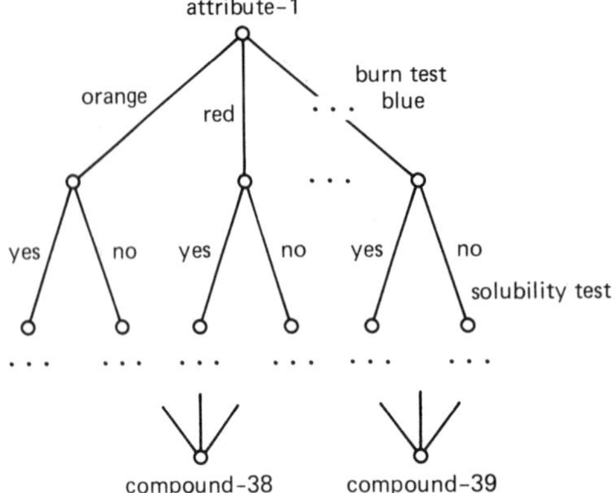

15.5 A segment of a decision tree structure.

are needed to further discriminate among new objects. As the system gains experience, the values associated with the branches can be modified for more accurate results.

Blackboard System Architectures

Blackboard architectures refer to a special type of knowledge-based system which uses a form of opportunistic reasoning. This differs from pure forward or pure backward chaining in production systems in that either direction may be chosen dynamically at each stage in the problem solution process. Other reasoning methods (model driven, for example) may also be used.

Blackboard systems are composed of three functional components as depicted in Figure 15.6.

1. There are a number of *knowledge sources* which are separate and independent sets of coded knowledge. Each knowledge source may be thought of as a specialist in some limited area needed to solve a given subset of problems. The sources may contain knowledge in the form of procedures, rules, or other schemes.
2. A globally accessible data base structure, called a *blackboard,* contains the current problem state and information needed by the knowledge sources (input data, partial solutions, control data, alternatives, final solutions). The knowledge sources make changes to the blackboard data that incrementally lead to a solution. Communication and interaction between the knowledge sources takes place solely through the blackboard.
3. *Control information* may be contained within the sources, on the blackboard, or possibly in a separate module. (There is no actual control unit specified as

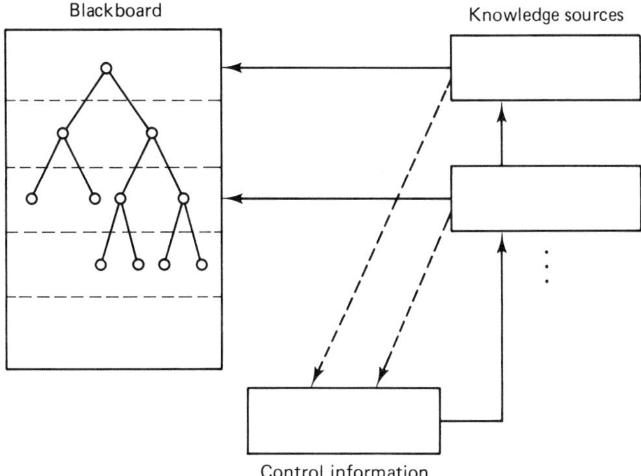

Figure 15.6 Components of blackboard systems.

part of a blackboard system.) The control knowledge monitors the changes to the blackboad and determines what the immediate focus of attention should be in solving the problem.

H. Penny Nii (1986a) has aptly described the blackboard problem solving strategy through the following analogy.

> Imagine a room with a large blackboard on which a group of experts are piecing together a jigsaw puzzle. Each of the experts has some special knowledge about solving puzzles (e.g., a border expert, a shape expert, a color expert, etc.). Each member examines his or her pieces and decides if they will fit into the partially completed puzzle. Those members having appropriate pieces go up to the blackboard and update the evolving solution. The whole puzzle can be solved in complete silence with no direct communication among members of the group. Each person is self-activating, knowing when he or she can contribute to the solution. The solution evolves in this incremental way with each expert contributing dynamically on an opportunistic basis, that is, as the opportunity to contribute to the solution arises.
>
> The objects on the blackboard are hierarchically organized into levels which facilitate analysis and solution. Information from one level serves as input to a set of knowledge sources. The sources modify the knowledge and place it on the same or different levels.

The control information is used by the control module to determine the focus of attention. This determines the next item to be processed. The focus of attention can be the choice of knowledge sources or the blackboard objects or both. If both, the control determines which sources to apply to which objects.

Problem solving proceeds with a knowledge source making changes to the blackboard objects. Each source indicates the contribution it can make to the new solution state. Using this information, the control module chooses a focus of attention. If the focus of attention is a knowledge source, a blackboard object is chosen as the context of its invocation. If the focus of attention is a blackboard object, a knowledge source which can process that object is chosen. If the focus of attention is both a source and an object, that source is executed within that context.

Blackboard systems have been gaining some popularity recently. They have been applied to a number of different application areas. One of the first applications was in the HEARSAY family of projects, which are speech understanding systems (Reddy et al., 1976). More recently, systems have been developed to analyze complex scenes, and to model the human cognitive processes (Nii, 1986b).

Analogical Reasoning Architectures

Little work has been done in the area of analogical reasoning systems. Yet this is one of the most promising areas for general problem solving. We humans make extensive use of our previous experience in solving everyday problems. This is because new problems are frequently similar to previously encountered problems.

Expert systems based on analogical architectures solve new problems like humans, by finding a similar problem solution that is known and applying the known solution to the new problem, possibly with some modifications. For example, if we know a method of proving that the product of two even integers is even, we can successfully prove that the product of two odd integers is odd through much the same proof steps. Only a slight modification will be required when collecting product terms in the result. Expert systems using analogical architectures will require a large knowledge base having numerous problem solutions and other previously-encountered situations or episodes. Each such situation should be stored as a unit in memory and be content-indexed for rapid retrieval. The inference mechanism must be able to extend known situations or solutions to fit the current problem and verify that the extended solution is reasonable. The author and one of his students has built a small toy analogical expert system in LISP to demonstrate many of the features needed for such systems (Patterson and Chu, 1988).

Neural Network Architectures

Neural networks are large networks of simple processing elements or nodes which process information dynamically in response to external inputs. The nodes are simplified models of neurons. The knowledge in a neural network is distributed throughout the network in the form of internode connections and weighted links which form the inputs to the nodes. The link weights serve to enhance or inhibit the input stimuli values which are then added together at the nodes. If the sum of all the inputs to a node exceeds some threshold value T, the node executes and produces an output which is passed on to other nodes or is used to produce some output response. In the simplest case, no output is produced if the total input is less than T. In more complex models, the output will depend on a nonlinear activation function.

Neural networks were originally inspired as being models of the human nervous system. They are greatly simplified models to be sure (neurons are known to be fairly complex processors). Even so, they have been shown to exhibit many ''intelligent'' abilities, such as learning, generalization, and abstraction.

A single node is illustrated in Figure 15.7. The inputs to the node are the values $x_1, x_2, \ldots, x_n$, which typically take on values of -1, 0, 1, or real values within the range $(-1,1)$. The weights $w_1, w_2, \ldots, w_n$, correspond to the synaptic strengths of a neuron. They serve to increase or decrease the effects of the corresponding x_i input values. The sum of the products $x_i * w_i$, $i = 1, 2, \ldots, n$, serve as the total combined input to the node. If this sum is large enough to exceed the

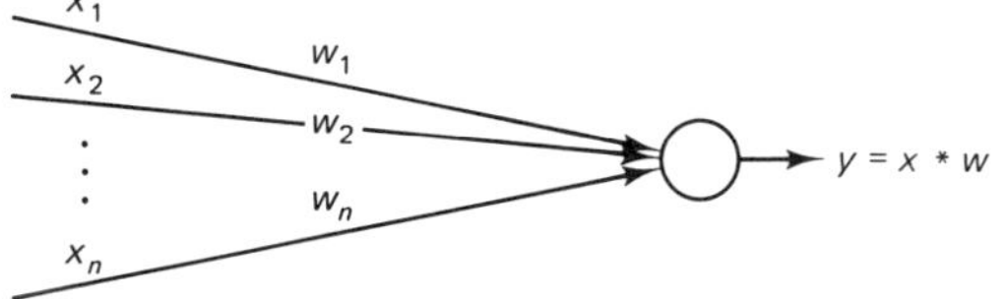

Figure 15.7 Model of a single neuron (node).

threshold amount T, the node fires, and produces an output y, an activation function value placed on the node's output links. This output may then be the input to other nodes or the final output response from the network.

Figure 15.8 illustrates three layers of a number of interconnected nodes. The first layer serves as the input layer, receiving inputs from some set of stimuli. The second layer (called the hidden layer) receives inputs from the first layer and produces a pattern of inputs to the third layer, the output layer. The pattern of outputs from the final layer are the network's responses to the input stimuli patterns. Input links to layer j ($j = 1, 2, 3$) have weights w_{ij} for $i = 1, 2, \ldots, n$.

General multilayer networks having n nodes (number of rows) in each of m layers (number of columns of nodes) will have weights represented as an $n \times m$ matrix **W.** Using this representation, nodes having no interconnecting links will have a weight value of zero. Networks consisting of more than three layers would, of course, be correspondingly more complex than the network depicted in Figure 15.8.

A neural network can be thought of as a black box that transforms the input vector **x** to the output vector **y** where the transformation performed is the result of the pattern of connections and weights, that is, according to the values of the weight matrix **W.**

Consider the vector product

$$\mathbf{x} * \mathbf{w} = \Sigma x_i w_i$$

There is a geometric interpretation for this product. It is equivalent to projecting one vector onto the other vector in n-dimensional space. This notion is depicted in Figure 15.9 for the two-dimensional case.

The magnitude of the resultant vector is given by

$$\mathbf{x} * \mathbf{w} = |\mathbf{x}||\mathbf{w}| \cos \theta$$

where $|\mathbf{x}|$ denotes the norm or length of the vector **x.** Note that this product is maximum when both vectors point in the same direction, that is, when $\theta = 0$. The

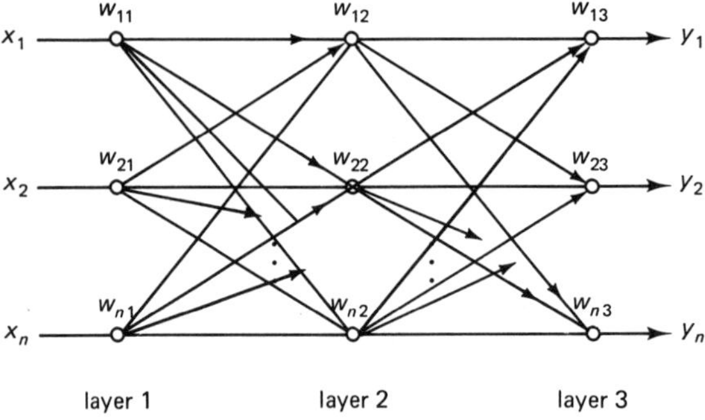

Figure 15.8 A multilayer neural network.

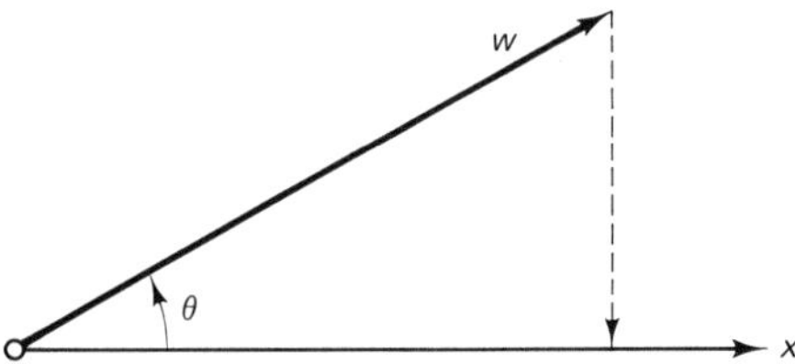

Figure 15.9 Vector multiplication is like vector projection.

product is a minimum when both point in opposite directions or when $\theta = 180$ degrees. This illustrates how the vectors in the weight matrix **W** influence the inputs to the nodes in a neural network.

Learning pattern weights. The interconnections and weights **W** in the neural network store the knowledge possessed by the network. These weights must be preset or learned in some manner. When learning is used, the process may be either supervised or unsupervised. In the supervised case, learning is performed by repeatedly presenting the network with an input pattern and a desired output response. The training examples then consist of the vector pairs $(\mathbf{x},\mathbf{y}')$, where **x** is the input pattern and $\mathbf{y}'$ is the desired output response pattern. The weights are then adjusted until the difference between the actual output response **y** and the desired response $\mathbf{y}'$ are the same, that is until $D = \mathbf{y} - \mathbf{y}'$ is near zero.

One of the simpler supervised learning algorithms uses the following formula to adjust the weights **W.**

$$\mathbf{W}_{\text{new}} = \mathbf{W}_{\text{old}} + a * D * \frac{\mathbf{x}}{|\mathbf{x}|^2}$$

where $0 < a < 1$ is a learning constant that determines the rate of learning. When the difference D is large, the adjustment to the weights **W** is large, but when the output response **y** is close to the target response $\mathbf{y}'$ the adjustment will be small. When the difference D is near zero, the training process terminates at which point the network will produce the correct response for the given input patterns **x**.

In unsupervised learning, the training examples consist of the input vectors **x** only. No desired response $\mathbf{y}'$ is available to guide the system. Instead, the learning process must find the weights w_{ij} with no knowledge of the desired output response. We leave the unsupervised learning description until Chapter 18 where learning is covered in somewhat more detail.

A neural net expert system. An example of a simple neural network diagnostic expert system has been described by Stephen Gallant (1988). This system diagnoses and recommends treatments for acute sarcophagal disease. The system is illustrated in Figure 15.10. From six symptom variables $u_1, u_2, \ldots, u_6$, one of two possible diseases can be diagnosed, u_7 or u_8. From the resultant diagnosis, one of three treatments, u_9, u_{10}, or u_{11} can then be recommended.

When a given symptom is present, the corresponding variable is given a value

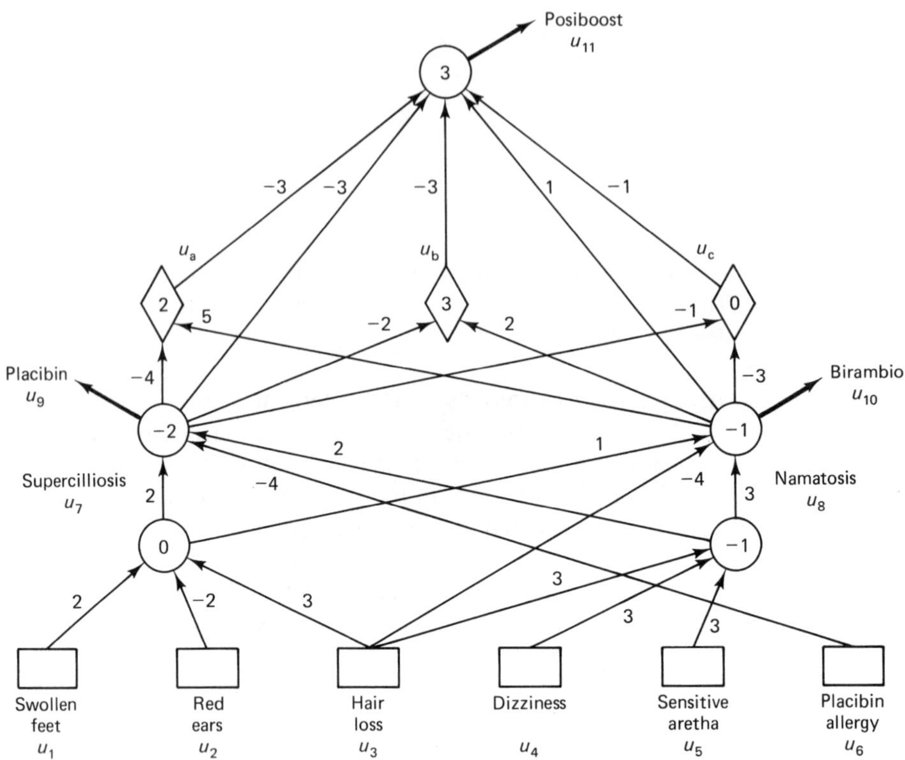

Figure 15.10 A simple neural network expert system. (From S. I. Gallant, ACM Communications, Vol. 31, No. 2, p. 152, 1988. By permission.)

of +1 (true). Negative symptoms are given an input value of −1 (false), and unknown symptoms are given the value 0. Input symptom values are multiplied by their corresponding weights w_{ij}. Numbers within the nodes are initial bias weights w_{i0}, and numbers on the links are the other node input weights. When the sum of the weighted products of the inputs exceeds 0, an output will be present on the corresponding node output and serve as an input to the next layer of nodes.

As an example, suppose the patient has swollen feet ($u_1 = +1$) but not red ears ($u_2 = -1$) nor hair loss ($u_3 = -1$). This gives a value of $u_7 = +1$ (since $0+(2)(1)+(-2)(-1)+(3)(-1) = 1$), suggesting the patient has superciliosis.

When it is also known that the other symptoms of the patient are false ($u_4 = u_5 = u_6 = -1$), it may be concluded that namatosis is absent ($u_8 = -1$), and therefore that birambio ($u_{10} = +1$) should be prescribed while placibin should not be prescribed ($u_9 = -1$). In addition, it will be found that posiboost should also be prescribed ($u_{11} = +1$).

The intermediate triangular shaped nodes were added by the training algorithm. These additional nodes are needed so that weight assignments can be made which permit the computations to work correctly for all training instances.

Deductions can be made just as well when only partial information is available. For example, when a patient has swollen feet and suffers from hair loss, it may be concluded the patient has superciliosis, regardless of whether or not the patient has red ears. This is so because the unknown variable cannot force the sum to change to negative.

A system such as this can also explain how or why a conclusion was reached. For example, when inputs and outputs are regarded as rules, an output can be explained as the conclusion to a rule. If placibin is true, the system might explain why with a statement such as

Placibin is TRUE due to the following rule:

IF Placibin Alergy (u_6) is FALSE, and
  Superciliosis is TRUE

THEN Conclude Placibin is TRUE.

Expert systems based on neural network architectures can be designed to possess many of the features of other expert system types, including explanations for how and why, and confidence estimation for variable deduction.

15.4 DEALING WITH UNCERTAINTY

In Chapters 5 and 6 we discussed the problem of dealing with uncertainty in knowledge-based systems. We found that different approaches were possible including probabilistic (Bayesian or Shafer-Dempster), the use of fuzzy logic, ad-hoc, and heuristic methods. All of these methods have been applied in some form of system, and many building tools permit the use of more than a single method. The ad-hoc method used in MYCIN was described in Section 6.5. Refer to that section to review how uncertainty computations are performed in a typical expert system.

15.5 KNOWLEDGE ACQUISITION AND VALIDATION

One of the most difficult tasks in building knowledge-based systems is in the acquisition and encoding of the requisite domain knowledge. Knowledge for expert systems must be derived from expert sources like experts in the given field, journal articles, texts, reports, data bases, and so on. Elicitation of the right knowledge can take several man years and cost hundreds of thousands of dollars. This process is now recognized as one of the main bottlenecks in building expert and other knowledge-based systems. Consequently, much effort has been devoted to more effective methods of acquisition and coding.

Pulling together and correctly interpreting the right knowledge to solve a set of complex tasks is an onerous job. Typically, experts do not know what specific knowledge is being applied nor just how it is applied in the solution of a given problem. Even if they do know, it is likely they are unable to articulate the problem solving process well enough to capture the low-level knowledge used and the inferring processes applied. This difficulty has led to the use of AI experts (called knowledge engineers) who serve as intermediaries between the domain expert and the system. The knowledge engineer elicits information from the experts and codes this knowledge into a form suitable for use in the expert system.

The knowledge elicitation process is depicted in Figure 15.11. To elicit the requisite knowledge, a knowlege engineer conducts extensive interviews with domain experts. During the interviews, the expert is asked to solve typical problems in the domain of interest and to explain his or her solutions.

Using the knowledge gained from the experts and other sources, the knowledge engineer codes the knowledge in the form of rules or some other representation scheme. This knowledge is then used to solve sample problems for review and validation by the experts. Errors and omissions are uncovered and corrected, and additional knowledge is added as needed. The process is repeated until a sufficient body of knowledge has been collected to solve a large class of problems in the chosen domain. The whole process may take as many as tens of person years.

Penny Nii, an experienced knowledge engineer at Stanford University, has described some useful practices to follow in solving acquisition problems through a sequence of heuristics she uses. They have been summarized in the book *The Fifth Generation* by Feigenbaum and McCorduck (1983) as follows.

> You can't be your own expert. By examining the process of your own expertise you risk becoming like the centipede who got tangled up in her own legs and stopped dead when she tried to figure out how she moved a hundred legs in harmony.
>
> From the beginning, the knowledge engineer must count on throwing efforts away. Writers make drafts, painters make preliminary sketches; knowledge engineers are no different.
>
> The problem must be well chosen. AI is a young field and isn't ready to take on every problem the world has to offer. Expert systems work best when the problem is well bounded, which is computer talk to describe a problem for which large amounts of specialized knowledge may be needed, but not a general knowledge of the world.
>
> If you want to do any serious application you need to meet the expert more than half way; if he's had no exposure to computing, your job will be that much harder.
>
> If none of the tools you normally use works, build a new one.
>
> Dealing with anything but facts implies uncertainty. Heuristic knowledge is not hard and fast and cannot be treated as factual. A weighting procedure has to be built into

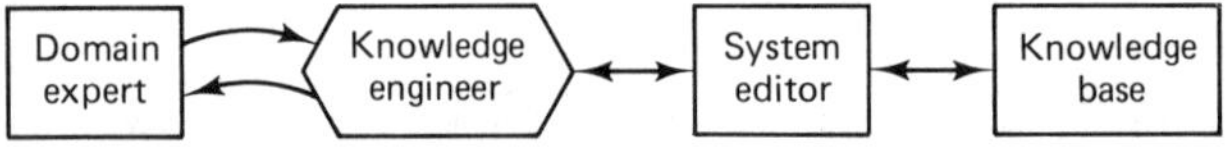

Figure 15.11 The knowledge acquisition process.

the expert system to allow for expressions such as "I strongly believe that . . ." or "The evidence suggests that. . . ."

A high-performance program, or a program that will eventually be taken over by the expert for his own use, must have very easy ways of allowing the knowledge to be modified so that new information can be added and out-of-date information deleted.

The problem needs to be a useful, interesting one. There are knowledge-based programs to solve arcane puzzles, but who cares? More important, the user has to understand the system's real value to his work.

When Nii begins a project, she first persuades a human expert to commit the considerable time that is required to have the expert's mind mined. Once this is done, she immerses herself in the given field, reading texts, articles, and other material to better understand the field and to learn the basic jargon used. She then begins the interviewing process. She asks the expert to describe his or her tasks and problem solving techniques. She asks the expert to choose a moderately difficult problem to solve as an example of the basic approach. This information is then collected, studied, and presented to other members of the development team so that a quick prototype can be constructed for the expert to review. This serves several purposes. First, it helps to keep the expert in the development loop and interested. Secondly, it serves as a rudimentary model with which to uncover flaws and other problems. It also helps both expert and developer in discovering the real way the expert solves problems. This usually leads to a repeat of the problem solving exercise, but this time in a step-by-step walk through of the sample problem. Nii tests the accuracy of the expert's explanations by observing his or her behavior and reliance on data and other sources of information. She is concerned more with the manipulation of the knowledge than with the actual facts. Keeping the expert focused on the immediate problem requires continual prompting and encouragement.

During the whole interview process Nii is mentally examining alternative approaches for the best knowledge representation and inferencing methods to see how well each would best match the expert's behavior. The whole process of elicitation, coding, and verification may take several iterations over a period of several months.

Recognizing the acquisition bottleneck in building expert systems, researchers and vendors alike have sought new and better ways to reduce the burden and reliance placed on knowledge engineers, and in general, ways to improve and speed up the development process. This has led to a number of sophisticated building tools which we consider next.

15.6 KNOWLEDGE SYSTEM BUILDING TOOLS

Since the introduction of the first successful expert systems in the late 1970s, a large number of building tools have been introduced, both by the academic community and industry. These tools range from high level programming languages to intelligent editors to complete shell environment systems. A number of commercial products are now available ranging in price from a few hundred dollars to tens of thousands of dollars. Some are capable of running on medium size PCs while others require larger systems such as LISP machines, minis, or even main frames.

When evaluating building tools for expert system development, the developer should consider the following features and capabilities that may be offered in systems.

1. Knowledge representation methods available (rules, logic-based network structures, frames, with or without inheritance, multiple world views, object-oriented, procedural, and the methods offered for dealing with uncertainty, if any).
2. Inference and control methods available (backward chaining, forward chaining, mixed forward and backward chaining, blackboard architecture approach, logic driven theorem prover, object-oriented approach, the use of attached procedures, types of meta-control capabilities, forms of uncertainty management, hypothetical reasoning, truth maintenance management, pattern matching with or without indexing, user functions permitted, linking options to modules written in other languages, and linking options to other sources of information such as data bases).
3. User interface characteristics (editor flexibility and ease of use, use of menus, use of pop-up windows, developer provided text capabilities for prompts and help messages, graphics capabilities, consistency checking for newly entered knowledge, explanation of how and why capabilities, system help facilities, screen formatting and color selection capabilities, network representation of knowledge base, and forms of compilation available, batch or interactive).
4. General system characteristics and support available (types of applications with which the system has been successfully used, the base programming language in which the system was written, the types of hardware the systems are supported on, general utilities available, debugging facilities, interfacing flexibility to other languages and databases, vendor training availability and cost, strength of software support, and company reputation).

In the remainder of this section, we describe a few representative building tool systems. For a more complete picture of available systems, the reader is referred to other sources.

Personal Consultant Plus

A family of Personal Consultant expert system shells was developed by Texas Instruments, Inc. (TI) in the early 1980s. These shells are rule-based building tools patterned after the MYCIN system architecture and developed to run on a PC as well as on larger systems such as the TI Explorer. The largest and most versatile of the Personal Consultant family is Personal Consultant Plus.

Personal Consultant Plus permits the use of structures called frames (different from the frames of Chapter 7) to organize functionally related production rules into subproblem groups. The frames are hierarchically linked into a tree structure which is traversed during a user consultation. For example, a home electrical appliance diagnostic system might have subframes of microwave cooker, iron, blender, and toaster as depicted in Figure 15.12.

When diagnosing a problem, only the relevant frames would be matched, and the rules in each frame would address only that part of the overall problem. A feature of the frame structure is that parameter property inheritance is supported from ancestor to descendant frames.

The system supports certainty factors both for parameter values and for complete rules. These factors are propagated throughout a chain of rules used during a consultation session, and the resultant certainty values associated with a conclusion are presented. The system also has an explanation capability to show how a conclusion was reached by displaying all rules that lead to a conclusion and why a fact is needed to fire a given rule.

An interactive dialog is carried out between user and system during a consultation session. The system prompts the user with English statements provided by the developer. Menu windows with selectable colors provide the user parameter value selections. A help facility is also available so the developer can provide explanations and give general assistance to the user during a consultation session.

A system editor provides a number of helpful facilities to build, store, and print a knowledge base. Parameter and property values, textual prompts, help messages, and debug traces are all provided through the editor. In addition, user defined functions written in LISP may be provided by a developer as part of a rule's conditions and/or actions. The system also provides access to other sources of information, such as dBase II and dBase III. An optional graphics package is also available at extra cost.

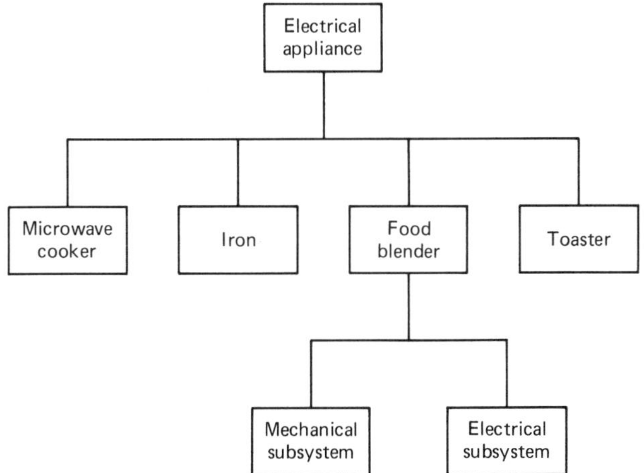

Figure 15.12 Hierarchical frame structure in PC Plus.

Radian Rulemaster

The Rulemaster system developed in the early 1980s by the Radian Corporation was written in C language to run on a variety of mini- and microcomputer systems. Rulemaster is a rule-based building tool which consists of two main components: Radial, a procedural, block structured language for expressing decision rules related to a finite state machine, and Rulemaker, a knowledge acquisition system which induces decision trees from examples supplied by an expert. A program in Rulemaster consists of a collection of related modules which interact to affect changes of state. The modules may contain executable procedures, advice, or data. The building system is illustrated in Figure 15.13.

Rulemaster's knowledge can be based on partial certainty using fuzzy logic or heuristic methods defined by the developer. Users can define their own data types or abstract types much the same as in Pascal. An explanation facility is provided to explain its chain of reasoning. Programs in other languages can also be called from Rulemaster.

One of the unique features of Rulemaster is the Rulemaker component which has the ability to induce rules from examples. Experts are known to have difficulty in directly expressing rules related to their decision processes. On the other hand, they can usually come up with a wealth of examples in which they describe typical solution steps. The examples provided by the expert offer a more accurate way in

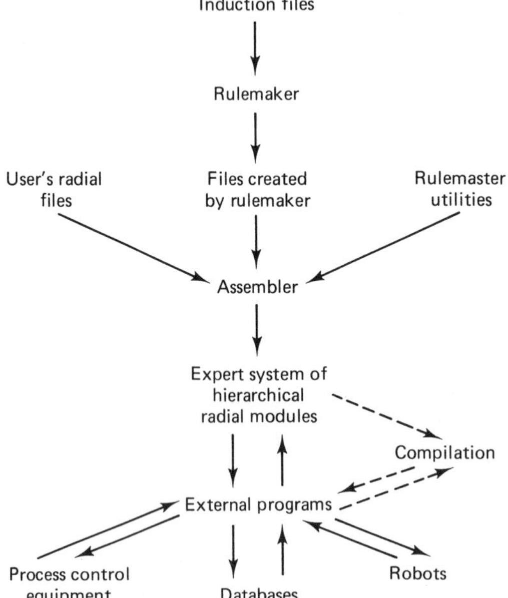

Figure 15.13 Rulemaster building system.

which the problem solving process is carried out. These examples are transformed into rules by Rulemaker through an induction process.

KEE (Knowledge Engineering Environment)

KEE is one of the more popular building tools for the development of larger-scale systems. Developed by Intellicorp, this system employs sophisticated representation schemes structured around frames called units. The frames are made up of slots and facets which contain object attribute values, rules, methods, logical assertions, text, or even other frames. The frames are organized into one or more knowledge bases in the form of hierarchical structures which permit multiple inheritance down hierarchical paths. Rules, procedures, and object oriented representation methods are also supported.

Inference is carried out through inheritance, forward-chaining, backward-chaining, or a mixture of these methods. A form of hypothetical reasoning is also provided through different viewpoints which may be explored concurrently. The viewpoints represent different aspects of a situation, views of the same situation taken at different times, hypothetical situations, or alternative courses of action. This feature permits a user to compare competing courses of action or to reason in parallel about partial solutions based on different approaches.

KEE's support environment includes a graphics-oriented debugging package, flexible end-user interfaces using windows, menus, and an explanation capability with graphic displays which can show inference chains. A graphics-based simulation package called SimKit is available at additional cost.

KEE has been used for the development of intelligent user interfaces, genetics, diagnosis and monitoring of complicated systems, planning, design, process control, scheduling, and simulation. The system is LISP based, developed for operation on systems such as Symbolics machines, Xerox 1100s, or TI Explorers. Systems can also be ported to open architecture machines which support Common LISP without extensive modification.

OPS5 System

The OPS5 and other OPS building tools were developed at Carnegie Mellon University in conjunction with DEC during the late 1970s. This system was developed to build the R1/XCON expert system which configures Vax and other DEC minicomputer systems. The system is used to build rule-based production systems which use forward chaining in the inference process (backward and mixed chaining is also possible). The system was written in C language to run on the DEC Vax and other minicomputers. It uses a sophisticated method of indexing rules (the Rete algorithm) to reduce the matching times during the match-select-execute cycle. Examples of OPS5 rules were given above in Section 15.2, and a description of the Rete match algorithm was given in Section 10.6.

15.7 SUMMARY

Expert and other knowledge-based systems are usually composed of at least a knowledge base, an inference engine, and some form of user interface. The knowledge base, which is separate from the inference and control components, contains the expert knowledge coded in some form such as production rules, networks of frames or other representation scheme. The inference engine manipulates the knowledge structures in the knowledge base to perform a type of symbolic reasoning and draw useful conclusions relating to the current task. The user interface provides the means for dialog between the user and system. The user inputs commands, queries, and responses to system messages, and the system, in turn, produces various messages for the user. In addition to these three components, most systems have an editor for use in creating and modifying the knowledge base structures and an explanation module which provides the user with explanations of how a conclusion was reached or why a piece of knowledge is needed. A few systems also have some learning capability and a case history file with which to record complete consultation traces.

A variety of expert system architectures have been constructed including rule-based systems, frame-based systems, decision tree (discrimination network) systems, analogical reasoning systems, blackboard architectures, theorem proving systems, and even neural network architectures. These systems may differ in the direction of rule chaining, in the handling of uncertainty, and in the search and pattern matching methods employed. Rule and frame based systems are by far the most popular architectures used.

Since the introduction of the first expert systems in the late 1970s, a number of building tools have been developed. Such tools may be as unsophisticated as a bare high level language or as comprehensive as a complete shell development environment. A few representative building tools have been described and some general characteristics of tools for developers were given.

The acquisition of expert knowledge for knowledge-based systems remains one of the main bottlenecks in building them. This has led to a new discipline called knowledge engineering. Knowledge engineers build systems by eliciting knowledge from experts, coding that knowledge in an appropriate form, validating the knowledge, and ultimately constructing a system using a variety of building tools.

EXERCISES

15.1. What are the main advantages in keeping the knowledge base separate from the control module in knowledge-based systems?

15.2. Why is it important that an expert system be able to explain the why and how questions related to a problem solving session?

15.3. Give an example of the use of metaknowledge in expert systems inference.

15.4. Describe and compare the different types of problems solved by four of the earliest expert systems DENDRAL, MYCIN, PROSPECTOR, and R1.

15.5. Identify and describe two good application areas for expert systems within a university environment.

15.6. How do rules in PROLOG differ from general production system rules?

15.7. Make up a small knowledge-base of facts and rules using the same syntax as that used in Figure 15.2 except that they should relate to an office working environment.

15.8. Name four different types of selection criteria that might be used to select the most relevant rules for firing in a production system.

15.9. Describe a method in which rules could be grouped or organized in a knowledge base to reduce the amount of search required during the matching part of the inference cycle.

15.10. Using the knowledge base of Problem 15.7, simulate three match-select-execute cycles for a query which uses several rules and/or facts.

15.11. Explain the difference between forward and backward chaining and under what conditions each would be best to use for a given set of problems.

15.12. Under what conditions would it make sense to use both forward and backward chaining? Give an example where both are used.

15.13. Explain why you think associative networks were never very popular forms of knowledge representations in expert systems architectures.

15.14. Suppose you are diagnosing automobile engines using a system having a frame type of architecture similar to PIP. Show how a trigger condition might be satisfied for the distributor ignition system when it is learned that the spark at all spark plugs is weak.

15.15. Give the advantages of expert system architectures based on decision trees over those of production rules. What are the main disadvantages?

15.16. Two of the main problems in validating the knowledge contained in the knowledge bases of expert systems are related to completeness and consistency, that is, whether or not a system has an adequate breadth of knowledge to solve the class of problems it was intended to solve and whether or not the knowledge is consistent. Is it easier to check decision tree architectures or production rule systems for completeness and consistency? Give supporting information for your conclusions.

15.17. Give three examples of applications for which blackboard architectures are well suited.

15.18. Give three examples of applications for which the use of analogical architectures would be suitable in expert systems.

15.19. Consider a simple fully connected neural network containing three input nodes and a single output node. The inputs to the network are the eight possible binary patterns 000, 001, . . . , 111. Find weights w_i for which the network can differentiate between the inputs by producing three distinct outputs.

15.20. For the preceding problem, draw projection vectors on the unit circle for the eight different inputs using the weights determined there.

15.21. Explain how uncertainty is propagated through a chain of rules during a consultation with an expert system which is based on the MYCIN architecture.

15.22. Select a problem domain that requires some special expertise and consult with an expert in the domain to learn how he or she solves typical problems. After collecting enough knowledge to solve a small subset of problems, create rules which could be used in a knowledge base to solve the problems. Test the use of the rules on a few problems which have been suggested by the expert and then get his or her confirmation.

15.23. Relate each of the heuristics given by Penny Nii in Section 15.5 to a real expert system solving problem.

15.24. Discuss how each of the features of expert system building tools given in Section 15.6 can affect the performance of the systems developed.

15.25. Obtain a copy of an expert system building tool such as Personal Consultant Plus and create an expert system to diagnose automobile engine problems. Consult with a mechanic to see if your completed system is reasonably good.

PART 5
Knowledge Acquisition

16
General Concepts in Knowledge Acquisition

The success of knowledge-based systems lies in the quality and extent of the knowledge available to the system. Acquiring and validating a large corpus of consistent, correlated knowledge is not a trivial problem. This has given the acquisition process an especially important role in the design and implementation of these systems. Consequently, effective acquisition methods have become one of the principal challenges for the AI research community.

16.1 INTRODUCTION

The goals in this branch of AI are the discovery and development of efficient, cost effective methods of acquisition. Some important progress has recently been made in this area with the development of sophisticated editors and some impressive machine learning programs. But much work still remains before truly general purpose acquisition is possible. In this chapter, we consider general concepts related to acquisition and learning. We begin with a taxonomy of learning based on definitions of behavioral learning types, assess the difficulty in collecting and assimilating large quantities of well correlated knowledge, describe a general model for learning, and examine different performance measures related to the learning process.

Definitions

Knowledge acquisition is the process of adding new knowledge to a knowledge base and refining or otherwise improving knowledge that was previously acquired. Acquisition is usually associated with some purpose such as expanding the capabilities of a system or improving its performance at some specified task. Therefore, we will think of acquisition as goal oriented creation and refinement of knowledge. We take a broad view of the definition here and include autonomous acquisition, contrary to many workers in the field who regard acquisition solely as the process of knowledge elicitation from experts.

Acquired knowledge may consist of facts, rules, concepts, procedures, heuristics, formulas, relationships, statistics, or other useful information. Sources of this knowledge may include one or more of the following.

Experts in the domain of interest
Textbooks
Technical papers
Databases
Reports
The environment

We will consider machine learning as a specialized form of acquisition. It is any method of autonomous knowledge creation or refinement through the use of computer programs.

Table 16.1 depicts several types of knowledge and possible representation structures which by now should be familiar. In building a knowledge base, it is

TABLE 16.1 TYPES OF KNOWLEDGE AND POSSIBLE STRUCTURES

Type of Knowledge	Examples of Structures
Facts	(snow color white)
Relations	(father_of john bill)
Rules	(if (temperature>200 degrees) (open relief_valve))
Concepts	(forall (x y) (if (and (male x) ((brother_of x) (or (father_of y) (mother_of y))) (uncle x y)]
Procedures, Plans, etc.	. . . .

necessary to create or modify structures such as these for subsequent use by a performance component (like a theorem prover or an inference engine).

To be effective, the newly acquired knowledge should be integrated with existing knowledge in some meaningful way so that nontrivial inferences can be drawn from the resultant body of knowledge. The knowledge should, of course, be accurate, nonredundant, consistent (noncontradictory), and fairly complete in the sense that it is possible to reliably reason about many of the important conclusions for which the system was intended.

16.2 TYPES OF LEARNING

We all learn new knowledge through different methods, depending on the type of material to be learned, the amount of relevant knowledge we already possess, and the environment in which the learning takes place. It should not come as a surprise to learn that many of these same types of learning methods have been extensively studied in AI.

In what follows, it will be helpful to adopt a classification or taxonomy of learning types to serve as a guide in studying or comparing differences among them. One can develop learning taxonomies based on the type of knowledge representation used (predicate calculus, rules, frames), the type of knowledge learned (concepts, game playing, problem solving), or by the area of application (medical diagnosis, scheduling, prediction, and so on). The classification we will use, however, is intuitively more appealing and one which has become popular among machine learning researchers. The classification is independent of the knowledge domain and the representation scheme used. It is based on the type of inference strategy employed or the methods used in the learning process.

The five different learning methods under this taxonomy are

Memorization (rote learning)
Direct instruction (by being told)
Analogy
Induction
Deduction

Learning by memorization is the simplest form of learning. It requires the least amount of inference and is accomplished by simply copying the knowledge in the same form that it will be used directly into the knowledge base. We use this type of learning when we memorize multiplication tables, for example.

A slightly more complex form of learning is by direct instruction. This type of learning requires more inference than rote learning since the knowledge must be transformed into an operational form before being integrated into the knowledge base. We use this type of learning when a teacher presents a number of facts directly to us in a well organized manner.

The third type listed, analogical learning, is the process of learning a new concept or solution through the use of similar known concepts or solutions. We use this type of learning when solving problems on an exam where previously learned examples serve as a guide or when we learn to drive a truck using our knowledge of car driving. We make frequent use of analogical learning. This form of learning requires still more inferring than either of the previous forms, since difficult transformations must be made between the known and unknown situations.

The fourth type of learning is also one that is used frequently by humans. It is a powerful form of learning which, like analogical learning, also requires more inferring than the first two methods. This form of learning requires the use of inductive inference, a form of invalid but useful inference. We use inductive learning when we formulate a general concept after seeing a number of instances or examples of the concept. For example, we learn the concepts of color or sweet taste after experiencing the sensations associated with several examples of colored objects or sweet foods.

The final type of acquisition is deductive learning. It is accomplished through a sequence of deductive inference steps using known facts. From the known facts, new facts or relationships are logically derived. For example, we could learn deductively that Sue is the cousin of Bill, if we have knowledge of Sue and Bill's parents and rules for the cousin relationship. Deductive learning usually requires more inference than the other methods. The inference method used is, of course, a deductive type, which is a valid form of inference.

In addition to the above classification, we will sometimes refer to learning methods as either weak methods or knowledge-rich methods. Weak methods are general purpose methods in which little or no initial knowledge is available. These methods are more mechanical than the classical AI knowledge-rich methods. They often rely on a form of heuristic search in the learning process. Examples of some weak learning methods are given in the next chapter under the names of Learning Automata and Genetic Algorithms. We will be studying these and many of the more knowledge-rich forms of learning in more detail later, particularly various types of inductive learning.

16.3 KNOWLEDGE ACQUISITION IS DIFFICULT

One of the important lessons learned by AI researchers during the 1970s and early 1980s is that knowledge is not easily acquired and maintained. It is a difficult and time-consuming process. Yet expert and other knowledge-based systems require an abundant amount of well correlated knowledge to achieve a satisfactory level of intelligent performance. Typically, tens of person years are often required to build up a knowledge base to an acceptable level of performance. This was certainly true for the early expert systems such as MYCIN, DENDRAL, PROSPECTOR, and XCON. The acquisition effort encountered in building these systems provided the impetus for researchers to search for new efficient methods of acquisition. It helped to revitalize a new interest in general machine learning techniques.

Early expert systems initially had a knowledge base consisting of a few hundred rules. This is equivalent to less than 10^6 bits of knowledge. In contrast, the capacity of a mature human brain has been estimated at some 10^{15} bits of knowledge (Sagan, 1977). If we expect to build expert systems that are highly competent and possess knowledge in more than a single narrow domain, the amount of knowledge required for such knowledge bases will be somewhere between these two extremes, perhaps as much as 10^{10} bits.

If we were able to build such systems at even ten times the rate these early systems were built, it would still require on the order of 10^4 person years. This estimate is based on the assumption that the time required is directly proportional to the size of the knowledge base, a simplified assumption, since the complexity of the knowledge and the interdependencies grow more rapidly with the size of the knowledge base.

Clearly, this rate of acquisition is not acceptable. We must develop better acquisition and learning methods before we can implement such systems within a realistic time frame. Even with the progress made in the past few years through the development of special editors and related tools, more significant breakthroughs are needed before truly large knowledge bases can be assembled and maintained. Because of this, we expect the research interest in knowledge acquisition and machine learning to continue to grow at an accelerated rate for some years in the future.

It has been stated before that a system's performance is strongly dependent on the level and quality of its knowledge, and that "in knowledge lies power." If we accept this adage, we must also agree that the acquisition of knowledge is of paramount importance and, in fact, that "the real power lies in the ability to acquire new knowledge efficiently." To build a machine that can learn and continue to improve its performance has been a long time dream of mankind. The fulfillment of that dream now seems closer than ever before with the modest successes achieved by AI researchers over the past twenty years.

We will consider the complexity problem noted above again from a different point of view when we study the different learning paradigms.

16.4 GENERAL LEARNING MODEL

As noted earlier, learning can be accomplished using a number of different methods. For example, we can learn by memorizing facts, by being told, or by studying examples like problem solutions. Learning requires that new knowledge structures be created from some form of input stimulus. This new knowledge must then be assimilated into a knowledge base and be tested in some way for its utility. Testing means that the knowledge should be used in the performance of some task from which meaningful feedback can be obtained, where the feedback provides some measure of the accuracy and usefulness of the newly acquired knowledge.

A general learning model is depicted in Figure 16.1 where the environment has been included as part of the overall learner system. The environment may be regarded as either a form of nature which produces random stimuli or as a more

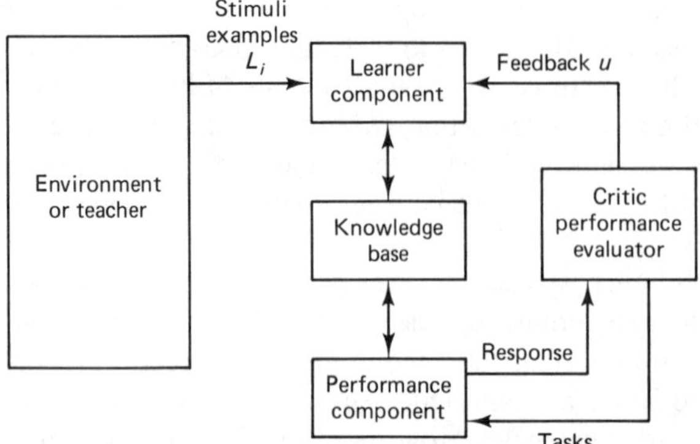

Figure 16.1 General learning model.

organized training source such as a teacher which provides carefully selected training examples for the learner component. The actual form of environment used will depend on the particular learning paradigm. In any case, some representation language must be assumed for communication between the environment and the learner. The language may be the same representation scheme as that used in the knowledge base (such as a form of predicate calculus). When they are chosen to be the same, we say the single representation trick is being used. This usually results in a simpler implementation since it is not necessary to transform between two or more different representations.

For some systems the environment may be a user working at a keyboard. Other systems will use program modules to simulate a particular environment. In even more realistic cases, the system will have real physical sensors which interface with some world environment.

Inputs to the learner component may be physical stimuli of some type or descriptive, symbolic training examples. The information conveyed to the learner component is used to create and modify knowledge structures in the knowledge base. This same knowledge is used by the performance component to carry out some tasks, such as solving a problem, playing a game, or classifying instances of some concept.

When given a task, the performance component produces a response describing its actions in performing the task. The critic module then evaluates this response relative to an optimal response.

Feedback, indicating whether or not the performance was acceptable, is then sent by the critic module to the learner component for its subsequent use in modifying the structures in the knowledge base. If proper learning was accomplished, the system's performance will have improved with the changes made to the knowledge base.

The cycle described above may be repeated a number of times until the performance of the system has reached some acceptable level, until a known learning goal has been reached, or until changes cease to occur in the knowledge base after some chosen number of training examples have been observed.

There are several important factors which influence a system's ability to learn in addition to the form of representation used. They include the types of training provided, the form and extent of any initial background knowledge, the type of feedback provided, and the learning algorithms used (Figure 16.2).

The type of training used in a system can have a strong effect on performance, much the same as it does for humans. Training may consist of randomly selected instances or examples that have been carefully selected and ordered for presentation. The instances may be positive examples of some concept or task being learned, they may be negative, or they may be a mixture of both positive and negative. The instances may be well focused using only relevant information, or they may contain a variety of facts and details including irrelevant data.

Many forms of learning can be characterized as a search through a space of possible hypotheses or solutions (Mitchell, 1982). To make learning more efficient, it is necessary to constrain this search process or reduce the search space. One method of achieving this is through the use of background knowledge which can be used to constrain the search space or exercise control operations which limit the search process. We will see several examples of this in the next three chapters.

Feedback is essential to the learner component since otherwise it would never know if the knowledge structures in the knowledge base were improving or if they were adequate for the performance of the given tasks. The feedback may be a simple yes or no type of evaluation, or it may contain more useful information describing why a particular action was good or bad. Also, the feedback may be completely reliable, providing an accurate assessment of the performance or it may contain noise; that is, the feedback may actually be incorrect some of the time. Intuitively, the feedback must be accurate more than 50% of the time; otherwise the system would never learn. If the feedback is always reliable and carries useful information, the learner should be able to build up a useful corpus of knowledge quickly. On the other hand, if the feedback is noisy or unreliable, the learning process may be very slow and the resultant knowledge incorrect.

Finally, the learning algorithms themselves determine to a large extent how successful a learning system will be. The algorithms control the search to find and build the knowledge structures. We then expect that the algorithms that extract much of the useful information from training examples and take advantage of any background knowledge outperform those that do not. In the following chapters we

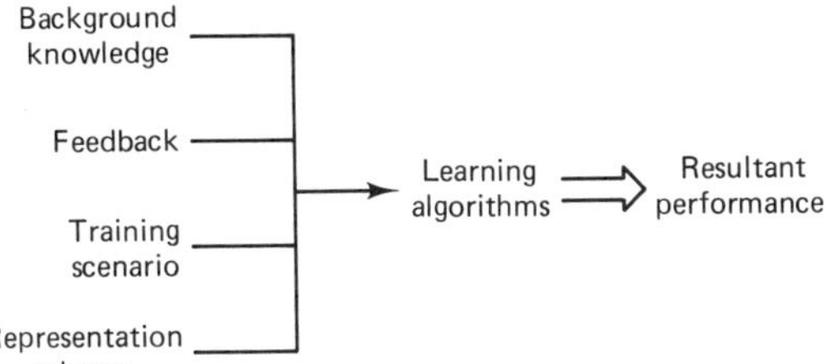

Figure 16.2 Factors affecting learning performance.

will see examples of systems which illustrate many of the above points regarding the effects of different factors on performance.

16.5 PERFORMANCE MEASURES

In the following four chapters, we will be investigating systems based on different learning paradigms and having different architectures. How can we evaluate the performance of a given system or compare the relative performance of two different systems? We could attempt to conduct something like a Turing test on a system. But would this tell us how general or robust the system is or how easy it is to implement? Clearly, such comparisons are possible only when standard performance measures are available. For example, it would be useful to establish the relative efficiencies or speed with which two systems learned a concept or how robust (noise tolerant) a system is under different training scenarios. Although little work has been done to date in this area, we will propose some informal definitions for performance measures in this section. These definitions will at least permit us to establish estimates of some relative performance characteristics among the different learning methods we will be considering.

Generality. One of the most important performance measures for learning methods is the generality or scope of the method. Generality is a measure of the ease with which the method can be adapted to different domains of application. A completely general algorithm is one which is a fixed or self adjusting configuration that can learn or adapt in any environment or application domain. At the other extreme are methods which function in a single domain only. Methods which have some degree of generality will function well in at least a few domains.

Efficiency. The efficiency of a method is a measure of the average time required to construct the target knowledge structures from some specified initial structures. Since this measure is often difficult to determine and is meaningless without some standard comparison time, a relative efficiency index can be used instead. For example, the relative efficiency of a method can be defined as the ratio of the time required for the given method to the time required for a purely random search to find the target structures.

Robustness. Robustness is the ability of a learning system to function with unreliable feedback and with a variety of training examples, including noisy ones. A robust system must be able to build tentative structures which are subject to modification or withdrawal if later found to be inconsistent with statistically sound structures. This is nonmonotonic learning, the analog of nonmonotonic reasoning discussed in Chapter 5.

Efficacy. The efficacy of a system is a measure of the overall power of the system. It is a combination of the factors generality, efficiency, and robustness. We say that system A is more efficacious than system B if system A is more efficient, robust, and general than B.

Ease of implementation. Ease of implementation relates to the complexity of the programs and data structures and the resources required to develop the given learning system. Lacking good complexity metrics, this measure will often be somewhat subjective.

Other performance terms that are specific to different paradigms will be introduced as needed.

16.6 SUMMARY

Knowledge acquisition is the purposeful addition or refinement of knowledge structures to a knowledge base for use by knowledge-based systems. Machine learning is the autonomous acquisition of knowledge through the use of computer programs. The acquired knowledge may consist of facts, concepts, rules, relations, plans, and procedures, and the source of the knowledge may be one or more of the following: data bases, textbooks, domain experts, reports, or the environment.

A useful taxonomy for learning is one that is based on the behavioral strategy employed in the learning process, strategies like rote (memorization), being told, analogy, induction, or deduction. Rote learning requires little inference, while the other methods require increasingly greater amounts.

An important lesson learned by expert systems researchers is that knowledge acquisition is difficult, often requiring tens of person years to assemble several hundred rules. This problem helped to revive active research in more autonomous forms of acquisition or machine learning.

Any model of learning should include components which support the basic learner component. These include a teacher or environment, a knowledge base, a performance component which uses the knowledge, and a critic or performance evaluation unit which provides feedback to the learner about the performance.

Factors which affect the performance of a learner system include (1) the representation scheme used, (2) the training scenario, (3) the type of feedback, (4) background knowledge, and (5) the learning algorithm.

Performance measures provide a means of comparing different performance characteristics of learning algorithms (systems). Some of the more important performance measures are generality, efficiency, robustness, efficacy, and ease of implementation. Lacking formal metrics for some measures will require that subjective estimates be used instead.

EXERCISES

16.1. Give a detailed definition of knowledge acquisition complete with an example.

16.2. Give an example for each of the following types of knowledge: (a) a fact, (b) a rule, (c) a concept, (d) a procedure, (e) a heuristic, (f) a relationship.

16.3. How is machine learning distinguished from general knowledge acquisition?

16.4. The taxonomy of learning methods given in this chapter is based on the type of behavior or inference strategy used. Give another taxonomy for learning methods and illustrate with some examples.

16.5. Describe the role of each component of a general learning model and why it is needed for the learning process.

16.6. Explain why a learning component should have scope.

16.7. What is the difference between efficiency and efficacy with regard to the performance of a learner system?

16.8. Review the knowledge acquisition section in Chapter 15 and explain why elicitation of knowledge from experts is so difficult.

16.9. Consult a good dictionary and describe the difference between induction and deduction. Give examples of both.

16.10. Explain why inductive learning should require more inference than learning by being told (instruction).

16.11. Try to determine whether inductive learning requires more inference than analogical learning. Give reasons for your conclusion. Which of the two types of learning, in general, would be more reliable in the sense that the knowledge learned is logically valid?

16.12. Give examples of each of the different types of learning as they relate to learning you have recently experienced.

16.13. Give an estimate of the number of bits required to store knowledge for 500 if . . . then rules, where each rule has five conjunctive terms or conditions in the antecedent. Can you estimate what fraction of your total knowledge is represented in some set of 500 rules?

16.14. Try to give a quantitative measure for knowledge. Explain why your measure is or is not reasonable. Give examples to support your arguments.

16.15. Explain why robustness in a learner is important in real world environments.

17

Early Work in Machine Learning

17.1 INTRODUCTION

Attempts to develop autonomous learning systems began in the 1950s while cybernetics was still an active area of research. These early designs were self-adapting systems which modified their own structures in an attempt to produce an optimal response to some input stimuli. Although several different approaches were pursued during this period, we will consider only four of the more representative designs. One approach was believed to be an approximate model of a small network of neurons.

A second approach was initially based on a form of rote learning. It was later modified to learn by adaptive parameter adjustment. The third approach used self-adapting stochastic automata models, while the fourth approach was modeled after survival of the fittest through population genetics.

In the remainder of this chapter, we will examine examples of the four methods and reserve our descriptions of more classical AI learning approaches for Chapters 18, 19, and 20. The systems we use as examples here are famous ones that have received much attention in the literature. They are Rosenblatt's perceptrons, Samuel's checkers playing system, Learning Automata, and Genetic Algorithms.

17.2 PERCEPTRONS

Perceptrons are pattern recognition or classification devices that are crude approximations of neural networks. They make decisions about patterns by summing up evidence obtained from many small sources. They can be taught to recognize one or more classes of objects through the use of stimuli in the form of labeled training examples.

A simplified perceptron system is illustrated in Figure 17.1. The inputs to the system are through an array of sensors such as a rectangular grid of light sensitive pixels. These sensors are randomly connected in groups to associative threshold units (ATU) where the sensor outputs are combined and added together. If the combined outputs to an ATU exceed some fixed threshold, the ATU unit executes and produces a binary output.

The outputs from the ATU are each multiplied by adjustable parameters or weights w_i ($i = 1, 2, \ldots, k$) and the results added together in a terminal comparator unit. If the input to the comparator exceeds a given threshold level T, the perceptron produces a positive response of 1 (yes) corresponding to a sample classification of class-1. Otherwise, the output is 0 (no) corresponding to an object classification of non-class-1

All components of the system are fixed except the weights w_i which are adjusted through a punishment-reward process described below. This learning process contin-

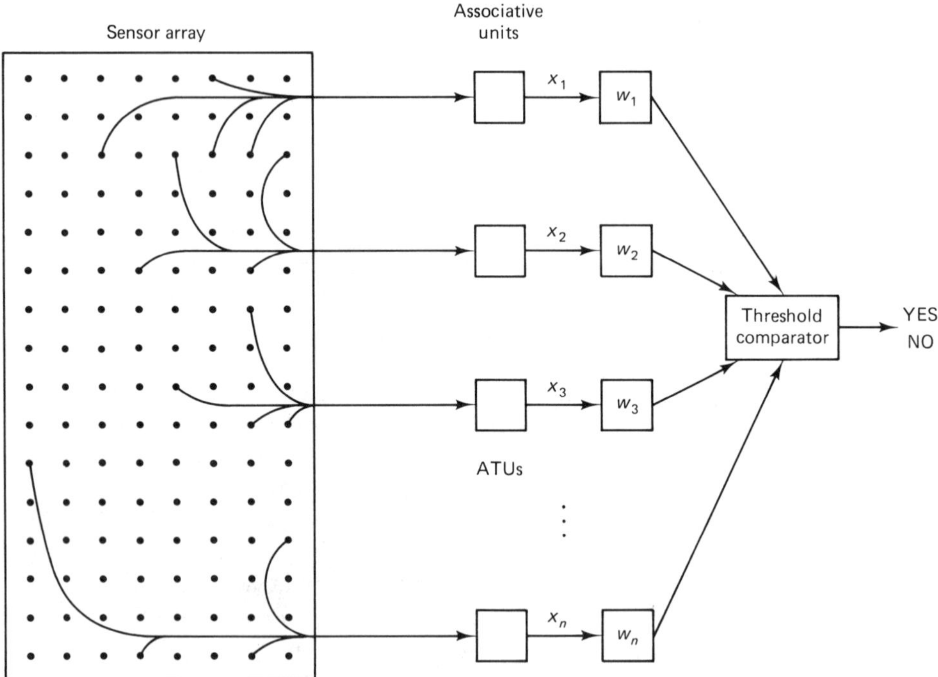

Figure 17.1 A simple perceptron.

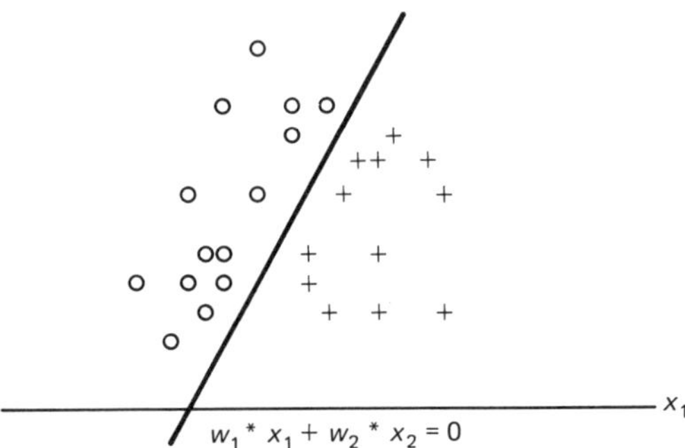

Figure 17.2 Geometrical illustration of separable space.

ues until optimal values of w_i are found at which time the system will have learned the proper classification of objects for the two different classes.

The light sensors produce an output voltage that is proportional to the light intensity striking them. This output is a measure of what is known in pattern recognition as the object representation space parameters. The outputs from the ATUs which combine several of the sensor outputs (x_i) are known as feature value measurements. These feature values are each multiplied by the weights w_i and the results summed in the comparator to give the vector product $\mathbf{r} = \mathbf{w} * \mathbf{x} = \Sigma_i w_i x_i$. When enough of the feature values are present and the weight vector is near optimal, the threshold will be exceeded and a positive classification will result.

Finding the optimal weight vector value **w** is equivalent to finding a separating hyperplane in k-dimensional space. If there is some linear function of the x_i for which objects in class-1 produce an output greater than T and non-class-1 objects produce an output less than T, the space of objects is said to be linearly separable (see Chapter 13 for example). Spaces which are linearly separable can be partitioned into two or more disjointed regions which divide objects based on their feature vector values as illustrated in Figure 17.2. It has been shown (Minsky and Papert, 1969) that an optimal **w** can always be found with a finite number of training examples if the space is linearly separable.
One of the simplest algorithms for finding an optimum **w** (**w***) is based on the following perceptron learning algorithm. Given training objects from two distinct classes, class-1 and class-2

1. Choose an arbitrary initial value for **w**

2. After the mth training step set

$$\mathbf{w}_{m+1} = \mathbf{w}_m + d * \mathbf{x}_m$$

where

$$d = +1 \text{ if } r = \mathbf{w} * \mathbf{x} < 0 \quad \text{and} \quad \mathbf{x}_m \text{ is type class-1}$$

$$d = -1 \text{ if } r > 0 \quad \text{and} \quad \mathbf{x}_m \text{ is type class-2}$$

Otherwise set $\mathbf{w}_{m+1} = \mathbf{w}_m$ ($d = 0$)

3. When $\mathbf{w}_m = \mathbf{w}_m +_j$, (for all $j >= 1$) stop, the optimum **w*** has been found.

It should be recognized that the above learning algorithm is just a method for finding a linear two-class decision function which separates the feature space into two regions. For a generalized perceptron, we could just as well have found multiclass decision functions which separate the feature space into c regions. This could be done by terminating each of the ATU outputs at $c > 2$ comparator units. In this case, class j would be selected as the object type whenever the response at the jth comparator was greater than the response at all other $j - 1$ comparators.

Perceptrons were studied intensely at first but later were found to have severe limitations. Therefore, active research in this area faded during the late 1960s. However, the findings related to this work later proved to be most valuable, especially in the area of pattern recognition. More recently, there has been renewed interest in similar architectures which attempt to model neural networks (Chapter 15). This is partly due to a better understanding of the brain and significant advances realized in network dynamics as well as in hardware over the past ten years. These advances have made it possible to more closely model large networks of neurons.

17.3 CHECKERS PLAYING EXAMPLE

During the 1950s and 1960s Samuel (1959, 1967) developed a program which could learn to play checkers at a master's level. This system remembered thousands of board states and their estimated values. They provided the means to determine the best move to make at any point in the game.

Samuel's system learns while playing the game of checkers, either with a human opponent or with a copy of itself. At each state of the game, the program checks to see if it has remembered a best-move value for that state. If not, the program explores ahead three moves (it determines all of its possible moves; for each of these, it finds all of its opponent's moves; and for each of those, it determines all of its next possible moves). The program then computes an advantage or win-value estimate of all the ending board states. These values determine the best move for the system from the current state. The current board state and its corresponding value are stored using an indexed address scheme for subsequent recall.

The best move for each state is the move value of the largest of the minimums, based on the theory of two-person zero-sum games. This move will always be the best choice (for the next three moves) against an intelligent adversary.

As an example of the look-ahead process, a simple two move sequence is illustrated in Figure 17.3 in the form of a tree. At board state K, the program looks ahead two moves and computes the value of each possible resultant board state. It then works backward by first finding the minimum board values at state $K + 2$ in each group of moves made from state $K + 1$ (minimums = 4, 3, and 2).

These minimums correspond to the moves the opponent would make from each position when at state $K + 1$. The program then chooses the maximum of these minimums as the best (minimax) move it can make from the present board

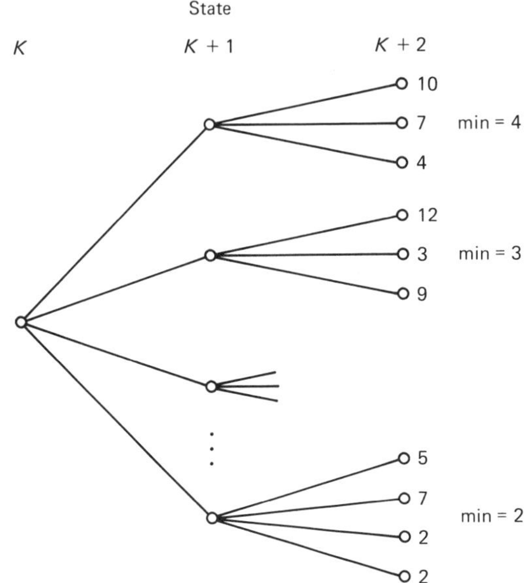

Figure 17.3 A two-move look-ahead sequence.

state K (maximum = 4). By looking ahead three moves, the system can be assured it can do no worse than this minimax value. The board state and the corresponding minimax value for a three-move-ahead sequence are stored in Samuel's system. These values are then available for subsequent use when the same state is encountered during a new game.

The look ahead search process could be extended beyond three moves; however, the combinatorial explosion that results makes this infeasible. But, when many board states have been learned, it is likely that any given state will already have look-ahead values for three moves, and some of those moves will in turn have look-ahead values stored. Consequently, as more and more values are stored, look-ahead values for six, nine, or even more moves may be prerecorded for rapid use. Thus, when the system has played many games and recorded thousands of moves, its ability to look ahead many moves and to show improved performance is greatly increased.

The value of a board state is estimated by computing a linear function similar to the perceptron linear decision function. In this case, however, Samuel selected some 16 board features from a larger set of feature parameters. The features were typically checkers concepts such as piece advantage, the number of kings and single piece units, and the location of pieces. In the original system, the weighting parameters were fixed. In subsequent experiments, however, the parameters were adjusted as part of the learning process much like the weighting parameters were in the perceptrons.

17.4 LEARNING AUTOMATA

The theory of learning automata was first introduced in 1961 (Tsetlin, 1961). Since that time these systems have been studied intensely, both analytically and through simulations (Lakshmivarahan, 1981). Learning automata systems are finite state adaptive systems which interact iteratively with a general environment. Through a probabilistic trial-and-error response process they learn to choose or adapt to a behavior which produces the best response. They are, essentially, a form of weak, inductive learners.

In Figure 17.4, we see that the learning model for learning automata has been simplified to just two components, an automaton (learner) and an environment. The learning cycle begins with an input to the learning automata system from the environment. This input elicits one of a finite number of possible responses from the automaton. The environment receives and evaluates the response and then provides some form of feedback to the automaton in return. This feedback is used by the automaton to alter its stimulus-response mapping structure to improve its behavior in a more favorable way.

As a simple example, suppose a learning automata is being used to learn the best temperature control setting for your office each morning. It may select any one of ten temperature range settings at the beginning of each day (Figure 17.5). Without any prior knowledge of your temperature preferences, the automaton randomly selects a first setting using the probability vector corresponding to the temperature settings.

Since the probability values are uniformly distributed, any one of the settings will be selected with equal likelihood. After the selected temperature has stabilized, the environment may respond with a simple good-bad feedback response. If the response is good, the automata will modify its probability vector by rewarding the probability corresponding to the good setting with a positive increment and reducing all other probabilities proportionately to maintain the sum equal to 1. If the response is bad, the automaton will penalize the selected setting by reducing the probability corresponding to the bad setting and increasing all other values proportionately. This process is repeated each day until the good selections have high probability values and all bad choices have values near zero. Thereafter, the system will always choose the good settings. If, at some point, in the future your temperature preferences change, the automaton can easily readapt.

Learning automata have been generalized and studied in various ways. One

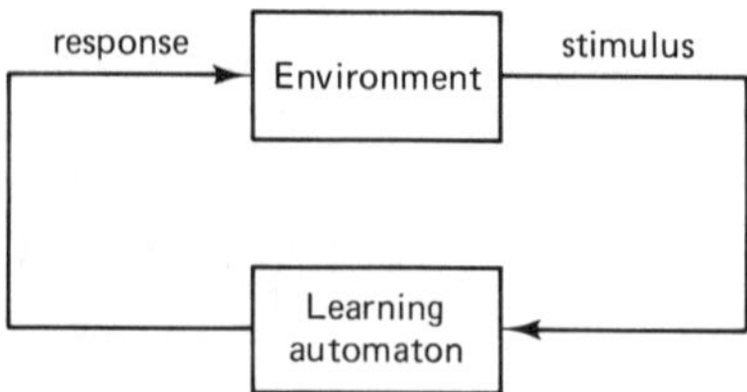

Figure 17.4 Learning automaton model.

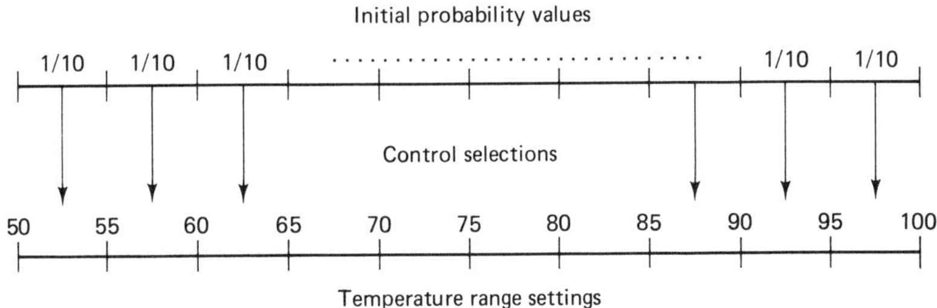

Figure 17.5 Temperature control model.

such generalization has been given the special name of collective learning automata (CLA). CLAs are standard learning automata systems except that feedback is not provided to the automaton after each response. In this case, several collective stimulus-response actions occur before feedback is passed to the automaton. It has been argued (Bock, 1976) that this type of learning more closely resembles that of human beings in that we usually perform a number or group of primitive actions before receiving feedback on the performance of such actions, such as solving a complete problem on a test or parking a car. We illustrate the operation of CLAs with an example of learning to play the game of Nim in an optimal way.

Nim is a two-person zero-sum game in which the players alternate in removing tokens from an array which initially has nine tokens. The tokens are arranged into three rows with one token in the first row, three in the second row, and five in the third row (Figure 17.6).

The first player must remove at least one token but not more than all the tokens in any single row. Tokens can only be removed from a single row during each player's move. The second player responds by removing one or more tokens remaining in any row. Players alternate in this way until all tokens have been removed; the loser is the player forced to remove the last token.

We will use the triple (n_1,n_2,n_3) to represent the states of the game at a given time where n_1, n_2, and n_3 are the numbers of tokens in rows 1, 2, and 3, respectively. We will also use a matrix to determine the moves made by the CLA for any given state. The matrix of Figure 17.7 has heading columns which correspond to the state of the game when it is the CLA's turn to move, and row headings which correspond to the new game state after the CLA has completed a move. Fractional entries in the matrix are transition probabilities used by the CLA to execute each of its moves. Asterisks in the matrix represent invalid moves.

Beginning with the initial state (1,3,5), suppose the CLA's opponent removes two tokens from the third row resulting in the new state (1,3,3). If the CLA then

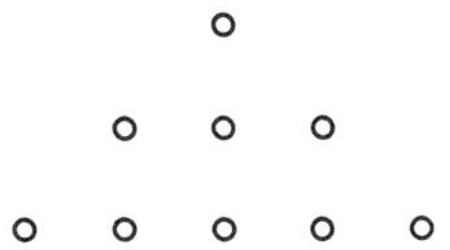

Figure 17.6 Nim initial configuration.

removes all three tokens from the second row, the resultant state is (1,0,3). Suppose the opponent now removes all remaining tokens from the third row. This leaves the CLA with a losing configuration of (1,0,0).

At the start of the learning sequence, the matrix is initialized such that the elements in each column are equal (uniform) probability values. For example, since there are eight valid moves from the state (1,3,4) each column element under this state corresponding to a valid move has been given an initial value of $\frac{1}{8}$. In a similar manner all other columns have been given uniform probability values corresponding to all valid moves for the given column state.

The CLA selects moves probabilistically using the probability values in each column. So, for example, if the CLA had the first move, any row intersecting with the first column not containing an asterisk would be chosen with probability $\frac{1}{9}$. This choice then determines the new game state from which the opponent must select a move. The opponent might have a similar matrix to record game states and choose moves. A complete game is played before the CLA is given any feedback, at which time it is informed whether or not its responses were good or bad. This is the collective feature of the CLA.

If the CLA wins a game, all moves made by the CLA during that game are rewarded by increasing the probability value in each column corresponding to the winning move. All nonwinning probabilities in those columns are reduced equally to keep the sum in each column equal to 1. If the CLA loses a game, the moves leading to that loss are penalized by reducing the probability values corresponding to each losing move. All other probabilities in the columns having a losing move are increased equally to keep the column totals equal to 1.

After a number of games have been played by the CLA, the matrix elements

Current state

	135	134	133	132	. . .	125	. . .
135	*	*	*	*	. . .	*	
134	1/9	*	*	*	. . .	*	. . .
133	1/9	1/8	*	*	. . .	*	
132	1/9	1/8	1/7	*	. . .	*	. . .
⋮	⋮	⋮	⋮	⋮			
124	*	1/8	*	*	. . .	1/8	. . .
⋮	⋮	⋮					

Figure 17.7 CLA internal representation of game states.

which correspond to repeated wins will increase toward one, while all other elements in the column will decrease toward zero. Consequently, the CLA will choose the winning moves more frequently and thereby improve its performance.

Simulated games between a CLA and various types of opponents have been performed and the results plotted (Bock, 1985). It was shown, for example, that two CLAs playing against each other required about 300 games before each learned to play optimally. Note, however, that convergence to optimality can be accomplished with fewer games if the opponent always plays optimally (or poorly), since, in such a case, the CLA will repeatedly lose (win) and quickly reduce (increase) the losing (winning) move elements to zero (one). It is also possible to speed up the learning process through the use of other techniques such as learned heuristics.

Learning systems based on the learning automaton or CLA paradigm are fairly general for applications in which a suitable state representation scheme can be found. They are also quite robust learners. In fact, it has been shown that an LA will converge to an optimal distribution under fairly general conditions if the feedback is accurate with probability greater than 0.5 (Narendra and Thathachar, 1974). Of course, the rate of convergence is strongly dependent on the reliability of the feedback.

Learning automata are not very efficient learners as was noted in the game playing example above. They are, however, relatively easy to implement, provided the number of states is not too large. When the number of states becomes large, the amount of storage and the computation required to update the transition matrix becomes excessive.

Potential applications for learning automata include adaptive telephone routing and control. Such applications have been studied using simulation programs (Narendra et al., 1977). Although they have been given favorable recommendations, few if any actual systems have been implemented, however.

17.5 GENETIC ALGORITHMS

Genetic algorithm learning methods are based on models of natural adaptation and evolution. These learning systems improve their performance through processes which model population genetics and survival of the fittest. They have been studied since the early 1960s (Holland, 1962, 1975).

In the field of genetics, a population is subjected to an environment which places demands on the members. The members which adapt well are selected for mating and reproduction. The offspring of these better performers inherit genetic traits from both their parents. Members of this second generation of offspring which also adapt well are then selected for mating and reproduction and the evolutionary cycle continues. Poor performers die off without leaving offspring. Good performers produce good offspring and they, in turn, perform well. After some number of generations, the resultant population will have adapted optimally or at least very well to the environment.

Genetic algorithm systems start with a fixed size population of data structures which are used to perform some given tasks. After requiring the structures to execute the specified tasks some number of times, the structures are rated on their performance, and a new generation of data structures is then created. The new generation is created by mating the higher performing structures to produce offspring. These offspring and their parents are then retained for the next generation while the poorer performing structures are discarded. The basic cycle is illustrated in Figure 17.8.

Mutations are also performed on the best performing structures to insure that the full space of possible structures is reachable. This process is repeated for a number of generations until the resultant population consists of only the highest performing structures.

Data structures which make up the population can represent rules or any other suitable types of knowledge structure. To illustrate the genetic aspects of the problem, assume for simplicity that the population of structures are fixed-length binary strings such as the eight bit string 11010001. An initial population of these eight-bit strings would be generated randomly or with the use of heuristics at time zero. These strings, which might be simple condition and action rules, would then be assigned some tasks to perform (like predicting the weather based on certain physical and geographic conditions or diagnosing a fault in a piece of equipment).

After multiple attempts at executing the tasks, each of the participating structures would be rated and tagged with a utility value *u* commensurate with its performance. The next population would then be generated using the higher performing structures as parents and the process would be repeated with the newly produced generation. After many generations the remaining population structures should perform the desired tasks well.

Mating between two strings is accomplished with the *crossover* operation which randomly selects a bit position in the eight-bit string and concatenates the head of

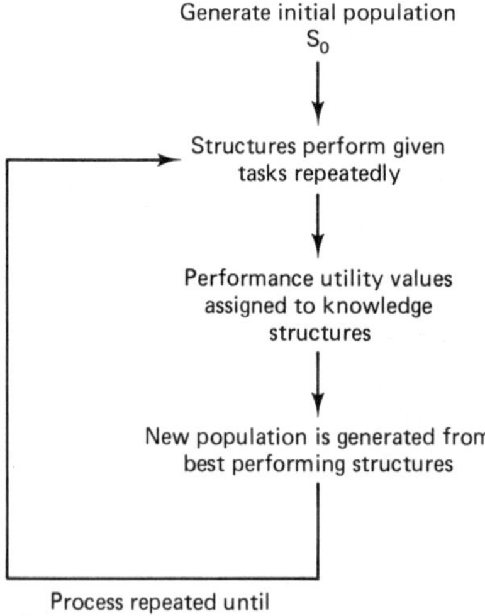
Generate initial population
S_0
Structures perform given
tasks repeatedly
Performance utility values
assigned to knowledge
structures
New population is generated from
best performing structures
Process repeated until
desired performance reached

Figure 17.8 Genetic algorithm.

one parent to the tail of the second parent to produce the offspring. Suppose the two parents are designated as xxxxxxxx and yyyyyyyy respectively, and suppose the third bit position has been selected as the crossover point (at the position of the colon in the structure xxx:xxxxx). After the crossover operation is applied, two offspring are then generated, namely xxxyyyyy and yyyxxxxx. Such offspring and their parents are then used to make up the next generation of structures.

A second genetic operation often used is called *inversion*. Inversion is a transformation applied to a single string. A bit position is selected at random, and when applied to a structure, the inversion operation concatenates the tail of the string to the head of the same string. Thus, if the sixth position were selected ($x_1x_2x_3x_4x_5x_6{:}x_7x_8$), the inverted string would be $x_7x_8x_1x_2x_3x_4x_5x_6$.

A third operator, *mutation*, is used to insure that all locations of the rule space are reachable, that every potential rule in the rule space is available for evaluation. This insures that the selection process does not get caught in a local minimum. For example, it may happen that use of the crossover and inversion operators will only produce a set of structures that are better than all local neighbors but not optimal in a global sense. This can happen since crossover and inversion may not be able to produce some undiscovered structures. The mutation operator can overcome this by simply selecting any bit position in a string at random and changing it. This operator is typically used only infrequently to prevent random wandering in the search space.

The genetic paradigm is best understood through an example. To illustrate similarities between the learning automaton paradigm and the genetic paradigm we use the same learning task of the previous section, namely learning to play the game of nim optimally. We use a slightly different representation scheme here since we want a population of structures that are easily transformed. To do this, we let each member of the population consist of a pair of triplets augmented with a utility value u, $((n_1,n_2,n_3)\ (m_1,m_2,m_3)u)$, where the first pair is the game state presented to the genetic algorithm system prior to its move, and the second triple is the state after the move. The u values represent the worth or current utility of the structure at any given time.

Before the game begins, the genetic system randomly generates an initial population of K triple-pair members. The population size K is one of the important parameters that must be selected. Here, we simply assume it is about 25 or 30, which should be more than the number of moves needed for any optimal play. All members are assigned an initial utility value of 0. The learning process then proceeds as follows.

1. The environment presents a valid triple to the genetic system.
2. The genetic system searches for all population triple pairs which have a first triple that matches the input triple. From those that match, the first one found having the highest utility value u is selected and the second triple is returned as the new game state. If no match is found, the genetic system randomly generates a triple which represents a valid move, returns this as the new state,

and stores the triple pair, the input, and newly generated triple as an addition to the population.

3. The above two steps are repeated until the game is terminated, in which case the genetic system is informed whether a win or loss occurred. If the system wins, each of the participating member moves has its utility value increased. If the system loses, each participating member has its utility value decreased.
4. The above steps are repeated until a fixed number of games have been played. At this time a new generation is created.

The new generation is created from the old population by first selecting a fraction (say one half) of the members having the highest utility values. From these, offspring are obtained by application of appropriate genetic operators.

The three operators, crossover, inversion, and mutation, randomly modify the parent moves to give new offspring move sequences. (The best choice of genetic operators to apply in this example is left as an exercise). Each offspring inherits a utility value from one of the parents. Population members having low utility values are discarded to keep the population size fixed.

This whole process is repeated until the genetic system has learned all the optimal moves. This can be determined when the parent population ceases to change or when the genetic system repeatedly wins.

The similarity between the learning automaton and genetic paradigms should be apparent from this example. Both rely on random move sequences, and the better moves are rewarded while the poorer ones are penalized.

17.6 INTELLIGENT EDITORS

In the previous chapter, we considered some of the difficulties involved in acquiring and assembling a large corpus of well-correlated knowledge. Expert systems sometimes require hundreds or even thousands of rules to reach acceptable levels of performance. To help alleviate this problem, the development of special editors such as TEIRESIAS (Davis and Lenat, 1982) were initiated during the mid 1970s. Since that time a number of commercial editors have been developed. These intelligent editors have made it possible to build expert systems without strong reliance on knowledge engineers.[1]

An intelligent editor acts as an interface between a domain expert and an expert system. They permit a domain expert to interact directly with the system without the need for an intermediary to code the knowledge (Figure 17.9). The expert carries on a dialog with the editor in a restricted subset of English which includes a domain-specific vocabulary. The editor has direct access to the knowledge in the expert system and knows the structure of that knowledge. Through the editor,

[1] For additional details related to the overall process of eliciting, coding, organizing, and refining knowledge from domain experts, see Chapter 15 which examines expert system architectures and building tools.

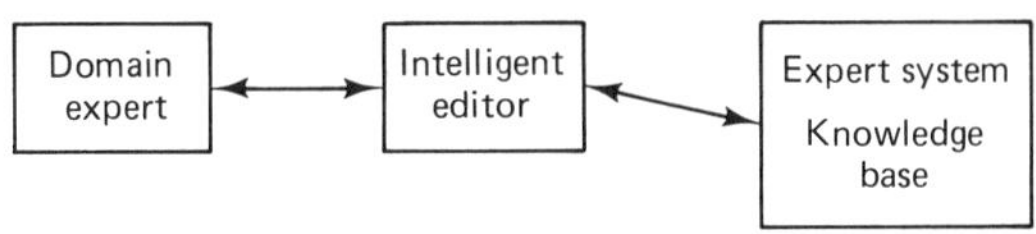

Figure 17.9 Acquisition using an intelligent editor.

an expert can create, modify, and delete rules without a knowledge of the internal structure of the rules.

The editor assists the expert in building and refining a knowledge base by recalling rules related to some specific topic, and reviewing and modifying the rules, if necessary, to better fit the expert's meaning and intent. Through the editor, the expert can query the expert system for conclusions when given certain facts. If the expert is unhappy with the results, a trace can be obtained of the steps followed in the inference process. When faulty or deficit knowledge is found, the problem can then be corrected.

Some editors have the ability to suggest reasonable alternatives and to prompt the expert for clarifications when required. Some editors also have the ability to make validity checks on newly entered knowledge and detect when inconsistencies occur. More recently, a few commercial editors have incorporated features which permit rules to be induced directly from examples of problem solutions. These editors have greatly simplified the acquisition process, but they still require much effort on the part of domain experts.

17.7 SUMMARY

We have examined examples of early work done in machine learning including perceptrons which learn through parameter adjustment, by looking at Samuel's checkers playing system which learns through a form of rote learning as well as parameter adjustment. We then looked at learning automata which uses a reward and punishment process by modifying their state probability transformation mapping structures until optimal performance has been achieved. Genetic algorithm systems learn through a form of mutation and genetic inheritance. Higher performing knowledge structures are mated and give birth to offspring which possess many of their parents' traits. Generations of structures are created until an acceptable level of performance has been reached. Finally, we briefly discussed semiautonomous learning systems, the intelligent editors. These systems permit a domain expert to interact directly in building and refining a knowledge base without strong support from a knowledge engineer.

EXERCISES

17.1. Given a simple perceptron with a 3-x-3 input sensor array, compute six learning cycles to show how the weights w_i change during the learning process. Assign random weights to the initial w_i values.

17.2. For the game of checkers with an assumed average number of 50 possible moves per board position, determine the difference in the total number of moves for a four move look-ahead as compared to a three move look-ahead system.

17.3. Design a learning automaton that selects TV channels based on day of week and time of day (three evening hours only) for some family you are familiar with.

17.4. Write a computer program to simulate the learning automaton of the previous problem. Determine the number of training examples required for the system to converge to the optimal values.

17.5. Describe how a learning automaton could be developed to learn how to play the game of tic-tac-toe optimally. Is this a CLA or a simple learning automaton system?

17.6. Describe the similarities and differences between learning automata and genetic algorithms. Which learner would be best at finding optimal solutions to nonlinear functions? Give reasons to support your answer.

17.7. Explain the difference of the genetic operators inversion, crossover, and mutation. Which operator do you think is most effective in finding the optimal population in the least time?

17.8. Explain why some editors can be distinguished as "intelligent."

17.9. Read an article on TEIRESIUS and make a list of all the intelligent functions it performs that differ from so called nonintelligent editors.

18

Learning by Induction

18.1 INTRODUCTION

Consider playing the following game. I will choose some concept which will remain fixed throughout the game. You will then be given clues to the concept in the form of simple descriptions. After each clue, you must attempt to guess the concept I have chosen. I will continue with the clues until you are sure you have made the right choice.

Clue 1. A diamond ring.

For your first guess did you choose the concept beautiful? If so you are wrong.

Clue 2. Dinner at Maxime's restaurant.

What do clues 1 and 2 have in common? Perhaps clue 3 will be enough to reveal the commonality you need to make a correct choice.

Clue 3. A Mercedes-Benz automobile.

You must have discovered the concept by now! It is an expensive or luxury item.

The above illustrates the process we use in inductive learning, namely, inductive inference, an invalid, but useful form of inference.

In this chapter we continue the study of machine learning, but in a more focused manner. Here, we study a single learning method, learning by inductive inference.

Inductive learning is the process of acquiring generalized knowledge from examples or instances of some class. This form of learning is accomplished through inductive inference, the process of reasoning from a part to a whole, from particular instances to generalizations, or from the individual to the universal. It is a powerful form of learning which we humans do almost effortlessly. Even though it is not a valid form of inference, it appears to work well much of the time. Because of its importance, we have devoted two complete chapters to the subject.

18.2 BASIC CONCEPTS

When we conclude that October weather is always pleasant in El Paso after having observed the weather there for a few seasons, or when we claim that all swans are white after seeing only a small number of white swans, or when we conclude that all Scots are tough negotiators after conducting business with only a few, we are learning by induction. Our conclusions may not always be valid, however. For example, there are also black Australian swans and some weather records show that October weather in El Paso was inclement. Even so, these conclusions or rules are useful. They are correct much or most of the time, and they allow us to adjust our behavior and formulate important decisions with little cognitive effort.

One can only marvel at our ability to formulate a general rule for a whole class of objects, finite or not, after having observed only a few examples. How is it we are able to make this large inductive leap and arrive at an accurate conclusion so easily? For example, how is it that a first time traveler to France will conclude that all French people speak French after having spoken only to one Frenchman named Henri? At the same time, our traveler would not incorrectly conclude that all Frenchmen are named Henri!

Examples like this emphasize the fact that inductive learning is much more than undirected search for general hypotheses. Indeed, it should be clear that inductive generalization and rule formulation are performed in some context and with a purpose. They are performed to satisfy some objectives and, therefore, are guided by related background or other world knowledge. If this were not so, our generalizations would be on shaky ground and our class descriptions might be no more than a complete listing of all the examples we had observed.

The inductive process can be described symbolically through the use of predicates P and Q. If we observe the repeated occurrence of events $P(a_1)$, $P(a_2)$, . . . , $P(a_k)$, we generalize by inductively concluding that $\forall x\, P(x)$, i.e. if (canary_1 color yellow), (canary_2 color yellow), . . . , (canary_*k* color yellow) then (forall *x* (if canary *x*)(*x* color yellow)). More generally, when we observe the implications

$$P(a_1) \rightarrow Q(b_1)$$
$$P(a_2) \rightarrow Q(b_2)$$
$$\cdot$$
$$\cdot$$
$$\cdot$$
$$P(a_k) \rightarrow Q(b_k)$$

we generalize by concluding $\forall xy\ P(x) \rightarrow Q(y)$.

In forming a generalized hypothesis about a complete (possibly infinite) class after observing only a fraction of the members, we are making an uncertain conclusion. Even so, we have all found it to be a most essential form of learning.

Our reliance on and proven success with inductive learning has motivated much research in this area. Numerous systems have been developed to investigate different forms of such learning referred to as learning by observation, learning by discovery, supervised learning, learning from examples, and unsupervised learning. We have already seen two examples of weak inductive learning paradigms in the previous chapter: learning automata and genetic algorithms. In this chapter we will see different kinds of examples which use the more traditional AI architecture.

In the remainder of this and the following chapter, we will study the inductive learning process and look at several traditional AI learning systems based on inductive learning paradigms. We begin in the next two sections with definitions of important terms and descriptions of some essential tools used in the learning systems which follow.

18.3 SOME DEFINITIONS

In this section we introduce some important terms and concepts related to inductive learning. Many of the terms we define will have significance in other areas as well.

Our model of learning is the model described in Section 16.4. As you may recall, our learner component is presented with training examples from a teacher or from the environment. The examples may be positive instances only or both positive and negative. They may be selected, well-organized examples or they may be presented in a haphazard manner and contain much irrelevant information. Finally, the examples may be correctly labeled as positive or negative instances of some concept, they may be unlabeled, or they may even contain erroneous labels. Whatever the scenario, we must be careful to describe it appropriately.

Given (1) the observations, (2) certain background domain knowledge, and (3) goals or other preference criteria, the task of the learner is to find an inductive assertion or target concept that implies all of the observed examples and is consistent with both the background knowledge and goals. We formalize the above ideas with the following definitions (Hunt et al., 1966, and Rendell, 1985).

Definitions

Object. Any entity, physical or abstract, which can be described by a set of attribute (feature) values and attribute relations is an object. We will refer to an object either by its name o_i or by an appropriate representation such as the vector of attribute values $\mathbf{x} = (x_1, x_2, \ldots, x_n)$. Clearly, the x_i can be very primitive attributes or higher level, more abstract ones. The choice will depend on the use being made of the representations. For example, a car may be described with primitives as an entity made from steel, glass, rubber, and its other component materials or, at a higher level of abstraction, as an object used for the transportation of passengers at speeds ranging up to 250 miles per hour.

Class. Given some universe of objects U, a class is a subset of U. For example, given the universe of four-legged animals, one class is the subset horses.

Concept. This is a description of some class (set) or rule which partitions the universe of objects U into two sets, the set of objects that satsisfy the rule and those that do not. Thus, the concept of horse is a description or rule which asserts the set of all horses and excludes all nonhorses.

Hypothesis. A hypothesis H is an assertion about some objects in the universe. It is a candidate or tentative concept which partitions the universe of objects. One such hypothesis related to the concept of horse is the class of four-legged animals with a tail. This is a candidate (albeit incomplete) for the concept horse.

Target concept. The target is one concept which correctly classifies all objects in the universe.

Positive instances. These are example objects which belong to the target concept.

Negative instances. These are examples opposite to the target concept.

Consistent classification rule. This is a rule that is true for all positive instances and false for all negative instances.

Induction. Induction is the process of class formation. Here we are more interested in the formation of classes which are goal-oriented; therefore, we will define induction as purposeful class formation. To illustrate, from our earlier example, we concluded that all Scotsmen are tough negotiators. Forming this concept can be helpful when dealing with any Scot. The goal or purpose here is in the simplification of our decisions when found in such situations.

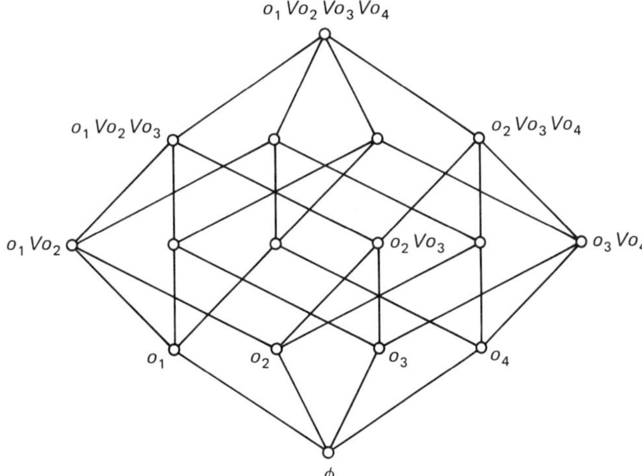

Figure 18.1 Lattice of object classes. Each node represents a disjunction of objects from a universe of four objects.

Selective induction. In this form of induction class descriptions are formed using only the attributes and relations which appear in the positive instances.

Constructive induction. This form of induction creates new descriptors not found in any of the instances.

Expedient induction. This is the application of efficient, efficacious inductive learning methods which have some scope, methods which span more than a single domain. The combined performance in efficiency, efficacy, and scope has been termed the inductive power of a system (Rendell, 1985).

In this chapter we are primarily interested in learners which exhibit expedient induction. Our reason for this concern will become more apparent when we examine the complexity involved in locating a target concept, even in a small universe. Consider, for example, the difficulty in locating a single concept class in a universe consisting of only four objects. Since the universe of all dichotomous sets (the concept C and U-C) containing n objects can be represented as a lattice structure having 2^n nodes, we see that this is an exponential search problem (Figure 18.1).

18.4 GENERALIZATION AND SPECIALIZATION

In this section we consider some techniques which are essential for the application of inductive learning algorithms. Concept learning requires that a guess or estimate of a larger class, the target concept, be made after having observed only some fraction of the objects belonging to that class. This is essentially a process of generalization, of formulating a description or a rule for a larger class but one which is still consistent with the observed positive examples. For example, given the three positive instances of objects

(blue cube rigid large)
(small flexible blue cube)
(rigid small cube blue)

a proper generalization which implies the three instances is blue cube. Each of the instances satisfies the general description.

Specialization is the opposite of generalization. To specialize the concept blue cube, a more restrictive class of blue cubes is required such as small blue cube or flexible blue cube or any of the original instances given above. Specialization may be required if the learning algorithm over-generalizes in its search for the target concept. An over-generalized hypothesis is inconsistent since it will include some negative instances in addition to the positive ones.

There are many ways to form generalizations. We shall describe the most commonly used rules below. They will be sufficient to describe all of the learning paradigms which follow. In describing the rules, we distinguish between two basic types of generalization, comparable to the corresponding types of induction (Section 18.2), selective generalization and constructive generalization (Michalski, 1983). Selective generalization rules build descriptions using only the descriptors (attributes and relations) that appear in the instances, whereas constructive generalization rules do not. These concepts are described further below.

Generalization Rules

Since specialization rules are essentially the opposite of rules for generalization, to specialize a description, one could change variables to constants, add a conjunct or remove a disjunct from a description, and so forth. Of course, there are other means of specialization such as taking exceptions in descriptions (a fish is anything that swims in water but does not breathe air as do dolphins). Such methods will be introduced as needed.

These methods are useful tools for constructing knowledge structures. They give us methods with which to formulate and express inductive hypotheses. Unfortunately, they do not give us much guidance on how to select hypotheses efficiently. For this, we need methods which more directly limit the number of hypotheses which must be considered.

Selective Generalization

Changing Constants to Variables.

An example of this rule was given in Section 18.1. Given instances of a description or predicate $P(a_1)$, $P(a_2)$, . . . , $P(a_k)$ the constants a_i are changed to a variable which may be any value in the given domain, that is, $\forall x\ P(x)$.

Dropping Condition.

Dropping one or more conditions in a description has the effect of expanding or increasing the size of the set. For example, the set of all small red spheres is less general than the set of small spheres. Another way of stating this rule when the conjunctive description is given is that a generalization results when one or more of the conjuncts is dropped.

Adding an Alternative.

This is similar to the dropping condition rule. Adding a disjunctive term generalizes the resulting description by adding an alternative to the possible objects. For example, transforming red sphere to (red sphere) $\vee$ (green pyramid) expands the class of red spheres to the class of red spheres or green pyramids. Note that the *internal disjunction* could also be used to generalize. An internal disjunction is one which appears inside the parentheses such as (red $\vee$ green sphere).

Climbing a Generalization Tree.

When the classes of objects can be represented as a tree hierarchy as pictured in Figure 18.2, generalization is accomplished by simply climbing the tree to a node which is higher and, therefore, gives a more general description. For example, moving up the tree one level from elephant we obtain the more general class description of mammal. A greater generalization would be the class of all animals.

Closing an Interval.

When the domain of a descriptor is ordered ($d_1 < d_2 < \ldots < d_k$) and a few values lie in a small interval, a more restricted form of generalization than changing constants to variables can be performed by generalizing the values to a closed interval. Thus, if two or more instances with values $D = d_i$ and $D = d_j$

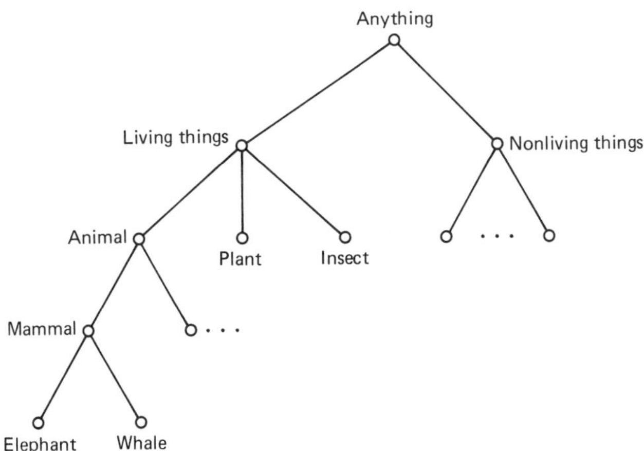

Figure 18.2 Generalization tree for the hierarchy of All Things.

where $d_i < d_j$ have been observed, the generalization $D = [d_i \ . \ . \ . \ d_j]$ can be made; that is, D can be any value in the interval d_i to d_j.

Constructive Generalization

Generating Chain Properties.

If an order exists among a set of objects, they may be described by their ordinal position such as first, second, . . . , n^{th}. For example, suppose the relations for a four story building are given as

$$\text{above}(f_2,f_1) \ \& \ \text{above}(f_3,f_2) \ \& \ \text{above}(f_4,f_3)$$

then a constructive generalization is

$$\text{most\_above}(f_4) \ \& \ \text{least\_above}(f_1).$$

The most above, least above relations are created. They did not occur in the original descriptors.

Other forms of less frequently used generalization techniques are also available including combinations of the above. We will introduce such methods as we need them.

18.5 INDUCTIVE BIAS

Learning generalizations has been characterized as a search problem (Mitchell, 1982). We saw in Section 18.2 that learning a target concept is equivalent to finding a node in a lattice of 2^n nodes when there are n elementary objects. How can one expect to realize expedient induction when an exponential space must be searched? From our earlier exposure to search problems, we know that the naive answer to this question is simply to reduce the number of hypotheses which must be considered. But how can this be accomplished? Our solution here is through the use of *bias*.

Bias is, collectively, all of those factors that influence the selection of hypotheses, excluding factors directly related to the training examples. There are two general types of bias: (1) restricting hypotheses from the hypothesis space and (2) the use of a preferential ordering among the hypotheses or use of an informed selection scheme. Each of these methods can be implemented in different ways. For example, the size of the hypothesis space can be limited through the use of syntactic constraints in a representation language which permits attribute descriptions only. This will be the case with predicate calculus descriptions if only unary predicates are allowed, since relations cannot be expressed easily with one place predicates. Of course, such descriptions must be expressive enough to represent the knowledge being learned.

Representations based on more abstract descriptions will often limit the size of the space as well. Consider the visual scene of Figure 18.3. When used as a training example for concepts like on top of, the difference in the size of the hypothesis space between representations based on primitive pixel values and more abstract

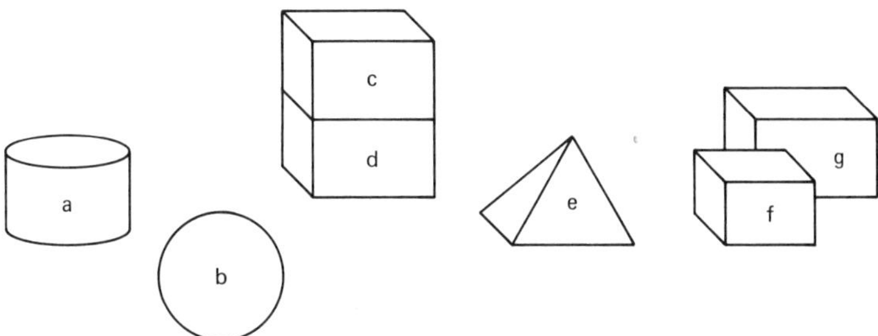

Figure 18.3 Blocks world scene.

descriptions based on a semantic net can be very large. For example, a representation using only two levels of gray (light and dark) in a 1024 by 1024 pixel array will have a hypothesis space in excess of 2^{10^6}. Compare this with the semantic net space which uses no more than 10 to 20 objects and a limited number of position relationships. Such a space would have no more than 10^4 or 10^5 object-position relationships. We see then that the difference in the size of the search space for these two representations can be immense.

Another simple example which limits the number of hypotheses is illustrated in Figure 18.4. The tree representation on the left contains more information and, therefore, will permit a larger number of object descriptions to be created than with the tree on the right. On the other hand, if one is only interested in learning general descriptions of geometrical objects without regard to details of size, the tree on the right will be a superior choice since the smaller tree will result in less search.

Methods based on the second general type of bias limit the search through preferential hypotheses selection. One way this can be achieved is through the use of heuristic evaluation functions. If it is known that a target concept should not contain some object or class of objects, all hypotheses which contain these objects can be eliminated from consideration. Referring again to Figure 18.1, if it is known

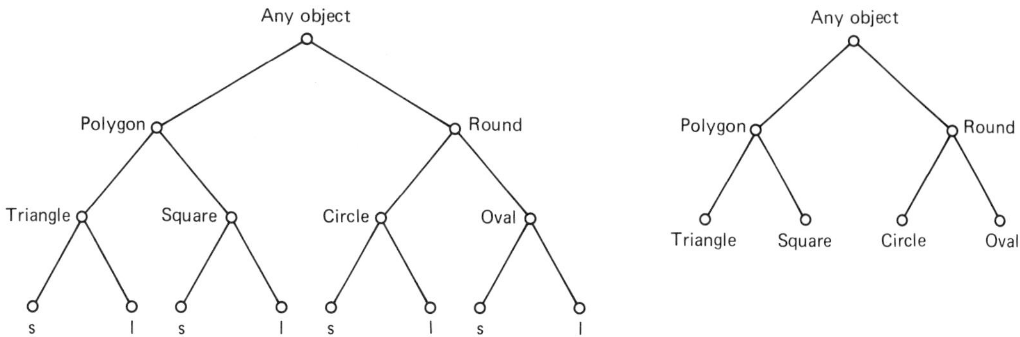

Figure 18.4 Tree representation for object descriptions (s = small, l = large).

that object o_3 (or the description of o_3) should not be included in the target set, all nodes above o_3 and connected to o_3 can be eliminated from the search. In this case, a heuristic which gives preferential treatment would not choose descriptions which contain o_3.

Another simple example which relates to learning an optimal play of the game of Nim might use a form of preference which introduces a heuristic to block consideration of most moves which permit an opponent to leave only one token. This eliminates a large fraction of the hypotheses which must be evaluated (see Chapter 17).

Bias can be strong or weak, correct or incorrect. A strong bias is one which focuses on a relatively small number of hypotheses. A weak bias does not. A correct bias is one which allows the learner to consider the target concept, whereas an incorrect bias does not. Obviously, a learner's task is simplified when the bias is both strong and correct (Utgoff, 1986). Bias can also be implemented in a program as either static or dynamic. When dynamic bias is employed, it is shifted automatically by the program to improve the learner's performance. We will see different forms of bias used in subsequent sections.

18.6 EXAMPLE OF AN INDUCTIVE LEARNER

Many learning programs have been implemented which construct descriptions composed of conjunctive features only. Few have been implemented to learn disjunctive descriptions as well. This is because conjunctive learning algorithms are easier to implement. Of course, a simple implementation for a disjunctive concept learner would be one which simply forms the disjunction of all positive training instances as the target concept. Obviously, this would produce an awkward description if there were many positive instances.

There are many concepts which simply cannot be described well in conjunctive terms only. One of the best examples is the concept of uncle since an uncle can be *either* the brother of the father *or* the brother of the mother of a child. To state it any other way is cumbersome.

The system we describe below was first implemented at M.I.T (Iba, 1979). It is a more traditional AI type of learner than the systems of the previous chapter in that it builds symbolic English-like descriptions and the learning process is more algorithmic in form. This system learns descriptions which are essentially in disjunctive normal form. Consequently, a broad range of descriptions is possible. Furthermore, the system can learn either concept descriptions from attribute values or structural descriptions of objects.

The training set we use here consists of a sequence of labeled positive and negative instances of the target concept. Each instance is presented to the learner as an unordered list of attributes together with a label which specifies whether or not the instance is positive or negative.

For this first example, we require our learner to learn the disjunctive concept "something that is either a tall flower or a yellow object." One such instance of

```
concept_name:(tall flower or yellow object)
    positive_part:
        cluster:description: ______________________
                  examples: ______________________
                            ______________________
                                      .
                                      .
                                      .
        cluster:description: ______________________
                  examples: ______________________
                            ______________________
                                      .
            .                         .
            .
            .
    negative_part:
                  examples: ______________________
                            ______________________
                                      .
                                      .
                                      .
```

Figure 18.5 Frame-like knowledge structure.

this concept is represented as (short skinny yellow flower +), whereas a negative instance is (brown fat tall weed −). Given a number of positive and negative training instances such as these, the learner builds frame-like structures with groups of slots we will call clusters as depicted in Figure 18.5.

The target concept is given in the concept name. The actual description is then built up as a group of slots labeled as clusters. All training examples, both positive and negative, are retained in the example slots for use or reuse in building up the descriptions. An example will illustrate the basic algorithm.

Garden World Example

Each cluster in the frame of Figure 18.5 is treated as a disjunctive term, and descriptions within each cluster are treated as conjuncts. A complete learning cycle will clarify the way in which the clusters and frames (concepts) are created. We will use the following training examples from a garden world to teach our learner the concept "tall flower or yellow object."

(tall fat brown flower +)
(green tall skinny flower +)
(skinny short yellow weed +)
(tall fat brown weed −)
(fat yellow flower tall +)

After accepting the first training instance, the learner creates the tentative concept hypothesis "a tall fat brown flower." This is accomplished by creating a cluster in the positive part of the frame as follows:

```
concept_name:(tall flower or yellow object)
 positive_part:
        cluster:description:(tall fat brown flower)
               :examples:(tall fat brown flower)
 negative_part: ______________________________
```

With only a single example, the learner has concluded the tentative concept must be the same as the instance. However, after the second training instance, a new hypothesis is created by merging the two initial positive instances. Two instances are merged by taking the set intersection of the two. This results in a more general description, but one which is consistent with both positive examples. It produces the following structure.

```
concept_name:(tall flower or yellow object)
 positive_part:
        cluster:description:(tall, flower)
               :examples:(tall fat brown flower)
                         (green tall skinny flower)
 negative_part:
     examples: ______________________________
```

The next training example is also a positive one. Therefore, the set intersection of this example and the current description is formed when the learner is presented with this example. The resultant intersection and new hypothesis is an over generalization, namely, the null set, which stands for anything.

```
concept_name:(tall flower or yellow object)
 positive_part:
        cluster:description:()
               :examples:(tall fat brown flower)
                         (green tall skinny flower)
                         (skinny short yellow weed)
 negative_part:
               :examples: ________________________
```

The fourth instance is a negative one. This instance is inconsistent with the current hypothesis which includes anything. Consequently, the learner must revise its hypothesis to exclude this last instance.

It does this by splitting the first cluster into two new clusters which are then both compatible with the negative instance. Each new cluster corresponds to a disjunctive term in this description.

To build the new clusters, the learner uses the three remembered examples from the first cluster. It merges the examples in such a way that each merge produces new consistent clusters. After merging we get the following revised frame.

```
concept_name:(tall flower or yellow object)
 positive_part:
        cluster:description:(tall flower)
               :examples:(tall fat brown flower)
                          (green tall skinny flower)
        cluster:description:(skinny short yellow weed)
               :examples:(skinny short yellow weed)
 negative_part:
               :examples:(tall fat brown weed)
```

The reader should verify that this new description has now excluded the negative instance.

The next training example is all that is required to arrive at the target concept. To complete the description, the learner attempts to combine the new positive instance with each cluster by merging as before, but only if the resultant merge is compatible with all negative instances (one in this case). If the new instance cannot be merged with any existing cluster without creating an inconsistency, a new cluster is created.

Merging the new instance with the first cluster results in the same cluster. Merging it with the second cluster produces a new, more general cluster description of yellow. The final frame obtained is as follows.

```
concept_name:(tall flower or yellow object)
 positive_part:
        cluster:description:(tall flower)
               :examples:(tall fat brown flower)
                          (green tall skinny flower)
                          (fat yellow flower tall)

        cluster:description:(yellow)
               :examples:(skinny short yellow weed)
                          (fat yellow flower tall)
 negative_part:
               :examples:(tall fat brown weed)
```

The completed concept now matches the target concept ''tall flower or yellow object.''

The above example illustrates the basic cycle but omits some important factors. First, the order in which the training instances are presented to the learner is important. Different orders, in general, will result in different descriptions and may require different numbers of training instances to arrive at the target concept.

Second, when splitting and rebuilding clusters after encountering a negative example, it is possible to build clusters which are not concise or maximal in the sense that some of the clusters could be merged without becoming inconsistent. Therefore, after rebuilding new clusters it is necessary to check for this maximality and merge clusters where possible without violating the inconsistency condition.

Blocks World Example

Another brief example will illustrate this point. Here we want to learn the concept "something that is either yellow or spherical." For this, we use the following training instances from a blocks world.

(yellow pyramid soft large +)
(blue sphere soft small +)
(yellow pyramid hard small +)
(green large sphere hard +)
(yellow cube soft large +)
(blue cube soft small −)
(blue pyramid soft large −)

After the first three training examples have been given to the learner, the resultant description is the empty set.

```
concept_name:(yellow or spherical object)
 positive_part:
      cluster:description:()
             :examples:(yellow pyramid soft large)
                       (blue sphere soft small)
                       (yellow pyramid hard small)
negative_part:
             :examples:____________________
```

Since the next two examples are also positive, the only change to the above frame is the addition of the fourth and fifth training instances to the cluster examples. However, the sixth training instance is negative. This forces a split due to the inconsistency. In rebuilding the clusters this time, we rebuild starting with the last positive (fifth) example and work backwards as though the examples were put on a stack. This is actually the order used in the original system. After the fifth and fourth examples are processed, the following frame is produced.

```
concept_name:(yellow or spherical object)
  positive_part:
          cluster:description:(large)
                 :examples:(yellow cube soft large)
                           (green large sphere hard)

 negative_part:
                 :examples: ________________
```

Next, when an attempt is made to merge the third example, an inconsistency results. Therefore, this example must be put into a separate cluster. The same applies when an attempt is made to merge the second example with either of the new clusters; merging with the first cluster results in the empty set, while merging with the second cluster results in the set (small) which is also inconsistent with the negative example (blue cube soft small). This forces the creation of a third cluster. Finally, after attempts are made to merge the first example (it merges with the first two clusters), we obtain the frame

```
concept_name:(yellow or spherical object)
  positive_part:
          cluster:description:(large)
                 :examples:(yellow cube soft large)
                          :(green large sphere hard)
                          :(yellow pyramid soft large)
          cluster:description:(yellow pyramid)
                 :examples:(yellow pyramid hard small)
                           (yellow pyramid soft large)
          cluster:description:(blue sphere soft small)
                 :examples:(blue sphere soft small)
 negative_part:
                 :examples:(blue cube soft small)
```

Note that we still have not arrived at the target concept. The last training instance, a negative one,

(blue pyramid soft large −)

is needed to do the trick. The first cluster is inconsistent with this instance. Therefore, it must be split. After completing this split we get the new frame

```
concept_name:(yellow or spherical object)
 positive_part:
        cluster:description:(yellow soft large)
               :examples:(yellow cube soft large)
                         (yellow pyramid soft large)
        cluster:description:(green large sphere hard)
               :examples:(green large sphere hard)
        cluster:description:(yellow pyramid)
               :examples:(yellow pyramid hard small)
                         (yellow pyramid soft large)
        cluster:description:(blue sphere soft small)
               :examples:(blue sphere soft small)
 negative_part:
               :examples:(blue cube soft small)
                         (blue pyramid soft large)
```

All of the new clusters are now consistent with the negative examples. But the clusters are not maximal, since it is possible to merge some clusters without violating the inconsistency condition. To obtain maximality, the clusters must be rewritten and merged where possible. This rewrite is accomplished by copying the first cluster and then successively merging or copying the other clusters in combination. Of course, a merge can be completed only when an inconsistency does not result.

The first two clusters cannot be merged as we know from the above. The first and third clusters can be merged to give yellow. The second and fourth clusters can also be merged to produce sphere. These are the only merges that can be made that are compatible with both negative examples. The final frame then is given as

```
concept_name:(yellow or spherical object)
 positive_part:
        cluster:description:(yellow)
               :examples:(yellow cube soft large)
                         (yellow pyramid hard
                         small)
                         (yellow pyramid soft
                         large)
        cluster:description:(sphere)
               :examples:(green large sphere hard)
                         (blue sphere soft small)
 negative_part:
               :examples:(blue cube soft small)
                         (blue pyramid soft large)
```

It may have been noticed already by the astute reader that there is no reason why negative-part clusters could not be created as well. Allowing this more symmetric structure permits the creation of a broader range of concepts such as ''neither yellow nor spherical'' as well as the positive type of concepts created above. This is implemented by building clusters in the negative part of the frame using the negative examples in the same way as the positive examples. In building both descriptions concurrently, care must be taken to maintain consistency between the positive and negative parts. Each time a negative example is presented, it is added to the negative part of the model, and a check is made against each cluster in the positive part of the model for inconsistencies. Any of the clusters which are inconsistent are split into clusters which are maximal and consistent and which contain all the original examples among them. We leave the details as an exercise.

Network Representations

It is also possible to build clusters of network representation structures and to learn structural descriptions of objects. For example, the concept of an arch can be learned in a manner similar to the above examples. In this case our training examples could be represented as something like the following where, as in earlier chapters, ako means a kind of.

```
((nodes (a b c)
 (links (ako a brick)
        (ako b brick)
        (ako c brick)
        (supports a c)
        (supports b c) +)
```

Since an arch can support materials other than a brick, another positive example of the concept arch might be identical to the one above except for the object supported, say a wedge. Thus, substituting (ako c wedge) for (ako c brick) above we get a second positive instance of arch. These two examples can now be generalized into a single cluster by simply dropping the differing conjunctive ako terms to get the following.

```
((nodes (a b c)
 links  (ako a brick)
        (ako b brick)
        (supports a c)
        (supports b c))
```

This is an over generalization. It can be corrected by a negative training example which uses some nonvalid object such as a sphere as the supported item.

```
((nodes (a b c)
 links  (ako a brick)
        (ako b brick)
        (ako c sphere)
        (supports a c)
        (supports b c) -)
```

This example satisfies the current description of an arch. However, it has caused an inconsistency. Therefore, the cluster must be split into a disjunctive description as was done before in the previous examples. The process is essentially the same except for the representation scheme.

In a similar manner the concept of uncle can be learned with instances presented and corresponding clusters created using a network representation as follows.

```
((nodes (a b c)
 links  (ako a person)
        (ako b person)
        (ako c person)
        (male c)
        (parent_of b a)
        (brother_of c b) +)
```

Again, we leave the remaining details as an exercise.

Before leaving these examples, the reader should consider what learning methods and tools have been used from the previous two sections, what types of bias have been used to limit the search, and what methods of generalization have been employed in the learning process.

18.7 SUMMARY

Inductive learning is accomplished through inductive inference, the process of inferring a common class from instances, reasoning from parts to the whole or from the individual to the universal. Learning a concept through induction requires generalization, a search through a lattice of hypotheses. Practical induction is based on the use of methods that constrain or direct the search process. This is made possible through the use of bias which is used to reduce the size of the hypothesis space or to impose preferential selection on the hypotheses.

A number of techniques are available for either selective or constructive generalization, including changing constants to variables, dropping conjunctive conditions, adding a disjunctive alternative, closing the interval, climbing a generalization tree, and generating chain properties, among others. Specialization is achieved through the inverse operation to generalization as well as some other methods like including exceptions.

An example of an inductive learning system was presented in some detail. This system constructs concept descriptions from positive and negative examples presented as attribute lists. The descriptions are created as clusters or disjuncts by first generalizing conjunctive descriptions from the positive training examples until an inconsistent negative example is experienced. This separates the clusters to produce compatible, disjunctive descriptions. The system can also learn structural descriptions in the form of network representations. It is possible to build negative disjunctive descriptions as well, building clusters in the negative part of the frame structure or both positive and negative descriptions.

EXERCISES

18.1. Define inductive learning and explain why we still use it even though it is not a "valid" form of learning.

18.2. What is the difference between a class and a concept?

18.3. What is the difference between selective, constructive, and expedient induction? Give examples of each.

18.4. What is the purpose of inductive bias?

18.5. Give three examples in which inductive bias can be applied to constrain search.

18.6. Use the following training examples to simulate learning the concept "green flower or skinny object." Build up the concept description in clusters using the same method as that described in Section 18.6.
(green tall fat flower +)
(skinny green short flower +)
(tall skinny green flower +)
(red skinny short weed +)
(green short fat weed −)
(tall green flower skinny +)

18.7. Work out an example of concept learning using network structures. The concept to be learned is the concept wife. Create both positive and negative training examples.

18.8. Write a computer program in LISP to build concept descriptions in the form of clusters like the examples of Section 18.7.

18.9. The method described in Section 18.7 for learning concepts depends on the order in which examples are presented. State what modifications would be required to make the learner build the same structures independent of the order in which training examples are presented.

18.10. Compare each of the generalization methods described in Section 18.4 and explain when each method would be appropriate to use.

18.11. Referring to the previous problem, rank the generalization methods by estimated computation time required to perform each.

18.12. Give an example of learning the negative of the concept ''tall flower or red object,'' that is, something that is ''neither a tall flower nor a red object.''

19

Examples of Other Inductive Learners

19.1 INTRODUCTION

In this chapter we continue with our study of inductive learning. Here, we review four other important learning systems based on the inductive paradigms.

Perhaps the most significant difference among these systems is the type of knowledge representation scheme and the learning algorithms used. The first system we describe, ID3, constructs a discrimination tree for use in classifying objects. The second system, LEX, creates and refines heuristic rules for carrying out symbolic integrations. The third system, INDUCE, constructs descriptions in an extended form of predicate calculus. These descriptions are then used to classify objects such as soybean diseases. Our final system, Winston's Arch, forms conjunctive network structures similar to the ones described in the previous chapter.

19.2 THE ID3 SYSTEM

ID3 was developed in the late 1970s (Quinlan, 1983) to learn object classifications from labeled training examples. The basic algorithm is based on earlier research programs known as Concept Learner Systems or CLSs (Hunt et al., 1966). This system is also similar in many respects to the expert system architecture described in Section 15.3.

The CLS algorithms start with a set of training objects $O = \{o_1, o_2, \ldots, o_n\}$ from a universe U, where each object is described by a set of m attribute values. An attribute A_j having a small number of discrete values $a_{j1}, a_{j2}, \ldots, a_{jk}$ is selected and a tree node structure is formed to represent A_j. The node has k_j branches emanating from it where each branch corresponds to one of the a_{ji} values (Figure 19.1). The set of training objects O are then partitioned into at most k_j subsets based on the object's attribute values. The same procedure is then repeated recursively for each of these subsets using the other $m - 1$ attributes to form lower level nodes and branches. The process stops when all of the training objects have been subdivided into single class entities which become labeled leaf nodes of the tree.

The resulting discrimination tree or decision tree can then be used to classify new unknown objects given a description consisting of its m attribute values. The unknown is classified by moving down the learned tree branch by branch in concert with the values of the object's attributes until a leaf node is reached. The leaf node is labeled with the unknown's name or other identity.

ID3 is an implementation of the basic CLS algorithm with some modifications. In the ID3 system, a relatively small number of training examples are randomly selected from a large set of objects O through a window. Using these training examples, a preliminary discrimination tree is constructed. The tree is then tested by scanning all the objects in O to see if there are any exceptions to the tree. A new subset or window is formed using the original examples together with some of the exceptions found during the scan. This process is repeated until no exceptions are found. The resulting discrimination tree can then be used to classify new objects.

Another important difference introduced in ID3 is the way in which the attributes are ordered for use in the classification process. Attributes which discriminate best are selected for evaluation first. This requires computing an estimate of the expected information gain using all available attributes and then selecting the attribute having the largest expected gain. This attribute is assigned to the root node. The attribute having the next largest gain is assigned to the next level of nodes in the tree and so on until the leaves of the tree have been reached. An example will help to illustrate this process.

For simplicity, we assume here a single-class classification problem, one where all objects either belong to class C or U-C. Let h denote the fraction of objects

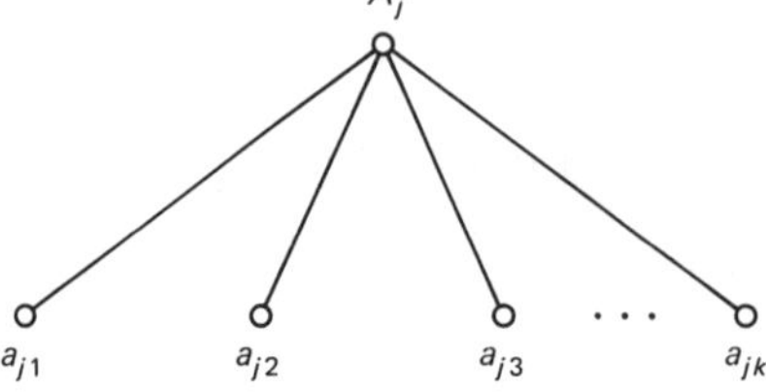

Figure 19.1 A node created for attribute A_j (color) with k discrete values, $a_{j1}, a_{j2}, \ldots, a_{jk}$ (red, orange, . . . , white).

that belong to class C in a sample of n objects from O; h is an estimate of the true fraction or probability of objects in U that belong to class C. Also let

c_{jk} = number of objects that belong to C and have value a_{jk}
d_{jk} = number of objects *not* belonging to C and having value a_{jk}
$p_{jk} = (c_{jk} + d_{jk}) / n$ be the fraction of objects with value a_{jk} (we assume objects have all attribute values so that $\Sigma_j p_{jk} = 1$)
$f_{jk} = c_{jk} / (c_{jk} + d_{jk})$, the fraction of objects in C with attribute value a_{jk}, and
$g_{jk} = 1 - f_{jk}$, the fraction of objects *not* in C with value a_{jk}.

Now define

$$H_c(h) = -h * \log_2 h - (1 - h) * \log_2(1 - h)$$

with $H_c(0) = 0$, and

$$H_{jk} = -f_{jk} * \log_2 f_{jk} - g_{jk} * \log_2 g_{jk}$$

as the information content for class C and attribute a_{jk} respectively. Then the expected value (mean) of H_{jk} is just

$$E(H_{jk}) = \Sigma p_{jk} * H_{jk}$$

We can now define the gain G_j for attribute A_j as

$$G_j = H_c - H_{jk}$$

Each G_j is computed and ranked. The ones having the largest values determine the order in which the corresponding attributes are selected in building the discrimination tree.

In the above equation, quantities computed as

$$H = -\Sigma p_i * \log_2 p_i \quad \text{with} \quad \Sigma_i p_i = 1$$

are known as the information theoretic entropy where p_i is the probability of occurrence of some event i. The quantities H provide a measure of the dispersion or surprise in the occurrence of a number of different events. The gains G_j measure the information to be gained in using a given attribute.

In using attributes which contain much information, one should expect that the size of the decision tree will be minimized in some sense, for example, in total number of nodes. Therefore, choosing those attributes which contain the largest gains will, in general, result in a smaller attribute set. This amounts to choosing those attributes which are more relevant in characterizing given classes of objects.

In concluding this section, an example of a small decision tree for objects described by four attributes is given in Figure 19.2. The attributes and their values are horned = {yes, no}, color = {black, brown, white, grey}, weight = {heavy, medium, light}, and height = {tall, short}. One training set for this example consists

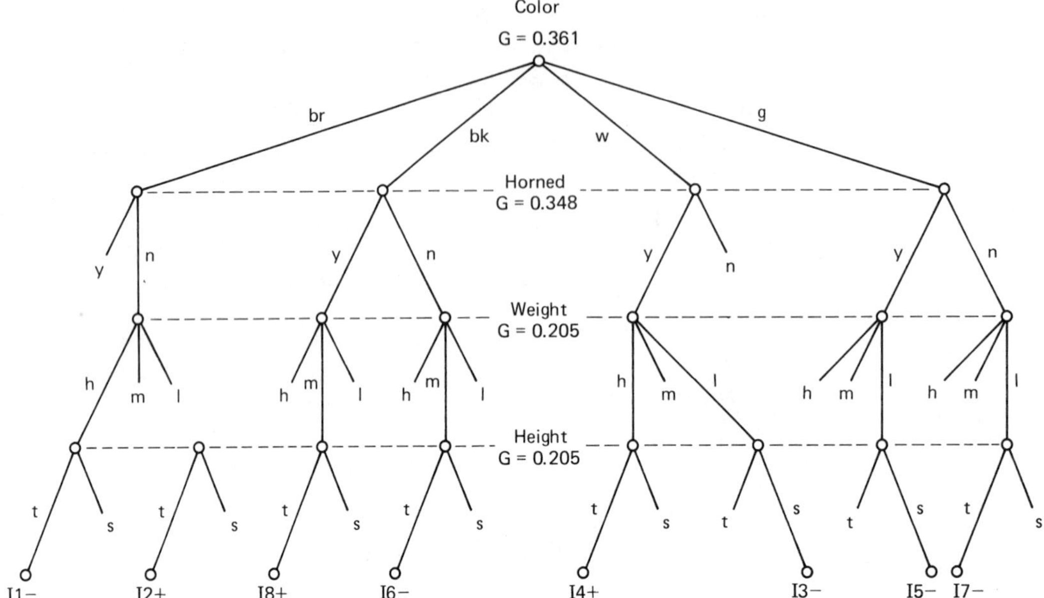

Figure 19.2 Discrimination tree for three attributes ordered by information gain. Abbreviations are br = brown, bk = black, w = white, g = gray, y = yes, n = no, h = heavy, m = medium, l = light, t = tall, and s = short.

of the eight instances given below where members of the class *C* have been labeled with + and nonmembers with −. (Class *C* might, for example, be the class of cows).

I1 (brown heavy tall no −)
I2 (black heavy tall yes +)
I3 (white light short yes −)
I4 (white heavy tall yes +)
I5 (grey light short yes −)
I6 (black medium tall no −)
I7 (grey heavy tall no −)
I8 (black medium tall yes +)

The computations required to determine the gains are tabulated in Table 19.1. For example, to compute the gain for the attribute color, we first compute

$$H_c = -3 / 8 * \log_2 3 / 8 - 5 / 8 * \log_2 5 / 8 = 0.955$$

TABLE 19.1 SUMMARY OF COMPUTATIONS REQUIRED FOR THE GAIN VALUES.

		c_{jk}	$c_{jk} + d_{jk}$	f_{jk}	$\log f_{jk}$	$\log g_{jk}$	I_{jk}	G_j
$k = 1$	brown	0	1	0	—	—	0	
2	black	2	3	2/3	−0.585	−1.585	0.918	
3	white	1	2	1/2	−1.0	−1.0	1.0	0.361
4	grey	0	2	0	—	—	0	
$k = 1$	tall	3	6	1/2	−1.0	−1.0	1.0	
2	short	0	2	0	—	—	0	0.205
$k = 1$	heavy	2	4	1/2	−1.0	−1.0	1.0	
2	medium	1	2	1/2	−1.0	−1.0	1.0	0.205
3	light	0	2	0	—	—	0	
$k = 1$	yes	3	5	3/5	−0.737	−1.322	0.971	
2	no	0	3	0	—	—	0	0.348

The information content for each color value is then computed.

$$H(\text{brown}) = 0$$

$$H(\text{black}) = -2 / 3 * \log_2 2 / 3 - 1 / 3 * \log_2 1 / 3 = 0.918$$

$$H(\text{white}) = -1 / 2 * \log_2 1/ 2 - 1 / 2 * \log_2 1 / 2 = 1.0$$

$$H(\text{grey}) = 0$$

$$E(H_{\text{color}}) = 1 / 8 * 0 + 3 / 8 * 0.918 + 1 / 4 * 1.0 + 0 = 0.594.$$

Therefore, the gain for color is

$$G = H_c - H_{\text{color}} = 0.955 - 0.594 = 0.361$$

The other gain values for horned, weight, and height are computed in a similar manner.

19.3 THE LEX SYSTEM

LEX was developed during the early 1980s (Mitchell et al., 1983) to learn heuristic rules for the solution of symbolic integration problems. The system is given about 40 integration operators which are expressed in the form of rewrite rules. Some of the rules are shown in Figure 19.3a. Internal representations for some typical integral expressions are given in Figure 19.3b.

Each of the operators has preconditions which must be satisfied before it can be applied. For example, before OP6 can be applied, the general form of the integrand must be the product of two real functions, that is $udv = f_1(x) * f_2(x)dx$. Each operator also has associated with it the resultant states that can be produced by that operator. For example, OP6 can have

OP1 $1 * f(x) \rightarrow f(x)$ ($f(x)$ is any real function of x)
OP2 $\int r * f(x) \rightarrow r \int f(x)\, dx$ (r is any real number)
OP3 $\int \sin(x)\, dx \rightarrow -\cos(x)\, dx$
OP4 $\int \cos(x)\, dx \rightarrow \sin(x)$
OP5 $\int [f_1(x) + f_2(x)] dx \rightarrow \int f_1(x)\, dx + \int f_2(x)\, dx$
OP6 $\int u dv \rightarrow uv - \int v du$ (integration by parts)
. .
. .
. .

Figure 19.3a Typical calculus operators.

$\int [\sin(x) + \cos(x)] dx$ (int((+ sin cos) x))
$\int \cos^2(x)\, dx$ (int(↑ cos 2) x))
$\int x * e^x\, dx$ (int((* id(↑ e id)) x))

Figure 19.3b Typical calculus representations.

the result obtained from the opposite bindings. The choice of the result obtained with u bound to f_1 and dv to f_2 or of an incorrect or poor operator at a given stage in the solution will lead to failure or possibly to a lengthy solution. The learning problem then is to create or refine heuristic rules which suggest when an operator should be used.

All heuristics in LEX are of the form

If: The integrand pattern is P
Then: Apply OPn with bindings B.

For example, a typical heuristic for OP6 would be

$\int f(x) * \text{trig}(x)\, dx \rightarrow$ Apply OP6 with bindings $u = f(x)$, and $dv = \text{trig}(x)\, dx$

Part of the refinement problem is the generalization or specialization of the heuristics to apply to as many consistent instances as possible. Generalization and specialization are achieved in LEX through the use of a hierarchical description tree. A segment of this tree is depicted in Figure 19.4. Thus, when a rule applies to more than a single trig function such as to both sin and cos, the more general term trig would be substituted in the rule. Likewise, when a rule is found which applies to both log and exp functions, the exp_log description would be used.

LEX is comprised of four major components as illustrated in Figure 19.5. The Problem Generator selects and generates informative integration problems which are submitted to the Problem Solver for solution. The Generator was included as part of the system to provide well-ordered training examples and to make the system a fully automatic learner. The Problem Solver attempts to find a solution to this problem using available heuristics and operators. (A solution has been found when an operator produces an expression not containing an integral.)

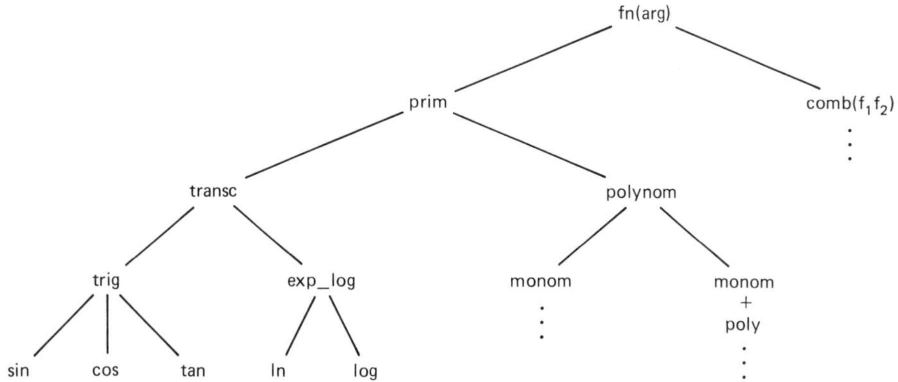

Figure 19.4 A segment of the LEX generalization tree grammar.

Output from the Problem Solver is some solution together with a complete trace of the solution search. This is presented to the Critic unit for evaluation. The Critic then analyzes the solution trace, comparing it to a least-cost path and passes related positive or negative training instances to the Generalizer. A positive instance is an operator which lies on the least-cost path, while a negative instance is one lying off the path. Given these examples, the Generalizer modifies heuristics to improve the selection of operators for best application during an attempted solution.

During the learning process each operator is given a *version space* of heuristic rules associated with it. Rules in the version space give the conditions under which the operator applies as well as the domain of states that can be produced. The version space is actually stored as two bounding rules, a rule G which gives the most general conditions of application and a rule S which gives the most specific conditions. Between these two bounds are implicitly contained all plausible versions of the heuristic. As the system learns, the bound S is made more general to include all positive instances presented by the Critic while the bound G is made more specific to exclude all negative instances. When the two bounds become equal ($G = S$), the correct heuristic has been learned.

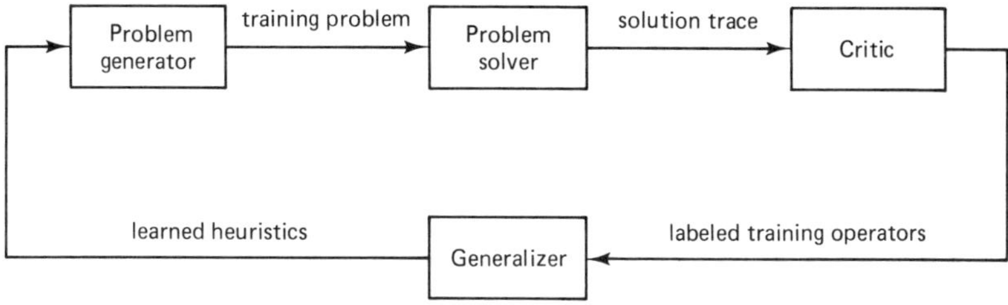

Figure 19.5 LEX learning model.

As an example of heuristic refinement for the operator OP6, suppose the Problem Generator has submitted the following two integrals for solution.

$$\int 2x * \sin(x)\, dx$$

$$\int 2x * \cos(x)\, dx$$

Let the version space for the OP6 heuristic be initialized to the G and S bounds illustrated in Figure 19.6. The functions $f_1(x)$ and $f_2(x)$ are any real-valued functions of x, and S has been set to the first specific problem instance. (Operators between G and S are implicitly contained in the version space.)

In solving the first integral above, the Problem Solver finds that operator OP6, integration by parts, is applicable. For this operator, two different bindings are possible

$$(a)\quad u = 2x \qquad\qquad (b)\quad u = \sin(x)$$
$$dv = \sin(x)\, dx \qquad\qquad dv = 2x\, dx$$

If the bindings given by a are used, OP6 produces the new expression

$$2x * (-\cos(x)) - \int 2 * (-\cos(x))dx$$

which can be further reduced using OP2, OP4 and other simplification operators to give the correct solution

$$-2x * \cos(x) + 2 * \sin(x) + C$$

For this binding, the Critic will label this as a positive instance.

On the other hand, if the variable bindings given in b are used, OP6 produces the more complex expression

$$x^2 * \sin(x) - \int x^2 * \cos(x)\, dx$$

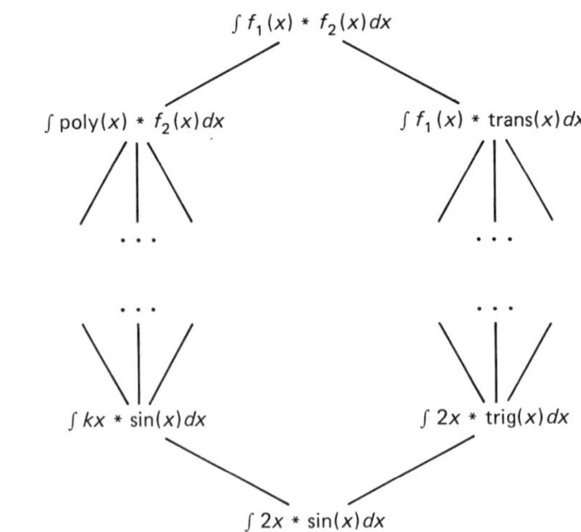

Figure 19.6 Version space with bounds G and S.

In this case the Critic will label that instance as a negative one. This negative instance will be used to adjust the version space to exclude this instance by specializing the G integrand to either

$$\text{poly}(x) * f_2(x)\,dx \qquad \text{or to} \qquad f_1(x) * \text{tran}(x)\,dx$$

with corresponding bindings

$$\begin{aligned} u &= \text{poly}(x) \\ dv &= f_2(x)\,dx \end{aligned} \qquad \text{and} \qquad \begin{aligned} u &= f_1(x) \\ dv &= \text{tran}(x)\,dx \end{aligned}$$

both of which exclude the negative instance.

After the Problem Solver attempts to solve the second integral, $\int 2x * \cos(x)\,dx$, the Critic labels the binding $u = 2x$, $dv = \cos(x)\,dx$ as positive. However, this example is not yet included in the version space. Consequently, S must be generalized to include this instance. The bound S is generalized by finding the least general function in the description hierarchy which includes both sin and cos (Figure 19.4). This generalization produces the new version space

$$G\text{: } \int f_1(x) * \text{tran}(x)\,dx$$

$$S\text{: } \int 2x * \text{trig}(x)\,dx$$

Through repeated attempts at solving such well organized problems, LEX is able to create and refine heuristics for each operator which designate when that operator should be applied. Thus, the refined heuristics reduce the class of problems to those producing acceptable solutions.

19.4 THE INDUCE SYSTEM

Several versions of the INDUCE system were developed beginning in the late 1970s (Larson and Michalski, 1977, and Dietterich and Michalski, 1981). INDUCE is a system which discovers similar patterns among positive examples of objects and formulates generalized descriptions which characterize the class patterns. The description language and the internal representation used in the system are an extension of first order predicate calculus. This is one of the unique features of INDUCE.

Before outlining how the system operates, we introduce a few new terms:

Selector. A relational statement defined by either a predicate or a function together with the values it assumes. Typical selectors used to describe objects or events in INDUCE are [shape = square V rectangular], [color = green], [size <= 4], [number_spots = 3 . . 8], [ontop(a,b)], and so on.

Complex. A logical product of selectors. A complex is a conjunctive description of some object (each selector in brackets is regarded as a conjunct). For example, a plant leaf might be represented as

Leaf_1 [contains(Leaf_1,spots)][color(Leaf_1) = yellow]&
[shape(Leaf_1 = curled)][length(Leaf_1) = 4][width(Leaf_1 = 2.3]

This expression states that a particular leaf contains spots, is yellow, curled at the sides, is 4 cm in length and 2.3 cm wide.

Cover. A cover of a set of events E is a set of complexes which describe or contain all events in E. A cover of the set E_1 against the set E_2, where E_1 and E_2 are disjointed is a set of complexes which cover all events in E_1 and no event in E_2. For example, the complex [shape = circle] [color = red] [size $<$ 5] covers the set of all red circles of size less than 5 and none of the set of circles greater than 5.

Characteristic description. A description of a class of objects which uses descriptive facts that are true for all objects in the class and thus discriminates between objects in the class and all other objects. A characteristic description of a house is one which sets houses apart from all nonhouses.

Discriminant description. A description of a class given in the context of a fixed set of other classes. A fruit tree that bears apples is a discriminant description of an apple tree within the context of fruit trees.

Given specifications for object descriptions and the type of inductive assertions desired, INDUCE can discover and formulate general class descriptions of the objects. We give here only a brief outline of the basic steps followed when inducing a single-class description.

1. The user initially makes a determination of all descriptor types (attributes or relations) needed to describe the objects. This requires a specification of type, the domains, and if appropriate, the conditions of applicability. For example, in describing living cells, number_of_tails would apply only to cells with objects possessing tails. Next, each object is described using the given descriptors and the class to which it belongs. In addition, general rules and descriptors which apply for constructive induction are specified, and finally, the type of output description desired, the characteristic and/or discriminant descriptors.

2. Given the above information, INDUCE breaks down the object descriptions into new descriptors or complexes by dropping a single selector from each description; it then places them in a list. Each of these new structures represents a generalization of the object description (dropping condition rule). Clearly, some of these new descriptors will cover negative objects as well. Consequently, the descriptors are ordered giving highest rank to ones that cover the greatest number of positive objects and the fewest number of negative objects.

3. New descriptions are also created by applying inference rules to the original ones. The inference rules use constructive generalization, heuristics, and other information to create the new descriptors. These are then added to the ranked list at their appropriate locations.

4. Each of the descriptions in the list is then tested for consistency and completeness. A description is consistent if it does not cover any negative object. It is complete if it covers all the (positive) objects. Those that pass the test are removed from the ranked list and put on a solutions list. Incomplete but consistent descriptions are put on a consistent list. Any descriptors remaining are specialized by appending selectors from the original list. These modified descriptions are tested for consistency and completeness and the process is repeated until predefined list size limits are exceeded or until all descriptors have been put on either the solutions or the consistent list.

5. Each of the descriptors on the consistent list is made more generic using generalizations such as climbing a generalization tree or closing an interval. The generalizations are then ranked and pruned using a Lexicographic Evaluation Function (LEF) and the best *m* of these are chosen as the description. The LEF uses criteria established by the user such as maximum examples covered, simplest decriptions (fewest terms), or user defined least cost. The final descriptions on the solutions list are the induced (generalized) descriptions which cover all the training instances. The following example will illustrate this process.

Assume the following three descriptions have been given for the object instances displayed in Figure 19.7.

$\exists o_1,o_2$ [color(o_1) = green][shape(o_1) = sphere][size(o_1) = large]
[color(o_2) = red][shape(o_2) = box][size(o_2) = large]
[supports(o_2, o_1)]

$\exists o_3,o_4$ [color(o_3) = red][shape(o_3) = cylinder][size(o_3) = small]
[color(o_4) = red][shape(o_4) = cube][size(o_4) = large]
[supports(o_4,o_3)]

$\exists o_5,o_6$ [color(o_5) = blue][shape(o_5) = pyramid][size(o_5) = small]
[color(o_6) = red][shape(o_6) = cylinder][size(o_6) = large]
[supports(o_6,o_5)]

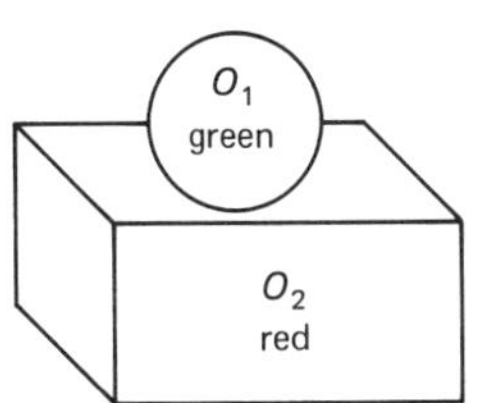

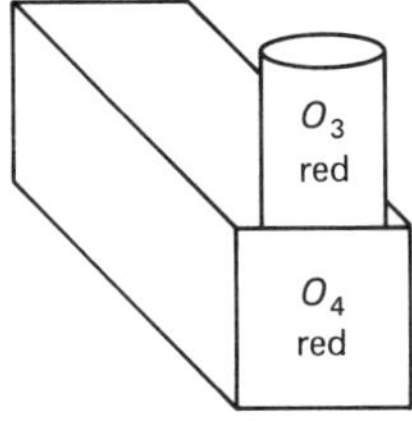

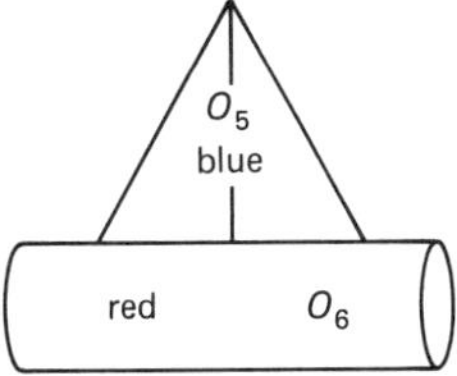

Figure 19.7 Three positive examples for training.

Using the procedure outlined above, INDUCE would discover the generalized description for the examples as "a red object supports another object," that is

$$\exists x,y\ [\text{color}(x) = \text{red}][\text{supports}(x,y)]$$

19.5 LEARNING STRUCTURAL CONCEPTS

Winston's Arch system was developed early in 1970 (Winston, 1975). This work has been noted as one of the most influential projects in recent AI research and has been cited as being responsible for stimulating renewed research in the area of machine learning.

The Arch system learns concepts in the form of associative network representations (Figure 19.8) much like the cluster network representations of the previous chapter. The Arch system, however, is not able to handle disjunctive descriptions.

Given positive and negative training examples like the ones in Figures 19.9 and 19.10, the system builds a generalized network description of an arch such as

(if (and (has_parts x (x_1 x_2 x_3))
        (ako brick x_1)
        (ako brick x_2)
        (ako prism x_3)
        (supports x_1 x_3)
        (supports x_2 x_3))
    (isa x arch))

Each training example is presented as a blocks world line drawing which is converted to a network representation. The first positive example is taken as the

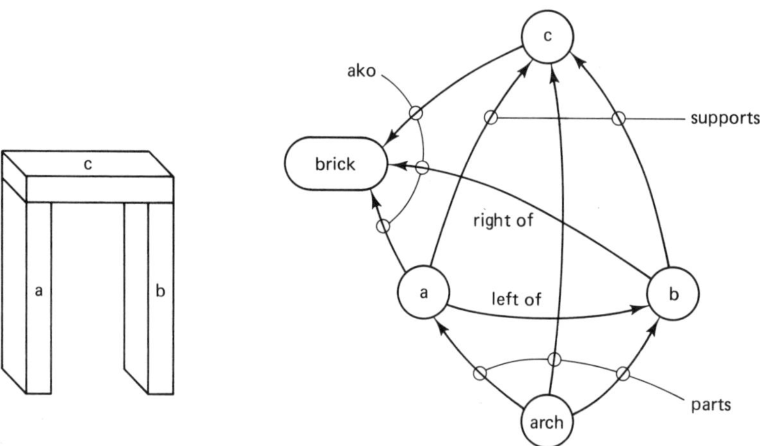

Figure 19.8 An arch and its network representation.

```
((arch(nodes(a b c)      (arch(nodes(a b c)        (arch(nodes a b c)
  (links(ako a brick)     (links(ako a brick)        (links(ako a brick)
     (ako b brick)            (ako b brick)              (ako b brick)
     (ako c brick)            (ako c wedge)              (ako c prism)
     (supports a c)     +     (supports a c)     ⇒      (supports a c)
     (supports b c)           (supports b c)             (supports b c)
     (right_of b a)           (right_of b a)             (right_of b a)
     (left_of a b)))          (left_of a b)))            (left_of a b)))

  Positive Example          Positive Example           Generalization
```

Figure 19.9 Generalized description for two positive examples.

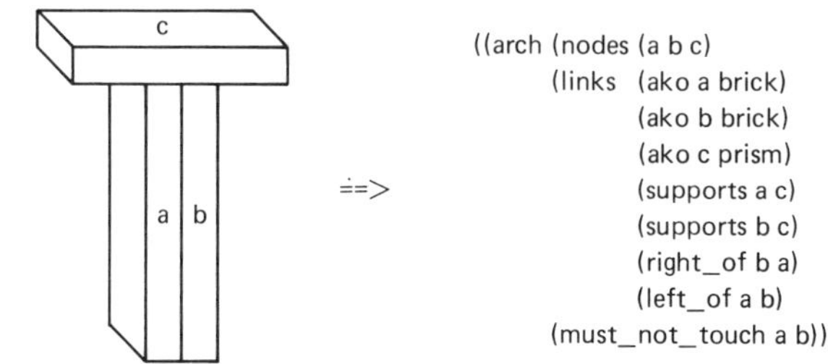
c
a
b
==>
((arch (nodes (a b c)
(links (ako a brick)
(ako b brick)
(ako c prism)
(supports a c)
(supports b c)
(right_of b a)
(left_of a b)
(must_not_touch a b)))

Negative example — near miss

Specialized exception

Figure 19.10 A nonarch and the resulting specialized representation.

initial concept description. The next example is then matched against this description using a graph-matching algorithm. This produces a common subgraph and a list of nodes and links which differ. The unmatched nodes and links are tagged with comments which are used to determine how the current description should be modified. If the new example is positive, the description is generalized (Figure 19.9) by either dropping nodes or links or replacing them with more generalized ones obtained from a hierarchical generalization tree. If the new example is a negative one, the description is specialized to exclude that example (Figure 19.10).

The negative examples are called *near misses*, since they differ from a positive example in only a single detail. Note the form of specialization used in Figure 19.10. This is an example of specialization by taking exception. The network representation for these exceptions are *must* and *must not* links to emphasize the fact that an arch must not have these features.

19.6 SUMMARY

Examples of four different inductive learning paradigms were presented in this chapter. In the first paradigm, the ID3 system, classifications were learned from a set of positive examples only. The examples were described as attribute values of objects. The classifications were learned in the form of discrimination tree. Once created, the ID3 system used the tree to classify new unknown objects. Attributes are selected on the basis of the information Gain expected. This results in a minimal tree size. LEX, the second system described, learned heuristics to choose when certain operators should be used in symbolic integration problems. One of the interesting features of LEX is the use of a version space which bounds the set of plausible heuristics that are applicable in a given problem state. LEX uses a syntactic form of bias, its grammar, to limit the size of the hypothesis space. In LEX, generalizations are found by climbing a hierarchical description tree.

The third system considered, INDUCE, formed generalized descriptions of a class of objects in an extended form of predicate calculus. This system builds both attribute and structural types of descriptions. One weakness of this system, however, is the amount of processing required when creating descriptions by removing the selectors in all possible ways. When the number of object descriptions becomes large, the computation becomes excessive.

The fourth and final inductive learner described in this chapter was Winston's Arch. This system builds associative net representations of structural concepts. One of the unique aspects of this system is the use of near miss negative examples which differ from positive examples in only a single feature. This simplifies the learning process somewhat. This system is similar in some ways to the one described in the previous chapter. It is not able to build disjunctive descriptions like that system, however.

Similar features shared by all of these systems include the use of symbolic representations, and the methods of generalization and specialization. The principal differences among these paradigms are the forms of symbolic representation schemes used and the algorithms employed for generalizing and specializing.

EXERCISES

19.1. Derive the discrimination tree of Figure 19.2 using attributes arranged in the following order: height, weight, horned, and color.

19.2. Prove that the entropy H is maximum when $p_i = p_j$ for all $i, j = 1, 2, \ldots, n$, where

$$H = -\Sigma_i \, p_i * \log_2 p_i$$

19.3. Plot the entropy as a function of p for the case $n = 2$; that is, plot H as p ranges from 0 to 1.

19.4. Describe how LEX generalizes from tan, cos, ln, and log to transc (transcendental).

19.5. Use the concepts related to version space bounding to illustrate how a system can learn the concept of a large circle from both positive and negative examples of objects described by the attributes shape (circle, square, triangle), size (small, medium, large), and color (red, blue, green).

19.6. What is the difference between a standard disjunction and an internal disjunction?

19.7. What is the significance of a cover, and how does it relate to a concept?

19.8. What steps, if any, are taken by INDUCE to avoid overgeneralization?

19.9. Compare the methods of induction used by ID3, LEX and INDUCE. Which of the methods is most efficient? Which is most robust? Which has greatest scope; that is, which is most domain independent?

19.10. Compare Winston's Arch learning system with the system developed by Iba (see Chapter 18). Which is most versatile?

19.11. What is the inductive leap used in inductive learning? Why is it potentially dangerous, but still useful? At what point can it be taken?

20

Analogical and Explanation-Based Learning

In this last chapter on autonomous acquisition, we investigate two of the most promising approaches to artificial learning, analogical and explanation-based learning. These approaches are both potentially powerful forms of learning, yet to date, they have received less attention than other methods. We expect this will change because of the great promise they both offer.

20.1 INTRODUCTION

Unlike inductive or similarity-based learning which is based on the observance of a number of training examples, analogical and explanation-based learning (EBL) can be accomplished with only a single example. In analogical learning, one example in the form of a known solution or a past experience is often sufficient knowledge for learning a new solution. In EBL, one positive training example is all that is needed to develop an explanation of a target concept. Of course, multiple examples may be used in both of these learning types, but in general, only a single example is required.

Analogies play an important role in our reasoning processes. We frequently explain or justify one phenomenon with another. A previous experience can often serve as a framework or pattern for a new, analogous experience. We use the familiar experience as a guide in dealing with the new experience. And, since so many of our acts are near repetitions of previous acts, analogical learning has gained a prominant place in our learning processes.

EBL methods of learning differ from other methods in that the learned knowledge is valid knowledge. It is derived from a set of facts through a deductive reasoning process and, therefore, is justified, consistent knowledge. These EBL methods will most likely find use in conjunction with other learning paradigms where it is important to validate newly learned knowledge.

20.2 ANALOGICAL REASONING AND LEARNING

Analogies are similarities or likenesses between things otherwise different. Things which are similar in some respects tend to be similar in other respects. The things or participants in analogies are unlimited. They may be physical objects, concepts, problems and their solutions, plans, situations, episodes, and so forth.

Analogies play a dominant role in human reasoning and learning processes. Previously remembered experiences are transformed and extended to fit new unfamiliar situations. The old experiences provide scenarios or explanations which tend to match the new situation in some aspects and, therefore, offer the promise of suggesting a solution to the new situation. The old and new situations need not be in the same domain. Frequently, the two domains, the base and target domains, will be entirely different, but similarities between the relationships of objects remain strong, a likely consequence of the regularity of nature. For example, consider the solar planetary system and the Rutherford model of an atom or the flow of liquids in pipes and the flow of electricity in conducting wires. In the first case, both consist of a system of smaller bodies being attracted to and revolving around a more massive nucleus. In the second case, the flow behaviors are governed by the force of the sources, the resistance of the medium, and other properties of the respective flow in networks.

Analogical reasoning is probably the form of reasoning we are most dependent upon for all of our decisions and actions. Its use spans such mundane tasks as finding one's way home from work, to more complex tasks such as playing chess or writing a technical paper. As suggested by Carbonell and Minton (1983), this form of reasoning requires less cognitive effort than more formal types of reasoning, which could explain why analogical reasoning is so prevelant in human thought processes.

Analogies appear in different guises and at varied levels of abstraction. Simpler analogies are the word-object or geometric ones often found in SAT or GRE tests. They take the form

$A \sim B$ (A is like B) or more generally

$A{:}B :: C{:}D$ (A is to B as C is to D)

where one of the components is missing. For example, the type of word-object and geometrical analogies typically found in aptitude or GRE tests are given by

(a)	(b)
house : hut tree : _____	(b) water : dam _____ : battery
(c)	(d)
green : go red : _____	# 0 * 0 * * # 0

Examples of more abstract analogies are the planetary system or atomic model noted above, the proof of a theorem based on a similar known proof, solving a new problem from knowledge of an old familiar problem solving technique, learning to play the card game of bridge from a knowledge of hearts, or producing a new algorithm for a program using previously learned programming examples and concepts.

Although applications of analogical methods have received less attention in AI than other methods, some important results have been published including (Burstein, 1986, Carbonell, 1983 and 1986, Greiner, 1988, Kling, 1971, McDermott, 1979, and Winston, 1980). Researchers in related fields have also made important contributions: cognitive science (Gentner, 1983), and psychology (Rumelhart and Norman, 1981). Several of the researchers in AI have produced working programs based on their models of the analogical process. We examine some of these models in the following section. In the remainder of this section we investigate the analogical reasoning process in some detail.

The Analogical Reasoning Process

Analogical reasoning was briefly described in Chapter 4 as a nonvalid form of inference. This follows from the fact that conclusions based on analogies are not necessarily logical entailments of the source knowledge. Analogy is a form of plausible reasoning. It is based on previously tested knowledge that bears a strong resemblance to the current situation.

There are five essential steps involved in the analogical learning process. A central step is the mapping process which is illustrated in Figure 20.1 and described below.

Analogical Learning Process

1. Analogue recognition: A new problem or situation is encountered and recognized as being similar to a previously encountered situation.

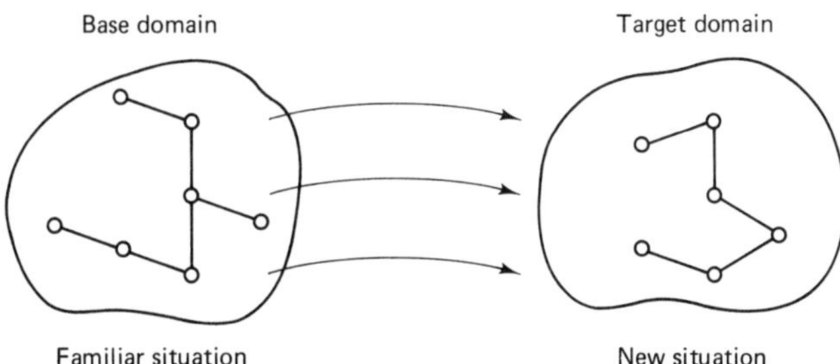

Figure 20.1 The analogical mapping process.

2. Access and recall: The similarity of the new problem to previously experienced ones serves as an index with which to access and recall one or more candidate experiences (analogues).
3. Selection and mapping: Relevant parts of the recalled experiences are selected for their similarities and mapped from the base to the target domain.
4. Extending the mapped experience: The newly mapped analogues are modified and extended to fit the target domain situation.
5. Validation and generalization: The newly formulated solution is validated for its applicability through some form of trial process (such as theorem provers or simulation). If the validation is supported, a generalized solution is formed which accounts for both the old and the new situations.

Implementation of the above process requires that several important issues be addressed. These issues are recurrent ones that appeared several times in other problems.

First, there is the question of representation. For analogical reasoning, it is desirable that knowledge be stored in a form that is easily accessed, retrieved, and evaluated for possible use as a candidate solution. This implies that self-contained, interrelated pieces of knowledge comprising a particular situation, episode, proof, plan, concept, and other unit of knowledge should be indexed and stored for simultaneous recall. Object attributes and relationships should be bound together with identifiers and other descriptive information for ease of use.

Second, it is desirable that an appropriate similarity measure be used to insure that only candidate analogues bearing a strong similarity to the new situation be considered.

Third, it is important that the mapping process from base to target domain be flexible enough to capture and import only the appropriate parts of the descriptions. The mapping should be able to transform objects, attributes, and predicates into corresponding ones which best meet the requirements of the target domain situation. For a general analogical system, this means that the transformation process should be dynamically adaptable to map between different domains and at different levels of abstraction.

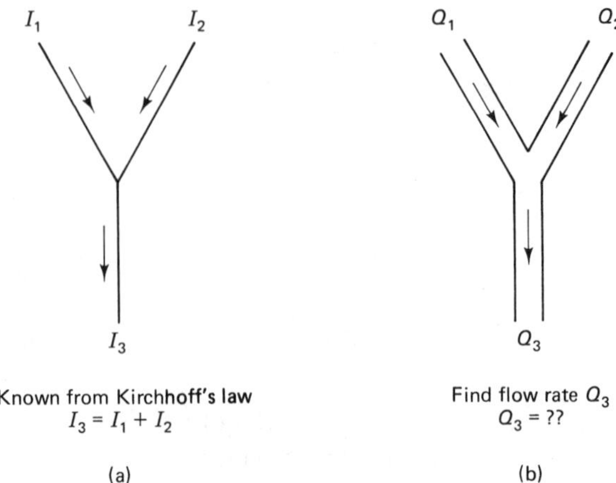

Figure 20.2 Analogical problem solving example.

Next, the newly created solution must be tested for its suitability. This test can be as informal as a simulated solution trial in the target domain or as formal as a deductive test of logical entailment.

Finally, having found an analogy and tested it successfully, the resultant episode should be generalized if possible and then summarized, encoded, indexed and stored for subsequent use in reasoning or learning.

A simple example will help to illustrate this process. Suppose we are given the problem of determining the flow rate of a fluid from a simple Y junction of pipes (Figure 20.2b). We are asked to determine the value of Q_3 given only knowledge of the flow rates Q_1 and Q_2. A description of this unknown problem reminds us of a similar known problem, that of finding the flow rate of electrical current in a circuit junction. We recall the solution method to the electrical problem as being that based on Kirchhoff's current flow law, namely, that the sum of the currents at a junction is zero. We use this knowledge in an attempt to solve the hydraulic flow problem using the same principles; that is, we map the electrical flow solution to the hydraulic flow problem domain. This requires that corresponding objects, attributes and relations be suitably mapped from the electrical to the hydraulic domain. We then test the conjectured solution in some way.

In the reminding process, we may alternatively be given a direct hint from a teacher that the hydraulic flow problem is like the electrical flow problem. Otherwise, we must infer this likeness in some way and proceed with the conjecture that they are alike, justifying the likeness on the basis of the consistency of nature or some other means.

Next, we examine some representative examples of analogical learning systems.

20.3 EXAMPLES OF ANALOGICAL LEARNING SYSTEMS

Winston's System

Patrick Winston (1980) developed programs that reason about relationships, motives, and consequent actions that occur among people. Using relationships and acts of actors in one story (such as *Macbeth*) the program was able to demonstrate that analogous results occurred in different stories (such as *Hamlet*) when there were similarities among the relationships and motives of the second group of characters. The programs could also learn through the analogical reasoning process. For example, when a teacher declared that voltage, current, and resistance relationships were like those of water pressure, flow, and pipe resistance, the system was able to learn basic results in electrical circuits and related laws such as Ohm's law (the opposite of the learning problem described above).

The analogical mapping and learning process for this example is illustrated in Figure 20.3. The items in the figure labeled as voltage-value-3, current-value-3, and resistance-value-3 represent specific values of voltage, current, and resistance, respectively.

The important features of Winston's system can be summarized as follows:

1. Knowledge representation: Winston's system used frame structures as part of the Frame Representation Language (FRL) developed by Roberts and Goldstein (1977). Slots within the frames were given special meanings, such as AKO, appears-in, and the like. Individual frames were linked together in a network for easy access to related items.

2. Recall of analogous situations: When presented with a current situation, candidate analogues were retrieved from memory using an hierarchical indexing scheme. This was accomplished by storing a situations (frame) name in the slots of all object frames that appeared in the situation. For example, in the Cinderella story, the prince is one of the central parts. Therefore, prince would be used as a node in a hierarchical tree structure with sublinks

prince→AKO-man→AKO-person

and the Cinderella label CI would be stored in an appears-in slot of the frames belonging to the prince, the man, and the person. These slots were always searched as part of the recall reminding process when looking for candidate analogues.

3. Similarity matching: In selecting the best of the known situations during the reminding process described above, a similarity matching score is computed for each of the recalled candidates. A score is computed for all slot pairings between two frames, and the pairing having the highest score is selected as the proper analogue. The scoring takes into account the number of values that match between slots as

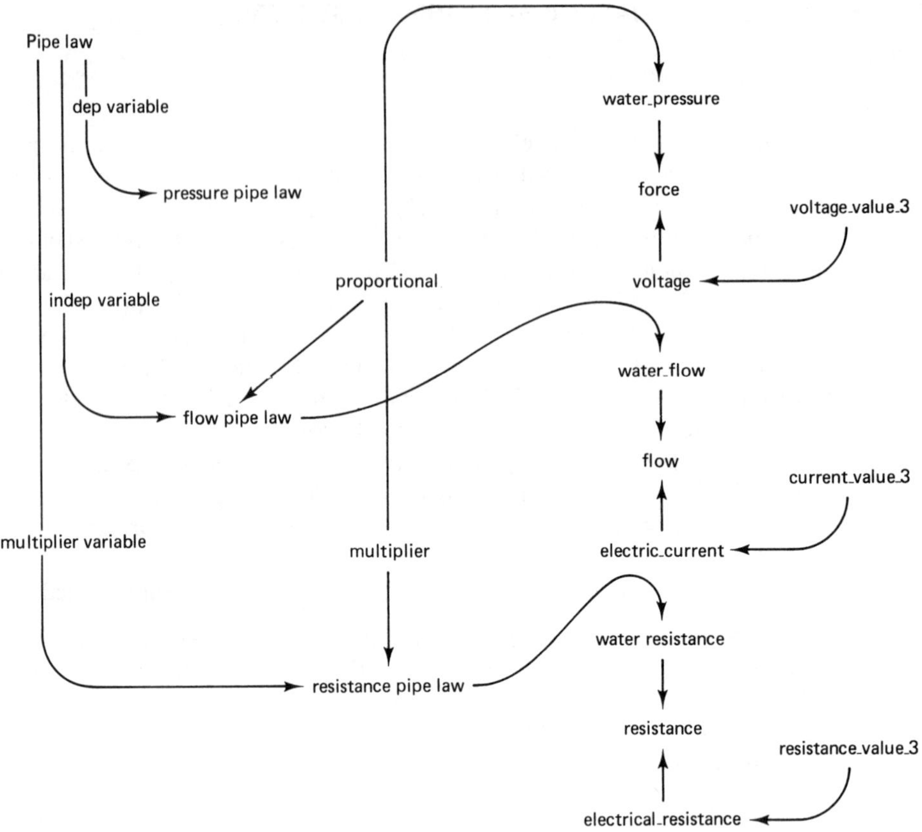

Figure 20.3 Learning electrical laws from hydraulics.

well as matching relationships found between like parts having causal relations as noted in comment fields.

4. Mapping base-to-target situations: The base-to-target analogue mapping process used in this system depends on the similarity of parts between base and target domains and role links that can be established between the two. For example, when both base and target situations share the same domain, such as water-flow in pipes, parts between the two are easily matched for equality. A specific pipe, pipel, is matched with a general pipe, pipe#, specific water-flow, with general flow, and so forth. The relationships from the general case are then mapped directly to the specific case without change.

In cases where base and target are different domains, the mapping is more difficult as parts, in general, will differ. Before mapping is attempted, links are established between corresponding parts. For example, if the two domains are water-flow and electricity-flow (it is known the two are alike), determining the electrical resistance in a circuit is achieved by mapping the pipe-water-flow laws to the electrical domain. Before mapping, a link between the pressure and voltage laws and the water-flow and current-flow laws is established. The link is determined from a hierarchical tree connecting the two parts, where voltage-2 is a specific voltage.

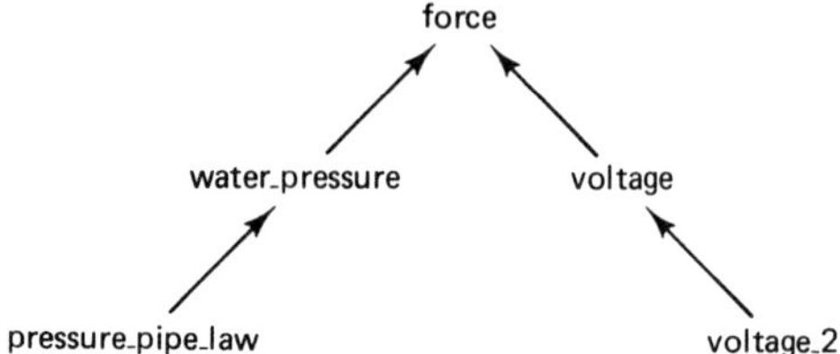

In all of the above components, matching plays a dominant role. First, in recall, matching is used to determine candidate situations. Second, matching is used for scoring to select the best analogue. Finally, matching is used to determine how parts and relationships are mapped from base to target domains.

Greiner's NLAG System

Russell Greiner (1988) developed an analogical learning system he called NLAG using Stanford University's MRS logic development language. The system requires three inputs and produces a single output. The inputs are an impoverished theory (a theory lacking in knowledge with which to solve a given problem), an analogical hint, and the given problem for solution. The output from the system is a solution conjecture for the problem based on the analogical hint.

Using Greiner's notation, the process can be described as follows. The analogical inference process described here is represented by the operator $\mid\!\sim$. This operator takes three inputs.

1. A finite collection of consistent propositions (rules, facts, and the like) called a theory (*Th*).
2. An analogical hint about the source and target analogues *A* and *B* respectively, written $A \sim B$ (*A* is like *B*). Here $A = \{a_1, \ldots, a_n\}$ and $B = \{b_1, \ldots, b_n\}$ are sets of arbitrary formulae or knowledge related to some problem situations.
3. A problem to be solved in the target domain (target problem) denoted as *PT*.

The output from the system is a set of new propositions or conjectures $\phi(A)$ related to the set *B* that can be used to solve *PT*.

The above process can be summarized as follows:

$$Th, A \sim B \models_{PT} \phi(A)$$

The NLAG system was designed to perform useful, analogical learning. We define the *learning* part here as the process of determining or creating one or more formulas f which are not initially in the deductive closure of Th, that is, such that

$$Th \not\models f \text{ holds,}$$

(so f is not initially derivable from Th), and such that

$$Th \not\models \sim f,$$

that is, f is not known to be false; so the augmented theory

$$Th' = Th \cup \{f\} \text{ is consistent.}$$

We specialize this type of learning to be *analogical learning* by requiring that the process use the operator $\mid\!\sim$ and have as inputs both the theory Th as well as the hint $A \sim B$. Also, the new formulae f should be about the target analogue A ($f = \phi(A)$ where ϕ is some set of arbitrary formulae). The source analogue B should also satisfy the analogy formulae. Thus, we must also have $Th \models \phi(B)$.

Finally, we specialize the definition further to *useful analogical learning* by requiring that the conjectured formulae $\phi(A)$ returned by the system be limited to those formulae that are useful in the sense that the ϕ, together with Th, can solve PT, that is

$$Th \cup \{\phi(A)\} \models PT.$$

This definition of useful analogical learning is summarized in Figure 20.4 where we have named the conditions described in the above definition as unknown, consistent, common, and useful.

These notions are illustrated in terms of our earlier example for the hydraulics or electrical flow problem (Figure 20.2). Thus, B here corresponds to the known theory Th that given an electrical Y junction as in Figure 20.2a, then $I_3 = I_1 + I_2$. The problem PT is to find Q_3, the fluid flow rate in a similar Y junction of pipes when Q_1 and Q_2 are known. The analogical hint, $A \sim B$, is that the hydraulics flow problem is like the electrical current flow problem. The useful formula needed to solve the problem is of course $Q_3 = Q_1 + Q_2$. A more complex example would, of course, require more than a single formula.

Since many analogies may satisfy the theory and the analogical hint, it is necessary to restrict the analogies considered to those which are useful. For this, NLAG uses heuristics to select only those formulae which are likely to be useful.

One heuristic used by the system is based on the idea that relationships in

$$Th, A \sim B \mid\!\sim_{PT} \phi(A)$$

where

UNKNOWN:	$Th \not\models \phi(A)$
CONSISTENT:	$Th \not\models \sim\phi(A)$
COMMON:	$Th \models \phi(B)$
USEFUL:	$Th \cup \{\phi(A)\} \models_{PT}$

Figure 20.4 Summary of useful analogical inference.

one domain should hold in other, similar domains (in two domains governed by physical laws). In our example, this is the law related to zero flow rates into a junction and the corresponding reusable zero-sum formula for general, physical flows. Thus, only those uninstantiated abstract formulas found in the base analogue would be permitted as conjectures in the target analogue solution. Furthermore, this same heuristic requires that the selected formulae be atomic; formulae of the form $f(a_1, a_2, \ldots, a_k)$ are permitted, whereas formulae containing multiple conjunctive or disjunctive terms such as

$$f_1(a,b) \ \& \ f_2(b,c) \lor f_3(a,c,d,e)$$

are not permitted. These formulae must also satisfy the usefulness condition (Figure 20.4).

A heuristic which helps to further prune the abstract solutions described above uses the target domain problem *PT*, to suggest a related query in the source domain. The corresponding source domain query *PS* is then used in turn to select only those formulae which are both abstractions (as selected above) and are also relevant. For example, the target query *PT* = "Find the flowrate in the given pipe structure" is used to find the analogous source domain query *PS* = "Find the current in the given electrical structure." This query is then used to determine which facts are used to solve *PS*. These facts are then used as a guide in selecting facts (formulae) for the target domain to solve *PT*.

Other system heuristics require that formulae must all come from the same domain, that more general abstractions be preferred over less general ones, and that for a given abstraction, instances which require the fewest conjectures be chosen. In general, these heuristics are all based on choosing only enough new information about the target analogue to solve *PT* and then stop.

Carbonell's Systems

Carbonell developed two analogical systems for problem solving, each based on a different perception of the analogical process (1983 and 1986). The first system was based on what he termed transformational analogy and the second on derivational analogy. The major differences between the two methods lie in the amount of details remembered and stored for situations such as problem solution traces and the methods used in the base-to-target domain transformational process.

Both methods used a knowledge representation and memory indexing and recall scheme similar to the memory organization packets or MOPs of Roger Schank (Chapter 11). Both methods also essentially followed the five-step analogical learning process outlined in the previous section. The main differences between the two methods can be summarized as follows:

Transformational Analogy. Problem solving with this approach is based on the use of means-end analysis (MEA) as described in Chapter 9. Known problem solutions are indexed and stored for later retrieval. The solutions are stored as an initial state, a goal state, and a sequence of actions (operators) which, when applied to the initial and intermediate states, result in a transformation to the goal state. When a new problem is encountered, it is matched against potentially relevant known ones using a suitable similarity measurement. The partial match producing the highest similarity measure is transformed to satisfy the requirements of the new problem. In finding a solution to the new problem using the known mapped solution, it is often necessary to disturb some states to find operators which reduced the current-to-goal state differences. With this method, the focus is on the sequence of actions in a given solution, and not on the derivation process itself.

Derivational Analogy. This approach requires the storage of much more information than the transformational approach. It is intended that the analogies here be made more on the basis of the complete reasoning process than on the sequence of solution states for the past problem solutions. In solving newly encountered problems, a plan is formulated using the complete solution trace of the analogue. This plan includes a list of all subgoals derived, alternative solution paths generated and those rejected, each step of the solution process and the decisions made at each step, pointers to knowledge which proved to be useful in the solution, and detailed failure information when a solution cannot be found. This plan is modified to fit the new problem domain. If it cannot produce a solution, other methods are applied such as MEA.

Both of the systems developed by Carbonell are useful as analogical research tools. And both worked reasonably well in more than one domain.

20.4 EXPLANATION-BASED LEARNING

One of the most active areas of learning research to emerge during the early 1980s is explanation-based learning (also known as explanation-based generalization). This is essentially a form of deductive generalization. It has been successfully demonstrated for the general area of concept learning.

In EBL, four kinds of information must be known to the learner in advance.

1. A formal statement of the goal concept to be learned,
2. At least one positive training example of the concept,
3. Domain theory, which relates to the concept and the training example, and
4. Criteria for concept operationality.

The notion of operationality in item 4 requires some explanation. We say a procedure is operational if, for some agent and task, the procedure can be applied by the agent to solve the task. Thus, if the concept to be learned is one related to the recognition of pencils, operational criteria in this case would be given as a structural definition which could serve to uniquely identify pencils. If the concept is related to the function or use of pencils, the operational criteria would be given as a functional definition.

The objective of EBL is to formulate a generalized explanation of the goal concept. The explanation should prove how the training example satisfies the concept definition in terms of the domain theory.

The EBL method constructs an explanation of the concept based on the given example in terms of the domain theory. The explanation is a deductive proof of how the example satisfies the goal concept definition. Once an explanation has been developed, it is generalized by regressing the goal concept through the explanation structure. We illustrate these ideas with an example given by Mitchell, Keller, and Kedar-Cabelli (1986).

The concept to be learned in this example is the conditions under which it is safe to stack one item on top of another item. The training example is given as a description of a pair of objects; one object is a box which is stacked on top of the other object, an end table. The domain knowledge needed by the system consists of some structural attributes and relationships between physical objects such as volume, density, weight, lighter-than, fragile, and so on. The operational criteria in this case requires that the concept definition be expressed in terms of the predicates used to describe the example. The objective of the learning process here is to develop a generalization of the training example that is a sufficient concept definition for the goal concept which satisfies the operationality criteria. These definitions are summarized in Figure 20.5.

In carrying out the EBL method, the system must first construct an explanation of how the training example satisfies the goal concept. This requires that it select those attributes and relations which are relevant and which satisfy the operational criteria. From the goal concept definition it is seen that it is safe-to-stack an object x on an object y if and only if either y is not fragile or x is lighter than y. A search through the domain theory for the predicate FRAGILE fails; therefore, a search is then made for the predicate LIGHTER. This predicate is found in the rule

$$\text{WEIGHT}(p_1,v_1)\ \&\ \text{WEIGHT}(p_2,w_2)\ \&\ \text{LESS}(w_1,w_2) \rightarrow \text{LIGHTER}(p_1,p_2)$$

Matching obj1 to x (to p_1 in the above rule) and obj2 to y (to p_2 in the above rule) we can form the following partial explanation for safe-to-stack.

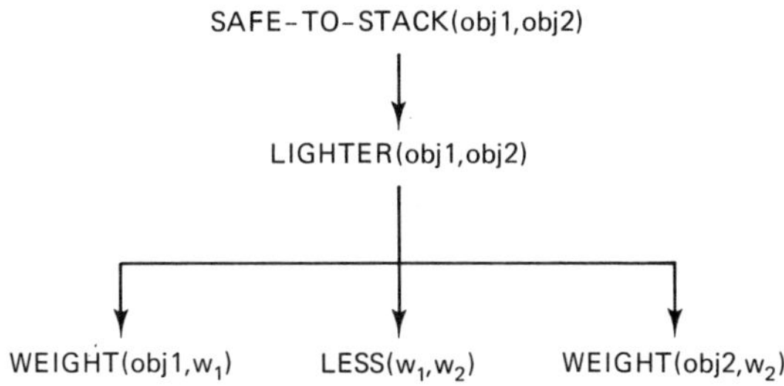

Continuing with the explanation process, we find rules relating the weights with volume and density and to an endtable. After instantiation of these terms, we

Known:

Concept Definition:

Pairs of objects <x,y> are SAFE-TO-STACK when
SAFE-TO-STACK(x,y)↔ ~FRAGILE(y) V LIGHTER(x,y).

Training Example:

ON(obj1,obj2)
ISA(obj1,box)
ISA(obj2,endtable)
COLOR(obj1,red)
COLOR(obj2,blue)
VOLUME(obj1,1)
DENSITY(obj1,0.1)
. . .

Domain Theory:

VOLUME(p_1,v_1) & DENSITY(p_1,d_1) → WEIGHT(p_1,v_1*d_1)
WEIGHT(p_1,w_1) & WEIGHT(p_2,w_2) & LESS(w_1,w_2) →
LIGHTER(p_1,p_2)

ISA(p_1,endtable) → WEIGHT(p_1,5) (i.e. a default)
LESS(0.1,5)
. . .

Operationality Criteria:

The learned concept should be expressed in terms of the same predicates used to describe the example, i.e. COLOR, DENSITY, VOLUME, etc. or simple predicates from the domain theory (e.g. LESS).

Determine:

A generalization of the training example that is a sufficient goal concept definition which satisfies the operationality criteria.

Figure 20.5 Safe-to-stack example for EBL.

are led to the complete explanation tree structure given below in which the root terms are seen to satisfy the operationality criteria.

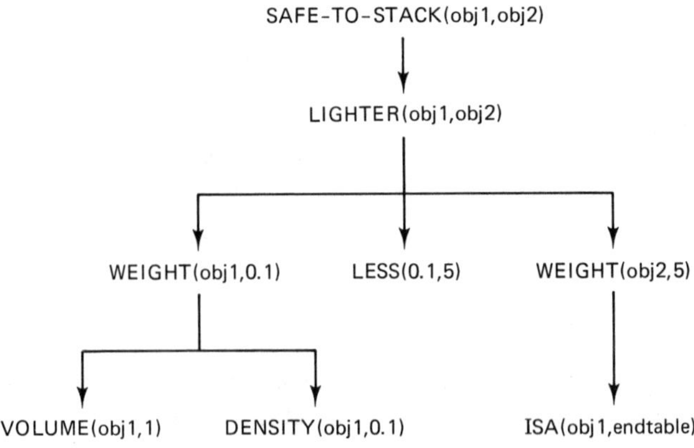

The next step in developing the final target concept is to generalize the above structure by regressing or back-propagating formulae through rules in the above structure step by step, beginning with the top expression SAFE-TO-STACK and regressing SAFE-TO-STACK(x,y) through the goal rule (the ˜ FRAGILE disjunct is omitted since it was not used). LIGHTER$(p_1,p_2) \rightarrow$ SAFE-TO-STACK(p_1,p_2) yields the term LIGHTER(x,y) as a sufficient condition for inferring SAFE-TO-STACK(x,y). In a similar way LIGHTER(x,y) is regressed back through the next step to yield WEIGHT(x,w_1) & WEIGHT(y,w_2) & LESS(w_1,w_2). This expression is then regressed through the final steps of the explanation structure to yield the following generalized, operational, definition of the safe-to-stack concept.

```
VOLUME(x,v1)
& DENSITY(x,d1)
& LESS(v1*d1,5)
& ISA(y,endtable) → SAFE-TO-STACK(x,y)
```

The complete regression process is summarized in Figure 20.6 where the underlined expressions are the results of the regression steps and the substitutions are as noted within the braces.

In summary, the process described above produces a justified generalization of a single training example as a learned concept. It does this in a two step process. The first step creates an explanation that contains only relevent predicates. The second step uses the explanation structure to establish constraints on the predicate values that are sufficient for the explanation to apply in general. This differs from inductive learning in that a single training example is adequate to learn a valid description of the concept. Of course there is a trade-off here. The EBL method also requires appropriate domain knowledge as well as a definition of the target concept.

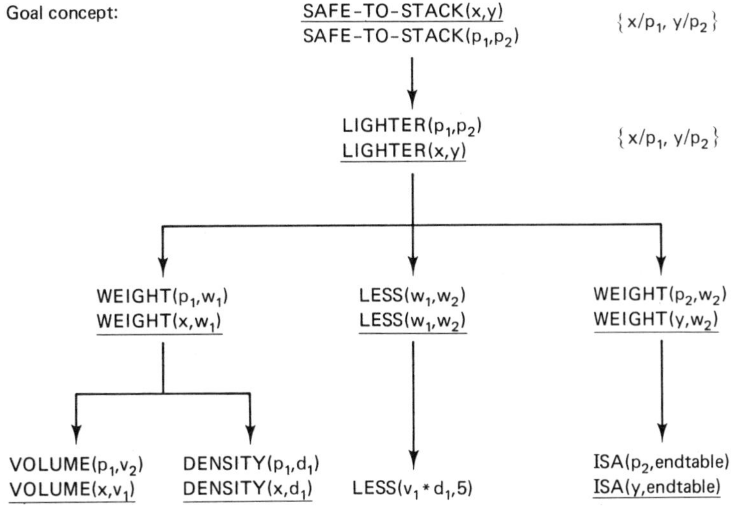

Figure 20.6 Generalization by regression through the explanation structure.

There is an apparent paradox in the EBL method in that it may appear that no actual learning takes place since the system must be given a definition of the very concept to be learned! The answer to this dilemma is that a broader, generalized, and more useable definition is being learned. With the EBL method, existing knowledge is being transformed to a more useful form. And, the learned concept applies to a broader class than the supplied definition. This newly learned concept is a valid definition since it has been logically justified through the explanation process. The same claim cannot be made of other nondeductive learning techniques like inductive or analogical learning.

The notion of operationality used in EBL systems should depend on the purpose of the learning system. As such, it should be treated as a dynamic property. For example, a robot may need to learn the concept of a pencil in order to recognize pencils. In this case, operationality should be interpreted in terms of the structural properties of the pencil. On the other hand, if the purpose of learning the pencil concept relates to design, the robot would be better served with a functional definition of a pencil. Keller (1988) discusses the operationality problem and its application in a program called MetaLEX (a successor to LEX described in Chapter 19).

20.5 SUMMARY

We have described two of the more promising approaches to machine learning, the analogical and explanation-based learning paradigms. These methods, unlike similarity-based methods, are capable of creating new knowledge from a single training example. Both methods offer great potential as autonomous learning methods.

Learning by analogy requires that similar, known experiences be available for use in explaining or solving newly encountered experiences. The complete process can be described in five steps: (1) a newly encountered situation serves as a reminder of a known situation, (2) the most relevent of the reminded situations are accessed and recalled, (3) the appropriate parts of the recalled analogues are mapped from the base domain to the target domain, (4) the mapped situation or solution is extended to fit the current problem, and (5) the extended solution is tested, generalized, and stored for subsequent recall.

A number of analogical research learning systems have been developed. Four representative systems have been described in this chapter.

Explanation-based learning is a form of deductive learning where the learner develops a logical explanation of how a positive training example defines a concept. The explanation is developed using the example, the concept definition, and relevant domain theory. A key aspect of the explanation is that it satisfy some operational criteria, possibly through the use of only attributes and predicates that are used in the domain theory and/or the example.

The EBL method is a two step process. In the first step, an explanation of the concept is formulated using the training example and domain theory. In the second, this explanation is generalized by regressing formulae step-by-step back through rules in the explanation structure. The final concept, if successful, is a definition which both satisfies the operationality criteria and is also a valid definition of the concept.

EXERCISES

20.1. Describe two examples of analogical learning you have experienced recently.

20.2. Why is it that things similar in some ways tend to be similar in other ways?

20.3. Consult a good dictionary and determine the differences between the definitions of analogies, metaphors, and similes.

20.4. Make up three new analogies like the examples given in Section 20.2.

20.5. Relate each of the five steps followed in analogical learning to the following example: Riding a motorcycle is like riding a bicycle with an engine in it.

20.6. Compare the analogical system of Winston to that of Greiner. In what ways do they differ?

20.7. What appears to be more important in mapping from base to target domain, object attributes, object relationships, or both? Give examples to support your conclusions.

20.8. What are the main differences between Carbonell's transformational and derivational systems?

20.8. Define operationality as it applies to explanation-based learning and give an example of it as applied to some task.

20.10. Explain why each of the four kinds of information (concept definition, positive training example, domain theory, and operational criteria) is needed in EBL.

20.11. If the end table in the Safe-to-Stack example had not been given a default weight value, what additional steps would be required in the explanation to complete the tree structure?

20.12. What is the purpose of the regression process in EBL?

20.13. Work out a complete explanation for the concept safe to cross the street. This requires domain theory about traffic lights, and traffic, a positive example of a safe crossing, and operational criteria.

20.14. The learning methods described in Part V have mostly been single paradigm methods, yet we undoubtedly use combined learning for much of our knowledge learning. Describe how analogical learning could be combined with EBL as well as inductive learning to provide a more comprehensive form of learning.

REFERENCES

ANDERBERG, M. R. 1973. *Cluster Analysis for Applications.* New York: Academic Press.

ANDERSON, J. R., AND G. H. BOWER. 1980. *Human Associative Memory.* Washington, D.C.: Winston.

ANDREWS, H. C. 1972. *Introduction to Mathematical Techniques in Pattern Recognition.* New York: Wiley Interscience.

APPELT, D. 1985. "Planning English Referring Expressions." *Artificial Intelligence* 26.

BALLARD, D. H., AND C. M. BROWN. 1982. *Computer Vision.* Englewood Cliffs: Prentice Hall.

BOBROW, D. G., AND T. WINOGRAD. 1977. "An Overview of KRL, a Knowledge Representation Language." *Cognitive Science*, 1,3.

BOCK, P. 1985. "The Emergence of Artificial Intelligence: Learning to Learn." *AI Magazine*, 6, 3 (Fall).

BRACHMAN, R. J. 1978. "A Structural Paradigm for Representing Knowledge." Report No. 3605, Bolt Beranek and Newman, Inc. Cambridge, Mass.

———. 1979. "What's in a Concept? Structural Foundations for Semantic Networks." In *Associative Networks,* ed. N. V. Findler. New York: Academic Press.

BRATKO, IVAN. 1986. *PROLOG: Programming for Artificial Intelligence.* Menlo Park, CA: Addison-Wesley.

BROOKS, R. A. 1981. *Model-Based Computer Vision*, Ann Arbor: UMI Research Press.

BROWNSTON, L., R. FARRELL, E. KANT, AND N. MARTIN. 1985. *Programming Expert Systems in OPS5: An Introduction to Rule-Based Programming.* Reading, MA: Addison-Wesley.

BUCHANAN, B. G., AND E. H. SHORTLIFFE. 1984. *Rule-Based Expert Systems: The MYCIN Experiments of the Stanford Heuristic Programming Project.* Reading, MA: Addison-Wesley.

BUDD, T. 1987. *A Little Smalltalk.* Reading, MA: Addison-Wesley.

BURSTEIN, M. H. 1983. "A Model of Learning by Incremental Analogical Reasoning and Debugging." 45–48 in *Proceedings of AAAI-83*, Washington, D.C.

———. 1986. "Incremental Analogical Reasoning." In *Machine Learning: An Artificial Intelligence Approach*, Vol. II, eds. R. S. Michalski, J. G. Carbonell, and T. M. Mitchell. Los Altos: Morgan Kaufmann.

CARBONELL, J. G. 1983. "Learning by Analogy: Formulating and Generalizing Plans from Past Experience." In *Machine Learning: An Artificial Intelligence Approach*, eds. R. S. Michalski, J. G. Carbonell, and T. M. Mitchell. Palo Alto: Tioga.

———. 1983a. "Derivational Analogy and Its Role in Problem Solving." 64–69 in *Proceedings of AAAI-83*, Washington, D.C.

———. 1983b. "Analogy in Problem Solving." In *Machine Learning: An Artificial Intelligence Approach*, Vol. II, eds. R. S. Michalski, J. G. Carbonell, and T. M. Mitchell. Los Altos: Morgan Kaufmann.

———. 1986. "Derivational Analogy: A Theory of Reconstructive Problem Solving and Expertise Acquisition." In *Machine Learning*, Vol II, eds. R. S. Michalski, J. G. Carbonell, and T. M. Mitchell. Los Altos: Morgan Kaufmann Publishers, Inc.

———., AND S. MINTON. 1983. "Metaphor and Common-Sense Reasoning." 83–110 in *Technical Report CMU-CS-83-110*. Carnegie-Mellon University, Pittsburgh.

CHOMSKY, NOAM. 1965. *Aspects of the Theory of Syntax.* Cambridge: MIT Press.

Clowes, M. B. 1971. "On Seeing Things." *Artificial Intelligence*, 2, 1.

Cohen, P. R. 1985. *Heuristic Reasoning About Uncertainty: An Artificial Intelligence Approach*. Boston: Pitman Publishing.

———., and E. A. Feigenbaum, eds. 1982. *The Handbook of Artificial Intelligence*, Vol. 3. Los Altos: Morgan Kaufmann.

Davis, R., and D. B. Lenat. 1982. *Knowledge-Based Systems in Artificial Intelligence*. New York: McGraw-Hill.

DeJong, G. 1981. "Generalizations Based on Explanations." 67–69 in *Proceedings of the Seventh IJCAI*, Vancouver, B.C.

———., and R. Mooney. 1986. "Explanation-Based Learning: An Alternative View." *Machine-Learning* 1: 145–76.

de Kleer, J. 1986. "An Assumption-Based TMS," *Artificial Intelligence* 28,2.

———. 1986a. "Problem Solving with the ATMS," *Artifical Intelligence* 28,2.

Dempster, A. P. 1968. "A Generalization of Baysian Inference." *Journal of the Royal Statistical Society*, Series B, 30,2.

Devijver, P., and J. Kittler. 1982. *Pattern Recognition: A Statistical Approach*. Englewood Cliffs: Prentice Hall.

Dietterich, T. C., and R. S. Michalski. 1981. "Inductive Learning of Structural Descriptions: Evaluation Criteria and Comparative Review of Selected Methods." *Artificial Intelligence* 16,3: 257–94.

———, 1983. "A Comparative Review of Selected Methods for Learning from Examples," In *Machine Learning*: *An Artificial Intelligence Approach*, eds. R. S. Michalski, J. G. Carbonell and T. M. Mitchell. Palo Alto: Tioga.

Doyle, J. 1979. "A Truth Maintenance System." *Artificial Intelligence* 12,3 (Nov): 231–72.

Duda, R. O., and P. E. Hart. 1973. *Pattern Classification and Scene Analysis*. New York: Wiley.

Ernst, G. W., and A. Newell. 1969. *GPS: A Case Study in Generality and Problem Solving*. New York: Academic.

Eshera, M. A., and King-Sun Fu. 1984. "A Graph Distance Measure for Image Analysis." *IEEE Transactions on Systems, Man, and Cybernetics* SMC-14,3.

Feigenbaum, E. A. 1985. Paper presented at the Fifth International Joint Conference on Artificial Intelligence, Los Angeles, CA.

———., and P. McCorduck. 1983. *The Fifth Generation*. Reading, MA: Addison-Wesley.

Fikes, R. E., and N. J. Nilsson. 1971. "STRIPS: A New Approach to the Application of Theorem Proving to Problem Solving." *Artificial Intelligence* 2:189–208.

Fillmore, C. J. 1968. *The Case for Case in Universals in Linguistic Theory*. Eds. E. Bach and R. Harms. New York: Holt, Rinehart, and Winston.

———. 1977. *The Case for Case Reopened in Syntax and Semantics 8: Grammatical Relations*. Ed. P. Cole and J. Sadock. New York: Academic Press.

Fischler, M. A., and R. A. Elschlager. 1973. "The Representation and Matching of Pictorial Structures." *IEEE Transactions on Computers* 22,1.

Fu, K. S. 1968. *Sequential Methods in Pattern Recognition and Machine Learning*. New York: Academic.

———. 1970. "Statistical Pattern Recognition." 35–80 in *Adaptive, Learning, and Pattern Recognition Systems*, eds. J. M. Mendel and K. S. Fu. New York: Academic.

———. 1970a. "Stochastic Automata as Models of Learning Systems." 393–432 in *Adaptive, Learning, and Pattern Recognition Systems*, eds. J. M. Mendel and K. S. Fu. New York: Academic.

———. 1974. *Syntactic Methods in Pattern Recognition*. New York: Academic.

———. 1975. "Grammatical Inference: Introduction and Survey." 95–111, 409–23 in *IEEE Transactions on Systems, Man, and Cybernetics*, Vol 5.

GALLANT, S. I. 1988. "Connectionist Expert Systems." *Communications of the ACM* 31,2.

GARVEY, T. D., J. D. LOWRANCE, AND M. A. FISCHLER. 1981. "An Inference Technique for Integrating Knowledge from Disparate Sources." *Proceedings of the Seventh International Joint Conference on Artificial Intelligence*, Vancouver B.C.

GENTNER, D. 1983. "Structure Mapping: A Theoretical Framework for Analogy." *Cognitive Science* 7,2(April-June): 155–170.

GOLDBERG, A., AND D. ROBSON. 1983. *Smalltalk-80: The Language and Its Implementation*. Reading, MA: Addison-Wesley.

GOLDSTEIN, I. P., AND R. B. ROBERTS. 1977. "Nudge, a Knowledge-Based Scheduling Program." 257–63 in Proceedings of the *Fifth International Joint Conference on Artificial Intelligence*.

GONZALEZ, R. C., AND M. G. THOMPSON. 1978. *Syntactic Pattern Recognition*. Reading, MA: Addison-Wesley.

GREINER, R. 1988. "Learning by Understanding Analogies." *Artificial Intelligence* 35: 81–125.

GUPTA, M. M., A. KANDEL, W. BANDLER, AND J. B. KISZKA, EDS. 1985. *Approximate Reasoning in Expert Systems*. New York: North-Holland.

GUZMAN, A. 1969. "Decomposition of a Visual Scene into Three-Dimensional Bodies." In *Automatic Interpretation and Classification of Images*, ed. A. Grasseli. New York: Academic.

HALLIDAY, M. A. K. 1961. "Categories of the Theory of Grammar." *Word* 17: 241–292.

HAYES-ROTH, F., AND J. MCDERMOTT. 1977. "Knowledge Acquisition from Structural Description." 356–62 in *Proceedings of IJCAI-5*.

———. "An Interference Matching Technique for Inducing Abstractions." *Communications of the ACM* 26: 401–10.

HAYES-ROTH, F., D. A. WATERMAN, AND D. B. LENAT, eds. 1983. *Building Expert Systems*. Reading, MA: Addison-Wesley.

HENDRIX, G. G. 1978. *Semantic Knowledge in Understanding Spoken Language*. Ed. D. E. Walker. New York: North-Holland.

———. 1979. "Encoding Knowledge in Partitioned Networks." 51–120 in *Associative Networks: Representation and Use of Knowledge by Computers*, ed. N. V. Findler. New York: Academic.

———., E. D. SACERDOTI, D. SAGALOWICZ, AND J. SLOCUM. 1986. "Developing a Natural Language Interface to Complex Data." 563–84 in *Readings in Natural Language Processing*, eds. B. J. Grosz, K. S. Jones, B. L. Webber. Los Altos: Morgan Kaufmann.

Huffman, D. A. 1971. ''Impossible Objects as Nonsense Sentences.'' In *Machine Intelligence* 6, eds. B. Meltzer and D. Michie. Edinburgh: Edinburgh UP.

Hughes, G. E., and M. J. Cresswell. 1968. *An Introduction to Modal Logic*. London: Methuen.

Hunt, E. B., J. Marin, and P. J. Stone. 1966. *Experiments in Induction*. New York: Academic.

Iba, G. A. 1979. Learning Disjunctive Concepts from Examples. Master's thesis, MIT, 1979.

Kaeler, T., and D. Patterson. 1986. *A Taste of Smalltalk*. New York: W. W. Norton.

Kandel, A. 1982. *Fuzzy Techniques in Pattern Recognition*. New York: Wiley.

Keller, R. M. 1987. ''Defining Operationality for Explanation-Based Learning.'' *Proceedings of the Sixth National Conference on Artificial Intelligence*, Seattle, WA.

Klahr, P., and W. S. Faught. 1980. ''Knowledge-based Simulation.'' *Proceedings of the First Annual National Conference on Artificial Intelligence*, Palo Alto, CA.

———., D. McArthur, and R. Narain. 1982. ''SWIRL: An Object-Oriented Air Battle Simulator.'' *Proceedings of the Second Annual Conference on Artificial Intelligence*, Pittsburgh.

Kling, R. E. 1971. ''A Paradigm for Reasoning by Analogy.'' *Artificial Intelligence* 2,2(Fall): 147–78.

Kolodner, J. L. 1983a. ''Maintaining Memory Organization in a Dynamic Long Term Memory.'' *Cognitive Science* 7,4.

———. 1983b. ''Reconstructive Memory: A Computer Model, *Cognitive Science*.'' 7,4.

———. 1984. *Retrieval and Organizational Strategies in Conceptual Memory: A Computer Model*. Hillsdale, NJ: Lawrence Erlbaum Associates.

Korf, R. E. 1983. *Learning to Solve Problems by Searching for Macro-Operators*. Marshfield, MA: Pitman.

———. 1985. ''Depth-first Iterative Deepening: An Optimal Admissible Tree Search.'' *Artificial Intelligence* 27: 97–109.

Langley, P. W., H. A. Simon, and G. L. Bradshaw. 1983. ''Rediscovering Chemistry with the BACON System.'' In *Machine Learning: An Artificial Intelligence Approach*, eds. R. S. Michalski, J. G. Carbonell, and T. M. Mitchell. Palo Alto: Tioga.

Larson, J., and R. S. Michalski. 1977. ''Inductive Inference in the Variable Valued Predicate Logic System VL2: Methodology and Computer Implementation.'' Report No. 869, Computer Science Dept., University of Illinois, Urbana, Ill.

Lenat, D. B. 1980. ''The Nature of Heuristics.'' Report No. HPP-80–26, Heuristic Programming Project, Computer Science Department, Stanford University.

———. 1982. ''The Nature of Heuristics.'' *Artificial Intelligence* 19,2 (Oct): 189–249.

———. 1983. ''Theory Formation by Heuristic Search: The Nature of Heuristics II: Background and Examples.'' *Artificial Intelligence* 21,1–2 (Mar): 31–59.

———. 1983a. ''EURISKO: A Program That Learns New Heuristics and Domain Concepts: The Nature of Heuristics III: Program Design and Results.'' *Artificial Intelligence* 21,1–2 (Mar): 61–98.

Lenat, D. B., and J. S. Brown. 1984. ''Why AM and Eurisko Appear to Work.'' *Artificial Intelligence* 23.

LOVELAND, D. 1978. *Automatic Theorem Proving: A Logical Basis*. Amsterdam: North Holland.

MARR, D. 1982. *Vision*. New York: Freeman.

———., and E. C. Hildreth. 1980. "Theory of Edge Detection." *Proc. Royal Society of London*, Ser. B, 207.

MCCARTHY, J. 1968. "Programs with Common Sense." 403–09 in *Semantic Information Processing*, ed. M. Minsky. Cambridge: MIT Press.

———. 1980. "Circumscription: A Form of Nonmonotonic Reasoning." *Artificial Intelligence* 13: 27–39.

MCCORDUCK, P. 1979. *Machines Who Think*. San Francisco: W. H. Freeman and Co.

MCDERMOTT, J. 1979. "Learning to Use Analogies." 568–76 in *Proceedings of the Sixth IJCAI*, Tokyo.

MICHALSKI, R. S. 1980. "Pattern Recognition as Rule-Guided Inductive Inference." *IEEE Transactions on Pattern Analysis and Machine Intelligence* PAMI-2,4 (July): 349–61.

———. 1980a. "Knowledge Acquisition Through Conceptual Clustering: A Theoretical Framework and an Algorithm for Partitioning Data into Conjunctive Concepts." *Policy Analysis and Information Systems* 4,3 (Sept): 219–44.

———. 1983. "A Theory and Methology of Inductive Learning." *Artificial Intelligence* 20,2 (Feb): 111–61.

———. 1986. "Understanding the Nature of Learning." In *Machine Learning: An Artificial Intelligence Approach*, Vol II, eds. R. S. Michalski, J. G. Carbonell, and T. M. Mitchell. Los Altos: Morgan Kaufmann.

———., AND R. STEPP. 1983. "Learning from Observation: Conceptual Clustering." In *Machine Learning: An Artificial Intelligence Approach*, eds. R. S. Michalski, J. G. Carbonell, and T. M. Mitchell. Palo Alto: Tioga.

MINSKY, M. L., ed. 1968. *Semantic Information Processing*. Cambridge: MIT Press.

———. 1975. "A Framework for Representing Knowledge." In *The Psychology of Computer Vision*. ed. P. H. Winston. New York: McGraw-Hill.

———., AND S. PAPERT. 1969. *Perceptrons; An Introduction to Computational Geometry*. Cambridge: MIT Press.

MITCHELL, T. M. 1977. "Version Spaces: A Candidate Elimination Approach to Rule Learning." 305–10 in *Proceedings of the Fifth IJCAI*.

———. 1982. "Generalization as Search." *Artificial Intelligence* 18,2, (Mar): 203–26.

———., R. M. KELLER, AND S. T. KEDAR-CABELLI. 1986. "Explanation-Based Generalization: A Unifying View." *Machine Learning* 1.

———., S. MAHADEVAN, AND L. STEINBERG. 1985. "LEAP: A Learning Apprentice for VLSI Design." 573–80 in *Proceedings of the Ninth IJCAI*, Los Angeles, CA.

———., P. E. UTGOFF, AND R. B. BANERJI. 1983. "Learning by Experimentation: *Acquiring and Refining Problem-Solving Heuristics*." *Machine Learning: An Artificial Intelligence Approach*, eds. R. S. Michalski, J. G. Carbonell, and T. M. Mitchell. Palo Alto: Tioga.

MOSTOW, D. J. 1983b. "Operationalizing Advice: A Problem-Solving Model." 110–16 in *Proceedings of the International Machine Learning Workshop*, ed. R. S. Michalski. Allerton House, University of Illinois at Urbana-Champaign, June 22–24.

Narendra, K., and M. Thathachar. 1974. "Learning Automata: A Survey." *IEEE Transactions on Systems, Man, and Cybernetics* SMC-4,4.

Newell, A., and H. A. Simon. 1972. *Human Problem Solving*. Englewood Cliffs: Prentice Hall.

Nii, H. P. 1986a. "Blackboard Systems: The Blackboard Model of Problem Solving and the Evolution of Blackboard Architectures." *AI Magazine* 7,2.

———. 1986b. "Blackboard Systems: Blackboard Application Systems, Blackboard Systems from a Knowledge Engineering Perspective." *AI Magazine* 7,3.

Nilsson, N. J. 1971. *Problem Solving Methods in Artificial Intelligence*. New York: McGraw-Hill.

———. 1980. *Principles of Artificial Intelligence*. Palo Alto: Tioga.

———. 1986. "Probabilistic Logic." *Artificial Intelligence* 28,1.

Ohta, Y. 1985. *Knowledge-based Interpretation of Outdoor Natural Color Scenes*. Boston: Pitman.

Patterson, D. W., and K. Chu. 1987. "GIDES: An Expert System that Learns." UTEP Report CS-101–87, University of Texas at El Paso, El Paso, TX.

Pearl, J. 1986. "Fusion, Propagation, and Structuring in Belief Networks." *Artificial Intelligence* 29: 241–288.

———. 1987. "Distributed Revision of Composite Beliefs." *Artificial Intelligence* 33: 173–215.

Prewitt, J. M. S. 1970. *Object Enhancement and Extraction in Picture Processing and Psychopictorics*. Eds. B. S. Lipkin and A. Rosenfeld. New York: Academic.

Quillian, M. 1968. "Semantic Memory." In *Semantic Information Processing*, ed. M. Minsky, Cambridge: MIT Press.

Quinlân, J. R. 1983. "Inductive Inference as a Tool for the Construction of High-Performance Programs." In *Machine Learning: An Artificial Intelligence Approach*, eds. R. S. Michalski, J. G. Carbonell, and T. M. Mitchell. Palo Alto: Tioga.

Reddy, R., L. Erlman, R. Fennel, and R. Neeley. 1973. "The HEARSAY Speech Understanding System." *IEEE Transactions on Computers* C-25.

Reiter, R. 1980. "A Logic for Default Reasoning." *Artificial Intelligence* 13: 81–132.

Rendell, L. A. 1985. "Toward a Unified Approach for Conceptual Knowledge Acquisition." *AI Magazine* 4,4 (Winter): 19–27.

———. 1985. "A General Framework for Induction and a Study of Selective Induction." *Machine Learning* 1.

Roberts, L. G. 1965. "Machine Perception of Three Dimensional Solids." In *Optical and Electro-Optical Information Processing*, eds. J. T. Tippett et al. Cambridge: MIT Press.

Roberts, R. B., and I. P. Goldstein. 1977. "The FRL Primer." AI Memo #408, MIT AI Lab, Cambridge.

Rosenblatt, F. 1962. *Principles of Neurodynamics: Perceptrons and the Theory of Brain Mechanisms*. Washington: Spartan Books.

Rumelhart, W. R., and D. A. Norman. 1981. "An Activation-Trigger-Schema Model for the Simulation of Skilled Typing." *Proceedings of the Third Annual Conference of the Cognitive Science Society*, Berkeley CA.

SAGAN, C. 1977. *The Dragons of Eden.* New York: Random House.

SAMMUT, C., AND R. B. BANERJI. 1983. "Learning Concepts by Asking Questions." In *Machine Learning: An Artificial Intelligence Approach*, Vol. II, eds. R. S. Michalski, J. G. Carbonell, and T. M. Mitchell. Los Altos: Morgan Kaufmann.

SAMUEL, A. L. 1959. "Some Studies in Machine Learning Using the Game of Checkers." *IBM Journal of Research and Development* 3.

———. 1963. "Some Studies in Machine Learning Using the Game of Checkers." In *Computers and Thought*, eds. E. A. Feigenbaum and J. Feldman. New York: McGraw-Hill.

———. 1963. "Some Studies in Machine Learning Using the Game of Checkers. II-Recent Progress." *IBM Journal of Research and Development* 11: 601–17.

SCHANK, R. C. 1972. "Conceptual Dependency: A Theory of Natural Language Understanding." *Cognitive Psychology* 3.

———. 1982. *Dynamic Memory: A Theory of Reminding and Learning in Computers and People.* Cambridge: Cambridge UP.

———., AND R. P. ABELSON. 1977. *Scripts, Plans, Goals and Understanding.* Hillsdale, NJ: Lawrence Erlbaum.

———., AND P. G. CHILDERS. 1984. *The Cognitive Computer.* Menlo Park, CA: Addison-Wesley.

———., N. GOLDMAN, C. REIGER, AND C. RIESBECK. 1973. "MARGIE: Memory, Analysis, Response Generation, and Inference in English." *Proceedings of the Third International Joint Conference on Artificial Intelligence*, Stanford, CA.

SCHUBERT, L. K., R. G. GOEBEL, AND N. J. CERCONE. 1979. "The Structure and Organization of a Semantic Net for Comprehension and Inference." In *Associative Networks*, ed. N. V. Findler. New York: Academic.

SELFRIDGE, M. A. 1981. "A Computer Model of Child Language Acquisition." 92–95 in *Proceedings of the Seventh IJCAI*, Vancouver, B.C.

SHAFER, G. A. 1979. *Mathematical Theory of Evidence.* Princeton: Princeton UP.

SHANNON, C. E. 1955. "A Chess Playing Machine: In *The World of Mathematics*, Vol 4, ed. J. R. Newman. New York: Simon and Schuster.

———., AND W. WEAVER. 1963. *The Mathematical Theory of Communication.* Urbana: University of Illinois Press.

SHAPIRO, S. C. 1979. "The SNePS Semantic Network Processing System." In *Associative Networks*, ed. N. V. Findler. New York: Academic.

SHORTLIFFE, E. H. 1976. *Computer-based Medical Consultations: MYCIN.* New York: American Elsevier.

SIMON, J. C. 1986. *Patterns and Operators.* New York: McGraw-Hill.

Smalltalk/V Tutorial and Programming Handbook. 1987. Los Angeles: Digitalk, Inc.

SOBEL, I. 1970. "Camera Models and Machine Perception." AIM-21 Stanford, CA.

SOWA, J. F. 1984. *Conceptual Structures: Information Processing in Mind and Machine.* Reading, MA: Addison-Wesley.

SPATH, H. 1980. *Cluster Analysis Algorithms for Data Reduction and Classification of Objects.* Chichester, Eng.: Ellis Horwood LTD.

STEFIK, M., AND D. BOBROW. 1986. "Object-Oriented Programming: Themes and Variations." *AI Magazine* 6,4.

STEPP, R. E., AND R. S. MICHALSKI. 1986. "Conceptual Clustering: Inventing Goal-Oriented Classifications of Structured Objects." In *Machine Learning: An Artificial Intelligence Approach*, Vol II, eds. R. S. Michalski, J. G. Carbonell, and T. M. Mitchell. Los Altos: Morgan Kaufmann.

SZOLOVITS, P., AND S. PAUKER. 1978. "Categorical and Probabilistic Reasoning in Medical Diagnosis." *Artificial Intelligence* 11,1–2.

TOU, J. T., AND R. C. GONZALEZ. 1974. *Pattern Recognition Principles*. Reading, MA: Addison-Wesley.

TVERSKY, A. 1977. "Features of Similarity." *Psychological Review* 84,4.

UTGOFF, P. E. 1984. Shift of Bias for Inductive Concept Learning. Ph.D. Diss., Department of Computer Science, Rutgers University.

———. 1986. "Shift of Bias for Inductive Conceptive Learning." In *Machine Learning: An Artificial Intelligence Approach*, Vol II, eds. R. S. Michalski, J. G. Carbonell, and T. M. Mitchell. Los Altos: Morgan Kaufmann.

VALIANT, L. G. 1984. "A Theory of the Learnable." *Communications of the ACM* 27,11 (Nov): 1134–42.

VERE, S. A. 1978. "Inductive Learning of Relational Productions." 281–96 in *Pattern-Directed Inference Systems*, ed. D. A. Waterman and F. Hayes-Roth. New York: Academic.

WALZ, D. 1975. "Understanding Line Drawings of Scenes with Shadows." In *The Psychology of Computer Vision*, ed. P. H. Winston. New York: McGraw-Hill.

WEAVER, W. 1955. "Translation." In *Machine Translation of Languages*, ed. W. N. Locke and A. D. Booth. New York: Wiley.

WEISS, S. M., C. A. KULIKOWSKI, A. AMAREL, AND A. SAFIR. 1978. "A Model-Based Method for Computer-Aided Medical Decision-Making." *Artificial Intelligence* 11.

WINOGRAD, T. 1972. *Understanding Natural Language*. New York: Academic.

———. 1986. "A Procedural Model of Language Understanding." 249–66 in *Readings in Natural Language Processing*, eds. B. J. Grosz, K. S. Jones, and B. L. Webber. Los Altos: Morgan Kaufmann.

WINSTON, P. H. 1975. "Learning Structural Descriptions from Examples." In *The Psychology of Computer Vision*, ed. P. H. Winston. New York: McGraw-Hill.

———. 1977. *Artificial Intelligence*. New York: Addison-Wesley.

———. 1980. "Learning and Reasoning by Analogy." *Communications of the ACM* 23,12 (Dec): 689–702.

———. 1986. "Learning by Augmenting Rules and Accumulating Censors." In *Machine Learning: An Artificial Intelligence Approach*, Vol II, eds. R. S. Michalski, J. G. Carbonell, and T. M. Mitchell. Los Altos: Morgan Kaufmann.

WOODS, W. A. 1970. "Transition Network Grammars for Natural Language Analysis." *Communication of the ACM* 13(Oct).

———. 1972. "Speech Understanding Systems. Final Report, BBN Report 3438, Bolt, Berenek, and Newman, Cambridge, MA.

———. 1986. "Transition Network Grammars for Natural Language Analysis." 71–99 in

Readings in Natural Language Processing, ed. B. J. Grosz, K. S. Jones, and B. L. Webber. Los Altos: Morgan Kaufmann.

ZADEH, L. A. 1977. "Fuzzy Sets and Their Application to Pattern Classification and Clustering Analysis." 251–99 in *Classification and Clustering*, ed. Van Ryzin. New York: Academic.

———. 1983. "The Role of Fuzzy Logic in the Management of Uncertainty in Expert Systems." In *Fuzzy Sets and Systems* 11,3.

ZIMMERMAN, H. J. 1985. *Fuzzy Set Theory and Its Applications*. Dordrecht: Kluwer Nijhoff.

Index

A

B

C

D

E

F

G

H

I

J

K

L

M

N

O

P

Q

R

S

T

U

V

W

X

Z